Overview
(see page 7 for detailed Table of Contents)

MW01096774

Preface   13

Features   17

Acknowledgments   25

Chapter 1: What Is Philosophy?   28
   1.1   What Is a Philosopher?   33
   1.2   The Practical Value of Philosophy   41
   1.3   Fields of Philosophy   46
   1.4   Approaches to Philosophy   51

Chapter 2: Understanding Arguments, Claims, and Fallacies of Reasoning   72
   2.1   What Is an Argument?   81
   2.2   Deductive Arguments   98
   2.3   Non-Deductive Arguments   109
   2.4   Evaluating Claims   113
   2.5   Informal Logical Fallacies   118

Chapter 3: Philosophies of Life   132
   3.1   Stoicism: A Prescription for Peace of Mind   139
   3.2   Existentialism: Born Free, Let Me Be Me   152
   3.3   The Meaning of Life   161
   3.4   Hedonism: Pleasure Is the Measure   169
   3.5   Buddhism as a Philosophy of Life   181

Chapter 4: Epistemology, Metaphysics, and God   212
   4.1   Preliminary Questions and Definitions   220
   4.2   Plato's Metaphysical Epistemology   221
   4.3   René Descartes's Rational Method of Doubt   236
   4.4   John Locke's Empiricist Theory of Ideas   251
   4.5   David Hume's Radical Skepticism   257

   4.6   Immanuel Kant's Synthesis of Reason and Sensory Experience   270
   4.7   Critiques of Traditional Western Approaches to Epistemology and Metaphysics   285
   4.8   Proofs for the Existence of God   291

Chapter 5: Ethics and Moral Decision Making   312
   5.1   Plato's Character Ethics   322
   5.2   Aristotle's Virtue Ethics   338
   5.3   Jeremy Bentham's Utilitarian Ethics   353
   5.4   Immanuel Kant's Deontological Ethics   365
   5.5   Carol Gilligan's and Nel Noddings's Care Ethics—Two Critiques of Male Moral Bias   379
   5.6   Friedrich Nietzsche's Will to Power   394
   5.7   Religion and Ethics: Islamic, Hindu, and Christian Perspectives   405

Chapter 6: Political Philosophy   428
   6.1   Political Philosophy versus Politics and Political Science   436
   6.2   Plato's *Republic*   439
   6.3   Thomas Hobbes's and John Locke's Social Contract Theories   453
   6.4   Karl Marx's Socialism   474
   6.5   Martin Luther King Jr.'s Philosophy of Nonviolence   492

Answers to Progress Checks   521

Endnotes   527

Index   545

Experiencing Philosophy

SECOND EDITION

Anthony Falikowski
with Susan Mills

broadview press

BROADVIEW PRESS – www.broadviewpress.com
Peterborough, Ontario, Canada

Founded in 1985, Broadview Press remains a wholly independent publishing house. Broadview's focus is on academic publishing; our titles are accessible to university and college students as well as scholars and general readers. With over 800 titles in print, Broadview has become a leading international publisher in the humanities, with world-wide distribution. Broadview is committed to environmentally responsible publishing and fair business practices.

Library and Archives Canada Cataloguing in Publication

Title: Experiencing philosophy / Anthony Falikowski with Susan Mills.
Names: Falikowski, Anthony F., author. | Mills, Susan (Professor), author.
Description: Second edition. | Includes bibliographical references and index.
Identifiers: Canadiana (print) 20220429308 | Canadiana (ebook) 20220429324 |
    ISBN 9781554815258 (softcover) | ISBN 9781770488410 (PDF) | ISBN 9781460407882
    (EPUB)
Subjects: LCSH: Philosophy—Introductions.
Classification: LCC BD21 .F35 2022 | DDC 100—dc23

Broadview Press handles its own distribution in North America:
PO Box 1243, Peterborough, Ontario K9J 7H5, Canada
555 Riverwalk Parkway, Tonawanda, NY 14150, USA
Tel: (705) 743-8990; Fax: (705) 743-8353
email: customerservice@broadviewpress.com

For all territories outside of North America, distribution is handled by Eurospan Group.

Canada Broadview Press acknowledges the financial support of the Government of Canada for our publishing activities.

Edited by Robert M. Martin
Book Design by Em Dash Design

FSC MIX Paper from responsible sources FSC® C016245

PRINTED IN CANADA

Dedicated with gratitude to all my former students who, with curious-mind and open-heart, shared with me their experience of philosophy.

Also dedicated to Pamela, Heather, Michael, and Michelle. All of you have brought me enormous fun, love, and joy in my life. Thank you!

Detailed Table of Contents

Preface   13

Features   17

Acknowledgments   25

CHAPTER 1

What Is Philosophy?   28

Take It Personally   30

Know Thyself: My Preconceptions about Philosophy   32

1.1 What Is a Philosopher?   33
Philosophy and Philosophers: Caricatures, Myths, and Realities   33
The Philosopher's Profile   34
ORIGINAL SOURCE: Sor Juana Inés de la Cruz, *Reply to Sor Filotea*   37
Wisdom: The Object of Love   40

1.2 The Practical Value of Philosophy   41
Philosophy's Relevance in an Age of Technology   43
Therapeutic Applications of Philosophy   44

1.3 Fields of Philosophy   46
Metaphysics   47
Epistemology   48
Logic   48
Ethics   48
Axiology   49
Social/Political Philosophy   50
Foundational and Disciplinary Philosophies   50
Philosophies of Life   50

1.4 Approaches to Philosophy   51
Western Philosophy   51

Historical Approaches   52
Non-Traditional and Non-Western Approaches   52
Feminist Approaches   53
ORIGINAL SOURCE: Lee Hester, "Truth and Native American Epistemology"   54
Spiritually-Based Philosophical Traditions   55
ORIGINAL SOURCE: Abu Hamid al-Ghazali, *Al-Munqidh min al-Dalal* (*Deliverance from Error*)   57
Modern Western Philosophy   60
ORIGINAL SOURCE: Bertrand Russell, "The Value of Philosophy"   62

Progress Check   66

Study Guide   67

CHAPTER 2

Understanding Arguments, Claims, and Fallacies of Reasoning   72

Take It Personally   74

Know Thyself: How Rational Am I?   77

2.1 What Is an Argument?   81
Arguments vs. Opinions and Other Non-Arguments   81
Attitude Adjustments for Argument   84
Benefits of Argument   86
The Socratic Method   86
ORIGINAL SOURCE: Plato, *Euthyphro*, featuring the Socratic Method   88

2.2 Deductive Arguments 98
Modus Ponens 99
Modus Tollens 101
Hypothetical Syllogisms/Chain Arguments 102
Disjunctive Syllogisms 103
Categorical Syllogisms or Syllogisms of Class
Membership 105
Validity, Truth, and Soundness 106

2.3 Non-Deductive Arguments 109
Argument from Past Experience 110
Argument by Analogy 111
Argument by Inductive Generalization 112

2.4 Evaluating Claims 113
Factual Statements 113
Value Judgments 114
Conceptual Claims 116

2.5 Informal Logical Fallacies 118
Ad Hominem Fallacy 118
Straw Person Fallacy 118
Circular Reasoning/Begging the Question
Fallacy 119
Two Wrongs Fallacy 120
Slippery Slope Fallacy 120
Appealing to Authority Fallacy 120
Red Herring Fallacy 121
Guilt by Association Fallacy 122

Progress Check 126

Study Guide 127

CHAPTER 3

Philosophies of Life 132

Take It Personally 134

**Know Thyself: The Philosophy of Life Preference
Indicator 136**

3.1 Stoicism: A Prescription for Peace of Mind 139
Stoicism's Cynical Origins 139
The Stoic Universe 140
How to Live in a Fated Universe 140

Freedom and Value 142
Purpose of Life 142
Emotions in Life 145
How to Progress Morally 146
ORIGINAL SOURCE: Marcus Aurelius, *The
Meditations of Marcus Aurelius* 147

3.2 Existentialism: Born Free, Let Me Be Me 152
Methods 153
Philosophers Associated with Existentialism 153
Existentialism as a Revolt 154
Essence versus Existence 155
Individuality and Subjective Experience 156
Existential Freedom 157
ORIGINAL SOURCE: Jean-Paul Sartre, *Existentialism
Is a Humanism* 159

3.3 The Meaning of Life 161
Meaningful Lives 162
ORIGINAL SOURCE: Susan Wolf, "The Meanings of
Lives" 165
Viktor Frankl and the Will-to-Meaning 168

3.4 Hedonism: Pleasure Is the Measure 169
Psychological versus Ethical Hedonism 169
Aristippus of Cyrene 170
Epicurus 171
Momentary versus Enduring Pleasures 172
Kinetic versus Static Pleasures 173
Ataraxia: The Ultimate End of Life 173
Natural Desires 174
Impediments to *Ataraxia* 175
Virtue in the Pleasant Life 176
The Role of Friendship 177
ORIGINAL SOURCE: Epicurus, "Letter to
Menoeceus" 179

3.5 Buddhism as a Philosophy of Life 181
The Four Noble Truths 183
The Noble Eight-Fold Path 189
ORIGINAL SOURCE: Buddha,
Dhammacakkappavattana Sutta (*Setting in Motion
the Wheel of Truth*) 198

Progress Check 201

Study Guide 203

CHAPTER 4

Epistemology, Metaphysics, and God   212

Take It Personally   214

Know Thyself: My Philosophical Presuppositions about Knowledge and Reality   217

4.1 Preliminary Questions and Definitions   220

4.2 Plato's Metaphysical Epistemology   221
  Divided Line Theory   224
  Theory of Forms   226
  Simile of the Sun   227
  ORIGINAL SOURCE: Plato, Simile of the Sun   228
  Allegory of the Cave   230
  ORIGINAL SOURCE: Plato, Allegory of the Cave   231

4.3 René Descartes's Rational Method of Doubt   236
  Historical Context   236
  The Quest for Certainty   237
  Method of Doubt   239
  ORIGINAL SOURCE: René Descartes, First Meditation   241
  Cogito Ergo Sum—I Think, Therefore I Am   244
  ORIGINAL SOURCE: René Descartes, Second Meditation, featuring the *Cogito*   245
  ORIGINAL SOURCE: René Descartes, Second Meditation, featuring The Wax Example   249

4.4 John Locke's Empiricist Theory of Ideas   251
  Tabula Rasa   253
  Criticisms of Innate Ideas   253
  Primary and Secondary Qualities of Objects   254

4.5 David Hume's Radical Skepticism   257
  On the Origin of Ideas   260
  Rejection of the *Cogito*   260
  Association of Ideas   262
  Critique of Causality   262
  "Hume's Fork" and Types of Reasoning   265
  ORIGINAL SOURCE: David Hume, *An Enquiry Concerning Human Understanding*   267
  David Hume's Origins and Limits of Knowledge: A Summary   270

4.6 Immanuel Kant's Synthesis of Reason and Sensory Experience   270
  The Role of the Senses in Knowledge   271
  The Copernican Revolution in Epistemology   274
  A Priori Elements of Knowledge   275
  Kantian versus Platonic Forms   277
  The Categories of *Cause* and *Substance*   277
  Metaphysics and the Regulative Function of Transcendental Ideas   279
  ORIGINAL SOURCE: Immanuel Kant, *Prolegomena to Any Future Metaphysics*   283

4.7 Critiques of Traditional Western Approaches to Epistemology and Metaphysics   285
  Standpoint Epistemology   285
  ORIGINAL SOURCE: Patricia Hill Collins, *Black Feminist Thought*   287
  Mind-Body Metaphysics   289
  ORIGINAL SOURCE: Yasuo Yuasa, *Toward an Eastern Mind-Body Theory*   290

4.8 Proofs for the Existence of God   291
  St. Anselm's Ontological Proof   293
  St. Thomas Aquinas's "Five Ways": Proofs for the Existence of God   295
  ORIGINAL SOURCE: St. Thomas Aquinas, Whether God Exists   300

Progress Check   302

Study Guide   304

CHAPTER 5

Ethics and Moral Decision Making   312

Take It Personally   314

Know Thyself: The Ethical Perspective Indicator   319

5.1 Plato's Character Ethics   322
  Plato's Teleology   323
  Vision of the Soul   323
  Moral Balance and Plato's Functional Explanation of Morality   324

ORIGINAL SOURCE: Plato, Virtue and Justice in the Individual and in the State   325

Know Thyself: Platonic Character Type Index (PCTI)   329

Plato's Character Types   331

5.2 Aristotle's Virtue Ethics   338

Aristotle's Teleology   338

Happiness (*Eudaimonia*) and the Ends of Human Life   339

Kinds of Lifestyles   342

Virtue and the Virtuous Lifestyle   345

ORIGINAL SOURCE: Aristotle, *Nicomachean Ethics*   350

5.3 Jeremy Bentham's Utilitarian Ethics   353

The Principle of Utility   354

Is-Ought Fallacy   355

The Hedonic Calculus   356

The Theory of Sanctions   360

ORIGINAL SOURCE: Jeremy Bentham, *An Introduction to the Principles of Morals and Legislation*   362

5.4 Immanuel Kant's Deontological Ethics   365

The Rational Basis of Morality   365

Concept of the Good Will   366

Notion of Duty   367

Maxims and Moral Behavior   370

The Categorical Imperative   371

Autonomy versus Heteronomy of the Will   373

ORIGINAL SOURCE: Immanuel Kant, On Pure Moral Philosophy   375

The Impermissibility of Lying: Maria von Herbert's Correspondence with Kant   377

5.5 Carol Gilligan's and Nel Noddings's Care Ethics— Two Critiques of Male Moral Bias   379

Gilligan on Male Bias in Moral Research   379

Gilligan's Ethic of Care   384

Nel Noddings and Care Ethics   386

ORIGINAL SOURCE: Nel Noddings, *Caring: A Feminine Approach to Ethics and Moral Education*   391

5.6 Friedrich Nietzsche's Will to Power   394

God Is Dead   394

Will to Power   395

ORIGINAL SOURCE: Friedrich Wilhelm Nietzsche, *The Gay Science*   398

Master versus Slave Morality   399

Traditional (Herd) Morality and the Revaluation of All Values   401

Evaluating Values   402

The Superman/*Übermensch*   403

5.7 Religion and Ethics: Islamic, Hindu, and Christian Perspectives   405

Islamic Ethics   405

ORIGINAL SOURCE: Riffat Hassan, "Islamic View of Peace"   408

Hindu Ethics   410

ORIGINAL SOURCE: Ashok Kumar Malhotra, *Transcreation of the Bhagavad Gita*   412

Christian Ethics   414

ORIGINAL SOURCE: Brian Berry, Roman Catholic Ethics: Three Approaches   416

Progress Check   420

Study Guide   422

CHAPTER 6

Political Philosophy   428

Take It Personally   430

Know Thyself: My Political Outlook   432

6.1 Political Philosophy versus Politics and Political Science   436

6.2 Plato's *Republic*   439

The Individual and the State   440

Plato's Class System   442

Imperfect Societies   445

Women, Marriage, and Family in the Republic   446

ORIGINAL SOURCE: Plato, The Nature of Woman   448

6.3 Thomas Hobbes's and John Locke's Social Contract Theories   453

Thomas Hobbes   453
ORIGINAL SOURCE: Thomas Hobbes, "Of the Causes, Generation, and Definition of a Commonwealth"   461
John Locke   463
ORIGINAL SOURCE: John Locke, "Of the Ends of Political Society and Government"   472

6.4 Karl Marx's Socialism   474
Marx's Metaphysics and Dialectical Materialism   478
Class Conflict   479
Alienation as a Byproduct of Capitalism   482
Idolatry/Fetishism of Commodities   485
Division of Labor   486
After Capitalism   489
ORIGINAL SOURCE: Karl Marx, *Economic and Philosophic Manuscripts*   490

6.5 Martin Luther King Jr.'s Philosophy of Nonviolence   492
Influences on King   492
Logic of Nonviolence   496

ORIGINAL SOURCE: Martin Luther King Jr.'s "I Have a Dream" Speech   497
ORIGINAL SOURCE: Martin Luther King Jr., *Where Do We Go from Here?*   504

Progress Check   511

Study Guide   513

Answers to Progress Checks   521

A Note on Citations   525

Endnotes   527

Sources   537

Image Sources   541

Index   545

Preface

THIS BOOK BEGINS WITH THE ASSUMPTION that philosophy is not simply something you know or do, but something you *experience*. There is a human side to philosophy that, unfortunately, is too often neglected in traditional approaches to philosophical teaching. Philosophy needn't be seen as something that is completely theoretical and dry or something that is totally impractical and outdated. Rather, the study of philosophy has the potential to transform lives. Acceptance of a metaphysical belief in God, for example, or a philosophical commitment to materialistic atheism, will take individuals down very different roads in life.

In this book, we explore philosophy with frequent references to its personal and practical relevance. The subject is presented in its rich diversity to an audience that demands accessibility. Convoluted, impenetrable language will therefore be regarded as an academic vice, not as a virtue of philosophic expression. And on the subject of language, please note that while this revised work is a collaborative venture, the personal pronoun "I" will sometimes be used when I, Tony, share some of my own thoughts or personal experiences to help clarify or illustrate points made. This practice, carried over from the first edition, is certainly not meant to exclude my new contributing author for the second edition, Susan Mills, and in no way should it discount the fact that she fully collaborated with me on all aspects of this work. Further, while the use of personal pronouns may not be considered by some as consistent with established academic norms, it does have the advantage of serving to humanize what potentially could be a sterile and purely theoretical presentation. It's nice to be reminded on occasion that there is actually a real life person behind the prose.

Experiencing Philosophy is an *applied* text. Though the applied nature of the book does not adequately reveal itself in the Table of Contents, the practical experiential relevance shows up in the "Know Thyself" diagnostics and in the "Take It Personally" chapter introductions. The personal and practical elements of the text also present themselves in the "Thinking about Your Thinking" self-reflections, as well as in the "Philosophers in Action" feature scattered throughout. "Reading Questions," that accompany original writings by important authors in the field, combine with these other book elements to provide multiple occasions for students to actually *do* philosophy and *experience* it in practice for themselves.

While the book often does focus on the personal and experiential, it is important to note that efforts have been made to ensure it is also technically accurate and appropriately detailed. This text is written to be theoretically sound and philosophically sophisticated.

As part of content coverage, actual writings of philosophers are included in a repeating feature throughout the book titled "Original Sources." Any one excerpt is relatively short so as not to discourage beginning students, but, cumulatively, the original writings constitute a significant exposure to some of the major works with which introductory philosophy students should be familiar. For the most part, though, significant topics and important philosophers' writings are paraphrased, summarized, and explained for those students who would find an entire course based exclusively on the classical works inappropriate.

Experiencing Philosophy is written in recognition of the fact that there are levels of difficulty. Most students don't plan to major in philosophy. Furthermore, it's appreciated that beginning students should not be expected to master material often assigned in philosophy graduate courses. To capture the point metaphorically, let us say that before one can run a marathon, one must first learn to walk.

In response to learners' needs, this text contains a substantial pedagogical apparatus designed to encourage and motivate students as well as to maximize their chances of success. No philosophy instructor wants their students' first philosophy course to be their last. Little is accomplished if the syllabus is covered, but nobody cares to learn or remember what was taught. Systematically covering the contents of philosophy, but failing to motivate and inspire students to pursue it further, is like saying, "the operation was a success, but the patient died."

In this book, we'll be focusing on the *philosophical patient* as much as on following the strict operational procedures demanded by the doctors of philosophy. The aim is to make philosophy student-friendly—to give it S.O.U.L.—a *S*tudent *O*rientation for *U*nderstanding and *L*earning. The goal here is to make this text interesting and exciting for students. The hope is to challenge and inspire them. Anyone using this book can expect to do the same.

Chapter 1 begins with a discussion of the nature, purpose, and scope of philosophy, examining a number of myths and misconceptions about it. This is done while at the same time exploring its personal and therapeutic value. In this section, we make efforts to motivate students in their studies by pointing out that philosophy can help to clarify values and assist them in making important life decisions. We observe that people can find greater direction through an examination of perennial wisdom; so too can they achieve an enhanced sense of personal well-being. In this regard, it's claimed that philosophy may in fact turn out to be the most important and practical subject the student will ever study—truly a startling claim for many. As part of the introduction to philosophy, we also cover the major sub-disciplines and discuss the various approaches to philosophy that have been taken in the past.

In Chapter 2, there's coverage of reasoning and logic and its place in philosophical thinking. So many introductory textbooks make the point that philosophy is more of a method of thinking than a body of knowledge and then, surprisingly, neglect to deal with the method or forget to give students a chance to practice it. In this book, students are indeed encouraged to *do* philosophy, especially when completing reasoning exercises and evaluative critiques. Focusing as well on the human side of philosophy, the necessity of making certain *attitude adjustments* is underscored if people are to do philosophy properly. In efforts to engage students, the benefits of philosophical argument are discussed, as well as how arguing is different from opinionating.

In this chapter, we also look at inductive and deductive logic, learning the differences among concepts like *validity*, *truth*, *soundness*, and *argumentative strength*. We examine a number of informal logical fallacies that make use of emotional and psychological appeals. Students are given opportunities here to practice their logical reasoning skills necessary for further philosophical analysis and rational debate.

Chapter 3 is titled "Philosophies of Life." In order to engage students with the practical *existential relevance* of philosophy, they are invited to reconsider their own personal philosophies in light of some others that have been developed throughout the ages. We learn in this section how differing philosophical ideas and worldviews are captured by Hedonism, Stoicism, Existentialism, and Buddhism—four starkly contrasting visions of reality. We also see how life takes on different value priorities, depending on which philosophical worldview is adopted. Students are encouraged to reflect on their own values, goals, and perceptions of the world. An awareness is generated of how people's unconscious philosophical assumptions can have real life consequences.

In this chapter, a consideration of 'meaning' is also provided, giving students an opportunity to think about the meaning of life and how they might find it. The work of Viktor Frankl and Susan Wolf are covered in this regard. The notion that meaning is found in work, love, suffering, or in things having objective value beyond oneself is discussed. Wolf argues that even if there is no ultimate *meaning of life*, there still can be *meaning in life*.

Once students understand what philosophy is all about, once they can begin to think as philosophers using cogent arguments and sound reasoning, and having engaged in a preliminary examination of their own personal philosophies, we move ahead in Chapter 4 to explore epistemology and metaphysics, including a section on God.

Coverage of Plato, René Descartes, John Locke, David Hume, and Immanuel Kant reveals how claims regarding the nature of knowledge (epistemology) are often based on beliefs and assumptions about reality and the physical universe (metaphysics). Conversely, one's views on reality can also impact how one sees or conceptualizes the nature of knowledge. Chapter 4 concludes with a presentation of rational proofs for the existence of God, one that can help students on a personal level, especially if they are grappling with religious questions at this time in their lives.

In Chapter 5, we proceed to the study of ethics and moral philosophy. Perspectives to be covered include Character Ethics, Virtue Ethics, Utilitarian Ethics, Deontological Ethics, Care Ethics, and what can be seen as a kind of precursor to Existentialist Ethics, namely Friedrich Nietzsche's conception of morality explained in terms of the will to power. This coverage will expose students to ancient and modern thinkers, to male and female theorists, and to rational and non-rational approaches. We will also introduce students to the relationship between religion and ethics, enhancing the inclusive nature of this text by juxtaposing secular and religious viewpoints. Upon successful completion of this chapter, students will be able to make better-informed, intelligent, and rationally justifiable moral decisions—certainly an important practical life skill.

Chapter 6, the final one, takes us into the territory of political philosophy. Plato's utopian *Republic* is discussed, as are the social contract theorists Thomas Hobbes and John Locke, the latter of whom had a particularly significant impact on the philosophical foundations of Western liberal democracy. In addition, a perspective critical of this democracy, namely Marxism, is also covered. Karl Marx works very effectively as an *intellectual alarm clock*, as it were, waking us from what some might term our *dogmatic capitalist slumbers*.

As a follow-up to Marx, a treatment of Martin Luther King's action-oriented philosophy of nonviolence is presented. King adopts a number of Marxist insights and incorporates them into his version of a revised capitalism, one that seeks to eradicate structural inequalities, especially those faced by racialized or otherwise marginalized communities.

Coverage of Chapter 6 should enable students to better appreciate alternative political systems. It should also help to inject a dose of calm, rational objectivity when discussing political issues and ideologies. Successful efforts in this regard will have the effect of liberating students from political bias and ethnocentric dogmatism and thereby enable them to function better as rational patriots and citizens of the world.

Features

Pedagogical Elements

Take It Personally

"The hottest places in hell are reserved for those who, in times of great moral crisis, maintain their neutrality."
ANONYMOUS*

* Widely attributed to Dante Alighieri, but found nowhere in his writing.

Of all the sub-disciplines of philosophy outlined in Chapter 1, the study of ethics is perhaps the most strikingly relevant and practical, especially given that so much of our life is awash in morality. For example, after the death of George Floyd on May 25, 2020,* some called for blood vengeance, others for reform, and still others for calm adherence to the rule of law. There were those who wanted immediate criminal prosecution, while many advocated complete defunding of police departments. When events like these occur, people are stunned into a new ethical awareness, frequently characterized by confusion and moral self-doubt. Questions are asked: "What *should* we do?" "What is the *right* response?"

Not only in such extreme cases as George Floyd's death, but also with respect to world events in general, a moral response is demanded from all of us. In plain view of poverty, hunger, global injustice or the inequitable treatment of minorities, for example, we may choose as moral agents to accept responsibility and take action. Quite possibly, however, we may do nothing by ignoring the problem, defensively rationalizing our noninvolvement, or blaming the victims who suffer. One should note, though, that even choosing not to respond is itself a moral response needing justification.

When it comes to the mistreatment and abuse suffered by racialized minorities, for instance, many concerned citizens have protested, yelling, "Silence is violence!" Doing nothing or standing on the sidelines while injustices are being perpetrated is tantamount to collusion or at least tacit approval, in the estimation of many people. So, even if neutrality is an ethical position that has consequences and requires justification, it would appear that there is, in fact, no escaping moral responsibility. What is more, an examined life—a life *worth living*—cannot be lived in a moral vacuum.

Given this, let's apply here in this context a metaphor used in Chapter 2: Recall the notion that we can either stay afloat in our *philosophical lifeboats*, by making ongoing repairs to our damaged and leaking *moral planks*, or we can break apart and capsize in a whirlpool of moral confusion and indecision. If we don't wish to be uncontrollably pushed this way and that by the turbulent waters of life, and if we wish to steer properly and maintain the integrity of our existential vessels with any success, morality is not something that should be left unattended. Our own safe travels on life's journey depend upon our having a working moral compass. We all need to know when to make proper directional adjustments in and during the course of our lives.

In view of the fact that morality is unavoidable and so important, the question arises as to why so many people still try to sidestep it. Part of the reason, perhaps, is because of morality's serious, difficult, and sometimes overwhelming nature. Morality often deals with the *big issues* of life, things like war, capital punishment, and euthanasia—favorite topics covered in many applied ethics textbooks.

Because most of us are not in the military, on death row, or dying from a terminal illness, however, these enormously important moral issues and others like them can sometimes appear like distant hypothetical concerns, things we needn't worry about while commuting to school in rush hour traffic or stocking the shelves at work. Nevertheless,

* George Floyd was an African American who was killed by a police officer in Minneapolis. The officer, Derek Chauvin, knelt on Floyd's neck for over nine minutes while Floyd was lying face down and handcuffed. Chauvin was sentenced to 22.5 years in prison.

Take It Personally

To illustrate how philosophy can be useful and relevant to individuals, each chapter of *Experiencing Philosophy* begins by placing the material to be covered in a personal context. Students are shown how philosophical questions and concerns are often built into their daily life experiences. Grounding philosophical inquiry in the context of real life serves to motivate students and thereby helps instructors to teach more effectively.

Quotations

Inspirational and thought-provoking quotations are sprinkled throughout the text as a way of generating interest and providing opportunities for personal reflection and meditation. They may be taken to heart by some readers or possibly remembered for purposes of finding personal meaning and direction in life. At other times, the quotations may simply be useful to capture the essence of points that are made in a much more detailed way in the main text. These philosophical zingers should give us all pause for thought.

Know Thyself Diagnostics

This book takes seriously, as did Socrates, the Delphic Oracle's dictum to *Know thyself*. To this end, students are provided self-diagnostics in each of the chapters to explore further their own philosophical values, ideals, and beliefs pertaining to truth, reality, ethics, the existence of God, the nature of knowledge, metaphysics, and the best system of political organization. By means of these diagnostics, students are given a chance to identify their underlying personal philosophies of life and to compare them with other worldviews that have been articulated over the centuries. Students are also able to assess their current logical thinking abilities so that they can establish how much work they will need to do in order to think more rationally.

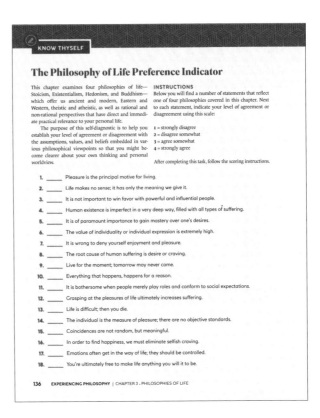

The Philosophy of Life Preference Indicator page (page 136):

KNOW THYSELF

The Philosophy of Life Preference Indicator

This chapter examines four philosophies of life—Stoicism, Existentialism, Hedonism, and Buddhism—which offer us ancient and modern, Eastern and Western, theistic and atheistic, as well as rational and non-rational perspectives that have direct and immediate practical relevance to your personal life.

The purpose of this self-diagnostic is to help you establish your level of agreement or disagreement with the assumptions, values, and beliefs embedded in various philosophical viewpoints so that you might become clearer about your own thinking and personal worldview.

INSTRUCTIONS

Below you will find a number of statements that reflect one of four philosophies covered in this chapter. Next to each statement, indicate your level of agreement or disagreement using this scale:

1 = strongly disagree
2 = disagree somewhat
3 = agree somewhat
4 = strongly agree

After completing this task, follow the scoring instructions.

1. _____ Pleasure is the principal motive for living.
2. _____ Life makes no sense; it has only the meaning we give it.
3. _____ It is not important to win favor with powerful and influential people.
4. _____ Human existence is imperfect in a very deep way, filled with all types of suffering.
5. _____ It is of paramount importance to gain mastery over one's desires.
6. _____ The value of individuality or individual expression is extremely high.
7. _____ It is wrong to deny yourself enjoyment and pleasure.
8. _____ The root cause of human suffering is desire or craving.
9. _____ Live for the moment; tomorrow may never come.
10. _____ Everything that happens, happens for a reason.
11. _____ It is bothersome when people merely play roles and conform to social expectations.
12. _____ Grasping at the pleasures of life ultimately increases suffering.
13. _____ Life is difficult; then you die.
14. _____ The individual is the measure of pleasure; there are no objective standards.
15. _____ Coincidences are not random, but meaningful.
16. _____ In order to find happiness, we must eliminate selfish craving.
17. _____ Emotions often get in the way of life; they should be controlled.
18. _____ You're ultimately free to make life anything you will it to be.

Philosopher Profile page (page 182):

PHILOSOPHER PROFILE

Siddhartha Gautama, the Buddha

The person we have come to know as the Buddha was born circa 563 BCE as Siddhartha Gautama, the only son of a ruling king in what is now Nepal. The details of Siddhartha's life are sketchy since no complete biography of the Buddha was compiled until centuries after his death. Much of the information we have comes from tradition and myth, and it's difficult, therefore, to distinguish between fact and legend. What we do know is that his people were called the Sakyas; for this reason, the Buddha is sometimes referred to as *Sakyamuni*, or "the sage of the Sakyas." "Buddha" is not a personal name but an honorific title meaning *the awakened one*. Siddhartha Gautama (his clan name) did not actually become the Buddha until his mid-thirties, when he achieved enlightenment.

As the son of a royal ruler, the young Siddhartha led a life of luxury and pleasure. Legend has it that soon after his birth, a wise sage came to visit and noticed that there were 32 special markings on Siddhartha's tiny body. For the sage, this was a sign that Siddhartha was destined for glory. He would either become a universal monarch or great religious teacher.

Siddhartha's father, Suddhodana, was not entirely thrilled by this. The king wanted his son to succeed him, since if the prince abandoned his position in the royal palace, Suddhodana would be without an heir. Believing that the ugly, unpleasant, and painful things of life would turn Siddhartha's mind toward religion, Suddhodana decided he should raise his son in a completely protected environment of comfort, beauty, and pleasure.

Three splendid marble palaces were built—one for each of the hot, cool, and rainy seasons. Siddhartha was confined to the upper stories of these palaces and provided with every kind of pleasure and luxury to prevent boredom from setting in. He lazed around the palace in fine silks, ate the most delicious foods, and enjoyed armies of musicians, dancing girls, and the most sensuous courtesans who were on hand to amuse and entertain him. Shielded from him were illness and old age. Presumably, if Buddha never experienced the pains and miseries of life, he would never be drawn to religion and could therefore fulfill his father's wishes. At age 16, Siddhartha married his cousin Yasodhara, who bore him a son (Rahula) when he was 29.

Before the birth of his son, Siddhartha had already fallen prey to restless boredom, notwithstanding all of the efforts of his father. Ironically perhaps, unproductive self-indulgence simply could not make life satisfying for him. With his hired guardian, friend, and charioteer, Channa, Siddhartha made secret trips outside the palace walls. Channa became a tour guide of sorts, answering many of Siddhartha's questions about the harsh realities of life beyond his protected environment. It was during these secret trips that Siddhartha saw "the four signs" that would change his life forever.

On the first trip, Siddhartha encountered an old man; on the second trip, a sick man; and on the third trip, a corpse being carried away for cremation. Because Siddhartha had lived such a cloistered life for almost 30 years, these three encounters were quite traumatic for him. He had no concept of the true human condition: that all human beings are susceptible to sickness, old age, and death—including Siddhartha himself. Disturbed by this, he wondered how anyone could find happiness since, in the end, there is no escape from suffering and loss, with all of the associated sadness and disappointment. After witnessing the first three signs, all the pleasures and delights of palace life quickly lost their charm: Siddhartha had lost his innocence.

On a fourth trip outside the palace walls, Siddhartha and Channa came upon a wandering holy man. Alone, dressed in rags and possessing nothing, this ascetic monk displayed a demeanor that thoroughly impressed

Philosopher Profiles

The student-centeredness of *Experiencing Philosophy* is evidenced again by putting names and faces to the ideas covered in the book. Pictures of influential and historically important philosophers are presented along with biographical information. Abstract ideas contained within the book are tied to real people with interesting real-life personal histories. This helps to bring the textbook material alive.

PHILOSOPHERS IN ACTION

Does Buddhism make sense to you as a practical philosophy of life? How so, or why not? What, if anything, about Buddhism do you like most? What, if any, Buddhist notion is most challenging or most difficult for you to accept?

After thinking about this, imagine a conversation between Siddhartha Gautama and the Hedonist Aristippus. What would they say to each other? Would they agree with each other's philosophy? Explain and elaborate, creating a kind of dialogue or debate that might transpire between them. You might even wish to stage a theatrical scene for the benefit of the class!

you. Perhaps a sudden outburst of anger soured your relationship with somebody for days, weeks, or possibly even years. Maybe a brilliant political career was ruined by a momentary moral lapse. Whatever the case, karma does not involve a punishing judge heaping on retribution; it's about the individual creating the consequences of his or her own future. Buddha teaches that

If a person speaks or acts with unwholesome mind, pain pursues him, even as the wheel follows the hoof of the ox that draws the cart. (*The Dhammapada*)

Another way of explaining karma is to say, "What goes around comes around." In this respect, *giving is indeed receiving*. Give unwholesomeness, and you get it back in return. Give wholesomeness, and you receive it in kind.

The notion of karma extends beyond current existence to past lives and future ones. For instance, your own karma has determined such matters as the species into which you were born (human), your beauty, intelligence, longevity, wealth, and social status. What you do in this life will, in turn, affect the karma of your next life. If you have been born with "bad karma," not to worry. There is a modifiability of the karma you've inherited. Furthermore, if you have already engaged in some unwholesome activities to this point in your life, it is not necessarily true that bad karma will result. It can be mitigated. On the subject of the modifiability of karma, the Buddhist monk Nyanaponika Thera writes:

A particular karma, either good or bad, may sometimes have its result strengthened by supportive karma, weakened by counter-active karma, or even annulled by destructive karma.⁴⁹

For Nyanaponika Thera, a bad action, or any karmic actions for that matter, must be viewed from the total qualitative structure of the mind from which the action issues:

It is an individual's accumulation of good or evil karma and also his dominating character traits, good or evil, which affect the karmic result. They determine the greater or lesser weight of the result and may even spell the difference between whether or not it occurs at all.⁵⁰

Appreciating that karmic results are modifiable frees us from the bane of determinism. It teaches moral and spiritual responsibility for oneself and others. It helps us to recognize that karmic action affects the doer of the deed. Even if bad words and deeds,

196   EXPERIENCING PHILOSOPHY | CHAPTER 3 · PHILOSOPHIES OF LIFE

Philosophers in Action

Philosophy is often described as more of a method of thinking than as a body of knowledge. From this perspective, philosophy is something you *do*, not simply something you know. With this in mind, students are given many opportunities to practice doing philosophy. Students using this text are frequently asked to think critically and analytically in response to questions posed in the *Philosophers in Action* feature. These questions require them to conduct thought experiments, analyze concepts, as well as to discuss and debate controversial points.

Thinking about Your Thinking

Thinking about Your Thinking is an exciting new feature inserted into this second edition of the book. Metacognitive prompts require students to engage in higher-order thinking, not only about presented readings and ideas, but also with respect to their own values, assumptions, and beliefs. This type of *self-conscious thinking* or way of *thinking with self-awareness* reinforces learning about philosophy. It also helps students to develop a general understanding about themselves as learners and as rational agents in the world.

When students begin to think more about the content and structure of their own thinking, they are able to think more creatively, analytically, and objectively. Also, when they can bring to conscious awareness what was previously and unreflectively accepted or assumed, distortions due to psychological defensiveness can be reduced; at the same time, more objective attitudes can be cultivated. The ultimate result is a more expansive, nuanced, and open-minded view of the world, not to mention a richer experience of life.

THINKING ABOUT YOUR THINKING

Make a list of 5-10 of your current desires that you've not yet satisfied, and 5-10 of your past desires that you've already satisfied at some earlier time. Why do you desire what you desire now? What, if anything, stands in the way of you satisfying your desires? Turning now to desires that you have successfully satisfied in the past, was the satisfaction of some of your desires more pleasing than the satisfaction of others? If so, why do you think that was?

According to Epicurus, the natural child, in its untutored state, would not desire logic and math as something pleasurably good. The Epicurean does not, therefore, glorify the contemplative life or the life of reason, as Plato and Aristotle did, for example. Mental pleasures are not any better or higher than bodily pleasures. Both are natural.

Natural Desires

On this note, Epicurus instructs us to follow our **natural desires**. As Julia Annas, a scholarly expert on Epicurus, puts it in her excellent book about Stoicism and Epicureanism, *The Morality of Happiness*, "Natural desires ... do not produce mental rather than bodily pleasures; rather, the natural/not natural distinction cuts right across that of mental and bodily. Natural desires are those we cannot help having, so that in fulfilling them we are following, rather than forcing, our nature."⁵¹ Thus, bodily desires for food and drink are, for Epicurus, as natural as the mental desire for tranquility of the soul (what some of us today would call peace of mind).

If we are to fulfill our natural desires, it is important that we not rely on **empty beliefs**, that is, on those that are false and harmful. Vain or unnatural desires based on empty beliefs do not come from nature but rather are products of teaching and acculturation. Their falsity results from the incorrect evaluative beliefs that ground them. Empty beliefs have a tendency to be vain and self-defeating, since they typically reach out for boundless objects that can provide no stability or long-term satisfaction. Natural desires, by contrast, can be well-satisfied because they do have limits.

By trying to satisfy artificial and limitless desires, we end up sabotaging our own *ataraxia*. Suppose, for instance, you are hungry. Simple bread could ease your hunger pangs. But if you believe that, given your station in life, you truly deserve beluga caviar, then if the caviar is unavailable, you will still remain troubled in your soul with frustration, even though you quiet your body's craving with bread. You will believe that you didn't get what you deserve and be upset by this belief. Needing food is natural; craving caviar is not. Though eating caviar may be pleasurable (if you like that sort of thing), not every pleasure is worthy of being pursued or troubled about if it's not available. Believing you deserve caviar and developing a desire for it are things you have been taught or introduced to, not things natural or necessary to the human organism. If we don't rid ourselves of empty beliefs like the one about caviar, we may end up satisfying our basic physical needs, but in ways that perpetuate our mental disturbances.

In his "Letter to Menoeceus," Epicurus classified the various kinds of human desires. Some are **vain desires**, meaning that they are not rooted in nature. Becoming famous or owning jewels are things you may desire, but they do not come with being born human. Such vain desires are conditioned by false beliefs of what is required to make one happy.

Natural desires, by contrast, may be either necessary or unnecessary. The desire for sex is natural, yet many people live a celibate life without much, if any, frustration. Desiring delicious foods is also natural but unnecessary, for we could easily live on a bland diet. Those desires that are both natural and necessary are required for comfort, happiness, and life itself. Epicurus believed that practical wisdom and friendship contrib-

174   EXPERIENCING PHILOSOPHY | CHAPTER 3 · PHILOSOPHIES OF LIFE

Original Sources

Experiencing Philosophy seeks to balance accessibility and relevance with academic rigor. While introducing some beginning students to philosophy entirely by means of original writings might be regarded as inappropriate for a variety of reasons, doing so without any exposure at all to the primary works of the philosophers could be seen as equally misguided. To say that one has completed an introductory course in philosophy, but has not read any philosophy in the original, seems wrong somehow.

In efforts to strike an appropriate balance for beginning students, the bulk of this text will be comprised of descriptive outlines of philosophers and their theories. In addition, however, numerous *Original Source* reading selections—usually shorter excerpts from longer original texts—will be included as well to give readers exposure to the *real thing*, so to speak. Follow-up reading questions accompany the works included.

Reading Questions and Metacognition: While some reading questions aim to promote analysis and further comprehension, other questions are formulated as metacognitive prompts. These prompts draw students' awareness to the activity of reading itself, in order to develop their philosophical literacy in particular, and their skills for reading independently more generally. Together, both types of questions afford students the opportunity to engage in more self-reflection, to enhance their reading and learning strategies, to *do* more philosophy, and to practice their logical, critical-analytical thinking skills in a more directed, rigorous fashion.

Other Features

Various summary tables, figures, and highlighted features are presented throughout the text as a way of illustrating or underscoring important points. These items add relevance by relating philosophical theory to real-world applications, experiences, and current events.

ORIGINAL SOURCE

Jean-Paul Sartre, *Existentialism Is a Humanism*[12]

Sartre originally delivered Existentialism Is a Humanism *as a public lecture at Club Maintenant in Paris in 1945. The following year, Simone de Beauvoir edited the lecture for publication.*[13]

PART I

What, then, is "existentialism"?

Most people who use this word would be at a loss to explain what it means. For now that it has become fashionable, people like to call this musician or that painter an "existentialist." A columnist in *Clartés* goes by the pen name "The Existentialist." Indeed, the word is being so loosely applied to so many things that it has come to mean nothing at all. It would appear that, for lack of an avant-garde doctrine analogous to surrealism, those who thrive on the latest scandal or fad have seized upon a philosophy that hardly suits their purpose. The truth is that of all doctrines, this is the least scandalous and the most austere: it is strictly intended for specialists and philosophers. Yet it can be easily defined. What complicates the matter is that there are two kinds of existentialists: on one hand, the Christians, among whom I would include Karl Jaspers and Gabriel Marcel, both professed Catholics; and, on the other, the atheistic existentialists, among whom we should place Heidegger, as well as the French existentialists and myself. What they have in common is simply their belief that existence precedes essence; or, if you prefer, that subjectivity must be our point of departure. What exactly do we mean by that? If we consider a manufactured object, such as a book or a paper knife,* we note that this object was produced by a craftsman who drew his inspiration from a concept: he referred both to the concept of what a paper knife is, and to a known production technique that is a part of that concept and is, by and large, a formula. The paper knife is thus both an object produced in a certain way and one that, on the other hand, serves a definite purpose. We cannot suppose that a man would produce a paper knife without knowing what purpose it would serve. Let us say, therefore, that the essence of the paper knife—that is, the sum of formulae and properties that enable it to be produced and defined—precedes its existence. Thus the presence before my eyes of that paper knife or book is determined. Here, then, we are viewing the world from a technical standpoint, whereby we can say "production precedes essence."

When we think of God the Creator, we usually conceive of him as a superlative artisan. Whatever doctrine we may be considering, say Descartes's or Leibniz's, we always agree that the will more or less follows understanding, or at the very least accompanies it, so that when God creates he knows exactly what he is creating. Thus the concept of man, in the mind of God, is comparable to the concept of the paper knife in the mind of the manufacturer: God produces man following certain techniques and a conception, just as the craftsman, following a definition and a technique, produces a paper knife. Thus each individual man is the realization of a certain concept within the divine intelligence. Eighteenth-century atheistic philosophers suppressed the idea of God, but not, for all that, the idea that essence precedes existence. We encounter this idea nearly everywhere: in the works of Diderot, Voltaire, and even Kant. Man possesses a human nature; this "human nature," which is the concept of that which is human, is found in all men, which means that each man is a particular example of a universal concept—man. In Kant's works, this universality extends so far as to encompass forest dwellers—man in a state of nature—and the bourgeois,† meaning that they all possess the same basic qualities. Here again, the essence of man precedes his historically primitive existence in nature.

Atheistic existentialism, which I represent, is more consistent. It states that if God does not exist, there is at least one being in whom existence precedes essence—a being whose existence comes before its essence, a being who exists before he can be defined by any concept of

---

* A knife designed for cutting the pages of a book, necessary then for reading French publications.

† The contemporary conformist middle-class member.

3.2 EXISTENTIALISM: BORN FREE, LET ME BE ME   159

Stoicism and Stress Management

The psychologically healing powers of Stoic wisdom have managed to trickle down into contemporary society through psychotherapeutic practices of stress management. **Albert Ellis**, the internationally recognized developer of Rational-Emotive Behavior Therapy, has found through research and clinical practice that people feel largely the way they do because of how they think. Ellis says, "What we label our emotional reactions are mainly caused by our conscious and unconscious evaluations, interpretations and philosophies."[5] When we feel anxious, worried, or stressed, it is frequently due to the irrational assumptions we make and the foolish beliefs to which we cling.

Consistent with Stoic thinking, Ellis argues that things and events, in themselves, don't *make us unhappy*; rather, our *interpretations* of them do. Therefore, if we could identify our irrational assumptions and beliefs and then abandon them, we would then begin to live a more rational lifestyle, one with significantly less stress and less negative emotion. By clinging to irrationality, we become architects of our own emotional disturbance and "dis-ease."

To illustrate how this is so, Ellis has conceptualized an A–B–C Model of psychological functioning which he incorporated into his therapeutic methods (Figure 3.2). The *A* represents the activating event—the real-life occurrence that is potentially stressful, although not necessarily so. The activating event could be a failure, loss, hurt, or anything else that could produce stress in your life. Intuitively, some of us think that such events automatically cause a stress response. However, the emotional consequence C—of failure, loss, or hurt—is not necessarily determined by such things. Coming between the activating event (A) and the ultimate emotional response or consequence (C) is the belief (B) about what just happened (A). The cognitive interpretation and appraisal of the activating event will ultimately determine the emotional response. Besides serving as an explanatory illustration for Ellis, Figure 3.2 also serves to underscore the stoic insight of Epictetus that *Men are not disturbed by things, but by the view that they take of them.*

FIGURE 3.2 Albert Ellis's "A–B–C" model

Emotions in Life

Given the lengthy history of Stoicism and its many variations from different periods and geographic locations (Athens and Rome), academic interpretations regarding the Stoic position on **emotion** are not entirely consistent. Some analysts claim the Stoics rejected all emotions to the extent it was humanly possible; others contend that such a claim is only a half-truth, asserting that what the Stoics wished to abolish were the "excessive passions" that led to mental disturbance.[6]

The discrepancy seems to come from the fact that interpreters cite different sources in their translations from the Greek that either distinguish, or fail to distinguish, between the notions of *emotion* and *passion*. Where emotion is totally dismissed, the distinction between emotion and passion appears not to be made; where some expressions of emotion are permitted, the difference is recognized.

"Things themselves touch not the soul, not in the least degree."
MARCUS AURELIUS

3.1 STOICISM: A PRESCRIPTION FOR PEACE OF MIND   145

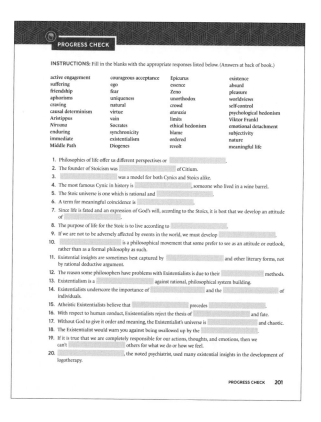

PROGRESS CHECK

INSTRUCTIONS: Fill in the blanks with the appropriate responses listed below. (Answers at back of book.)

active engagement	courageous acceptance	Epicurus	existence
suffering	ego	essence	absurd
friendship	fear	Zeno	pleasure
aphorisms	uniqueness	unorthodox	worldviews
craving	natural	crowd	self-control
causal determinism	virtue	*ataraxia*	psychological hedonism
Aristippus	vain	limits	Viktor Frankl
Nirvana	Socrates	ethical hedonism	emotional detachment
enduring	synchronicity	blame	subjectivity
immediate	existentialism	ordered	nature
Middle Path	Diogenes	revolt	meaningful life

1. Philosophies of life offer us different perspectives or ⬚⬚⬚.
2. The founder of Stoicism was ⬚⬚⬚ of Citium.
3. ⬚⬚⬚ was a model for both Cynics and Stoics alike.
4. The most famous Cynic in history is ⬚⬚⬚, someone who lived in a wine barrel.
5. The Stoic universe is one which is rational and ⬚⬚⬚.
6. A term for meaningful coincidence is ⬚⬚⬚.
7. Since life is fated and an expression of God's will, according to the Stoics, it is best that we develop an attitude of ⬚⬚⬚.
8. The purpose of life for the Stoic is to live according to ⬚⬚⬚.
9. If we are not to be adversely affected by events in the world, we must develop ⬚⬚⬚.
10. ⬚⬚⬚ is a philosophical movement that some prefer to see as an attitude or outlook, rather than as a formal philosophy as such.
11. Existential insights are sometimes best captured by ⬚⬚⬚ and other literary forms, not by rational deductive argument.
12. The reason some philosophers have problems with Existentialism is due to their ⬚⬚⬚ methods.
13. Existentialism is a ⬚⬚⬚ against rational, philosophical system building.
14. Existentialists underscore the importance of ⬚⬚⬚ and the ⬚⬚⬚ of individuals.
15. Atheistic Existentialists believe that ⬚⬚⬚ precedes ⬚⬚⬚.
16. With respect to human conduct, Existentialists reject the thesis of ⬚⬚⬚ and fate.
17. Without God to give it order and meaning, the Existentialist's universe is ⬚⬚⬚ and chaotic.
18. The Existentialist would warn you against being swallowed up by the ⬚⬚⬚.
19. If it is true that we are completely responsible for our actions, thoughts, and emotions, then we can't ⬚⬚⬚ others for what we do or how we feel.
20. ⬚⬚⬚, the noted psychiatrist, used many existential insights in the development of logotherapy.

Progress Checks

Completion of the *Progress Check* at the end of each chapter can help to verify one's mastery of the material. Answers to the Progress Checks are found in the *Answers to Progress Checks* at the back of the book.

Summary of Major Points

1. What is the historical background of Stoicism?
- flourished in ancient Rome and Greece for about five centuries (third century BCE–second century CE)
- founded by Zeno; co-founded by Chrysippus
- well-known Stoics: Epictetus, Marcus Aurelius, Seneca
- influenced by Socrates and the Cynics

2. What is the Stoic universe like?
- ordered, rational, structured, and shaped by design
- synchronistic, fated
- monistic (God is immanent in all things)

3. How should we live in a fated universe?
- Be reassured; God orders things for the best.
- See beyond evils and misfortunes; in a larger context, they make sense.
- Appreciate your freedom to choose your attitudes and make your judgments.
- Develop an attitude of courageous acceptance.
- Live according to nature.
- Try to develop Stoic apathy to live in *eudaimonia*.
- Look upon the world with emotional detachment to develop peace of mind.
- Abolish excessive passions.

4. How do we progress morally?
- Know thyself.
- Engage in daily self-examinations.
- Monitor your thoughts, feelings, and actions.
- Substitute good habits for bad ones.
- Avoid temptations and wayward companions.
- Become master in your own psychological home.
- Eliminate disturbing passions and excessive emotions.
- Forgive others.
- Live up to some ideal of virtue (e.g., Socrates, Jesus, Buddha).
- Perform your duties in accordance with right reason.

5. Why is Existentialism difficult to define?
- It is something like an attitude or outlook; not a formal system
- It comprises several different perspectives (atheist, theist, apolitical, Marxist)
- It uses unorthodox methods (literary and artistic)

6. Who are the major figures associated with Existentialism?
- Friedrich Nietzsche
- Karl Jaspers
- Gabriel Marcel
- Jean-Paul Sartre
- Simone de Beauvoir
- Martin Heidegger
- Albert Camus
- Fyodor Dostoyevsky
- Franz Kafka

7. How is Existentialism a revolt?
- It is a reaction against pure rationality and philosophical system-building.
- It emphasizes subjective experience.
- It uses literary forms and other unorthodox methods.

8. What are some central themes of Existentialism?
- essence versus existence
- freedom of choice
- individuality and subjective experience
- possibility and contingency
- authenticity
- negation
- personal responsibility

9. What constitutes a meaningful life according to Susan Wolf?
- It is a life that is actively and at least somewhat successfully engaged in one or more projects of positive objective value, as opposed to projects of subjective value.

Study Guides

Experiencing Philosophy is designed to maximize student chances for success. Before students can properly analyze, discuss, and debate subtle and sometimes esoteric philosophical material, they must first master basic vocabulary and be able to grasp fundamental concepts. The study guide built into the end of each chapter is designed to help them do this. It contains a glossary of key terms and summaries of major points.

By enabling students to gain basic knowledge and understanding of the fundamental ideas contained within any one chapter, the book helps them to be better prepared to do philosophy when it comes to conceptual analysis, theoretical application, or critical evaluation. Note that the chapter end study guides themselves are part of a larger system of SQ3R learning incorporated into the text and described in what follows.

The SQ3R System of Learning

This book incorporates the *SQ3R system of learning*. Its elements are listed and described below. SQ3R is the acronym for *survey, question, read, recite, and review*.

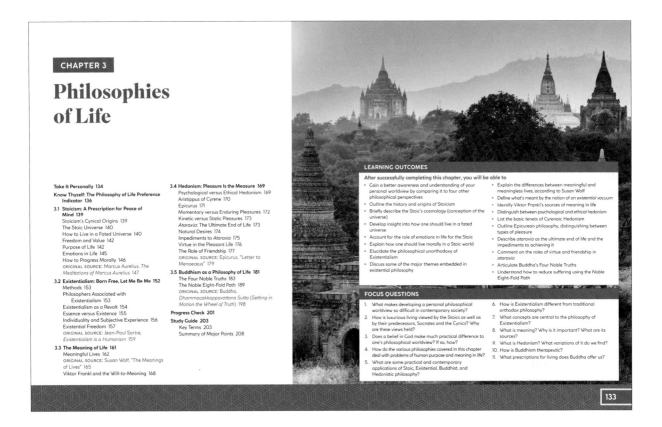

CHAPTER 3

Philosophies of Life

Take It Personally 134
Know Thyself: The Philosophy of Life Preference Indicator 136
3.1 Stoicism: A Prescription for Peace of Mind 139
  Stoicism's Cynical Origins 139
  The Stoic Universe 140
  How to Live in a Fated Universe 140
  Freedom and Value 141
  Purpose of Life 142
  Emotions in Life 145
  How to Progress Morally 146
  ORIGINAL SOURCE: Marcus Aurelius, *The Meditations of Marcus Aurelius* 147
3.2 Existentialism: Born Free, Let Me Be Me 152
  Methods 153
  Philosophers Associated with Existentialism 153
  Existentialism as a Revolt 154
  Essence versus Existence 155
  Individuality and Subjective Experience 157
  Existential Freedom 157
  ORIGINAL SOURCE: Jean-Paul Sartre, *Existentialism Is a Humanism* 159
3.3 The Meaning of Life 161
  Meaningful Lives 162
  ORIGINAL SOURCE: Susan Wolf, "The Meanings of Lives" 165
  Viktor Frankl and the Will-to-Meaning 168

3.4 Hedonism: Pleasure Is the Measure 169
  Psychological versus Ethical Hedonism 169
  Aristippus of Cyrene 170
  Epicurus 171
  Momentary versus Enduring Pleasures 172
  Kinetic versus Static Pleasures 173
  Ataraxia: The Ultimate End of Life 173
  Natural Desires 174
  Impediments to *Ataraxia* 175
  Virtue in the Pleasant Life 176
  The Role of Friendship 177
  ORIGINAL SOURCE: Epicurus, "Letter to Menoeceus" 179
3.5 Buddhism as a Philosophy of Life 181
  The Four Noble Truths 183
  The Noble Eight-Fold Path 189
  ORIGINAL SOURCE: Buddha, *Dhammacakkappavattana Sutta (Setting in Motion the Wheel of Truth)* 198
Progress Check 201
Study Guide 203
  Key Terms 203
  Summary of Major Points 208

LEARNING OUTCOMES

After successfully completing this chapter, you will be able to

- Gain a better awareness and understanding of your personal worldview by comparing it to four other philosophical perspectives
- Outline the history and origins of Stoicism
- Briefly describe the Stoic's cosmology (conception of the universe)
- Develop insight into how one should live in a fated universe
- Account for the role of emotions in life for the Stoic
- Explain how one should live morally in a Stoic world
- Elucidate the philosophical unorthodoxy of Existentialism
- Discuss some of the major themes embedded in existential philosophy
- Explain the differences between meaningful and meaningless lives, according to Susan Wolf
- Define what's meant by the notion of an *existential vacuum*
- Identify Viktor Frankl's sources of meaning in life
- Distinguish between psychological and ethical hedonism
- List the basic tenets of Cyrenaic Hedonism
- Outline Epicurean philosophy, distinguishing between types of pleasure
- Describe *ataraxia* as the ultimate end of life and the impediments to achieving it
- Comment on the roles of virtue and friendship in *ataraxia*
- Articulate Buddha's Four Noble Truths
- Understand how to reduce suffering using the Noble Eight-Fold Path

FOCUS QUESTIONS

1. What makes developing a personal philosophical worldview so difficult in contemporary society?
2. How is luxurious living viewed by the Stoics as well as by their predecessors, Socrates and the Cynics? Why are these views held?
3. Does a belief in God make much practical difference to one's philosophical worldview? If so, how?
4. How do the various philosophies covered in this chapter deal with problems of human purpose and meaning in life?
5. What are some practical and contemporary applications of Stoic, Existential, Buddhist, and Hedonistic philosophy?
6. How is Existentialism different from traditional orthodox philosophy?
7. What concepts are central to the philosophy of Existentialism?
8. What is meaning? Why is it important? What are its sources?
9. What is Hedonism? What variations of it do we find?
10. How is Buddhism therapeutic?
11. What prescriptions for living does Buddha offer us?

133

STEP ONE: Survey

Each chapter of the book begins with a list of *Learning Outcomes* and *Focus Questions*. Students are asked to survey these things to find out what is included in the chapter to determine what they will be expected to know and do upon successful completion of it. Think of outcomes as objectives or goals to be achieved. Study of the chapter is not really done until one demonstrates mastery of all of the outcomes listed up front in any particular chapter.

STEP TWO: Question

Every chapter of *Experiencing Philosophy* contains *Focus Questions*. As you might guess, they are intended to focus one's attention while reading. Knowing what to look for helps one to be selective and to separate what needs to be known from what is nice to know or what is less important.

STEP THREE: Read

Once students know what to look for and what they are supposed to accomplish by a study of the chapter, reading can begin. Of course, reading philosophy is not like reading the newspaper or a popular graphic novel. Philosophy contains a lot of technical vocabulary and terms with which students may not be familiar.

We recommend that individual students read each section slowly, repeatedly, and with an online or physical philosophical dictionary handy nearby. Some may find it helpful to highlight important sections of the text with a marker or pen. One should not be discouraged if a first reading leaves one bewildered sometimes. Philosophy requires everyone to pay attention to difficult matters and to think in a way that is not always encouraged by popular culture, social media, or mainstream news outlets.

While reading, students should take notice of the **boldfaced** terms and *italicized* passages. They indicate that an especially important concept or idea is being addressed. Footnotes (indicated by * and † in the text, and found at the bottom of some pages) add some parenthetical bits. Numbered endnotes refer to bibliographical references at the end of the book.

STEP FOUR: Recite and Review

After completing the chapter reading, it's time to begin the review and recitation process. Students are asked to look over the list of *Key Terms* and make sure they can understand and define each one. Another thing students may wish to do is to go back to the sections of the chapter that were highlighted and make notes from them by paraphrasing what was written in a language that is more easily remembered and understood. Chapter headings and subtitles can serve as organizational guides for note taking.

As part of the recitation and review process, students should also refer to the *Summary of Major Points*. Captured in each of the chapter summaries is the essential content to be grasped. Once students have studied their notes in light of the summaries provided, they can then go back to review the list of learning outcomes at the beginning of the chapter. They can also see whether they are able to answer the Focus Questions presented.

Some students may wish to complete the Progress Checks that help to comprise the SQ3R system immediately after reading, prior to going over the summaries of key points and before reviewing key terms; others may wish to do them afterwards. Regardless, answers to the Progress Checks can be found at the end of this book. Note that mastery of more advanced philosophical reasoning will require individuals to practice logical, critical-analytical thinking skills covered in Chapter 2 and addressed in several of the pedagogical features included in the book, e.g., *Philosophers in Action* and *Thinking about Your Thinking*. *Reading Questions* that accompany each of the original philosophical sources presented in the text often require higher-order thinking as well.

In conclusion, success in the study of philosophy is going to require a lot of hard work and active involvement on the part of students. Quick or cursory reading and mere passive listening during lectures is not likely to be enough to ensure that they achieve at optimum levels. The SQ3R learning method and other pedagogical elements integrated into this text require students to interact with the material that is presented. It prepares the way for higher-order philosophical inquiry and critical-analytical discussion by facilitating a mastery of basic knowledge and understanding. While this learning method cannot guarantee success, it can pave the way for the first step toward achieving it.

Acknowledgments

IT'S SAFE TO SAY THAT NO BOOK is ever published without the efforts of a whole team of people. This fact certainly applies here. The production of *Experiencing Philosophy*, second edition, was initially made possible by Stephen Latta, the philosophy acquisitions editor at Broadview Press. He saw value and merit in the book as he shepherded this project from beginning to end with impressive professionalism; for that I am extremely grateful. Stephen displayed excellent philosophical instincts and meticulous attention to detail in making the recommendations and comments that he did. I especially liked Stephen's thoughtful and mild manner, as he managed to coordinate everyone's efforts in a clear and straightforward fashion. Completing the project was both interesting and pleasant due to Stephen's masterful handling of it.

As part of the team, Bob Martin deserves many thanks for his helpful copyediting, comments, and substantive contributions. I very much appreciated his addition of examples that often helped to clarify points made in the text. Overall, Bob's efforts made the book much clearer and more accurate than it otherwise would have been. Of course, I take full responsibility for any remaining deficiencies.

Another person deserving acknowledgment for his contributions to this project is Dr. Michel Pharand. His proofreading efforts helped to clean up the manuscript in numerous ways, reminding me of the fact that even after decades of academic writing, I still have not mastered the proper use of the comma!

The inviting and creative aesthetic of this text can be attributed to Liz Broes and Matthew Jubb, both of *Em Dash Design*. Liz looked after the interior design elements, while Matthew was responsible for the cover. I'm sure students will enjoy the layout and physical features of the book as much as its content.

Tara Lowes served as production coordinator on this project. She arranged the designers' work on the book's typesetting, coordinated proofreading and corrections, and she reviewed the text multiple times for accuracy of formatting. Tara also arranged for printing, doing her job impressively well, keeping the rest of the team on track and on deadline.

A shout out is also warranted to Mary King, the Digital Instructional Materials Editor for Broadview. Her efforts along with those of proofreader Joe Davies and index producer Tere Mullin are greatly appreciated.

Finally, special thanks also go out to Dr. Susan Mills, my contributing co-author for this second edition of the book. Many of the improvements to the first edition of *Experiencing Philosophy* come from her efforts. Susan enhanced the inclusivity of the text by incorporating materials dealing with historically important female thinkers such as Sor Juana Inés de la Cruz and Maria von Herbert. Her inclusion of Susan Wolf's contemporary work on meaning also served to augment this text's personalized treatment of philosophy.

Faculty and students alike should enjoy Susan's new metacognitive pedagogical feature, found under the heading "Thinking about Your Thinking." This tool helps students develop skills of critical self-reflection and takes them beyond mere knowledge acquisition and application. Susan's many excellent "Reading Questions" following "Original Sources" in the text also help to focus students' attention and will no doubt give rise to some interesting classroom discussions.

I should add as well that Susan provided chapter readings with very useful contextual introductions and improved on a number of Philosopher Profiles in the book, bringing more personal biographical information and thus greater humanity to the philosophers showcased. She also made many good editorial suggestions, improved theoretical linkages, and helped to re-organize a number of elements in the text, improving the flow of material. Susan's substantive contributions to the discussions on Descartes, Locke, and Hume in Chapter 4 were especially appreciated. So too were her additions involving critiques of traditional epistemological and metaphysical approaches. This new edition of *Experiencing Philosophy* is certainly much improved because of Susan's valued contributions.

Thank you Dr. Mills!

Anthony Falikowski

With Gratitude

The first edition of *Experiencing Philosophy* is a captivating celebration of philosophical thought and an impressive achievement by Anthony Falikowski. It is also distinctively and indisputably in Tony's voice. His personality, interests, and love of philosophy are on every page, and they are very much *his*. Nevertheless, when it came to preparing this second edition of *Experiencing Philosophy*, he welcomed me to the project and encouraged me to use my voice to bring some new voices to these pages and to enhance the ones that were already there. Thank you, Tony, for the wealth of generosity and support that you shared with me. Your kindness, humor, selflessness, care, and wonder are exemplary of someone who lives an examined life, and it is entirely fitting that you have created something that encourages and assists others to do the same.

Stephen Latta at Broadview Press had terrific vision for this project and the expertise to make it happen. He is a puzzle master of ideas and people, who saw each perfect fit before the rest of us did, and his coordination and input throughout the process allowed the second edition to flow into formation with ease and enjoyment. Thank you, Stephen, for your guidance and assistance. Whether it was trusting me and Tony to play to our individual strengths or nudging us towards improvements, every strength in this second edition of *Experiencing Philosophy* can be traced back to you.

Lastly, many of my contributions to this project come from my teaching and would not be what they are without colleagues who enjoy and value conversations about curriculum as much as I do and students who approach philosophy with an inspiring amount of curiosity and courage. Of particular note, I am grateful to Kate Moran for introducing me to Maria von Herbert and to Lisa Shapiro and Marcy Lascano for introducing me to Sor Juana Inés de la Cruz. To everyone who has listened and let me listen so that I could learn, thank you very much. I am eager for whatever lessons come next.

Susan Mills

CHAPTER 1

What Is Philosophy?

Take It Personally 30

Know Thyself: My Preconceptions about
   Philosophy 32

1.1 What Is a Philosopher? 33
   Philosophy and Philosophers: Caricatures,
      Myths, and Realities 33
   The Philosopher's Profile 34
   ORIGINAL SOURCE: Sor Juana Inés de la Cruz,
      Reply to Sor Filotea 37
   Wisdom: The Object of Love 40

1.2 The Practical Value of Philosophy 41
   Philosophy's Relevance in an Age of
      Technology 43
   Therapeutic Applications of Philosophy 44

1.3 Fields of Philosophy 46
   Metaphysics 47
   Epistemology 48
   Logic 48
   Ethics 48
   Axiology 49
   Social/Political Philosophy 50
   Foundational and Disciplinary Philosophies
      50
   Philosophies of Life 50

1.4 Approaches to Philosophy 51
   Western Philosophy 51
   Historical Approaches 52
   Non-Traditional and Non-Western
      Approaches 52
   Feminist Approaches 53
   ORIGINAL SOURCE: Lee Hester, "Truth and
   Native American Epistemology" 54
   Spiritually-Based Philosophical Traditions 55
   ORIGINAL SOURCE: Abu Hamid al-Ghazali,
   Al-Munqidh min al-Dalal (*Deliverance from
   Error*) 57
   Modern Western Philosophy 60
   ORIGINAL SOURCE: Bertrand Russell, "The
   Value of Philosophy" 62

Progress Check 66

Study Guide 67
   Key Terms 67
   Summary of Major Points 69
   Additional Resources 70

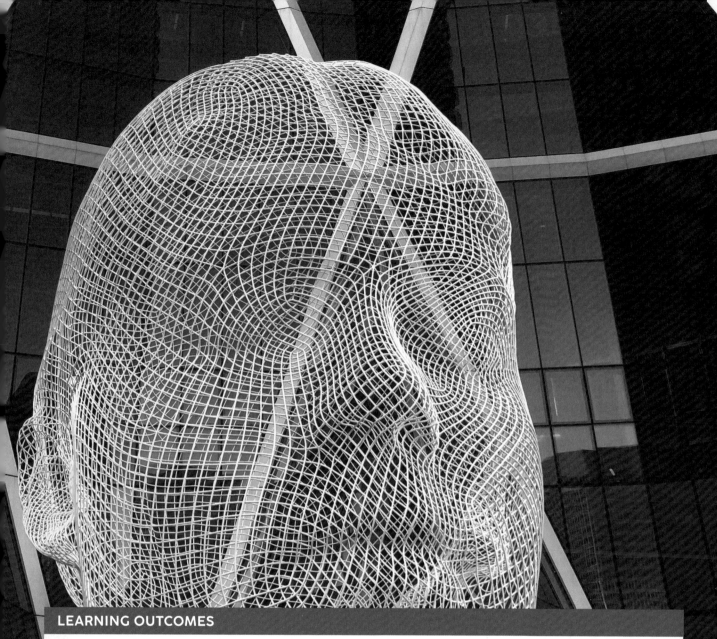

LEARNING OUTCOMES

After successfully completing this chapter, you will be able to

- Describe various caricatures associated with philosophers
- Provide a general profile of the Western philosopher
- Define 'wisdom'
- Appreciate the practical value of philosophy
- Point to the therapeutic applications of philosophy

- Show how philosophy is relevant in a technological age
- Outline the internal boundaries of Western philosophy
- Describe some non-Western and spiritual approaches to philosophy
- List the historical periods of philosophy

FOCUS QUESTIONS

1. What thoughts come to mind when the subject of philosophy is raised? What images are evoked?

2. What do philosophers try to be like? What do they do?

3. What is meant by 'wisdom'? What good is it?

4. What practical value could philosophy possibly have? How is it relevant for us in the twenty-first century?

5. What constitutes the discipline of philosophy? What are its sub-disciplines?

Take It Personally

"The unexamined life is not worth living."
SOCRATES

As someone who has already experienced the joys of philosophy for many years, I'm excited about what's in store for you as we embark together on our travels into the philosophical domain. This journey into the realm of philosophy promises to be one of the most rewarding explorations you will ever undertake. Although the philosophical landscape can sometimes be slippery and difficult to navigate, previous climbs to the tops of metaphysical mountain peaks reveal breathtaking horizons stretching across alternative realities and differing conceptions of the universe.

Our philosophical quest will be no trivial pursuit, but one of significant import. In fact, philosophy may turn out to be *the* most relevant, practical, and important course you will ever take in your lifetime! The questions and issues raised in this book will not disappear with fad and fashion. They will not become dated or obsolete like last year's Internet meme. The philosopher's tune is not like the musician's one-hit wonder. Philosophy's soothing and sometimes haunting eternal themes have echoed for centuries and will continue to play in our minds throughout our lives—quietly in good times, but with startling bombast in situations of calamity and disappointment.

We are embarking here on a very important task, my fellow journeyer, one that takes us down many difficult but previously traveled roads. Proceed with caution, then, respecting the twists and turns ahead. Your safe journey to philosophical enlightenment depends upon it. St. Teresa of Avila, a Christian mystical writer, prepares us for our journey to enlightenment, or what she calls heaven, with the following words:

> Do not be frightened, [sons and] daughters, by the many things you need to consider in order to begin this divine journey which is the royal road to heaven. A great treasure is gained by traveling this road; no wonder we have to pay what seems to us a high price. The time will come when you will understand how trifling everything is next to so precious a reward.
>
> To those who want to journey on this road and continue until they reach the end, which is to drink from this water of life, I say that how they are to begin is very important—in fact, all important. They must have a great and very resolute determination to persevere until reaching the end, come what may, happen what may, whatever work is involved, whatever criticism arises, whether they arrive or whether they die on the road, or even if they don't have courage for the trials that are met, or if the whole world collapses.[1]

Finding the "resolute determination to persevere" that St. Teresa talks about may not be easy, especially given the misguided preconceptions many people have regarding philosophy and those who engage in its practice. I suppose that as a philosopher, I could try to prove to you, using reason and logic alone, that philosophy does matter and that it should be important to you, whether you believe it or not. Because I have tried this strategy before—not surprisingly with something less than perfect success—I appreciate how opting for this approach is analogous to trying to get people to believe in a creator-God by simply offering them logical proofs for God's existence. Anyone with deep religious convictions probably already knows that faith goes far beyond mere rational assent. Some might even argue that a genuine belief in God requires a personal encounter with the

Divine at some existential, heart-felt level, perhaps in a conversion experience. In this case, the experience of God serves as the proof.

In the same vein, let me suggest that an appreciation of the value of philosophy and its practical relevance to you will gradually unfold as we proceed through this text. I'll let your experience of philosophy be the judge of its ultimate worth, asking only that you not make up your mind in advance before sampling the many tasty philosophical delicacies that will be offered to you for your intellectual consumption along the way. The proof that philosophy is worthwhile will be in the philosophical food for thought you'll be invited to sample. I'm confident that you'll enjoy philosophy, for so much of it relates directly to your experience of everyday life.

To illustrate this point, let me ask this: Have you ever wondered what you should do with your life or what sort of person you should strive to become? If so, then you may find some helpful direction in Chapter 3, where we cover different philosophies of life. You may also find guidance in Chapter 5, dealing with ethics, where character and virtue are discussed.

Further, do people who dress or act like everyone else bother you for some unknown reason? You might find some deep insights on this matter in sections of the book dealing with Marxist alienation and Nietzsche's slave morality. How about your annoyance when it comes to all the fighting you witness on television talk shows? Is it bothersome that people just seem to be filibustering or screaming their opinions at each other without really listening and without actually putting forward any reasoned arguments in a legitimate debate? Well then, have a look at Chapter 2, where you learn to distinguish between unfounded opinions and valid arguments, and discover what's better about the latter. You needn't be one of the screaming opinionators. Learn how to put your own proper arguments together, displaying if not the wisdom of Socrates, then at least his humility.

And what about an afterlife? Is this all there is, or is there another reality beyond the material realm of sensory experience? Check out Plato in the metaphysics chapter, for example, to discover what he says about the spaceless, timeless realm of forms. Further, does God exist? Read about St. Anselm and St. Thomas Aquinas, who provide what they take to be proofs that there is indeed a God. You might also wish to consider those proofs in light of what atheistic philosophers say. Maybe religion is just an "opium of the people," as Karl Marx charges, or perhaps God is nothing more than a psychological invention of fearful and neurotic individuals? You'll get the opportunity to think about such things later in the text.

Lastly, are you completely convinced that socialism is bad, that American capitalist democracy is unconditionally good, or that economic globalization should be encouraged or discouraged? Are there moral consequences at stake? Is it possible that human rights are being violated? If so, then what constitutes a violation of rights? What is justice? What is the individual's proper relation to the state? You can read more about rights and justice in the final chapter on political philosophy to find out. In the process, you can become a more intelligent, critically-minded rational citizen.

The point, as you can plainly see by the questions just raised, is that philosophical concerns are an inextricable part of life. You can make vain efforts to ignore them in your daily living, but in the end they cannot be escaped. It's highly unfortunate, therefore, that so much confusion surrounds the nature and purpose of philosophy. If we properly understood philosophy and used it to our advantage, much in life could be improved.

My Preconceptions about Philosophy

AIM

The purpose of this self-diagnostic is to help you develop an awareness of your preconceptions about philosophy. Just as attitudes like anger or suspicion can interfere with productive dialogue, so too can uncritically accepted misunderstandings of philosophy interfere with proper learning and application. In order to be fully open to the experience of philosophy, any prejudgments about it should first be exposed and then critically examined.

INSTRUCTIONS

Below are ten statements pertaining to philosophy. Indicate which are true (T) and which are false (F).

1.　T　F　The vast majority of philosophers today are hermits and monks, either living in monasteries, caves, deserts, or mountainside retreats.

2.　T　F　If you are a philosopher, you must be an atheist, since reason necessarily contradicts faith.

3.　T　F　Philosophy is essentially useless and outdated, serving no practical purpose.

4.　T　F　Most philosophers are either unemployed, driving cabs, or working in the gig economy.

5.　T　F　Few women study or teach philosophy today.

6.　T　F　In order to be a philosopher, you must have a beard, smoke a pipe, and wear elbow patches on your jacket.

7.　T　F　Philosophers are rarely grounded in reality; usually living impractical lives with their heads in the clouds.

8.　T　F　Philosophers are a dysfunctional bunch because they are hypercritical and like to argue about everything.

9.　T　F　Philosophers, by profession, are always wise individuals.

10.　T　F　Practically speaking, the study of philosophy will most likely get you nowhere.

INTERPRETATION OF RESULTS

All of the preceding statements about philosophy and philosophers are *false*. To the extent you agreed with any of them, you may have fallen prey to some popular, uncritically held misconceptions of who philosophers are, what philosophers do and what philosophy is all about. Not to fear, however, for the rest of this chapter will dispel any of your misguided preconceptions and help you to gain a clearer, more accurate understanding of philosophers and philosophical inquiry.

Before we proceed any further, you are invited to complete the preceding *Know Thyself* diagnostic. It will enable you to get a preliminary indication of how accurate or inaccurate your current understanding of philosophy is. In case you have developed any distorted views, the sections that follow the self-diagnostic should help to clarify the true nature and purpose of philosophy, its history, sub-disciplines, and approaches, as well as its personal and practical relevance. Let the experience of philosophy begin!

1.1 What Is a Philosopher?

Philosophy and Philosophers: Caricatures, Myths, and Realities

For first-time travelers into the philosophical domain, directions can be found by turning to the wisdom of the philosophical immortals, those whose ideas have stood the test of time and whose rational reflections have changed our conceptions of reality, human nature, truth, beauty, and goodness. Don't be discouraged by the anti-intellectual crowd or by defensive individuals fearful of embarking on the philosophical journey. They have opted for ignorance over illumination and have tended to trivialize the pursuit of wisdom by stereotyping and caricaturing those most actively engaged in it.

These caricatures and stereotypes portraying the philosopher's weird irrelevance are often amusingly perpetuated in popular culture by cartoonists, comedians, and Hollywood moviemakers. For instance, the term *philosopher* has come to evoke, in many minds, the stereotypic image of a bearded old man, a detached hermit who wanders the desert wilderness or dwells in a mountainside cave. Perhaps the term *philosopher* conjures up a mental picture of someone who works in an ivory tower, occupying a comfortable wingback chair in an oak-walled den or library. Of course, pipe in mouth and book in hand are mandatory, along with a distant pensive gaze. Still another image may be that of a sandaled and toga-clad ancient Greek making a nuisance of himself by asking unquestioned authorities unanswerable questions.

In spite of the stereotypes you may apply to **philosophers**, as revealed if you marked any of the statements above as T, you can rest assured that philosophers are not necessarily male, aged, toga-clad, or bearded. Their dwelling place is probably not a cave or desert, but a neighborhood apartment or house. Although lots of professional philosophers do, in fact, make a living today teaching at colleges and universities, many more lay-philosophers discuss philosophical issues at informal places such as pubs, parties, and family gatherings; still some others tend to be the quiet type who privately write down their ideas in journals and read books on their own.

In short, philosopher types are unpredictable. They are varied in appearance and may show up almost anywhere. For all you know, the student sitting next to you in class may, in fact, be a *philosopher-in-waiting* ready to come out at the first invitation. So, to all of you philosophers, I extend your long-awaited invitation to embark on the philosophical quest together. Let's all join in our efforts as we face the amazing adventure that awaits us!

THINKING ABOUT YOUR THINKING

Do you think of yourself as a philosopher? Why or why not? While answering these questions, consider what idea of a philosopher you have in mind. Describe the qualities and characteristics that belong to that idea. Where did your idea of a philosopher come from?

The Philosopher's Profile

If it's erroneous to see philosophers as hermits, cave dwellers, or toga-clad renegades, then we're still left wondering who or what a philosopher is. Throughout this book, we will examine a variety of different philosophies, and I will introduce you to different noteworthy philosophers who support them. For the moment, however, let me give you a rough sketch of the Western philosopher's psychological profile.

"I have said that the love of study is the passion most necessary to our happiness. It is an unfailing resource against misfortunes, it is an inexhaustible source of pleasure."

ÉMILIE DU CHÂTELET

Our first clue about the philosopher's identity comes from the origins of the word **philosophy** itself. Etymologically, the word 'philosophy' derives from the Greek words '*philos*', meaning love, and '*sophia*', meaning the exercise of one's intelligence in practical affairs. However, as historian-philosopher John Passmore explains, most English-speaking philosophers have chosen to translate *sophia* more narrowly as wisdom.[2] Consequently, we often speak of philosophy as the love of wisdom and philosophers as *lovers of wisdom*. But having said this, we still don't know what the typical philosopher is like as a person or what the ideal philosopher should be like.

Recognizing that philosophers are not clones of one another and that they express a variety of styles and orientations, permit me, nonetheless, at the risk of making my own gross generalizations, to describe them in the following fashion. I believe many philosophers, but certainly not all, would accept my depiction of them. To begin with, professionally trained philosophers aspire to be **reasonable** individuals. In fact, reason is the primary tool used in conducting their work. It is their *modus operandi* or way of operating. I'm not suggesting that all philosophers can be described as rationalists or that reason is necessarily given primacy of place for all of them—only that philosophers tend to take a rational approach to life and human inquiry.

By using this rational approach, philosophers seek to make sense of themselves, others, and the world. Using reason, they aim to arrive at clear understandings of things by reducing vagueness and ambiguity as much as possible. If philosophers didn't, or couldn't, make sense to each other—that is, if their use of language were so imprecise and their reasoning so scattered that nobody could figure out what they were saying—then philosophical discourse would be impossible. Even "non-rational" existentialist philosophers (see Chapter 3) and feminist critics of rational morality (see Chapter 5) must still use language and rational thought to express their objections to the supremacy of pure rationality. Paradoxically, then, reason must be used to criticize its own applications.

The remarks just made point to the critical function of philosophers. Philosophers, as a group, tend to be **critically minded**. They choose to adopt a questioning attitude toward most things, accepting little on authority or blind faith. Philosophers are typically curious, frequently asking "Why?" and demanding *rational justifications* for the positions people take on issues and for the actions they perform. The ancient philosopher Socrates asked many questions and called himself a "gadfly"[3]—literally a kind of fly that attacks cattle, but figuratively a person who irritates everybody with annoying questions and criticisms.

Good philosophers who are also good people try to minimize the irritation, and although most philosophers are not as irritating as Socrates, they do bug us sometimes, due to a kind of positive addiction manifested as an unquenchable thirst for knowledge and understanding. Their questions just never seem to end. Don't get me wrong; the critical mindedness of philosophers is not intended to be unproductively confrontational or dangerously subversive, but rather to reflect caution and a desire for clarity and precision in thought.

Unlike people who are critical simply for the sake of opposition, philosophers are critical with a legitimate purpose. They do not want unfounded assumptions to go unchallenged. They do not want unsubstantiated or unverified factual claims to pass notice; nor do they wish illogical conclusions to follow from invalid reasoning. Philosophers are not only lovers of wisdom but also **seekers of truth**.

As seekers of truth, philosophers make efforts to be *open-minded*. They are prepared to entertain propositions that, at first glance, may seem disturbing, counter-intuitive, or wrong. Philosophers also raise basic questions about reality, truth, beauty, and goodness. Is the material world all there is? Does beauty exist in things themselves, or does it exist only in the eye of the beholder? Are morality and knowledge merely matters of opinion, or can the truth or falsity of moral and factual beliefs be objectively determined?

Philosophers are willing to inquire into what many of us might accept unreflectively as *self-evident* truths. For instance, you might loudly declare your firm conviction in a classroom debate that all human beings are created equal. But how do you know this for sure? Did a supreme being create humans and then bestow equality upon them, or have they evolved according to evolutionary laws of nature?; and if they evolved, then how does that make them equal? If, as equals, we all have the same rights, then what is a right? Do we share all rights or only basic rights? What then is a basic right? Which rights do we not share? Do some of us have rights that others don't? Can rights be taken away once they are given to us? Are rights earned, or are they somehow inherent in our being? How big or broad is a right? Is it ever justifiable to violate somebody's rights? Why or why not?

As you can tell from this line of questioning, philosophers don't take things for granted just because they make us feel good, because the majority holds a particular point of view, or because common sense dictates. Philosophers are like intellectual miners, digging deeply beneath the surface of life to find diamonds of truth that must be polished by the friction of argument and analysis before they can radiate their true brilliance.

A number of attitude adjustments necessary to conduct proper philosophical argument and debate are discussed in the next chapter on logic and philosophical method, but for now, suffice it to say that philosophers like to probe, analyze, reflect, consider alternatives, question authority, display healthy skepticism and doubt, while at the same time remaining objective, impartial, respectful of others, and cognizant of differing and divergent points of view. Certainly, the ideal Western rational philosopher can be described as detached and unbiased, someone who suspends judgment before all the philosophical facts are in, so to speak. As we travel along on our philosophical journey, you will get to know many different philosophers, as well as their ideas and methods, a little better, and you should begin to develop an appreciation of philosophers that is more elaborate than the thumb-nail sketch I have provided you here.

Sor Juana Inés de la Cruz [4]

Nun, poet, playwright, and defender of the humanities, **Sor Juana Inés de la Cruz** (1648–1695) is not standardly mentioned in philosophical circles. Perhaps that is because she does not fit the caricature of a philosopher! Arguably, however, her commitment to living a life of intellectual curiosity, thought, and expression makes her the portrait of a true philosopher.

Born in a small town near Mexico City, Juana showed signs of a great intellect from a very early age. Denied a formal education, she was largely self-taught from the books that she had access to in her grandfather's library. Although she later lamented the absence of teachers or fellow students in her youth, the intellectual independence and self-reliance that she cultivated as a child served her well.

When young Juana was sent to live with relatives in Mexico City, word of her intellectual talents spread, and by the time she was a teenager, she was welcomed into the court of the viceroy of New Spain and his wife. So impressed by her intelligence and learnedness, the viceroy arranged a formal debate between Juana and various theologians, biblical scholars, philosophers, mathematicians, historians, poets, and other intellectuals. In a brilliant and legendary performance, she answered their questions and replied to their arguments with ease.

At age 19, Juana left the court for the convent, becoming Sor (Sister) Juana. Given the options available to her, it was a decision based on faith as much as her repugnance of marriage and desire to pursue her studies. She had a comfortable life in the Convent of Santa Paula of the Order of San Jerónimo with private living quarters and her own library of books and collection scientific instruments. She spent time reading, studying, and writing, becoming an acclaimed and well-known

author of poetry and plays, which, despite her being a nun, were on secular topics.

Even though she lived as a cloistered nun, Sor Juana's life was far from limited to the convent. She kept active correspondence with intellectuals in Spain and Spanish America and hosted conversational gatherings with the political and intellectual elite of Mexico City. In one of those gatherings, Sor Juana gave an oral critique of a 40-year-old sermon by a famous Portuguese Jesuit preacher. Afterwards, she received a request for a written copy of her speech. She obliged and, without her permission, her critique was published along with an admonishing letter addressed to Sor Juana and signed by Sor Filotea de la Cruz. The letter praised Sor Juana's intellectual talents but reprimanded her choice of secular, rather than sacred, subjects of study. The concern was not exactly that she was a woman engaging in intellectual activity but that the subject of her activity might make her less obedient and subordinate.

In truth, "Sor Filotea" was a pseudonym for the Bishop of Puebla, an occasional participant in the gatherings of intellectuals that Sor Juana hosted. In response, Sor Juana wrote a lengthy letter that begins with great deference to "Sor Filotea" but gives way to a spirited defense of an educated and examined life for women and, indeed, for anyone who seeks to understand the world. Challenging the view that philosophy is an exclusive activity reserved for only some, she offers this quotation from a poet: "one can philosophize very well and prepare supper."[5]

Eventually, under pressure and punishment, Sor Juana repented and renounced her intellectual pursuit of worldly knowledge. She spent the last two years of her life in complete silence.

Sor Juana Inés de la Cruz, *Reply to Sor Filotea*[6]

The following text comes from the letter Sor Juana wrote in 1691 in response to an admonishing letter signed under the pseudonym "Sor Filotea de la Cruz." In fact, the author of the admonishment was the Bishop of Puebla, Manuel Fernández de Santa Cruz. In her reply, Sor Juana defends herself against the criticism that she was misspending her time studying philosophy and other "human letters" rather than Scripture or "divine letters": "Your Grace has spent a good deal of time studying philosophers and poets; now is the proper moment for you to perfect your pursuits and improve the books you read."[7]

———

I

Continuing the narration of my inclination, about which I want to give you a complete account, I say that before I was three years old my mother sent an older sister of mine to learn to read in one of the primary schools for girls called *Friends*, and, led by affection and mischief, I followed after her; and seeing that she was being taught a lesson, I was so set ablaze by the desire to know how to read that in the belief I was deceiving her, I told the teacher my mother wanted her to give me a lesson too. She did not believe it, because it was not believable, but to go along with the joke, she taught me. I continued to go and she continued to teach me, in earnest now, because with experience she realized the truth; and I learned to read in so short a time that I already knew how when my mother found out, for the teacher hid it from her in order to give her complete gratification and receive her reward at the same time; and I kept silent believing I would be whipped for having done this without her knowledge. The woman who taught me is still alive (may God keep her), and she can testify to this.

I remember at this time, my appetite being what is usual at that age, I abstained from eating cheese because l had heard it made people stupid, and my desire to learn was stronger in me than the desire to eat, despite this being so powerful in children. Later, when I was six or seven years old and already knew how to read and write, along with all the other skills pertaining to sewing and needlework learned by women, I heard there was a university and schools in Mexico City where sciences were studied; as soon as I heard this I began to pester my mother with insistent, inopportune pleas that she send me, dressed as a boy, to the home of some relatives she had in Mexico City, so I could study and attend classes at the university; she refused, and rightly so, but I satisfied my desire by reading many different books owned by my grandfather, and there were not enough punishments and reprimands to stop me, so that when I came to Mexico City, people were surprised not so much by my intelligence as by my memory and the knowledge I possessed at an age when it seemed I had barely had enough time to learn to speak.

I began to learn Latin and believe I had fewer than twenty lessons; my seriousness was so intense that since the natural adornment of hair is so admired in women—especially in the flower of one's youth—I would cut off four to six inches, first measuring how long it was and then imposing on myself the rule that if, when it had grown back, I did not know whatever I had proposed to learn while it was growing, I would cut it again as a punishment for my stupidity. And when it grew back and I did not know what I had determined to learn, because my hair grew quickly and I learned slowly, then in fact I did cut it as punishment for my stupidity, for it did not seem right for my head to be dressed in hair when it was so bare of knowledge, which was a more desirable adornment. I entered the convent although I knew the situation had certain characteristics (I speak of secondary qualities, not formal ones) incompatible with my character, but considering the total antipathy I had toward matrimony, the convent was the least disproportionate and most honorable decision I could make to provide the certainty I desired for my salvation, and the first (and in the end the most important) obstacle to overcome was to relinquish all the minor defects in my character, such as wanting to live alone, and not wanting any obligatory occupation that would limit the freedom of my studies, or the noise of a community that would interfere with the tranquil silence of my books. These made me hesitate somewhat in my determination, until learned persons enlightened me, saying they were a temptation, which I overcame with Divine Grace and entered into the state I so unworthily am in now....

I returned to (no, I am wrong, for I never stopped): I mean to say I continued my studious effort (which for me was repose whenever I had time away from my obligations) to read and read some more, to study and study some more, with no teacher other than the books themselves. I learned how difficult it is to study those soulless characters without the living voice and explanations of a teacher; yet I gladly endured all this work for the sake of my love of letters. Oh, if it had only been for the sake of my love of God, which is the correct love, how meritorious it would have been! I did attempt to elevate it as much as I could and turn it to His service, because the goal to which I aspired was the study of theology, for, being Catholic, it seemed a foolish lack in me not to know everything that can be learned in this life, by natural means, about the Divine Mysteries; and being a nun and not a layperson, according to my ecclesiastical state I should profess vows to letters, and even more so, as a daughter of a Saint Jerome and a Saint Paula, for it seemed a deterioration if such learned parents produced an idiot child. I proposed this to myself and it seemed correct, if it was not (and this is most likely) flattery and applause of my own inclination, its enjoyment being proposed as an obligation.

In this way I proceeded, always directing the steps of my study to the summit of sacred theology, as I have said; and to reach it, I thought it necessary to ascend by the steps of human sciences and arts, because how is one to understand the style of the queen of sciences without knowing that of the handmaidens? How, without logic, was I to know the general and particular methods used in the writing of Holy Scripture? How, without rhetoric, would I understand its figures, tropes, and locutions? How, without physics, comprehend the many inherent questions concerning the nature of the animals used for sacrifices, in which so many stated subjects, as well as many others that are undeclared, are symbolized? How to know whether Saul healing at the sound of David's harp came from the virtue and natural power of music or the supernatural ability God wished to place in David? How, without arithmetic, understand so many computations of years, days, months, hours, and weeks

as mysterious as those in Daniel, and others for whose deciphering one must know the natures, concordances, and properties of numbers? How, without geometry, can one measure the Holy Ark of the Covenant and the holy city of Jerusalem, whose mysterious measurements form a cube with all its dimensions, a marvelous proportional distribution of all its parts? How, without architecture, fathom the great temple of Solomon, where God Himself was the artificer, conceiving the proportion and design, and the wise king merely the overseer who executed it; where there was no base without a mystery, no column without a symbol, no cornice without an allusion, no architrave without a meaning, and so on in all its parts, so that even the smallest fillet was placed not for the service and complement of art alone but to symbolize greater things? How, without great knowledge of the rules and parts that constitute history, can the historical books be understood? Those recapitulations in which what happened earlier often is placed later in the narration and seems to have occurred afterward? How, without great familiarity with both kinds of law, can one apprehend the legal books? How, without great erudition, approach so many matters of profane history mentioned in Holy Scripture, so many Gentile customs, so many rites, so many ways of speaking? How, without many rules and much reading of the Holy Fathers, can one grasp the obscure expression of the prophets? And without being very expert in music, how are we to understand the musical proportions and their beauty found in so many places, especially in the petition of Abraham to God on behalf of the cities? ... In the Book of Job, God says: *Shalt thou be able to join together the shining stars the Pleiades, or canst thou stop the turning about of Arcturus? Canst thou bring forth the day star in its time and make the evening star to rise upon the children of the earth?* The terms, without knowledge of astronomy, would be impossible to comprehend. And not only these noble sciences, but there is no mechanical art that is not mentioned. In short, it is the book that encompasses all books, and the science that includes all sciences, which are useful for its understanding: even after learning all of them (which clearly is not easy, or even possible), another consideration demands more than all that has been said, and that is constant prayer and purity in one's life, in order to implore God for the purification of spirit and enlightenment of mind necessary for comprehending these lofty matters; if this is lacking, the rest is useless.

… Therefore, having attained a few elementary skills, I continually studied a variety of subjects, not having an inclination toward one in particular but toward all of them in general; as a consequence, having studied some more than others has not been by choice but because, by chance, I had access to more books about those subjects, which created the preference more than any decision of mine. And since I had no special interest that moved me, and no time limit that restricted my continuing to study one subject because of the demands of formal classes, I could study a variety of subjects or abandon some for others, although I did observe a certain order, for some I called study and others diversion, and with these I rested from the first, with the result that I have studied many subjects and know nothing, because some have interfered with my learning others. True, I say this regarding the practical aspect of those subjects that have one, because it is obvious that while one moves a pen, the compass does nothing, and while one plays the harp, the organ is silent, and so on; because since a great deal of physical practice is necessary to acquire a practical skill, the person who is divided among various exercises can never achieve perfection; but the opposite happens in formal and speculative areas, and I would like to persuade everyone with my experience that this not only does not interfere but helps, for one subject illuminates and opens a path in another by means of variations and hidden connections—placed in this universal chain by the wisdom of its Author—so that it seems they correspond and are joined with admirable unity and harmony….

As for me, I can state that what I do not understand in an author from one discipline I usually can understand in a different author from another discipline that seems quite distant from the first; and in their explanations, these authors offer metaphorical examples from other arts, as when logicians say that the mean is to the terms as a measurement is to two distant bodies, in order to determine whether they are equal; and that the statement of a logician moves, like a straight line, along the shortest path, while that of a rhetorician follows, like a curve, the longest, but both travel to the same point; and when it is said that expositors are like an open hand

and scholastics like a closed fist. This is not an excuse for having studied a diversity of subjects, nor do I offer it as such, for these subjects contribute to one another, but my not having benefitted from them has been the fault of my ineptitude and the weakness in my understanding, not of their variety.

II

… I do confess that my work has been interminable, which means I cannot say what I enviously hear others say: that they have not had to work for knowledge. How fortunate for them! For me, not the knowing (for I still know nothing) but only the desire to know has been so difficult that I could say with my father Saint Jerome (although not with his achievements): The labour it has cost me, the difficulties I have endured, the times I have despaired, and the other times I have desisted and begun again, all because of my determination to learn, to what I have suffered my conscience is witness and the conscience of those who have lived with me. Except for the companions and witnesses (for I have lacked even that solace), I can affirm the truth of the rest. And that my unfortunate inclination has been so great it has overcome everything else!

READING QUESTIONS

1. In this letter, Sor Juana defends her intellectual activities. Have you ever criticized someone for being "too bookish"? Have you ever had to defend yourself for having intellectual interests or spending too much time on your studies? Why do you think these criticisms arise in the first place?

2. Identify one of the points that Sor Juana raises in defense of her intellectual activities. Is it a compelling point in her favor? Why or why not?

3. Based on what Sor Juana writes in this letter, what advice do you think she would give to an undergraduate student selecting courses? How does that advice compare or contrast with your own approach to educational planning? Has Sor Juana made you rethink any of your educational plans? If so, how? If not, why not?

Wisdom: The Object of Love

Now that you have some idea of what philosophers are like, we can turn to **wisdom**, the object of their affection. In *The Encyclopedia of Philosophy*, Brand Blanshard defines wisdom in the following way:

> Wisdom in its broadest and commonest sense denotes sound and serene judgment regarding the conduct of life. It may be accompanied by a broad range of knowledge, by intellectual acuteness and by speculative depth, but it is not to be identified with any of these and may appear in their absence. It involves intellectual grasp or insight, but it is concerned not so much with the ascertainment of fact or the elaboration of theories as with the means and ends of practical life.[8]

Blanshard's conception of wisdom reminds us of philosophy's usefulness. Wisdom concerns the practical conduct of life—how we choose to live our lives on an everyday basis. Wisdom requires that we exercise good judgment when making choices and import- ant life decisions. As Blanshard explains, wisdom can be accompanied by **knowledge** and **intelligence**, but not necessarily so. Having a high IQ doesn't necessarily make you wise. You could be a clever crook who uses your "smarts" to cheat other people out of what is rightfully theirs. You could also use those same smarts in imprudent ways or as an evil genius. Ted Kaczynski, the infamous Unabomber, who spent nearly two decades mailing bombs to innocent people in the United States, was described by many as brilliant, yet despite his obvious intelligence as a Harvard graduate, he displayed demonically bad judgment and made many wrong choices.

Clearly, the lesson we learn from Kaczynski is that being smart doesn't necessarily make you wise. Needless to say, perhaps, is that intelligent people are not necessarily excluded from wisdom. Intelligent people can indeed be wise as well, even if Kaczynski wasn't.

Blanchard also distinguishes between wisdom and knowledge. He understands that knowing a lot doesn't necessarily make you wise either. You may have extensive knowl- edge of theoretical physics or a photographic memory, for example, and be able to recall so much information that you become a veritable walking encyclopedia, yet this still wouldn't be a confirmation of wisdom. You could memorize the great ideas of all the important philosophers throughout history and ace all of your philosophy exams and still be a fool. Wisdom would be reflected by your ability to put that knowledge and all those ideas to practical use.

Having distinguished wisdom from knowledge and intelligence, perhaps we should note that wisdom is often connected to experience, although again, not necessarily so. As previously suggested, wisdom goes beyond mere book learning and intellectual activity. It is associated with maturity, life experience, and the virtue of putting into practice what is truly valuable. Of course, experience guarantees nothing. Some young people are *wise beyond their years*, while others are remarkably foolish, given their mature age. Experience is a great teacher, but unfortunately, not every student of life learns the lessons it has to teach.

Wisdom has an all-encompassing feature: people displaying wisdom seem to have a **sense of perspective**. They are somehow able to find unity in separate and seemingly disconnected things. Hence, wise people tend not to live compartmentalized, fragmented lives. They present solid priorities, which somehow rationally cohere into a distinguishable worldview or *integrated mode of existence*. As a result, wise people's lives are far less subject to whim and fancy. While exceptions no doubt exist, they are not typically like leaves tossed about by the winds of life, since at a deep level, they tend to be more solidly rooted. Of course, wise people are not always happy and effervescent souls, as life can sometimes be unkind. Nonetheless, despite their trials and tribulations, you will often notice a joyful serenity in the demeanor of those people you would describe as wise.

Lastly, on the subject of wisdom, a study of intellectual history reveals a **perennial wisdom** that crops up again and again in different cultures and during different epochs. We call this the *wisdom of the ages*. This wisdom takes on different expressions depending on time and place, but it often reflects remarkably similar insightful truths. As we proceed in this text, you'll come across some of this perennial wisdom as embedded in different philosophies of life and as expressed by various philosophers in their theories and philosophical outlooks. Such encounters give rise to fruitful thought and self-reflection. They also disturb and challenge, waking us from our dogmatic slumbers. That's the value of wisdom—it awakens us to new visions of reality and to fresh perceptions of life.

THINKING ABOUT YOUR THINKING

Think of someone that you regard as wise. It could be someone you know in real life or it could be a character from a TV show or book. What is it about that person or character that displays wisdom? Take note that in order to give particular examples of wisdom you need to have an idea of what wisdom is in general. What is your idea of wisdom in general? Do you find it more challenging to explain what wisdom is in general than to give a particular example of it? If so, why do you think that is?

1.2 The Practical Value of Philosophy

In view of the preceding discussion of wisdom, we need to question one widely accepted commonsense notion—namely, that philosophy has little or no practical value. Tell people you're studying philosophy or, heaven forbid, majoring in it, and you'll often be asked, "Why study that?" or "What's that going to get you?"

The fact is that much practical value can come from philosophical studies. For example, government policy analysts are often asked to use their critical-analytical thinking skills, the kind that can be learned in philosophy class, when completing reports or when justifying policy recommendations to other politicians or government officials. Research officers in many fields of scientific endeavor may need to know something about ethics when determining whether subjects in a particular study are being treated in an ethical fashion. Educators can benefit as well from understanding the philosophical underpinnings supporting their pedagogical practice. Lawyers and judges often engage in interpretations of laws and statutes requiring what philosophers would call *conceptual analysis*, a method of clarifying the specific meaning of a term or phrase and determining whether its application is proper in this case or that. In short, the skills of logical, critical-analytical thinking developed through the study of philosophy can have useful and far-ranging applications.

Despite the practical value of philosophy, as just alluded to, many if not most philosophers find **intrinsic value** in the study of philosophy. The value of pursuing knowledge or wisdom *for its own sake* is not something the vast majority of philosophers need to be arm-twisted about. Indeed, for some philosophers, deliberate efforts to make philosophy practical or applied are not appreciated. I can only guess their objection to making philosophy practical is not based so much on rational objection but more on the fear that the profound and important endeavors of philosophers will be watered down or distorted

to appeal to the masses who often demand instant intellectual gratification—something leading to gross oversimplifications of philosophical subtleties.

In the academic world, there is often tension between *pure* and *applied* research. The former is usually given more status than the latter. Sometimes, "applied" efforts are looked upon with derision as somehow less academic. But one could argue that the pursuit of philosophy is both valuable in itself, and also **instrumentally valuable** as a means to an end. Nicely capturing the sentiment about the value of putting philosophical theory into personal practice is the Armenian-Russian mystic George Gurdjieff, who writes: *Books are like maps, but there is also the necessity of traveling.*

"Research is formalized curiosity. It is poking and prying with a purpose."
ZORA NEALE HURSTON

The suggestion made earlier that philosophy is inescapable doesn't mean that we are somehow imprisoned by it. Indeed, the study of philosophy can be a liberating experience. As the saying goes, "The truth shall set you free." By studying philosophy, we can burst the bubble of **ethnocentrism** and **subjective bias** and release all of our hot air pretensions. Philosophy can help us to emerge from our socially conditioned prejudices to see other perspectives and worldviews in objective terms.

How many people do you know whose lives are severely constricted by their narrow-minded or, even worse, close-minded attitudes? Some people simply refuse to know, inquire, or understand. Communicating with such people is quite difficult, as you may have already discovered. Do you wish to be like them? Do you wish to be blind to reality, shielded from the truth and willfully ignorant of life? Is this freedom and the good life? Philosophical questioning offers you intellectual freedom. It is your way out of the prison of darkness and your guiding light to existential liberation!

Philosophy's Relevance in an Age of Technology

In the first few decades of the twenty-first century, it is fairly safe to say that we are still firmly ensconced in the *information age*. High-speed Internet access, social media platforms, satellites, 5-G networks, and smart phones are just a few of the things that make the worldwide transmission of information quick and efficient. It seems, sometimes, that we're relentlessly moving at a frenzied pace to acquire and process ever-increasing amounts of information. Computers become faster, hard drives increase their capacity, while modems send and receive data in amounts and at speeds that boggle the mind.

Every day, as we approach the altar of information technology, many of us are humbled and awestruck by the miracles performed there. The gurus of digital animation create graphic images and virtual realities never dreamed of before or thought only possible by divine intelligence. In our frozen and dazed state, brought on by the glare of computer pixel lights, many of us do not always appreciate the philosophical questions raised by the frenzied rush to know more and more. Surely, gathering and organizing information has positive value, but to what end?

Professors often lament the fact that students can research and gather information from the Internet but often do not understand the information they've gained. Furthermore, there's no guarantee, even if they understand the information they've acquired, that they'll know how to put it to use wisely. As suggested earlier, it's possible to gain all the knowledge in the world and still be a fool. It's curious, isn't it, how preoccupied we are with acquiring information (electronically and otherwise), but how little we focus on understanding what we've acquired, and how little emphasis we place on putting what we know to proper use? Information without understanding and wise application is oftentimes useless and may sometimes be potentially dangerous. Social media platforms can increase interconnectedness in a good way or they can also spread massive amounts of propaganda and disinformation, things that undermine both truth and democracy.

Insofar as philosophy can help us make sense of the information we dig up, and assist us in putting that information to good use, it is indeed highly practical, relevant, and important. History reveals to us that misapplications of knowledge and technology can have disastrous consequences. Without trying to overly dramatize the situation, one could say that philosophical wisdom may be required to save future generations and maintain the security of the world.

Faced with the many innovative technologies emerging in the twenty-first century, philosophers are sometimes called out of the halls of academe to help with real-life ethical and philosophical problems. For example, with the modern genetic engineering techniques evidenced by the cloning of Dolly the sheep in 1996, the question has arisen as to whether we should allow humans to be cloned as well. Should cloning research continue to be funded, or should a moratorium be called? Just because we are able to do something in terms of genetic engineering, does this necessarily mean that it should be done?

With respect to other reproductive technologies, such as *in vitro* fertilization and artificial insemination, should we now encourage, or at least countenance, childbirth outside the boundaries of traditional marriage? For example, should lesbian women involved in same-sex relationships be allowed to be artificially inseminated or undergo *in vitro* fertilization with sperm purchased from the local sperm bank in order to have families and raise children of their own? Today, this is possible, but is it right? Who should decide? Should the government? How about the private individuals involved? Do the rights of the yet unborn children matter? Is encouraging the advancement of reproductive technology in an era of world overpopulation and diminishing resources for health care a good thing? These are all excellent questions requiring moral and ethical considerations: the domain of philosophy.

It's important to underscore the point again that just because we are able to do certain things doesn't necessarily mean that we should. As you'll learn later in the book, you can't justifiably derive a philosophical or moral "ought" from an "is" of experience. This constitutes a kind of reasoning error or logical mistake called the **is-ought fallacy**. Normative issues (that is, matters of value and morality) require rational, philosophical treatment, not scientific or technological solutions. Science and technology expand our knowledge and what we *can* do, but they don't tell us what we *should* do. It would appear that, yet again, philosophy serves as a practical aid in the affairs of everyday life.

Therapeutic Applications of Philosophy

Many years ago, when I began my undergraduate university studies as a psychology major, I was interested in matters of human nature, morality, emotion, mental dysfunction, and the meaning of life. It wasn't very long into my psychology program before I began studying hormones and human physiology, neural synaptic transmissions, mechanisms of perception, rats in Skinner boxes, dominance hierarchies in primates, and so on. To use a philosophical term, I felt quite **alienated** as a result. At the time, I didn't see much of a connection between the kind of insight and self-understanding I was looking for and studying reinforcement schedules used to condition rats.

"We move about the earth with unprecedented speed, but we do not know, and have not thought, where we are going, or whether we shall find any happiness there for our harassed souls."
WILL DURANT

I'm not suggesting that scientific, experimental psychology has no value; it certainly does. Nonetheless, for me, it was unsatisfying. In retrospect, I see I was hungering for something in my life, which in the end turned out to be the fruits of philosophical inquiry. Philosophers asked the same questions I experienced as most pressing in my early adult life. As a seeker of sorts, trying to make sense of myself, others, and the world around me, philosophy became the key to wisdom and understanding. My elective course in introductory philosophy opened the door to a whole new way of seeing life and the world.

After only preliminary study, I realized that a subject so important had never been taught to me before in high school, and I felt cheated. I thought everybody should study philosophy as a required course. Had the adult world conspired to hide something from me, or was it that only a few enlightened individuals had access to the sweet wisdom that philosophy clearly had to offer? I didn't know for sure. What I did know is that after the study of philosophy, I would never be the same. Philosophy was to become an exercise of self-transformation, an experience of existential rebirth and, for a lost soul like me, a way out of the woods. (By the way, after graduating in psychology, I transferred to the philosophy program.)

For centuries, philosophers have recognized the healing and therapeutic powers of **philosophical counseling**. The therapy here is not so much ministered to the body, as to the mind—what the ancients sometimes referred to as "soul." Some philosophers, certainly those belonging to the **Hellenistic tradition** (Epicureans, Skeptics, and Stoics, circa 400 BCE–350 CE) thought of philosophy as a way of dealing with the most painful problems of human life. As Martha Nussbaum reminds us in her excellent book, *The Therapy of Desire: Theory and Practice in Hellenistic Ethics* (1994), the Hellenistic philosophical schools in Greece and Rome

> ... practiced philosophy not as a detached intellectual technique dedicated to the display of cleverness, but as an immersed and worldly art of grappling with human misery. They focused their attention, in consequence, on issues of daily and urgent human significance—the fear of death, love and sexuality, anger and aggression— issues that are sometimes avoided as embarrassingly messy and personal by the more detached varieties of philosophy.[9]

The therapeutic dimension of Hellenistic philosophy points again to philosophy's surprising practicality in real life. The thinking of philosophers such as Epicurus and Marcus Aurelius can help people to reduce stress and anxiety, especially where things like misfortune and heightened passions are concerned.

For centuries Hellenistic philosophers were very much concerned with the practical matters of life, and for hundreds of years following the Hellenistic era, philosophers continued trying to make a difference in people's lives, especially where morality and religious beliefs were concerned. Immanuel Kant's efforts in the 18th century to give morality a solid and secure foundation were certainly no useless endeavor (see Chapter 5). The influence of Stoicism on some cognitive-behavioral techniques of modern psychological counseling is also undeniable (see Chapter 3). So, the personal and practical therapeutic role of philosophy is neither new nor innovative. One could even make the case that to neglect the practical contributions of the ancients, and to ignore the enduring influence

"Vain is the word of a philosopher which does not heal any suffering of man. For just as there is no profit in medicine if it does not expel the diseases of the body, so there is no profit in philosophy either if it does not expel the suffering of the mind."
EPICURUS

of their therapeutic mission is, in fact, to provide a distorted picture of what the history of philosophy is all about.

However, just so you don't develop any misunderstandings about the therapeutic role of philosophy, and just so you don't confuse it with psychology or psychotherapy, I should quickly add at this juncture that Western philosophy during the past two centuries has not made much use of Hellenistic philosophy.[10] Most Western philosophers nowadays approach topics like ethics in a more detached and theoretical way, trying to keep personal matters to the side.

In view of this tendency, the present focus on philosophy's practical and therapeutic function appears strangely new and innovative—again, largely because it does not reflect the prevailing interests, activities, and preoccupations of most contemporary philosophers. Nevertheless, in view of some very recent developments within the field, it appears that a number of philosophers are now willing to revisit the Hellenistic period to see where philosophy might be going in this new millennium. For example, Tom Morris, a former Notre Dame professor and founder of The Morris Institute for Human Values, wrote the following:

> We live in a time suddenly hungry for wisdom. In a culture that has been celebrating material success for a century, we're ready for a reassessment of what really matters. As we move into a new millennium, we're witnessing a new global openness to ancient wisdom, a personal concern for meaning on a broad scale, and a widespread quest to understand what truly constitutes the good life.
>
> We want to get our bearings. Money, fame, power, and status have been found elusive by some, empty by others. They structure our societies and permeate our minds, but never deliver all they promise. And so we find ourselves searching for something more.
>
> The ancient Stoic thinkers had something more. These practical philosophers say that inner strength is the secret to personal effectiveness; that inner peace is, for most of us, the missing link to personal happiness; and that a nobility of self-possession and emotional self-control can make all the difference for living a life in full command of its own resources, and with a full enjoyment of its deepest inner rewards. The Stoics saw what we need. And they left us powerful advice about how to find it in our own lives.[11]

1.3 Fields of Philosophy

Another way to understand and approach philosophy, apart from focusing on its practical and therapeutic dimensions, is to examine philosophy in terms of its specialized fields of inquiry. There is some disagreement about how to divide philosophy into special subjects, but the general view is that there are six major specializations: **metaphysics**, **epistemology**, **logic**, **ethics**, **axiology** (aesthetics and the study of non-moral values), and **social/political philosophy.** Less fundamental, perhaps, but still important are the philosophical subdivisions I call **foundational and disciplinary philosophies** and the **philosophies of life.**

"There is no truth ... to the promise that technology does away with human drudgery ... it merely does away with human purpose."
GEORGE GRANT

AIM

Philosophy is sometimes described as an activity, not as a body of knowledge. Let's *do* some philosophy now, even before we cover the section on philosophical reasoning in Chapter 2. Our less-than-professional efforts here will be compensated for by our enthusiasm and eagerness to start engaging in philosophical discussion.

INSTRUCTIONS

First, break up into pairs, or split into two groups. One individual or group will take the affirmative side, while the other individual or group will take the negative side of this proposition: "*Philosophy should be a required course for all post-secondary students.*" Each side will be given a few minutes to prepare its position. Arguments in favor of the proposition will be offered first; then arguments opposed will be presented. Subsequently, the affirmative side will be afforded an opportunity to critique the negative, and the negative side will be given the last word to critique the arguments made by the positive side. Once finished, have the instructor facilitate full-class discussion, evaluating the merits of both affirmative and negative positions. Decide which arguments turned out to be better. This will require objectivity and rational detachment—virtues of the true philosopher.

Several philosophies of life will be discussed in Chapter 3, and you'll be better able there to appreciate why I consider them less basic or fundamental than the six major specializations. For now, let me say the reason is that life philosophies incorporate ideas, values, principles, and understandings that ultimately come from the primary branches. For instance, as part of your personal philosophy of life, you may or may not believe in God (metaphysics); you may argue that no knowledge of anything beyond sensory experience is possible (epistemology); that the purpose of rational argument is simply to win, gain control, and persuade opponents (logic); that nobody has the right to make value judgments on the behavior of others (ethics); and that beauty is in the eye of the beholder (axiology-aesthetics). Of course, taking a position in one area of philosophy may influence what position you can reasonably take in another one. If your metaphysical stance is that only the material universe exists and nothing else, then you can't logically believe in an immaterial heaven, hell, God, or immortal soul, or rationally think that morality can have a supernatural foundation or divine architect behind it.

Metaphysics

Popular usage of the term 'metaphysics' might lead you to conclude that it has something to do with spiritualism and the occult. After all, metaphysical bookstores do specialize in selling things like astrological charts, Ouija boards, and crystals. However, this is *not* what philosophical metaphysics concerns itself with. In the context of academic philosophy, metaphysics is the study of ultimate reality—what really exists and what it really is.

Examples of metaphysical topics of study include the existence and nature of the self, matter, freedom, God, causality, space, and time. As elusive as metaphysics seems, it is quite common to ponder metaphysical questions: Is there some one basic substance that everything is composed of? Is there something beyond the physical? Is there an unchanging reality behind the world of perception and appearance? Do humans have free will, or are they determined? Is there a God and, if not, what are the implications? Do minds exist? Do souls? If so, what are they like? Is there a purpose to life, life after death, or a reason behind the existence of all things as we experience them?

Epistemology

The term 'epistemology' means *the theory or study of knowledge*. Philosophers are fascinated by the nature and limits of knowledge. They ask themselves what we, as humans, can know. How is knowledge possible? Is certainty required for knowledge? Is there such a thing as absolute knowledge, or is all knowledge relative to the individual? What are the possible sources of knowledge? How is knowledge similar to, or different from, belief? What constitutes truth? Is reason the only way to truth or are there other avenues leading to it (such as divine revelation)?

Logic

Logic is that branch of philosophy that concerns itself with correct reasoning and the structures of valid rational thought. Much like grammar that underlies language, when it comes to the use of deductive logic in conversation, say, we find that embedded in the content or substance of our arguments are the underlying structures or logical forms that give it shape, so to speak. These forms may or may not conform to the accepted norms of correct reasoning—analogous to the rules of grammar. The science or study of logic allows us to discern which arguments do, and which do not, conform to accepted norms; which arguments are valid, sound, cogent, and strong; and which arguments are invalid, unsound, uncogent, and weak.

In the next chapter we will learn what constitutes valid logic and sound reasoning. We will look at some of the differences between inductive and deductive reasoning before examining some informal logical fallacies—those unacceptable forms of reasoning using diversionary tactics, faulty assumptions, and psychological appeals. Logic is the primary tool for doing philosophy, understanding the discipline more as an activity than as a body of knowledge to be memorized.

Ethics

Ethics, as a branch of philosophy, can generally be understood as the study of morals in human conduct. Ethicists are concerned with concepts such as good and bad, right and wrong, better and worse. They evaluate people's actions and social institutions' structures, policies, and procedures as morally praiseworthy or blameworthy. Contemporary ethical philosophy has had a lot to say, for example, about abortion, euthanasia (mercy-killing), warfare, and social inequality.

Philosophers doing ethics also attempt to provide general principles of moral obligation, as well as guidelines for ethical conduct. They address ultimate life values, matters of virtue, normative concerns pertaining to personal behavior, and ideal character development. Philosophers have presented a variety of approaches to what they take to be the basic principles and methods for ethical decision-making. Such decision-making can be made, for example, from the perspective of utilitarianism or virtue ethics. (See Chapter 5 to learn more.)

Some philosophers go beyond immediate practical concerns to examine and evaluate the *ultimate foundations* of ethical systems of thought, asking, for example, "Should faith or reason constitute the ultimate foundation of morality?" Because they are one step removed from thinking about specific moral issues, they are called *meta*-ethicists. Whereas the moral philosopher could ask whether capital punishment is appropriate or right in this case or that, the meta-ethicist would ask what is meant by the concept of 'right'; they might also question the standard used to determine rightness.

Thinking Can Be Dangerous

The following story is from Donald Simanek and John Holden's *Science Askew: A Light-hearted Look at the Scientific World*.[12]

It started out innocently enough. I began to think at parties now and then to loosen up. Inevitably though, one thought led to another, and soon I was more than just a social thinker. I began to think alone—"to relax," I told myself; but I knew it wasn't true. Thinking became more and more important to me, and finally, I was thinking all the time. I began to think on the job. I knew that thinking and employment don't mix, but I couldn't stop myself. I began to avoid friends at lunchtime so I could read Thoreau and Kafka. I would return to the office dizzied and confused, asking, "What is it exactly we are doing here?" Things weren't going so great at home either. One evening I had turned off the TV and asked my wife about the meaning of life. She spent that night at her mother's. I soon had a reputation as a heavy thinker.

One day the boss called me in. He said, "Skippy, I like you, and it hurts me to say this, but your thinking has become a real problem. If you don't stop thinking on the job, you'll have to find another job." This gave me a lot to think about. I came home early after my conversation with the boss. "Honey," I confessed, "I've been thinking ... "

"I know you've been thinking," she said, lower lip aquiver. "You think as much as college professors, and college professors don't make any money, so if you keep on thinking we won't have any money!"

"That's a faulty syllogism," I said impatiently, and she began to cry.

I had enough. "I'm going to the library," I snarled as I stomped out the door. I headed for the library, in the mood for some Nietzsche, with a PBS station on the radio. I roared into the parking lot and ran up to the big glass doors ... they didn't open. The library was closed! To this day, I believe that a Higher Power was looking out for me that night. As I sank to the ground clawing at the unfeeling glass, whimpering for Zarathustra, a poster caught my eye. "Friend, is heavy thinking ruining your life?" it asked. You probably recognize that line. It comes from the standard Thinker's Anonymous poster. Which is why I am what I am today: a recovering thinker. I never miss a TA meeting. At each meeting we watch a non-educational video; last week it was "Caddyshack." Then we share experiences about how we avoided thinking since the last meeting. I still have my job, and things are a lot better at home. Life just seemed ... easier, somehow, as soon as I stopped thinking. Now that makes you think, doesn't it?

Axiology

Axiology is a field of philosophical inquiry dealing with values. Ethics can be considered a sub-field of axiology, but we'll use the term to refer to the study of values other than ethical.

A major component of axiology is **aesthetics**. Aesthetics concerns itself with artistic values, beauty, and aesthetic appreciation. In the realm of aesthetics, people make value judgments about visual art, music, dance, and theater. Is beauty merely in the eye of the beholder? Are there objective standards by which to judge artworks? Can we say justifiably that classical music is better than country and western, or hip-hop? These constitute just a tiny sampling of the kinds of questions that philosophers concerned with aesthetics might ask.

Social/Political Philosophy

"There is perhaps nothing worse than reaching the top of the ladder and discovering that you're on the wrong wall."
JOSEPH CAMPBELL

Sometimes divided into two categories, social/political philosophy can be seen as that part of philosophy drawing our attention to conceptions of how to live well together in society, as well as to the philosophical foundations of the state and its political institutions. Social/political philosophers examine the individual's relation to the state and argue in favor of or against specific social policies (for example, forced busing and integrated schools, quota systems, corporate welfare, public funding for medical treatments, preferential admissions, and graduated income tax). Social/political philosophers also analyze different forms of government and social arrangements to help establish what is best or ideal.

As you can probably intuit, the questions raised by social/political philosophers are likely to have ethical implications, especially where rights and social responsibilities are concerned. These philosophers ask the following sorts of questions: Is it ever justified to violate the rights of the individual or minority group for the benefit of the majority? Is capitalism inherently corrupt? What is the best form of government? What principles should constitute the basis of a free and well-ordered society? Are all people created equal? Should we recognize the collective rights of Native Americans, or in Canada, the First Nations, the Inuit, the Métis, or other Indigenous groups? Should we give them preferred treatment in order to rectify past injustices? Does legitimate reconciliation require some sort of compensation or reparation for historical injustices?

Foundational and Disciplinary Philosophies

Foundational and disciplinary philosophies serve as the theoretical and conceptual bases for different kinds of human activities and academic subjects of study. For example, the practice of education is typically founded on a particular educational philosophy; how we run a business may be tied to our business philosophy; and how we participate in athletic events may hinge on our philosophy of sport.

As an educator, you might value cooperation and therefore stress teamwork and group projects as a way of achieving your educational goals. As a business owner, you might apply the philosophy that "the customer is always right," even when it inconveniences you or cuts into your profits. As an athlete, you might choose to quietly "look out for number one," selfishly sacrificing the welfare of the team for the sake of personal advantage.

Whatever the activity or human endeavor, the underlying philosophy gives purpose, order, and direction to it. It defines what's acceptable and what's not; what should be done and what shouldn't. Academic discipline-related philosophies (such as the philosophy of science, law, or psychology) spell out the implicit assumptions, methods, and principles of inquiry used by scholars in the field.

Philosophies of Life

There are probably as many philosophies of life as there are intelligent thinking beings in the world. Your own philosophy may or may not be well thought out. It may or may not be something to which you have paid much attention. Regardless, your personal philosophy reveals itself in much of what you value, think, say, and do.

Probably the best indicator of your personal philosophy is captured by your current lifestyle. What do you own? What do you want? What do you hope to achieve? How do you spend your time? What do you consider most important? What are your ideals

and aspirations? What do you hate? For what things, if any, are you willing to sacrifice or even die? On what issues will you not bend? How do you see yourself as a person?

Answers to these and similar questions form your *philosophical worldview*. Perhaps you seek pleasure, and fall under the category of "hedonist." By contrast, maybe you're a "stoic," wishing to find peace of mind above all else. In Chapter 3, we examine different philosophies of life and give you an opportunity to reflect on your own. Maybe it's time for you to reconsider your lifestyle or perhaps to engage in a wholesale philosophical reorientation.

1.4 Approaches to Philosophy

Still another way to understand and appreciate philosophy is by examining different approaches that have been taken toward it. In this section, you will see how gender, ethno-racial, historical, and methodological considerations can influence the way we conceptualize philosophy and engage in the enterprise.

Western Philosophy

The **Western tradition** has a proud and venerable past, and most of the philosophers covered in this introductory text belong to it, including all of the philosophers mentioned in the historical divisions listed above. When referring to philosophers like Plato, Aristotle, Seneca, Kant, or Nietzsche, for example, we're talking about Western thought. As a student of philosophy, you should be aware, however, that there are many other philosophical traditions. Academic philosophy in North America tends to focus on the Western tradition, most likely for reasons of historical accident, but perhaps because of bias, or due to efforts to maintain some sort of internal coherence in the continuing dialogue among significant thinkers in the field. Traditional treatments of philosophy will largely influence this book's coverage and the decisions made about how to allocate space. Unfortunately, limited space allocations imposed by this book prevent anything like an adequate treatment of non-traditional philosophical perspectives.

Historical Approaches

Efforts to understand philosophy have sometimes led individuals to carve it up historically. In Western philosophy, there are different periods into which particular philosophers fit. Plato and Aristotle, for instance, would fall under the category of **ancient philosophy**, which ranges from the sixth century BCE to approximately the third century CE. Religious philosophers such as St. Augustine and St. Thomas Aquinas can be placed together under **medieval philosophy**, a period running from the fourth century to roughly the sixteenth century. **Modern philosophy** includes thinkers like Immanuel Kant and John Stuart Mill. It extends from about the end of the sixteenth century through to the nineteenth century. **Contemporary philosophy** incorporates twentieth-century thinkers such as Jean-Paul Sartre, Simone de Beauvoir, Bertrand Russell, and those involved in philosophy during the twenty-first century. Contemporary philosophers tend to be classed as either **analytic** or **continental**, a distinction based on the interests displayed and methods used. **Analytical philosophers** focus on **conceptual analysis**, while **continental philosophers**—existentialists and phenomenologists, for example—concentrate on matters of being, authenticity, freedom, and meaning. Still more recently, **postmodernism** has appeared as a new school of philosophical thought. Essentially, it rejects most of the cultural certainties on which life in the West has been structured over the past couple of centuries.

Non-Traditional and Non–Western Approaches

For our introductory purposes here, we must begin somewhere. Admittedly, focusing on the Western tradition does not give one a complete picture of the richness and diversity of all philosophical approaches when it comes to understanding life and the universe more broadly. Nonetheless, it can serve as a basis for later studies and comparisons to other non-traditional and/or non-Western ways of engaging in philosophical activity. A preliminary coverage of the traditional Western approach is useful, then, even if limited in scope.

But before we begin our coverage, let's briefly identify some other philosophies falling outside the boundaries of the Western canon. In East Asia, for instance, hundreds of millions of people profess some form of religious philosophy, be it Buddhism, Daoism, or classical Confucianism. In India and in parts of South Asia, you again have different philosophical worldviews, Hinduism in particular. In the Middle East, Islam and Judaism are the prevailing religious philosophies guiding the lives of millions.

Despite this work's primary focus on the Western canon, we will include some consideration of other traditions. In Chapter 3, we'll examine Buddhism as a philosophy of life, while the religious philosophies of Hinduism and Islam will be covered briefly in Chapter 5. In that same chapter, under the heading of "Religious Ethics," a treatment of Christianity will also be provided. This coverage should serve to underscore the overlap between philosophy and religion.

Africa too has rich philosophical traditions, though many are unwritten and difficult to make general statements about. For the past several decades, African philosophers have been trying to come to terms with past colonial oppression. They have faced a "deconstructive" challenge, trying to understand and respond to what some regard as a harmful Eurocentrism inherited from European colonists who culturally imposed themselves on indigenous Africans. They have also confronted the "reconstructive" challenge of trying to revitalize the modern reality of Africa's historical and cultural heritage. African (and African American) philosophers are now asking: What does and does not genuinely belong to African philosophy? Is it different from Western philosophy? And what does philosophizing as a black person really mean? In Chapter 6, we'll get some idea of what the answer to the last question could possibly be as we examine the philosophy of black minister and social activist Martin Luther King Jr.—an action-oriented social and political philosophy that can be distilled from his sermons and public orations.

Important to note as well is that the Indigenous peoples of North America have developed their own philosophical traditions independently from European, Middle Eastern, African, and Asian influences. In Saskatchewan, for example, the Moose Mountain Medicine Wheel, a 2000-year-old physical structure, is believed to have spiritual and astrological significance. As a teaching tool, the concept of the **medicine wheel** has been used for centuries by some of the Indigenous peoples of North America to help them gain self-awareness, spiritual nourishment, and guidance for living. However, little is recorded about it. Knowledge and information about the medicine wheel has been transmitted orally from one generation to the next.

Because Indigenous traditions tend to be oral rather than written, the best way for you to learn more is by actually speaking to a tribal elder. That being said, there are a growing number of resources that serve to introduce particular aspects of Indigenous North American philosophy.

Feminist Approaches

It was suggested earlier that philosophy can serve a liberating function, freeing us from our prejudices, ignorance, and subjectivity. It's a bit embarrassing, therefore, to have to admit that, in the past, many male philosophers have been guilty of their own gender bias and cognitive egocentrism. This is evidenced by the fact that women have traditionally been ignored in textbooks and histories of philosophy.

With the growing interest in women's thought and feminist political activism, however, the role of women within the field of philosophy is sure to expand. Alison Jaggar, for example, has made a significant philosophical contribution by reexamining the role of emotion in a newly re-framed feminist epistemology. As will be discussed in Chapter 5, Carol Gilligan has questioned the use of male norms as a basis for evaluating the adequacy of ethical judgment and determining the maturity levels of moral development in children and adolescents. More recently, initiatives such as New Narratives in the History of Philosophy and Project Vox are increasing the exposure of women philosophers who have traditionally received little to no attention in the history of philosophy.[13] The contributions of women to philosophy have for too long been underappreciated or unnoticed; gladly, philosophy only stands to be enriched by including the fresh new insights that a feminist perspective has to offer.

Lee Hester, "Truth and Native American Epistemology"[14]

Lee Hester, *a citizen of the Choctaw Nation, is Professor of American Indian Studies at the University of Science and Arts of Oklahoma. In the following passage, taken from an article he co-wrote with Jim Cheney, Hester describes some differences between Western philosophy and Indigenous (or Native American) thinking. Hester emphasizes the guiding role played by stories themselves, rather than any propositions or "truths" one might derive from them: "the narrative is as close to the truth as you can get."*

———

Knowledge is narrative of a life lived in the world. The individual stories are what you know. They may or may not provide a map of the world, but they do tell you about the consequences of your actions. You can learn much even if you believe little. You can even be taught. Here another short story might be useful.

After a long day's work I was supposed to help unload a bunch of tables and chairs at the new Choctaw center in Oklahoma City. Mr. Amos Dorsey, an older full-blood Cree and I were going to work together. There was quite a bit of work to do and I wanted to get home, so I threw myself into the work—busily hustling back and forth. Mr. Dorsey began to work too, but a bit slower and only after watching me for a second or two. Indeed, as he worked and watched me, I could almost swear he was actually going even slower. Eventually, it was as if he was going in slow-motion. Of course, part of that was due to my haste. As we worked and I fumed a bit at his slowness, I finally realized that somehow he was actually getting more done than I was. Mr. Dorsey respected the task, understood the context and set about working efficiently. However, I think it was also an instance of teaching. I cannot help but think he slowed down as he saw my thoughtless, disrespectful haste and then speeded up as he saw that I had learned my lesson and was working efficiently.

Now, we could assert some 'Truths' here. We might say that 'Haste makes waste'. Yet of course, the 'Early bird got the worm'. Just about any 'Truth' we might assert—particularly action guiding truths—are going to have contradictory 'Truths' that can be abstracted out of other stories. Thus we have the contradictory actions. This search for 'Truth' is the European tradition. The Native tradition does not abstract truths out of the stories, the stories are often abstract enough in themselves without further removing them from reality. The narrative is as close to the truth as you can get. In the end, I think that the two epistemic systems may converge. As the Euro-American tradition refines its truths, resolving the contradictions by adding more and more exceptions and greater and greater complexity, these truths may eventually more nearly resemble stories. In the meantime, Indian people will be waiting at the fire already telling some good ones.

READING QUESTIONS

1. Hester writes that the "search for 'Truth' is the European tradition." Does truth vary from one culture to another? Does the very idea of truth vary across cultures?

2. "The Native tradition does not abstract truths out of the stories.... The narrative is as close to the truth as you can get." Hester uses a story to convey his meaning in the passage above. Could the same meaning be conveyed through statements without a story? Is the narrative version indeed "close[r] to the truth"?

Spiritually-Based Philosophical Traditions

While the majority of academic philosophers are committed to the ideals of reason, religious existentialists such as Søren Kierkegaard contend that subjective truth cannot properly be understood by pure rational objectivity, and that certain higher levels of being are beyond reason, requiring "irrational" leaps of faith to arrive at them.

Many other world philosophies similarly place less emphasis on reason and argument than they do on faith and practice. Not all of philosophy is based on discursive reasoning, proceeding in a linear fashion from premises to logical conclusions. Specifically, we find traditions that make extensive use of *symbols* in their spiritual practices and in their philosophical efforts to understand the universe.

From the Middle East comes mystical Judaism with its Kabbalah, or *Tree of Life*—a diagram that functions as a kind of map illustrating the particular patterns and laws by which God is said to have created the manifest universe (see Figure 1.1). The "Sign of the Presence of God" has been used by Middle Eastern Islamic Sufi mystics to promote moral healing (see Figure 1.2). An adaptation of the Sign, called the *enneagram*, is now used by Jesuits and other mystically inclined Christians to understand the human condition in terms of man's fall from grace. The symbol illustrates and explains how we all inevitably detach from our human *essence* and what we must do to recapture our true selves in God

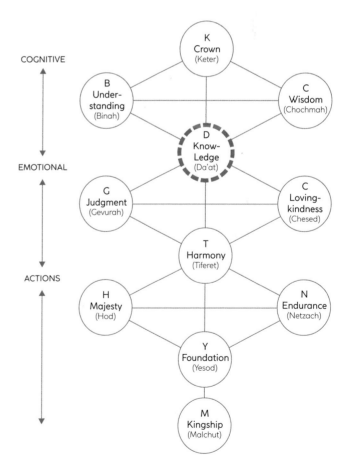

FIGURE 1.1 The Kabbalah[15]

Kabbalah means "given by the tradition," and the term refers to the oral, mystical, and esoteric traditions of the Jewish people. Many of its ideas and themes are present in other systems of thought, for example, Indian philosophy, Platonism, and Gnosticism. In the Kabbalah, the biblical tradition converges with these other systems "to produce a comprehensive philosophical and psychological vision of the nature of God and humankind that was only imperfectly represented in prior traditions."

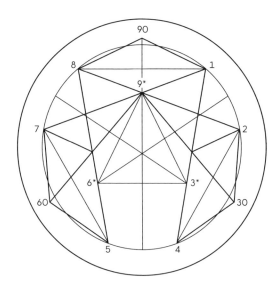

FIGURE 1.2 The Sign of the Presence of God (Wajh Allah)

The design was given this name by the Naqshbandi Sufi Order in Central Asia. It is used to help the "spiritual warrior" attain moral healing. The more familiar Enneagram, which symbolizes nine character types, derives from this sign. You can learn more about this by reading Laleh Bakhtiar's writings on Sufism.[16]

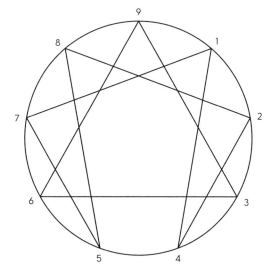

FIGURE 1.3 The Enneagram

The Enneagram is a symbol used to promote character development. Each number captures a different character type that constructs reality in accordance with type-specific fears, desires, and assumptions about the world. Use of the Enneagram helps one to achieve spiritual liberation, knowledge of oneself, and understanding of others.

(see Figure 1.3). Modern developers of the enneagram, like Oscar Ichazo and Claudio Naranjo, have made efforts to synthesize its traditional wisdom with modern psychiatry to get a better understanding of human character.

In some Eastern religious philosophies such as Buddhism, meditative practices and disciplined ritual take on a much more prominent role than do rational analysis and critique. (We'll get a chance to experiment with meditation shortly and learn more about Buddhism as a philosophy of life in Chapter 3.) But first, let's examine how spiritual and philosophical concerns can overlap and differ by looking at the work of **Abu Hamid al-Ghazali**, a Middle-Eastern Muslim thinker who believed that the traditional Islam of his day had become moribund. In the original source that follows, we learn how he adopted a faith in God philosophically, but at the same time without accepting any philosophical system.

Abu Hamid al-Ghazali, *Al-Munqidh min al-Dalal (Deliverance from Error)*[17]

Abu Hamid Muhammad Ibn Muhammad Ahmad al-Tusi al-Ghazali (1058–1111 CE) was an influential theologian, philosopher, and legal scholar of Islam. A prolific writer, al-Ghazali wrote many works, including the short but significant autobiography al-Munqidh min al-Dalal (Deliverance from Error). *In it, al-Ghazali uses the story of his own crisis of skepticism to support the book's main message that deliverance from error is achieved by religious faith and, more specifically, by mystical union with God. As he shares with his audience, intellectual doubts stirred up by his studies led him to resign from academic life and enter a period of intense solitude and spirituality. It was during this period that he achieved direct knowledge of God and the certainty which his traditional education in philosophy and theology lacked. In this way, al-Ghazali blends his reflections on philosophy and religion with autobiographical insights into his intellectual and spiritual experience.* Deliverance from Error *consists of an introduction and eight main sections. The following selection comes from the introduction and chapter one.*

———

QUOTH THE IMAM GHAZALI:

Glory be to God, whose praise should precede every writing and every speech! May the blessings of God rest on Mohammed, his Prophet and his Apostle, on his family and companions, by whose guidance error is escaped!

You have asked me, O brother in the faith, to expound the aim and the mysteries of religious sciences, the boundaries and depths of theological doctrines. You wish to know my experiences while disentangling truth lost in the medley of sects and divergencies of thought, and how I have dared to climb from the low levels of traditional belief to the topmost summit of assurance. You desire to learn what I have borrowed, first of all from scholastic theology; and secondly from the method of the Ta'limites, who, in seeking truth, rest upon the authority of a leader; and why, thirdly, I have been led to reject philosophic systems; and finally, what I have accepted of the doctrine of the Sufis, and the sum total

of truth which I have gathered in studying every variety of opinion. You ask me why, after resigning at Baghdad a teaching post which attracted a number of hearers, I have, long afterward, accepted a similar one at Nishapur. Convinced as I am of the sincerity which prompts your inquiries, I proceed to answer them, invoking the help and protection of God.

Know then, my brothers (may God direct you in the right way), that the diversity in beliefs and religions, and the variety of doctrines and sects which divide men, are like a deep ocean strewn with shipwrecks, from which very few escape safe and sound. Each sect, it is true, believes itself in possession of the truth and of salvation, "each party," as the Qur'an saith, "rejoices in its own creed"; but as the chief of the apostles, whose word is always truthful, has told us, "My people will be divided into more than seventy sects, of whom only one will be saved." This prediction, like all others of the Prophet, must be fulfilled.

From the period of adolescence, that is to say, previous to reaching my twentieth year to the present time when I have passed my fiftieth, I have ventured into this vast ocean; I have fearlessly sounded its depths, and like a resolute diver, I have penetrated its darkness and dared its dangers and abysses. I have interrogated the beliefs of each sect and scrutinized the mysteries of each doctrine, in order to disentangle truth from error and orthodoxy from heresy. I have never met one who maintained the hidden meaning of the Qur'an without investigating the nature of his belief. Nor a partisan of its exterior sense without inquiring into the results of his doctrine. There is no philosopher whose system I have not fathomed, nor theologian the intricacies of whose doctrine I have not followed out.

Sufism has no secrets into which I have not penetrated; the devout adorer of Deity has revealed to me the aim of his austerities; the atheist has not been able to conceal from me the real reason of his unbelief. The thirst for knowledge was innate in me from an early age; it was like a second nature implanted by God, without any will on my part. No sooner had I emerged from boy-hood than I had already broken the fetters of tradition and freed myself from hereditary beliefs.

Having noticed how easily the children of Christians become Christians, and the children of Muslims embrace Islam, and remembering also the traditional saying ascribed to the Prophet, "Every child has in him the germ of Islam, then his parents make him Jew, Christian, or Zarathustrian," I was moved by a keen desire to learn what was this innate disposition in the child, the nature of the accidental beliefs imposed on him by the authority of his parents and his masters, and finally the unreasoned convictions which he derives from their instructions.

Struck with the contradictions which I encountered in endeavoring to disentangle the truth and falsehood of these opinions, I was led to make the following reflec-tion: "The search after truth being the aim which I pro-pose to myself, I ought in the first place to ascertain what are the bases of certitude." In the next place I recognized that certitude is the clear and complete knowledge of things, such knowledge as leaves no room for doubt nor possibility of error and conjecture, so that there remains no room in the mind for error to find an entrance. In such a case it is necessary that the mind, fortified against all possibility of going astray, should embrace such a strong conviction that, if, for example, any one possess-ing the power of changing a stone into gold, or a stick into a serpent, should seek to shake the bases of this cer-titude, it would remain firm and immovable. Suppose, for instance, a man should come and say to me, who am firmly convinced that ten is more than three, "No; on the contrary, three is more than ten, and, to prove it, I change this rod into a serpent," and supposing that he actually did so, I should remain none the less convinced of the falsity of his assertion, and although his miracle might arouse my astonishment, it would not instil any doubt into my belief.

I then understood that all forms of knowledge which do not unite these conditions (imperviousness to doubt, etc.) do not deserve any confidence, because they are not beyond the reach of doubt, and what is not impregnable to doubt can not constitute certitude.

THE SUBTERFUGES OF THE SOPHISTS

I then examined what knowledge I possessed, and discov-ered that in none of it, with the exception of sense-per-ceptions and necessary principles, did I enjoy that degree of certitude which I have just described. I then sadly reflected as follows: "We can not hope to find truth except in matters which carry their evidence in them-selves—that is to say, in sense-perceptions and necessary principles; we must therefore establish these on a firm basis. Is my absolute confidence in sense-perceptions and on the infallibility of necessary principles analogous to the confidence which I formerly possessed in matters believed on the authority of others? Is it only analo-gous to the reliance most people place on their organs of vision, or is it rigorously true without admixture of illusion or doubt?"

I then set myself earnestly to examine the notions we derive from the evidence of the senses and from sight in order to see if they could be called in question. The result of a careful examination was that my confidence in them was shaken. Our sight, for instance, perhaps the best practiced of all our senses, observes a shadow, and finding it apparently stationary pronounces it devoid of movement. Observation and experience, however, show subsequently that a shadow moves not suddenly, it is true, but gradually and imperceptibly, so that it is never really motionless.

Again, the eye sees a star and believes it as large as a piece of gold, but mathematical calculations prove, on the contrary, that it is larger than the earth. These notions, and all others which the senses declare true, are subsequently contradicted and convicted of falsity in an irrefragable manner by the verdict of reason.

Then I reflected in myself: "Since I can not trust to the evidence of my senses, I must rely only on intellec-tual notions based on fundamental principles, such as the following axioms: 'Ten is more than three. Affirmation and negation can not coexist together. A thing can not both be created and also existent from eternity, living and annihilated simultaneously, at once necessary and impossible.'" To this the notions I derived from my senses made the following objections: "Who can guarantee you that you can trust to the evidence of reason more than to that of the senses? You believed in our testimony till it was contradicted by the verdict of reason, otherwise you would have continued to believe it to this day. Well, perhaps, there is above reason another judge who, if he appeared, would convict reason of falsehood, just as reason has confuted us. And if such a third arbiter is not yet apparent, it does not follow that he does not exist."

To this argument I remained some time without reply; a reflection drawn from the phenomena of sleep deepened my doubt. "Do you not see," I reflected, "that while asleep you assume your dreams to be indisputably real? Once awake, you recognize them for what they are—baseless chimeras. Who can assure you, then, of the reliability of notions which, when awake, you derive from the senses and from reason? In relation to your present state they may be real; but it is possible also that you may enter upon another state of being which will bear the same relation to your present state as this does to your condition when asleep. In that new sphere you will recognize that the conclusions of reason are only chimeras."

This possible condition is perhaps, that which the Sufis call "ecstasy" (hal), that is to say, according to them, a state in which, absorbed in themselves and in the suspension of sense-perceptions, they have visions beyond the reach of intellect. Perhaps also Death is that state, according to that saying of the prince of prophets: "Men are asleep; when they die, they wake." Our present life in relation to the future is perhaps only a dream, and man, once dead, will see things in direct opposition to those now before his eyes; he will then understand that word of the Qur'an, "To-day we have removed the veil from thine eyes and thy sight is keen."

Such thoughts as these threatened to shake my reason, and I sought to find an escape from them. But how? In order to disentangle the knot of this difficulty, a proof was necessary. Now a proof must be based on primary assumptions, and it was precisely these of which I was in doubt. This unhappy state lasted about two months, during which I was, not, it is true, explicitly or by profession, but morally and essentially, a thorough-going skeptic.

God at last deigned to heal me of this mental malady; my mind recovered sanity and equilibrium, the primary assumptions of reason recovered with me all their stringency and force. I owed my deliverance, not to a concatenation of proofs and arguments, but to the light which God caused to penetrate into my heart—the light which illuminates the threshold of all knowledge. To suppose that certitude can be only based upon formal arguments is to limit the boundless mercy of God. Some one asked the Prophet the explanation of this passage in the Divine Book: "God opens to Islam the heart of him whom he chooses to direct." "That is spoken," replied the Prophet, "of the light which God sheds in the heart." "And how can man recognize that light?" he was asked. "By his detachment from this world of illusion and by a secret drawing toward the eternal world," the Prophet replied.

On another occasion he said: "God has created his creatures in darkness, and then has shed upon them his light." It is by the help of this light that the search for truth must be carried on. As by his mercy this light descends from time to time among men, we must ceaselessly be on the watch for it. This is also corroborated by another saying of the Apostle: "God sends upon you, at certain times, breathings of his grace; be prepared for them." …

READING QUESTIONS

1. Take a closer look at al-Ghazali's ocean metaphor, where he compares his study of diverse beliefs and religions to diving into a "vast ocean." How does his use of ocean imagery help you understand what he did during his studies and why he did it? How does it help you understand his skepticism?

2. If you are certain that something is true, can anything make you doubt that belief, according to al-Ghazali? Consider the belief that the moon exists. Using al-Ghazali's conditions of certitude, is that a certain belief? If not, why not?

3. Formal argument, or God: of those two options, which cured al-Ghazali of his skeptical doubts, and how did it cure him? Next, which of those two options did not—and could not—cure al-Ghazali of his skeptical doubts, and why not? Use the text to explain your answers.

4. What lesson about philosophy do you take from al-Ghazali's story? What lesson about religion do you take from it? Compare and contrast those lessons.

EXPERIENCE MEDITATION

Before we become fully engaged in the typically Western rational pursuit of philosophical wisdom, let us pause and still the unsettled, indecisive, confused and out-of-control "monkey mind," as the Buddhists call it, with some Eastern-inspired meditation.

The idea is to narrow your focus and limit the stimuli bombarding your nervous system. To the extent you are successful, you will calm your mind in the process. Hindu gurus, highly trained in meditative practices, claim to be able to reach higher levels of cosmic consciousness transcending all rational forms of knowledge. Since we are neither gurus nor highly trained, we will be content for now just to still the mind for a few minutes. Your experience of meditation should quickly reveal to you how busy and agitated your mind really is, and how difficult such an apparently simple practice can be. If you're unsure about what to do for your first meditation, you could try the following:

1. First, find a quiet spot, dim the lights, and sit comfortably in a chair with a relatively straight back. Unfold your arms and uncross your legs.

2. Close your eyes and then take three or four deep breaths.

3. Pick a word, phrase, or affirmation that is quite simple or has special meaning to you.

4. Start to breathe through your nose, repeating the word or phrase in your mind in time with your breathing. Some people find counting breaths is useful. As you inhale, count *one*; when you exhale, count *two*; on the next inhalation count *one* again, and then *two* again when you exhale. Repeat. If and when distractions occur, release them and let them pass by. Don't feel like you've done something wrong or that the meditation hasn't worked. Be gentle with yourself.

5. Continue the meditation for about five minutes. Slowly regain normal awareness and then peacefully go about the rest of your day.[18]

FOR DISCUSSION

What was your experience of meditation like? Were you able to still the mad "monkey mind" and achieve inner calm? Describe that calm or explain what prevented you from attaining it.

Modern Western Philosophy

Whether reason, meditation, introspective character analysis, or something else should be your vehicle to philosophical enlightenment is a question that only you can answer. As mentioned, for our introductory purposes in this book, we'll be emphasizing the Western philosophical tradition.

As we've now learned, the Western philosophical tradition is only one of many different ways of doing, experiencing, or engaging in philosophy. And even within Western thought, there are various views and movements across its enduring run from ancient Greece to today. A particularly insightful account of what western philosophers *do* when they are doing philosophy, and of why they do it, is offered by Bertrand Russell, a notable Western thinker of the twentieth century.

Bertrand Russell

Bertrand Russell, a British philosopher, logician, and social critic, was born in Trelleck, Wales, in 1872. He lived a long life, dying in 1970 at age 97. Concerning how he lived that life, Russell wrote: "Three passions, simple but overwhelmingly strong, have governed my life: the longing for love, the search for knowledge, and unbearable pity for the suffering of mankind."[19]

Russell studied mathematics, logic, and philosophy at Trinity College at Cambridge University, where he later became a Lecturer in philosophy. Prior to that appointment, Russell had also studied and published in social and political thought; but it was his social and political activities that ended that appointment. In 1916, during World War I, Russell was fined for writing an anti-war document and subsequently dismissed from his position at Trinity College. Sanctions did not deter Russell from further activism. He spent months in prison in 1918 for more anti-war writings and decades later, in 1961, his anti-nuclear protests put him back in prison—albeit only for one week.

Although Russell was offered reinstatement to his position at Trinity College, he declined. Instead, he spent much of the 1920s occupied with travel, unsuccessful runs for Parliament, and lecturing in the United States. His views on educational philosophy were put into practice in his experimental Beacon Hill School, which he started in 1927 with Dora Russell, his second of four wives. In 1938, Russell moved to the United States, first teaching at the University of Chicago and then at the University of California at Los Angeles. In 1940, he accepted an invitation to join the philosophy department at the City College of New York. A local judge, however, found Russell "morally unfit" for the position, because his popular books advocated sex before marriage, temporary marriages, and homosexuality. For the protection of "public health, safety and morals," the position was revoked before it began. In 1944, almost 30 years after his dismissal from Cambridge, Russell was reappointed a Fellow of Trinity College.

Above all, Russell identified as a writer. What is more, despite an irreverence that offended many, Russell was a writer with an enormous audience who enjoyed widespread popularity. His first important book, *The Principles of Mathematics*, was a work in logic, but Russell also wrote about various social, moral, political, and ethical issues. Some books on these topics include *The Practice and Theory of Bolshevism*, *Why I Am Not a Christian*, *Education and the Social Order*, *Marriage and Morals*, *Religion and Science*, and *On Education, Especially in Early Childhood*. Russell was awarded the Nobel Prize for Literature in 1950. The Russell archives are currently housed at McMaster University in Hamilton, Ontario, Canada.

Bertrand Russell, "The Value of Philosophy"[20]

The following essay, titled "The Value of Philosophy," is the final chapter in Bertrand Russell's book, The Problems of Philosophy *(1912). As he puts it in the book's preface, Russell's approach to those problems is "positive and constructive, since merely negative criticism seemed out of place."*

——

Having now come to the end of our brief and very incomplete review of the problems of philosophy, it will be well to consider, in conclusion, what is the value of philosophy and why it ought to be studied. It is the more necessary to consider this question, in view of the fact that many men, under the influence of science or of practical affairs, are inclined to doubt whether philosophy is anything better than innocent but useless trifling, hair-splitting distinctions, and controversies on matters concerning which knowledge is impossible.

This view of philosophy appears to result, partly from a wrong conception of the ends of life, partly from a wrong conception of the kind of goods which philosophy strives to achieve. Physical science, through the medium of inventions, is useful to innumerable people who are wholly ignorant of it; thus the study of physical science is to be recommended, not only, or primarily, because of the effect on mankind in general. This utility does not belong to philosophy. If the study of philosophy has any value at all for other than students of philosophy, it must be only indirectly, through its effects upon the lives of those who study it. It is in these effects, therefore, if anywhere, that the value of philosophy must be primarily sought.

But further, if we are not to fail in our endeavor to determine the value of philosophy, we must first free our minds from the prejudices of what are wrongly called "practical" men. The "practical" man, as this word is often used, is one who recognizes only material needs, who realizes that men must have food for the body, but is oblivious of the necessity of providing food for the mind. If all men were well off, if poverty and disease had been reduced to their lowest possible point, there would still remain much to be done to produce a valuable society: and even in the existing world the goods of the mind are at least as important as the goods of the body. It is exclusively among the goods of the mind that the value of philosophy is to be found; and only those who are not indifferent to these goods can be persuaded that the study of philosophy is not a waste of time.

Philosophy, like all other studies, aims primarily at knowledge. The knowledge it aims at is the kind of knowledge which gives unity and system to the body of the sciences, and the kind which results from a critical examination of the grounds of our convictions, prejudices, and beliefs. But it cannot be maintained that philosophy has had any very great measure of success in its attempts to provide definite answers to its questions. If you ask a mathematician, a mineralogist, a historian, or any other man of learning, what definite body of truths has been ascertained by his science, his answer will last as long as you are willing to listen. But if you put the same question to a philosopher, he will, if he is candid, have to confess that his study has not achieved positive results such as have been achieved by other sciences. It is true that this is partly accounted for by the fact that, as soon as definite knowledge concerning any subject becomes possible, this subject ceases to be called philosophy and becomes a separate science. The whole study of the heavens, which now belongs to astronomy, was once included in philosophy; Newton's great work was called "the mathematical principles of natural philosophy." Similarly, the study of the human mind, which was, until very lately, a part of philosophy, has now been separated from philosophy and has become the science of psychology. Thus, to a great extent, the uncertainty of philosophy is more apparent than real: those questions which are already capable of definite answers are placed in the sciences, while those only to which, at present, no definite answer can be given, remain to form the residue which is called philosophy.

This is, however, only a part of the truth concerning the uncertainty of philosophy. There are many questions—and among them those that are of the profoundest interest to our spiritual life—which, so far as we can see, must remain insoluble to the human intellect unless its powers become of quite a different order from what they are now. Has the universe any unity of plan or purpose, or is it a fortuitous concourse of atoms? Is consciousness a permanent part of the universe, giving hope of indefinite growth in wisdom, or is it transitory accident on a small planet on which life must ultimately become impossible? Are good and evil of importance to the universe or only to man? Such questions are asked by philosophy, and variously answered by various philosophers. But it would seem that, whether answers be otherwise discoverable or not, the answers suggested by philosophy are none of them demonstrably true. Yet, however slight may be the hope of discovering an answer, it is part of the business of philosophy to continue the consideration of such questions, to make us aware of their importance, to examine all the approaches to them, and to keep alive that speculative interest in the universe which is apt to be killed by confining ourselves to definitely ascertainable knowledge.

Many philosophers, it is true, have held that philosophy could establish the truth of certain answers to such fundamental questions. They have supposed that what is of most importance in religious beliefs could be proved by strict demonstration to be true. In order to judge of such attempts, it is necessary to take a survey of human knowledge, and to form an opinion as to its methods and its limitations. On such a subject it would be unwise to pronounce dogmatically; but if the investigations of our previous chapters have not led us astray, we shall be compelled to renounce the hope of finding philosophical proofs of religious beliefs. We cannot, therefore, include as part of the value of philosophy any definite set of answers to such questions. Hence, once more, the value of philosophy must not depend upon any supposed body of definitely ascertainable knowledge to be acquired by those who study it.

The value of philosophy is, in fact, to be sought largely in its very uncertainty. The man who has no tincture of philosophy goes through life imprisoned in the prejudices derived from common sense, from the habitual beliefs of his age or his nation, and from convictions which have grown up in his mind without the cooperation or consent of his deliberate reason. To such a man the world tends to become definite, finite, obvious; common objects rouse no questions, and unfamiliar possibilities are contemptuously rejected. As soon as we begin to philosophize, on the contrary, we find as we saw in our opening chapters, that even the most everyday things lead to problems to which only very incomplete answers can be given. Philosophy, though unable to tell us with certainty what is the true answer to the doubts which it raises, is able to suggest many possibilities which enlarge our thoughts and free them from the tyranny of custom. Thus, while diminishing our feeling of certainty as to what things are, it greatly increases our knowledge as to what they may be; it removes the somewhat arrogant dogmatism of those who have never travelled into the region of liberating doubt, and it keeps alive our sense of wonder by showing familiar things in an unfamiliar aspect.

Apart from its utility in showing unsuspected possibilities, philosophy has a value—perhaps its chief value—through the greatness of the objects which it contemplates, and the freedom from narrow and personal aims resulting from this contemplation. The life of the instinctive man is shut up within the circle of his private interests: family and friends may be included, but the outer world is not regarded except as it may help or hinder what comes within the circle of instinctive wishes. In such a life there is something feverish and confined, in comparison with which the philosophic life is calm and free. The private world of instinctive interests is a small one, set in the midst of a great and powerful world which must, sooner or later, lay our private world in ruins. Unless we can so enlarge our interests as to include the whole outer world, we remain like a garrison in a beleaguered fortress, knowing that the enemy prevents escape and that ultimate surrender is inevitable. In such a life there is no peace, but a constant strife between the insistence of desire and the powerlessness of will. In one way or another, if our life is to be great and free, we must escape this prison and this strife.

One way of escape is by philosophic contemplation. Philosophic contemplation does not, in its widest survey, divide the universe into two hostile camps—friends and foes, helpful and hostile, good and bad—it views the whole impartially. Philosophic contemplation, when it is unalloyed, does not aim at proving that the rest of the universe is akin to man. All acquisition of knowledge is an enlargement of the Self, but this enlargement is best attained when it is not directly sought. It is obtained when the desire for knowledge is alone operative, by a study which does not wish in advance that its objects should have this or that character, but adapts the Self to the characters which it finds in its objects. This enlargement of Self is not obtained when, taking the Self as it is, we try to show that the world is so similar to this Self that knowledge of it is possible without any admission of what seems alien. The desire to prove this is a form of self-assertion, and like all self-assertion, it is an obstacle to the growth of Self which it desires, and of which the Self knows that it is capable. Self-assertion, in philosophic speculation as elsewhere, views the world as a means to its own ends; thus it makes the world of less account than Self, and the Self sets bounds to the greatness of its goods. In contemplation, on the contrary, we start from the not-Self, and through its greatness the boundaries of Self are enlarged, through the infinity of the universe the mind which contemplates it achieves some share in infinity.

For this reason greatness of soul is not fostered by those philosophies which assimilate the universe to man. Knowledge is a form of union of Self and not-Self; like all union, it is impaired by dominion, and therefore by any attempt to force the universe into conformity with what we find in ourselves. There is a widespread philosophical tendency towards the view which tells us that man is the measure of all things, that truth is man-made, that space and time and the world of universals are properties of the mind, and that, if there be anything not created by the mind, it is unknowable and of no account for us. This view, if our previous discussions were correct, is untrue; but in addition to being untrue, it has the effect of robbing philosophic contemplation of all that gives it value, since it fetters contemplation to Self. What it calls knowledge is not a union with the not-Self, but a set of prejudices, habits, and desires, making an impenetrable veil between us and the world beyond. The man who finds pleasure in such a theory of knowledge is like the man who never leaves the domestic circle for fear his word might not be law.

The true philosophic contemplation, on the contrary, finds its satisfaction in every enlargement of the not-Self, in everything that magnifies the objects contemplated, and thereby the subject contemplating. Everything, in contemplation, that is personal or private, everything that depends upon habit, self-interest, or desire, distorts the object, and hence impairs the union which the intellect seeks. By thus making a barrier between subject and object, such personal and private things become a prison to the intellect. The free intellect will see as God might see, without a *here* and *now*, without hopes and fears, without the trammels of customary beliefs and traditional prejudices, calmly, dispassionately, in the sole and exclusive desire of knowledge—knowledge as impersonal, as purely contemplative, as it is possible for man to attain. Hence also the free intellect will value more the abstract and universal knowledge into which the accidents of private history do not enter, than the knowledge brought by the senses, and dependent, as such knowledge must be, upon an exclusive and personal point of view and a body whose sense-organs distort as much as they reveal.

The mind which has become accustomed to the freedom and impartiality of philosophic contemplation will preserve something of the same freedom and impartiality in the world of action and emotion. It will view its purposes and desires as parts of the whole, with the absence of insistence that results from seeing them as infinitesimal fragments in a world of which all the rest is unaffected by any one man's deeds. The impartiality which, in contemplation, is the unalloyed desire for truth, is the very same quality of mind which, in action, is justice, and in emotion is that universal love which can be given to all, and not only to those who are judged useful or admirable. Thus contemplation enlarges not only the objects of our thoughts, but also the objects of our actions and our affections: it makes us citizens of the universe, not only of one walled city at war with all the rest. In this citizenship of the universe consists man's true freedom, and his liberation from the thralldom of narrow hopes and fears.

Thus, to sum up our discussion of the value of philosophy: Philosophy is to be studied, not for the sake of any definite answers to its questions, since no definite answers can, as a rule, be known to be true, but rather for the sake of the questions themselves; because these questions enlarge our conception of what is possible, enrich our intellectual imagination, and diminish the dogmatic assurance which closes the mind against speculation; but above all because, through the greatness of the universe which philosophy contemplates, the mind also is rendered great, and becomes capable of that union with the universe which constitutes its highest good.

READING QUESTIONS

1. What is not the value of philosophy, according to Russell? Justify your answer with textual evidence.

2. What is the value of philosophy, according to Russell? Justify your answer with textual evidence.

3. Russell describes philosophy as "self-enlarging." What does he mean by that?

4. Has Russell changed your thinking about what philosophers do? Has he changed your thinking about the value of doing philosophy? If so, how? If not, why not?

PROGRESS CHECK

INSTRUCTIONS: Fill in the blanks with the appropriate responses listed below. (Answers at back of book.)

historical periods	liberate	social/political philosophy
knowledge	depth	ethics
instrumental	rational	wisdom
Hellenistic tradition	conceptual analysis	therapeutic value
Western rational tradition	irrational leap	logic
epistemology	practical use	medicine wheel
disciplinary	axiology	

1. Philosophy means the love of _____.
2. Philosophers belonging to the _____ are curious, detached, objective, and critically minded.
3. Wisdom is not the same thing as _____ or intelligence.
4. Wisdom is captured by one's ability to put information and intelligence to _____.
5. Wise people exhibit _____ and a sense of perspective.
6. Because philosophy can help to reduce tensions and anxiety resulting from such things as moral indecision and meaninglessness, it has _____.
7. Philosophy has both intrinsic and _____ value.
8. The study of philosophy can _____ one from ethnocentrism and subjective bias.
9. The _____ deals most directly with the healing powers of philosophy.
10. _____ is the study of knowledge.
11. _____ is the study of values (aesthetic and non-moral).
12. The philosophy of sport is an example of a _____ philosophy.
13. _____ is the science of reasoning.
14. _____ is the study of morals in human conduct.
15. _____ is the study of the philosophical foundations of society and its institutions.
16. Not all world philosophies are _____ in nature.
17. The _____ is a conceptual device used by Indigenous North Americans as a tool for living wisely.
18. Some religious philosophers believe that a(n) _____ of faith is required to live life at the highest level of human existence.
19. Philosophy can be understood by dividing it up into _____.
20. Contemporary analytic philosophers focus on _____.

Key Terms

Abu Hamid al-Ghazali: medieval Persian scholar whose work heavily influenced Islamic thought   56

aesthetics: a field of philosophy dealing with beauty, art, and judgments of taste   49

alienated: isolated, alone, misunderstood, sense of estrangement or isolation from a group or activity to which one should belong or in which one should be involved   44

analytic philosophers: Anglo-American philosophy from the early twentieth century that emphasizes the study of language and the logical analysis of concepts   52

ancient philosophy: in the western tradition, typically associated with the thinking of Socrates, the Pre-Socratics, Plato, Aristotle, Hellenistic, as well as Roman philosophical thinking   52

axiology: the study of normative moral and non-moral values (e.g., aesthetic, political, or economic)   46

Bertrand Russell: British philosopher who produced influential work in 20th Century logic and wrote extensively on social issues   61

conceptual analysis: the analysis of concepts, words, or ideas for their clarity and meaning   52

contemporary philosophy: refers to the current era of philosophy, generally dealing with philosophers from the late nineteenth century through to the twenty-first   52

continental philosophers: primarily associated with the countries of the western European continent, especially Germany and France   52

critically minded: a questioning attitude; unwillingness to accept things on blind faith; predisposition to demand rational justifications for disputed claims   34

epistemology: the theory or study of knowledge—its sources, nature, and limits   46

ethics: the study of morals in human conduct; focuses on principles and rules of acceptable behavior in personal and public life   46

ethnocentrism: seeing and evaluating the customs and traditions, etc. of other countries or cultures using standards set by one's own national customs, traditions, and values usually deemed, consciously or unconsciously, to be better   43

foundational and disciplinary philosophies: the theoretical and conceptual bases for different human activities and academic subjects of study   46

Hellenistic tradition: the term 'Hellenistic' means *Greek-like* and comes from the word 'Hellene' describing the uniquely Greek culture that spread around the ancient world with the military campaigns of Alexander the Great, including Greek language, art, religion, and philosophy   45

instrumentally valuable: that which has value as a means to an end; description for something that is used to get something else beyond itself (e.g., money as a means to buy a car)   43

intelligence: the ability to acquire knowledge and apply it   40

intrinsic value: having worth in itself; valuable on its own merits; not valued as a means to something else   41

is-ought fallacy: faulty reasoning based on the assumption that one can derive an 'ought' from an 'is'; incorrectly concluding that just because something 'is' the case, that it 'should' be the case   44

knowledge: factual information or skills possessed by an individual; a theoretical or practical understanding of a subject matter   40

Lee Hester: Professor of American Indian Studies and member of the Choctaw Nation of Oklahoma   54

logic: the science of reasoning; can be formal (deductive) or informal (non-deductive)   46

medicine wheel: teaching tool used by Indigenous peoples of North America for purposes of self-awareness and spiritual enlightenment   53

medieval philosophy: the philosophy of Western Europe from about the fourth century to the sixteenth century, roughly the period between the fall of Rome and the Renaissance   52

metaphysics: the study of ultimate reality, human existence, personhood, freedom, God, causality, space, and time   46

modern philosophy: western European philosophy spanning the seventeenth and eighteenth centuries   52

perennial wisdom: repeated or similar truths and insights that are discovered at different times, in different places and cultures, by different thinkers; a perspective in spirituality that views all of the world's religious traditions as sharing a single, metaphysical truth or origin from which all esoteric and worldly knowledge has grown   41

philosophers: lovers of wisdom   33

philosophical counseling: the application of philosophical thinking for the purpose of trying to resolve a person's existential problems; used to come to terms with matters of meaning and value in the context of one's life predicaments; a kind of self-reflective worldview analysis   45

philosophies of life: worldviews or personal value systems providing meaning, purpose, and direction in choosing and acting   46

philosophy: term derived from Greek root words meaning 'love of wisdom'   34

postmodernism: attempt to rethink a number of concepts held dear by Enlightenment humanism and many modernists   52

reasonable: who, or that which, is consistent with the principles of logic, reason, and evidence-based thinking   34

seekers of truth: people who want to know what in fact is the case; open-minded; awe-struck by life; objective, rational, willing to raise basic questions about God, reality, truth, and the universe; not afraid to question accepted beliefs and assumptions   35

sense of perspective: the ability to keep all aspects of life in proper proportion; the skill to consider things in relation to each other in a fair and accurate fashion; knowing what's very important and what's not so much; having a reasonable, balanced, integrated mode of existence   40

social/political philosophy: theoretical study of how to live well together in society; an examination of the philosophical foundations of the state and its political institutions   46

Sor Juana Inés de la Cruz: seventeenth century Mexican nun who wrote in a variety of genres including poetry, drama, and philosophy   36

subjective bias: a distorted or slanted view of things based on personal values, interests, beliefs or assumptions leading to perceptual blind spots   43

Western Tradition: a philosophical tradition that has its origins in Greece and Rome; often broken down into approaches or historical periods: Pre-Socratic, Classical, Hellenistic, Roman, Medieval, Renaissance, Modern, Late Modern, Contemporary, Analytic, Continental, Existential, Marxist, etc.; tries to codify the rules of human thought; promotes rationality and the rigorous examination of ideas   51

wisdom: goes beyond intelligence and knowledge; primarily concerned with human conduct and the ends of practical life, not discovery of facts; involves depth and unity of experience   40

Summary of Major Points

1. What comic images and caricatures does the term philosopher evoke?
- bearded old man
- detached hermit
- cave dweller
- ivory-tower professor
- toga-clad Greek
- wandering nuisance

2. How could Western rational philosophers be more accurately portrayed?
- lovers of wisdom
- seekers of truth
- reasonable
- critically minded
- questioning
- curious
- objective, impartial
- respectful of others
- cognizant of differing and divergent points of view
- detached, unbiased

3. What is wisdom?
- Related to, but not the same as, intelligence and knowledge
- The ability to put one's knowledge and intelligence to good practical use
- Sometimes achieved by experience, though not necessarily so
- A sense of depth and perspective
- Reflected in an integrated mode of existence and in joyful serenity
- Perennial: arises again and again in different contexts and times

4. What is the practical value of philosophy?
- Unavoidable, so must be dealt with
- Intrinsically valuable: pleasure and insight from the pursuit of wisdom
- Instrumentally valuable: personally therapeutic and socially useful
- A liberating experience
- Removes subjective bias and ethnocentrism
- Enhances wisdom and understanding
- Offers guidance, direction, and meaning
- Helps people to cope with moral indecision, matters of purpose, lifestyle development, and psychological self-management
- Offers insight into the wise application of technology

5. What are the various specializations within the discipline of philosophy?
- Metaphysics: The study of ultimate reality, human existence, personhood, God, freedom
- Epistemology: The theory of the nature and limits of knowledge
- Logic: The science of reasoning
- Ethics: The study of morals in human conduct
- Axiology-Aesthetics: Philosophical inquiry dealing with (artistic) values
- Social/Political: The study of the philosophical foundations of society and its political institutions
- Foundational and Disciplinary: Theoretical and conceptual bases for different human activities and academic subjects of study
- Philosophies of Life: The underlying principles and values of one's lifestyle, belief system, and chosen actions

6. What are some basic approaches to philosophy?
- Regional (Eastern, Western, African, Indigenous American, etc.)
- Historical (divided into ancient, medieval, modern, contemporary, and postmodern)

Additional Resources

For interactive quizzes, stories, supplements, and other materials for study and review, visit:

sites.broadviewpress.com/experiencing-philosophy/chapter1
Passcode: w4822kj

Or scan the following QR code:

CHAPTER 2

Understanding Arguments, Claims, and Fallacies of Reasoning

Take It Personally 74

Know Thyself: How Rational Am I? 77

2.1 What Is an Argument? 81
Arguments vs. Opinions and Other Non-Arguments 81
Attitude Adjustments for Argument 84
Benefits of Argument 86
The Socratic Method 86
ORIGINAL SOURCE: Plato, *Euthyphro*, featuring the Socratic Method 88

2.2 Deductive Arguments 98
Modus Ponens 99
Modus Tollens 101
Hypothetical Syllogisms/Chain Arguments 102
Disjunctive Syllogisms 103
Categorical Syllogisms or Syllogisms of Class Membership 105
Validity, Truth, and Soundness 106

2.3 Non-Deductive Arguments 109
Argument from Past Experience 110
Argument by Analogy 111
Argument by Inductive Generalization 112

2.4 Evaluating Claims 113
Factual Statements 113
Value Judgments 114
Conceptual Claims 116

2.5 Informal Logical Fallacies 118
Ad Hominem Fallacy 118
Straw Person Fallacy 118
Circular Reasoning/Begging the Question Fallacy 119
Two Wrongs Fallacy 120
Slippery Slope Fallacy 120
Appealing to Authority Fallacy 120
Red Herring Fallacy 121
Guilt by Association Fallacy 122

Progress Check 126

Study Guide 127
Key Terms 127
Summary of Major Points 130

LEARNING OUTCOMES

After successfully completing this chapter, you will be able to

▸ Assess your current level of logical reasoning ability

▸ Explain the differences between arguments and different forms of non-argument

▸ Distinguish among factual statements, value judgments, and conceptual claims

▸ Identify examples of valid and invalid reasoning

▸ Create and complete syllogisms

▸ Understand and properly apply the process of non-deductive reasoning

▸ Distinguish among the concepts of validity, truth, and soundness

▸ Evaluate different kinds of claims

▸ Define and identify some common informal fallacies

▸ List some "Do's and Don'ts" when it comes to philosophical argument

FOCUS QUESTIONS

1. What is philosophical argument?

2. How is arguing different from opinionating?

3. What are some benefits of philosophical argument?

4. What are some valid and invalid forms of logic used in discussion and philosophical debate?

5. How are inductive and deductive logic different?

6. In what ways can normative arguments be evaluated?

7. What are some common informal fallacies? How do they work?

Take It Personally

It's been said that there are two unavoidable things in life: death and taxes. I would like to add a third item, namely, **disagreement**. If you think about it, it is virtually impossible to avoid having disagreements with others. Whether friends are discussing sports, entertainment, culture, religion, politics, art, education, business, morality, or, in this context, philosophy, we almost always find conflicting points of view.

For example, as we'll soon learn in the next chapter dealing with philosophies of life, Aristippus, the Ancient Greek Hedonist, presents the view that pleasure is good-in-itself and that it should be pursued without guilt. The venerable Buddha recommends, by contrast, that we loosen our worldly attachments to things, recognizing the impermanence of the ego. He reminds us that pleasures are always alloyed with negative emotions like fear, which result from the realization at some level that those things we take pleasure in will eventually change, decay, wither, or cease to be. Besides, the "me" that takes pleasure in things doesn't really exist in the first place, making our garden of earthly delights something of an illusion.

As for Existentialists and Stoics, we'll shortly discover how they clearly disagree about freedom. Sartre claims that individuals are utterly free, whereas the best the lenient Stoics offer us is a small degree of personal influence in an otherwise fated universe. The more stringent Stoic position doesn't even allow for that, maintaining that every little occurrence, however insignificant, is totally determined. If we ask, "Determined by what or by whom?" the Stoic would reply saying "by God" or "by the divine *Logos*." Tell that to the atheist Sartre, who would disagree!

In addition to these matters just mentioned, many more controversial issues and disputed philosophical positions will be raised as we proceed through this book. In Chapter 4, conflicting ideas will be presented regarding the sources and nature of knowledge. In Chapter 5, dealing with morality, you will encounter theorists who disagree among themselves about what should serve as the foundation for ethical action and moral decision-making. Should it be virtue, utility, duty, care, survival, or personal self-interest?

In Chapter 6, dealing with political philosophy, alternative conceptions of the state and the individual's proper relation to it will be presented: What degree of control should the state have over the individual? Should society be structured in terms of a class system, or should everyone be treated as equals? Historically, philosophers have disagreed among themselves when trying to answer such questions and they continue to do so today.

Making efforts to answer philosophical questions or resolve philosophical disputes can be as difficult as it is exhausting. Jonathan Glover, a contemporary English philosopher, once described doing philosophy as something akin to trying to stay afloat in a leaky boat. The leaks spring up on our voyage of philosophical discovery. They occur when we realize that some of our assumptions, values, beliefs, and ideas—*our planks*—that have kept us afloat in the past, are now rotting and thus require us to make some repairs. The rotting planks must be replaced so we don't sink, but since we're at sea, we don't wish to down our vessel in the process of making our alterations: tricky business! Finding the right planks and making the proper repairs takes significant time and effort, not to mention some of St. Teresa's "resolute determination to persevere," discussed in the introductory chapter.

Part of the reason why staying philosophically afloat is so difficult is that we are reluctant to let go of the rotting old planks, i.e., our previously held assumptions, values, and beliefs. Due to our conscious and often unconscious habits of thinking, we develop stubborn attachments to them. They become sources of *cognitive comfort*, so to speak, so we don't want to let go.

Once specific assumptions, thoughts, or ideas become ingrained in our way of understanding the world, they shape how we think. They hold a lot of sway over what we believe is true or what is right. When these assumptions, thoughts or ideas become *rotten*, when they are no longer applicable or are found to be faulty in some fashion, they interfere with our objective search for truth. It can be difficult to follow, let alone see, a better course on that search when our attachments to rotten thoughts and ideas, or faulty assumptions, fog the way. The best method of proceeding in those cases is to let go of our old ways of thinking and move on to new and better ones. Again, that's not easy, even if those old ways are wrong. Different ideas—different "planks"—challenge the comforting ones to which we've become habituated; the resulting *cognitive dissonance* can upset our whole system of thought.

Perhaps you know someone who would rather sink in a leaking vessel of faulty assumptions and false beliefs than change them in order to stay afloat. Perhaps *you* are someone like that. If so, be glad you are in the right place. You will soon learn in this chapter about the *Socratic Method*. As you will discover, this method and indeed philosophical reflection more broadly are exceptionally good at drawing our attention to the prejudices that we hold. As the term itself implies, 'prejudice' amounts to to *pre-judgments* that stand in the way of our achieving objective knowledge and practical wisdom, both necessary for enlightened living.

Still another part of the reason why staying afloat in our philosophical lifeboats is so difficult has to do with the nature of philosophical questions themselves. Philosophy asks *the big questions*, ones like "What constitutes human nature?" "Is there a God?" "What is the meaning of life?" or "What is worth living and dying for?" These types of questions cannot be answered by experiment, with a microscope, or by means of a lab test providing quick results. Instead, they are answered by thinking, and good thinking takes time and effort. As you will soon learn from the Socratic Method, the effort that it takes to answer the big questions, as well as other deceptively simple-sounding philosophical questions, is great, and for that reason one can begin to feel frustrated and sometimes hopeless in the search for answers. *But don't despair!*

The good news is that there are established ways to organize ideas into effective arguments using good reasoning. Later in this chapter you will learn about some of the strategies and rules of proper logic. As you begin to master them and the associated skills pertaining to critical analytical thinking, you're invited to reconsider your personal worldview. These skills will also come in handy when it comes to evaluating, accepting or rejecting the philosophies of life covered in Chapter 3. Analysis and evaluation are important, for one could argue that a philosophy of life is not really a philosophy at all if it isn't reached through rational reflection, careful analysis, and critical self-examination.

Many people have never received formal training in logic or philosophical argumentation. The result is that discussions about the big questions or controversial issues relating to matters of religion and politics, say, often degenerate into mindless opinionating and explosions of over-heated emotion. In view of this, people frequently avoid disputed subjects, preferring to keep things light. Some individuals would rather keep human discourse on a superficial level. The underlying assumption seems to be that if you say nothing important or controversial, everybody will get along just fine. If you personally adopt this psychologically defensive life strategy, your interpersonal communications may indeed be more friendly, but in the end will turn out to be less rewarding and meaningful than they otherwise could be—or do you disagree?

Further, if you wish to adopt this defensive strategy for yourself, this implies that you are willing in principle to agree with all points of view, however contradictory they are to each other, or however adverse their implications are for you or for others. The problem here may not only point to the possibility of rational inconsistencies; it could also involve agreeing to hurtful actions or harmful consequences just for the sake of getting along. But, if this is the case, are you really getting along with others? Moreover, refusing to take a position on significant issues could be taken as a sign of cowardice.

So, if mindless superficiality and ethical fence-sitting are not attractive options, and if you wish to make rational and responsible choices regarding important decisions in your life, then it will be necessary for you to learn how to argue and think philosophically. Referring back to Jonathon Glover's metaphor, we can say that among all the different philosophical planks and platforms to choose from, we must all select those which will enable us to make the necessary repairs and modifications to our existential lifeboats, those required for our rational and enlightened travels throughout life.

In order to determine what's worth accepting and what needs modifying or rejecting, we have to learn to weigh the value of opposing ideas and philosophical positions by determining their meaningfulness, coherence, and justifiability. We must become rational, critical, and analytical in our perspective. *Doing philosophy* requires that we engage in a structured process of thought using accepted norms of logic, a notion that underscores the idea that philosophy is sometimes considered more of a method of thinking than a body of knowledge. Very shortly we'll look into this method of thinking, but before we do, let's continue to take philosophical argument personally, bearing in mind that some attitude adjustments may be in order.

How Rational Am I?

Let's first make efforts to determine your current level of reasoning. The ability to think philosophically presupposes a number of sub-skills addressed in this diagnostic.

For instance, if you are going to think like a philosopher, you must be able to distinguish between mere opinions and *bona fide* arguments; you must know the difference between factual statements, value judgments, and conceptual claims and be able to identify them.

Furthermore, philosophical argumentation requires the proper use of logic. Philosophers must be able to spot invalid, unsound, and fallacious reasoning if they wish to argue in a rational fashion.

By completing this diagnostic, you will be able to get a sense of how much work you'll need to do before being able to properly engage in philosophical discussion and debate. After completing the chapter study, you may wish to do this self-diagnostic again to gauge your progress.

PART I

INSTRUCTIONS

The statements below are either factual, reflecting what is true or false, or they are value judgments requiring rational justification by appeals to standards and norms, or they are conceptual claims whose acceptability hinges on clarity of meaning or definition and their proper application.

▸ Write *F* next to the factual statements.
▸ Write *V* next to the value judgments.
▸ Write *C* next to conceptual claims.

1. _____ It is good to do what is in your rational self-interest.

2. _____ Marcus Aurelius was a Roman citizen.

3. _____ Neo-liberalism supports a free market.

4. _____ Karl Marx was banished from several countries during his lifetime.

5. _____ Martin Luther King professed a philosophy of nonviolence.

6. _____ Love is a form of selfishness.

7. _____ The Oracle at Delphi declared that Socrates was the wisest man in Athens.

8. _____ Trying to avoid anxiety by following fads or fitting in with the group is wrong.

9. _____ 'Education' means indoctrination into the status quo.

10. _____ You shouldn't worry about the future.

11. _____ Jean-Paul Sartre is an atheist.

12. _____ Cheerleading is not a sport.

13. _____ Hedonism is morally corrupt.

14. _____ People ought to seek philosophical enlightenment, as Buddha did.

15. _____ God is the manifest universe.

PART II

Philosophers need to be able to distinguish between arguments and non-arguments. The latter can present either as unfounded personal opinions or as a series of unrelated claims. They can also appear as descriptions, reports, commands, instructions, explanations, or expressions of emotion. Such things don't try to argue or *prove* anything.

Arguments involve arriving at conclusions that are based on *relevant* ideas and *evidence*. Though not always neatly sequential, good arguments often have a structured flow, starting from claims that are true or plausible and leading to conclusions that are *warranted* because they are justifiably inferred from those claims. Note that bad arguments are still arguments because they are attempts to show that a conclusion is warranted, even though they are defective in some way. For example, bad arguments may start from claims that are implausible, unlikely or demonstrably false, or the claims they start with do not support the conclusion they were intended to prove or justify.

INSTRUCTIONS

Distinguish below between reasoned arguments and opinions or other forms of non-argument.

▸ Write *A* next to reasoned *A*rguments.
▸ Write *O* next to *O*pinions and *O*ther non-arguments.

1. _____ Toll roads ought to be banned.

2. _____ Look here. Unrestricted immigration has to be stopped. Unlimited increases in the number of immigrants will surely cause higher levels of unemployment, and we all know that whatever causes people to be out of work should be ended as quickly as possible.

3. _____ Cosmetics research using animals is evil. Besides, face creams and hand lotions cost too much.

4. _____ The whole idea of a "space force" or some kind of "star wars" program involving an intercontinental missile defense system is indefensible. Next thing you know, we'll be looking for Martians.

5. _____ Globalization is a bad thing. Countries have a right to protect their national sovereignty for the good of their citizens. Whatever violates or threatens that right is wrong. All that economic globalization does is undermine the ability of countries to exercise their right to self-determination by putting undue political power in the hands of transnational corporations.

6. _____ The document reveals that the company showed a drastic decrease in net profits last year according to the latest figures. Also, we hired fewer people, but released many more temporary and part-time workers. Recent economic projections suggest we will have better results this year.

7. _____ The person I saw had fair skin, blue eyes, and was wearing blue jeans and a T-shirt with some sort of logo on it. I couldn't make it out.

8. _____ There is probably alien life somewhere in the universe. Recently, an American astronaut at the space station captured a UFO on time-lapse photography.

9. _____ Oh my goodness!

10. _____ Ravinder did not come to class today because she was sick.

PART III

"Doing philosophy" sometimes requires you to be able to think deductively. In this part of the self-diagnostic, see how good you are in providing the missing statements in the arguments that follow.

INSTRUCTIONS

Fill in the missing statements for each of the arguments below.

For example,

All toads are frogs.

_____

Therefore, all toads are amphibians.

In the above argument, the missing statement is "All frogs are amphibians."

1. That which pollutes the mind should be avoided.

   _____

   Therefore, alcohol should be avoided.

2. _____
   Seneca is a stoic.
   Therefore, Seneca values peace of mind.

3. If there is a God, then all misfortune is fated.
   There is a God.

   _____

4. If I make pleasure my number one priority, then I'll be happy.

   _____

   Therefore, I didn't make pleasure my number one priority.

5. _____
   If I am free, then I am responsible for my actions.
   Therefore, if there is no God, then I am responsible for my actions.

PART IV

From the vantage point of rational philosophy, individuals should try to remain objective, logical, and impartial whenever constructing arguments or debating with others. Unfortunately, individuals sometimes use rhetorical devices called *informal fallacies* to divert attention, introduce irrelevancies, personally attack, or intimidate in order to persuade others or win debates.

INSTRUCTIONS

▸ Place an **F** next to any of the following examples that are instances of *Fallacious* reasoning.
▸ Place an **A** (for *Acceptable*) next to those statements or arguments that are not fallacious.

1. _____ It's perfectly acceptable to cheat on exams since everybody else does.

2. _____ All people have a right to religious freedom, and so it's acceptable that you choose to be a Catholic.

3. _____ Smoking can't really be harmful; all of my favorite Hollywood actors smoke.

4. _____ You shouldn't accept anything he says, because he's just an idiot!

5. _____ Regardless of what the test results say, the quality of our educational system hasn't declined. After all, we've spent more on it than ever before.

ANSWER KEY

PART I

1. V	4. F	7. F	10. V	13. V
2. F	5. F	8. V	11. F	14. V
3. C	6. C	9. C	12. C	15. C

Score _____ /15

PART II

1. O	3. O	5. A	7. O	9. O
2. A	4. O	6. O	8. A	10. O

Score _____ /10

PART III

1. Alcohol pollutes the mind.
2. Stoics value peace of mind.
3. Therefore, all misfortune is fated.
4. I am not happy.
5. If there is no God, then I am free.

Score _____ /5

PART IV

1. *F* – Two wrongs fallacy; one wrong doesn't justify another.
2. *A* – This is a valid inference.
3. *F* – Invalid inference because the supporting claim is irrelevant and thus insufficient to prove the conclusion; this fallacy of relevance also reflects a hasty conclusion.
4. *F* – *Ad hominem* fallacy; attacking the person rather than the person's argument is improper reasoning.
5. *F* – Red herring fallacy; here, attention is diverted from quality issues to budget issues in order to avoid addressing the concern about educational deterioration.

Score: _____ /5

Total Score: _____ /35 (add sub-totals for each part of this diagnostic to determine Total Score)

INTERPRETATION OF RESULTS

In view of the fact that this diagnostic is only suggestive and that it depends in part on your prior exposure to the process and terminology of argumentation, don't be overly concerned about the final result. The goal of this chapter is to help you improve your thinking and better understand some of the important distinctions made above.

2.1 What Is an Argument?

What is an argument? And why should we bother arguing? In this section, we turn our attention to the various dimensions of arguments themselves, distinguishing them from opinions and other forms of non-argument.

"... isn't anyone with a true but unthinking opinion like a blind man on the right road?"
PLATO

Arguments vs. Opinions and Other Non-Arguments

ARGUMENTS

From a philosophical perspective, an **argument** is not an interpersonal event, a screaming match, or a confrontation of egos; rather, it is a combination of related statements leading to a conclusion. A single statement or set of statements can act as either a reason or set of supporting **premises** that can be used to prove or justify some sort of **conclusion** or terminal claim.

By concentrating on the form of someone's argument, on its validity, strength, or soundness, and not on the person with whom we disagree, we can divest ourselves of the unpleasant feelings and contaminating psychological variables that often disrupt rational debate. We can then proceed to examine controversial philosophical positions with impartial objectivity.

"If you want to know whether you are thinking rightly, put your thoughts into words. In the very attempt to do this, you will find yourselves, consciously or unconsciously, using logical forms."
JOHN STUART MILL

OPINIONS

Most of us intuitively understand what an **opinion** is: it's a belief without sufficient justification. In view of the uncertainty surrounding opinions, we should be careful about accepting them. Not all opinions should be given equal weight, as some are more acceptable than others.

Judges and lawyers, for instance, may issue opinions on the legality of particular actions or public policies (e.g., adoption rights or hiring quotas). Medical doctors may offer considered opinions on the advisability of surgery or the best therapeutic procedures for a patient. Such *professional opinions* are usually based on extensive research, expert knowledge, and careful thought. Although these opinions do not always turn out to be right, it is usually reasonable to accept them. Admittedly, sometimes they might turn out false. But since they are largely reliable, and if that's the best we can get in any specific practice, area, or field of endeavor, then it's usually wise to accept them. If multiple professional opinions conflict, we might tend to go with majority rule, or remain undecided if we can.

By contrast to expert professional opinions, we often hear expressions of *personal opinion* in which we tend to place far less confidence. This is probably because we often perceive them to be baseless, emotionally charged, or sometimes biased, bigoted, and discriminatory. In some ways, personal opinions are cheap. We can all afford to have them on any subject, even if we know very little or nothing about the subject itself. Personal opinions are especially abundant when the issue is a controversial one, like immigration or gun control legislation, for instance.

In contrast to professional opinions, personal ones are not always accompanied by any solid reasons or concrete evidence. If no **grounds** are given for adopting them, then no process of thought supports or justifies them. Such personal opinions are simply blurted out in a spontaneous, knee-jerk fashion. They may be intended, either consciously or

unconsciously, to fill space in idle conversation, to express emotions, launch an attack, or to elicit reactions from others. Nonetheless, to the extent that personally stated opinions initiate discussion and give rise to serious thought, they can *potentially* be worthwhile.

In many cases, personal opinions can serve as the first step toward genuine philosophical argument and debate, acting as a catalyst for further analysis and deliberation. Unfortunately, all too often discussions begin and end with statements of unreasoned personal opinion. Emotions are vented and viewpoints are stridently expressed, but little progress is made by way of further insight, understanding, or clarification of the issues involved. Sadly, many people take great pleasure in forcing their opinions upon others, winning shouting matches, name calling, and making others look foolish or stupid. The truth is that screaming and one-upmanship do not take us very far down the road of sober thought and rational understanding.

OTHER NON-ARGUMENTS

Turning now to other forms of non-argument, we sometimes witness unproductive miscommunication because people confuse things like descriptions and reports with arguments when they are not. A **description**, for example, is meant to provide some sort of representative account of a person, place, object, or event. *No effort is made to prove or justify anything*. In describing, an individual may simply be relating their experience or perceptions of a situation they personally witnessed.

Reports are like this as well. If a professor asked you to go to the university quad to see what was going on and then report back to everyone what you found, there would be information relayed, but no case to be made. You wouldn't start *arguing* to prove what you saw. Reporting back that you witnessed protesters carrying signs, for instance, would not mean you favor the protest or condemn it, or that you're supporting it or wanting to suppress it. If someone took issue with you over the fact that a protest was going on, that person would be missing the point of your communication, confusing a merely descriptive report with what was wrongly interpreted as an argument. On this note, how many times in your life have you been forced to say something like, *I'm not arguing; I'm just telling you what they said!*

Explanations are another form of non-argument, though they can sometimes read and sound a lot like real arguments. One reason is due to the fact that the word *because* features prominently in explanations, as it does in arguments. In arguments, the word 'because' serves to introduce a *supporting reason* for accepting another claim. This reason is meant to prove a point or establish a fact, say.

By contrast, in explanations the word 'because' is not meant to prove or justify anything, but typically to clarify and provide insight into *why* or *how* something is the case. Very often what's at issue is accepted fact, so there's no need for proof. If we were to say, for example, that "The man's coughing *because* he has a cold," we're just explaining the reason for the cough. We're not trying to prove that coughing is happening or that the person has a cold. Here, we're connecting two things for purposes of providing a *causal explanation*. The reason given is explanatory, not justificatory.

In the same vein, if someone were to say the sun rises in the east and sets in the west *because of* the rotation of the earth, this common knowledge would not likely be taken as an argument. Nobody would be trying to prove that the earth rotates or that the sun rises and sets where it does. Again, since both explanations and arguments give reasons and often introduce those reasons with the word *because*, they can be easily confused. (By the way, I just gave you an explanation for how and why explanations and arguments are different, yet sound similar! I wasn't trying to prove *that* they are different. That's understood.)

It's also worth noting that *commands* and *instructions* don't fall under the category of argument either. Yelling, "Shut the door!" at someone is an order; it doesn't prove or justify anything. So too is the case with following assembly instructions for electronic devices, say, or for furniture from big box stores. When conveying instructions, nobody is trying to prove a point. Nobody is trying to justify the claim that you *should* put anything together or that you have an *obligation* to do A, B, and C. Assembly instructions are informational, not argumentative.

QUESTIONS

When someone asks a question, it is generally understood that they are *not* trying to present an argument, or even an argumentative claim for that matter. Asking, for instance, "Can penguins fly?" is not to draw any kind of conclusion. The sentence is interrogatory; it is not a declarative statement that something is or is not the case. Since no claim or any inference is made, no actual argument is present.

Sometimes, however, someone will ask a question that *implies* an argument, but leaves one to fill in the missing pieces. How so?

Unstated argument often results from the fact that it is possible to indirectly express claims as either loaded or rhetorical questions—sometimes both. Such questions typically contain questionable assumptions that the questioner treats as reasons to draw a certain conclusion.

"Are you ever going to smarten up and quit ignoring global warming?" could be one of those indirect arguments by question. In that example, the questioner is, in effect, arguing that smart people don't ignore global warming and you should agree with smart people, so, therefore, you should not ignore global warming. Here's another example you might have heard from someone criticizing your behavior: "How would you like it if someone did that to you?" The question implies that you wouldn't like it but that you ought to treat others the way that you would like to be treated; thus, you shouldn't have done what you did.

However, if a questioner leaves it up to others to make explicit what was implicit, and *to decide for themselves the nature of the precise inference that was vaguely implied by the question*, and the context of argument provides no clue what those unstated assumptions might be, then arguably no concrete argument was actually ever made. Those on the receiving end of loaded questions, fronting as vaguely fragmented implied arguments, shouldn't be responsible for filling in the missing pieces of the suggested inferences.

It is important to recognize, however, that what's missing is sometimes clear, so leaving out all the implicit details, either in questions or in fully formed arguments, is frequently permissible. For example, suppose I argue, "Look, it's not true that all birds can fly, because penguins can't." I haven't explicitly stated one assumption in this argument, which is that penguins are birds, but in ordinary conversation, leaving out the obvious is permissible.

In Part III of this chapter's *Know Thyself* diagnostic, you were asked to supply premises or conclusions that are obvious but not stated. Notice that, in everyday talk, and even in most philosophical writing, almost every argument has missing bits of this sort, but it's easy for the hearer to fill them in because it's obvious what the arguer had in mind—or at least obvious in that particular context. There's nothing wrong with this sort of short-cut in ordinary communication. (Think of how tedious things would get without it!) But when very careful and detailed evaluation of an argument is called for, we would want to fill in, as above, the important or controversial missing parts.

Attitude Adjustments for Argument

If people are going to argue in constructive ways about what's true, valuable or right, it's important to cultivate a particular mind-set. We should welcome properly conducted arguments, not avoid them. This does not mean that we should get into serious arguments with everyone we meet, as this would be highly impractical and time consuming.

On the other hand, opportunities for meaningful discussion should not be missed. Rather than become defensively belligerent about conflicting viewpoints, we should see them as opportunities for intellectual growth. If these viewpoints are presented in an honest and sincere fashion, then they pose legitimate challenges that we can use for building philosophical insight. If our opponent's disagreements are ill-founded, we can bring this to light. If they are justified, then we are given an opportunity to modify our views or, if necessary, abandon our positions entirely. It's an admirable philosophical trait to be able to change one's thinking under the weight of contrary evidence or in response to legitimate criticism. Refusing to do so makes one irrational, or possibly arrogant, bigoted, and stubbornly dogmatic.

As well as opening up to arguments, we should try to develop an attitude of **rational disinterestedness**—remaining as objective and impartial as possible. This attitude requires that we stop trying to impose our viewpoints on others. Properly conducted argument is not really about winning and losing; nor is it a matter of looking good at someone else's expense; proper argument is not about *one-upping* another person.

The problem is that many people view argument and debate as a competition where there are winners and losers. Some people will say or do almost anything rather than concede a disputed point. Losing an argument can be personally embarrassing or a threat to self-esteem. For instance, in the middle of a heated discussion, have you ever invented statistics to support your argument? Be honest, now! Have you ever magically manufactured *alternative facts*, or made unsupportable claims as a way of winning and not losing face? If you have, then you can well appreciate how psychological factors can affect rational thinking processes.

If you or the person you're arguing with are making things up, then no wonder arguments are often seen as useless and something to avoid. Before we can engage in productive debate, we have to get our psychological acts in order. This is part of the human experiential dimension of philosophy that so often gets overlooked.

An important recommendation for us in this context comes from the example of Plato's mentor, Socrates. Centuries ago, the Oracle at Delphi declared Socrates to be the wisest man in Athens. Aware of his ignorance, Socrates set out to disprove the Oracle by finding someone wiser. After searching long and hard, he concluded that everyone he encountered was ignorant, just like him. If he possessed greater wisdom, it must have come from the awareness of his own ignorance. Others were apparently unaware of theirs. They pretended to know what they did not.

In light of this historical example, you might wish to reduce your own pretensions to knowledge. If you have no ignorance to hide, because you freely and openly admit when you do not know something, then you greatly reduce the need to communicate

Socrates

The ancient Greek thinker **Socrates** (c. 469–399 BCE) is one of the most renowned yet enigmatic philosophers belonging to the Western rational tradition. He has been a model and source of inspiration for many philosophers throughout the centuries. Yet, Socrates actually wrote no philosophy himself. Instead, what we know about him as a philosopher is limited to what his contemporaries wrote about him, including **Plato** (c. 427–347 BCE).

Plato was strongly influenced by his mentor Socrates and wrote many dialogues with Socrates as the main speaker. We have to take care, however, to treat those texts for what they are—namely, philosophical dialogues of Plato's creation, and not historical transcripts of Socrates's actual words. As many commentators point out, it is difficult to know exactly how to separate Socrates the person from Socrates the character in Plato's dialogues. Nevertheless, in Plato's *Apology* we likely find a fairly accurate account of the real Socrates. This dialogue offers us a look at the extraordinary force of the human being behind the lasting legacy.

The *Apology* takes place in 399 BCE during Socrates's trial for corruption and impiety. In his defense speech against these charges and, moreover, against the slanderous opinions about him, Socrates describes himself as someone who does not care about wealth or his body but cares greatly about the state of his soul. Unlike those who measure themselves by the external aspects of their lives, for Socrates, self-control, not self-indulgence, makes for the good life. To that end, he declares daily discussions of virtue as the greatest good and eschews material "goods" as frivolous trappings.

In his manner of philosophical questioning, Socrates went around trying to convince others to do the same, even to the neglect of his own affairs, the detriment of his popularity, and the danger of death. It is from Socrates that we get the saying, "The unexamined life is not worth living." Refusing, on principle, to manipulate the jury with lies or emotional pleas, Socrates is sentenced to death and carries out the penalty by drinking hemlock, a poisonous plant. Unmoved by a fear of death, Socrates died for the philosophical life that he boldly and courageously lived for.

PHILOSOPHERS IN ACTION

Socrates's execution was part of a pattern of harsh reactions to philosophy in ancient Greece. Other philosophers of this time were executed, killed, expelled, imprisoned, or had prices put on their heads, making philosophy "an extremely dangerous activity."[1] If philosophy is irrelevant and useless, as many claim, then why would any of these philosophical thinkers be considered dangerous? What does the persecution of philosophers indicate about the nature and value of the philosophical life? Discuss.

Logic: another thing that penguins aren't very good at.

defensively. If you reduce defensiveness, you can then engage in more fruitful dialogue without having to prove yourself or convince everybody else that you are always right. Rather than trying to one-up others or embarrass them, you should display **Socratic humility**, making efforts to listen carefully and then responding intelligently and thoughtfully to what others have to say. Constructive attitudes toward disagreement can provide enormous benefits. Let's see what some of those benefits are.

Benefits of Argument

If engaged-in properly, philosophical argument can open minds. It can rid us of ignorance and the evils of blind prejudice. Without argument, people are free to rest on a bed of unexamined beliefs. Lies may be taken for truths. Gross injustices may be accepted as normal or what nature intended. For instance, before some thoughtful and morally sensitive people began to question and to seriously disagree with the values of their contemporaries, women and people of color were regarded as inferior beings and were unfairly denied their basic human rights. In part because of the philosophical challenges raised in protest, many moral advances have been made, even if current legislation and policing practices often fall short. Admittedly, much work remains to be done in this regard. Nonetheless, argument and rational criticism can serve a social purpose. Such things can expose and help to rectify prejudice and injustice. In short, philosophical argument can have positive social value.

Argument also has advantages for personal growth. When challenged by argument, we are not allowed the questionable luxury of mindless response. Saying things without thinking becomes more difficult when people disagree with us. This should not discourage us, for by engaging in productive dialogue with those who dispute what we claim or believe, we may, in the end, strengthen our viewpoints, modify them to make them more acceptable, or discard them when they are no longer supportable.

When people argue and disagree with us, we could choose to see this as a kind of compliment. If our views were regarded as totally insignificant, or if others did not take us seriously, then nobody would waste their time on us. They would simply ignore us. So, when someone chooses to debate with us, we can safely assume that the other individual has at least heard and acknowledged us. Being recognized is important—a good first step.

The Socratic Method

The spirit of Socratic humility, recommended for all philosophical discussions, is perhaps best captured in the writings of Plato, especially in the Platonic dialogues where the character of Socrates is featured. In the dialogue entitled *Euthyphro*, Socrates engages a man by that name in conversation. The dialogue is set outside the king-archon's court.

In ancient Athens, there were laws protecting the city from the gods' displeasure. The king-archon was the magistrate who oversaw legal cases involving alleged offenses against the gods, deciding whether or not those cases would

THINKING ABOUT YOUR THINKING

What is something that you know a lot about? It could be anything: a person, an object, an activity, a pastime, a vocation, a value. It could even be you! Have you ever asked yourself what that thing really is? Can you identify its core features? Can you describe what it is without just giving examples of it? For example, what is a person, a celebrity, a car, a game, food, music, beauty, goodness? If you struggle to know what something is, can you honestly speak knowledgeably or authoritatively about it?

go to trial by jury. In that vein, Socrates is at the court because he has been charged with the crime of *impiety* by a man named Meletus. Coincidentally, another man, Euthyphro, is there because he has charged his own father with the murder of a slave. Slave-murdering at the time was a religious offense, a form of impiety or pollution, which, if not ritually purified, would offend the gods.

In charging his father, Euthyphro believes that he is acting on knowledge about the gods and their wishes, and thus about the general topic of impiety. His family disagrees with the charges, but Euthyphro is firm in his convictions and confident in his expertise, even going so far as to compare himself with Zeus. Socrates wishes to gain this special knowledge of impiety from Euthyphro so that he can mount a defense for himself. Or so he says.

In his usual manner, Socrates engages in conversation with someone who professes to be an expert in some subject.[2] In this situation, Socrates inquires into Euthyphro's knowledge of the nature of piety and piety—what the pious *is* and *is not*—and, as usual, Socrates's questions generate confusion for his **interlocutor** and reveal the bluster of his supposed expertise.

As you will read in the dialogue below, Euthyphro cannot answer Socrates's questions about piety to Socrates's satisfaction or even his own. Much to his frustration, Euthyphro is unable to make clear what piety is, even though he is confident that he is acting piously by charging his father with a crime. When Socrates presses Euthyphro to express his knowledge of impiety, he leaves with the excuse of business elsewhere. For a very brief period Euthyphro was willing to engage in philosophical thinking that challenged his assumptions and beliefs, but in the end, he hastily returned to the safety of his everyday affairs and to his everyday way of thinking.

Even though Plato wrote the *Euthyphro* dialogue with no final answer to the question "What is piety?" he nonetheless presents a valuable lesson in how to conduct that search, beginning with the realization of one's own faulty beliefs and flawed thinking.

Turn now to the excerpt from *Euthyphro* to get a flavor of philosophical discussion from the master Socrates himself. You may wish to apply the Socratic method in your next philosophical discussion, but do so with Socratic humility, of course!

Basic Elements of the Socratic Method

1. Engage someone in a conversation about a controversial issue.
2. Turn the conversation in the direction of some concept or term of philosophical significance or central importance to the issue discussed.
3. Ask for a definitional clarification of the key philosophical concept or term.
4. Uncover the inadequacies of the definition provided and help your opponent develop a new, more adequate definition.
5. Critically examine the new, improved version of the previously unacceptable definition, showing how it still fails or is inconsistent.
6. Repeat steps 4 and 5 several times until a clear definition is articulated to everyone's satisfaction. (In the Platonic dialogues, the other party engaged by Socrates often becomes irritated or upset in the end, usually finding an excuse for terminating the conversation or suggesting that the search for a proper definition continue at some other time.)

Plato, *Euthyphro*, featuring the Socratic Method[3]

Euthyphro is one of many philosophical dialogues by Plato that feature Socrates as the main speaker. It is always important to remember that these dialogues are not transcripts of conversations that took place but, rather, presentations of Plato's philosophy in which Plato pays homage to his mentor, the real Socrates. The dialogue format also shows us something about philosophy, namely, that it is an activity.

...

Socrates: So tell me, what do you say the pious is, and what is the impious?

Euthyphro: Well then, I claim that the pious is what I am doing now, prosecuting someone who is guilty of wrongdoing—either of murder or temple robbery or anything else of the sort, whether it happens to be one's father or mother or whoever else—and the impious is failing to prosecute. For observe, Socrates, how great a proof I will give you that this is how the law stands, one I have already given to others as well, which shows such actions to be correct—not yielding to impious people, that is, no matter who they happen to be. Because these very people also happen to worship Zeus as the best and most just of the gods, and agree that he put his own father in bonds because he unjustly swallowed his sons, and the father too castrated his own father for other similar reasons.* Yet they are sore at me because I am prosecuting my father for his injustice. And so they say contradictory things about the gods and about me.

Socrates: Maybe this, Euthyphro, is why I am being prosecuted for this crime, that whenever someone says such things about the gods, for some reason I find them hard to accept? For this reason, I suppose, someone will claim I misbehave. But now if you, with your expertise in such matters, also hold these beliefs, it's surely necessary, I suppose, that we too must accept them—for indeed what *can* we say, we who admit openly that we know nothing about these matters? But before the god of friendship tell me, do you truly believe these things happened like this?

Euthyphro: These and still more amazing things, Socrates, that most people are unaware of.

Socrates: And do you believe there is really a war amongst the gods, with terrible feuds, even, and battles and many other such things, such as are recounted by the poets and the holy artists, and that have been elaborately adorned for us on sacred objects, too, and especially the robe covered with such designs which is brought up to the acropolis at the great Panathenaea?† Are we to say that these things are true, Euthyphro?

Euthyphro: Not only these, Socrates, but as I said just now, I could also describe many other things about the gods to you, if you want, which I am sure you will be astounded to hear.

Socrates: I wouldn't be surprised. But you can describe these to me at leisure some other time. For the time being, however, try to state more clearly what I asked you just now, since previously, my friend, you did not teach me well enough when I asked what the pious was but you told me that what you're doing is something pious, prosecuting your father for murder.

Euthyphro: And I spoke the truth, too, Socrates.

Socrates: Perhaps. But in fact, Euthyphro, you say there are many other pious things.

Euthyphro: Indeed there are.

---

* *Zeus ... his own father ... his own father ...* For the stories of Zeus, Cronos, and Ouranos, see Hesiod, *Theogony*, 154–82 and 453–506. [This footnote and the others for *Euthyphro* were inserted by the editor of the Broadview Press edition.]

† *robe ... great Panathenaea?* The Panathenaea was a celebration of Athena's birthday, held annually, with a larger ("great") celebration every four years. A new robe would be presented to the statue of the goddess Athena.

Socrates: So do you remember that I did not request this from you, to teach me one or two of the many pious things, but to teach me the form itself by which everything pious is pious? For you said that it's by one form that impious things are somehow impious and pious things pious. Or don't you remember?

Euthyphro: I certainly do.

Socrates: So then tell me whatever this form itself is, so that, by looking at it and using it as a paradigm, if you or anyone else do anything of that kind I can say that it is pious, and if it is not of that kind, that it is not.

Euthyphro: Well if that's what you want, Socrates, that's what I'll tell you.

Socrates: That's exactly what I want.

Euthyphro: Well, what is beloved by the gods is pious, and what is not beloved by them is impious.

Socrates: Excellent, Euthyphro! And you have answered in the way I was looking for you to answer. Whether you have done so truly or not, that I don't quite know—but you will obviously spell out how what you say is true.

Euthyphro: Absolutely.

Socrates: Come then, let's look at what we said. An action or a person that is beloved by the gods is pious, while an action or person that is despised by the gods is impious. It is not the same, but the complete opposite, the pious to the impious. Isn't that so?

Euthyphro: Indeed it is.

Socrates: And this seems right?

Euthyphro: I think so, Socrates.

Socrates: But wasn't it also said that the gods are at odds with each other and disagree with one another and that there are feuds among them?

Euthyphro: Yes, it was.

Socrates: What is the disagreement about, my good man, that causes hatred and anger? Let's look at it this way. If we disagree, you and I, about quantity, over which of two groups is greater, would our disagreement over this make us enemies and angry with each other, or wouldn't we quickly resolve the issue by resorting to counting?

Euthyphro: Of course.

Socrates: And again, if we disagreed about bigger and smaller, we would quickly put an end to the disagreement by resorting to measurement?

Euthyphro: That's right.

Socrates: And we would weigh with scales, I presume, to reach a decision about heavier and lighter?

Euthyphro: How else?

Socrates: Then what topic, exactly, would divide us and what difference would we be unable to settle such that we would be enemies and angry with one another? Perhaps you don't have an answer at hand, so as I'm talking, see if it's the just and the unjust, the noble and the shameful, and the good and the bad. Isn't it these things that make us enemies of one another, any time that happens, whether to me and you or to any other men, when we quarrel about them and are unable to come to a satisfactory judgment about them?

Euthyphro: It is indeed this disagreement, Socrates, and over these things.

Socrates: And what about the gods, Euthyphro? If they indeed disagree over something, don't they disagree over these very things?

Euthyphro: It's undoubtedly necessary.

Socrates: Then some of the gods think different things are just—according to you, worthy Euthyphro—and noble and shameful, and good and bad, since they surely wouldn't be at odds with one another unless they were disagreeing about these things. Right?

Euthyphro: You're right.

Socrates: And so whatever each group thinks is noble and good and just, they also love these things, and they hate the things that are the opposites of these?

Euthyphro: Certainly.

Socrates: Then according to you the things some of them think are just, others think are unjust, and by disagreeing about these things they are at odds and at war with each other. Isn't this so?

Euthyphro: It is.

Socrates: The same things, it seems, are both hated by the gods and loved, and so would be both despised and beloved by them?

Euthyphro: It seems so.

Socrates: And the same things would be both pious and impious, Euthyphro, according to this argument?

Euthyphro: I'm afraid so.

Socrates: So you haven't answered what I was asking, you remarkable man! I didn't ask you for what is both pious and impious at once: what is beloved by the gods is also hated by the gods, as it appears. As a result, Euthyphro, it wouldn't be surprising if in doing what you're doing now—punishing your father—you were doing something beloved by Zeus but despised by Cronos and Uranus, and while it is dear to Hephaestus, it is despised by Hera, and if any other god disagrees with another on the subject, your action will also appear to them similarly.

Euthyphro: But I believe, Socrates, that none of the gods will disagree with any other on this matter at least:

that any man who has killed another person unjustly need not pay the penalty.

Socrates: What's that? Have you never heard any *man* arguing that someone who killed unjustly or did something else unjustly should not pay the penalty?

Euthyphro: There's no end to these arguments, both outside and inside the courts, since people commit so many injustices and do and say anything to escape the punishment.

Socrates: Do they actually agree that they are guilty, Euthyphro, and despite agreeing they nonetheless say that they shouldn't pay the penalty?

Euthyphro: They don't agree on that at all.

Socrates: So they don't do or say *everything*, since, I think, they don't dare to claim or argue for this: that if they are in fact guilty they should *not* pay the penalty. Rather, I think they claim that they're not guilty. Right?

Euthyphro: That's true.

Socrates: So they don't argue, at least, that the guilty person shouldn't pay the penalty, but perhaps they argue about who the guilty party is and what he did and when.

Euthyphro: That's true.

Socrates: Doesn't the very same thing happen to the gods, too, if indeed, as you said, they are at odds about just and unjust things, some saying that a god commits an injustice against another one, while others deny it? But absolutely no one at all, you remarkable man, either god or human, dares to say that the guilty person need not pay the penalty.

Euthyphro: Yes. What you say is true, Socrates, for the most part.

Socrates: But I think that those who quarrel, Euthyphro, both men and gods, if the gods actually quarrel, argue over the particulars of what was done. Differing over a certain action, some say that it was done justly, others that it was done unjustly. Isn't that so?

Euthyphro: Certainly.

Socrates: Come now, my dear Euthyphro. So that I can become wiser, teach me too what evidence you have that all gods think the man was killed unjustly—the one who committed murder while he was working for you, and was bound by the master of the man he killed, and died from his bonds before the servant could learn from the interpreters what ought to be done in his case, and is the sort of person on whose behalf it is proper for a son to prosecute his father and make an allegation of murder. Come, try to give me a clear indication of how in this case all the gods believe beyond doubt that this action is proper. If you could show me this satisfactorily I would never stop praising you for your wisdom.

Euthyphro: But this is probably quite a task, Socrates, though I could explain it to you very clearly, even so.

Socrates: I understand. It's because you think I'm a slower learner than the judges, since you could make it clear to *them* in what way these actions are unjust and how the gods all hate such things.

Euthyphro: Very clear indeed, Socrates, if only they would listen to me when I talk.

Socrates: Of course they'll listen, so long as they think you speak well. But while you were speaking the following occurred to me: I'm thinking to myself, "Even if Euthyphro convincingly shows me that every god thinks this kind of death is unjust, what more will I have learned from Euthyphro about what the pious and the impious are? Because while this particular deed might be despised by the gods, as is likely, it was already apparent, just a moment ago, that the pious and impious aren't defined this way, since we saw that what is despised by the gods is also beloved by them." So I acquit you of this, Euthyphro. If you want, let us allow that all gods think this is unjust and that all of them despise it. But this current correction to the definition—that what all the gods despise is impi-

ous while what they love is pious, and what some love and some hate is neither or both—do you want us to now define the pious and the impious in this way?

Euthyphro: Well, what is stopping us, Socrates?

Socrates: For my part nothing, Euthyphro, but think about whether adopting this definition will make it easiest for you to teach me what you promised.

Euthyphro: I do indeed say that the pious is what all the gods love, and the opposite, what all gods hate, is impious.

Socrates: Then let's look again, Euthyphro, to see whether it's well stated. Or will we be content to simply accept our own definition or someone else's, agreeing that it is right just because somebody says it is? Or must we examine what the speaker is saying?

Euthyphro: We must examine it. But I'm quite confident that what we have now is well put.

Socrates: We'll soon know better, my good man. Think about this: Is the pious loved by the gods because it's pious, or is it pious because it is loved?

Euthyphro: I don't know what you mean, Socrates.

Socrates: I'll try to express myself more clearly. We speak of something being carried and of carrying, and being led and leading, and being seen and seeing, and so you understand that all of these are different from one another and how they are different?

Euthyphro: I think I understand.

Socrates: So there's a thing loved and different from this there's the thing that loves?

Euthyphro: How could there not be?

Socrates: Then tell me whether what is carried is a carried thing because it is carried, or because of something else?

Euthyphro: No, it's because of this.

Socrates: And also what is led because it is led, and what is seen because it is seen?

Euthyphro: Absolutely.

Socrates: So it is not that because it is something seen, it is seen, but the opposite, that because it is seen it is something seen. And it is not because it is something led that it is led, but because it is led it is something led. And it is not because it is something carried that it is carried, but because it is carried, it is something carried. Is it becoming clear what I'm trying to say, Euthyphro? I mean this: that if something becomes or is affected by something, it's not because it is a thing coming to be that it comes to be; but because it comes to be it is a thing coming into being. Nor is it affected by something because it is a thing that is affected; but because it is affected, it is a thing that is being affected. Or don't you agree?

Euthyphro: I do.

Socrates: And is a loved thing either a thing coming to be or a thing affected by something?

Euthyphro: Certainly.

Socrates: And does the same apply to this as to the previous cases: it is not because it is a loved thing that it is loved by those who love it, but it is a loved thing because it is loved?

Euthyphro: Necessarily.

Socrates: So what do we say about the pious, Euthyphro? Precisely that it is loved by all the gods, according to your statement?

Euthyphro: Yes.

Socrates: Is it because of this: that it is pious? Or because of something else?

Euthyphro: No, it's because of that.

Socrates: Because it is pious, then, it is loved, rather than being pious because it is loved?

Euthyphro: It seems so.

Socrates: Then because it is loved by the gods, it is a loved thing and beloved by the gods?

Euthyphro: How could it not?

Socrates: So the beloved is not pious, Euthyphro, nor is the pious beloved by the gods, as you claim, but the one is different from the other.

Euthyphro: How so, Socrates?

Socrates: Because we agree that the pious is loved because of this—that is, because it's pious—and not that it is pious because it is loved. Right?

Euthyphro: Yes.

Socrates: The beloved, on the other hand, because it is loved by gods, is beloved due to this very act of being loved, rather than being loved because it is beloved?

Euthyphro: That's true.

Socrates: But if the beloved and the pious were in fact the same, my dear Euthyphro, then, if the pious were loved because of being the pious, the beloved would be loved because of being the beloved; and again, if the beloved was beloved because of being loved by gods, the pious would also be pious by being loved. But as it is, you see that the two are opposites and are completely different from one another, since the one, because it is loved, is the kind of thing that is loved, while the other is loved because it is the kind of thing that is loved.

So I'm afraid, Euthyphro, that when you were asked what in the world the pious is, you did not want to reveal its nature to me, but wanted to tell me some one of its qualities—that the pious has the quality of being loved by all the gods—but as for what it *is*, you did not say at all. So if I am dear to you, don't keep me in the dark but tell me again from the beginning what in the world the pious is. And we won't differ over whether it is loved by the gods or whatever else happens to it, but tell me without delay, what is the pious, and the impious?

Euthyphro: But Socrates, I have no way of telling you what I'm thinking, because somehow whatever we put forward always wanders off on us and doesn't want to stay where we put it.

Socrates: Your statements, Euthyphro, seem to belong to my ancestor Daedalus.* And if I were saying them and putting them forward, perhaps you would be joking about how, on account of my relationship to him, my works made of words run away even on me and don't want to stay wherever a person might put them. But at present these propositions are yours, and so we have to find some other joke, since they don't want to stay put for you, as even you yourself admit.

Euthyphro: It seems to me that pretty much the same joke applies to the statements, Socrates, since I am not the inspiration for their wandering off and their refusal to stay in the same place. Rather, it seems to me that you are the Daedalus, since they would stay in place just fine for me, at least.

Socrates: Then I'm afraid, my friend, that I've become more skilled in the craft than the man himself, to the extent that while he could only make his own works move, I can do so to others' works as well as my own. And to my mind this is the most exquisite thing about my skill, that I am unintentionally clever, since I wanted the words to stay put for me and to be fixed motionless more than to have the money of Tantalos† and the skill of Daedalus combined. But enough of this. Since I think you are soft, I myself will help you educate me about the

pious. So don't give up the task. See whether you believe that everything pious is necessarily just.

Euthyphro: I do.

Socrates: And is everything just pious? Or is every part of piety just but the just is not the whole of piety, but some part of it is pious, and some other part is different?

Euthyphro: I can't keep up with what you're saying, Socrates.

Socrates: And yet you are younger than me by at least as much as you are wiser than me! But, as I say, you are spoiled by your abundance of wisdom. Pull yourself together, you blessed man, since what I'm saying is not difficult to get your head around. I mean, of course, the opposite of what the poet meant when he wrote:

> Zeus who created it and who produced all of these
> You do not want to revile; for where there is fear
> there is also respect.‡

I disagree with this statement from the poet. Shall I tell you how?

Euthyphro: Yes indeed.

Socrates: I don't think that "where there is fear there is also respect" since I think many people who fear sickness, poverty and many other things feel fear, but they feel no respect at these things they fear. Don't you think so, too?

Euthyphro: Certainly.

Socrates: Where there is respect, though, there is also fear, for is there anyone who feels respect and is ashamed at some act who doesn't also feel fear and dread a reputation for cowardice?

Euthyphro: He does indeed dread it.

---

* *Daedalus* The statues made by the mythical Daedalus were said to be so lifelike that they appeared to move. Daedalus is most famous for making wings for himself and his son Icarus to use to escape from Crete.

† *money of Tantalos* Tantalos (or Tantalus) was a son of Zeus, and a king who derived great wealth from the mines he controlled. He murdered his son and tried to feed him to the gods as an offering. For this he was punished by being placed in the deepest part of the Underworld, where he was constantly offered food and drink, which then receded just outside his grasp when he tried to take them.

‡ The quotation is from Stanisos's *Cypria*, a collection of tales describing the events prior to the beginning of Homer's *Iliad*.

Socrates: So it's not right to claim that "where there is fear there is also respect," for respect is not in fact everywhere fear is, but instead where there is respect there is also fear. Because I think fear covers more than respect since respect is a part of fear, just as oddness is a part of number, so that it's not the case that where there is number there is also oddness, but where there is oddness, there is also number. Do you follow now, at least?

Euthyphro: I certainly do.

Socrates: This is the kind of thing I was talking about earlier when I was questioning you: where there is justice, is there also piety? Or is it that where there is piety, there is also justice, but piety is not everywhere justice is, since piety is a part of justice? Do you think we should speak in this way or in some other?

Euthyphro: No, in this way. I think you're speaking properly.

Socrates: Then see what follows this: if the pious is a part of the just, we must, it seems, discover what part of the just the pious might be. If, to go back to what we were just discussing, you now asked me something such as what part of number the even is, and what kind of number it happens to be, I would say that it would be the number that can be divided into two equal and not unequal parts.* Doesn't it seem so to you?

Euthyphro: It does.

Socrates: So try to teach me in this way, Euthyphro, what sort of part of the just piety is, so that we can also tell Meletus not to do us wrong and charge me with impiety, since I have already learned enough from you about what is holy and what is pious and what is not.

Euthyphro: It seems to me now, Socrates, that holiness and piety is the part of justice concerned with attending to the gods, while the remaining part of justice is concerned with attending to human beings.

---

* *divided into two equal and not unequal parts* Literally "isosceles and not scalene," presumably because isosceles triangles have two equal legs.

Socrates: I think you put that well, Euthyphro. But I still need just one small thing: I don't know quite what you mean by "attending." Surely you don't mean that attending to the gods is like the other kinds of attending, even though we do say so. We say, for example, that not everybody knows how to attend to a horse, just the horse-trainer. Right?

Euthyphro: Certainly.

Socrates: Since horse-training is attending to horses?

Euthyphro: Yes.

Socrates: And no one but the dog-trainer knows how to attend to dogs?

Euthyphro: Right.

Socrates: And dog-training is attending to dogs?

Euthyphro: Yes.

Socrates: And cattle-herding is to cattle?

Euthyphro: Absolutely.

Socrates: Naturally, then, piety and holiness are to the gods, Euthyphro? That's what you say?

Euthyphro: I do.

Socrates: Then does all attending bring about the same effect? Something of the following sort: the good and benefit of what is attended to, in just the way you see that horses, when attended to by horse-trainers, are benefited and become better? Or don't you think they are?

Euthyphro: They are.

Socrates: And dogs by the dog-trainer somehow, and cattle by the cattle-herder, and all the others similarly? Or do you think the attending is aimed at harming what is attended to?

Euthyphro: By Zeus, I do not.

Socrates: But at benefiting them?

Euthyphro: How could it not be?

Socrates: And since piousness is attending to the gods, does it benefit the gods and make the gods better? Do you agree to this, that whenever one does something pious it results in some improvement of the gods?

Euthyphro: By Zeus, no, I don't.

Socrates: Nor did I think that that's what you meant, Euthyphro—far from it, in fact—and that's why I was asking what you really meant by "attending to the gods," because I didn't think you mean this kind of thing.

Euthyphro: And you're right, Socrates. Because I mean no such thing.

Socrates: Alright then. But what kind of attending to the gods would piousness be, then?

Euthyphro: The kind, Socrates, when slaves attend to their masters.

Socrates: I understand. It would be a kind of service to gods, it seems.

Euthyphro: Certainly.

Socrates: Can you tell me about service to doctors, what end result is such service aimed at? Don't you think it's at health?

Euthyphro: I do.

Socrates: And what about service to shipbuilders? What end result is that service aimed at?

Euthyphro: Clearly it's aimed at a ship, Socrates.

Socrates: And service to house-builders, I suppose, is aimed at houses?

Euthyphro: Yes.

Socrates: Tell me then, best of men, what end result is service to the gods aimed at? It's obvious that you know, since you claim to have the finest religious knowledge—of any human, at least.

Euthyphro: And as a matter of fact, Socrates, I speak the truth.

Socrates: So tell me, by Zeus, what in the world is that magnificent task which the gods accomplish by using us as servants?

Euthyphro: Many fine tasks, Socrates.

Socrates: Well, and so do the generals, my friend. But nevertheless one could easily say what their key purpose is: that they achieve victory in war. Is that not so?

Euthyphro: How else could it be?

Socrates: And I think the farmers accomplish many fine tasks. And yet their key purpose is nourishment from the soil.

Euthyphro: Very much so.

Socrates: So what, then, about the many fine things that the gods accomplish? What is the key purpose of their labor?

Euthyphro: As I said a little earlier, Socrates, it is a great task to learn exactly how all these things are. But I will put it for you generally: if a man knows how to speak and act pleasingly to the gods in his prayers and sacrifices, those are pious, and such things preserve both his own home and the common good of the city. But the opposites of these pleasing things are unholy, and they obviously overturn and destroy everything.

Socrates: If you were willing, Euthyphro, you could have told me the heart of what I was asking much more briefly. But in fact you are not eager to teach me, that much is clear—since now when you were just about to do so, you turned away. If you had given your answer, I would already have a satisfactory understanding of piousness from you. But for the present, the lover must follow his beloved wherever he might lead. So what do you say the pious and piousness are, again? Aren't you saying it's a certain kind of knowledge, of how to sacrifice and pray?

Euthyphro: I am.

Socrates: And sacrificing is giving to the gods, while praying is making a request of the gods?

Euthyphro: Very much so, Socrates.

Socrates: Based on this, piousness would be knowledge of making requests and giving things to the gods?

Euthyphro: You have understood my meaning very well, Socrates.

Socrates: It's because I am eager for your wisdom, my friend, and pay close attention to it, so that nothing you might say falls to the ground. But tell me, what is this service to the gods? You say it is making requests of them and giving to them?

Euthyphro: I do.

Socrates: And proper requests would be requests for what we need from them, asking them for these things?

Euthyphro: What else?

Socrates: And again, giving properly would be giving what they happen to want from us, to give these things to them in return? Since to give a gift by giving someone what he has no need of would not be too skillful, I suppose.

Euthyphro: That's true, Socrates.

Socrates: So piousness for gods and humans, Euthyphro, would be some skill of trading with one another?

Euthyphro: If naming it that way is sweeter for you, call it "trading."

Socrates: As far as I'm concerned, nothing is sweeter unless it is true. Tell me, how do the gods benefit from the gifts they receive from us? What they give us is clear to everyone, since every good we have was given by them. But what they receive from us, what good is it? Or do we fare so much better than them in the trade that we get everything that's good from them, while they get nothing from us?

Euthyphro: But do you think, Socrates, that the gods are benefited by what they receive from us?

Socrates: Well then what in the world would they be, Euthyphro, these gifts from us to the gods?

Euthyphro: What else, do you think, but honor and admiration and, as I said just now, gratitude?

Socrates: So being shown gratitude is what's pious, Euthyphro, but it is neither beneficial to the gods nor dear to them?

Euthyphro: I think it is dear to them above everything else.

Socrates: So the pious is once again, it seems, what is dear to gods.

Euthyphro: Very much so.

Socrates: Are you at all surprised, when you say such things, that your words seem not to stand still but to move around? And you accuse me of making them move around like a Daedalus when you yourself are much more skilled than Daedalus, even making things go around in circles? Or don't you see that our discussion has gone around and arrived back at the same place? You remember, no doubt, that previously the pious and the beloved by the gods seemed to us not to be the same but different from one another. Or don't you remember?

Euthyphro: I certainly do.

Socrates: Well, don't you realize now that you're saying that what is dear to the gods is pious? But this is nothing other than what is beloved by the gods, isn't it?

Euthyphro: It certainly is.

Socrates: So either what we decided then was wrong, or, if we were right then, we are wrong now.

Euthyphro: So it seems.

Socrates: Then we must examine again from the beginning what the pious is, as I am determined not to give up until I understand it. Do not scorn me, but by applying your mind in every way, tell me the truth now more than ever. Because you know it if anybody does and, like Proteus,* you cannot be released until you tell me. Because unless you knew clearly about the pious and impious there is no way you would ever have, on behalf of a hired laborer, tried to pursue your aging father for murder. Instead you would have been afraid before the gods, and ashamed before men, to run the risk of conducting this matter improperly. But as it is, I am sure that you think you have clear knowledge of the pious and the impious. So tell me, great Euthyphro, and do not conceal what you think it is.

Euthyphro: Well, some other time, Socrates, because I'm in a hurry to get somewhere and it's time for me to go.

Socrates: What a thing to do, my friend! By leaving, you have cast me down from a great hope I had: that I would learn from you what is pious and what is not, and moreover would free myself from Meletus's charge by showing him that, thanks to Euthyphro, I had already become wise in religious matters and that I would no longer speak carelessly and innovate about these things due to ignorance, and most of all that I would live better for the rest of my life.

READING QUESTIONS

1. Socrates begins by asking Euthyphro the question, "What is piety?" and Euthyphro quickly answers. What is Euthyphro's answer and why is Socrates dissatisfied with it? Reflecting on this exchange between the characters, what does Socrates's problem with Euthyphro's immediate answer reveal about the question? In other words, what exactly is Socrates asking for when he inquires, "What is piety?"

2. Socrates "catches" Euthyphro in a number of contradictions. What is one of the contradictions in Euthyphro's thinking? Based on the text, why do you think Euthyphro is caught holding contradictory beliefs?

3. What did you enjoy about reading this philosophical dialogue? What did you find challenging? What strategies, if any, did you come up with for working through what you found challenging?

---

* *Proteus* A mythical sea god who could change shape. Menelaus had to hold on to Proteus as he changed shape in order to get him to prophesy. (See Homer, *Odyssey* 4.398–463.)

Next up, we'll learn to construct arguments ourselves. There are two basic types of argument that we will cover here: *deductive* and *non-deductive*.

2.2 Deductive Arguments

A **deductive argument** is one that attempts to *guarantee* the truth of its conclusion. When you offer a deductive argument, you are saying "If my assumptions and reasoning are correct, then this conclusion *must* be true." This is in contrast to non-deductive (or inductive) arguments, which we will discuss in the next section. If this book were designed for a course in deductive logic, it would be appropriate to examine the many subtleties, nuances, and intricate forms of this kind of reasoning. Since, however, this text is meant primarily for philosophical beginners, our brief coverage of logic will be limited to some of the basics, including treatment of some *invalid* forms of deduction. As just mentioned, after covering formal deductive logic, we will move on to *informal logic* or *non-deductive reasoning*, another type of thinking that is important to master for our philosophical purposes. For now, it is helpful to refer to Table 2.1 to get an initial understanding of how both forms of reasoning differ from each other.

TABLE 2.1 Comparing Inductive and Deductive Arguments

Example of a Deductive Argument	Example of an Inductive Argument
Deductive arguments are either completely valid or invalid. All birds have wings. Every swan is a bird. Therefore, every swan has wings.	*Inductive arguments are better or worse by degree.* Every swan that has ever been observed has wings. Therefore, every swan has wings.
If the form of the argument is valid and the premises are true, then the conclusion *must* also be *necessarily* true.	If the premises are true, then the conclusion is *likely*, though *not necessarily* true. (A negation of the conclusion does not constitute a logical contradiction.)

To understand the nature of deductive arguments, it is helpful to distinguish between their **form** and **content**. Arguments can refer to just about anything—whether moral, epistemological, social or political, for example. They typically address some subject matter, topic, or controversial issue. These things make for the *content* of arguments.

Regardless of the content or subject matter under debate, if the deductive arguments involved are to be considered valid, they must display an acceptable **logical form**. Underlying the content or substance comprising any rational deductive argument is a formal structure that can be abstracted, and thereby evaluated. A 'formal structure' here means a structure that has one of a variety of accepted *forms*. 'Formal' does not have its more usual meaning here. The more common forms have been given standardized names, some of which have Latin origins like the first one we will examine: *modus ponens*, meaning *mode that affirms*.

Modus Ponens

Many of the arguments that you will come across in philosophical writings or hear expressed in your daily conversations contain the **modus ponens** logical form. Arguments of this type are valid, and so this logical structure can be used to test arguments for their validity.

Of course, *modus ponens* is not the *only* valid form of reasoning, and therefore, an argument not displaying the *modus ponens* form is not necessarily invalid. As you will see, there is more than one type of **valid reasoning**.

Below are two valid *modus ponens* arguments containing different content but sharing identical forms.

1. If the economy goes into a recession, then church attendance increases. Since we are currently in an economic recession, we can conclude that church attendance has increased or that it will do so shortly.
2. If a person is a Democrat, then the person is liberal minded. Linda is a democrat, so we can conclude that Linda is liberal minded.

If we abstract from the content of these two very different arguments, we can see that they still share the same formal structure expressed below. (*Note*: There is nothing significant about the selection of the letters "p" and "q"; any letters would do.)

If p, then q
p
So, q

The analysis leading to our conclusion that both arguments display the same formal structure, regardless of their differing content, can be found below. Notice what's labeled 'p' and 'q'.

Example One:

If the economy goes into a recession (p), then church attendance increases (q).
We are currently in an economic recession (p).
So, (q) we can conclude that church attendance has increased or will increase shortly.

Example Two:

If a person is a Democrat (p), then the person is liberal minded (q).
Linda is a democrat (p).
So, (q) Linda is liberal minded.

The proper logical procedure in *modus ponens* reasoning involves something called **affirming the antecedent**. In "If ... then" statements such as in the examples above, the

antecedent is the first part or first clause (before the "then"). It is represented by 'p'. The **consequent** is the second part or second clause (after the "then"). It is represented by 'q'.

Modus ponens reasoning includes two premises: an "If … then" premise, a premise stating the antecedent of the "If … then" premise, and a conclusion stating the consequent of the "If … then" premise. So, when we *affirm the antecedent*, we're saying that the first part of the "if, then" statement (the antecedent 'p') is true. On the basis of that affirmation, we then conclude that the second part of the statement (the consequent 'q') is true. This is how a *modus ponens* argument works and is structured.

When working with "if, then" statements as found in *modus ponens* argumentation, you should be careful not to make a common mistake. As explained, the proper thing to do is to affirm the antecedent; this makes for a valid form of argument. If, however, you **affirm the consequent**, an *invalid faulty form* of argument results. Formally expressed, affirming the consequent looks like this:

If p, then q
q
So, p

If we provide some content to the formal expression above, we can easily see how affirming the consequent constitutes an invalid form of reasoning.

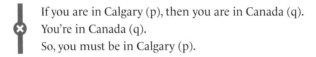

If you are in Calgary (p), then you are in Canada (q).
You're in Canada (q).
So, you must be in Calgary (p).

In the example above, where the consequent (q) is affirmed, we find an example of invalid reasoning. Sure, being in Calgary *necessarily means* you are in Canada, but being in Canada *does not necessarily mean* that you are in Calgary. You could be in Vancouver or Montréal. What's important to note is that in valid deductive logic, *a single conclusion necessarily* follows from preceding premises, something not so in this case. Here, being in Canada *might* mean one is in Calgary, but *not necessarily so*. The conclusion is only possibly, not necessarily, true.

When testing arguments for their validity, one thing you can try to do is construct an obviously invalid counterexample containing the identical logical form of the first example. Clearly seeing how the counterexample is invalid will enable you to appreciate what's wrong in the first instance.

Let's look at another pair of examples. First, a valid modus ponens argument:

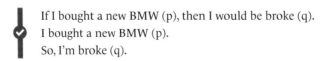

If I bought a new BMW (p), then I would be broke (q).
I bought a new BMW (p).
So, I'm broke (q).

As you can well imagine, buying an expensive BMW could leave one broke or strapped for cash. This is not hard to understand. Whether or not this is always or ever true is not in question here. It's the *form of the reasoning* on the basis of the assumptions—the premises—that is at issue in validity, not the truth of the premises.

Okay, so assume that both premises are true. Notice, and this is the important point, that given this, the conclusion would have to be true too. It would be logically inconsistent to accept both premises but deny the conclusion. It's impossible for any argument with this form to have true premises but a false conclusion.

But consider the next example, and notice how it differs from the BMW argument just presented above. It's an example of affirming the consequent, and is invalid reasoning. Notice also how it has the same logical form as the invalid Calgary argument.

If I bought a new BMW (p), then I would be broke (q).
I am broke (q).
So, I must have bought a new BMW (p).

Imagine both premises are true. Would it be logically inconsistent to deny the conclusion? Is it possible that the premises are both true, while the conclusion is false? Yes, it's possible. Buying a new BMW would make me broke; I am broke. But I haven't bought a new BMW. So, while buying a BMW may leave you broke, being broke does not logically, and *necessarily*, entail that you bought a BMW. Perhaps a business deal fell through or a declaration of personal bankruptcy due to excessive credit card debt caused you to lose most or all of your monetary assets. The conclusion about the BMW purchase does not necessarily follow from the preceding premises included in the argument. Thus, affirming the consequent here results in invalid logic.

We have shown this argument is invalid by imaging a situation in which those premises are true, but the conclusion is false. Another way to show an argument invalid is by creating another argument—a counterexample—having the same form but with clearly true premises and a clearly false conclusion. That's what we did earlier.

Consider, however, what would happen to this argument by *denying* the consequent, not affirming it. What conclusion would follow from denying (q)? That is, what conclusion would follow if you were *not* broke? Would you be the owner or a shiny new BMW or not? Give it some thought. Once you have your answer, continue reading to learn more about the logical structure that involves *denying the consequent*.

Modus Tollens

Modus tollens is a second form of valid logic. Translated, *modus tollens* means *mode that denies*. In a *modus tollens* argument, an inference results by **denying the consequent**. Formally, *modus tollens* is expressed in the following fashion:

If p, then q
not q
So, not p

Example:

If it rains (p), then the streets get wet (q).
The streets did not get wet (not q).
So, it has not rained (not p).

In this example, we start off with the first premise stating that, *if it rains, the streets get wet.* If we accept this premise, and agree with the second claim that the streets did not get wet, then we can rationally conclude with certainty that it *must not* have rained. To argue that the streets didn't get wet, but that it rained, wouldn't make any sense given our acceptance of the first two premises of the argument.

Now, let's look at another formal error in reasoning—what might be described as the invalid form of *modus tollens*. It involves **denying the antecedent**. In this instance, the wrong thing is denied.

If p, then q
not p
So, not q

Sticking with the "rain and wet streets" example, we can understand how the form just expressed is invalid. (See below.) Even if we accept the premise that, "If it rains, then the streets get wet," it still is possible that the streets can get wet *from something other than rain*. A fire hydrant could have burst or municipal workers could have hosed them down. The conclusion that the streets are not wet *does not necessarily follow* simply from the fact it is not raining. There can be more than one cause for a wet street. Put another way, *rain may "guarantee" wet streets, but lack of rain cannot "guarantee" the streets didn't get wet for other reasons.*

If it rains (p) then the streets get wet (q).
It did not rain (not p).
So, the streets didn't get wet (not q).

In case you still can't see how the preceding argument is invalid, examine a similar example below. It will help you to better intuit how denying the antecedent constitutes invalid logic.

If the US capital were Philadelphia, (p), then the capital would be an eastern city (q). (TRUE)
The US capital is not Philadelphia (not p). (TRUE)
So, the capital is not in an eastern city (not q). (FALSE)

Again we see in this argument that this invalid form does not necessitate a true conclusion even when the premises are true.

Hypothetical Syllogisms/Chain Arguments

Hypothetical syllogisms in the form of **chain arguments** comprise two "if-then" premises, connected in a "chain," and a conclusion. Because this type of syllogism contains "conditional" premises it is referred to as *hypothetical*. An example of a hypothetical chain argument is the following:

If you obtain a pass on this test (p), then you will successfully complete your last course (q). On top of that, if you successfully complete your last course (q), then you will earn your diploma (r). So, if you pass the test (p), then you will earn your diploma (r).

Expressed formally,

If p, then q
If q, then r
Therefore, if p, then r

One *invalid* form of a hypothetical chain syllogism, among others, is the **fallacy of common antecedent**:

If p, then q
If p, then r
Therefore, if q, then r

To appreciate why the form above is invalid, here's a counter-example:

If you smoke (p), then you will be popular (q).
If you smoke, (p), then you will get lung cancer (r).
Therefore, if you become popular (q), then you will get lung cancer (r).

Even if we accept the first two premises of this argument, the conclusion does not *necessarily* follow. On the face of it, this argument actually doesn't make sense. In this syllogism, smoking entails popularity, but popularity does not *necessarily* entail smoking or the lung cancer that results from smoking. Even if it were true that smoking makes one popular, it's not true that smoking is the only way to become popular. Smoking may mean you're popular, but being popular doesn't mean you smoke. It's possible that some popular people don't smoke and hence are not likely to develop lung cancer. So, the chain argument here concluding that *popularity necessarily leads to lung cancer* is irrational and unsound.

Disjunctive Syllogisms

Like the chain argument syllogism, the **disjunctive syllogism** is made up of three statements. Unlike the former, however, which deals with a logical chain of entailments or consequences, this one typically involves an *either/or choice*. An example of a disjunctive syllogism is the following:

Either Mary has a raincoat (p), or she has an umbrella (q). Since she does *not* have an umbrella (not q), she therefore has a raincoat (p).

Expressed formally,

Either p or q
not q
Therefore, p

This argument form works so long as either one of 'p' or 'q' is false—it doesn't matter which. For example, if we knew that Mary doesn't have a raincoat, we could instead conclude that she has an umbrella:

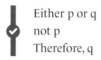

Either p or q
not p
Therefore, q

Sometimes disjunctive arguments can have more than two alternatives. Instead of just 'p' and 'q' say, there could also be 'r'. We might even have 's' and 't'. For simplicity's sake, let's limit ourselves to only one more alternative disjunct, 'r'. In this case, denying 'p' does not allow us to conclude 'q' *necessarily* as 'r' remains a possibility as well. Similarly, denying 'p' does not permit us to conclude 'r' since 'q' is possible. If we deny 'q' instead, then both 'p' and 'r' still remain as two possible conclusions. Remember that when a single conclusion does not follow necessarily in a deductive argument, the argument is invalid. The error of **ignoring an alternative disjunct** is presented below.*

Either p, q, or r   Either p, q, or r
Not p   Not q
So, q   So, p

TABLE 2.2 Some Valid and Invalid Forms of Deductive Logic

Valid Logical Forms	Invalid Logical Forms
Modus Ponens	**Affirming the Consequent**
If p, then q p So, q	If p, then q q So, p
Modus Tollens	**Denying the Antecedent**
If p, then q not q So, not p	If p, then q not p So, not q
Hypothetical Syllogism	**Hypothetical Fallacy (Fallacy of Common Antecedent)**
If p, then q If q, then r So, if p, then r	If p, then q If p, then r So, if q, then r
Disjunctive Syllogism (two versions)	**Ignoring an Alternative Disjunct**
Either p or q Either p or q not q not p So, p So, q	Either p, q, or r not p So, q

---

* I thank Susan Mills for suggesting and labeling this form of invalid reasoning.

Categorical Syllogisms or Syllogisms of Class Membership

Not all formal deductive arguments are of the "If ... then" or "Either ... or" variety. Sometimes we draw conclusions based on inferences pertaining to classes, groups, or categories. In such cases, **categorical syllogisms or syllogisms of class membership** are used. See below:

Premise: All A are B
Premise: C is A
Conclusion: Therefore, C is B

Adding some content to this formal structure, we come up with the following example:

Premise: All men (A) are mortal (B).
Premise: Socrates (C) is a man (A).
Conclusion: Therefore, Socrates (C) is mortal (B).

Another variation of a categorical syllogism is provided below.

All A are B.
Some C are A.
Therefore, some C are B.

Content Example:

All bankers (A) are conservative (B).
Some people (C) are bankers (A).
Therefore, some people (C) are conservative (B).

An invalid form of categorical syllogism can be expressed in the following symbolic fashion:

All A is B.
C is B.
Therefore, C is an A.

At first glance, you might be a bit bewildered as to how the syllogism above is invalid. After all, if all A's are B's, and C is also a B, then why shouldn't C be an A? Both are B's, after all. Adding some content to the invalid logical form above, we can find a counterexample with true premises and a false conclusion. You can easily see that the conclusion of an argument with this form is not necessitated by the premises.

All cats (A) are animals (B).
A dog (C) is an animal (B).
Therefore, a dog (C) is a cat (A).

Validity, Truth, and Soundness

In everyday conversations, you often hear people say things like, "That's a valid point," or "That's a valid statement" or perhaps, "Your criticism is valid." In strict logical terms, however, 'points,' 'statements,' and 'criticisms' are not called 'valid' or 'invalid.' Deductive arguments are. Statements may be true or false or more or less likely; criticisms may be justified or unjustified; and good points may be based on accurate observations or be supported by good reasoning. But when it comes to logic, **validity** refers to arguments with correct deductive forms only. The premises and the corresponding conclusion of any deductive argument may be true or false, but that's irrelevant to validity—except, as we've seen, a valid argument cannot have true premises and a false conclusion.

Validity should be clearly distinguished from another logical notion, namely, **soundness**. The concept of soundness also refers to deductive arguments. A **sound argument** is one that is valid in form *and* contains true (or acceptable) premises. An **unsound argument**, by contrast, can be valid in form, but because its premises are untrue or unacceptable, the conclusion that follows from them is not rationally acceptable.

So, it's important to recognize that in deductive arguments, **truth** refers to the veracity of the individual statements contained within the syllogism itself; validity refers to an argument's form or structure; and soundness involves a combination of both truth *and* validity. A deductive argument is sound, therefore, if it is comprised of true premises and is valid in form. *True premises and a valid form lead to a necessary and true conclusion.*

It's also important to remember here that *necessary* conclusions are found only in deductive logic, not in inductive reasoning. Thus, *soundness* is a concept appropriately applied to the former and not the latter type of thinking process. Inductive logic is *better or worse—weaker or stronger by degree.*

It is also important to keep in mind that *valid arguments are sometimes unsound.* To appreciate why, look at the following example:

All birds (A) are blue (B).	All A is B.
The Dalai Lama (C) is a bird (A).	C is A.
The Dalai Lama (C) is blue (B).	Therefore, C is B.

What you have here is a valid categorical syllogism. The logical form of the argument is found to the right of it. What is obvious about this valid syllogism is that the conclusion is obviously false. The Dalai Lama is not blue. You should note as well that the premises are both false; the Dalai Lama is not a bird; some birds are black, others are red, and so on.

This example serves to underscore the point that *valid arguments containing false premises can lead to false conclusions,* and so they are unsound and must be rejected.

Note as well that *invalid arguments can contain true conclusions,* even with all true premises. Here is an example:

All chickens are egg-layers. (True)
All birds are egg-layers. (True)
So all chickens are birds. (True)

Although every statement in this argument is true, the premises don't provide support for the conclusion because of its invalidity. This argument has the logical form: All C are E; all B are E; therefore all C are B. This can be shown to be invalid by imagining or producing another argument with this same form, but with true premises and a false conclusion:

> All dachshunds are mammals. (True)
> All corgis are mammals. (True)
> All dachshunds are corgis. (False)

By contrast, when an argument is valid in form, and when it possesses true premises, it must contain a true conclusion. It is sound and rationally compelling.

EVALUATING DEDUCTIVE ARGUMENTS

For each of the reasoning examples below, indicate whether the argument is valid or invalid and note the argument type (hypothetical syllogism, disjunctive syllogism, etc.). Then display its logical form; for example:

If p, then q
p
Therefore, q

1. If George lost his wallet, then he lost his student identification. If he lost his student identification, then he will not be allowed to join any varsity teams. Therefore, if Fred lost his wallet, then he will not be allowed to join any varsity teams.

Valid or Invalid?

Argument Type

Logical Form:

2. Either I will sleep in or I'll wake up early for work tomorrow. I know I won't sleep in. Therefore, I'll be waking up early for work tomorrow.

Valid or Invalid?

Argument Type

Logical Form:

3. If we go to war, I will be very upset. I am very upset. So, we went to war.

Valid or Invalid?

Argument Type

Logical Form:

4. If you lie to people, then they will not trust you. People do trust you. So you have not lied.

Valid or Invalid?

Argument Type

Logical Form:

5. All humans are sentient beings. Jonas is a human. Jonas is a sentient being.

Valid or Invalid?

Argument Type

Logical Form:

6. All Olympic athletes are team members. All professional athletes are team members. So, all Olympic athletes are professional athletes.

Valid or Invalid?

Argument Type

Logical Form:

ANSWER KEY

1. Valid
Hypothetical Syllogism / Chain argument
Form:　If p, then q
　　　　If q, then r
　　　　Therefore, if p then r

2. Valid
Disjunctive Syllogism
Form:　Either p or q
　　　　not p
　　　　Therefore, q

3. Invalid
(You can become upset for reasons other than going to war; the conclusion does not follow *necessarily*.)
Affirming the Consequent
Form: If p, then q
         q
        So, p

4. Valid
(Note: The consequent is denied; the denial of the consequent here, "not trust you," is *to trust you*. The double negative [i.e., to not, "not trust you"] may cause some initial confusion. As you've probably learned, *two negatives make a positive*.)
Modus Tollens
Form: If p, then q
        not q
        So, not p

5. Valid
Categorical Syllogism
Form: All H are S
        J is H
        So, J is S
Expressed alternatively: All A are B; C is A; C is B.

6. Invalid
(Note: the second premise should be "All P are O" and the conclusion should be "All P are T" in order for the argument to have the valid form of a categorical syllogism. The truth of each claim is irrelevant when considering only validity.)
Categorical Syllogism
Form: All O are T
        All P are T
        So, all O are P

2.3 Non-Deductive Arguments

In addition to deductive logic, philosophers also use *non-deductive reasoning*, in the form of **inductive arguments**. Unlike valid deductive logic, which always leads to *necessary* conclusions, non-deductive reasoning or inductive logic can yield only *probable* conclusions. One reason is because inductive arguments often use past experience to support conclusions about what will *probably* be the case but is *not necessarily* so. Experience teaches us that the past is often a good predictor of the future, but it is certainly no guarantor.

While admittedly there's no deductive logical force that pressures us to accept conclusions reached by inductive reasoning, experience nonetheless compels us to draw the conclusion that the world works in a regular fashion. The events we don't observe frequently have the same characteristics as the similar events we do observe or have observed. The more consistent our experiences, the firmer our convictions become. The eighteenth-century philosopher David Hume will have more to say about this in Chapter 4, but for now let's say this: Although it's a *logical possibility* that the sun might not rise tomorrow, we strongly believe on the basis of prior experience that it will! We're *probably* right.

Important to note is the fact that non-deductive conclusions are *weaker or stronger by degree* and need not necessarily be accepted or rejected in an all-or-nothing fashion. Thus, in contrast to formal arguments, examples of non-deductive reasoning are never said to be 100% valid or invalid. To see why, let us take the following illustration.

Suppose, for instance, that we know that Wendy has a long history of lying. She has lied on her job application, on her income tax return, and to her husband. We might then conclude that she has lied about her medical history required to purchase a new life insurance policy. Because she has lied many times before in many other instances, we conclude that she has *probably* lied this time as well. Here, we are using past experience to support a current conclusion.

Since our inductive conclusion about Wendy is based on the facts of experience, and because these facts are never complete, however, or because new facts can have the effect of weakening, changing, or contradicting today's assumptions, we can never be absolutely sure about our conclusion. Perhaps Wendy has experienced some kind of religious or moral conversion that has led to a complete character transformation. Maybe Wendy was indeed a liar, but is now an honest and responsible citizen. Maybe she thought she'd be caught this time. Many variables could weaken the strength of the inductive inference made here.

Though it can never provide absolute certainty, we routinely rely on inductive logic to navigate the world in our everyday lives and in our scientific methods and investigations. It may not be valid reasoning, in the purely formal sense, but it is a powerful and important way of thinking. Non-deductive reasoning comes in numerous forms. We look briefly at three of them for our introductory purposes.

Argument from Past Experience

We've already touched on one **argument from past experience** using the Wendy illustration. Let's now look at another example for a better understanding of the reasoning dynamics involved.

If, say, you developed a rash every time you ate strawberries in the past, would you expect to be rash-free the next time you eat a strawberry? Probably not. If, in every year on record, it has snowed in the Rocky Mountains, is it reasonable to conclude that it will snow in the Rocky Mountains next year? Probably so. These are just a couple of examples using inductive reasoning based on past experience to predict the future. The basic structure is as follows:

> In all past observed instances, event A has coincided with event B.
> Therefore, in the future, event A will (likely) coincide with event B.

For example,

> In every recent election my street has been littered with campaign signs.
> So, in this coming election, my street will likely also be littered with campaign signs.

Inductive reasoning of this form is *predictive*. The conclusion is a statement about what *will happen*, and it is based on what *has happened*. Since we cannot know the future in advance, inductive reasoning of this form is how we formulate our expectations and prepare for future outcomes. Of course, it is not necessary that the past experience be your own experience for you to use it in this kind of argument. If reliable sources tell you that in the past things have consistently been a certain way, it is reasonable to take their word and anticipate that they will be that way in the future.

For example, you don't need your own firsthand experience of poking sharks to know that they will bite if they are provoked. Plenty of other people have made numerous observations of shark behavior for you to base that conclusion on. Similarly—but one would hope not too similarly—you may have asked other people about their experiences in the courses they took in the past in order to help you decide what to enroll in this semester or in the future. In fact, their reported experiences might be the reason you're taking this course and learning about philosophy right now!

That said, peoples' experiences can offer no absolute certainty about how things will be or how they will turn out; the next time *could* be different. The past is a good predictor of the future, but it is not a guarantee. Conclusions about what will happen are probable conclusions only, no matter how many past experiences have been reliably recorded. Like all forms of inductive logic, this form yields probable conclusions, not necessary ones.

As with formal logic, faulty reasoning is also possible with inductive logic—in this case, with arguments from past experience. If, say, reliable sources are completely lacking or if past experience with something or someone is inconsistent, then inferences drawn in such cases may be unwarranted and hence indicative of a **hasty conclusion**—an informal fallacy of reasoning. If such conclusions drawn on the basis of past experience are less likely, rather than more likely to any degree, then the argument can be deemed weak and uncogent. Arguments based on hasty conclusions are flawed arguments. Successful inductive arguments are weaker or stronger by degree; but their conclusions are more likely true than not. Note that one successful argument could be weaker or stronger than another successful argument. The argument having the *greatest likelihood of truth* in its conclusion is the strongest.

> "There is nothing in which an untrained mind shows itself more hopelessly incapable than in drawing the proper conclusions from its own experience."
> JOHN STUART MILL

Argument by Analogy

A second type of non-deductive reasoning involves **argument by analogy**. Analogical arguments proceed from the similarities of two or more things in certain respects to their similarity in some additional respect. Analogical arguments have the following form:

A, B and C have characteristics X and Y.
A and B have characteristic Z.
Therefore, C probably has characteristic Z also.

For example,

Chimpanzees and gorillas have similar brain structures and evolutionary histories.
Chimpanzees can learn to use some elements of sign language.
Therefore, it's likely that gorillas can learn some elements of sign language.

This analogical form of non-deductive reasoning is the type used to argue, for example, for the probable existence of life on other planets. If significant similarities can be found between Earth and other celestial bodies, and if Earth supports life, then one might wish to argue by analogy that those other celestial bodies also support life. Notice again, there is no absolute certainty or deductive necessity about this conclusion; there is only lesser or greater probability.

When gauging the strength of the analogy, look for relevant similarities and dissimilarities. If relevant similarities are numerous and/or significant, the strength of the analogy is increased. If relevant differences are numerous and/or significant, then the strength is diminished. When two things aren't really comparable, we often say, "That's like comparing apples and oranges." In this instance, though both things are fruit and similar in that respect, they are different in other relevant respects (i.e., texture, fiber, and vitamin C content). Here's an example of a **weak analogy**:

"Faced with the choice between changing one's mind and proving there is no need to do so, almost everyone gets busy on the proof."
JOHN KENNETH GALBRAITH

> Facebook, Twitter, and newspapers such as *The Guardian* are all platforms for distributing information.
> Facebook and Twitter spread fake news.
> Therefore, newspapers such as *The Guardian* also spread fake news.

Here, the differences between newspapers like *The Guardian* and social media platforms such as Facebook and Twitter should be intuitively clear. Newspapers are informative and edited by journalists and experienced news staff, not to mention a vital element of democracy, often referred to as the Fourth Estate of government. So, while it is true that both social media platforms and newspapers are "platforms" and that they both "spread information," making them similar in a couple of trivial respects, the differences are far more significant and thus make the conclusion unjustified. *The Guardian* is a trusted British newspaper with a long history of respected journalism. It is known to corroborate its facts and base its articles on legitimate, reliable sources, something that Facebook posts and Twitter tweets often do not do, allowing for the spread of false information.

Argument by Inductive Generalization

A third form of non-deductive reasoning is argument by **inductive generalization**. When we make an inductive generalization, we make a statement about *all, some, or none of a class* based on our examination of *only a part of that class*. These arguments have the following form:

> In an observed *sample* of cases of population A, X% had characteristic Z.
> Therefore, in the *total* population or in all cases of population A, close to X% has characteristic Z.

For example,

> In an observed sample of cases, 1500 post-secondary students (A), 65% (X) were liberal minded (Z).
> Therefore, in the total population of post-secondary students (all cases of population A), 65% (X) are liberal minded (have characteristic Z).

It is important not to confuse inductive generalizations with **generalized descriptions**. Suppose, for instance, that we surveyed an introductory ethics class on its views about abortion and found that 88% of class members were against it. In stating this, one would simply be presenting a general statement or generalized description of what is true for that group. If we were to conclude, however, that 88% of *all* post-secondary students in North America were opposed to abortions, then we would be making an inductive generalization.

As you can well appreciate in this example, inductive generalizations can easily be prone to error unless certain precautions are taken. For instance, when making inductive generalizations, it is important to work from *large samples*. Basing a conclusion about millions of students in North America on a limited sample of one class is no guarantee that the findings are truly *representative* of the whole group about which a conclusion is being made.

Important to note as well is that large samples alone do not guarantee that generalizations based on them will be representative. If the larger sample we need were drawn exclusively from Catholic colleges, say, then the results might tend to be more reflective of the specific religious views held by a special subgroup of students and not representative of the entire post-secondary student population of North America. The views of students at Catholic colleges might not represent those of the majority attending secular institutions.

In addition to being large, then, samples must also be *fair*. All members within a class (in this case, post-secondary students in North America) must have an equal chance of being included in a *randomized* survey sample. Otherwise, inductive generalizations are likely to be *skewed*. Arguments by inductive generalization based on biased or skewed samples are less acceptable than those based on fair and large ones that are more representative of the group under study. The kind of reasoning error identified here is labeled a faulty or **hasty generalization**.

However, you should understand that even a perfectly randomized survey sample can sometimes give bad information, because it may, simply *by chance*, happen to pick out a percentage of the variable under study that is very different from the general group or population. Imagine a pot containing 100 red marbles and 200 green ones. One could pick out a sample of ten, blindfolded, shaking the pot with each pick. Just by chance, nine out of those 10 might be red! Concluding that 90% of the marbles in the pot are red would be clearly wrong, notwithstanding the random sample.

"I must govern my mind with care, giving it agreeable objects, for the least laziness makes it fall back onto those subjects, all too readily available, which afflict it."
PRINCESS ELISABETH OF BOHEMIA

2.4 Evaluating Claims

In assessing or evaluating claims, we should recognize that there are different ways of doing so. How to determine whether a claim or premise is true or acceptable depends on the nature of the claim itself. *Factual statements*, *value judgments*, and *conceptual claims* are all different in kind and thus need to be handled in different ways. Let's now learn how.

Factual Statements

A **factual statement** is a statement that attempts to describe some aspect of the world and is either true or false. The name is slightly misleading, because a "factual" statement can sometimes be false. For instance, "Pigs can fly" is a factual but false statement. Its falsehood depends on the observable way the world is. "There is a red rock sitting on the North Pole of Mars" is also a factual statement; but this one can be known to be true or false only given observations which haven't happened yet.

The simple point about factual statements is that they are **empirical**: sensory experience and observation can serve to determine their truth or falsity—*in principle*, though sometimes not yet, sometimes not ever. "The number of stars in our galaxy is divisible by 3" is a factual statement whose truth or falsity we'll never discover.

Whenever you make a claim about the way things are now, you are making a factual statement. But there are also factual statements about the past and the future. Of course, if you are making an assertion about the past, you could refer to old newspapers, magazines, historical documents, and so on to determine the accuracy and truth of your claim. If, on the other hand, you are making a claim about how things will be in the future, you could always wait to see how things turn out. You could also refer to past experience or do some kind of statistical, scientific, or empirical study to prove your point or to support your prediction about what you claim will happen. During the COVID-19 crisis, for example, epidemiological charts from the past were used to predict that cases of the virus would significantly rise in the fall and winter seasons when more people tend to stay indoors due to inclement weather. The predictions proved accurate.

Value Judgments

Value judgments are very different in kind from factual claims. First of all, they are *normative* as opposed to empirical. That is, they make statements about what *should or should not be done*, or what is *good or bad, right or wrong, praiseworthy or blameworthy, better or worse, obligatory or prohibited*. Examples of value judgments include the following: "Liberal democracy is better than fascism"; "Country music is good, classical music is snobbish"; "You shouldn't trespass"; "Single motherhood is unacceptable"; "You ought to give to charity"; and "People who pay income tax are suckers."

A feature of normative statements (value judgments) is that they cannot be *proven* or *verified* in the same way that empirical, factual statements can. You can't look into a microscope or perform an experiment to see whether one form of music is better or worse than another. Whether people should scribble graffiti on walls cannot be decided by observing what they actually do. If most kids in a particular neighborhood vandalize with graffiti, maybe they shouldn't. If most people don't donate to charity, maybe they should. The point is that telling me what people actually do does not tell me whether what they are doing (or not doing) is right.

In the context of philosophy, we try to justify value judgments by appeals to reason. In doing so, we try to account for our value judgments relating to particular actions, events, policies, or people through more general principles, rules of conduct, ideals, or other normative standards that apply to the particular cases under judgment. Whether or not the standards that we base our value judgments on are acceptable is a matter of rational scrutiny.

If our general principles and standards are unjustifiable, then any specific value judgments issuing from them will also be unacceptable. If they are vague, then we will not know for sure whether they apply in a given case. If our standards are inconsistent, then our value judgments will not make any sense. We could say, therefore, that the acceptability of a particular value judgment hinges on the justifiability of the normative principle or standard on which it is based, and on the proper application of that principle or standard in any given instance. Thus, if we say that Person P is a bad person, we probably have in mind some standard or ideal of what constitutes a good person. Perhaps "good people" are honest and kind. In view of the fact that Person P is dishonest and unkind, we make a negative character evaluation.

Several tests can be used to determine the justifiability of a value premise that serves as the basis of a rational argument, and much more will be said about these tests and standards in Chapter 5. For now, though, you can begin by asking, "Is the principle or value premise logically coherent?" A value premise suggesting, for example, that "We should make promises with the intention of breaking them" doesn't make any logical sense. By definition, promise making entails the intention of keeping one's word. The principle as stated here reflects deceptive intent or just plain lying, not promise-making at all.

Another way of determining the acceptability of a value premise is by using the **role-exchange test**. This test requires us to ask ourselves whether we ourselves would be willing to exchange places with the person or persons most disadvantaged by the application of a particular moral rule or principle in a given set of circumstances. If we are not prepared to be the ones most disadvantaged by the application of the rule or principle in question, then it is probably unjustified or inadequate in some fashion.

Suppose, for instance, a shopkeeper frequently shortchanged customers operating on the principle that: *It's okay to cheat people when you can get away with it*. Presumably the shopkeeper would not want to be cheated. If so, there's something wrong with the normative principle guiding the shopkeeper's behavior. In general, then, if a guiding principle leads you to *do unto others what you wouldn't want done to you*, then there's something wrong with that principle.

Another traditionally emphasized method for testing value premises is to try to think of them as a universal rule. Value premises can be rejected if they cannot reasonably and consistently be *universalized*. For instance, if you are wondering about the policy of accepting help but never offering it, imagine that it were a universal moral principle for everyone. If nobody ever offered help, then clearly there wouldn't be any help to accept, rendering the principle irrational and incoherent. So this could not be a morally right policy.

Another principle that becomes unacceptable when universalized is the following: "Everybody else, but me, should pay their income taxes." If such a principle were universalized, then nobody would pay taxes and "everybody else" arguably wouldn't even exist in a sense, since *nobody* would be paying taxes. Whenever you test a value premise by asking, "What if everyone accepted and acted upon this principle?" you are using the **universalizability** criterion. (To learn more about one version of this test, see Section 5.4 on Immanuel Kant's ethics.)

Sometimes what we need to do when evaluating arguments is critically examine a particular value premise in view of the **higher-order principle** that supports it. A value premise stating that *Trespassing is wrong*, for example, could be justified by the higher-order principle that "*We shouldn't violate other people's basic rights.*" Since trespassing involves violating someone's property rights, the conclusion can be drawn that trespassing is unacceptable. In this example, we can see how a more narrowly expressed normative claim about trespassing can be justified by a more broadly stated one about rights.

In addition to rights, *justice, goodness, honesty, fairness, freedom,* and *happiness* are other higher-order values that figure in principles one might wish to describe as 'ultimate' in the sense that they do not usually require justification themselves. They typically serve as the final basis of justification for other lower-order principles and rules of conduct. Of course, if an individual articulates a higher-order principle using any of these normative

TESTING VALUE PREMISES

Evaluate the value premises stated below. Discuss your evaluations with classmates. Are they acceptable from a rational, philosophical point of view? Why or why not?

1. You should take advantage of others when it is in your material self-interest to do so.

2. Killing is always wrong.

3. It's okay to cut across your neighbor's lawn on your way to work.

4. A nation has the right to enforce its borders by any means necessary.

5. The government never has a right to limit personal freedoms to act or not act.

6. You should never use people solely as a means to get what you want out of life.

concepts, but does so in a way that is incoherent, inconsistent, or self-contradictory, then any particular value conclusion that follows from it needn't be accepted.

Lastly, if a principle, standard, or value premise is considered acceptable in one case, then it should apply to other similar cases. Making sure it does involves using what might be called the **new cases test**. However, if other similar instances can be provided where the value premise clearly does not apply or intuitively cannot be justified, then the principle is weakened, if not made entirely unacceptable.

Conceptual Claims

A third kind of statement or claim is conceptual in nature. **Conceptual claims** can be *purely* conceptual or *mixed* with empirical or normative elements. Let's begin with an example of a purely conceptual claim: *Dairy-free ice cream contains no milk*. Note that no effort is made here to examine the contents of individual samples of ice cream. The term 'dairy-free' simply means "contains no milk (or milk-products)," and so the claim is true by virtue of the concepts themselves. No statistical or empirical means are relevant to investigating the claim. Only a consideration of language is required.

Some statements involve a mix of elements; and sometimes statements are ambiguous, and it's difficult to determine how to treat a statement until it is clarified. The justifiability of an ambiguous claim such as "Red hair is abnormal" depends on how *abnormal* is understood. If taken as a statistical statement of fact (meaning "unusual"), one might be inclined to accept it. If taken as an expression of taste-evaluation, one might not. The precise definition of "abnormal" here is the determining factor of the claim's acceptability.

Generally speaking, conceptual claims raise matters that deal with definition and meaning. Concepts and ideas in arguments that are defined too narrowly, too broadly, too vaguely, or too ambiguously generally weaken them. Claims displaying the aforementioned flaws are considered less acceptable than claims containing concepts and ideas that are well defined in a precise, consistent, and clear way and applied appropriately given the articulated criteria and the particular context or circumstances under consideration.

DISTINGUISHING AMONG FACTUAL STATEMENTS, VALUE JUDGMENTS, AND CONCEPTUAL CLAIMS

Being able to distinguish among factual statements, value judgments, and conceptual claims is important to philosophical argument. As you've learned, factual statements are those that can in principle be proven to be either true or false by sensory observation, by experience, or by some type of empirical investigation. Value judgments, by contrast, tell us what is good or bad, right or wrong, praiseworthy or blameworthy, better or worse, obligatory or prohibited, nice or awful, tasty or yucky, cute or ugly, etc. Conceptual claims are true or false merely because of matters of meaning and definition.

In the list below, see if you can identify the

factual statements (**F**)
value judgments (**V**)
conceptual claims (**C**).

Any mixed claims should be treated as conceptual (C).

1. _____ Introductory philosophy is a good course.

2. _____ Most students select job-related programs of study.

3. _____ An SUV is not a truck.

4. _____ The Catholic Church condemns abortion.

5. _____ Imported cars are better than domestic ones.

6. _____ A married man donating sperm for purposes of artificial insemination is adulterous.

7. _____ Immigration to this country should be reduced.

8. _____ The Earth is flat.

9. _____ Fair treatment is identical treatment.

10. _____ On average, taller people earn more money than shorter people.

11. _____ Corporations do not pay enough taxes.

12. _____ Happiness is pleasure.

13. _____ Before traveling abroad, you should travel through your own country.

14. _____ Electric vehicles will reduce climate change.

15. _____ Gender identity is the same as sexual orientation.

ANSWER KEY

1. V	4. F	7. V	10. F	13. V
2. F	5. V	8. F	11. V	14. F
3. C	6. C	9. C	12. C	15. C

2.5 Informal Logical Fallacies

People who fail to appreciate the benefits of argument often feel threatened when their viewpoints are challenged. If there has been a lot of ego investment in a particular philosophical position or a deep involvement of personal feelings, improper forms of reasoning called **informal logical fallacies** may be used to perform the emotional rescue of the threatened self. Informal fallacies are irrational. They are designed to persuade emotionally and psychologically, not rationally.

Informal fallacies can also be used as *forms of intimidation*. Defensive people worried about being wrong may respond aggressively toward others, engaging in *personal attacks*. Putting someone else on the defensive requires you to be less defensive about yourself.

Informal fallacies can also work through *diversion* and the introduction of *irrelevancies* to the argument. As instruments of persuasive rhetoric, they are, unfortunately, sometimes very effective. As ways of correct thinking, however, they are always wrong.

Logical fallacies are sometimes committed unconsciously and without malicious intent. Some people are simply unaware of their poor reasoning or the poor reasoning of others. In view of this fact, lct us now look at some common fallacies you will need to guard against in your own *logical self-defense*.

Ad Hominem Fallacy

When you disagree with someone, the proper response is to criticize your opponent's position. If, instead of debating the issues or questioning the claims, you attack your opponent personally, you then commit the ***ad hominem* fallacy**. For example, a person who resents the costs brought about by carbon offset programs might refuse to support the arguments presented by climate advocacy groups on the grounds that all environmentalists are "dirty hippies" or "emotional basket cases." Of course, the merits of an argument should not be judged by when its advocates were born, by what generation they come from, or by what their emotional state is. Carbon offset is either a good or bad idea, to be decided independently of such irrelevant considerations.

Straw Person Fallacy

In formal debate or in informal conversations with others, we do not always like what we hear. In response, we may sometimes misrepresent or distort what others have said so we can make their arguments appear obviously unacceptable. If we do this, and then proceed to argue against the unsatisfying versions we've ourselves created, in order to reject their original, but unaddressed, positions, we commit the **straw person fallacy.**[*]

A caution may be in order here. Occasionally, it happens that people responding to others' claims do not accurately understand what was intended by those claims. They may then respond to what was never meant or intended. This kind of honest mistake may reflect a communication problem of listening or comprehension. It is unlike the straw person fallacy, where one individual *deliberately misrepresents* the argument of another. We get into foggy territory when misrepresentations occur unconsciously in psy-

---

[*]   An imitation person made of straw is easy to attack. This name may have been derived from military training, where straw men provided easy practice targets.

chological efforts to reduce anxiety. Conscious or unconscious, however, straw person fallacies are irrational distortions of the truth of what was argued or claimed.

Circular Reasoning/Begging the Question Fallacy

Have you ever been involved in an argument that seemed to go around in circles? If you have, perhaps someone was using **circular reasoning**, also known as the **fallacy of begging the question**.* In circular reasoning, people use the conclusion they are trying to establish as a starting premise of their argument. In other words, people assume to be true in the beginning what they intend to prove logically at the end. Thus, the "logical" argument does not take you anywhere except back to what was assumed to be true at the outset. The following is an example of circular reasoning in a religious context.

B. LEVER:	God exists.
I.M. AGNOSTIC:	How do you know God exists?
B. LEVER:	Because it says so in the Bible.
I.M. AGNOSTIC:	How do you know the Bible is telling you the truth?
B. LEVER:	Because it's the inspired word of God.

In this example, B. Lever begins by concluding that God exists. In fact, he uses the Bible to prove this. However, the authority of the Bible carries absolute truth value or weight only if one *already accepts* the premise or presupposition that God inspired it in the first place. In other words, to use the Bible as proof that God exists, one must assume from the very beginning that God actually does exist as the inspirational Source—but this is the disputed point under debate.

If B. Lever begins by assuming to be true at the beginning of his argument what he is trying to prove in the end, then nothing has, in fact, been proven, and we have just gone around in a big circle. This is not to suggest that rational proofs cannot be offered for the existence of God, only that circular ones do not work. (To learn more about other efforts to prove that God exists, read Section 4.8 "Proofs for the Existence of God.")

---

* People nowadays who say "begging the question" often mean *raising the question*. This usage is now so common that it might no longer be counted as a mistake. But you now know what the original "correct" meaning of this phrase is.

Two Wrongs Fallacy

Committing the **two wrongs fallacy** involves defending a particular wrongdoing by drawing attention to another instance of the same behavior that apparently went un-challenged and was, therefore, accepted by implication. For instance, I remember how back in my student days, there were traditional initiation rituals for first-year students at the University of Toronto. One ritual required first-year students to commit minor acts of vandalism (painting a certain statue in Queen's Park). Confronted about the justifi-ability of such acts, a student (guess who) responded by saying that freshmen had been committing these acts for years. Apparently, for this poor misguided soul, the previous years' vandalism served as a justification for his own wrongdoing. Trying to justify one wrongdoing by referring to an instance of another is not rational or justified. If you don't believe this, try convincing a highway patrol officer not to give you a ticket for speeding, arguing that you were just keeping up with the other speeders in traffic. Good luck!

Slippery Slope Fallacy

People who commit the **slippery slope fallacy** display this form of illogic when they ob-ject to something because they incorrectly assume that it will necessarily lead to a chain of other consequences, eventually undesirable ones. The alleged *negative end consequences* are used as a basis for rejecting the initial claim, proposal, or suggestion, etc. This is bad reasoning when the end consequences are not necessary or even very likely to happen. For example, you may claim that smoking marijuana is wrong, and try to justify that by arguing that such behavior can often lead to harder drug usage, addiction, and eventu-ally to a life of crime. Because a life of crime is undesirable, you conclude that smoking marijuana is therefore wrong. But the supposition that these are frequent results may well be mistaken.

The point is that smoking marijuana is a separate and distinct act from harder drug use, addiction, and crime. Connections may be non-existent or tenuous at best. Each must be considered independently and evaluated on its own terms. Although it may be that many drug-addicted criminals began their lives of crime by smoking marijuana, not everybody who smokes marijuana becomes a criminal addict. Many law-abiding, non-ad-dicted people have experimented with marijuana; therefore, there is no necessary *causal connection* between marijuana and criminality. Claims about a connection are rather du-bious. One does not have to lead to the other. In general, if you can find a break in the causal chain that presumably links two unrelated acts, you can uncover the presence of a slippery slope, as we have here.

On the other hand, this sort of chain reasoning is fully acceptable when the act un-der evaluation really does have bad eventual consequences.

Appealing to Authority Fallacy

When people get into debates or disagreements with one another, they frequently com-mit the **fallacy of appealing to authority** to justify their positions. The authority could simply be an *individual, a select few*, or perhaps *majority opinion*. Some appeals to au-thority are proper, while others are not. Proper appeals can be made to support factual claims within larger arguments. If, in the previous example about marijuana, someone had wanted to condemn its use on medical grounds, scientific and empirical research data could have been presented to support claims about marijuana's adverse physical effects. As long as the data presented were based on the recognized contributions of medical researchers in the field, and were accepted after peer review and evaluation, such data could have been justifiably used to support factual claims embedded in the broader argument.

When questions of value are at issue, however, it is much more difficult, and often unjustifiable, to make authoritative appeals. Normative assumptions and principles of conduct cannot be proven true or false by empirical observation or by scientific experiment. So observing how someone in a position of power or status actually does behave does not tell us whether that person—and the rest of us—should behave in that way.

Where matters of value are concerned, we must carefully consider what is really good and right and not just take someone's words and actions as the truth. That's the case even if that person is a supposed authority in values. It is ill-advised, for example, to make appeals to religious authority when justifying moral claims. For one thing, appeals to religious authorities may not make compelling arguments for all audiences. Since nobody has a *moral duty* to belong to any one religion, or any religion for that matter, judgments issued by religious authorities need not necessarily carry any weight for the nonreligious or for those outside one's faith community.

Furthermore, the fact that different religious authorities and faith communities sometimes disagree among themselves on basic issues of moral principle means that authoritative appeals become problematically inconsistent. If we don't wish to foster religious intolerance and bigotry in a pluralistic democratic society, authoritative appeals must be discouraged. Better yet, a deeper, non-authoritative understanding of shared and common values should be fostered.

Red Herring Fallacy

The **red herring fallacy** is another favorite form of ill-logic often used in arguments and debates. The name of this fallacy comes from the sport of rabbit hunting. Specifically, it comes from the technique of dragging smelly herring in a direction away from the track of a fleeing rabbit in order to distract pursuing hounds from the scent of their prey.

Just as some hounds might be prevented from catching their prey by the smelly herring diverting them and getting them off course, someone might try to prevent another individual from proving their point by distracting the advocate away from their original claim or position with a tangential issue, one irrelevant to that point. Consider the tangential issue as equivalent to the smelly herring. In this case, the critic switches to something that is more beneficial to their own criticism—but not so good for the original claim or position presented by the advocate. Efforts are made to sidetrack the discussion to matters that work better for the critic's irrational attack.

THINKING ABOUT YOUR THINKING

Think about the last time you were frustrated by a disagreement you had with someone. You were trying to make a point, but somehow that point was not coming through to your interlocutor.

Now that you know more about the logical forms of arguments and fallacious reasoning, think back to that discussion. What point were you trying to make? What claims, principles, or assumptions were included in it? Were you offering reasons in a logical form? Did you support and verify your claims? Did the value premises pass the tests of adequacy discussed earlier in this chapter?

Without being too quick to blame the other party, why do you think your interlocutor was not agreeing with you? Was the other party guilty of being stubbornly dogmatic or defensive? Were you? Were your claims, principles, or assumptions clear, consistent, and well supported? Was your reasoning free of any fallacies?

Take some time now to rationally reflect. If you were to have that discussion again, what would you change about what you said? What would you say differently and how would you say it instead?

Of course, if it were the case that a critic made a good argument against the position taken by an advocate, that advocate might divert attention and change the subject to something more favorable to them. Red herring fallacies are not the exclusive preserve of critics.

Guilt by Association Fallacy

This form of ill logic is used in adversarial situations in an attempt to discredit an opponent or that opponent's position. It draws attention to the opponent's alleged association with some group, idea, or individual that has already been discredited. When people are involved, the attempt to discredit is not direct, as in *ad hominem* arguments, but is indirect. The guilt of the discredited individual or group is transferred onto the opponent.

Let's suppose, hypothetically, that a new Socialist Party of America has been formed and is running candidates in the next federal election. A friend of yours says he refuses to vote "socialist" on principle, and therefore he will not support the newly formed party. His reason is that "Socialists almost sent England and France into bankruptcy." The unspoken claim is that, if elected here, they will bankrupt this country too.

Apparently, for this voter, socialist mismanagement across the ocean is enough to convict socialists here of incompetence. They are found guilty prior to doing anything wrong. It is possible, of course, that a socialist government could mismanage a country like the United States; some argue that the Democrats and Republicans have been doing so for years! But seriously, actions and policies of foreign socialist governments alone cannot serve as an adequate basis of judgment on domestic socialism. This socialism may be different in significant ways.

For example, the new socialists may have learned from the mistakes of their European counterparts. Perhaps contemporary North American socialism has evolved into something more akin to capitalism. Simply put, you cannot pin incompetence on American socialists because of what foreign socialists have done. To do so is to commit the **guilt by association fallacy**. Nonetheless, by using this diversionary tactic, fear can be created in the minds of unreflective voters, and it may work as a means of persuasion. Creating fear is not very rational, but against people lacking the skills of logical self-defense, it often works.

On the other hand, in certain cases, it might sometimes be rational to find guilt by association. Imagine that you're the mayor of a town where the local chapter of the Ku Klux Klan has asked for a permit for a rally. The Klan representative insists that the speeches will be tolerant of all groups and will advocate nonviolence. This is the first time anyone in town has heard anything about the local Klan; in this case, bringing to attention their association with other Klan chapters seems sufficient reason to judge their promise of tolerance and nonviolence to be one of those "false promises" (i.e., lies) discussed above.

In conclusion to this treatment of logic and philosophical argument, I invite you now to review some useful "Do's and Don'ts for Argument's Sake." They will help you to become more rational the next time you get involved in any sort of philosophical debate (see Table 2.3). Also, now that we have covered a number of the most frequently used informal logical fallacies, practice your skill of identifying them in the exercise that follows.

TABLE 2.3 Some Do's and Don'ts for Argument's Sake

DO	DON'T
‣ Adopt the proper attitude	‣ Attack or intimidate
‣ Make sure your writing is rational instead of merely emotional, no matter how strongly you feel	‣ Divert attention from the real issues
‣ Stay objective	‣ Present mere opinions, personal preferences, or prejudices
‣ Listen to opposing viewpoints with openness	‣ Build false or questionable claims into your argument
‣ Analyze conflicting positions fairly and impartially	‣ Use invalid logic
‣ Appraise factual claims with evidence and facts	‣ Use unjustifiable premises
‣ Evaluate premises	‣ Make questionable assumptions
‣ Examine the logical thinking behind particular conclusions	‣ Confuse valid logic with truth
‣ Look for fallacious reasoning	‣ Take disagreements personally
‣ Appeal to higher-order values to justify your viewpoints	‣ Appeal to authorities unjustifiably
‣ Distinguish among arguments, opinions, and other non-arguments	‣ Attribute to others what they didn't say
‣ Stick to the issues	‣ Make illegitimate associations
‣ Use proper processes of inductive and deductive logic	‣ Contradict yourself
‣ Base your positions on sound arguments	‣ Change the subject when challenged
‣ Avoid diverting and intimidating using fallacious reasoning	‣ Be inconsistent
	‣ Use faulty causal reasoning
	‣ Justify one wrongdoing with another

IDENTIFYING THE FALLACY

This exercise will give you an opportunity to apply your knowledge and understanding of fallacious reasoning. Practice here will help you to develop your skills of logical self-defense. Being able to identify fallacious reasoning will protect you against illogical attacks and irrational attempts to manipulate your thinking. Recognizing informal fallacies will also help you to minimize them in your own arguments.

INSTRUCTIONS

Below are some examples of fallacious reasoning. Identify the fallacies in each. This exercise can be done individually or in groups. For classroom purposes, be prepared to provide explanations for each identification.

ad hominem fallacy
straw person fallacy
circular reasoning/begging the question
fallacy of two wrongs
slippery slope fallacy
fallacy of appealing to authority
red herring fallacy
fallacy of guilt by association

	FALLACY

1. You shouldn't accept the city counselor's arguments in favor of legalized gambling. After all, he's a godless communist.

2. I can't believe you're thinking about sleeping with your boyfriend. It's obviously wrong. The Pope says so.

3. Two students were arguing about cars. The first student said, "I can prove to you that Fords are faster than Chevys. My cousin Bill owns a Ford, and he told me that he has beaten every Chevy that he has ever raced on the highway." The second student asked, "How do you know your cousin is telling you the truth?" The first replied, "Someone who drives the fastest car wouldn't have to lie."

4. We cannot allow hashish to be legalized. If we do, then sooner or later everyone will become addicted to fentanyl, then crack cocaine, and after that the streets will be filled with "crack-heads."

5. It's perfectly all right to run red lights; everybody in town does it.

6. The business consultant recommended that we switch to voice mail only for receiving and sending internal messages. She claims this change will make our operations more secure. I can't believe this woman. She thinks every problem in the world has an electronic solution. Computers and telephones and voice mail messages cannot improve the economy or morale at work. I think we should reject her recommendation.

7. You don't really believe that guy do you? Don't you know his uncle was caught stealing cars? I wouldn't accept anything he says.

8. You say everyone should support the Black Lives Matter movement and other such groups protesting against racial inequality. You argue it's the right and just thing to do. Give me a break. You're the one who failed the first test last week on Black History. There's nothing I can learn from you. So, no, I won't support BLM.

ANSWER KEY

1. *ad hominem* fallacy
2. fallacy of appealing to authority
3. circular reasoning/begging the question
4. slippery slope fallacy

5. fallacy of two wrongs
6. straw person fallacy
7. fallacy of guilt by association
8. red herring fallacy

PROGRESS CHECK

INSTRUCTIONS: Fill in the blanks with the appropriate responses listed below. (Answers at back of book.)

groundless
form
rational disinterestedness
necessary
appealing to authority
straw person
premises

value
conceptual claims
syllogisms
inductive generalization
factual
modus ponens
inductive

content
two wrongs
sound
arguments
logical fallacies
modus tollens
ad hominem

1. _____ statements make empirical claims, whereas _____ judgments make normative assertions.

2. _____ make statements that are acceptable or not acceptable on the basis of their clarity, definition, and application.

3. Everyday opinions, expressed without serious thought, tend to be _____ and little more than a statement of personal preference.

4. _____ involve a process of thought in which conclusions are derived from preceding premises.

5. If we remain objective and impartial in our disagreements with others, we display an attitude of _____.

6. The two statements, "If she's home, then we can talk to her" and "If the test is next week, I'll be prepared," have the same _____ but different _____.

7. Arguments with the form "If p, then q; p; So, q" are given the label of _____.

8. "If p, then q; not q; So, not p" is the form of a _____ argument.

9. _____ may be either hypothetical, disjunctive, or categorical.

10. _____ logic can only provide probability, not certainty.

11. When we make a(n) _____, we make a statement about all, some, or none of a class based on an empirical examination of only a part of the class.

12. Valid deductive arguments with true premises lead to _____ conclusions.

13. A(n) _____ argument is valid in form and contains true premises.

14. Value _____ can be tested using the role-exchange, new cases, and higher-order principle tests, as well as the consistency and universalizability test.

15. People who try to win arguments by resorting to diversion and intimidation tactics are guilty of using informal _____.

16. Attacking the person, rather than criticizing the person's argument, is the definition of the _____ fallacy.

17. When we misrepresent someone's argument in order to reject what someone really did argue, we are guilty of committing the _____ fallacy.

18. Arguing that it's all right to commit a wrongdoing just because others are committing the same wrongdoing is to fall prey to the _____ fallacy.

19. Arguing that something is right or wrong / good or bad simply because the majority says so is evidence of the fallacy of _____.

Key Terms

ad hominem fallacy: faulty reasoning whereby one attacks the person making an argument rather than properly dealing with the argument itself   118

affirm the antecedent: the process of thought in *modus ponens* arguments   99

affirm the consequent: a form of invalid reasoning   100

antecedent: that which is affirmed in *modus ponens* arguments; the first half of a hypothetical proposition (e.g., in the case of: If p, then q, 'p' is the antecedent)   100

argument: comprises a conclusion based on at least one supporting claim   81

argument by analogy: form of non-deductive reasoning; two things seen as similar in some respects are concluded to be similar in other respects   111

argument from past experience: inductive logic using prior experience as a way of drawing a conclusion   110

categorical syllogisms / syllogisms of class membership: arguments having three categorical propositions (two premises and a conclusion) in which there appear a total of exactly three categorical terms, each of which is used exactly twice; the premises and the conclusion state that one, some, or all members of one category are, or are not, members of another category   105

circular reasoning: erroneous logic; assuming at the beginning of an argument what one hopes to prove in the end as the conclusion   119

conceptual claims: statements or premises the acceptability of which depends on clarity of meaning and/or the proper application of concepts or ideas in those statements and premises   116

conclusion: the endpoint that an argument is used to prove or justify   81

consequent: that which is denied in *modus tollens*; the second half of a hypothetical proposition (e.g., in the case of: If p, then q, 'q' is the consequent)   100

content: the substance of an argument (i.e., the subject matter)   98

deductive argument: reasoning leading to a necessary conclusion   98

denying the antecedent: asserting that the first half of a hypothetical proposition is not true   102

denying the consequent: asserting that the second half of a hypothetical proposition is not true   101

description: account of a person, place, thing, or event   82

disagreement: lack of consensus   74

disjunctive syllogism: a deductive argument beginning with an "Either-or" structure   103

empirical: relating to the facts of the world, especially those whose truth can (in principle) be determined through sensory observation   113

explanation(s): used to give clarifying reasons for *why* or *how* something is the case; *not* an effort to prove *that* something is the case   82

factual statements: claims that assert something is the case; claims that are true or false in principle; claims dealing with matters of fact; proven by verification   113

fallacy of appealing to authority: inappropriately referring to the judgments, pronouncements, or teachings of an authoritative individual or body when there is no objective way of determining the truth, given the nature of the concern at hand, or when there is no consensus among authorities   120

fallacy of begging the question: circular reasoning; can also involve basing an argument on an assumption that is more problematic than the conclusion one hopes to prove   119

fallacy of common antecedent: error of reasoning in which two premises with a common antecedent are used to mistakenly derive an "if...then" conclusion that connects the premises' consequents   103

form: structure of an argument   98

generalized description: a general statement, not involving any generalization about a larger group or population   112

grounds: basis or support   81

guilt by association fallacy: inappropriately rejecting an individual or that individual's claim or argument by drawing an association between that individual and someone or something already discredited; the association does not exist, is distorted, or is not relevant to the acceptance or rejection of the individual or that individual's claim or argument   122

hasty conclusion: an inductive reasoning error arising from insufficient evidence   111

hasty generalization: results when using a biased, skewed, or unrepresentative sample to draw an inference about a larger group or population   113

higher-order principle test: a way of determining the acceptability of a rule or proposed action by reference to a broader or more general principle   115

hypothetical syllogisms / chain argument: an "If-then" deductive argument involving a chain   102

ignoring an alternative disjunct: error made when the affirmation of a disjunct in a conclusion is not necessary because at least one other alternative disjunct is also a possible conclusion   104

inductive argument: reasoning leading to a probable but not necessary conclusion   109

inductive generalization: the process of drawing a conclusion about all, some, or none of a class based on an empirical examination of only a part of that class   112

informal logical fallacies: errors in non-deductive reasoning based on faulty assumptions, personal attacks, irrelevancies, and diversionary tactics   118

interlocutor: a person who takes part in a dialogue or conversation   87

logical form: structure of an argument that can be abstracted from its content   98

modus ponens (MP): valid form of deductive logic; affirms the antecedent   99

modus tollens: a valid form of deductive logic which denies the consequent as a basis of inference   101

new cases test: a way to determine whether a value premise deemed acceptable in one case is still acceptable when applied in other similar and relevant cases; if not, then the value premise is not acceptable   116

opinion: unsupported claim or assertion; judgment or belief without evidence   81

Plato: Greek philosopher and founder of the Academy; student of Socrates and teacher of Aristotle   85

premise: a statement within an argument that is used to prove or justify a conclusion   81

rational disinterestedness: impartial and objective stance   84

red herring fallacy: wrongly trying to defend a contentious or problematic claim by diverting attention to some other irrelevant matter and using it as a basis of support for the initial claim; can also be used to wrongly criticize a justifiable claim by directing attention away to something else more easily criticized and using that as a way of rejecting the original justifiable claim   121

role-exchange test: a way to determine the acceptability of a normative judgment by asking whether one would be willing to change places and accept being the person most adversely affected by the application of the judgment in question   115

slippery slope fallacy: a faulty argument with the built-in assumption that if we allow for something (A), it will lead to a necessary chain of events ending in something unwanted or undesirable (Z); since we don't want the undesirable endpoint of the chain (Z), we should not allow or be in favor of the original something (A); there is a break somewhere between (A) and (Z)   120

Socrates: ancient Greek philosopher who is sometimes said to be the founder of Western philosophy; influenced Plato, but wrote nothing.   85

Socratic humility: the humble trait displayed by Socrates; admission of ignorance; openness to the better judgment or knowledge of others   86

sound argument: an argument that is valid in form and which contains true premises   106

soundness: a characteristic of deductive arguments that have true claims, a valid form, and result in a logically necessary conclusion.   106

straw person fallacy: faulty reasoning whereby one criticizes an argument never made by a person to reject the argument that was actually and originally presented   118

truth: that which corresponds to reality; a feature of claims in sound deductive arguments   106

two wrongs fallacy: inappropriately trying to justify one wrongdoing by pointing to other instances of the same wrongdoing that went unpunished   120

universalizability: a criterion of acceptability that can be used to test the value premise of a practical syllogism—if something is deemed obligatory or acceptable for one person, it must also be so universally, for everyone, in order to be accepted   115

unsound argument: an argument with a false claim, an invalid structure, or both   106

valid reasoning: logical reasoning that displays a valid deductive structure   99

validity: feature of a deductive argument that guarantees the necessity of the conclusion   106

value judgments: normative statements about what is good or bad, right or wrong, better or worse, praiseworthy or blameworthy, obligatory or prohibited; justified by appeals to values, standards, principles, ideals, and norms   114

weak analogy: a faulty inference based on insufficient and/or insignificant similarities between or among two or more things; like comparing *apples and oranges*   112

Summary of Major Points

1. Are arguments beneficial?
Yes. They can open minds and contribute to social progress.

2. What attitudes are useful for productive argument?
Rational disinterestedness, Socratic humility, openness, reduction of personal defensiveness, and willingness to change our position in view of counter-evidence and justified criticism are all useful if we are to engage in productive argument.

3. What are the differences between factual statements, value judgments, and conceptual claims?
Factual statements refer to what is or is not the case; value judgments make reference to what is good or bad, right or wrong, better or worse, obligatory or prohibited. The former would be verified (when possible) by means of observation or other empirical means; the latter are often justified by reference to rules, standards, and ideals. Conceptual claims are those whose acceptability depends on things such as definition, clarity of meaning, and appropriateness of application.

4. In what ways are personal opinions different from arguments?
Opinions are groundless. They express personal tastes, preferences, and beliefs without any basis in fact or carefully reasoned thought. Arguments involve a process of rational thought whereby conclusions are derived from preceding premises. Arguments can be based on inductive or deductive logic.

5. What are the general characteristics of deductive arguments?
They come in various forms (e.g., *modus tollens*, categorical syllogisms). They are either valid or invalid. Valid arguments lead to necessary conclusions derived from preceding premises.

6. How is the "form/content" distinction to be understood in the context of philosophical argument?
Underlying the content or substance of any deductive argument is some kind of formal structure that is either valid or invalid.

7. How do inductive and deductive logic differ?
Inductive logic leads to probable conclusions, whereas deductive logic leads to necessary conclusions. Inductive reasoning is weaker or stronger; deductive logic is valid or invalid.

8. What are some forms of deductive logic?
Modus ponens, *modus tollens*, hypothetical syllogisms, disjunctive syllogisms, and syllogisms of class membership are all forms of deductive logic.

9. What are some forms of inductive logic?
They are arguments from past experience, arguments by analogy, and arguments by inductive generalization.

10. In the context of logical argument, how are validity, truth, and soundness different?
Validity refers to the form of an argument. Truth refers to the veracity of premises and the conclusion. Soundness pertains to valid arguments having true premises leading to necessary conclusions.

11. Do valid arguments always have to be accepted?
No. If a valid argument contains faulty or incorrect premises, then we do not have to accept the conclusion even though it follows logically.

12. What is an informal logical fallacy?
An informal logical fallacy is an irrational rhetorical device designed to persuade through emotional and psychological appeals. Fallacies divert attention, introduce irrelevancies, attack or intimidate others, or make questionable assumptions in efforts to win arguments.

13. What are some common fallacies?
Some common fallacies are the straw person, circular reasoning/begging the question, two wrongs, slippery slope, appealing to authority, red herring, guilt by association, and the *ad hominem* attack.

Additional Resources

For interactive quizzes, stories, supplements, and other materials for study and review, visit:

sites.broadviewpress.com/experiencing-philosophy/chapter2
Passcode: w4822kj

Or scan the following QR code:

CHAPTER 3

Philosophies of Life

Take It Personally 134

Know Thyself: The Philosophy of Life Preference Indicator 136

3.1 Stoicism: A Prescription for Peace of Mind 139
Stoicism's Cynical Origins 139
The Stoic Universe 140
How to Live in a Fated Universe 140
Freedom and Value 142
Purpose of Life 142
Emotions in Life 145
How to Progress Morally 146
ORIGINAL SOURCE: Marcus Aurelius, *The Meditations of Marcus Aurelius* 147

3.2 Existentialism: Born Free, Let Me Be Me 152
Methods 153
Philosophers Associated with Existentialism 153
Existentialism as a Revolt 154
Essence versus Existence 155
Individuality and Subjective Experience 156
Existential Freedom 157
ORIGINAL SOURCE: Jean-Paul Sartre, *Existentialism Is a Humanism* 159

3.3 The Meaning of Life 161
Meaningful Lives 162
ORIGINAL SOURCE: Susan Wolf, "The Meanings of Lives" 165
Viktor Frankl and the Will-to-Meaning 168

3.4 Hedonism: Pleasure Is the Measure 169
Psychological versus Ethical Hedonism 169
Aristippus of Cyrene 170
Epicurus 171
Momentary versus Enduring Pleasures 172
Kinetic versus Static Pleasures 173
Ataraxia: The Ultimate End of Life 173
Natural Desires 174
Impediments to *Ataraxia* 175
Virtue in the Pleasant Life 176
The Role of Friendship 177
ORIGINAL SOURCE: Epicurus, "Letter to Menoeceus" 179

3.5 Buddhism as a Philosophy of Life 181
The Four Noble Truths 183
The Noble Eight-Fold Path 189
ORIGINAL SOURCE: Buddha, *Dhammacakkappavattana Sutta* (*Setting in Motion the Wheel of Truth*) 198

Progress Check 201

Study Guide 203
Key Terms 203
Summary of Major Points 208

After successfully completing this chapter, you will be able to

▸ Gain a better awareness and understanding of your personal worldview by comparing it to four other philosophical perspectives

▸ Outline the history and origins of Stoicism

▸ Briefly describe the Stoic's cosmology (conception of the universe)

▸ Develop insight into how one should live in a fated universe

▸ Account for the role of emotions in life for the Stoic

▸ Explain how one should live morally in a Stoic world

▸ Elucidate the philosophical unorthodoxy of Existentialism

▸ Discuss some of the major themes embedded in existential philosophy

▸ Explain the differences between meaningful and meaningless lives, according to Susan Wolf

▸ Define what's meant by the notion of an *existential vacuum*

▸ Identify Viktor Frankl's sources of meaning in life

▸ Distinguish between psychological and ethical hedonism

▸ List the basic tenets of Cyrenaic Hedonism

▸ Outline Epicurean philosophy, distinguishing between types of pleasure

▸ Describe *ataraxia* as the ultimate end of life and the impediments to achieving it

▸ Comment on the roles of virtue and friendship in *ataraxia*

▸ Articulate Buddha's Four Noble Truths

▸ Understand how to reduce suffering using the Noble Eight-Fold Path

1. What makes developing a personal philosophical worldview so difficult in contemporary society?

2. How is luxurious living viewed by the Stoics as well as by their predecessors, Socrates and the Cynics? Why are these views held?

3. Does a belief in God make much practical difference to one's philosophical worldview? If so, how?

4. How do the various philosophies covered in this chapter deal with problems of human purpose and meaning in life?

5. What are some practical and contemporary applications of Stoic, Existential, Buddhist, and Hedonistic philosophy?

6. How is Existentialism different from traditional orthodox philosophy?

7. What concepts are central to the philosophy of Existentialism?

8. What is meaning? Why is it important? What are its sources?

9. What is Hedonism? What variations of it do we find?

10. How is Buddhism therapeutic?

11. What prescriptions for living does Buddha offer us?

Take It Personally

Have you ever been overwhelmed by the many choices you've been faced with in life? Have your options been so numerous that you simply couldn't decide? Or, could it be that you've already made some important decisions in life, but are now regretful or worried about the future consequences likely to result from them? Are we talking just about specific things like shopping at the mall, choosing a career, buying a car, picking an academic program, or selecting next year's vacation destination? Well, yes and no. We're actually focusing attention on the *fundamental choices* you've already made regarding *your guiding life principles and cherished values*. These prior philosophical choices may have been made consciously or unconsciously. They may also have been made in a consistent or inconsistent fashion. Either way, they have an impact on your life right now.

One could say it's your underlying philosophy of life—what some might call your *worldview*—that guides all of the particular choices you make on a daily basis. Knowing what's worthwhile, choosing what to do in this circumstance or that, or deciding how to live (e.g., as a minimalist or unapologetic materialist), all come from your basic perspective on the world. What you value, believe, assume, or think to be true, all inform and influence your choices and activities. Given this, consciously establishing a consistent life philosophy is what can give solid direction and coherence to all of your personal and practical decision-making. Your general outlook on life can provide rationales or rationally inform the specific choices you make.

Here's a complicating factor, however: Every day, especially through advertising and the media, we are bombarded with endless messages telling us how we ought to live our lives: Buy this! Don't buy that! Go here! Don't go there! Look like so-and-so! Be authentic! Play for fun! Beat the competition! Stay in school! Go to work! Feed the hungry! Pig out! Get even! Turn the other cheek! Take control! Serve others! Chill! Get pumped!

© XKCD

For many of us, these countless and conflicting messages leave us wondering, "What, exactly, is the good life?" "What am I here for?" "How should I live in order to find happiness and self-fulfillment?" or "What's the best philosophy of life to live by?" Such questions, while deceptively simple in statement, are exceedingly difficult to answer. In fact, they belong to a class of timeless questions that philosophers have asked for centuries. In some instances, these answers have coalesced to form different philosophical worldviews that people have used to find personal guidance and direction in their lives.

In what follows, we will try to find some more of that personal guidance and direction by examining the role that *meaning* plays in human existence, particularly as discussed in the works of Susan Wolf and Viktor Frankl. We will also look at several historically significant philosophies of life that philosophers have articulated. Specifically, we will examine Stoicism, Existentialism, Hedonism, and Buddhism. These four were chosen because of their personal relevance as well as their starkly contrasting outlooks. Do you think, for example, that everything happens for a reason and that the world makes sense? If so, you might be surprised to learn that the ancient Stoic philosophers claimed much the same thing centuries ago. Reading about the Stoics will give you the chance to reflect upon your cosmological belief, hopefully clarifying it in the process.

On the other hand, maybe you think that all of this destiny, fate, or preordained purpose stuff is for the birds, that there is no God to determine anything, and that essentially life is irrational and absurd. Well, then, the coverage of atheistic existentialist philosophy here should help you understand this philosophical stance a little better. What exactly are the personal and ethical implications of believing that life makes no inherent sense, that no moral order exists, and that there is no underlying purpose to anything? Read on to find out.

Now, how about lifestyle? Do you buy into the notion of the American Dream: a spouse, two kids, a dog, and a house in the suburbs? Is this your definition of the good life, or would you prefer to indulge yourself, live for the moment, and satisfy your every wandering desire? Is this sort of life really good living? A number of philosophers, known as Cyrenaic Hedonists, would largely say yes. In this chapter you'll come to appreciate the value of pleasure and learn more about its types and pursuit.

It is possible of course that you may have come to the conclusion that living for things like pleasure, money, or status is really a morally bankrupt proposition, leading only to gross dissatisfaction in the end. Perhaps you grew up in a highly secured mansion or were protected in a gated community, lest any *undesirables* penetrate your protective bubble of idealistic existence. If this rings true for you, then you might be interested to learn about the life and philosophy of Siddhartha Gautama—better known in the West as the Buddha.

Buddha escaped the walls of the luxurious palace that his father built to protect him. He gave up his worldly attachments and chose to live simply, with a compassionate heart, devoting himself entirely to helping the suffering people of the world find *Nirvana* and peace of mind. He renounced the material values of his princely station in life and became the Enlightened One.

Maybe you're looking for a little enlightenment yourself, especially given what may seem to be the terrible or challenging conditions that surround you. If you're experiencing mental agitation or dissatisfaction resulting from frustrated desires, perhaps you'll find solace in the teachings of the Buddha. He has much guidance and direction to offer you.

As we proceed through this chapter, no one philosophical outlook will be presented as *the* way to go. That decision will ultimately be yours. You may, or may not, be influenced by what you are about to learn. Whatever the case, the following discussion should at least get you thinking about your personal philosophy of life, however clear or unclear it is at this time. The naked truth is that you are responsible for your life and whatever direction it takes. Even allowing others, whoever they may be, to tell you what to do is still a personal choice for which you are accountable. It would be prudent, then, to make an intelligent and informed choice, don't you think? The quality of your life hinges on it.

Oh, by the way, did I ever suggest that philosophy might be an important subject of study?

To learn which philosophy of life presented here most resembles your current worldview, complete the following self-reflective diagnostic instrument.

The Philosophy of Life Preference Indicator

This chapter examines four philosophies of life—Stoicism, Existentialism, Hedonism, and Buddhism—which offer us ancient and modern, Eastern and Western, theistic and atheistic, as well as rational and non-rational perspectives that have direct and immediate practical relevance to your personal life.

The purpose of this self-diagnostic is to help you establish your level of agreement or disagreement with the assumptions, values, and beliefs embedded in various philosophical viewpoints so that you might become clearer about your own thinking and personal worldview.

INSTRUCTIONS

Below you will find a number of statements that reflect one of four philosophies covered in this chapter. Next to each statement, indicate your level of agreement or disagreement using this scale:

1 = strongly disagree
2 = disagree somewhat
3 = agree somewhat
4 = strongly agree

After completing this task, follow the scoring instructions.

1. _____ Pleasure is the principal motive for living.

2. _____ Life makes no sense; it has only the meaning we give it.

3. _____ It is not important to win favor with powerful and influential people.

4. _____ Human existence is imperfect in a very deep way, filled with all types of suffering.

5. _____ It is of paramount importance to gain mastery over one's desires.

6. _____ The value of individuality or individual expression is extremely high.

7. _____ It is wrong to deny yourself enjoyment and pleasure.

8. _____ The root cause of human suffering is desire or craving.

9. _____ Live for the moment; tomorrow may never come.

10. _____ Everything that happens, happens for a reason.

11. _____ It is bothersome when people merely play roles and conform to social expectations.

12. _____ Grasping at the pleasures of life ultimately increases suffering.

13. _____ Life is difficult; then you die.

14. _____ The individual is the measure of pleasure; there are no objective standards.

15. _____ Coincidences are not random, but meaningful.

16. _____ In order to find happiness, we must eliminate selfish craving.

17. _____ Emotions often get in the way of life; they should be controlled.

18. _____ You're ultimately free to make life anything you will it to be.

19. _____ Hollywood films are better than independently produced avant-garde productions because they're much more enjoyable to the audience.

20. _____ Peace of mind ultimately derives from compassion and showing loving-kindness toward others.

21. _____ "Eat, drink and be merry" should be everyone's motto in life.

22. _____ Peace of mind through acceptance of life is the greatest good any individual can achieve.

23. _____ People are responsible for their actions; you shouldn't blame your past, your parents, or anybody or anything else for what you do or have done.

24. _____ Giving and receiving are ultimately connected: "What goes around, comes around."

25. _____ Individuals are quite different and unique; there is no single human nature.

26. _____ Life is all about minimizing pain and maximizing fun and enjoyment.

27. _____ Everything that has happened to you until now has been a perfect preparation for where you're currently at in your life.

28. _____ Enlightenment requires that we reduce suffering in our lives through wisdom, morality, and concentration.

SCORING

Statement numbers are listed under each of the philosophical headings below. Next to each statement number, write in the value you gave it using the scale provided. Display your results visually by filling in the Philosophy of Life Sphere accordingly (see Figure 3.1).

Stoicism	Existentialism	Hedonism	Buddhism
3: ▨	2: ▨	1: ▨	4: ▨
5: ▨	6: ▨	7: ▨	8: ▨
10: ▨	11: ▨	9: ▨	12: ▨
15: ▨	13: ▨	14: ▨	16: ▨
17: ▨	18: ▨	19: ▨	20: ▨
22: ▨	23: ▨	21: ▨	24: ▨
27: ▨	25: ▨	26: ▨	28: ▨

TOTALS:

▨　　　▨　　　▨　　　▨

My highest total is ▨ under the philosophy of ▨ .

INTERPRETATION OF RESULTS

By completing this informal instrument, you have been able to compare your own values, beliefs, and philosophical presuppositions with four major worldviews. Be cautioned that your highest score doesn't necessarily make you a Stoic, an Existentialist, a Hedonist, or a Buddhist—though you could be. It may be that your pre-reflective philosophy is simply similar to one of them.

As you go through the chapter, consider more seriously your agreements and disagreements with the philosophies of life outlined. Nothing final or scientifically conclusive is intended by this self-diagnostic. It merely serves as a tool to stimulate thought.

You should note that the statements I've included under Existentialism reflect atheistic Existentialism, while those under Hedonism are consistent with the views of a philosopher named Aristippus. Including statements consistent with religious forms of Existentialism or the Hedonism of other thinkers such as Epicurus would have blurred the relatively clear-cut distinctions I have tried to incorporate into this measure. Therefore, as you learn about variations in hedonistic and existential philosophy, your identified preferences may change somewhat. Read the brief descriptions of each philosophy of life below. Greater detail for each position is provided in the chapter.

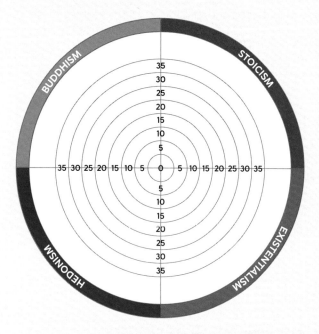

FIGURE 3.1 Philosophy of Life Sphere

HEDONISM

Cyrenaic Hedonism, the type used for the purposes of this comparative diagnostic, states that *pleasure is the principal motive for living*. Pleasure is always good, regardless of its source. There are no qualitative distinctions among pleasures. All pleasures are equally good. The only way to distinguish between pleasures is by their intensity. The greatest or most intense pleasure is the best. The pursuit of pleasure gives meaning to life. We ought to pursue our natural desires openly, without guilt or apology, and learn to enjoy ourselves. It is wrong to deny ourselves pleasure. The only pleasurable pursuits that are wrong are those which are enslaving and prevent the pursuit of other pleasures.

STOICISM

Stoics believe that true goodness does not lie in pleasure or in external objects, but in the state of the soul. *Peace of mind is found in wisdom and self-control*, by which people restrain passions and desires that disturb them in daily life. Stoicism adheres to the notion of fate or destiny, attributing the ultimate design of the universe to a divine being. Your mission in life is not to choose your role, but to play well the one you've been assigned.

EXISTENTIALISM

Atheistic Existentialism is a philosophy focusing on concepts such as *individuality*, *freedom*, and *human existence*. For the Existentialist, there is no such thing as human nature. We are simply thrust into the world without reason, and once there, we are held responsible for creating ourselves and making ourselves what we are. This is not an option, for we are "condemned to be free." Efforts to conform, follow, or fit in are merely attempts to escape the frightening realities of our uniqueness, free will, and the absurdity of life. No God has made us, and no objective moral laws can tell us what to do. We are abandoned and alone in the world. We find meaning by living freely and responsibly in ways true to ourselves.

BUDDHISM

Buddhism is an Eastern religion but often regarded in the West as a philosophy of life because it involves no worship of a creator god, as with Christianity, Judaism, and Islam. Based on the teachings of Siddhartha Gautama, Buddhism tries to reduce suffering in life through *spiritual discipline* and *meditative practices*. Enlightenment is achieved through psychological detachment, loving-kindness, and the development of a compassionate heart—all things reflective of *Buddha consciousness*. According to this worldview, nothing is fixed; all volitional actions have consequences (karmic results). That which we call the ego or self is impermanent, and hence ultimately unreal.

3.1 Stoicism: A Prescription for Peace of Mind

Stoicism's Cynical Origins

Stoicism is a school of philosophy that flourished in ancient Rome and Greece for approximately five centuries. It was founded in Cyprus by the merchant **Zeno** of Citium who, in the aftermath of being shipwrecked, took up philosophical studies in Athens. Initially, he became a pupil of the Cynic Crates, a Socratic model of sorts, but later went on to found his own school. Only fragments of Zeno's writings remain.

The term *stoic*, a name for adherents to Zeno's philosophy, is derived from the fact that he lectured at the great central square of Athens, at the location of the *Stoa Poikile* or *Painted Porch* (colonnade). At first called Zenonians, followers of Zeno later came to be dubbed **Stoics**, or "men of the porch." Other notable Stoics include the slave **Epictetus**, the Roman emperor **Marcus Aurelius**, and the statesman **Seneca**. **Chrysippus**, following Zeno and Cleanthes, eventually took over the Athenian Stoa academy and is sometimes considered the co-founder of this school of thought. He is credited with over 700 writings, but unfortunately none have survived.

Stoic philosophy owes its origins to **Cynicism**, whose Greek architect, **Antisthenes**, had been a disciple of Socrates. Antisthenes was so impressed by Socrates that he walked almost five miles a day just to hear him speak. Antisthenes was apparently less impressed with Socratic ideas than with Socrates himself. While Antisthenes did agree with Socrates that life should be based on reason, it was more Socrates's character and lifestyle that drew Antisthenes to him. Socrates showed contempt for fashion. He had no desire to impress people with shallow appearances. Rather, he opted for ragged functional clothing, choosing to walk without shoes. It was said that Socrates could go long periods of time without eating or sleeping. He displayed a physical toughness and forthright honesty that made a significant impact on Antisthenes.

After the death of Socrates, Antisthenes founded a school that came to be called the **Cynosarges**, which means *the silver dog*. The term *cynic* was derived from Cynosarges and later applied to perhaps the most famous Cynic in history, namely **Diogenes**. As the story goes, Diogenes lived in a wine barrel, preferring the company of dogs to the weakening corruptions of luxurious and sophisticated living. For him, trying to win favor with important and influential people was degrading. While many of us dream of the day when we can participate in *high society*, from the Cynic's perspective, high society is by its very nature corrupt.

Withdrawing from society, the Cynics came to regard luxury and wealth as a trap, requiring phony manners, dishonesty, flattery, and attention to fashion, things ultimately resulting in frustrating, but avoidable, complications. Cynics argued that happiness was possible only to the extent that one could develop self-discipline. The aim was to gain rational control over one's desires. If one chose to remain uncorrupted, then contact with conventional society had to be minimized.

The sarcastic hostility displayed by some of the early Cynics toward social conventions eventually led them to be held in disrepute. Their legacy, perhaps, is that when someone today is described as "cynical," we think of a person who is arrogant and condescending toward others. Whereas the archetypical philosophical Cynic offered reasoned argument and penetrating social critique, so-called cynics of today are more likely to spew their venom of contemptuous scorn much more indiscriminately and, quite possi-

"You may not control all the events that happen to you, but you can decide not to be reduced by them."
MAYA ANGELOU

bly, in a psychologically dishonest fashion. As you can well appreciate, rejecting people or their proposals out of fear, insecurity, or animus is a lot different from principled rational objection. It is important, therefore, not to confuse the philosophical Cynic, whose views trace back to Antisthenes, with the cynical "rebel without a cause"—someone who simply hates life or hates themself.

Lastly, it's worth noting that Stoics shared the Cynics' admiration for Socrates. They accepted the fundamental Cynical premise that excessive desires are a prescription for unhappiness, and that the best form of life is characterized by detachment, courage, dignity, and self-control. Though Socrates was neither a Cynic nor a Stoic, he was a model for both.

The Stoic Universe

"Events do not just happen, but arrive by appointment."
EPICTETUS

A great source of anxiety for some people is the prospect that life could be meaningless, that things might occur by fluke or happenstance, and that the future offers only chaos and dangerous unpredictability. In an uncertain world, people can often feel hopelessly alone and abandoned. If, indeed, you feel this way yourself, you might find some sort of psycho-spiritual help in the therapeutic philosophy of the Stoics, who hold the opposite view.

According to the Stoics, we live in an **ordered universe**. This means the universe is rational, structured, and shaped by design. Nothing that happens is random or serendipitous. For example, when two old friends bump into each other on the street, apparently by chance, they really don't; their meeting is evidence of what twentieth-century psychiatrist and psychoanalyst Carl Jung calls **synchronicity**, or meaningful coincidence. There is a reason behind it.

As Chrysippus argued, everything that happens is **fated**, predetermined, and according to plan. For Stoics, the power behind the plan is God. Be careful, however, how you interpret the notion of God. Depending on your religious belief system, if you have one, you may see God in essentially superhuman terms, as some kind of extraordinary being. Some Christians believe we are created in God's image as humans, only less than perfect.

The Stoics, by contrast, made God synonymous with Zeus, creative fire, ether, the Word (*Logos*), World Reason, Fate, Providence, Destiny, and the Law of Nature. In fact, in their **monistic universe**, there is no difference between God and all the things in the world: they are one. Thus, God, Zeus, the *Logos* (or whatever you choose to call this elemental force) is not somehow above or beyond us. God is **immanent** in everything. God is the determining element in all physical objects and events. As for humans, because we possess the power of reason, we have the spark of divinity emanating from our original Source. Under the guidance of the divine *Logos*, the universe displays a rational order. Everything is connected and happens for a reason—one that is divinely ordained.

How to Live in a Fated Universe

From the philosophical notion of Stoic determinism follow a number of practical, moral, and behavioral prescriptions for action. These prescriptions ultimately derive from the belief that God orders all things for the best. This Stoic belief offers us a great measure of reassurance. Whatever is, or whatever happens, is or does so by design and with a purpose. Nothing in the Stoic universe is out of place. This, of course, raises questions about the existence of evil in the world, to which Stoicism has the following reply: Good

TABLE 3.1 Periods and Proponents of Stoicism

Early Stoa (third century BCE)

Zeno (336–264 BCE)

Founder of Stoicism; lectured at the Painted Porch (*Stoa Poikile*) in Athens; emphasized strength of character in ethical and political action

Cleanthes of Assos (331–232 BCE)

Successor to Zeno; poet and religious visionary

Chrysippus of Soloi (279–206 BCE)

Third leader of the stoa at Athens; successor to Cleanthes; advocated living in accordance with reason; saw emotions as great obstacles to happiness that required eradication

Middle Stoa (second and first centuries BCE)

Panaetius of Rhodes (185–110 BCE)

Softened asceticism of early stoa; attached moral value to external goods; spoke in terms of gradual moral progress

Posidonius of Apamea (135–51 BCE)

Pupil of Panaetius; brought rigor and detail to the Stoic system; developed Stoic belief in the indivisibility of the cosmos

Late Stoa (first and second centuries CE)

Seneca (4 BCE–65 CE)

Most sympathetic to Posidonius; minister of Nero; writer of tragedies; developer of Stoic ethics: tranquility and social duty

Epictetus (50–138 CE)

Freed slave; member of Nero's bodyguard; distinguished between what we can and cannot control; believed in innate moral predispositions

Marcus Aurelius (121–180 CE)

Last of the great Stoics; emphasized inward self-control and useful citizenship in the cosmopolis

---

cannot exist without evil; evil throws the good into greater relief in the same way that the contrast of light and shadow is pleasing in a picture. In a similar vein, Chrysippus said, "Comedies have in them ludicrous verses which, though bad in themselves, nevertheless lend a certain grace to the whole play."[1] So, just like a discordant note in a song can contribute to the beauty of the music or a bad meal makes the good ones taste all the more delicious, the tragedies in life can make for a better life overall.

I'm reminded here of a former student of mine who transferred into the General Arts and Science program after flunking out of a sports injury management course. She was severely anxious and depressed by her removal from that course. In time, however, this student discovered she had an aptitude for philosophy. Subsequently, she decided to proceed with future university studies to become a lawyer. The last time we spoke, she was delighted by this "twist of fate" which, at the outset, was extremely painful for her, but now seemed for the best. Her originally perceived "failure" was simply a preparation for a new beginning, though she couldn't recognize and appreciate that fact at the time of her ejection. Just think, every joy, success, setback, disappointment, trauma, or failure that you've experienced constitutes, in a Stoic universe, simply the perfect preparation for what you're doing right now in your life. Past so-called "failures" make ever more sweet the "successes" of today and tomorrow.

Freedom and Value

Because things happen as they should in the **cosmology** of the Stoics, no act is evil or reprehensible in itself. As Stoics point out, it is "the intention, the moral condition of the agent from whom the act proceeds, that makes the act evil; the act as a physical entity is indifferent."[2] Moral evil manifests itself when the human will is out of harmony with right reason. Personal freedom in a Stoic universe does not come from doing anything you want, but from choosing to act according to nature.

A form of **interior freedom** is possible when individuals alter their *judgments* on events and *attitudes* toward them, perceiving them and welcoming them as the expressions of God's will. The Stoic's advice is that we develop a psychological posture of **courageous acceptance**. Although we cannot control world events, we have complete *interior freedom* to respond emotionally and psychologically. We cannot choose life's roles (being born male or female, into a rich or poor family); we can only choose how well to play the roles assigned us. As I read on a bumper sticker once, *Attitude is everything*. (I didn't know a Stoic was driving the car ahead of me—likely one of those everyday philosopher types we learned about Chapter 1!)

Purpose of Life

In the Stoic universe, the ultimate goal of life is to live according to nature. Doing so will lead to a state of spiritual peace and well-being, sometimes referred to as **Stoic apathy**. The Greek word *apatheia* translated here does not have the negative "I just don't care" connotations 'apathy' does. It means *without disturbance by passions*. 'Equanimity'—calmness, evenness of mind—is perhaps a better translation. At other times the Stoics characterized their goal as **eudaimonia**. The notion of *eudaimonia*, sometimes loosely translated as 'happiness.' should not be interpreted as mere pleasure, however, but rather as *living well*.

According to Stoicism, the *eudaimon*, one who has achieved happiness, is someone who flourishes from Stoic apathy, living the virtuous life. This person, whose human will accords with Divine Reason, lives life according to nature. Nothing else besides virtue has value in itself. External goods are neither parts of *eudaimonia*, nor necessary for it.[3] Things like health, wealth, pleasure, or absence of pain are, in fact, morally indifferent to the virtuous life. *Eudaimonia* is possible with or without them. One person can be sick and poor and still be virtuous. Another can be healthy and wealthy and yet be disturbed and miserably corrupt. Of course, given the choice, health is to be preferred over sickness, wealth over poverty, and freedom from pain over suffering. We should all try to conduct our affairs and influence events in our lives to enhance the former and to minimize the latter.

Things like health and wealth do possess a "second grade worth" within the Stoic hierarchical scale of values. What the Stoic recognizes, however, is that such things are ultimately beyond our control. You may choose to live a healthy lifestyle, for instance, but suddenly be hit by a car, leaving you permanently disabled. You may also have made prudent financial investments for years, only to discover one morning that the stock market has crashed and left you personally bankrupt. As devastating as such events may seem, according to Stoicism, they should not be cause for psychological disturbance. They only affect you if you let them, and you only let them if you allow yourself to become attached to worldly things. This Stoic insight is immensely liberating. Just think, nothing that happens in your life—no misfortune, accident, trauma, or tragedy—can ever prevent you from living your life as it should be lived. That is still in your control!

THINKING ABOUT YOUR THINKING

Take a moment to think about a time when you were upset by a setback or disappointment in your life. It could have occurred at home, with your friends, at work, at school, or anywhere else. What happened exactly? Why were you so upset by it? If it happened again, what could you do differently so that you wouldn't be upset about it? Assuming the view of a Stoic, what could you change about your judgments and attitudes in order to achieve courageous acceptance in that situation?

When "the good life" is equated with the virtuous life, one which accords with the *Logos* or God's will, a certain self-possession and emotional detachment from worldly affairs can manifest itself in tranquility and peace of mind. If you are currently upset by life, then, from a Stoic vantage point, you probably exhibit bad thinking and poor character development, confusing what you can and cannot control, placing value in things that have no intrinsic, ultimate worth. If you are unhappy, it is not because something has happened to you or because something has failed to happen; it is because *you* are the problem.

To illustrate how the problem is "in you," not "out there," consider the fact that not everybody is upset by the same insult. You may become infuriated, while someone else could be left unaffected. News of a job loss could depress you but exhilarate someone elated by the prospect of challenging new opportunities. Insults and bad news affect different people in different ways. The upset is therefore not in the insult or the bad news, but in the person. What is important to recognize is that nothing or nobody can make you feel glad, mad, or sad without your permission. When it comes to your attitudes and emotions, the Stoic maintains that you are ultimately in control. Marcus Aurelius says, *If you are pained by any external thing, it is not the thing that disturbs you, but your judgment about it. And it is in your power to wipe out this judgment now.*

Marcus Aurelius

Marcus Aurelius is the second-century emperor of Rome known by the nickname "the philosopher." In his youth, Marcus received an impressive education from tutors of great renown and significance. One of those tutors, the prominent lawyer and rhetorician named Fronto, tried to discourage Marcus from pursuing his interest in philosophy, but his warnings did not deter the future emperor. Instead, other teachers cultivated Marcus's philosophical tendencies and interest in ideas, including the Stoic philosopher Rusticus, who Marcus thanks in Book I of his *Meditations* in the following manner:

> From Rusticus I received the impression that my character required improvement and discipline; and from him I learned not to be led astray to sophistic emulation, nor to writing on speculative matters, nor to delivering little hortatory orations, nor to showing myself off as a man who practises much discipline, or does benevolent acts in order to make a display; and to abstain from rhetoric, and poetry, and fine writing; and not to walk about in the house in my outdoor dress, nor to do other things of the kind; and to write my letters with simplicity, like the letter which Rusticus wrote from Sinuessa to my mother; and with respect to those who have offended me by words, or done me wrong, to be easily disposed to be pacified and reconciled, as soon as they have shown a readiness to be reconciled, and to read carefully, and not to be satisfied with a superficial understanding of a book; nor hastily to give my assent to those who talk overmuch; and I am indebted to him for being acquainted with the discourses of Epictetus, which he communicated to me out of his own collection.[4]

In short, Marcus thanks Rusticus for being a Stoic influence on him.

Marcus reigned as emperor of Rome from 161 CE until his death in 180 CE. During this time, he faced challenges and turbulence in the forms of invasion, rebellion, and plague, but he ruled well enough to earn his legacy as the last of the so-called Five Good Emperors of Rome and a symbol of the prosperous Golden Age of the Roman Empire.

It was during years spent on military campaigns in various locations that Marcus wrote his famous book, *Meditations*. In that book, he seeks to put Stoic thought into action in his life. That is, within the context of his experiences, concerns, and irritations, Marcus truly sought to live the good life as a Stoic life, that is, a life that accords with nature.

Stoicism and Stress Management

The psychologically healing powers of Stoic wisdom have managed to trickle down into contemporary society through psychotherapeutic practices of stress management. **Albert Ellis**, the internationally recognized developer of Rational-Emotive Behavior Therapy, has found through research and clinical practice that people feel largely the way they do because of how they think. Ellis says, "What we label our emotional reactions are mainly caused by our conscious and unconscious evaluations, interpretations and philosophies."[5] When we feel anxious, worried, or stressed, it is frequently due to the irrational assumptions we make and the foolish beliefs to which we cling.

Consistent with Stoic thinking, Ellis argues that things and events, in themselves, don't *make us unhappy*; rather, our *interpretations* of them do. Therefore, if we could identify our irrational assumptions and beliefs and then abandon them, we would then begin to live a more rational lifestyle, one with significantly less stress and less negative emotion. By clinging to irrationality, we become architects of our own emotional disturbance and "dis-ease."

To illustrate how this is so, Ellis has conceptualized an A–B–C Model of psychological functioning which he incorporated into his therapeutic methods (Figure 3.2). The *A* represents the activating event—the real-life occurrence that is potentially stressful, although not necessarily so. The activating event could be a failure, loss, hurt, or anything else that could produce stress in your life. Intuitively, some

of us think that such events automatically cause a stress response. However, the emotional consequence *C*—of failure, loss, or hurt—is not necessarily determined by such things. Coming between the activating event (*A*) and the ultimate emotional response or consequence (*C*) is the belief (*B*) about what just happened (*A*). The cognitive interpretation and appraisal of the activating event will ultimately determine the emotional response. Besides serving as an explanatory illustration for Ellis, Figure 3.2 also serves to underscore the stoic insight of Epictetus that *Men are not disturbed by things, but by the view that they take of them.*

FIGURE 3.2 Albert Ellis's "A–B–C" model

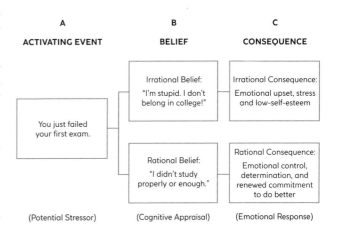

Emotions in Life

Given the lengthy history of Stoicism and its many variations from different periods and geographic locations (Athens and Rome), academic interpretations regarding the Stoic position on **emotion** are not entirely consistent. Some analysts claim the Stoics rejected all emotions to the extent it was humanly possible; others contend that such a claim is only a half-truth, asserting that what the Stoics wished to abolish were the "excessive passions" that led to mental disturbance.[6]

The discrepancy seems to come from the fact that interpreters cite different sources in their translations from the Greek that either distinguish, or fail to distinguish, between the notions of *emotion* and *passion*. Where emotion is totally dismissed, the distinction between emotion and passion appears not to be made; where some expressions of emotion are permitted, the difference is recognized.

"Things themselves touch not the soul, not in the least degree."
MARCUS AURELIUS

On this latter interpretation, some emotions are acceptable, while others can be described as **excessive passions**. Excessive passions are unreasonable and unnatural. However, a parent's love for a child, for instance, is an acceptable emotion that is natural and consistent with the divine order. Feelings of love for humanity and the attractions of friendship are also natural, so not necessarily to be avoided. By contrast, fear is an exaggerated emotion (a passionate disturbance), to be eliminated because it is contrary to reason.

When people experience fear of the future, they may exhibit symptoms such as nervous trembling, excessive perspiration, or heart palpitations. Such physical effects of fear result because of the belief that something bad is about to happen. However, in a fated Stoic universe, nothing that happens can be described as bad, for it occurs as a function of God's will. Even things like death, pain, and ill-repute are morally indifferent. The experience of fear is the result of exaggerating their importance—*catastrophizing* to use Ellis's terminology—and believing that they will bring real harm when, in truth, they leave our essential moral being unaffected.

Other disturbing passions to be avoided include *desire for revenge*, *envy*, *jealousy*, *grief*, and even *pity*. The desire for revenge contains a disquieting element of hatred, whereas envy, grief, and jealousy possess some fairly obvious negative qualities of their own, leading to their own *dis-ease*. As for pity, although it may sound like an admirable emotion, it too should be eliminated for it is based on the (false) belief that something "bad" has happened to someone else. Since no sorrow or resentment should follow from one's own suffering, it should not accompany another's. In the grand scheme of things—that is, from a universal and timeless perspective beyond one's own personal concerns and particular circumstances—*all that happens is for the best and by design*.

How to Progress Morally

Stoic wisdom offers us not only tranquility and freedom from fear, but also some suggestions for achieving such things. If we wish to develop morally as persons, we must behave in certain ways. First of all, we should live by the Socratic injunction to "Know Thyself." Seneca and Epictetus recommend that we engage in *daily self-examinations*, monitoring our thoughts, feelings, and actions.[7] This will help us to substitute good habits for bad ones. In this regard, we should try to avoid temptations and wayward companions.

Further, we must become masters in our own psychological homes—controlling, avoiding, or eliminating those excessive emotions contributing to passionate disturbances in our lives. Recognizing the role of divine Providence in all events and seeing how most things desired by people in life are morally indifferent, we should also learn to forgive those who we erroneously thought hurt us or took from us what we once believed was valuable, but now recognize as worthless.

From the Stoic perspective, it is advantageous to set before our eyes some ideal of virtue (Socrates, for example) and then try to live up to it. As aspiring Stoics, we should order our desires and perform our duties in accordance with right reason. Epictetus would recommend that we become indifferent to external goods. If instead we choose to seek happiness in goods that do not depend entirely on ourselves, we fall into the abyss of never-ending psychological dissatisfaction. Temperance and abstinence are more likely to result in happiness than ceaseless efforts directed toward self-gratification.

Further Stoic insights into how life should be lived can be gained in *The Meditations of Marcus Aurelius*.

Marcus Aurelius, *The Meditations of Marcus Aurelius*[8]

Marcus Aurelius (121–180 CE) wrote the Meditations *for himself in order to reflect on his experiences and reinforce the Stoic doctrines by which he led his life. The following excerpt comes from part five of the twelve parts comprising the* Meditations.[9]

——

1. In the morning when you rise unwillingly, let this thought be present—I am rising to the work of a human being. Why then am I dissatisfied if I am going to do the things for which I exist and for which I was brought into the world? Or have I been made for this, to lie in the bed-clothes and keep myself warm?—But this is more pleasant.—Do you exist then to take your pleasure, and not at all for action or exertion? Do you not see the little plants, the little birds, the ants, the spiders, the bees working together to put in order their several parts of the universe? And are you unwilling to do the work of a human being, and do you not make haste to do that which is according to your nature?—But it is necessary to take rest also.—It is necessary: however nature has fixed bounds to this too: she has fixed bounds both to eating and drinking, and yet you go beyond these bounds, beyond what is sufficient; yet in your acts it is not so, but you stop short of what you can do. So you love not yourself, for if you did, you would love your nature and her will. But those who love their several arts exhaust themselves in working at them unwashed and without food; but you value your own nature less than the engraver values the engraving art, or the dancer the dancing art, or the lover of money values his money, or the vainglorious man his little glory. And such men, when they have a violent affection to a thing, choose neither to eat nor to sleep rather than to perfect the things which they care for. But are the acts which concern society more vile in your eyes and less worthy of your labor?

2. How easy it is to repel and to wipe away every impression which is troublesome or unsuitable, and immediately to be in all tranquility.

3. Judge every word and deed which are according to nature to be fit for you; and be not diverted by the blame which follows from any people, nor by their words, but if a thing is good to be done or said, do not consider it unworthy of you. For those persons have their peculiar leading principle and follow their peculiar movement; which things do not you regard, but go straight on, following your own nature and the common nature; and the way of both is one.

4. I go through the things which happen according to nature until I shall fall and rest, breathing out my breath into that element out of which I daily draw it in, and falling upon that earth out of which my father collected the seed, and my mother the blood, and my nurse the milk; out of which during so many years I have been supplied with food and drink; which bears me when I tread on it and abuse it for so many purposes.

5. You say, men cannot admire the sharpness of your wits.—Be it so; but there are many other things of which you can not say, I am not formed for them by nature. Show those qualities then which are altogether in your power: sincerity, gravity, endurance of labor, aversion to pleasure, contentment with your portion and with few things, benevolence, frankness, no love of superfluity, freedom from trifling magnanimity. Do you not see how many qualities you are immediately able to exhibit, in which there is no excuse of natural incapacity and unfitness, and yet you still remain voluntarily below the mark? Or are you compelled through being defectively furnished by nature to murmur, and to be stingy, and to flatter, and to find fault with your poor body, and to try to please men, and to make great display, and to be restless in your mind? No, by the gods: but you might have been delivered from these things long ago. Only if in truth you can be charged with being rather slow and dull of comprehension, you must exert yourself about this also, not neglecting it nor yet taking pleasure in your dullness.

6. One man, when he has done a service to another, is ready to set it down to his account as a favour conferred. Another is not ready to do this, but still in his own mind he thinks of the man as his debtor, and he knows what he has done. A third in a manner does not even know what he has done, but he is like a vine which

has produced grapes, and seeks for nothing more after it has once produced its proper fruit. As a horse when he has run, a dog when he has tracked the game, a bee when it has made the honey, so a man when he has done a good act, does not call out for others to come and see, but he goes on to another act, as a vine goes on to produce again the grapes in season.—Must a man then be one of these, who in a manner act thus without observing it?—Yes.—But this very thing is necessary, the observation of what a man is doing; for it may be said, it is characteristic of the social animal to perceive that he is working in a social manner, and indeed to wish that his social partner also should perceive it.—It is true what you say, but you do not rightly understand what is now said; and for this reason you will become one of those of whom I spoke before, for even they are misled by a certain show of reason. But if you will choose to understand the meaning of what is said, do not fear that for this reason you will omit any social act.

7. A prayer of the Athenians: Rain, rain, O dear Zeus, down on the plowed fields of the Athenians and on the plains.—In truth we ought not to pray at all, or we ought to pray in this simple and noble fashion.

8. Just as we must understand when it is said, That Æsculapius prescribed to this man horse-exercise, or bathing in cold water, or going without shoes, so we must understand it when it is said, That the nature of the universe prescribed to this man disease or mutilation or loss or anything else of the kind. For in the first case prescribed means something like this: he prescribed this for this man as a thing adapted to procure health; and in the second case it means, That which happens to [or suits] every man is fixed in a manner for him suitably to his destiny. For this is what we mean when we say that things are suitable to us, as the workmen say of squared stones in walls or the pyramids, that they are suitable, when they fit them to one another in some kind of connection. For there is altogether one fitness [harmony]. And as the universe is made up out of all bodies to be such a body as it is, so out of all existing causes necessity [destiny] is made up to be such a cause as it is. And even those who are completely ignorant understand what I mean, for they say, It [necessity, destiny] brought this to such a person.—This then was brought and this was prescribed to him. Let us then receive these things, as well as those which Æsculapius* prescribes. Many, as a matter of course, even among his prescriptions, are disagreeable, but we accept them in the hope of health. Let the perfecting and accomplishment of the things, which the common nature judges to be good, be judged by you to be of the same kind as your health. And so accept everything which happens, even if it seem disagreeable, because it leads to this, to the health of the universe and to the prosperity and felicity of Zeus [the universe]. For he would not have brought on any man what he has brought, if it were not useful for the whole. Neither does the nature of anything, whatever it may be, cause anything which is not suitable to that which is directed by it. For two reasons, then, it is right to be content with that which happens to you; the one, because it was done for you and prescribed for you, and in a manner had reference to you, originally from the most ancient causes spun with your destiny; and the other, because even that which comes severally to every man is to the power which administers the universe a cause of felicity and perfection, nay even of its very continuance. For the integrity of the whole is mutilated, if you cut off anything whatever from the conjunction and the continuity either of the parts or of the causes. And you do cut off, as far as it is in your power, when you are dissatisfied, and in a manner try to put anything out of the way.

9. Be not disgusted, nor discouraged, nor dissatisfied, if you do not succeed in doing everything according to right principles; but when you have failed, return back again, and be content if the greater part of what you do is consistent with man's nature, and love this to which you return; and do not return to philosophy as if she were a master, but act like those who have sore eyes and apply a bit of sponge and egg, or as another applies a plaster, or drenching with water. For thus you will not fail to obey reason and you will repose in it. And remember that philosophy requires only the things which your nature requires; but you would have something else which is not according to nature. It may be objected, Why, what is more agreeable than this [which I am doing]? But is not this the very reason why pleasure deceives us? And consider if magnanimity, freedom, simplicity, equanimity, piety are not more agreeable.

_____

* The ancient Greek god of medicine.

For what is more agreeable than wisdom itself, when you think of the security and the happy course of all things which depend on the faculty of understanding and knowledge?

10. Things are in such a kind of envelopment that they have seemed to philosophers, not a few nor those common philosophers, altogether unintelligible; nay even to the Stoics themselves they seem difficult to understand. And all our assent is changeable; for where is the man who never changes? Carry your thoughts then to the objects themselves, and consider how short-lived they are and worthless, and that they may be in the possession of a filthy wretch or a whore or a robber. Then turn to the morals of those who live with you, and it is hardly possible to endure even the most agreeable of them, to say nothing of a man being hardly able to endure himself. In such darkness, then, and dirt, and in so constant a flux, both of substance and of time, and of motion, and of things moved, what there is worth being highly prized, or even an object of serious pursuit, I cannot imagine. But on the contrary it is a man's duty to comfort himself, and to wait for the natural dissolution and not to be vexed at the delay, but to rest in these principles only: the one, that nothing will happen to me which is not conformable to the nature of the universe; and the other, that it is in my power never to act contrary to my god and demon:* for there is no man who will compel me to this.

11. About what am I now employing my own soul? On every occasion I must ask myself this question, and inquire, what have I now in this part of me, which they call the ruling principle? and whose soul have I now? that of a child, or of a young man, or of a feeble woman, or of a tyrant, or of a domestic animal, or of a wild beast?

12. What kind of things those are which appear good to the many, we may learn even from this. For if any man should conceive certain things as being really good, such as prudence, temperance, justice, fortitude, he would not after having first conceived these endure to listen to anything which should not be in harmony with what is really good. But if a man has first conceived as good the things which appear to the many to be good,

he will listen and readily receive as very applicable that which was said by the comic writer. Thus even the many perceive the difference. For were it not so, this saying would not offend and would not be rejected [in the first case], while we receive it when it is said of wealth, and of the means which further luxury and fame, as said fitly and wittily. Go on then and ask if we should value and think those things to be good, to which after their first conception in the mind the words of the comic writer might be aptly applied—that he who has them, through pure abundance has not a place to ease himself in.

13. I am composed of the formal and the material; and neither of them will perish into non-existence, as neither of them came into existence out of non-existence. Every part of me then will be reduced by change into some part of the universe, and that again will change into another part of the universe, and so on forever. And by consequence of such a change I too exist, and those who begot me, and so on forever in the other direction. For nothing hinders us from saying so, even if the universe is administered according to definite periods [of revolution].

14. Reason and the reasoning art [philosophy] are powers which are sufficient for themselves and for their own works. They move then from a first principle which is their own, and they make their way to the end which is proposed to them; and this is the reason why such acts are named *catorthóseis* or right acts, which word signifies that they proceed by the right road.

15. None of these things ought to be called a man's which do not belong to a man, as man. They are not required of a man, nor does man's nature promise them, nor are they the means of man's nature attaining its end. Neither then does the end of man lie in these things, nor yet that which aids to the accomplishment of this end, and that which aids toward this end is that which is good. Besides, if any of these things did belong to man, it would not be right for a man to despise them and to set himself against them; nor would a man be worthy of praise who showed that he did not want these things, nor would he who stinted himself in any of them be good, if indeed these things were good. But now the more of these things a man deprives himself of, or of other things like them, or even when he is deprived of

---

* An inner directing spirit associated with a particular person. In this context, the word lacks its usual negative connotation.

any of them, the more patiently he endures the loss, just in the same degree he is a better man.

16. Such as are your habitual thoughts, such also will be the character of your mind; for the soul is dyed by the thoughts. Dye it then with a continuous series of such thoughts as these: for instance, that where a man can live, there he can also live well. But he must live in a palace—well then, he can also live well in a palace. And again, consider that for whatever purpose each thing has been constituted, for this it has been constituted, and toward this it is carried; and its end is in that toward which it is carried; and where the end is, there also is the advantage and the good of each thing. Now the good for the reasonable animal is society; for that we are made for society has been shown above. Is it not plain that the inferior exist for the sake of the superior? but the things which have life are superior to those which have not life, and of those which have life the superior are those which have reason.

17. To seek what is impossible is madness: and it is impossible that the bad should not do something of this kind.

18. Nothing happens to any man which he is not formed by nature to bear. The same things happen to another, and either because he does not see that they have happened or because he would show a great spirit he is firm and remains unharmed. It is a shame then that ignorance and conceit should be stronger than wisdom.

19. Things themselves touch not the soul, not in the least degree; nor have they admission to the soul, nor can they turn or move the soul: but the soul turns and moves itself alone, and whatever judgments it may think proper to make, such it makes for itself the things which present themselves to it.

20. In one respect man is the nearest thing to me, so far as I must do good to men and endure them. But so far as some men make themselves obstacles to my proper acts, man becomes to me one of the things which are indifferent, no less than the sun or wind or a wild beast. Now it is true that these may impede my action, but they are no impediments to my affects and disposition, which have the power of acting conditionally and changing: for the mind converts and changes every hindrance to its activity into an aid; and so that which is

a hindrance is made a furtherance to an act; and that which is an obstacle on the road helps us on this road.

21. Reverence that which is best in the universe; and this is that which makes use of all things and directs all things. And in like manner also reverence that which is best in yourself; and this is of the same kind as that. For in yourself also, that which makes use of everything else, is this, and your life is directed by this.

22. That which does no harm to the state, does no harm to the citizen. In the case of every appearance of harm apply this rule: if the state is not harmed by this, neither am I harmed. But if the state is harmed, you must not be angry with him who does harm to the state. Show him where his error is.

23. Often think of the rapidity with which things pass by and disappear, both the things which are and the things which are produced. For substance is like a river in a continual flow, and the activities of things are in constant change, and the causes work in infinite varieties; and there is hardly anything which stands still. And consider this which is near to you, this boundless abyss of the past and of the future in which all things disappear. How then is he not a fool who is puffed up with such things or plagued about them or makes himself miserable? for they vex him only for a time, and a short time.

24. Think of the universal substance, of which you have a very small portion; and of universal time, of which a short and indivisible interval has been assigned to you; and of that which is fixed by destiny, and how small a part of it you are.

25. Does another do me wrong? Let him look to it. He has his own disposition, his own activity. I now have what the universal nature wills me to have; and I do what my nature now wills me to do.

26. Let the part of your soul which leads and governs be undisturbed by the movements in the flesh, whether of pleasure or of pain; and let it not unite with them, but let it circumscribe itself and limit those affects to their parts. But when these affects rise up to the mind by virtue of that other sympathy that naturally exists in a body which is all one, then you must not strive to resist the sensation, for it is natural: but let not the ruling part of itself add to the sensation the opinion that it is either good or bad.

27. Live with the gods. And he does live with the gods who constantly shows to them that his own soul is satisfied with that which is assigned to him, and that it does all that the demon wishes, which Zeus has given to every man for his guardian and guide, a portion of himself. And this is every man's understanding and reason.

28. Are you angry with him whose arm-pits stink? Are you angry with him whose mouth smells foul? What good will this anger do you? He has such a mouth, he has such arm-pits: it is necessary that such an emanation must come from such things—but the man has reason, it will be said, and he is able, if he takes pains, to discover wherein he offends—I wish you well of your discovery. Well then, and you have reason: by your rational faculty stir up his rational faculty; show him his error, admonish him. For if he listens, you will cure him, and there is no need of anger.

29. As you intend to live when you are gone out, ... so it is in your power to live here. But if men do not permit you, then get away out of life, yet so as if you were suffering no harm. The house is smoky, and I quit it. Why do you think that this is any trouble? But so long as nothing of the kind drives me out, I remain, am free, and no man shall hinder me from doing what I choose; and I choose to do what is according to the nature of the rational and social animal.

30. The intelligence of the universe is social. Accordingly it has made the inferior things for the sake of the superior, and it has fitted the superior to one another. You see how it has subordinated, coordinated and assigned to everything its proper portion, and has brought together into concord with one another the things which are the best.

31. How have you behaved hitherto to the gods, your parents, brethren, children, teachers, to those who looked after your infancy, to your friends, kinsfolk, to your slaves? Consider if you have hitherto behaved to all in such a way that this may be said of you:

Never has wronged a man in deed or word.

And call to recollection both how many things you have passed through, and how many things you have been able to endure: and that the history of your life is now complete, and your service is ended: and how many beautiful things you have seen: and how many pleasures and pains you have despised; and how many things called honorable you have spurned; and to how many ill-minded folks you have shown a kind disposition.

32. Why do unskilled and ignorant souls disturb him who has skill and knowledge? What soul then has skill and knowledge? That which knows beginning and end, and knows the reason which pervades all substance and through all time by fixed periods [revolutions] administers the universe.

33. Soon, very soon, you will be ashes, or a skeleton, and either a name or not even a name; but name is sound and echo, and the things which are much valued in life are empty and rotten and trifling, and [like] little dogs biting one another, and little children quarrelling, laughing, and then straightway weeping. But fidelity and modesty and justice and truth are fled

Up to Olympus from the wide-spread earth.
Hesiod, Works, etc., v. 197.

What then is there which still detains you here? if the objects of sense are easily changed and never stand still, and the organs of perception are dull and easily receive false impressions; and the poor soul itself is an exhalation from blood. But to have good repute amid such a world as this is an empty thing. Why then do you not wait in tranquility for your end, whether it is extinction or removal to another state? And until that time comes, what is sufficient? Why, what else than to venerate the gods and bless them, and to do good to men, and to practice tolerance and self-restraint; but as to everything which is beyond the limits of the poor flesh and breath, to remember that this is neither thine nor in your power.

34. You can pass your life in an equable flow of happiness, if you can go by the right way, and think and act in the right way. These two things are common both to the soul of God and to the soul of man, and to the soul of every rational being, not to be hindered by another; and to hold good to consist in the disposition to justice and the practice of it, and in this to let your desire find its termination.

35. If this is neither my own badness, nor an effect of my own badness, and the commonweal* is not injured, why am I troubled about it? and what is the harm to the commonweal?

36. Do not be carried along inconsiderately by the appearance of things, but give help [to all] according to your ability and their fitness; and if they should have sustained loss in matters which are indifferent, do not imagine this to be a damage. For it is a bad habit. But as the old man, when he went away, asked back his foster-child's top,† remembering that it was a top, so do you in this case also.

When you are calling out on the Rostra, have you forgotten, man, what these things are? Yes; but they are objects of great concern to these people—will you too then be made a fool for these things? I was once a fortunate man, but I lost it, I know not how. But fortunate means that a man has assigned to himself a good fortune; and a good fortune is good disposition of the soul, good emotions, good actions.

_____

* The general welfare of people within a state or community.
† The old man gets his child's lost toy top back to him, even though he knows it's really a very unimportant thing.

READING QUESTIONS

1. Marcus Aurelius asks you to "Think of the universal substance, of which you have a very small portion; and of universal time, of which a short and indivisible interval has been assigned to you; and of that which is fixed by destiny, and how small a part of it you are." Does thinking those thoughts change any of your other thoughts, for example, your thoughts about what matters to you or your thoughts about what is important?

2. Marcus Aurelius writes that, "Things themselves touch not the soul, not in the least degree." What does this mean? What does it imply about our freedom and responsibility?

3. According to Marcus Aurelius, "How easy it is to repel and wipe away every impression which is troublesome or unsuitable, and immediately to be in all tranquility." You might very well disagree. What are some obstacles in your thinking that stand in the way of your achieving Stoic serenity? What statement or idea in the _Meditations_ is most useful for overcoming those obstacles?

3.2 Existentialism: Born Free, Let Me Be Me

Existentialism is a philosophical movement that some prefer to see as an attitude or outlook rather than as a formal philosophy. We regard it as a philosophy of life for our purposes here. Existentialism is difficult to define precisely because there doesn't exist any common body of doctrine to which all Existentialists would subscribe. For example, within the existential movement, you find **atheists** and **theists** (primarily Christian and Jewish), as well as **political conservatives**, **Marxists**, **humanitarians**, at least one **fascist**, and those who are **anti-political**. Some are optimistic, while others tend toward pessimism. Certain Existentialists have emphasized issues of **freedom** in their writing, whereas others have focused on **absurdity** or on the world of the **interpersonal**. To complicate things even further, some philosophers associated with Existentialism predate the use of the term itself, while others simply refuse to be called Existentialists at all. To belong to a "school of thought" and be labeled as a member, or to subordinate one's individuality and adhere to some shared philosophical doctrine, would not be very "existential." You'll understand why shortly.

Methods

Existentialism adopts some **unorthodox methods** of investigation for probing the human condition; consequently, some don't see Existentialism as a legitimate philosophy at all. Existential insights are often best communicated in **aphorisms**, **dialogues**, **parables**, and other **literary forms** such as novels and plays. Poignant existential statements are often found in poetic verse and in visual art, and not necessarily in the context of systematic rational argument and debate. Also, given that prominent Existentialists like **Jean-Paul Sartre** practiced his philosophy in Parisian cafés, far removed from the hallowed halls of academe and the lecture podium of the university professor, many initially regarded Existentialism as little more than a passing fad. The unorthodox existential approach to philosophical inquiry is certainly different from traditional philosophy and often the source of much confusion and bewilderment. Nonetheless, Existentialism remains a useful umbrella term under which it is possible to gather together a number of recurrent themes and philosophical preoccupations. Some basic existential questions pertaining to you include the following: *"What am I to do?" "To what can I commit my life?" "What does my life mean?"*

Philosophers Associated with Existentialism

Søren Kierkegaard (1813–1855) is generally regarded as the father of Existentialism, though elements of existential thinking can be found in the works of earlier writers such as **Michel de Montaigne** (1533–1592) and **Blaise Pascal** (1623–1662). When discussing Existentialism, other notable names certainly come to mind: **Friedrich Nietzsche** (1844–1900), **Karl Jaspers** (1883–1969), **Gabriel Marcel** (1889–1973), and of course **Jean-Paul Sartre** (1905–1980), who coined the term in 1946 in his famous essay, often translated from the French as *Existentialism Is a Humanism*. **Simone de Beauvoir**, lover and colleague of Sartre, was certainly a significant Existentialist too. She critically read and approved many of Sartre's works and became a celebrated writer herself. A noted feminist, she authored *The Second Sex* and *The Ethics of Ambiguity*. **Martin Heidegger**'s (1899–1976) works are often discussed under Existentialism, given that he exerted such an important influence on it. Nevertheless, he expressly indicated that he wished to be disassociated from Sartre.[10] **Albert Camus**, winner of the Nobel Prize for Literature in 1957, is usually tagged with the existentialist label as well, though he always refused it.[11] A good example of existential fiction is his novel *L'Étranger* (translated as *The Stranger* or *The Outsider*). See also **Fyodor Dostoyevsky**'s *Notes from Underground* (1864) and **Franz Kafka**'s *The Trial* (1925) for further examples of existential literary works.

> *"Whatever its ultimate meaning, the universe into which we have been thrown cannot satisfy our reason—let us have the courage to admit it once and for all."*
> GABRIEL MARCEL

Jean-Paul Sartre and Simone de Beauvoir

Jean-Paul Sartre (1905–1980) was a famous—if not the *most* famous—philosopher, novelist, and playwright of the twentieth century. Born in Paris, he spent most of his life there, holding court over French intellectual life for decades.

The so-called father of Existentialism, Sartre's attraction to philosophy began when he was a teenager at prestigious schools. He spent six years of study at the Sorbonne for his *agrégation*, the highly competitive philosophy exam that would launch his academic career as a philosophy teacher. His first attempt, however, was not successful. In 1928, Sartre failed the *agrégation*, coming last in his class. This setback resulted in his meeting Simone de Beauvoir (1908–1986) and the beginning of a celebrated yet unconventional companionship that would last until Sartre's death.

The next time Sartre wrote the *agrégation*, he was awarded first place, de Beauvoir second. Coincidental perhaps but fitting nonetheless, de Beauvoir went on to write a book titled *The Second Sex*, which is arguably the most important work of feminist thought in the last century. In it, the French philosopher and novelist asks the question, "What is woman?" In a similar spirit to Sartre's existentialist claim that "existence precedes essence," de Beauvoir writes that "one is not born, but rather becomes, a woman."

A preeminent existentialist philosopher in her own right, de Beauvoir provided us with a conception of existential ethics, something Sartre never did. So, even though they both greatly emphasized freedom, de Beauvoir paired it with morality, making her own original and important contribution to philosophical research.

Sartre's major philosophical opus is *Being and Nothingness*; his literary works include the novel *Nausea* and the play *No Exit*. Other notable works by de Beauvoir include *Pyrrhus and Cinéas*, *The Mandarins*, *Memoirs of a Dutiful Daughter*, and *America Day by Day*.

Existentialism as a Revolt

If Existentialism is unorthodox in its approach, this is largely because it represents a revolt against **rationality** and **philosophical system-building**. Perhaps one commonality shared by all Existentialists is the belief that human existence cannot be dissected into discrete categories or packaged into some kind of neatly arranged interlocking system. Certainly, Existentialists appreciate the fact that reason and rational inquiry are appropriate to mathematics and the natural sciences, but that such approaches are able to produce only disappointing vague generalities regarding real living persons. If you've ever read about a personality theory in your psychology class, for example, and then asked, "But how does this apply to me?" then you've experienced the existential disappointment referenced here.

As a protest against rationalism and the kinds of elaborate systems found in the works of thinkers such as Plato and **Hegel**, Existentialists argue that the individual self is lost in **abstract universals**. As far back as Plato, many rational philosophers have held the view that everyday experience cannot provide a secure and sound foundation for knowledge. Plato argued that the material world is, in fact, a shadow world of illusion, and that ultimate reality or truth can be found only beyond the experienced spatio-temporal plane in the **realm of forms** (see Section 4.2 on Plato). From the perspective of Platonic rationality, the body is to be held in contempt, since it houses the corrupting emotions and disquieting passions. **Sense Perception** is regarded as untrustworthy, while reason and deductive thinking are prized above all else. Since, for Plato, truth must be universal, immutable, and eternal, and because sense perception is notoriously inaccurate and frequently deceptive, no certainty can be found in the world of everyday experience. It should be viewed with suspicion.

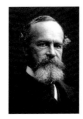

"Probably a crab would be filled with a sense of personal outrage if it could hear us class it without apology as a crustacean, and thus dispose of it. 'I am no such thing,' it would say, 'I am myself, myself alone.'"
WILLIAM JAMES

From an existential perspective, unquestioned adherence to reason and rational inquiry does violence to humanity by obliterating the **uniqueness of individuals** and their **subjective experience**. If you've ever been offended because someone drew conclusions about you based on some kind of broad sociological generalization, then you've experienced first-hand existential violence committed against your uniqueness and individuality. Your upset at being "typed," "pigeon-holed," "classed," "put in a box," or "scientifically figured-out" manifests the same spirit of protest that the Existentialists display toward faith in science and rationality as methods for understanding human existence.

Essence versus Existence

For an Existentialist such as Jean-Paul Sartre, **existence** precedes **essence**. This means that the *experience* of being human, and of having the freedom to choose how we act and to define our purpose, is fundamental. We do not have an inherent identity prior to these choices, and we are not *merely* a product of God's creation or of natural selection, or of the genetic structure we were born with, or of our experiences, training, and education. We were not born perfect, but neither were we born imperfect, stained with original sin. We are not good, nor are we evil by nature. Whatever we are, we are that by choice. To paraphrase Sartre, *we are nothing else but what we make of ourselves*.

The existential universe is very different from the stoic universe we learned about earlier. In the cosmology of the Stoic, we found a reality that is ordered, fated, and purposeful. We are taught by the Stoics to quiet the disturbing passions and to control the emotions in order to live a tranquil life in accordance with nature. Peace of mind is found not by choosing one's role (that is the task of God or the divine *Logos*), but by playing it well without complaint. A certain serenity can be found in the belief that the universe unfolds itself by design, and that whatever happens does so for a reason.

In the atheistic existential universe no such Stoic comfort is to be found. Physical suffering and mental anxiety serve as the origin of human consciousness and become the starting point for existential philosophy. Existentialists deny the *thesis of causal determinism* or *fate*, most clearly where psychological matters are concerned. For instance, traumatic events in your past weren't destined. They don't necessarily "make" you behave in this way or that. What someone said cannot "force" you to become mad, glad, or sad. The values you live by are not written in the sky or somehow indelibly ingrained in your mind from on high. How you respond to what others have said or done is a choice. Whatever has value has it only because you personally bestow worth upon it. In existential reality, nothing is good or bad in itself. Who would make it so?

In a godless universe, everything is permissible, and it is you who are personally responsible for everything you think, say, feel, or do. Since existence precedes essence and there is no creator God to preside over the universe, life is therefore meaningless in itself. Rather than display rational order, life is absurd and chaotic, without purpose or design. Simply put, the universe doesn't make inherent sense. Everything that happens is contingent and unpredictable. Thus, when a particular misfortune befalls you, it's silly to ask "why" it happened or what "meaning" is contained in the event. Being in the wrong place at the wrong time just happens—period. If there's any meaning, it is invented by you, not imposed from above. There are no hidden messages in life that some kind of divine presence transmits to you in times of struggle and adversity. Human beings themselves are the creators of meaning. The lessons of life are self-taught.

In view of the preceding discussion, it should be clear that atheistic Existentialists reject other-worldly religious realms or anything resembling Plato's picture of ultimate reality as perfect, unchanging, and comprising pure essences or forms. Existence is not somehow less real than essence for, in fact, essences don't exist—either within or separate from human reality. The saying, 'existence precedes essence' contains an ironic sense of 'essence': when we make ourselves one way or another, and decide on the natures and values and meanings of externals, they get "essence" only in the sense of receiving characteristics we create and give them. But these are not permanent characteristics: they change if we want them to. The psychological point is that if existence precedes essence, then we as individuals carry the burden of making meaning in life. In itself, human existence is contingent and insecure. There is no "answer" or ultimate meaning to be discovered *out there* somewhere.

> *"No one is born fully-formed: it is through self-experience in the world that we become what we are."*
> PAULO FREIRE

Individuality and Subjective Experience

The belief that systems, universals, and general categories cannot explain the nature of human existence leads Existentialists to emphasize the **uniqueness** of individuals. Though we are human, no two of us are exactly the same. Even identical twins are distinguishable by virtue of their behavioral patterns, differing beliefs, and so on. For Existentialists, the fundamental drive within us is the urge to exist and to be recognized as individuals. By creating a sense of individuality, we find meaning and significance in life. To reduce us to the *cogito* (or thinking thing) of René Descartes is limiting and unperceptive. (For a discussion of Descartes's *cogito*, see Chapter 4.) We are not pure thinkers but existing individuals with passions, commitments, fears, hopes, and dreams. Our existence is full, vital, rich, self-conscious, and something for which we, as individuals, are personally responsible.

As part of its protest against traditional rational philosophy, Existentialism glorifies the individual and subjective experience. It encourages us to go our own ways and to become truly unique individuals. It also cautions us against the dehumanizing influences of modern society. In an age of mass production, mass markets, impersonal bureaucracies, personal subjugation in service to science and technology, and the pressure to follow fads and conform to others' standards and expectations, the **individual** continues to be under attack.

Existentialists would encourage you to resist being swallowed up by the crowd. They advocate that you do not follow the herd or mindlessly go along with the masses. To do so is to rob yourself of your special uniqueness as an individual—a fatal mistake for

Is the Existentialist's preoccupation with individual uniqueness legitimate or merely reflective of some neurotic desire to be considered "special"? Explain why. If the Existentialist is correct that no objective reality exists and that no general statements can be made about human beings, then what are the consequences for morality? Discuss.

living an authentic and genuine lifestyle, the kind in which you express yourself in a personally responsible way. In this regard, E.E. Cummings writes, "*To be nobody but yourself—in a world which is doing its best, night and day, to make you everybody else—means to fight the hardest battle which any human being can fight, and never stop fighting.*"

Existential Freedom

Another major theme of great importance to Existentialists is **freedom of choice**. For Existentialists, to be conscious is to be free. The only thing we're not free about is the choice to be unfree. Even if we wish to follow the totalitarian leader or conform to the crowd, we have still *chosen* to give up our individuality and personal freedom. It seems obvious that coercive circumstances can seriously limit freedom, but for the Existentialist, one is (paradoxically) completely free even under duress.

Let's suppose, for instance, that you are held up at gunpoint by a would-be thief demanding that you surrender your wallet. Whatever you do, the consequences are precariously uncertain. Nonetheless, you still have a choice. You could hand over your wallet or refuse. In a very real example much like this one, an individual was once confronted in the night by a robber but refused to give up his billfold. Fortunately for him, the robber was a coward and ran away at the refusal. Of course, the innocent man could just as easily have been killed. The point is that he was ultimately free to choose. He chose to take a risk and won. (Such risks are generally not recommended!) We must therefore be careful to distinguish between having difficult choices and having no choices at all. Making a free choice at gunpoint is difficult, though not impossible.

Fortunately for most of us, the choices we have to make on a daily basis are not so dangerous. In fact, life sometimes becomes so routine that we're not even aware that we're making choices at all. When the phone rings, we automatically pick it up, or when the light turns red, we stop. Yet in both cases, it's important to note that we do have choices to make. Just because you reflexively and unthinkingly pick up the phone when it rings doesn't mean you have to do so; if you would rather be left alone, you could let it ring forever. If you are in an emergency and rushing to the hospital, you could also choose to run a red light. If securing the health and safety of someone is more important to you than concern about violating a traffic regulation, then you might very well choose to break the law to get to your destination quicker. Of course, if a police officer lacking compassion catches you, you may also be ticketed. Again, the point is that environmental stimuli like red lights and telephone rings don't *cause* your behavior or *determine* you in any way. You are free. Indeed, Sartre suggests that "you are condemned to be free." There is no way out of personal responsibility for your actions. The blame-game is therefore not something you can honestly play. You are personally accountable for everything you do.

In the Existentialist's universe of **possibility** and **contingency**, human freedom is guaranteed. It is the central fact of human existence. The only authentic and genuine way of life becomes, therefore, the one chosen by the individual. Responses, attitudes, purposes, values, feelings, beliefs, and thoughts are consciously or unthinkingly chosen by persons themselves. Saying "I did X because that's the way I was raised," or "You made me mad; that's why I'm screaming," are instances of attempted escapes from personal responsibility and hence from freedom. If you chose not to value what someone said or did, then they couldn't "make" you mad. If you chose to reject what you were taught when growing up, then you wouldn't behave as conditioned. Even emotion is not outside the control of our wills. We are responsible for how we feel and respond to the world. When we are able to make our individual choices with full awareness that nothing else determines them for us, we are then in a position to live with **authenticity**.

One last point to be made about existential freedom involves its relationship to the concept of **negation**. Don't assume that this term implies anything dismissive, evaluative, or pejorative. Rather, put it into the context of existence—what is and what is not. An essential component of existential freedom is the ability to conceive of what is *not* the case, what does not yet exist. If it helps, think of this in contrast with what must be the case, what can*not not* exist.

Social fairness and equality, for example, may not *now* exist between the sexes or among the various ethnic and racial groups living in a particular society, but we can imagine what life would be like if such things did obtain. In fact, by imagining to ourselves what is not now the case, we could commit our lives to working toward making it the case. Unlike purely instinctive organisms that have necessary reactions to stimuli, we can act freely, consciously, and intentionally to realize our visions, hopes, and aspirations. Consciously being able to make the possible a reality is a distinctively human characteristic. It is what makes us human. Thus, while having no escape from freedom in an absurd and contingent world may instill dread in the hearts of some, for others, this same freedom may serve as the impetus for taking personal action and living responsibly. How freedom is viewed is a choice—your choice!

If you agree with Existentialists like Sartre, that to be human is to be free, then an awesome burden of responsibility is placed upon your shoulders. You cannot hide behind excuses and blame others for what you say, do, think, or feel. To do this would require you to live inauthentically, in *bad faith*, to use the existentialist expression. For Existentialists, our intended actions belong exclusively to us. We have not been somehow programmed in advance; nor are we fulfilling some kind of preordained purpose. Nothing can control our attitudes or our will. There is simply nowhere to hide. We are naked and exposed, and the whole world is watching to see how we're going to respond to life's challenges.

Let us now consolidate our learning about the foundations of atheistic Existentialism by turning to an excerpt from Sartre's *Existentialism Is a Humanism*. You can also refer to a discussion of existentialist ethics in Chapter 5, where Friedrich Nietzsche's work is presented.

Jean-Paul Sartre, *Existentialism Is a Humanism*[12]

Sartre originally delivered Existentialism Is a Humanism *as a public lecture at Club Maintenant in Paris in 1945. The following year, Simone de Beauvoir edited the lecture for publication.*[13]

——

PART I

What, then, is "existentialism"?

Most people who use this word would be at a loss to explain what it means. For now that it has become fashionable, people like to call this musician or that painter an "existentialist." A columnist in *Clartés* goes by the pen name "The Existentialist." Indeed, the word is being so loosely applied to so many things that it has come to mean nothing at all. It would appear that, for lack of an avant-garde doctrine analogous to surrealism, those who thrive on the latest scandal or fad have seized upon a philosophy that hardly suits their purpose. The truth is that of all doctrines, this is the least scandalous and the most austere: it is strictly intended for specialists and philosophers. Yet it can be easily defined. What complicates the matter is that there are two kinds of existentialists: on one hand, the Christians, among whom I would include Karl Jaspers and Gabriel Marcel, both professed Catholics; and, on the other, the atheistic existentialists, among whom we should place Heidegger, as well as the French existentialists and myself. What they have in common is simply their belief that existence precedes essence; or, if you prefer, that subjectivity must be our point of departure. What exactly do we mean by that? If we consider a manufactured object, such as a book or a paper knife,* we note that this object was produced by a craftsman who drew his inspiration from a concept: he referred both to the concept of what a paper knife is, and to a known production technique that is a part of that concept and is, by and large, a formula. The paper knife is thus both an object produced in a certain way and one that, on the other hand, serves a definite

purpose. We cannot suppose that a man would produce a paper knife without knowing what purpose it would serve. Let us say, therefore, that the essence of the paper knife—that is, the sum of formulae and properties that enable it to be produced and defined—precedes its existence. Thus the presence before my eyes of that paper knife or book is determined. Here, then, we are viewing the world from a technical standpoint, whereby we can say "production precedes essence."

When we think of God the Creator, we usually conceive of him as a superlative artisan. Whatever doctrine we may be considering, say Descartes's or Leibniz's, we always agree that the will more or less follows understanding, or at the very least accompanies it, so that when God creates he knows exactly what he is creating. Thus the concept of man, in the mind of God, is comparable to the concept of the paper knife in the mind of the manufacturer: God produces man following certain techniques and a conception, just as the craftsman, following a definition and a technique, produces a paper knife. Thus each individual man is the realization of a certain concept within the divine intelligence. Eighteenth-century atheistic philosophers suppressed the idea of God, but not, for all that, the idea that essence precedes existence. We encounter this idea nearly everywhere: in the works of Diderot, Voltaire, and even Kant. Man possesses a human nature; this "human nature," which is the concept of that which is human, is found in all men, which means that each man is a particular example of a universal concept—man. In Kant's works, this universality extends so far as to encompass forest dwellers—man in a state of nature—and the bourgeois,† meaning that they all possess the same basic qualities. Here again, the essence of man precedes his historically primitive existence in nature.

Atheistic existentialism, which I represent, is more consistent. It states that if God does not exist, there is at least one being in whom existence precedes essence—a being whose existence comes before its essence, a being who exists before he can be defined by any concept of

---

* A knife designed for cutting the pages of a book, necessary then for reading French publications.

† The contemporary conformist middle-class member.

it. That being is man, or, as Heidegger put it, the human reality. What do we mean here by "existence precedes essence"? We mean that man first exists: he materializes in the world, encounters himself, and only afterward defines himself. If man as existentialists conceive of him cannot be defined, it is because to begin with he is nothing. He will not be anything until later, and then he will be what he makes of himself. Thus, there is no human nature since there is no God to conceive of it. Man is not only that which he conceives himself to be, but that which he wills himself to be, and since he conceives of himself only after he exists, just as he wills himself to be after being thrown into existence, man is nothing other than what he makes of himself. This is the first principle of existentialism.

It is also what is referred to as "subjectivity," the very word used as a reproach against us. But what do we mean by that, if not that man has more dignity than a stone or a table? What we mean to say is that man first exists; that is, that man primarily exists—that man is, before all else, something that projects itself into a future, and is conscious of doing so. Man is indeed a project that has a subjective existence, rather unlike that of a patch of moss, a spreading fungus, or a cauliflower. Prior to that projection of the self, nothing exists, not even in divine intelligence, and man shall attain existence only when he is what he projects himself to be—not what he would like to be. What we usually understand by "will" is a conscious decision that most of us take after we have made ourselves what we are. I may want to join a party, write a book, or get married—but all of that is only a manifestation of an earlier and more spontaneous choice than what is known as "will." If, however, existence truly does precede essence, man is responsible for what he is. Thus, the first effect of existentialism is to make every man conscious of what he is, and to make him solely responsible for his own existence. And when we say that man is responsible for himself, we do not mean that he is responsible only for his own individuality, but that he is responsible for all men.

The word "subjectivism" has two possible interpretations, and our opponents play with both of them, at our expense. Subjectivism means, on the one hand, the freedom of the individual subject to choose what he will be, and, on the other, man's inability to transcend human subjectivity. The fundamental meaning of existentialism resides in the latter. When we say that man chooses himself, not only do we mean that each of us must choose himself, but also that in choosing himself, he is choosing for all men. In fact, in creating the man each of us wills ourselves to be, there is not a single one of our actions that does not at the same time create an image of man as we think he ought to be. Choosing to be this or that is to affirm at the same time the value of what we choose, because we can never choose evil. We always choose the good, and nothing can be good for any of us unless it is good for all. If, moreover, existence precedes essence and we will to exist at the same time as we fashion our image, that image is valid for all and for our whole era. Our responsibility is thus much greater than we might have supposed, because it concerns all mankind. If I am a worker and I choose to join a Christian trade union rather than to become a Communist, and if, by that membership, I choose to signify that resignation is, after all, the most suitable solution for man, and that the kingdom of man is not on this earth, I am not committing myself alone—I am choosing to be resigned on behalf of all—consequently my action commits all mankind. Or, to use a more personal example, if I decide to marry and have children—granted such a marriage proceeds solely from my own circumstances, my passion, or my desire—I am nonetheless committing not only myself, but all of humanity, to the practice of monogamy. I am therefore responsible for myself and for everyone else, and I am fashioning a certain image of man as I choose him to be. In choosing myself, I choose man.

READING QUESTIONS

1. Does the example of the paper-cutter help you understand what existentialism is not and, in contrast, what it is? If so, how? If not, why not?

2. In a universe where "existence precedes essence," what are we responsible for? How does that responsibility reflect our freedom? How does it also establish our limitations?

3.3 The Meaning of Life

Our trek into the philosophical domain began in this chapter with an expansive view of an ordered Stoic universe. We found security and peace of mind in the knowledge that nothing that happens is random or out of place. We also learned how, in the Stoic's world, the divine *Logos* is immanent in all physical objects and events. We saw how things happen for a reason which, in the end, is for the best. Fate, which determines life, and Providence, which assures us it's good, are but different aspects of God. The moral lesson we were able to take away from this Stoic belief is that we should not balk at what life has to offer, but rather adopt an attitude of courageous acceptance, assenting to reality as an expression of God's will. There is a teleological purpose to all that happens.

No sooner did we gain some peaceful Stoic reassurance about the universe and our place in it, when the Existentialists exploded our cosmic complacency to bits. The atheist Sartre put "existence before essence," denying human beings a providential Godhead who would create, benevolently control, and look after things in the world. Suddenly, life became horribly confused in a whirlwind of existential doubt, chaos, and absurdity. There was no divine mission to complete, neither was there an ultimate meaning inherent in human experience for us to discover and progress toward. We were left aimless. No ultimate reason could be provided for why things happened as they did and not in some other fashion. No objective standard could be used to assure us that we were on the right track or that the ultimate purpose of life could be found. It felt as if we were thrown into some kind of dark abyss or horrifying maelstrom of meaninglessness, without any destiny or any real reason for being. Our Stoic calm was abruptly replaced by a dreadful existential anxiety resulting from the realization that we are condemned to be free. No wonder Sartre concluded that freedom is like a prison sentence—with no chance of parole until we die, I might add!

Anxiety and dread are thus likely to arise as we look at the dark sky of atheistic existential nothingness and infinite possibility. We are but mere specks in a godless universe and we must choose our futures without even so much as a psychological north star to guide us on our journeys. Anything is possible, and this horrifies us. What is particularly horrifying is the fact that, without God to structure reality, all possibility of objective standards blows away like dust in the wind. Without a divine designer determining the natures of things, there is no way things absolutely should be rather than not, no path we ought to take rather than not. Existence precedes essence; purpose is imposed by us. Life is meaningless unto itself.

"The only thing that makes life possible is permanent, intolerable uncertainty: not knowing what comes next."
URSULA K. LE GUIN

Susan Wolf

Susan Wolf (b. 1952) is currently the Edna J. Koury Distinguished Professor of Philosophy at the University of North Carolina at Chapel Hill. Previously, she taught at Johns Hopkins University (1986–2002), the University of Maryland (1981–86), and at Harvard University (1978–81).

During her own time as a university student, Wolf started out studying mathematics, and eventually her study of logic led her to philosophy. Although she entered graduate school with the intention to pursue philosophy with a specialization in logic, she ended up drawn to the study of ethics instead.[14] Now a well-regarded philosopher of ethics, Wolf's work focuses on topics that deal with freedom, responsibility, morality, value, and love.

Wolf explores these topics with thoughtful consideration of both the moral and non-moral aspects of a good human life. On that distinction, she opens her essay "Moral Saints" with this striking and provocative assertion: "I don't know whether there are any moral saints. But if there are, I am glad that neither I nor those about whom I care most are among them."[15] Wolf's inspiration for that essay was her realization that there were aspects of herself that she liked and took pride in

that nonetheless were in tension with various ideals of moral perfection.[16] From there, she became interested in the place moral *and* non-moral virtues should have in our lives.

In her work on meaningfulness, Wolf emphasizes the non-moral reasons that make life valuable and worth living, writing, "Meaning arises from living objects worthy of love and engaging with them in a positive way."[17] This sentence appears in Wolf's book *Meaning in Life and Why It Matters*. With respect to this book, one reviewer writes, "Susan Wolf is one of the clearest, most thoughtful, and most incisively elegant writers in contemporary ethics. She has an uncanny knack for putting her finger on important points and expressing them in ways that capture the imagination. In this book, she develops her ideas about meaningfulness in life with considerable subtlety, creating a work of genuine depth and importance."[18]

A prolific author, her other works include her book of essays, *The Variety of Values: Essays on Morality, Meaning, and Love*; the co-edited book, with Christopher Grau, *Understanding Love: Philosophy, Film, and Fiction*; and her book on problems of responsibility and freedom, *Freedom within Reason*.

Meaningful Lives

All of this might seem very depressing and anxiety producing. You might have started your philosophical journey expecting to learn what the meaning of life is only now to lament that atheistic Existentialism appears to undo any attempt at an ultimate answer. But don't despair. As present-day philosopher Susan Wolf tries to show us in her inspiring essay, "The Meanings of Lives," life can have meaning *in* it even if there is no meaning *to* life as such.[19]

To appreciate Wolf's distinction between meaning *in* life and meaning *to* life, first consider the question, "What is the meaning of life?" You have probably heard that question before or maybe you have thought about it and tried to answer it. But what exactly is the question even asking?

Wolf points out that we typically treat the question "What is the meaning of life?" as a question about the purpose of life. In that case, the standard response among many philosophers is that "it all depends on God": if God exists, then it might be true that life has a divinely-determined purpose and, hence, meaning; however, if God does not exist, then arguably life has no meaning. As the atheistic Existentialist claims, in the absence of a Creator who planned this universe with a purpose in mind, there is no ultimate point to life as a whole. Life, as such, does not have an objective meaning. Indeed, by this perspective, asking what the objective meaning of life is doesn't even make sense to begin with, since there is no such meaning to be found. All to say that the standard philosophical view is that the question of life's meaning gives way to the even bigger question of God's existence.

Wolf, however, does not try to settle the issue of life's meaning by arguing for or against God's existence. Instead, she points out that many people continue to care about meaning and search for meaning against the atheistic backdrop of a universe without God. That makes sense, according to Wolf. Specifically, it makes sense to inquire into meaning in a Godless universe if we understand the question "What is the meaning of life?" as a question about *what makes life meaningful* rather than *what is the purpose of life*. Wolf argues that while there may be no purpose to being alive, life's meaningfulness is a separate issue that can be assessed on its own. As such, even if the universe is nothing but a network of purposeless physical processes, it's entirely appropriate, according to Wolf, to want and seek meaningful lives for ourselves or be disappointed if we realize that we're living our lives without meaning. The attitudes are intelligible because having meaning in life is not the same as there being meaning to life. In short, *life can have meaningfulness in it without any meaning to it*.

To arrive at her account of what a meaningful life is, Wolf has us think of different types of lives that are *not* meaningful: *a life of* **passive disengagement**, *of frivolous activities*, *of pointless preoccupation*, *of failed projects*. Their meaninglessness is not because there is no God-ordained purpose to these lives and it's not because there is no reason why these lives exist at all. Rather, it is because these meaning*less* lives are lived in ways that lack what other lives—meaning*ful* lives—have in them. In particular, they lack the **active engagement**, *success*, and *positively valuable projects* that meaningful lives have.

Putting all of that together, a **meaningful life**, according to Wolf, is a life that is actively and at least somewhat successfully engaged in one or more projects of *positive objective value*, as opposed to projects of subjective value. Among other things, that means that your subjective impressions or feelings about a project are not what makes it meaningful. For Wolf, one might be perfectly happy and yet live a meaningless life.

To think otherwise is to overestimate the importance of, well, *you*. It is to treat yourself as the center of the universe and the source of all value, when in fact you

THINKING ABOUT YOUR THINKING

Think of two objects, one of which you believe to be better than the other. For example, maybe you think a tub of chocolate ice cream is better than one of strawberry; or maybe you think the Great Pyramid of Giza is better than the Eiffel Tower; or that an iPhone is better than an Android phone. *Why* do you think that the better object is better? *Why* do you think that the worse object is worse? Try to articulate your reasons, as if you had to justify your preference to someone else. *What* values underlie your preference? *Why* do you hold those values?

Now, do the same exercise, but instead of thinking about objects, think about activities. Identify one activity that you think is better than another. Why is it better? If you were to compare both of those activities to the activity of philosophizing, how would they rank?

"... it was only by hitching my wagon to something larger than myself that I was ultimately able to locate a community and purpose for my life."
BARACK OBAMA

hold no such privileged position. It is to fail to acknowledge that you are no more than a small speck in a vast universe. What is more, there is so much more worth caring about in that universe than *you*.

As Wolf sees it, the universe is vast and filled with **non-subjective values**. These are the objects, events, activities, and features of the world that have their source of value in something other than us and, arguably, even other than God. In other words, these *objective values are worthwhile regardless of whether or not someone gives them value*. They are meaningful despite any preferences, feelings, or attitudes a particular someone might have, and we lead meaningful lives when we actively and successful engage with them.

Wolf's main point is that one can have meaningfulness *in* one's life despite the absence of an overall meaning *to* life. To actively and successfully engage in accordance with objective values, and in recognition of the fact of your own "speckness" or insignificance, is to live life meaningfully. As such, **meaningfulness** involves getting over ourselves and any egoistic concern for subjectively-sourced values that we might have. Only then would we be engaging in the kinds of positive projects that factor into meaningful lives. Viktor Frankl calls this a process of **self-transcendence**. Similar to Wolf, Frankl believes that in order to find meaning, we have to engage in that process of looking beyond our personal interests and invest ourselves in something bigger. We'll learn more about Frankl shortly, but first let us read a brief passage by Susan Wolf.

Susan Wolf, "The Meanings of Lives"[20]

"The Meanings of Lives" is one of many important essays by American philosopher Susan Wolf (b. 1952). Originally published in 2007, it also appears in Wolf's book of essays titled The Variety of Values: Essays on Morality, Meaning, and Love *(2015).*

———

What does meaningfulness in life amount to? It may be easier to make progress by focusing on what we want to avoid. In that spirit, let me offer some paradigms, not of meaning*ful* but of meaning*less* lives.

For me, the idea of a meaningless life is most clearly and effectively embodied in the image of a person who spends day after day, or night after night, in front of a television set, drinking beer and watching situation comedies. Not that I have anything against television or beer. Still the image, understood as an image of a person whose life is lived in hazy passivity, a life lived at a not unpleasant level of consciousness, but unconnected to anyone or anything, going nowhere, achieving nothing—is, I submit, as strong an image of a meaningless life as there can be. Call this case The Blob.

If any life, any human life, is meaningless, the Blob's life is. But this doesn't mean that any meaningless life must be, in all important respects, like the Blob's. There are other paradigms that highlight by their absences other elements of meaningfulness.

In contrast to the Blob's passivity, for example, we may imagine a life full of activity, but silly or decadent or useless activity. (And again, I have nothing against silly activity, but only against a life that is wholly occupied with it.) We may imagine, for example, one of the idle rich who flits about, fighting off boredom, moving from one amusement to another. She shops, she travels, she eats at expensive restaurants, she works out with her personal trainer.

Curiously, one might also take a very un-idle rich person to epitomize a meaningless life in a slightly different way. Consider, for example, the corporate executive who works twelve-hour, seven-day weeks, suffering great stress, for the sole purpose of the accumulation of personal wealth. Related to this perhaps is David Wiggins's example of the pig farmer who buys more land to grow more corn to feed more pigs to buy more land to grow more corn to feed more pigs.[21]

These last three cases of the idle rich, the corporate executive, and the pig farmer are in some ways very different, but they all share at least this feature: They can all be characterized as lives whose dominant activities seem pointless, useless, or empty. Classify these cases under the heading Useless.

A somewhat different and I think more controversial sort of case to consider involves someone who is engaged, even dedicated, to a project that is ultimately revealed as bankrupt, not because the person's values are shallow or misguided, but because the project fails. The person may go literally bankrupt: For example, a man may devote his life to creating and building up a company to hand over to his children, but the item his company manufactures is rendered obsolete by technology shortly before his planned retirement. Or consider a scientist whose life's work is rendered useless by the announcement of a medical breakthrough just weeks before his own research would have yielded the same results. Perhaps more poignantly, imagine a woman whose life is centered around a relationship that turns out to be a fraud. Cases that fit this mold we may categorize under the heading Bankrupt.

The classification of this third sort of case as an exemplification of meaninglessness may meet more resistance than the classification of the earlier two. Perhaps these lives should not be considered meaningless after all. Nonetheless, these are cases in which it is not surprising that an argument of some sort is needed—it is not unnatural or silly that the subjects of these lives should entertain the thought that their lives have been meaningless. Even if they are wrong, the fact that their thoughts are not, so to speak, out of order, is a useful datum. So, of course, would be the sort of thing one would say to convince them, or ourselves, that these thoughts are ultimately mistaken.

If the cases I have sketched capture our images of meaninglessness more or less accurately, they provide clues to what a positive case of a meaningful life must contain. In contrast to the Blob's passivity, a person who lives a meaningful life must be actively engaged. But, as the Useless cases teach us, it will not do to be engaged in just anything, for any reason or with any goal—one must be engaged in a project or projects that have some positive value, and in some way that is nonaccidentally related to what gives them value. Finally, in order to avoid Bankruptcy, it seems necessary that one's activities be at least to some degree successful (though it may not be easy to determine what counts as the right kind or degree of success). Putting these criteria together, we get a proposal for what it is to live a meaningful life: A meaningful life is one that is actively and at least somewhat successfully engaged in a project (or projects) of positive value.

Several remarks are needed to qualify and refine this proposal. First, the use of the word "project" is not ideal: It is too suggestive of a finite, determinate task, something one takes on and, if all goes well, completes. Among the things that come to mind as projects are certain kinds of hobbies or careers, or rather, specific tasks that fall within the sphere of such hobbies or careers: things that can be seen as accomplishments, like the producing of a proof or a poem or a pudding, the organizing of a union or a high school band. Although such activities are among the things that seem intuitively to contribute to the meaningfulness of people's lives, there are other forms of meaningfulness that are less directed, and less oriented to demonstrable achievement, and we should not let the use of the word "project" distort or deny the potential of these things to give meaningfulness to life. Relationships, in particular, seem at best awkwardly described as projects. Rarely does one deliberately take them on and, in some cases, one doesn't even have to work at them—one may just have them and live, as it were, within them. Moreover, many of the activities that are naturally described as projects—coaching a school soccer team, planning a surprise party, reviewing an article for a journal—have the meaning they do for us only because of their place in the non-projectlike relationships in which we are enmeshed and with which we identify. In proposing that a meaningful life is a life actively engaged in projects, then, I mean to use "projects" in an unusually broad sense, to encompass not only goal-directed tasks but other sorts of ongoing activities and involvements as well.

Second, the suggestion that a meaningful life should be "actively engaged" in projects should be understood in a way that recognizes and embraces the connotations of "engagement." Although the idea that a meaningful life requires activity was introduced by contrast to the life of the ultra-passive Blob, we should note that meaning involves more than mere, literal activity. The alienated housewife, presumably, is active all the time—she buys groceries and fixes meals, cleans the house, does the laundry, chauffeurs the children from school to soccer to ballet, arranges doctors' appointments and babysitters. What makes her life insufficiently meaningful is that her heart, so to speak, isn't in these activities. She does not identify with what she is doing—she does not embrace her roles as wife, mother, and homemaker as expressive of who she is and wants to be. We may capture her alienated condition by saying that though she is active, she is not actively engaged. (She is, one might say, just going through the motions.) In characterizing a meaningful life, then, it is worth stressing that living such a life is not just a matter of having projects (broadly construed) and actively and somewhat successfully getting through them. The projects must engage the person whose life it is. Ideally, she would proudly and happily embrace them, as constituting at least part of what her life is about.*

Finally, we must say more about the proposal's most blatantly problematic condition—viz., that the projects engagement with which can contribute to a meaningful life must be projects "of positive value." The claim is that meaningful lives must be engaged in projects of positive value—but who is to decide which projects have positive value, or even to guarantee that there is such a thing?

---

* [Wolf's footnote] It seems to me there is a further condition or qualification on what constitutes a meaningful life, though it does not fit gracefully into the definition I have proposed, and is somewhat peripheral to the focus of this essay: Namely, the projects that contribute to a meaningful life must be of significant duration, and contribute to the unity of the life or of a significant stage of it. A person who is always engaged in some valuable project or other, but whose projects don't express any underlying core of interest and value is not, at least, a paradigm of someone whose *life* is meaningful. Here perhaps there is something illuminating in making analogies to other uses of "meaning," for what is at issue here has to do with there being a basis for "making sense" of the life, of being able to see it as a narrative.

I would urge that we leave the phrase as unspecific as possible in all but one respect. We do not want to build a theory of positive value into our conception of meaningfulness. As a proposal that aims to capture what most people mean by a meaningful life, what we want is a concept that "tracks" whatever we think of as having positive value. This allows us to explain at least some divergent intuitions about meaningfulness in terms of divergent intuitions or beliefs about what has positive value, with the implication that if one is wrong about what has positive value, one will also be wrong about what contributes to a meaningful life. (Thus, a person who finds little to admire in sports—who finds ridiculous, for example, the sight of grown men trying to knock a little ball into a hole with a club, will find relatively little potential for meaning in the life of an avid golfer; a person who places little stock in esoteric intellectual pursuits will be puzzled by someone who strains to write, much less read, a lot of books on supervenience.)

The exception I would make to this otherwise maximally tolerant interpretation of the idea of positive value is that we exclude merely subjective value as a suitable interpretation of the phrase.

It will not do to allow that a meaningful life is a life involved in projects that seem to have positive value from the perspective of the one who lives it. Allowing this would have the effect of erasing the distinctiveness of our interest in meaningfulness; it would blur or remove the difference between an interest in living a meaningful life and an interest in living a life that feels or seems meaningful. That these interests are distinct, and that the former is not merely instrumental to the latter can be seen by reflecting on a certain way the wish or the need for meaning in one's life may make itself felt. What I have in mind is the possibility of a kind of epiphany, in which one wakes up—literally or figuratively—to the recognition that one's life to date has been meaningless. Such an experience would be nearly unintelligible if a lack of meaning were to be understood as a lack of a certain kind of subjective impression. One can hardly understand the idea of waking up to the thought that one's life to date has seemed meaningless. To the contrary, it may be precisely because one did not realize the emptiness of one's projects or the shallowness of one's values until that moment that the experience I am imagining has the poignancy it does. It is the sort of experience that one might describe in terms of scales falling from one's eyes. And the yearning for meaningfulness, the impulse to do something about it, will not be satisfied (though it may be eliminated) by putting the scales back on, so to speak. If one suspects that the life one has been living is meaningless, one will not bring meaning to it by getting therapy or taking a pill that, without changing one's life in any other way, makes one believe that one's life has meaning.

To care that one's life is meaningful, then, is, according to my proposal, to care that one's life is actively and at least somewhat successfully engaged in projects (understanding this term broadly) that not just seem to have positive value, but that really do have it. To care that one's life be meaningful, in other words, is in part to care that what one does with one's life is, to pardon the expression, at least somewhat objectively good....

READING QUESTIONS

1. For Wolf, how do her examples of meaningless lives fail to be meaningful lives? Do you agree with her assessment that the lives in the examples are in fact meaningless? Compare and contrast your own ideas about what a meaningful life is with Wolf's account of meaningfulness.

2. Reflecting on Wolf's analysis of meaningfulness in life, consider whether or not a philosophical life is a meaningful life. What thoughts come to your mind about philosophy and value?

Viktor Frankl and the Will-to-Meaning

Viktor Frankl

Like Susan Wolf, the late Viktor Frankl, a noted psychiatrist, was also very much interested in the notion of meaning. In formulating his views on it, he adopted a number of existential insights and incorporated them into a form of psychological counseling called **logotherapy**. Consistent with the Stoics, he was able to see the overlap between psychological health and personal philosophy. During his lifetime of work, Frankl was able to identify a kind of spiritual malaise prevalent in contemporary society. He called it the **existential vacuum**.

According to Frankl, we are all born with a fundamental need to make sense of the world, and we manifest this need in a *will-to-meaning*. Unfortunately, this basic need is often frustrated or left unsatisfied, with the result that we begin to suffer from a type of existential frustration. If this existential frustration is constant and excessive, then what results is a new type of psychological disturbance labeled **noögenic neurosis.***

Frankl believed that meaninglessness comes essentially from a couple of sources. To begin with, unlike other animals, we are not governed by drives and instincts. Evolutionary biology has seen to it that we can, as autonomous beings, override biological urges. Therefore, biology no longer tells us what we *must do*. Secondly, in contrast to earlier times, conventions and traditional values relating to authority and the nuclear family are on the wane. What was once unquestionably valued is now oftentimes viewed with doubt and skepticism. Moral guidelines and acceptable practices are no longer clear. Therefore, we no longer know for sure what we *should do*.

So, not knowing what we must do (by force of instinct), nor knowing what we should do (according to traditional values and norms), we no longer know what we wish to do or what is truly rewarding and meaningful for us in life. The result is that we fall prey to the existential vacuum, feeling a sense of emptiness and futility.

> *"We must not wish for the disappearance of our troubles but for the grace to transform them."*
> SIMONE WEIL

To remedy the existential vacuum, Frankl recommends that we get beyond ourselves through a process of *self-transcendence*. He suggests we look for meaning outside of our petty egoistic preoccupations. For him, meaning is found in *love*, *work*, and potentially, though not necessarily, through *suffering*. It is when we invest ourselves in something *other than ourselves* that we find meaning. We all need a mission in life. By serving a cause greater than ourselves or by loving another, we can live a fulfilling life. Also, by overcoming misfortune or illness in our own unique style, we can lend dignity to life and transform any tragedy into a personal triumph. As Frankl points out, no animal besides the human can do this. Rather than live as if we were personally entitled to happiness, Frankl says, "man should not ask what he may expect from life, but rather understand that life expects something from him."

At this point in the discussion on meaning, you might think, unlike Frankl, that your *non-self-transcendent* egoistic preoccupations are far from petty. Perhaps you disagree as well with Wolf as to what kinds of projects are truly meaningful. In particular, you might take issue with her position that living a life solely devoted to your subjective happiness is a meaningless way to live. Instead, you might think that things outside of

---

* This is a kind of "existential" disorder, stemming from the lack of a sense of meaning in one's life.

you are not worth caring about because your happiness is all that really matters. You may have even read Wolf's description of the person who throws her wealth at amusing and pleasurable things and thought that it is far from a meaning*less* life. You may have thought it is the epitome of a meaning*ful* life. If so, you may have a personal philosophy of life that resembles the hedonistic worldview that we will turn to in the next section. In that case, if it pleases you, read on!

3.4 Hedonism: Pleasure Is the Measure

The third philosophy of life we'll cover in this chapter is called **hedonism**. Quite likely, you already have a vague familiarity with it. In fact, a cursory glance at popular culture might easily lead you to conclude that hedonism is the prevailing philosophy of the day, if not the last six or seven decades—from the post-World War II period until now. Before we get a more technical and detailed understanding of what philosophical hedonism entails, let's begin by defining it broadly as the doctrine that pleasure is worth pursuing and that, in the end, *pleasure is the ultimate goal of life*.

"The achievement of his own happiness is man's highest moral purpose."
AYN RAND

Whether or not you are a hedonist yourself, it's difficult to deny that vast amounts of time, energy, and money are spent on the pursuit of pleasure. Theme parks across the nation are visited annually by millions with the express purpose of having fun and seeking thrills. Millions more attend sporting events to cheer on their favorite teams. Race tracks and gambling casinos, not to mention state and provincial lotteries, hold out the hope that you too could win large sums of money and buy anything you want, making your life much happier than presumably it is right now. Travel agents, as well, hold out the promise of pleasure and excitement by showing you pictures of exotic vacation destinations, sumptuous meals, and luxurious hotel rooms that promise pleasure and relaxation.

On this note, many people say that they live for weekends, a time when work ends and the fun begins. Others fantasize about their early retirement and the prospect of endless hours on the golf course or at the beach, doing nothing but soaking up the mid-day sun. In a humorous vein, you often hear fun-loving adults who joke about the time of death, saying, "The one with the most toys wins!" Others find the greatest pleasure in sexual activity, in cultivating friendships, or in shopping for clothes and luxury items. Surely, all this pervasive and frenetic pursuit of pleasure points to our widespread hedonistic tendencies. What you may not know, however, is that hedonists have existed for centuries and have had much to say on the subject of pursuing pleasure as the ultimate end of life.

Psychological versus Ethical Hedonism

For purposes of philosophical understanding, it is important to note that there are two basic types of hedonism: psychological and ethical. **Psychological hedonism** is a motivational theory. It explains *why* we do the things we do. According to the psychological hedonist, actions and desires are determined by their pleasure-producing properties. People are motivated to produce one state of affairs over another if, and only if, they think it will be more pleasant, or less unpleasant, for themselves. Psychological hedonism posits that people wish to reduce and, if possible, to eliminate pain and displeasure as much as they want to give rise to its opposite. American philosopher Richard Brandt describes this concept of psychological hedonism as the "goal is pleasure" theory.[22]

By contrast to psychological hedonism, **ethical hedonism** is not a motivational theory or explanation of why we value or want the things we do. Rather, ethical hedonism is a *moral theory* that asserts that if you don't pursue pleasure in life, you should. It's wrong not to.

From the perspective of ethical hedonism, pleasure is the only thing that is *intrinsically valuable*—that is, valuable in itself. A corollary to this idea is the proposition that only displeasure is intrinsically undesirable, or undesirable in itself. In whatever we do, we should always strive to create states of affairs that produce pleasure and reduce pain or displeasure. If what you're doing right now (namely reading) is painful, then you should stop. However, if failing your philosophy course would cause more pain than the pain of reading on, then you should continue.

Ethical hedonism, understood as a theory of value and a moral prescription for living, has been defended by a long line of distinguished philosophers from the early Greeks to the present. Some see pleasure as ethical egoists, arguing that pleasure should be maximized for oneself. Others have been more altruistic in their hedonism, arguing that the right thing to do is to maximize the pleasure or happiness of the greatest number of people.

Aristippus of Cyrene

Aristippus (430–350 BCE) was the first Western philosopher we know of to make a direct and uncompromising statement of hedonism. Originally living in Cyrene, a town in what is now Libya in North Africa, he traveled to Athens and became a close friend of Socrates. Like his friend, he was interested almost exclusively in practical ethics, the end of which, Aristippus believed, is the enjoyment of present pleasures.

After spending a number of years in Aegina, Aristippus relocated to the court of Dionysius of Syracuse where, from 389 to 388 BCE, he earned his living teaching and writing. At the court, he also came into contact with Plato. Eventually, Aristippus returned to his home in Cyrene, where he opened his own school of philosophy, promoting what we now call **Cyrenaic hedonism**, named after his hometown. Unfortunately, his writings have been lost, and only lists of his works remain. Nonetheless, a number of his hedonistic ideas have survived and immortalized Aristippus, making him relevant for us even today.

The ideas of Aristippus can be summarized as a number of basic tenets. (Consider whether you agree with any of them.) First, according to Aristippus, *pleasure is the principal motive for living*. **Pleasure** is always to be considered good, regardless of where it originates. Second, no *qualitative* distinctions can be made among pleasures themselves. **Intensity** is the only criterion that can be used to determine which action or state of affairs is best. Those things producing the greatest or most intense pleasure should be preferred. However, since physical, sensory pleasures are more intense than mental or emotional ones, they become, for Aristippus, the best of all. Pursuing physical, sensory pleasure is therefore a higher good than the pursuit of knowledge, goodness, or truth.

Third, Aristippus contends that pleasure contributes greatly to the **meaning of life**. He recommends that we follow our natural desires without guilt or apology. Our mission in life is to learn how to enjoy ourselves most fully. Through the pursuit of sensory pleasures we can make our individual lives exciting, dynamic, and worth living. Don't take this to mean that Aristippus suggested that we should become enslaved by our cravings and appetites. He is not implying this at all. Rather, he advocates *Socratic self-control*, which he interpreted not as self-denial, but as rational control over pleasure, not slavery to it. For Aristippus, no pleasure or personal enjoyment can be wrong. No passion is evil in itself. Pleasures are misguided or sick only when we lose control and are victimized by them. Loss of self-control can lead to less pleasure in the long run, so self-restraint can sometimes be necessary.

A key element of Cyrenaic hedonism was the character example of Aristippus himself. Superimposed on Socratic self-control and freedom from debilitating desires was an uninhibited *capacity for enjoyment*. Aristippus could revel in luxury or be content with the simplest enjoyments, choosing each as he deemed fit and as the circumstances demanded. For Aristippus, since all acts were indifferent except in their capacity to provide immediate pleasure, the science of life translated into a calculated adaptation of the self to one's circumstances, along with the ability to use people and situations for self-gratification.

Another tenet of Cyrenaic hedonism is that **actual pleasures** are more desirable than **potential pleasures**. Some people deny pleasures to themselves now in hopes of gaining greater pleasures later on. Cyrenaics do not recommend such a strategy. You may deprive yourself now and save an entire lifetime to enjoy your retirement, for example, only to die shortly after you finish work. You may sacrifice or give up things now for promises of future rewards, only to find those promises empty and misleading. Furthermore, it's possible that you could change your mind and no longer want what you worked so long and so hard to achieve, once you get it. In this case, disappointment and regret are surely to follow. Thus, it is better to enjoy yourself today than to dream of achieving pleasurable rewards in the future.

The notion that all pleasures are equal and that they differ only in intensity points to the subjective element in Cyrenaic hedonism. Since pleasures cannot be objectively compared as better or worse, if I like watching cat videos on YouTube more than reading Shakespeare, then watching those videos is the higher good—for me. If you feel the reverse, that is better, for you. *The individual becomes the measure of pleasure.*

A last point to be made about Cyrenaic hedonism involves participation in society. According to Aristippus, participation in public life gives rise to avoidable hassles. Involved citizenship is almost certain to interfere with one's pursuit of pleasure. To remain free and detached from sociopolitical entanglements was therefore good, so that the individual could fulfill his or her ultimate obligation, namely, to enjoy every moment in life.

Epicurus

Epicureanism is another expression of hedonistic philosophy given form and substance by its originator, **Epicurus** (341–270 BCE), after whom it was obviously named. Epicurus was born in Samos in Asia Minor. He was a prolific writer, having produced over 300 works, most of which are lost today. Fortunately, **Diogenes Laertius** provides us with summaries of Epicurean doctrine. The Latin poet **Lucretius** also expresses many Epicurean ideas in his poem *De Rerum Natura* (*On the Nature of Things*). Sayings of Epicurus are found as well in the works of **Seneca** and **Cicero**.

"Pleasure is the absence of pain in the body and trouble in the soul."
EPICURUS

Epicurus

Epicurus chose to focus his attention on ethics, considering mathematics and all purely scientific pursuits as essentially useless, given that such studies have little connection with the conduct of everyday life. Though Epicurus studied with followers of **Plato** and **Aristotle**, he rejected both in the end as overly theoretical and irrelevant when it comes to the practical concerns of daily living. In reaction to both Plato and Aristotle, as well as to the Stoics, who had all set up their own schools of philosophy, so too did Epicurus in 306 BCE. He called his school **The Garden**, which was very appropriate given its secluded surroundings in Athens.

The Garden served as a retreat from the sociopolitical and philosophical turmoil of Athens. Everyone was welcome at The Garden and was treated equally. Epicurus admitted men, women, courtesans, slaves, and aristocrats, making no distinctions among people based on social status, gender, or race—a very progressive policy for the thinking and values of the day. The Garden developed a reputation not only for its operating philosophy, but also for its good living and pleasant social surroundings.

Disciples of Epicurus, called Epicureans, actively competed with other philosophers for the hearts and minds of followers. They ventured out into the great centers of the eastern Mediterranean to establish new communities modeled after The Garden. Epicureanism even took hold in the Roman Empire, where it reached its height of influence from 60 to 30 BCE.

Today, calling someone an 'Epicurean' means something different from what Epicurus actually believed in; it now normally refers to the *aesthete*—someone who lives a life devoted to the pursuit of beauty, physical pleasures, and the expression of discriminating and exquisite taste. Eating exotic foods, surrounding oneself with beautiful things, wearing only the finest clothes, and traveling to remote and exclusive destinations are often thought of as expressions of Epicureanism. The fact is that all of these things are more akin to Cyrenaic hedonism—not exactly what Epicurus had in mind.

Momentary versus Enduring Pleasures

To appreciate the pleasures that Epicurus would actually have us seek, it is first necessary to distinguish between **momentary pleasures** and **enduring pleasures**. Although Epicurus grants that all pleasure is good and all pain is evil, it's not the case that pleasure should always be chosen over painful or unpleasant activities. As Epicurus says, "Every pleasure is therefore good on account of its own nature, but it does not follow that every pleasure is worthy of being chosen; just as every pain is an evil, and yet every pain must not be avoided."[23]

For example, a particular pleasure might be very intense for the moment, but it might also lead to ill health or enslavement to a habit, thereby producing greater pain. Unprotected sex with a risky partner may lead to momentary orgasmic ecstasy, but it could also result in a sexually transmitted infection or disease, an enduring pain for such a brief episode of pleasure. So too, for a momentary high, some people will experiment with addictive drugs, only to find that they become enslaved to the high feeling produced and the ceaseless craving for more that must then be continually satisfied before panic and a frenzied preoccupation for physical satisfaction set in. Even intense pleasure without other bad consequences may lead to a "downer" when it ends.

From an Epicurean perspective, the pleasures of dangerous sex and addictive drugs should not be chosen, even if pain results from "missing out" or from not experiencing the physical high. On the other hand, sometimes pains should be chosen over pleasures. Undergoing surgery in a hospital is often painful, yet it produces the greater good—health—in the long run. Suffering momentary pain or short-lived pain thus may be the best choice for long-term well-being.

Living the good life, then, is not about the mindless pursuit of immediate pleasure; the exercise of *practical wisdom* is required. Practical wisdom enables one to measure pleasures against pains, accepting pains that lead to greater pleasures and rejecting pleasures that lead to greater pains.[24] Epicurus's willingness to delay immediate gratification for longer term benefits and the value he places on the exercise of practical wisdom both point to a kind of hedonism that can be distinguished from Aristippus's Cyrenaic version, which used intensity of pleasure as the main criterion of evaluative judgment. Unlike Aristippus, Epicurus would not necessarily conclude that the most immediate and intense pleasures are *always* the best.

Kinetic versus Static Pleasures

In the pursuit of pleasure, Epicurus would have us make a second distinction among pleasures, namely between **kinetic pleasures** and **static pleasures**. In the former case, pleasure is experienced through some kind of action. Drinking a cold glass of orange juice or ice water on a hot, humid day is quite satisfying. The body's craving for liquid, experienced as a need or deficiency, is removed, and drinking feels good. Likewise, the felt need for food (hunger) can be removed by eating. In short, there is kinetic pleasure whenever a want is satisfied or a pain is removed. Kinetic pleasures accompany some sort of motion or activity and cease when the motion or activity ceases.

Static ("*catastematic*") pleasures are not pleasures found in movement or in activity but in the *pleasurable states* resulting when pains, lacks, deficiencies, or frustrations have been removed. Static pleasure is the state of having no pain, whereas kinetic pleasure is the pleasure of getting to this state. Static pleasures give rise to a stable condition capable of indefinite prolongation. They are therefore characterized by an enduring nature not found in kinetic pleasures, which are momentary or short-lived, lasting only as long as the accompanying action.

Ataraxia: The Ultimate End of Life

For Epicurus, the ultimate end or *telos* of life is static pleasure, not kinetic. He calls this end ***ataraxia*** (often translated as tranquility), the state of not having ***tarachai*** (troubles).

To say that *ataraxia* is a state of being is not to suggest that it involves a total absence of activity. *Ataraxia* is not about being passive, doing nothing, or remaining motionless in some kind of transcendental blissful state. When *ataraxia* is achieved, one is functioning normally without painful interference. The goal of *ataraxia* is positive and substantial. It is about unimpeded activity of the human organism in its natural condition. In a state of Epicurean *ataraxia*, individuals use all their faculties without strain and without obstruction from fear, hunger, and disease. In *ataraxia*, the mind (or reason) works with an awareness of bodily functioning. It aims to keep things working smoothly.

Epicurus considers the specialized use of reason in logic and mathematics as only instrumentally valuable. Such use is not necessary for *ataraxia*, nor for a fulfilling life.

THINKING ABOUT YOUR THINKING

Make a list of 5-10 of your current desires that you've not yet satisfied, and 5-10 of your past desires that you've already satisfied at some earlier time. Why do you desire what you desire now? What, if anything, stands in the way of you satisfying your desires? Turning now to desires that you have successfully satisfied in the past, was the satisfaction of some of your desires more pleasing than the satisfaction of others? If so, why do you think that was?

According to Epicurus, the natural child, in its untutored state, would not desire logic and math as something pleasurably good. The Epicurean does not, therefore, glorify the contemplative life or the life of reason, as Plato and Aristotle did, for example. Mental pleasures are not any better or higher than bodily pleasures. Both are natural.

Natural Desires

On this note, Epicurus instructs us to follow our **natural desires**. As Julia Annas, a scholarly expert on Epicurus, puts it in her excellent book about Stoicism and Epicureanism, *The Morality of Happiness*, "Natural desires ... do not produce mental rather than bodily pleasures; rather, the natural/not natural distinction cuts right across that of mental and bodily. Natural desires are those we cannot help having, so that in fulfilling them we are following, rather than forcing, our nature."[25] Thus, bodily desires for food and drink are, for Epicurus, as natural as the mental desire for tranquility of the soul (what some of us today would call peace of mind).

If we are to fulfill our natural desires, it is important that we not rely on **empty beliefs**, that is, on those that are false and harmful. Vain or unnatural desires based on empty beliefs do not come from nature but rather are products of teaching and acculturation. Their falsity results from the incorrect evaluative beliefs that ground them. Empty beliefs have a tendency to be vain and self-defeating, since they typically reach out for boundless objects that can provide no stability or long-term satisfaction. Natural desires, by contrast, can be well-satisfied because they do have limits.

By trying to satisfy artificial and limitless desires, we end up sabotaging our own *ataraxia*. Suppose, for instance, you are hungry. Simple bread could ease your hunger pangs. But if you believe that, given your station in life, you truly deserve beluga caviar, then if the caviar is unavailable, you will still remain troubled in your soul with frustration, even though you quiet your body's craving with bread. You will believe that you didn't get what you deserve and be upset by this belief. Needing food is natural; craving caviar is not. Though eating caviar may be pleasurable (if you like that sort of thing), not every pleasure is worthy of being pursued or troubled about if it's not available. Believing you deserve caviar and developing a desire for it are things you have been taught or introduced to, not things natural or necessary to the human organism. If we don't rid ourselves of empty beliefs like the one about caviar, we may end up satisfying our basic physical needs, but in ways that perpetuate our mental disturbances.

In his "Letter to Menoeceus," Epicurus classified the various kinds of human desires. Some are **vain desires**, meaning that they are not rooted in nature. Becoming famous or owning jewels are things you may desire, but they do not come with being born human. Such vain desires are conditioned by false beliefs of what is required to make one happy.

Natural desires, by contrast, may be either necessary or unnecessary. The desire for sex is natural, yet many people live a celibate life without much, if any, frustration. Desiring delicious foods is also natural but unnecessary, for we could easily live on a bland diet. Those desires that are both natural and necessary are required for comfort, happiness, and life itself. Epicurus believed that practical wisdom and friendship contribute greatly to happiness; things like shelter from the elements and adequate clothing contribute to comfort, while food and water are necessary to sustain life.

Distinguishing between what is natural and necessary from what is empty, vain, and unnecessary, Epicurus and his followers chose to live simple and frugal lives. It is truly a misreading of Epicureanism to suggest that it advocates that we all "Eat, drink, and be merry." In truth, Epicurus recommended suppression of desires that go beyond natural needs and moderation in those desires of the natural sort. Neither overindulgence of natural desires (gluttony with regard to food) nor strict **asceticism** (excessive fasting or physically wasting away) can lead to a pleasurable life.

For Epicurus, happy is the person who displays **prudence** (practical wisdom), **simple tastes**, **bodily health**, **freedom from physical need**, **powers of discrimination** (to distinguish between natural and vain desires), and **tranquility of the soul**. Because happy people are not deluded by vain and empty beliefs, constantly trying to satisfy limitless and unnecessary cravings, they possess a sober **self-sufficiency**. See Figure 3.3 for a classification of Epicurean desires.

Impediments to *Ataraxia*

The road to achieving *ataraxia* is not an easy one according to Epicurus. Society and the acculturation process do severe damage to human desire and natural, unimpeded functioning. To begin with, religious teachers in Epicurus's day taught people to fear the gods and to fear death because of an uncertain afterlife. In ancient Greece, the gods were thought to intervene in the lives of humans. They could reward people as easily as they could take revenge on them. Thus, humans were constantly trying to appease the gods in order not to elicit their vengeful wrath.

For some people today, belief in "the gods" seems antiquated, heathen, or even barbaric given the monotheistic traditions of Christianity, Islam, and Judaism. Nonetheless,

> *"Frugal meals deliver a pleasure that is equal to that of an expensive diet, when once all the pain of need is removed; and bread and water give the very summit of pleasure, when a needy person takes them in."*
> EPICURUS

FIGURE 3.3 A Classification of Epicurean Desires

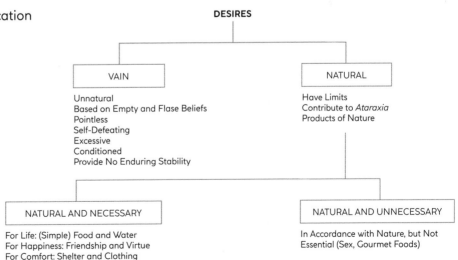

experience informs us that many people today still believe in divine intervention in earthly affairs, often *making deals* with God, promising in prayer to be more virtuous, for example, so that God may grant them their wishes: *Oh God, just do this for me and I promise to....* Some people continue to morbidly fear death, worrying about the prospects of hell-fire damnation if life is not lived according to God's will.

The belief that God rewards and punishes or that He intervenes in our lives is even evident in professional sports. Watch athletes on television after they score touchdowns or win games; religious gestures and prayers of thanks are frequently offered, as if God blessed the fortunate player or the player's team. We're left wondering how God feels about the losers. Are they being punished for something they did? Maybe God is a Buffalo Bills' fan and hates the Miami Dolphins?

When we pray for things to happen, aren't we just reducing God to some kind of errand boy whose task it is to satisfy our wandering desires? When we fear God, aren't we choosing to see Him as a vengeful judge who sentences his creations to an eternity in hell if they don't do His jealous bidding? To the extent we're forced to answer yes, fear of God and the fear of death appear to be no less real today than they were during the times of Epicurus.

If Epicurus were living now, I suspect he would strongly recommend that we stop making questionable assumptions about God and attributing to God our own imperfect, human qualities such as vengefulness and jealousy. Epicurus might speculate that seeing God as judgmental is nothing more than a human projection of our own feelings of guilt. No matter what utterances we make about God, what is certain is that they are not based on any actual perceptions or direct experience of Him. We have never seen or met God. In whatever way we conceptualize Him (or Her or It), we are merely projecting our own human qualities upon this divinity.

Epicurus would thus instruct us to show piety and reject popular superstitious beliefs about God—beliefs largely created out of fear. We ought to accept the blessedness and immortality of God (the gods) and recognize that He, She, or They are too preoccupied to trouble themselves with the problems of this world. As for our own mortality, we should be undisturbed, for with death comes the end of all physical sensation, the pleasant as well as the painful. Rather than yearn for the impossible (life forever), we should enjoy our present life all the more, understanding that our lifetime is not limitless. Every moment is precious and should be enjoyed to the fullest. Desiring the impossible and fearing the inevitable can only disturb the soul.

Virtue in the Pleasant Life

The role **virtue** plays for Epicurus in the development of *ataraxia* and the pleasant life is not entirely unambiguous. Some passages taken from Epicurus's writings seem to suggest that virtue possesses only a secondary instrumental value next to pleasure. In other words, if acting virtuously contributes to pleasure, then we should act virtuously. However, if virtuous acts stand in the way of personal pleasure, then virtuous acts should be overridden. In one passage, Epicurus states:

> It is because of pleasure that we choose even the virtues, not for their own sake, just as we choose medicine for the sake of health. (Diogenes X, 138)

In another passage, though, Epicurus says something quite different:

> ... it is impossible to live pleasantly without also living prudently, honestly, and justly; [nor is it possible to lead a life of prudence, honor, and justice] and not live pleasantly. For the virtues are closely associated with the pleasant life and cannot be separated from them.

I guess as long as there are different translators, analysts, and commentators on Epicurus's works, there will be conflicting opinions about what he really meant. Julia Annas, in her scholarship on Epicureanism, suggests that it's possible that hostile critics of Epicurus have tended to downplay the inextricable link he makes between virtue and pleasure, and that they have quoted Epicurus out of context and with the most damaging interpretation of his apparent inconsistencies. A more lenient interpretation allows for the inconsistencies to serve a rhetorical, albeit innovative, way for Epicurus to awaken his listeners to Epicurean insights. As Annas points out, and as some passages seem to support, pleasure and virtue appear to be inseparable for Epicurus, if life is taken as a whole. Each one entails the other. According to some interpretations, it would appear that the virtues become part of happiness, and that part of the pleasant life is formed by acting and living according to the virtues.[26]

The Role of Friendship

Ataraxia, as the final end of life, must be complete and self-sufficient, or else it is not the final end. In this respect, virtue must, for Epicurus, be included under *ataraxia*, for virtuous acts are pleasurable and *ataraxia* incorporates all that is pleasurable. As friendship, too, is pleasurable, any concept of *ataraxia* that is complete and self-sufficient must include it as well.

The value placed on **friendship** by Epicurus is evident from how The Garden was organized. Remember, it was a placid, apolitical world devoted to the values of companionship and solidarity. Life in The Garden community was to replace prior familial, societal, and civic relationships in order that all might grow together in philosophy. People were expected to leave their former positions in society and join in a common purpose at The Garden. On the subject of friendship from an Epicurean perspective, Cicero writes:

> Isolation and a life without friends are full of hidden traps and fears, so that reason itself advises us to secure friendships; when these are obtained our spirits are strengthened and cannot be parted from the hope of getting pleasures.
>
> So, since we cannot in any way keep a continuing pleasantness in life without friendship, and since we cannot have friendship itself unless we love our friends equally with ourselves—this is in fact brought about in friendship, and friendship is linked with pleasure.[27]

As Cicero points out, Epicurean friendship would have us love our friends as much as ourselves and have equal concern for their pleasures as our own. Friendship is not about using others to get pleasure for oneself; we get genuine pleasure from being concerned about, and caring for, others. Thus, our final end, *ataraxia*, must include friendship.

Sigmund Freud's Debt to Epicurus

"The poets and philosophers before me discovered the unconscious. What I discovered was the scientific method by which the unconscious can be studied."

SIGMUND FREUD

In a marvelous book titled *The Therapy of Desire: Theory and Practice in Hellenistic Ethics*, Martha C. Nussbaum points to Epicurus's greatness as a psychologist. In fact, she attributes the discovery of the unconscious to him. In The Garden, Epicurus emphasized memorization and repetition of Epicurean principles as a way of internalizing his teachings and giving them the transformative power required to overcome society's harmful teaching of false and empty beliefs. Epicurus understood how socially conditioned beliefs, causing disturbances in life, do not all lie on the surface of consciousness and may even show up in dreams.

Epicurus held that the self is not entirely transparent to itself and that false beliefs and vain desires can exercise their influence, often without our conscious awareness. As a consequence, he saw the limitations of a purely rational, critical, or dialectical scrutiny of the self. Rational understanding does not guarantee personal change. Knowing what is good does not necessarily mean that one will do it, according to Epicurus, no matter what Socrates thought. False beliefs are often buried deep in the soul and exert their troubling influence beneath the level of the conscious mind. By rote memory and repetition of Epicurean principles (based on natural and necessary desires), those vain desires based on

empty and false beliefs could be driven down so deeply that their influence would be minimized.

To help followers of The Garden become aware of their vain desires and false beliefs, Epicurus started something new in the Greek philosophical tradition: the *ritual of confession* or *personal narrative*. Philodemus, a student of Epicurus, wrote:

> The pupil must show him his failings without concealment and tell his defects in the open. For if he considers him the one guide of correct speech and deed, the one whom he calls the only savior and to whom saying 'with him at my side,' he gives himself over to be therapeutically treated, then how could he not show the things in which he requires therapeutic treatment, and receive his criticism?[28]

Through confession and personal narrative, that is, by having the disturbed person describe his or her actions, thoughts, desires, and even dreams, Epicurus hoped to grasp the totality of the philosophical patient's disturbing symptoms and open them up for analysis and diagnosis, much like *Sigmund Freud* used free association to uncover repressed conflicts and unconscious motivations. Freud's recognition of the unconscious and his use of indirect means (like dream analysis) to gain access to the unconscious would appear, then, to have been predated by Epicurus many centuries before!

So that you might now formulate your own interpretations and draw your own conclusions about Epicureanism, let us now turn to a text in which Epicurus shares with us his conception of the happy life.

Epicurus, "Letter to Menoeceus"[29]

The "Letter to Menoeceus" is one of only three surviving letters by the ancient Greek philosopher Epicurus (c. 341 BCE–270 BCE). He wrote those letters on physical theory, astronomical and meteorological matters, and, in this case, ethics to his disciples in order to help them remember his doctrines.

———

121. Epicurus to Menoeceus, greetings:

122. Let no one delay the study of philosophy while young nor weary of it when old. For no one is either too young or too old for the health of the soul. He who says either that the time for philosophy has not yet come or that it has passed is like someone who says that the time for happiness has not yet come or that it has passed. Therefore, both young and old must philosophize, the latter so that although old he may stay young in good things owing to gratitude for what has occurred, the former so that although young he too may be like an old man owing to his lack of fear of what is to come. Therefore, one must practise the things which produce happiness, since if that is present we have everything and if it is absent we do everything in order to have it.

123. Do and practise what I constantly told you to do, believing these to be the elements of living well. First, believe that god is an indestructible and blessed living being, in accordance with the general conception of god commonly held, and do not ascribe to god anything foreign to his indestructibility or repugnant to his blessedness. Believe of him everything which is able to preserve his blessedness and indestructibility. For gods do exist, since we have clear knowledge of them. But they are not such as the many believe them to be. For they do not adhere to their own views about the gods. The man who denies the gods of the many is not impious, but rather he who ascribes to the gods the opinions of the many. **124.** For the pronouncements of the many about the gods are not basic grasps but false suppositions. Hence come the greatest harm from the gods to bad men and the greatest benefits [to the good]. For the gods always welcome men who are like themselves, being congenial to their own virtues and considering that whatever is not such is uncongenial.

Get used to believing that death is nothing to us. For all good and bad consists in sense-experience, and death is the privation of sense-experience. Hence, a correct knowledge of the fact that death is nothing to us makes the mortality of life a matter for contentment, not by adding a limitless time [to life] but by removing the longing for immortality. **125.** For there is nothing fearful in life for one who has grasped that there is nothing fearful in the absence of life. Thus, he is a fool who says that he fears death not because it will be painful when present but because it is painful when it is still to come. For that which while present causes no distress causes unnecessary pain when merely anticipated. So death, the most frightening of bad things, is nothing to us; since when we exist, death is not yet present, and when death is present, then we do not exist. Therefore, it is relevant neither to the living nor to the dead, since it does not affect the former, and the latter do not exist. But the many sometimes flee death as the greatest of bad things and sometimes choose it as a relief from the bad things in life. **126.** But the wise man neither rejects life nor fears death. For living does not offend him, nor does he believe not living to be something bad. And just as he does not unconditionally choose the largest amount of food but the most pleasant food, so he savours not the longest time but the most pleasant. He who advises the young man to live well and the old man to die well is simple-minded, not just because of the pleasing aspects of life but because the same kind of practice produces a good life and a good death. Much worse is he who says that it is good not to be born, "but when born to pass through the gates of Hades as quickly as possible."[30] **127.** For if he really believes what he says, why doesn't he leave life? For it is easy for him to do, if he has firmly decided on it. But if he is joking, he is wasting his time among men who don't welcome it. We must remember that what will happen is neither unconditionally within our power nor unconditionally outside our power, so that we will not unconditionally expect that it will occur nor despair of it as unconditionally not going to occur.

One must reckon that of desires some are natural, some groundless; and of the natural desires some are necessary and some merely natural; and of the necessary, some are necessary for happiness and some for freeing the body from troubles and some for life itself. **128.** The unwavering contemplation of these enables one to refer every choice and avoidance to the health of the body and the freedom of the soul from disturbance, since this is the goal of a blessed life. For we do everything for the sake of being neither in pain nor in terror. As soon as we achieve this state every storm in the soul is dispelled, since the animal is not in a position to go after some need nor to seek something else to complete the good of the body and the soul. For we are in need of pleasure only when we are in pain because of the absence of pleasure, and when we are not in pain, then we no longer need pleasure.

And this is why we say that pleasure is the starting-point and goal of living blessedly. **129.** For we recognized this as our first innate good, and this is our starting point for every choice and avoidance and we come to this by judging every good by the criterion of feeling. And it is just because this is the first innate good that we do not choose every pleasure; but sometimes we pass up many pleasures when we get a larger amount of what is uncongenial from them. And we believe many pains to be better than pleasures when a greater pleasure follows for a long while if we endure the pains. So every pleasure is a good thing, since it has a nature congenial [to us], but not every one is to be chosen. Just as every pain too is a bad thing, but not every one is such as to be always avoided. **130.** It is, however, appropriate to make all these decisions by comparative measurement and an examination of the advantages and disadvantages. For at some times we treat the good thing as bad and, conversely, the bad thing as good.

And we believe that self-sufficiency is a great good, not in order that we might make do with few things under all circumstances, but so that if we do not have a lot we can make do with few, being genuinely convinced that those who least need extravagance enjoy it most; and that everything natural is easy to obtain and whatever is groundless is hard to obtain; and that simple flavours provide a pleasure equal to that of an extravagant life-style when all pain from want is removed, **131.**

and barley cakes and water provide the highest pleasure when someone in want takes them. Therefore, becoming accustomed to simple, not extravagant, ways of life makes one completely healthy, makes man unhesitant in the face of life's necessary duties, puts us in a better condition for the times of extravagance which occasionally come along, and makes us fearless in the face of chance. So when we say that pleasure is the goal we do not mean the pleasures of the profligate or the pleasures of consumption, as some believe, either from ignorance and disagreement or from deliberate misinterpretation, but rather the lack of pain in the body and disturbance in the soul. **132.** For it is not drinking bouts and continuous partying and enjoying boys and women, or consuming fish and the other dainties of an extravagant table, which produce the pleasant life, but sober calculation which searches out the reasons for every choice and avoidance and drives out the opinions which are the source of the greatest turmoil for men's souls.

Prudence is the principle of all these things and is the greatest good. That is why prudence is a more valuable thing than philosophy. For prudence is the source of all the other virtues, teaching that it is impossible to live pleasantly without living prudently, honourably, and justly, and impossible to live prudently, honourably, and justly without living pleasantly. For the virtues are natural adjuncts of the pleasant life and the pleasant life is inseparable from them.

133. For who do you believe is better than a man who has pious opinions about the gods, is always fearless about death, has reasoned out the natural goal of life and understands that the limit of good things is easy to achieve completely and easy to provide, and that the limit of bad things either has a short duration or causes little trouble?

As to [Fate], introduced by some as the mistress of all, he is scornful, saying rather that some things happen of necessity, others by chance, and others by our own agency, and that he sees that necessity is not answerable [to anyone], that chance is unstable, while what occurs by our own agency is autonomous, and that it is to this that praise and blame are attached. **134.** For it would be better to follow the stories told about the gods than to be a slave to the fate of the natural philosophers. For the former suggests a hope of escaping bad things by honouring the gods, but the latter involves an inescapable and merciless necessity. And he [the wise man] believes that chance is not a god, as the many think, for nothing is done in a disorderly way by god; nor that it is an uncertain cause. For he does not think that anything good or bad with respect to living blessedly is given by chance to men, although it does provide the starting points of great good and bad things. And he thinks it better to be unlucky in a rational way than lucky in a senseless way; **135.** for it is better for a good decision not to turn out right in action than for a bad decision to turn out right because of chance.

Practise these and the related precepts day and night, by yourself and with a like-minded friend, and you will never be disturbed either when awake or in sleep, and you will live as a god among men. For a man who lives among immortal goods is in no respect like a mere mortal animal.

READING QUESTIONS

1. Who is the ideal audience for this letter? How might they benefit from reading it?

2. What is Epicurus's prescription for eliminating the fear of death? Try to outline his reasoning that "death is nothing to us." Can fear be reasoned away?

3. Before reading this letter, how would you have described a life of pleasure? After reading this letter, how would you describe a life of pleasure? Has Epicurus changed your mind about what pleasure is and what the life of pleasure involves? If so, how? If not, why not?

3.5 Buddhism as a Philosophy of Life

As we turn now to **Buddhism**, we find yet another philosophy which, like Hellenistic Stoicism, has great personal and practical relevance. It too has therapeutic applications for better functioning in the world. One needn't be a practicing Buddhist to benefit from the insights it has to offer. If nothing else, a study of Buddhist philosophy affords an opportunity to engage in a process of self-reflection, reevaluating the directions our lives have taken thus far.

In what follows, we will briefly cover **The Four Noble Truths** revealed to Buddha at the time of his enlightenment. We will also take a look at **The Noble Eight-Fold Path** which constitutes **The Middle Path** of living—the one recommended by Buddha for release from selfish craving. Without such release, true and lasting happiness is not possible, according to Buddhist teachings.

"Suffering I teach— and the way out of suffering."
THE BUDDHA

Siddhartha Gautama, the Buddha

The person we have come to know as the Buddha was born circa 563 BCE as Siddhartha Gautama, the only son of a ruling king in what is now Nepal. The details of Siddhartha's life are sketchy since no complete biography of the Buddha was compiled until centuries after his death. Much of the information we have comes from tradition and myth, and it's difficult, therefore, to distinguish between fact and legend. What we do know is that his people were called the Sakyas; for this reason, the Buddha is sometimes referred to as *Sakyamuni*, or "the sage of the Sakyas." "Buddha" is not a personal name but an honorific title meaning *the awakened one*. Siddhartha Gautama (his clan name) did not actually become the Buddha until his mid-thirties, when he achieved enlightenment.

As the son of a royal ruler, the young Siddhartha led a life of luxury and pleasure. Legend has it that soon after his birth, a wise sage came to visit and noticed that there were 32 special markings on Siddhartha's tiny body. For the sage, this was a sign that Siddhartha was destined for glory. He would either become a universal monarch or great religious teacher.

Siddhartha's father, Suddhodana, was not entirely thrilled by this. The king wanted his son to succeed him, since if the prince abandoned his position in the royal palace, Suddhodana would be without an heir. Believing that the ugly, unpleasant, and painful things of life would turn Siddhartha's mind toward religion, Suddhodana decided that he should raise his son in a completely protected environment of comfort, beauty, and pleasure.

Three splendid marble palaces were built—one for each of the hot, cool, and rainy seasons. Siddhartha was confined to the upper stories of these palaces and provided with every kind of pleasure and luxury to prevent boredom from setting in. He lazed around the palace in fine silks, ate the most delicious foods, and enjoyed armies of musicians, dancing girls, and the most sensuous courtesans who were on hand to amuse and entertain him. Shielded from him were illness and old age. Presumably, if Buddha never experienced the pains and miseries of life, he would never be drawn to religion and could therefore fulfill his father's wishes. At age 16, Siddhartha married his cousin Yasodhara, who bore him a son (Rahula) when he was 29.

Before the birth of his son, Siddhartha had already fallen prey to restless boredom, notwithstanding all of the efforts of his father. Ironically perhaps, unproductive self-indulgence simply could not make life satisfying for him. With his hired guardian, friend, and charioteer, Channa, Siddhartha made secret trips outside the palace walls. Channa became a tour guide of sorts, answering many of Siddhartha's questions about the harsh realities of life beyond his protected environment. It was during these secret trips that Siddhartha saw "the four signs" that would change his life forever.

On the first trip, Siddhartha encountered an old man; on the second trip, a sick man; and on the third trip, a corpse being carried away for cremation. Because Siddhartha had lived such a cloistered life for almost 30 years, these three encounters were quite traumatic for him. He had no concept of the true human condition: that all human beings are susceptible to sickness, old age, and death—including Siddhartha himself. Disturbed by this, he wondered how anyone could find happiness since, in the end, there is no escape from suffering and loss, with all of the associated sadness and disappointment. After witnessing the first three signs, all the pleasures and delights of palace life quickly lost their charm: Siddhartha had lost his innocence.

On a fourth trip outside the palace walls, Siddhartha and Channa came upon a wandering holy man. Alone, dressed in rags and possessing nothing, this ascetic monk displayed a demeanor that thoroughly impressed

Siddhartha. He seemed to possess a peaceful tranquility that other people lacked, however great their possessions or station in life. The monk appeared to be detached from the worries of the world, serene and quietly purposeful. This was the fourth sign.

Shortly after witnessing it, Siddhartha knew deep within himself that he would have to leave the comforts of home and live as a monk. On the very night that his son Rahula was to be born, Siddhartha rose from bed, woke Channa, saddled up his horse, and rode to the River Anoma, which divided the land of the Sakyas from the neighboring kingdom of Magadha. On the banks of the river, Siddhartha removed his jewelry, cut off his hair, exchanged his silken robe for the ragged saffron garb of a wandering holy man, and then bid farewell to Channa. Siddhartha walked off alone in his spiritual quest for the solution to the problem of suffering.

Renouncing earthly attachments, he embarked on his search by first adopting a lifestyle of radical asceticism: fasting, meditation, simple clothes, and plain food. Siddhartha showed so much discipline in his fasting that he almost wasted away. Eventually, he abandoned asceticism as fruitless and instead adopted *a middle path* between a life of self-indulgence (exemplified by palace life) and one of self-denial.

One day, at a place now called Bodh Gaya in the modern Indian state of Bihar, Siddhartha sat at the base of what was to become known as The Bodhi Tree or Tree of Wisdom, swearing to remain there until he either had an answer to the problem of suffering or was dead. Meditating and gradually rising through a series of higher states of consciousness, he finally attained the enlightenment he had been seeking. Siddhartha had undergone a transformation: a spoiled and naive young man had turned into *the awakened one*—the one we call the Buddha.

In the Deer Park at Isipatana (an open space near Benares) Buddha preached his first sermon on The Four Noble Truths. He also spoke about The Middle Path that he had discovered between the extremes of sensual indulgence and self-mortification. For the next 45 years, the Buddha was to wander from place to place, gathering disciples and organizing them into a monastic community known as the *sangha*.

At around the age of 80, the Buddha was having a meal at the humble home of a lowly blacksmith. He took ill soon thereafter. As an accidental result of eating either poisonous mushrooms or tainted pork, Buddha died (circa 480 BCE).

The teachings of Buddha were handed down orally for hundreds of years until monks began to transcribe them in the first century BCE. More recently, the Pali Text Society has collected and edited them into the so-called "Three Baskets": the rules for monks (*Vinaya Pitaka*), the basic teachings of the Buddha (*Sutta Pitaka*), and a commentary (*Abhidhamma Pitaka*). Today the teachings of Buddha serve as an inspiration and guide for millions throughout the world.

The Four Noble Truths

Introducing the topic of Buddhism into any casual conversation probably elicits, in many minds, the image of bald-headed monks in saffron robes wandering about in some distant foreign land where the inhabitants look different, speak different languages, and practice strange and different customs. From the vantage point of the modern Western mind-set, the Buddhist monk probably looks about as weird as the toga-clad philosopher haunting the streets of ancient Athens—somewhat bothersome and irrelevant to day-to-day affairs.

Yet a closer inspection of Buddhism reveals that it is eminently practical. It does not begin by posing grand metaphysical questions like "Who made the world?" or "What is the meaning of life?"[31] Nor does it expect its adherents to suspend reason, critical judgment, or commonsense experience. Its teachings are not dogmatic articles of faith that must be accepted blindly and without question. Furthermore, Buddhism is not pre-

Buddha: The Higher Reality Therapist

William Glasser (1925–2013), the internationally famed psychiatrist who initially developed Reality Therapy, aimed to help people live more productively by enabling them to get what they want out of life, namely, more power, fun, freedom, and love. You could say "attachments" to people and things were generally accepted and that the counseling process was designed essentially to work on effective strategies to get basic needs met.

Of course, Buddha is not concerned about getting what one wants, but with removing attachments to those selfish cravings that ultimately lead to suffering. The reality Buddha is concerned with is beyond Glasser's physical and material want satisfaction. Buddha would not have us satisfy our every want or desire; rather, he would have us transcend them if we wish to achieve personal enlightenment.

As a higher reality therapist, Buddha has his own program of personal development—The Four Noble Truths and The Noble Eight-Fold Path. He uses them as part of his medical model, as we've learned. As a spiritual practitioner, what Buddha did was this:

1. First, diagnose the universal ailment of humankind as suffering.
2. Second, isolate its root cause, namely, craving.
3. Third, identify the remedy to restore spiritual health.
4. Lastly, prescribe an eight-fold course of action for purposes of psycho-spiritual rehabilitation.

The life and teachings of the Buddha serve again to underscore a basic premise of this book: that philosophy is relevant for us because it has both practical and therapeutic applications.

> *"When the iron bird flies, and horses run on wheels, the Tibetan people will be scattered like ants across the world, and the Dharma [Buddha's teachings] will come to the land of red-faced people."*
> PADMA SAMBHAVA,
> EIGHTH-CENTURY
> INDIAN GURU

sented as a universally prescriptive model of truth. As devotees admit, Buddhism may not, in fact, be appropriate for you at all. In a spirit of tolerance and understanding, his Holiness, the Fourteenth Dalai Lama—the current spiritual leader for millions of Buddhists—writes:

A teaching may be very profound but if it does not suit a particular person, what is the use of explaining it? In this sense, the **Dharma** [Buddhist teaching] is like medicine. The main value of medicine is that it cures illness; it is not just a question of price. For example, one medicine may be very precious and expensive, but if it is not appropriate for the patient, then it is of no use.

Since there are different types of people in the world, we need different types of religion.[32]

Rather than present itself as dogmatic and otherworldly, then, Buddhism starts with the down-to-earth fact that human existence is imperfect in a very deep way. Understood as a pathway to wisdom, Buddhism offers us a method for retraining our minds so that we may experience a self-transformation, one that improves the quality of our lives. In this respect, Buddhism is very much a **therapeutic philosophy**. Indeed, The Four Noble Truths, which make self-transformation possible, follow a medical pattern. We shall learn more about this pattern as we discuss each of The Four Noble Truths in turn.

FIRST NOBLE TRUTH

> This, monks, is the Noble Truth of Suffering; birth is suffering; decay is suffering; illness is suffering; death is suffering; presence of objects we hate is suffering; separation from objects we love is suffering; not to obtain what we desire is suffering. In brief, the five aggregates which spring from grasping, they are painful.

DIAGNOSIS OF HUMANITY'S PROBLEM

Buddha diagnoses the basic problem of human life as **suffering**. In his teachings, Buddha gives a systematic analysis of the nature and causes of suffering, providing numerous means for overcoming it.

In his statement of the First Noble Truth, Buddha lists various types of suffering, which most of us can easily recognize and understand, such as decay, illness, death. The point should be appreciated, however, that suffering goes much deeper than these examples might have you conclude. Suppose, for instance, that you are currently experiencing a great deal of pleasure in your life. You may not think you are a victim of suffering at all, and Buddha's assessment that life is suffering may seem counterintuitive to you. Before you summarily dismiss the venerable Buddha as some kind of bleak pessimist, however, let us take a closer look at the pleasures you (and the rest of us) might be enjoying right now.

First of all, isn't it true that the objects and activities we enjoy carry with them an element of **attachment**? Don't we often say things like, "I'm very attached to this or that," or "I don't know what I would do without him or her," meaning some possession or person has sentimental value? Isn't it also true that we consciously or unconsciously experience anxiety from the possibility of separation from the object, person, or activity to which we're so attached? For instance, have you ever rejected the idea of owning a pet because you dread the day it will inevitably die, leaving you sad and unhappy? In other words, have you ever anticipated the short-lived and precarious nature of your pleasures? Haven't your pleasures always been alloyed with fear and insecurity at some level—conscious or unconscious?

Buddhists understand that the anxiety that results from change and the possibility of separation is like a hidden cancer in any pleasure, and therefore, a source of suffering. Whereas one can easily appreciate how illness or death can be a clear source of suffering, understanding how attachment to pleasure-producing things can be painful is not so obvious.

Pleasure can lead to suffering in yet another way. Many pleasures are not only self-perpetuating but also self-accelerating. Getting pleasure from engaging in some activities may not diminish the drive for the particular pleasure but rather strengthen it. Enjoying a cold alcoholic beverage on a hot day may be pleasurable, yet experience teaches us that one drink can often lead to another, and then to another, and still another, until one becomes physically ill or one passes out. Some people find drinking alcohol so pleasurable that they become attached to certain beer and whiskey brands, psychologically identifying with them all the way down the rocky road to addiction—something not so pleasurable.

On a somewhat less dramatic note, have you ever found that the more pleasure one achieves, the more one wants? I once heard a very wealthy businessman discuss his kitchen renovation, which cost an exorbitant amount of money. Given that his original kitchen had looked virtually new and was very tastefully designed, an onlooker asked why the ren-

"Avoid attachment to both what is pleasant

And what is unpleasant.

Losing the pleasant causes grief.

Dwelling on the unpleasant also causes grief."
THE BUDDHA

ovation was being undertaken, since there was no real practical need for it. The rich man answered, "When you get to my station in life, it's not what you need, but what you want!"

Now, before you find yourself impressed by all the extravagance and choice that wealth can bring, ask yourself what motivated the rich man to renovate the kitchen in the first place. Was it not his dissatisfaction, boredom, displeasure, or unhappiness with what he had? Is this not a form of suffering? "How long will it be?" we could ask, before the new kitchen ceases to provide satisfaction; the previous one certainly couldn't sustain the rich man's enthusiasm. Will the pleasure produced by subsequent renovations successfully hide the suffering below? The Buddhist insight here is that grasping at the pleasures of life ultimately increases suffering. The drive for pleasure is simply too shallow and insignificant to be fulfilling. It cannot provide true happiness.

The notion of suffering can reflect a wide spectrum of possibilities. Suffering can be mental or physical. It can relate to petty dislikes and frustrations, or, more seriously, to conflict, anxiety, and anger. Sometimes, suffering results from a dull feeling of malaise stemming from the perception that things are never quite right or how we would like them to be. Also, as we've learned, even beautiful, pleasurable experiences can have melancholy undertones because we know they will not last forever. The proverbial saying reminds us that *all good things must come to an end*.

What prevents us from healing on our human journeys is that we staunchly resist the dark side of life. No matter how dissatisfied we are by our pursuit of pleasure, we continue to believe that with just a few changes and minor adjustments, we can overcome the obstacles to our happiness and enjoy heaven on earth. The Buddhist, however, would describe this approach to life as **willful blindness**—a refusal to face the facts of the human condition. Life is suffering. This is not irrational pessimism, but an accurate reflection of how things are.

SECOND NOBLE TRUTH

> [Suffering] originates in that craving which causes the renewals of becomings, is accompanied by sensual delight, and seeks satisfaction now here, now there; that is to say, craving for pleasures, craving for becoming, craving for not becoming.

CRAVING—THE CAUSE OF HUMAN SUFFERING

In the First Noble Truth, Buddha diagnoses the *disease* of humanity as the universal plague of suffering. In the Second Noble Truth, he isolates its *cause*. For Buddha, the cause of suffering stems from a *generalized mentality of poverty*. We feel we are deficient, lacking or missing something in our lives; hence, we crave. Indeed, suffering originates in **craving**.

Craving can take many forms, some subtle, some not so subtle. We may have an obsessive lust for money or physical pleasure. We may crave health in times of illness or immortality when facing death. We may desire to develop a more secure self or possess an ego which we can satisfy, massage, inflate, or develop a positive concept around. We may also lust after the truth or desire to do good. Whatever form our craving takes, it reflects a gnawing dissatisfaction with what is and an associated *grasping for something outside of ourselves*. This incessant craving ensures that we can never be at rest. Like the young child who screams for the dangerous scissors that could seriously injure, we crave those things that in the end cause only suffering and pain. No matter what, we insist on being possessive, greedy, and above all, self-centered. We all seek to satisfy our "**self**"—a self whose egocentric cravings can never be fully or finally satiated.

Important to note is that things in the world do not of themselves cause suffering. It is the *self*, aware of changes in its condition, that suffers. Bricks and water don't experience pain. Suffering occurs when objective factors—events and situations related to the self—change, or do not change, as desired. It is the self that craves changes or craves to avoid them. When what is craved is not obtained, then suffering arises.

For Buddha, then, *craving is associated with the ego or self*. It is the ego-self that forms attachments and identifications with objects and things in the external world. When such things are threatened, the self suffers. Another way to say this is that our self-centeredness, or desire to create and satisfy ourselves, produces suffering because of its *partiality*. If, for example, I am suffering from boredom listening to you, it's because I wish you were addressing a topic of interest *to me*. It is my *self* that gets bored. Likewise, if I'm envious of the attention my sister is receiving from my parents, it's because I crave more attention *for me*. If I did not crave the attention I felt I deserved, I would not be upset, but rather delighted for her. We can plainly see, then, how attachment to the ego-self constitutes a large part of our malady. We are attached to the self—a self that suffers because it craves. Before moving on to the cure to our suffering in the Third Noble Truth, let us examine in a bit more detail Buddha's conception of the ego-self, given its central importance.

THE EGO-SELF AS FICTION

We see now how for the Buddha craving, the cause of suffering, is inextricably tied to the *self*. It is only when conditions or objective factors in the world are perceived as being related to a self that suffering occurs. The self may crave to realize those conditions or crave to avoid them. When the self cannot obtain what is craved, there is suffering.

In this context, it makes sense to ask what it means to attribute a "self" to a person. Who or what is the "I" or "self" that craves? According to Buddha, a self, as such, doesn't really exist. It is the craving for one that gives rise to suffering. This craving results in the invention and projection of a self. One's projected or fabricated self, being attached to the perceived elements making up one's own person, suffers when that identification is threatened by changes in the factors, elements, or conditions to which it is attached, whether these belong to that particular person, other persons, or other objects and activities in the world.

According to Buddha, if we analyze what it actually means to be a person, we find that the person is really just a bundle of

1. Activities constituting what we call the bodily or physical self
2. Sensing activities
3. Perceiving activities
4. Action impulses
5. Activities of consciousness

These activities are forever changing from one moment to the next. In our efforts to attach a permanent self to these ever-changing activities, we create a fiction—one produced by ignorant craving—and it is this craving for a fictitious self that underlies all suffering.

Changing conditions and impermanent objective factors constantly threaten the satisfaction of our cravings, and hence, our ego-identifications with them. One might say in this context that, "Although nothing lasts, suffering is everywhere, and the 'me' that suffers isn't even real." For Buddha, our mission in life is not to become a "somebody," but rather to become a selfless, egoless nobody. If this sounds unappetizing, perhaps it is because you are still attached to the illusion of the self.

THIRD NOBLE TRUTH

This, monks, is the Noble Truth concerning the Cessation of Suffering; verily, it is passionless, cessation without remainder of this very craving; the laying aside of, the giving up, the being free from, the harboring no longer of, this craving.

IDENTIFICATION OF A CURE

After diagnosing humanity's illness as suffering, and isolating its root cause, therapist-Buddha offers us good news in the Third Noble Truth, declaring that a remedy exists. Suffering can be extinguished by putting an end to the selfish craving that causes it. The cessation of suffering leads to a kind of supreme bliss or inner peace called **Nirvana**. "*Nirvana* is liberation, everlasting freedom, fulfillment, and enlightenment itself."[33] The concept of *Nirvana* has connotations of "blowing out" or "extinguishing"—the idea is that when it is attained, selfish craving is blown out like a flame. Heated and flickering emotions are replaced by a cool and undisturbed peacefulness.

The concept of *Nirvana* can be difficult to understand, for it cannot be grasped by sense experience; neither can the mind get hold of it by operating in terms of the usual categories of thought. *Nirvana* falls outside of our normal field of experience and can only be known through *direct insight*. This is reminiscent of Plato's *acquaintance with the forms*—a kind of special wisdom available only to the "philosopher rulers," those who have undergone intensive moral and intellectual training qualifying them to govern the ideal society. This philosophical enlightenment lies beyond rational understanding (see Section 4.2 in Chapter 4 on Plato's epistemology and metaphysics).

Fortunately for us, therapist-Buddha offers us a prescription for achieving *Nirvana*. This prescription requires the annihilation of the self-consciousness, judgmentalism, greed, and fear that characterize the **ego**. By severing our attachments, by showing compassion and loving-kindness, and by learning to control our thoughts, attitudes, and behaviors, we can escape the treadmill of suffering. As one writer puts it, "*Nirvana* is always trying to seep through the small chinks in our ego's armor. You can widen these openings by relinquishing some of the defenses and barricades of your personality, your holding on, your repetitive, addictive habitual behavior—in short, your psychological conditioning."[34] What we must do to achieve *Nirvana* is specified in the Fourth Noble Truth.

FOURTH NOBLE TRUTH

[Concerning the path which leads to the cessation of suffering, Buddha taught:] It is this Noble Eight-Fold Path, that is to say, right view, right thought, right speech, right action, right livelihood, right effort, right mindfulness, and right concentration.

The Radiant Buddha said:

Regard this fleeting world like this:

Like stars fading and vanishing at dawn,

like bubbles on a fast moving stream,

like morning dewdrops evaporating on blades of grass,

like a candle flickering in a strong wind,

echoes, mirages, and phantoms, hallucinations,

and like a dream.

"THE EIGHT SIMILES OF ILLUSION," FROM *THE PRAJNA PARAMITA SUTRAS*

Having declared that a remedy for suffering exists, the Buddha presents us in the Fourth Noble Truth with directions leading away from the dissatisfaction of conditional existence and toward the end of craving—*Nirvana*. These directions require us to take *The Noble Eight-Fold Path to Enlightenment*. Following Buddha's instructions enables us to purify our hearts and minds by living an impeccable and enlightened life.

The Noble Eight-Fold Path is all about living Buddha's teachings, known as the *Dharma*, daily in everything we do. It captures *The Middle Path* between asceticism and self-indulgence. You might view The Noble Eight-Fold Path as a guideline for a way of life, designed to transform us by changing our way of seeing things, or our consciousness. The path prescribed by Buddha can help us to abandon our egocentric sense of identity, replacing the self-centered *me* with a compassionate heart.

In essence, The Noble Eight-Fold Path constitutes a systematic strategy to uproot the defilements or foul corruptions that generate suffering in our lives. By developing **morality**, we can restrain defilements in their coarsest form, namely their outflow in unwholesome actions. Through methods of **concentration**, we can remove more refined defilements that manifest as distracting and restless thoughts. With the help of **wisdom** we can also eradicate defilements presenting themselves as subtle latent tendencies, "by penetrating with direct insight the three basic facts of existence, summed up by the Buddha in the three characteristics of **impermanence**, **suffering**, and **egolessness**."[35] The Noble Eight-Fold Path constituting The Middle Path comprises the following elements:

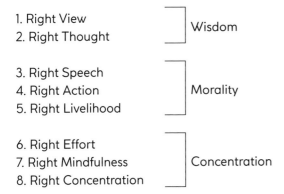

1. Right View
2. Right Thought

    Wisdom

3. Right Speech
4. Right Action
5. Right Livelihood

    Morality

6. Right Effort
7. Right Mindfulness
8. Right Concentration

    Concentration

Note that The Noble Eight-Fold Path is *not* to be thought of as hierarchical stages that one passes through sequentially, abandoning lower ones as more advanced ones are achieved. The eight factors specify the ways in which morality, wisdom, and concentration are to be cultivated on an integrated and continuous basis.[36]

The Noble Eight-Fold Path

THE TRAINING OF WISDOM

The first two elements of The Noble Eight-Fold Path deal with wisdom, that which involves correct understanding and the resolution to act in accordance with this understanding. Don't be misguided into thinking that wisdom is some kind of intellectual enterprise or theoretical form of knowledge; it is not. Wisdom derives from viewing things just as they are through a kind of *direct seeing*. In this kind of wisdom, there is an illumination of *things as they are in themselves*, something not limited by concepts and labels. The illumination of wisdom enables us to experience the relative and conditional nature of all things and to appreciate how suffering is caused by selfish grasping. We are wise when we resolve to overcome suffering by setting aside all of our selfish cravings. When wisdom is achieved, egoistic desires, ill-will, hatred, and violence are all abandoned.[37]

STEP ONE—RIGHT VIEW: To follow The Noble Eight-Fold Path, one must first become aware of the teachings of Buddha, and then come to accept them through *experimental confirmation*—not blind faith. As part of this acceptance, one develops the wisdom of clear vision, seeing the world as insubstantial and impossible to grasp. The first step reminds us to look at the world without any delusions, fabrications, or distortions about ourselves. Buddha was one of the first *spiritual psychotherapists*, so to speak, requiring us to engage in a kind of **reality testing**, looking out for **denial** and any other egoistic defensive distortions we might engage in as we produce delusional systems of thought.[38] The Buddha would have us move away from fantasy and illusion to directly see things as they really are.

STEP TWO—RIGHT THOUGHT OR RIGHT INTENTIONS: Following The Noble Eight-Fold Path requires that we develop **right intentions**, or to put it another way, correct motivation. In Step Two, we are asked to purify our thoughts and attitudes so that we may become totally straightforward and honest with ourselves. None of us possesses a perfect understanding of what makes us tick.

Through the practice of Buddhism, one gradually uncovers all sorts of blind spots and subtle forms of self-centeredness. The more we uncover, the more we become freed from our self-imposed bondage, becoming more able to express loving-kindness, empathy, and compassion toward all living creatures. Before achieving right thought, we fall prey to self-absorption, which acts as a veil of delusion destroying everything. Our self-absorption is so deeply ingrained that we can be fooled by its subtle manifestations.

For instance, even insecurity is a type of self-absorption—only an inverted expression of it. Worry and anxiety about our limitations or our inabilities is still worry about the self and what the self cannot do. If we didn't care so much about the self and how embarrassed we might become as a result of failure or exposed weaknesses, then we wouldn't have become insecure in the first place. So too with self-denial. Going through elaborate rituals of self-denial is to give importance to something that is significant enough that it must be denied—another example of inverted self-absorption.

When we have right thoughts and right intentions, things like winning, achieving, and looking good don't matter. When we understand how "selfish pleasures" are contaminated with ambivalent feelings, melancholy, and other disturbing defilements like anger, envy, and revenge, they no longer taste so sweet. What is really in our interest is to be less self-conscious and less selfish. As Buddhism scholar John Snelling puts it,

The unreformed (i.e., selfish) mind, like a mill in perpetual motion, is constantly devising plans, plots and strategies for advancing its own cause, outflanking rivals and undoing enemies. Or else it indulges itself in egoistic and hedonistic fantasies.[39]

When we achieve right thought, we switch over to other-directed mental modes. We adopt those that are more altruistic and benign. Rather than engage in self-promotion, we focus on being of service to the world.

THE TRAINING OF MORALITY

As we have seen thus far, there is no rigid or universally prescriptive moral code in Buddhism. Also, Buddhism does not seek to make evaluative judgments, ones which could arouse shame or guilt. For Buddhists, moral transgressions should be met with correction and instruction to overcome ignorance, not with punishment, condemnation, and blame.[40] When we fail to live up to an ethical principle, we should resolve to do better next time. Recognizing that we still have a long way to go before overcoming our faults breeds a healthy humility.

STEP THREE—RIGHT SPEECH: If you're someone who truly wishes release from suffering, then you should consider following Buddha's instructions regarding right speech. As everyone well knows, words can be used in a variety of ways: as gifts, weapons, or in magic, prayer, poetry, and song. Words enable us to put our thoughts and ideas into concrete terms. They enable us to define our priorities, express our views, and state our intentions. Through your words, you declare and confirm to the world and to yourself what you think is important. The compassionate Buddha would have us use words ideally as a reflection of our wish to help others. We should think kindly and speak in a gentle fashion. Words do indeed have power, and how you use them indicates how you have chosen to use yours.

Right speech requires that we "speak the truth and tell no lies." Never knowingly tell falsehoods to gain an advantage for yourself or others. Words spoken with guile or masked intentions muddy the clear waters of truth and complicate what is actually very simple. Like political spin-doctors who distort the truth to the advantage of their chosen leaders, we, as individuals, also embark on egotistical promotion campaigns, embellishing the truth to present ourselves in the best possible light. The consequence is that we create *false personas* that leave us feeling incomplete and alienated from our authentic selves. Ironically, perhaps, self-congratulatory words used to inflate the ego do violence to the self. In our relationships, we should therefore always try to be honest and forthright. We should try to let go of our elaborate defense mechanisms and be truthful and open about who we are and how we feel.

Another dimension of right speech involves refusing to gossip. Telling tales about others is a masked way for us to feel superior or part of the in-crowd. However, when we tell tales or make unkind jokes behind people's backs, we only create a greater distance between ourselves and others. We treat them disrespectfully as objects of our amusement. Thus, we must resist the urge to speak unkindly about others in their absence, as doing so is not kind.

Buddha also instructs us to "use words in helpful, not harmful ways." We should refrain from causing trouble with talk that is hurtful or unnecessarily disruptive. Pronouncing judgment on others increases interpersonal distance and alienation. Judgmentalism also obscures our higher view and distorts our direct appreciation of how things really are. Judgmental words and self-righteous tones seldom, if ever, help in any situation. So, to repeat a Tibetan proverb: "Don't notice the tiny flea in the other person's hair and overlook the lumbering yak on your own nose."[41]

Still on the subject of right speech, Buddha says we should "avoid harsh abusive language; always speaking kindly." You cannot find inner peace using abusive speech, which is associated with hostility and anger. Expressing arrogance and sarcasm may give you momentary pleasure, but at the expense of your long-term well-being. The challenge is to use words in ways that reflect acceptance, love, and compassion. A further challenge is to maintain a *noble silence* when appropriate. Sometimes the best thing or most helpful thing to say is nothing.

STEP FOUR—RIGHT ACTION: In a lovely book entitled *Awakening the Buddha Within*, Lama Surya Das sums up the fourth step of The Noble Eight-Fold Path with the following words: "The practice of **Right Action** is about cultivating goodness and virtue in the way we treat others; it's about creating harmony in our world, our home, in this very life, right now."[42] For practicing Buddhists like Lama Surya Das, life is an art form, and we are the artistic creators.

Though we are personally responsible for our own volitional actions, Buddhist teaching offers us five precepts that can be used in moral life. Blind obedience to these precepts is discouraged, since wisdom and discernment must accompany them. By pondering these precepts, we can come to see why refraining from certain actions is good. We can prepare the ground for our personal self-transcendence and enlightenment. We can *clear the weeds from the soil*, a wonderful metaphor that can be used to capture the idea of ordering the outer life before turning to the inner life.[43] The Five Precepts ask us to

1. Refrain from harming living things
2. Refrain from taking what is not given
3. Refrain from misuse of the senses
4. Refrain from wrong speech
5. Refrain from taking drugs or drinks that tend to cloud the mind

Each of the Five Precepts seems to have a fairly obvious, superficial meaning, but it should be understood that they all have deeper connotations. For example, the first precept is not just an injunction against hurting or killing, but it implies an awareness of the sanctity of life. It involves a reverence and respect for all life forms that we should incorporate into our daily behavior.

In the second precept, we are instructed to refrain from taking what is not given. Yes, we should not steal what does not belong to us. Moreover, we should not take more than our fair share or steal the spotlight as we try to become the center of attention. We should live patiently and generously without grasping to satisfy our own selfish desires.

The third precept would have us refrain from misuse of the senses. No doubt there is a directive about sexual misconduct here, but much more. We should refrain from any personal habits that lead to excess (e.g., over-eating), muscular deterioration, or any pollution of the body and its organs.

In the fourth precept, we should avoid lying, slander, gossip, and malicious talk. On the other hand, we should exhibit right speech whenever communicating with others, while engaged in activities such as promotion and advertising, or when giving political speeches. (Dirty political campaigns involving personal attacks violate this fourth precept.)

In the fifth precept, we are guided not to impair our mental functioning, for to do so is to create obstacles for enlightenment and illumination. As one writer puts it, "Anyone seriously interested in attaining the state of enlightened wisdom will refrain from indulgences that impair the clarity of mental vision, shroud doubts and uncertainties in a kind of euphoria, and encourage seeing things other than as they are."[44]

STEP FIVE—RIGHT LIVELIHOOD: If you are a college or university student, you are probably giving much thought to your future, especially where employment is concerned. What will be your chosen occupation? Will you pick the best job or most appropriate career? How will you know that you've made the right choice?

Again, the practical Buddha offers you some guidance in this aspect of your life. Step Five asks that we *express love in the world through our work*. We should not compromise our integrity by becoming involved in vocational activities that are likely to cause harm to people, animals, or the environment. For this reason we should avoid livelihoods that are deceitful, unwholesome, or corrupting in any fashion. Only occupations that enable you to earn a living while at the same time promoting peace and well-being are in accord with the requirement of **right livelihood**.[45] This doesn't mean you have to live a quiet life. Maybe your mission is to bring joy and laughter into the lives of others by becoming a comedian (who uses right speech). Or perhaps you should become a public philosopher, advancing wisdom and understanding around the world? Of course, there are many other professions that meet this test. What you should *not* do is choose a career based only on selfish considerations like a big paycheck or vacation perks; furthermore, you should not turn a blind eye to the harmful aspects of a career in order to feed your ego.

THE TRAINING OF CONCENTRATION

STEP SIX—RIGHT EFFORT: To live according to the teachings of the Buddha is going to require right effort. **Right effort**, in this context, means *spiritual effort*—working to elevate ourselves and to develop more wholesome states. In so doing, we strive to go deeper and live more fully. By our own efforts, we hope to open and awaken our hearts and minds, our bodies and souls.[46]

> "The mind is restless, unsteady, hard to guard, hard to control. The wise one makes it straight, like a fletcher* straightens an arrow. The mind is mercurial, hard to restrain, alighting where it wishes. It is good to tame and master this mind, for a disciplined mind brings happiness."
> THE BUDDHA
>
> * Arrow-maker.

Through meditation training, through introspection and contemplation, through mindfulness and through awareness practices, the devotee to Buddhism uses the tried and tested inner science of spiritual awakening and transformation. Clearly, effort is required to release old habits and patterns of behavior. It also takes effort to strengthen our mind so that it is not overcome by ignorance or easily swayed by craving or aversion. Accompanying all of this effort, we will certainly need commitment, patience, courage, and enthusiasm.

The method for exploring inner reality can start with *awareness of respiration*. This is the technique practiced by Buddha himself. You have to learn to focus your mind and fixate on a single object of attention (your breathing). By doing this you make the mind an instrument for examining the subtlest realities about yourself. Paying attention to your breath is a basic centering or grounding exercise you can practice anywhere. By training to pay attention, we can focus and pay attention to ourselves. (For some instructional tips on how to meditate, see the *Philosophers in Action* feature found in Section 1.4 of Chapter 1.)

STEP SEVEN—RIGHT MINDFULNESS: The human condition has sometimes been likened to a waking dream. From one day to the next, we live our lives largely distracted, lost in trains of unreflective thought and fantasy. Absent to immediate experience, we are by-passed by life without our conscious awareness. We mindlessly fall into bad habits and repetitive patterns of behavior. With all the predictability of conditioned Pavlovian dogs, we may become habitual grumblers who use any pretext to launch into angry and embittered diatribes.

Fortunately, there are ways of awakening to experience. Even if for only a few moments at a time, we can learn to detach from the ongoing drama of our lives and objectively examine the habitual patterns of behavior that entrap us. By doing this, we can begin to loosen their compulsive hold on us. In the process of *dis*-identifying with them, we can also start to see how those habitual thoughts, feelings, and actions are not *us*. They come along accidentally and so can be extinguished with effort. We are not necessarily slaves to our conditional existence.

By means of **right mindfulness**, we learn to awaken to reality and take what Lama Surya Das calls "the escalator to enlightenment." To live in a conscious, fully awake state, we must slow down, quiet the mad monkey mind, and be *present in the moment*. In our frenzy to get a job done, or to go here or there, or to meet with so-and-so, we forget to stay in touch with who we are, what we are, and what we are doing. We miss the truth of our experience as it passes us by from one fleeting moment to the next.

Going through life in a daze may, at first glance, not seem so bad. However, there are many negative consequences associated with semiconscious living. For instance, our lack of mindfulness can make us careless. How many times have you hurt someone without thinking or without even noticing that you did?

Not only can we hurt others by being asleep to reality, but we can also do damage to ourselves. If we fall asleep at the illumination switch of our lives, we leave ourselves vulnerable to all sorts of accidents, both physical and emotional. If we are not truly *with* our loved ones, not really *present* to them, we may discover one day that they have become distant and alienated from us. Make sure, then, that you mind your mindfulness!

STEP EIGHT—RIGHT CONCENTRATION: The final step of The Noble Eight-Fold Path is **right concentration**. In contrast to focusing on our breath in order to develop awareness of the present moment, right concentration demands that we maintain this awareness on an ongoing basis. Using right concentration, we harness energy so that every part of our being is integrated and working harmoniously toward the ultimate goal of enlightenment. Lama Surya Das puts it this way: "Buddha taught that in order to concentrate we need a combination of Right Effort and Right Mindfulness."[47] Concentration thus integrates all of the factors and aspects of mindful awareness into a coherent and vividly present, functioning whole. Right concentration involves recollection, remindfulness, vigilance, alertness, and perseverance; it thus brings us full circle back to the wisdom of Right View and authentic understanding.

Through right concentration, a person experiences oneness and a completeness in which everything fits. We feel "together," not "scatterbrained," entangled by numerous disjointed activities and thoughts. We are at one with the world.

Within Buddhism, four stages of concentration, which enable us to purify our mental activities as a means of achieving happiness, have been identified.[48]

1. The first stage involves getting rid of lust, ill-will, laziness, worry, anxiety, and doubt. These unwholesome mental activities are replaced by feelings of joy and happiness.
2. In stage two, one is able to see through and get beyond all mental activities, while still keeping an awareness of joy and happiness.
3. In the third stage of right concentration, one goes beyond the mental activity responsible for feelings of joy and attains an equanimity pervaded by happiness.
4. In the fourth and final stage of right concentration, complete equanimity and total awareness are achieved, both beyond happiness and unhappiness.

KARMA AND REBIRTH

It is important for adherents of Buddha's teachings to follow The Noble Eight-Fold Path because of its implications for **karma** and **rebirth**. Karma is the **law of moral causation**, which refers to all the willed actions of body, speech, and mind. According to this law, all such actions plant seeds which in time bear fruit, so to speak, spawning further consequences. *Karmic consequences* follow from actions that are either wholesome, unwholesome, or neutral. Lying, for example, is an unwholesome action producing unpleasant results. Giving money to charity or helping a neighbor, by contrast, are wholesome actions producing pleasant consequences. Neutral actions are intentional but have no beneficial or harmful effects either way.

Although karma is usually discussed as something one inherits from their actions in previous lives or what one passes on to future lives, there is a current dimension to it as well. You might wish to think of karma as something that *comes back on you*. For instance, maybe you told a lie or committed a misdeed that could come back to haunt

"These awakened ones,

Dedicated to meditation

Striving actively and vigorously,

Attain NIRVANA, the ultimate security."
THE BUDDHA

Does Buddhism make sense to you as a practical philosophy of life? How so, or why not? What, if anything, about Buddhism do you like most? What, if any, Buddhist notion is most challenging or most difficult for you to accept?

After thinking about this, imagine a conversation between Siddhartha Gautama and the Hedonist Aristippus. What would they say to each other? Would they agree with each other's philosophy? Explain and elaborate, creating a kind of dialogue or debate that might transpire between them. You might even wish to stage a theatrical scene for the benefit of the class!

you. Perhaps a sudden outburst of anger soured your relationship with somebody for days, weeks, or possibly even years. Maybe a brilliant political career was ruined by a momentary moral lapse. Whatever the case, karma does not involve a punishing judge heaping on retribution; it's about the individual creating the consequences of his or her own future. Buddha teaches that

> If a person speaks or acts with unwholesome mind, pain pursues him, even as the wheel follows the hoof of the ox that draws the cart. (*The Dhammapada*)

Another way of explaining karma is to say, "What goes around comes around." In this respect, *giving is indeed receiving*. Give unwholesomeness, and you get it back in return. Give wholesomeness, and you receive it in kind.

The notion of karma extends beyond current existence to past lives and future ones. For instance, your own karma has determined such matters as the species into which you were born (human), your beauty, intelligence, longevity, wealth, and social status. What you do in this life will, in turn, affect the karma of your next life. If you have been born with "bad karma," not to worry. There is a modifiability of the karma you've inherited. Furthermore, if you have already engaged in some unwholesome activities to this point in your life, it is not necessarily true that bad karma will result. It can be mitigated. On the subject of the modifiability of karma, the Buddhist monk Nyanaponika Thera writes:

> A particular karma, either good or bad, may sometimes have its result strengthened by supportive karma, weakened by counter-active karma, or even annulled by destructive karma.[49]

For Nyanaponika Thera, a bad action, or any karmic actions for that matter, must be viewed from the total qualitative structure of the mind from which the action issues:

> It is an individual's accumulation of good or evil karma and also his dominating character traits, good or evil, which affect the karmic result. They determine the greater or lesser weight of the result and may even spell the difference between whether or not it occurs at all.[50]

Appreciating that karmic results are modifiable frees us from the bane of determinism. It teaches moral and spiritual responsibility for oneself and others. It helps us to recognize that karmic action affects the doer of the deed. Even if bad words and deeds, or the thoughts that give rise to them, fail to harm others, they will not fail to have a damaging effect on the doer, speaker, or thinker.[51]

On a final cautionary note, don't confuse *rebirth* with *reincarnation*—the idea that there is a single soul that transmigrates or commutes from body to body down through the ages. The ego-identity of self-consciousness that you identify as "I" or "me" is not going to be transferred to an ant or weasel in the next life. Rebirth—a causal connection between one life and another—is perhaps best captured by metaphor: rebirth is a flame that is passed from one candle to the next. It is not exactly the same flame that moves on down the line, but it is not entirely different either. Another useful image involves billiard balls. As one ball strikes another, it stops dead on impact. The second ball moves on to strike a third and then stops dead; the third ball continues the process. There is a single movement passed on through a sequence of temporary vehicles.[52] The "you" with which you identify in life is simply one of these temporary vehicles.

Buddha, *Dhammacakkappavattana Sutta* (*Setting in Motion the Wheel of Truth*)[53]

After attaining enlightenment, the Buddha taught the Four Noble Truths and the Middle Path in his first sermon. This sermon, or sutta, is known as the Dhammacakkappavattana Sutta *or* The Setting in Motion the Wheel of Truth.

———

Thus have I heard:

On one occasion the Blessed One was living in the Deer Park at Isipatana (the Resort of Seers) near Varanasi (Benares). Then he addressed the group of five monks (*bhikkhus*):

"Monks, these two extremes ought not to be practiced by one who has gone forth from the household life. (What are the two?) There is addiction to indulgence of sense-pleasures, which is low, coarse, the way of ordinary people, unworthy, and unprofitable; and there is addiction to self-mortification, which is painful, unworthy, and unprofitable.

"Avoiding both these extremes, the Tathagata (The Perfect One)* has realized the Middle Path; it gives vision, gives knowledge, and leads to calm, to insight, to enlightenment and to *Nibbana* [the Pali term for *Nirvana*]. And what is that Middle Path realized by the *Tathagata* [how Buddha refers to himself in the Pali canon]? It is the Noble Eightfold path, and nothing else, namely: right understanding, right thought, right speech, right action, right livelihood, right effort, right mindfulness and right concentration. This is the Middle Path realized by the Tathagata which gives vision, which gives knowledge, and leads to calm, to insight, to enlightenment, and to Nibbana.

"The Noble Truth of Suffering (*dukkha*), monks, is this: Birth is suffering, aging is suffering, sickness is suffering, death is suffering, association with the unpleasant is suffering, dissociation from the pleasant is suffering, not to receive what one desires is suffering—in brief the five aggregates subject to grasping are suffering.

"The Noble Truth of the Origin (cause) of Suffering is this: It is this craving (thirst) which produces re-becoming (rebirth) accompanied by passionate greed, and finding fresh delight now here, and now there, namely craving for sense pleasure, craving for existence and craving for non-existence (self-annihilation).

"The Noble Truth of the Cessation of Suffering is this: It is the complete cessation of that very craving, giving it up, relinquishing it, liberating oneself from it, and detaching oneself from it.

"The Noble Truth of the Path Leading to the Cessation of Suffering is this: It is the Noble Eightfold Path, and nothing else, namely: right understanding, right

---

* The Perfect One, one attained to Truth. The Buddha used it when referring to himself. For details, see The Buddha's Ancient Path, Piyadassi Thera, Buddhist Publication Society, Kandy, Sri Lanka, p. 17, n. 4. [translator's note]

thought, right speech, right action, right livelihood, right effort, right mindfulness and right concentration.*

"'This is the Noble Truth of Suffering': such was the vision, the knowledge, the wisdom, the science, the light that arose in me concerning things not heard before. 'This suffering, as a noble truth, should be fully realized': such was the vision, the knowledge, the wisdom, the science, the light that arose in me concerning things not heard before. 'This suffering, as a noble truth has been fully realized': such was the vision, the knowledge, the wisdom, the science, the light that arose in me concerning things not heard before.

"'This is the Noble Truth of the Origin (cause) of Suffering': such was the vision, the knowledge, the wisdom, the science, the light that arose in me concerning things not heard before. 'This Origin of Suffering as a noble truth should be eradicated': such was the vision, the knowledge, the wisdom, the science, the light that arose in me concerning things not heard before. 'This Origin of suffering as a noble truth has been eradicated': such was the vision, the knowledge, the wisdom, the science, the light that arose in me concerning things not heard before.

"'This is the Noble Truth of the Cessation of Suffering': such was the vision, the knowledge, the wisdom, the science, the light that arose in me concerning things not heard before. 'This Cessation of suffering, as a noble truth, should be realized': such was the vision, the knowledge, the wisdom, the science, the light that arose in me concerning things not heard before. 'This Cessation of suffering, as a noble truth has been realized': such was the vision, the knowledge, the wisdom, the science, the light that arose in me concerning things not heard before.

"'This is the Noble Truth of the Path leading to the cessation of suffering': such was the vision, the knowledge, the wisdom, the science, the light that arose in me con-cerning things not heard before. 'This Path leading to the cessation of suffering, as a noble truth, should be developed': such was the vision, the knowledge, the wisdom, the science, the light that arose in me concerning things not heard before. 'This Path leading to the cessation of suffering, as a noble truth has been developed': such was the vision, the knowledge, the wisdom, the science, the light that arose in me concerning things not heard before.

"As long as my knowledge of seeing things as they really are, was not quite clear in these three aspects, in these twelve ways, concerning the Four Noble Truths,† I did not claim to have realized the matchless, supreme Enlightenment, in this world with its gods, with its Maras and Brahmas, in this generation with its recluses and brahmanas, with its Devas and humans. But when my knowledge of seeing things as they really are was quite clear in these three aspects, in these twelve ways, concerning the Four Noble Truths, then I claimed to have realized the matchless, supreme Enlightenment in this world with its gods, with its Maras and Brahmas, in this generation with its recluses and brahmanas, with its Devas and humans. And a vision of insight arose in me thus: 'Unshakable is the deliverance of my heart. This is the last birth. Now there is no more re-becoming (rebirth).'"

This the Blessed One said. The group of five monks was glad, and they rejoiced at the words of the Blessed One.

When this discourse was thus expounded there arose in the Venerable Koṇḍañña the passion-free, stainless vision of Truth (*dhamma-cakkhu*); in other words, he attained *sotapatti*, the first stage of sanctity, and realized: "Whatever has the nature of arising, has the nature of ceasing."

---

* For a very comprehensive account of the Four Noble Truths read *The Buddha's Ancient Path*, Piyadassi Thera, Buddhist Publication Society, Kandy, Sri Lanka (Ceylon). [translator's note]

† As the previous paragraphs indicate, there are three aspects of knowledge with regard to each of the Four Noble Truths: 1. The knowledge that it is the Truth (*sacca-ñana*). 2. The knowledge that a certain function with regard to this Truth should be performed (*kicca-ñana*). 3. The knowledge that the function with regard to this Truth has been performed (*kata-ñana*). The twelve ways or modes are obtained by applying these three aspects to each of the Four Noble Truths. [translator's note]

Now when the Blessed One set in motion the Wheel of Truth, the Bhummattha devas (the earth deities) proclaimed: "The Matchless Wheel of Truth that cannot be set in motion by recluse, brahmana, deva, Mara, Brahma, or any one in the world, is set in motion by the Blessed One in the Deer Park at Isipatana near Varanasi."

Hearing these words of the earth deities, all the Catummaharajika devas proclaimed: "The Matchless Wheel of Truth that cannot be set in motion by recluse, brahmana, deva, Mara, Brahma, or any one in the world, is set in motion by the Blessed One in the Deer Park at Isipatana near Varanasi." These words were heard in the upper deva realms, and from Catummaharajika it was proclaimed in Tavatimsa ... Yama ... Tusita ... Nimmanarati ... Paranimmita-vasavatti ... and the Brahmas of Brahma Parisajja ... Brahma Purohita ... Maha Brahma ... Parittabha ... Appamanabha ... Abhassara ... Parittasubha ... Appamana subha ... Subhakinna ... Vehapphala ... Aviha ... Atappa ... Sudassa ... Sudassi ... and in Akanittha: "The Matchless Wheel of Truth that cannot be set in motion by recluse, brahmana, deva, Mara, Brahma, or any one in the world, is set in motion by the Blessed One in the Deer Park at Isipatana near Varanasi."

Thus at that very moment, at that instant, the cry (that the Wheel of Truth is set in motion) spread as far as Brahma realm, the system of ten thousand worlds trembled and quaked and shook. A boundless sublime radiance surpassing the effulgence (power) of devas appeared in the world.

Then the Blessed One uttered this paean of joy: "Verily Kondañña has realized; verily Kondañña has realized (the Four Noble Truths)." Thus it was that the Venerable Kondañña received the name, "Añña Knondañña'—Kondañña who realizes."

READING QUESTIONS

1. Consider what insights the Tathagata (or Buddha) shares with his audience about the "Middle Path." Given what he says, what are the two extremes at either side of this path, and what is it like to be in the "middle" of those extremes? Where will the Middle Path take the one who follows it?

2. Among the things identified in the text as suffering are "birth ... aging ... sickness ... [and] death." What do all causes of suffering share in common, according to the Buddha? Seeing as how these are unavoidable aspects of a human life, how is it possible to detach from suffering?

INSTRUCTIONS: Fill in the blanks with the appropriate responses listed below. (Answers at back of book.)

active engagement	courageous acceptance	Epicurus	existence
suffering	ego	essence	absurd
friendship	fear	Zeno	pleasure
aphorisms	uniqueness	unorthodox	worldviews
craving	natural	crowd	self-control
causal determinism	virtue	*ataraxia*	psychological hedonism
Aristippus	vain	limits	Viktor Frankl
Nirvana	Socrates	ethical hedonism	emotional detachment
enduring	synchronicity	blame	subjectivity
immediate	existentialism	ordered	nature
Middle Path	Diogenes	revolt	meaningful life

1. Philosophies of life offer us different perspectives or _____.

2. The founder of Stoicism was _____ of Citium.

3. _____ was a model for both Cynics and Stoics alike.

4. The most famous Cynic in history is _____, someone who lived in a wine barrel.

5. The Stoic universe is one which is rational and _____.

6. A term for meaningful coincidence is _____.

7. Since life is fated and an expression of God's will, according to the Stoics, it is best that we develop an attitude of _____.

8. The purpose of life for the Stoic is to live according to _____.

9. If we are not to be adversely affected by events in the world, we must develop _____.

10. _____ is a philosophical movement that some prefer to see as an attitude or outlook, rather than as a formal philosophy as such.

11. Existential insights are sometimes best captured by _____ and other literary forms, not by rational deductive argument.

12. The reason some philosophers have problems with Existentialists is due to their _____ methods.

13. Existentialism is a _____ against rational, philosophical system building.

14. Existentialists underscore the importance of _____ and the _____ of individuals.

15. Atheistic Existentialists believe that _____ precedes _____.

16. With respect to human conduct, Existentialists reject the thesis of _____ and fate.

17. Without God to give it order and meaning, the Existentialist's universe is _____ and chaotic.

18. The Existentialist would warn you against being swallowed up by the _____.

19. If it is true that we are completely responsible for our actions, thoughts, and emotions, then we can't _____ others for what we do or how we feel.

20. _____, the noted psychiatrist, used many existential insights in the development of logotherapy.

21. _____ entails involvement in positively valuable projects.

22. A _____ is a life that is actively and at least somewhat successfully engaged in one or more projects of positive objective value, as opposed to projects of subjective value.

23. _____ is the thesis that human beings pursue pleasure and are motivated to do so.

24. _____ is the thesis that you ought to pursue pleasure and it is wrong for you not to do so.

25. _____ of Cyrene gave hedonism its strongest and most direct statement.

26. According to Cyrenaic hedonists, _____ is the principal motive for living.

27. For Cyrenaic hedonists, the only pleasures that should be avoided are those which are enslaving or cause us to lose _____.

28. Aristippus believed that _____ or actual pleasures are better than potential pleasures located in the future.

29. _____, another hedonist, founded his own philosophical school of thought at The Garden.

30. The selection of _____ pleasures over immediate ones may sometimes mean that one must opt for short-term pain for longer-term gain.

31. For Epicurus, the ultimate end of life is _____, a static pleasure reflected by tranquility of the soul.

32. According to Epicurus's classification, desires can either be _____ or vain.

33. Epicureans believe that peace of mind is disturbed by _____ of the gods and worry about the afterlife.

34. On some interpretations of Epicurus's writings, _____ is part of the pleasant life.

35. *Ataraxia* is an Epicurean notion that includes _____ and concern for others.

36. _____ desires are based on empty beliefs that are conditioned, false, and self-defeating.

37. Natural desires have _____ and can be satisfied.

38. The First Noble Truth of Buddhism states that life is _____

39. _____ is the source of human misery and unhappiness, according to Siddhartha Gautama.

40. With the attainment of _____, the hot flames of selfish desire are blown out like a lamp, resulting in a detached peacefulness for the individual.

41. To achieve enlightenment, it is necessary to follow the _____ captured by The Noble Eight-Fold Path.

42. In order to eliminate selfish craving, we must come to recognize the impermanence of the _____.

Key Terms

Stoicism

Albert Ellis: psychologist; founder of rational-emotive behavior therapy   145

Antisthenes: disciple of Socrates; architect of Cynicism   139

Chrysippus: Co-founder of the stoic school of philosophy   139

cosmology: the study of the physical universe   142

courageous acceptance: a psychological posture; recognition of interior freedom to respond emotionally and psychologically as we choose; accepting what we cannot change   142

Cynicism: school of philosophy founded by Antisthenes; recommends living a life of virtue in accordance with nature   139

Cynosarges: another name for Stoicism; means "the (white or) silver dog"   139

Diogenes: a famous Cynical philosopher   139

emotion: feeling or passion   145

Epictetus: Greek stoic philosopher; born a slave   139

eudaimonia: often translated as happiness; normative concept related to 'successful living'   142

excessive passions: unreasonable and unnatural emotions   146

fated: destined to happen; predetermined   140

immanent: inherent; operating or existing within; e.g., the divine encompasses or is manifest (is immanent) in the material world   140

interior freedom: psychological independence allowing one to determine one's attitudes and judgments about people, things, and events in the world   142

Marcus Aurelius: Roman emperor from 161 CE to 180 CE; stoic philosopher   139

monistic universe: the universe is one; all things are manifestations of the one   140

ordered universe: a universe that is rational and structured by design   140

Seneca: Roman stoic philosopher   139

Stoic apathy: a state of spiritual peace and well-being   142

Stoicism: Greek school of philosophy founded in Athens by Zeno of Citium   139

Stoics: followers of Zeno; so-called "men of the porch"   139

synchronicity: no causal relationship, but still a meaningful coincidence   140

Zeno: founder of Stoicism   139

Existentialism

abstract universals: that which is beyond material particulars (e.g., Plato's Forms)   155

absurdity: irrationality, unreasonableness, ridiculousness   152

Albert Camus: French philosopher, author, journalist, and 1957 Nobel Prize winner   153

anti-political: reaction or opposition to traditional politics and political policies   152

aphorisms: concise expressions of a general truth or principle   153

atheists: people who do not believe in God   152

authenticity: the degree or extent to which a person's actions and words are consistent with his or her true convictions and beliefs; honesty of expression   158

Blaise Pascal: French religious philosopher   153

cogito: Latin for "I think"; Descartes coined the phrase *cogito, ergo sum*: I think, therefore I am   156

contingency: a future event that is possible, but only conditional, not certain   158

dialogues: conversations between two people   153

essence: the inward nature, true substance, or constitution of anything, as opposed to what is accidental, phenomenal, illusory, etc.   155

existence: the state of living or having objective reality   155

Existentialism: an approach to philosophy that explores the nature of human existence; emphasizes the experience of the human subject, that is, not merely the thinking subject, but the flesh and blood acting, feeling, living human being   152

fascist: a political philosophy, movement, or regime that exalts nation and often race above the individual and that stands for a centralized autocratic government headed by a dictatorial leader, severe economic and social regimentation, and forcible suppression of opposition. Modern examples are the regimes of Hitler and Mussolini   152

Franz Kafka: Bohemian writer; his works expressed the anxieties and alienation felt by many people in twentieth-century Europe and North America   153

freedom: the condition of being free; absence of constraint or coercion   152

freedom of choice: ability to choose or decide as one pleases   157

Friedrich Nietzsche: Prussian philosopher; coined the expression "God is dead"   153

Fyodor Dostoyevsky: Russian writer whose works explore human psychology and a variety of philosophical and religious themes. His *Notes from Underground* (1864) is considered one of the first works of existentialist literature   153

Gabriel Marcel: French philosopher, playwright, music critic, and Christian Existentialist   153

Hegel: German post-Kantian idealist philosopher; attempted to elaborate a comprehensive and systematic philosophy   154

humanitarians: people who seek to promote human welfare   152

individual: single separate person; one who stands alone   156

interpersonal: that which involves relations between or among persons   152

Jean-Paul Sartre: French existentialist philosopher   153

Karl Jaspers: German-Swiss psychiatrist and philosopher who exercised considerable influence on a number of areas of philosophical inquiry, especially on epistemology, the philosophy of religion, and political theory   153

literary forms: genres of writing, (e.g., novel or play)   153

Martin Heidegger: German philosopher associated with phenomenology and Existentialism   153

Marxists: people whose social and political views are based on the writings of Karl Marx   152

Michel de Montaigne: French Renaissance philosopher; the first essayist   153

negation: the absence of something actual in the context of Existentialism   158

parables: short allegorical stories designed to illustrate or teach some truth or moral lesson   153

philosophical system-building: constructing theoretical models to help explain the nature of reality and knowledge; effort to connect concepts and ideas about life and the universe in a fashion that reflects an internal coherence and logical consistency   154

political conservatives: people who support traditional social institutions; importance is given to hierarchical authority and property rights   152

possibility: that which may happen or could be the case   158

rationality: a condition that is agreeable to reason; deductive and inductive reason have to do with increasing the likelihood of truth, and practical reason has to do with trying to base one's actions (or "practice") in part on truth and in part upon what one wants or values   154

realm of forms: the timeless and absolute dimension of non-material reality knowable only by the mind or direct intellectual acquaintance, not the senses   155

sense perception: experiencing or becoming aware of something through the senses (e.g., seeing a cat)   155

Simone de Beauvoir: French philosopher; colleague of Sartre; author of *The Second Sex*; contributed to the fields of ethics, politics, existentialism, phenomenology, and feminist theory   153

Søren Kierkegaard: Danish Existentialist; described as the father of Existentialism[54]   153

subjective experience: the emotional and cognitive elements of an individual person's experience; not objectively viewed, but personally experienced   155

theists: people who believe in one or more gods   152

uniqueness: special defining characteristic of something or somebody   156

uniqueness of individuals: that which makes one unlike anyone else   155

unorthodox methods: different or unusual ways of doing things   153

The Meaning of Life

active engagement: success, involvement in positively valuable projects; aspect of meaningful life   163

existential vacuum: notion developed by Viktor Frankl; results when we are frustrated in our fundamental need to make sense of the world or when our will-to-meaning is left unsatisfied; feelings of emptiness and futility   168

logotherapy: meaning-therapy developed by Viktor Frankl   168

meaningful life: a life that is actively and at least somewhat successfully engaged in one or more projects of positive objective value, as opposed to projects of subjective value   163

meaningfulness: involves getting over ourselves and any egoistic concern for subjectively-sourced values that we might have; results from engaging in positive projects that factor into meaningful lives   164

non-subjective values: related to things that are better than others despite how we feel about them; objects, events, activities, and features of the world that have their source of worth in something other than us   164

noögenic neurosis: a type of psychological disturbance discovered by Viktor Frankl. It's caused by existential anxiety over one's situation   168

passive disengagement: a life of frivolous activities, a life of pointless preoccupation, a life of failed projects   163

self-transcendence: that process of looking beyond our personal interests and investing in something bigger   164

Susan Wolf: contemporary American philosopher who writes on issues of meaning and the good life   162

Hedonism

actual pleasures: pleasures actually experienced in the moment   171

Aristotle: Greek philosopher; student of Plato; founder of The Lyceum   172

asceticism: the practice of strict self-denial or severe restraint from physical pleasures   175

ataraxia: tranquility; the state of not having troubles   173

bodily health: one's physical condition   175

Cicero: a Roman politician and Academic Skeptic   171

Cyrenaic hedonism: a school of hedonism; founded by Aristippus; named after his home town   170

Diogenes Laertius: biographer of ancient Greek philosophers   171

empty beliefs: beliefs that are false, harmful, and self-defeating   174

enduring pleasures: positive experiences that last a long time   172

Epicureanism: philosophy based on thinking of Epicurus   171

Epicurus: Athenian philosopher who founded The Garden, a school of philosophy dedicated to the pursuit of proper enduring pleasure   171

ethical hedonism: moral theory stating that one should pursue pleasure since pleasure is the only thing intrinsically valuable   170

freedom from physical need: having bodily or material needs met   175

friendship: a positive emotional relationship between friends   177

The Garden: school of philosophy in Athens founded by Epicurus   172

hedonism: the pursuit of pleasure   169

intensity: magnitude or strength of something   170

kinetic pleasures: pleasure obtained through some sort of action   173

Lucretius: Roman poet and philosopher   171

meaning of life: purpose for living; significance of existence; reason for being alive   170

momentary pleasures: brief positive physical or emotional experiences   172

natural desires: desires in accordance with nature; can be necessary or unnecessary   174

Plato: Greek philosopher; student of Socrates; founder of The Academy   172

pleasure: positive feeling related to experiences of joy, contentment, gratification, comfort, etc.   170

potential pleasures: future pleasures; those not yet experienced but anticipated   171

powers of discrimination: ability to discern (e.g., between vain and natural desires)   175

prudence: practical wisdom   175

psychological hedonism: motivational theory stating that actions are determined by their pleasure-producing properties   169

self-sufficiency: the state of needing nothing; emotional or intellectual independence   175

Seneca: a major philosophical figure of the Roman Imperial Period   171

simple tastes: preferences that are basic   175

static pleasures: pleasurable states resulting when pains, lacks, deficiencies, or frustrations have been removed   173

tarachai: troubles   173

tranquility of the soul: peace of mind   175

vain desires: desires not rooted in nature, in contrast to those which are natural and necessary   174

virtue: behavior exhibiting high moral excellence   176

Buddhism

attachment: the inability to practice detachment; the main obstacle to a serene and fulfilled life   185

Buddhism: a major faith founded by Siddhartha Gautama ("The Buddha") more than 2,500 years ago in India; a path of practice and spiritual development leading to insight into what is believed to be the true nature of reality   181

concentration: focus needed for right effort and right mindfulness   189

craving: the cause of human suffering; desire   186

denial: an egoistic or psychological defense mechanism   190

Dharma: the teachings of The Buddha   184

ego: self-consciousness characterized by judgmentalism, greed, and fear   188

egolessness: an emotional state where one feels no ego or self; state of having no distinct being apart from the world around oneself; a state of oneness   189

The Four Noble Truths: contain the essence of Buddhist teachings   181

impermanence: Buddhist teaching that all that exists is transitory and impermanent   189

karma: law of moral causation   195

law of moral causation: synonym for karma   195

The Middle Path: the avoidance of two extremes in practical life, i.e., indulgence in sensual pleasures on the one hand, and severe asceticism on the other   181

morality: comprised of right action and right livelihood   189

Nirvana: supreme bliss or inner peace   188

The Noble Eight-Fold Path: a positive, affirmative prescription for living   181

reality testing: ensuring that the ego is not engaging in defensive distortions of reality   190

rebirth: Buddhist doctrine of evolving consciousness passing from one being's aggregation to another   195

right action: goodness and virtue in the way we treat others; creating harmony   192

right concentration: involves recollection, remindfulness, vigilance, alertness, and perseverance   195

right effort: working to elevate ourselves to more wholesome states   193

right intentions: correct motivations   190

right livelihood: expressing love through work; a vocation with integrity   193

right mindfulness: a quiet mind, present to the moment   194

right speech: speaking the truth and telling no lies; not using words as weapons   191

self: our ego-identification; that which craves and forms attachments   187

suffering: pain; a basic characteristic of human life; can be physical, emotional or psychological   185, 189

therapeutic philosophy: philosophy that can have psychological and emotional benefits   184

willful blindness: a refusal to face the facts of the human condition   186

wisdom: in Buddhism it entails right view, right thought, and right speech   189

Summary of Major Points

1. What is the historical background of Stoicism?
- flourished in ancient Rome and Greece for about five centuries (third century BCE–second century CE)
- founded by Zeno; co-founded by Chrysippus
- well-known Stoics: Epictetus, Marcus Aurelius, Seneca
- influenced by Socrates and the Cynics

2. What is the Stoic universe like?
- ordered, rational, structured, and shaped by design
- synchronistic, fated
- monistic (God is immanent in all things)

3. How should we live in a fated universe?
- Be reassured; God orders things for the best.
- See beyond evils and misfortunes; in a larger context, they make sense.
- Appreciate your freedom to choose your attitudes and make your judgments.
- Develop an attitude of courageous acceptance.
- Live according to nature.
- Try to develop Stoic apathy to live in *eudaimonia*.
- Look upon the world with emotional detachment to develop peace of mind.
- Abolish excessive passions.

4. How do we progress morally?
- Know thyself.
- Engage in daily self-examinations.
- Monitor your thoughts, feelings, and actions.
- Substitute good habits for bad ones.
- Avoid temptations and wayward companions.
- Become master in your own psychological home.
- Eliminate disturbing passions and excessive emotions.
- Forgive others.
- Live up to some ideal of virtue (e.g., Socrates, Jesus, Buddha).
- Perform your duties in accordance with right reason.

5. Why is Existentialism difficult to define?
- It is something like an attitude or outlook; not a formal system
- It comprises several different perspectives (atheist, theist, apolitical, Marxist)
- It uses unorthodox methods (literary and artistic)

6. Who are the major figures associated with Existentialism?
- Friedrich Nietzsche
- Karl Jaspers
- Gabriel Marcel
- Jean-Paul Sartre
- Simone de Beauvoir
- Martin Heidegger
- Albert Camus
- Fyodor Dostoyevsky
- Franz Kafka

7. How is Existentialism a revolt?
- It is a reaction against pure rationality and philosophical system-building.
- It emphasizes subjective experience.
- It uses literary forms and other unorthodox methods.

8. What are some central themes of Existentialism?
- essence versus existence
- freedom of choice
- individuality and subjective experience
- possibility and contingency
- authenticity
- negation
- personal responsibility

9. What constitutes a meaningful life according to Susan Wolf?
- It is a life that is actively and at least somewhat successfully engaged in one or more projects of positive objective value, as opposed to projects of subjective value.

10. What for Wolf is a meaningless life?

▸ a life of passive disengagement
▸ a life of frivolous activities
▸ a life of pointless preoccupation
▸ a life of failed projects

11. What term did Viktor Frankl coin to capture our modern spiritual malaise? What does it involve?

▸ The spiritual malaise is called the existential vacuum.
▸ The existential vacuum arises when our will-to-meaning is frustrated or left unsatisfied.
▸ Existential frustration leaves us with feelings of emptiness and purposelessness.

12. What are sources of meaning in life for Frankl?

▸ work
▸ love
▸ suffering, if need be

13. What forms of hedonism are there?

▸ psychological versus ethical
▸ Cyrenaic versus Epicurean

14. Who founded Cyrenaic hedonism? What did he believe?

▸ The founder is Aristippus (430–350 BCE).
▸ Pleasure is the principle motive for living.
▸ Pleasure is always good; pain is always bad.
▸ Pleasures cannot be compared; the intensity of pleasure determines its value.
▸ The meaning of life is found in the pursuit of pleasure.
▸ One should control only those pleasures which become enslaving.
▸ Actual pleasures are preferable to potential pleasures.
▸ One should avoid public life to maximize personal pleasure.

15. Who is Epicurus? What did he found?

▸ Epicurus is a hedonistic philosopher.
▸ He founded The Garden as a challenge to the Stoa, Plato's Academy, and Aristotle's Lyceum.

16. What are some basic tenets of Epicureanism?

▸ Enduring pleasures are better than momentary pleasures.
▸ Kinetic pleasures (of motion) are different from static pleasures (states).
▸ *Ataraxia* is achieved when one functions normally without painful interference; it is freedom from bodily pain and tranquility of the soul.
▸ *Ataraxia* derives from the satisfaction of natural and necessary desires; vain desires are unnatural and based on empty and false beliefs; these latter desires cannot be satisfied and therefore offer no enduring stability.
▸ Pleasantness in life is also tied to virtue and friendship.

17. What are the obstacles to achieving *ataraxia*, or an enjoyable, tranquil life?

▸ Society and the acculturation process condition false beliefs, creating vain desires.
▸ People have wrongly learned to fear God and the afterlife.

18. How are the teachings of the Buddha therapeutic?

▸ The Buddha diagnoses the perennial problem of humanity as suffering.
▸ Second, he isolates the cause of suffering as selfish craving.
▸ Third, he identifies the remedy to restore psycho-spiritual health.
▸ Fourth, he prescribes an eight-fold course of action for personal healing involving right views, right thought, right speech, right action, right livelihood, right effort, right mindfulness, and right concentration.

Additional Resources

For interactive quizzes, stories, supplements, and other materials for study and review, visit:

sites.broadviewpress.com/experiencing-philosophy/chapter3
Passcode: w4822kj

Or scan the following QR code:

CHAPTER 4

Epistemology, Metaphysics, and God

Take It Personally 214

Know Thyself: My Philosophical Presuppositions about Knowledge and Reality 217

4.1 Preliminary Questions and Definitions 220

4.2 Plato's Metaphysical Epistemology 221
Divided Line Theory 224
Theory of Forms 226
Simile of the Sun 227
ORIGINAL SOURCE: Plato, Simile of the Sun 228
Allegory of the Cave 230
ORIGINAL SOURCE: Plato, Allegory of the Cave 231

4.3 René Descartes's Rational Method of Doubt 236
Historical Context 236
The Quest for Certainty 237
Method of Doubt 239
ORIGINAL SOURCE: René Descartes, First Meditation 241
Cogito Ergo Sum—I Think, Therefore I Am 244
ORIGINAL SOURCE: René Descartes, Second Meditation, featuring the Cogito 245
ORIGINAL SOURCE: René Descartes, Second Meditation, featuring The Wax Example 249

4.4 John Locke's Empiricist Theory of Ideas 251
Tabula Rasa 253
Criticisms of Innate Ideas 253
Primary and Secondary Qualities of Objects 254

4.5 David Hume's Radical Skepticism 257
On the Origin of Ideas 260
Rejection of the Cogito 260
Association of Ideas 262
Critique of Causality 262
"Hume's Fork" and Types of Reasoning 265

ORIGINAL SOURCE: David Hume, An Enquiry Concerning Human Understanding 267
David Hume's Origins and Limits of Knowledge: A Summary 270

4.6 Immanuel Kant's Synthesis of Reason and Sensory Experience 270
The Role of the Senses in Knowledge 271
The Copernican Revolution in Epistemology 274
A Priori Elements of Knowledge 275
Kantian versus Platonic Forms 277
The Categories of Cause and Substance 277
Metaphysics and the Regulative Function of Transcendental Ideas 279
ORIGINAL SOURCE: Immanuel Kant, Prolegomena to Any Future Metaphysics 283

4.7 Critiques of Traditional Approaches to Epistemology and Metaphysics 285
Standpoint Epistemology 285
ORIGINAL SOURCE: Patricia Hill Collins, Black Feminist Thought 287
Mind-Body Metaphysics 289
ORIGINAL SOURCE: Yasuo Yuasa, Toward an Eastern Mind-Body Theory 290

4.8 Proofs for the Existence of God 291
St. Anselm's Ontological Proof 293
St. Thomas Aquinas's "Five Ways": Proofs for the Existence of God 295
ORIGINAL SOURCE: St. Thomas Aquinas, Whether God Exists 300

Progress Check 302

Study Guide 304
Key Terms 304
Summary of Major Points 308

After successfully completing this chapter, you will be able to

▸ Define epistemology and metaphysics, identifying fundamental questions raised by each

▸ Outline Plato's "Divided Line Theory of Knowledge," understanding its metaphysical underpinnings

▸ Comprehend the Platonic concept of "goodness," using the Simile of the Sun

▸ Give an account of the ascent from illusion to philosophical illumination in terms of Plato's Allegory of the Cave

▸ Define rationalism and provide the historical context out of which it emerged

▸ Explain René Descartes's use of methodological doubt

▸ State the importance of the *cogito* in Descartes's rational philosophy

▸ Outline the basic ideas of British empiricism with reference to John Locke and David Hume

▸ Illustrate how Kant's epistemology represents a synthesis of reason and sensory experience

▸ Distinguish between Kantian and Platonic forms

▸ Discuss the regulative function of the Kantian transcendental ideas of 'self,' 'God' and 'cosmos'

▸ Understand how purely rational objective approaches to epistemology can be guilty of bias from the perspective of Black feminist epistemology

▸ Re-consider Descartes's dualism from the vantage point of Eastern mind-body theory

▸ Articulate ontological, cosmological, and teleological proofs for the existence of God

FOCUS QUESTIONS

1. How are epistemology and metaphysics related to each other?

2. What are some metaphysical worldviews implicit in the epistemological theories presented in this chapter?

3. What basic assumptions are built into rationalism and empiricism? What are Immanuel Kant's views on these assumptions?

4. What is meant by the suggestion that the human mind is either passive or active?

5. How can "detached" and "objective" approaches to the study of knowledge possibly be biased?

6. How do Eastern and Western philosophy differ on the issue of the mind-body relationship?

7. What proofs, if any, can be given for the existence of God?

Adam and Eve's desire to eat the forbidden fruit from the tree of knowledge led to their separation from God in the Garden of Eden. One could say that, in the beginning, there dawned on human consciousness an awareness of the connection between epistemology (knowledge) and metaphysics (God). That connection endures today and is the subject of this chapter.

Take It Personally

Our experience of philosophy began in Chapter 1 with a discussion of its nature and benefits, as well as with a brief outline of its historical periods and disciplinary subdivisions. In Chapter 2, we sought to amass the logical tools required to do the serious work that philosophers do. This necessitated that we learn a few essentials, such as distinguishing between types of claims and also between thoughtless opinions and genuine philosophical arguments. We mastered some basic forms of inductive and deductive logic as well, being careful to distinguish among notions of argumentative strength, validity, soundness, and truth. In addition, we spent some time studying a number of informal logical fallacies that are used as irrational rhetorical devices, not in the pursuit of wisdom, but for illegitimate purposes of persuasion, diversion, and psychological attack.

Once we gained a general understanding of what philosophy is all about and why it is important, and after mastering some basic skills of logic and reasoning, we proceeded in Chapter 3 to explore philosophy's existential relevance by comparing various philosophies of life with our own, taking the opportunity to re-evaluate our personal worldviews in light of these other alternatives, which in some cases have guided people for centuries.

Now that you know what philosophy is, have learned the basics of how to think critically and philosophically using proper methods of logic, and have reflected on where you currently stand with respect to your own personal philosophical worldview, we are finally prepared to engage in some heavy-duty philosophical deliberations pertaining to esoteric matters of epistemology, metaphysics, and God.

As we proceed through this section of the book, it might be interesting for you to reflect again on your personal philosophy of life. Discussions here on cause-and-effect relations and proofs given for the existence of God, for example, will have implications for everyone. Whether we are condemned to be free in an inherently meaningless and chaotic world, as Sartre claimed, or destined to be reunited with God, depends on the nature of reality—a matter of metaphysics.

This chapter will reinforce the point made in Chapter 1 that life philosophies are derivative of other primary branches of philosophical inquiry. As you go through this chapter, try to relate its content to your personal worldview or outlook on life—technically what's called, in German, your *Weltanschauung*.* What do the philosophers say about reality, God, and knowledge that has an impact on your own philosophical presuppositions?

---

* Pronounced *VELT-an-shao-oong*.

As a way of prefacing the important and overlapping concerns of epistemology and metaphysics, please allow me to take you back to my first geometry class in high school where, you could say, I *took it personally*. My own first experience with philosophy may strike a resonant chord with you.

In high school, I had the good fortune of being exposed to a very knowledgeable geometry teacher who appreciated the philosophical underpinnings of his discipline. I remember how, one day, he asked everyone in the class to imagine a point in space located just in front of him at the spot where his index finger met his thumb. Then, he directed us to imagine a second point in space using his other thumb and index finger. He proceeded to ask the class, "What is the shortest distance between these two imaginary points in space called?"

Though somewhat hesitant, believing this was a trick question of sorts, most students were finally able to reply, "A straight line." "Correct," responded the teacher. This all seemed simple enough until the next somewhat mysterious question was posed. The teacher asked, "What was important to note in my earlier directions to you?"

After some puzzlement, a student finally responded, "Imagine! You asked us to *imagine* two points in space." "Exactly," replied the teacher, "for in reality there are no such things as points in space. All we can do is represent them somehow, as located at our fingertips, or as two dots on the blackboard, for example."

If this wasn't intriguing enough, my instructor then went on to claim that perfectly straight lines, like points in space, do not really exist either. He challenged us to draw the straightest line that we could freehand, then using a ruler, the side of a book, or anything else we could find. He said that no matter how straight the line appeared, in truth it was still imperfect. Although the naked eye might not be able to detect the tiny imperfections, one glance at our lines through a powerful microscope would reveal that they were not straight and smooth-edged at all, but actually quite jagged in appearance. I accepted his contention that the best we can produce are rough approximations of perfection. Also, familiar with the methods of my teacher, I knew this insight was just a preliminary set-up for a grander revelation of some sort ... so I waited.

The teacher then drew a triangle on the board. He indicated that it contained one right angle and two equal sides (see Figure 4.1). He asked if anyone in the class knew the name of what he had drawn. A student shouted, "A right-angled isosceles triangle!" Again, "Correct," was the reply. Judging by the tone of his voice, I knew we were approaching the climactic point of the lesson when he asked if anyone could figure out the length of "c," which we learned was called the hypotenuse. I think it was the same student who blurted out that the hypotenuse squared is equal to the sum of both equal sides squared. He was even able to express it mathematically, saying, "$c^2 = a^2 + b^2$." "Excellent," said the teacher. "But does anyone know what right-angled isosceles triangles and straight lines have in common?"

On this one, everyone was stumped. After a lengthy pause, the teacher said that "both are perfect geometric forms that do not actually exist in the real world; they are both theoretical entities grasped only by the mind."

Furthermore, it was pointed out to us that the mathematical equation used to calculate the hypotenuse represented a necessary and undeniable truth. We couldn't say, for example, that $c^3 = a^2 + b^2$ or that $b^2 = c^3 + a^3$—the statement in its original form was the only one that was absolutely true: true unconditionally for everyone, and true for all time.

Putting *two and two* together, so to speak, I came up with the realization that by means of a mathematical equation I had attained *absolute and necessary truth about something that did not exist in the physical world*. I had achieved certain knowledge of something that was not materially real. Things were beginning to get spooky!

At the time, I didn't fully appreciate how I had been intellectually broadsided by some rather deep metaphysical and epistemological notions. It was only years later, through the study of philosophy, that I came to better understand those cryptic and puzzling questions of my geometry teacher.

In what follows, you too will explore some of the mysteries of the mind that pertain to unchanging eternal verities concerning immaterial things. Before we begin to unravel these mysteries, however, we will define epistemology and metaphysics as well as list some of the fundamental questions that they both raise.

In the interests of inclusiveness and diversity, we will take a critical look at traditional philosophical perspectives on knowledge and reality from the vantage points of Black feminist thought and Eastern thinking related to mind-body dualism. Although brief for the purposes of this chapter, this critical look should help us to reflect on any Western biases we might have in our own thinking.

Discussion of ideas about God will also be included in the theoretical discussions that follow. Indeed, several classical proofs for the existence of God are highlighted in the last section of the chapter. But before getting to the main text, you're invited to complete the *Know Thyself* diagnostic. It will help you to identify more clearly your pre-reflective assumptions about knowledge and reality.

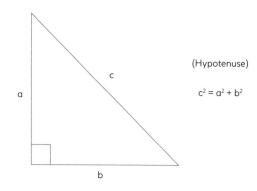

FIGURE 4.1 How to find the length of the hypotenuse of a right-angled triangle

(Hypotenuse)

$$c^2 = a^2 + b^2$$

My Philosophical Presuppositions about Knowledge and Reality

AIM

This diagnostic is designed to help you identify your pre-reflective assumptions about knowledge and reality.

INSTRUCTIONS

Indicate your level of agreement or disagreement with each of the statements below using the scale provided. Interpret any statements that you find difficult to understand in the best way you can. When finished, follow the scoring instructions and read about your metaphysical/epistemological outlook as encapsulated by one of the brief descriptions. (After finishing this chapter, you may wish to complete this self-diagnostic again, having a better understanding of the theories, terminology, and assumptions built into the statements comprising this measure.)

1 = strongly disagree
2 = disagree somewhat
3 = agree somewhat
4 = strongly agree

1. _____ There exists a reality beyond the world of sensory experience.

2. _____ All knowledge ultimately derives from our sensory experience of people, objects, and events.

3. _____ Because the senses can sometimes be misleading, reason is the ultimate source of knowledge.

4. _____ While not all knowledge is derived from experience, it begins with experience, interacting with the faculty of human reason.

5. _____ Behind the impermanence and transitoriness of life exists a timeless, spaceless, and changeless alternative reality.

6. _____ With respect to what is true or false, I can doubt many things; but I cannot doubt that I exist as a thinking thing.

7. _____ At birth, the human mind is like an empty blackboard slate, void of any information.

8. _____ Knowledge is the product of an active construction of the human mind assembling the sense data of experience into meaningful objects and events.

9. _____ The highest forms of knowledge are beyond logic and reason; they are attained only by immediate insight, pure thought, or by what might be called *direct intellectual apprehension*.

10. _____ It is possible to prove the existence of God using the methods of reason alone.

11. _____ Statements that are not logically true, not true by definition, nor verifiable as true by observation and experiment, are entirely meaningless statements.

12. _____ In order to gain knowledge, we should not conform our minds to objects in the external world, but rather try to understand how external objects conform to the mind.

13. _____ It is impossible for humans to have "certain" knowledge of that which is beyond space and time (e.g., God).

14. _____ Whatever we know about the universe ultimately comes from our sensory-based experiences of it.

15. _____ The concept of God must be an innate idea, since God has never been experienced by any of the senses.

16. _____ It is possible to have absolute and certain knowledge of things that do not exist in the material world.

17. _____ Perception and imagination can only yield opinion, whereas deductive reasoning and pure thought (i.e., intellectual intuition) can provide knowledge.

18. _____ Skeptical doubt is a good way of achieving rational certainty.

19. _____ Complex and imaginary ideas ultimately find their source in sensory experience.

20. _____ The reason we see things in the world in terms of cause-and-effect relationships is because our minds so organize our perceptions of reality.

SCORING

Record the values you gave for each of the numbered statements listed below. Add up each labeled column to discover your highest score. The column with the highest score points to your pre-reflective epistemological-metaphysical leanings.

Platonic Dualist	Cartesian Rationalist	Naturalistic Empiricist	Kantian Structuralist
1: ▢	3: ▢	2: ▢	4: ▢
5: ▢	6: ▢	7: ▢	8: ▢
9: ▢	10: ▢	11: ▢	12: ▢
16: ▢	15: ▢	14: ▢	13: ▢
17: ▢	18: ▢	19: ▢	20: ▢
TOTALS:			
▢	▢	▢	▢

INTERPRETATION OF RESULTS

According to my highest score, my present views on reality and knowledge are most closely aligned with the �▓▓▓▓▓▓▓▓▓▓▓▓▓.

This measure was designed to help you identify your pre-reflective assumptions about knowledge and reality. Not all epistemological (knowledge-related) and metaphysical perspectives are covered in this self-diagnostic, so the findings are only tentative. They need to be personally verified by you as we proceed through this chapter and later, as you continue your philosophical journey. It's quite possible that your views will change after greater thought and reflection or after further readings in these areas of study. For now, let's review the results with a certain playfulness and intellectual curiosity.

PLATONIC DUALIST

According to the Platonic Dualist, reality can be divided into two parts: the visible world of becoming and the intelligible world of being. ('Intelligible' means *able to be understood by operations of the intellect alone, without any contribution by the senses*.) The former yields opinion; the latter provides the highest forms of knowledge. Things in the physical world are merely imperfect approximations or copies of eternal spaceless and timeless forms. The highest knowledge is knowledge of *Goodness* (itself), achieved by a kind of immediate knowing or *direct intellectual apprehension*. Lacking such apprehension, most unenlightened people confuse opinions about transitory things with knowledge of eternal verities.

CARTESIAN RATIONALIST

The Cartesian (from the name "Descartes") Rationalist approaches questions of knowledge hoping to find certainty using the method of skeptical doubt. The senses are regarded as deceiving, so reason must be considered the ultimate source of truth. Conclusions about the nature of reality can be arrived at by means of logical deduction. Even the existence of God and the existence of the external world require rational justification. The one thing I can be absolutely sure of is that because I think, I must therefore exist.

NATURALISTIC EMPIRICST

The Naturalistic Empiricist argues that, given our human nature as beings who rely on sensations for ideas, whatever knowledge is possible is ultimately derived from our sensory experience of the world. On this view, much of metaphysics—such as talk about God's existence or an afterlife—should be abandoned as "metaphysical rubbish." Any claims about such things cannot be verified as either true or false, so no meaningful statement is being made, and hence, it doesn't make any sense to debate them.

KANTIAN STRUCTURALIST

According to the Kantian Structuralist, our experience of the world is a product of form and content. The mind brings to experience pure forms of sensory experience like space and time, by which all sensory impressions are structured. Human understanding makes judgments on the data of experience using intellectual forms like *Causality* and *Object*. Knowledge is therefore the result of an interaction between the rational subject's mind and the sense-data or sensible manifold of experience. Knowledge of super-sensible realities like God is impossible, for no sense impressions (content) can be provided for the mind to structure. Kantian theory represents a synthesis combining elements of both rationalism and empiricism.

4.1 Preliminary Questions and Definitions

Now that you have some idea of your epistemological and metaphysical presuppositions, as identified by the preceding self-diagnostic, let us define our terms and proceed with some preliminary questions relevant to the subject matter of this chapter. We'll start with 'epistemology.'

'**Epistemology**' is an impressive sounding term that comes from the Greek roots *episteme*, meaning *knowledge*, and *logos*, meaning *the study of* or *the theory of*. Hence, 'epistemology' is an abbreviated name for the theory or study of knowledge. Under this rubric fall a number of fundamental questions and concerns. Epistemologists are particularly interested in the nature, sources, limitations, and validity of knowledge. Specifically, they ask questions such as the following:

▸ What can we know? Where does our knowledge come from?
▸ Can we know anything for sure, or is all belief tentative?
▸ Are there different kinds of knowledge?
▸ What are the standards or criteria by which we can judge the reliability of knowledge claims?
▸ What roles do experience and reason play in the formation of knowledge?
▸ Are some things simply beyond human knowledge and comprehension?
▸ What assumptions are embedded in the knowledge claims that we make?

Metaphysics is another term derived from the Greek, only this time from *meta*, meaning "after" or "beyond," and *physikos*, pertaining to "nature," or *physis*, referring to what is "physical" or "natural." Metaphysics can thus be conceptualized as a sub-discipline of philosophy that addresses issues taking us beyond nature and the realm of the physical. In one dictionary of philosophy, metaphysics is defined as

▸ The attempt to present a coherent picture of reality
▸ The study of being
▸ The study of the characteristics of the universe: existence, space, time, substance, identity, and causality
▸ The study of ultimate reality
▸ The study of a transcendental reality that is the cause or source of all existence
▸ The critical examination of the underlying assumptions (presuppositions, basic beliefs) employed by our systems of knowledge in their claims about what is real.[1]

In light of these alternative definitions, metaphysicians ask questions like: "Is reality one or many?" "Can we be sure the world exists?" "Does God exist?" "Is the universe governed by laws of cause-and-effect, or is everything capricious and unpredictable?" "What do we mean by the notion of self?" "Does a self even exist?"

To answer these and other metaphysical and epistemological questions, philosophers over the centuries have developed ambitious systems of knowledge. Rather than trying to provide specific answers to specific questions that they justify in isolation from one another, philosophers including Plato, Descartes, Locke, Hume, and Kant developed extensive and unified systems of thought intended to offer consistent and coherent answers to an array of questions about knowledge and reality. Typically, no one answer is intended to stand apart from the rest, and particular justifications must take into account broader theoretical perspectives. Accordingly, it's important to understand these philosophies in a comprehensive fashion in order to critically examine a part.

As Descartes wrote in a note to readers of his *Meditations*, the book in which he establishes the foundations for his system of philosophy, one must take in the whole before attempting to tackle a point. In his words, "those who do not take the trouble to understand the order and the connections in my arguments and who are keen to chatter on only about individual conclusions, as many habitually do … will not harvest much fruit by reading this treatise. Although they may perhaps find in many parts an occasion to quibble, it will still not be easy for them to make a significant objection or any which merits a reply."[2]

For the purposes of introduction, this chapter covers the great philosophical system-builders mentioned above. We do not have the space or time to cover their entire systems, but we will certainly consider enough to appreciate their philosophical projects at large. Although the focus will be on their metaphysics and epistemologies, it is worth noting that none of the philosophers covered in this chapter stopped there. In their respective ways, these philosophers also worked on topics as diverse as political philosophy, education, medicine, moral philosophy, language, logic, and the emotions. Arguably, however, none constructed a system of philosophical thought with as much significance as **Plato** did. Appropriate to his place in history and in philosophy, we will begin with him.

As we work through Plato's epistemological and metaphysical theories and then continue on to Descartes, Locke, Hume, and Kant, try to appreciate the critical thinking that went into their systems. Notice how they build up from minimal foundations to great conclusions. To use the metaphor from Chapter 2, take note of how they cut, adjust, and fit the *planks of their philosophical lifeboats* in attempts to keep them afloat. Those planks are constituted by their assumptions about human nature, knowledge, and reality.

At the end of the chapter, we will consider criticisms that target some of those assumptions and, thus, open up even some of the most celebrated systems to challenging attacks on their integrity. Despite being in the hands of great builders, the work on watertight lifeboats is not guaranteed. Accordingly, we are reminded of the humility and perseverance required when doing philosophy or thinking philosophically.

4.2 Plato's Metaphysical Epistemology

In Plato's classic work, *The Republic*, we find not only a moral and social/political philosophy, but also a metaphysics and supporting epistemology.[3] It is difficult, if not impossible, to discuss Plato's theory of knowledge in isolation from his metaphysical conception of reality because the two are so inextricably linked. In order to understand what he means by knowledge, we have to appreciate how he conceptualizes the relationships between permanence and change, appearance and reality, as well as the visible and the intelligible worlds. In our efforts to gain this appreciation, let us turn for a moment to two other ancient philosophers whose ideas place these relationships in bolder relief.

Parmenides of Elea (circa 500 BCE) was a major influence on Plato. He was what is called in philosophical circles today a **monist**. Some philosophers are called monists

"When the mind's eye rests on objects illuminated by truth and reality, it understands and comprehends them, and functions intelligently; but when it turns to the twilight world of change and decay, it can only form opinions, its vision is confused and its beliefs shifting, and it seems to lack intelligence."
PLATO

because they believe that everything together, somehow, constitutes one entity. Other philosophers are called monists because they believe in many beings that all have the one same nature of being.

For Parmenides, monism means that everything in reality is one unchanging whole, which we can call "being." Being is singular, eternal, and indivisible. It is immutable—the "unchanging one." Being is also perfect, complete, and whole. It does not move or transform itself in any way. When we witness apparent variety and change in the world, we are observing only appearances that are not ultimately real. Behind the apparent change is a stable permanent reality not apprehended by the senses. True being is recognized by reason alone.

Heraclitus of Ephesus (circa 500 BCE) believed something very much different from Parmenides. He maintained that *change alone is unchanging*. Beneath the apparent permanence that accompanies our everyday perceptions and experiences of the world lies the hidden reality of continuous movement. Everything is always in a state of flux (flow, change). Even the solid table or desk your book may be resting on right now is changing and moving about. Just think, the atoms and molecules that comprise it are forever bouncing around, causing expansion and contraction in response to variations in temperature and humidity. The desk, as you see it now, is actually hurtling through space at thousands of miles per hour and will cease, in fact, to exist in centuries to come, as it is currently in the process of breaking down and decomposing like garbage in a dump. To capture this continual state of change, Heraclitus used what has now become an often-cited aphorism. "*One cannot step twice into the same river,*"[4] because the water into which you first step has flowed on.

Interestingly enough, this same insight is captured by Eastern Buddhist wisdom as well, which suggests that the "self" you were yesterday, five years ago, or the self you will become tomorrow is not the same self that you imagine yourself to be right now. The "self," like the river, is engaged in a continual process of change.

In a reconciliation of sorts between the worldviews presented by Heraclitus and Parmenides, and also in efforts to respond to the relativism put forward by early sophist philosophers, Plato accepts both the ideas of permanence and impermanence and also the ideas of appearance and reality, seeing them not so much at odds with each other, but rather reflecting different levels of knowledge and states of being within one larger conceptual scheme. What is perceived by the senses—that which changes and is characterized by impermanence—belongs to Plato's metaphysical realm of **becoming**. What is intellectually grasped to be permanent and unchanging belongs, by contrast, to the intelligible realm of **being**.

As far as the world of becoming is concerned, for Plato it constitutes the visible world, the world about which we form only opinions. The world of being, on the other hand, belongs to the intelligible world wherein human intelligence and understanding can achieve eternal and unchanging knowledge. It is in the context of this framework, which integrates being and becoming, knowledge and opinion, as well as the visible and the intelligible worlds that Plato spells out his **Divided Line Theory** of Knowledge.

As we go through this theory, you might find it helpful to refer to Figures 4.2 and 4.3. The latter figure highlights different states of mind associated with the ascending levels of knowledge and different levels of reality.

Plato

Plato (c. 427–347 BCE) was a philosopher of ancient Athens, and is arguably the most significant thinker of the western tradition. His monumental importance to intellectual history was underscored by Alfred North Whitehead, who once stated that all of western philosophy is but a series of footnotes to the work of Plato.

An exceptional writer, Plato's philosophical dialogues hold layered depths that include political thought, scathing commentary, provocative arguments, stirring storytelling, and playful language. The richness of his writings is remarkably impressive. He manages to capture readers with the drama of his dialogues, while their fluidity draws them into the activity of doing philosophy.

Part of that draw is attributable to his method. Plato shows the reader how to think philosophically rather than telling the reader what to think about knowledge, reality, politics, the cosmos, religion, love, death, the law, and the myriad topics covered in his approximately thirty dialogues.

Plato's own philosophical positions can be difficult to tease out of his writings and perhaps that is the point. Nevertheless, certain doctrines are associated with him on account of their prominence in his writings. Chief among them is the **Theory of Forms**, according to which there are two realms: the world of objects that we sense and the *more real* realm of perfect entities or "forms" that we grasp in thought alone. Another is the **Doctrine of Recollection**, which is based on the thesis that all learning is recollection. The soul already contains knowledge, and the right questions stir it up, bringing it to awareness.

The details of Plato's life are difficult to ascertain. Biographies from antiquity contain inconsistent information and there is no conclusive evidence to confirm what is correct. Among the facts that are known for certain is that Plato was born into a wealthy family that had political influence. His given name was actually Aristocles. "Plato," meaning "broad," is a nickname he acquired for some unsubstantiated reason that may have had something to do with his appearance—he supposedly had broad shoulders from his wrestling training. On a family note, several of his relatives appear as characters in his dialogues. Plato never married.

Not long after turning 40, Plato founded the Academy,* an independent institution of learning which continued to exist for almost nine hundred years until the Roman Emperor Justinian closed it in 529 CE. The Academy was a quiet and open retreat where teachers and students could meet to pursue knowledge. Students throughout Greece enrolled to partake in the adventure of learning and to experience personal growth toward wisdom. For many years, the famous philosopher Aristotle was one of them. True to his philosophical method, Plato did not assume the role of a teacher at the Academy but, rather, encouraged independent thinking through oral discourse.

Plato himself would likely have received a standard education, given his social status, until around the age of 20 when he met Socrates. It is unclear how close the two were, but in the eight years that Plato knew Socrates before the latter's tragic trial and death, Socrates clearly exerted an important influence. Most of Plato's dialogues feature Socrates as the principal speaker, engaging in a method of questioning similar to the method encouraged at the Academy.

Some argue that the early works of Plato are more reflective of Socratic thinking, while the later works begin to reflect Plato's own philosophical investigations. Regardless, it is important to read them for what they are, namely, Plato's literary and philosophical creations.

The most well-known of Plato's works is *The Republic*. Plato's *Euthyphro*, *Apology*, *Crito*, and *Phaedo* dialogues notably all take place in relation to Socrates's trial and death. Other dialogues by Plato include the *Symposium*, *Theaetetus*, *Meno*, and *Phaedrus*.

---

* Named after the grove where it was located, which in turn was named after an ancient mythological hero, Akademos. English names for any place or field of study are derived from the name of Plato's school.

Divided Line Theory

First of all, imagine a vertical line divided into two unequal parts. Now divide the top and bottom parts unequally again in the same proportion. Label the dividing lines A, B, C, and D starting at the top (see Figure 4.2). Having done this in your mind's eye, consider the segments as going from the lowest (D) to the highest (A). Furthermore, regard each level as having its own objects and its own method for knowing them.

The lowest level (D) is labeled **imagination**. It is at this level where mental activity is minimized, as is awareness of its objects. At the level of imagination, we carry illusions and hold opinions solely on the basis of appearances, unanalyzed impressions, uncritically inherited beliefs, and unevaluated emotions. For instance, when you go to the movies, you *suspend judgment*, as it were, allowing yourself to experience the combination of sights and sounds in a way that creates the illusion of reality, something which it clearly is not. We muse and sometimes worry when children cannot distinguish between fantasy and reality, yet we willingly fall prey to illusion ourselves when we pay the ticket price to go to the cinema.

At the lowest level of the divided line we really don't have knowledge as such but rather unfounded **opinions**. Our experience of persons and objects is not direct but secondhand. A movie scene containing a basket of fruit is not the fruit itself, only a reflection or image of it. Seeing film footage of Bora Bora is not the same as being there. Don't we sometimes disparage people for their inferior knowledge of something because they just *read it in a book* or *saw it online*, but never directly experienced it themselves? We respect more those who have actually done it, seen it, or had contact with the things of which they claim to have knowledge. This takes us to the next level.

Proceeding upward to the next higher level lands us at **perception** (C). Unlike imagination—where we experience illusory images and fantasies or where we observe re-

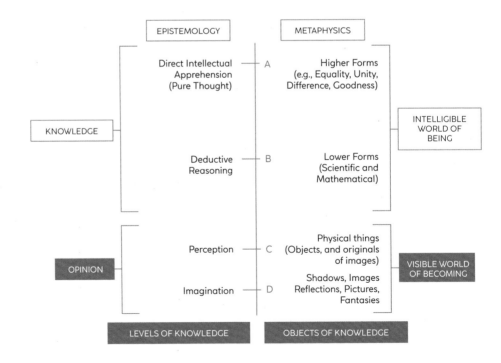

FIGURE 4.2 An illustration of Plato's Divided Line Theory

flections, pictures, and shadows of things—here the objects of our beliefs become the originals themselves. These original objects are physical and three-dimensional. They are things like cars, pets, trees, neighbors, fences, and so on. At the level of perception, classification and organization of objects can begin in a rudimentary way, but there is still no grasp of the abstract concept of the object(s) perceived. Being able to group red and green apples, for instance, is not the same as having a botanist's concept of 'apple,' which identifies the unchanging characteristics for each variety or species of it.

The second level from the bottom still belongs to the **visible world** of becoming. It constitutes the level of belief as captured by the saying "Seeing is believing." Just so that we don't limit our understanding here to visual perception, perhaps we should also say that hearing is believing, or, more generally, that "experiencing is believing."

The level of perception is of most interest to the common sense mind—the mind of the *person-in-the-street*. This type of person is wedded to what is perceived as concrete reality. Unfortunately, perception of objects in the physical world cannot give us true knowledge for a couple of reasons. First, what can be known by the senses belongs, for Plato, to the Heraclitian world of flux. At this level of reality, particular things are not stable. Whatever we believe is always liable to change. As a consequence, we can never be entirely certain. All we have are appearances of things based on our perceptions; we know nothing of their true nature or essential qualities. We are limited to opinion.

Second, sensory-based belief can never provide general, universal, unchanging, and abstract truth of the intelligible world. It can only give us specific ideas about *this* particular pet or *that* particular house, and so on. And, as just stated, because all particulars are in flux, we can derive no certainty from our direct sensory observations of them. "Knowledge" at the level of perception is insecure. It is still just opinion.

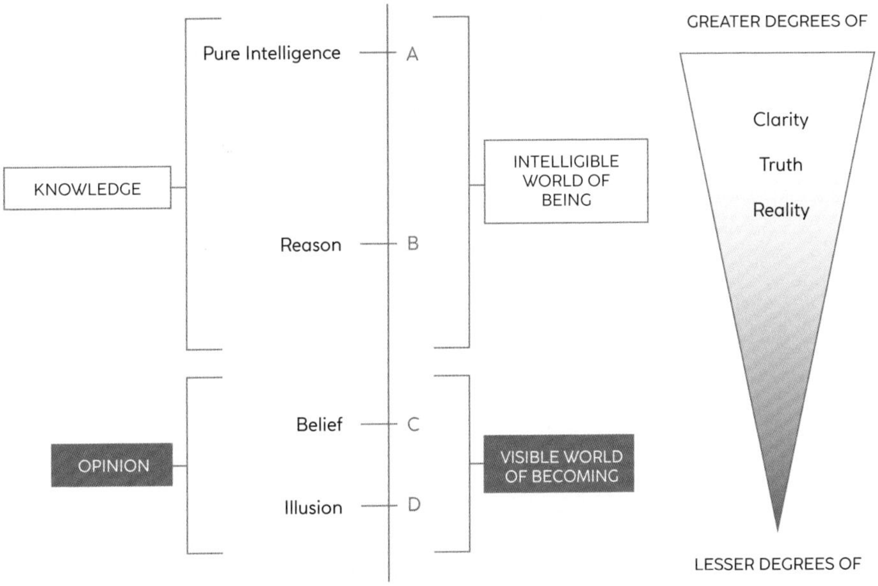

FIGURE 4.3 States of mind associated with the four levels of the divided line

As we move on to the second highest level along the divided line (B), we leave the realms of becoming and opinion and enter those of **being** and **knowledge**, both belonging to the **intelligible world**. At this level, scientific or mathematical knowledge is acquired through deductive reasoning. There is a movement away from belief in the concrete, changing, particular objects of perception and movement toward rational understanding and comprehension of abstract, unchanging universal concepts. Whereas at level (C) we have perception of this particular shape, at level (B), we gain an intellectual grasp of, for example, ideas of geometry, such as *circle*, *square*, or *triangle*. In other words, we grasp the nature or form *circularness*, *squareness*, or *triangularness* themselves. That knowledge allows us to solve geometrical problems involving these shapes. That is, we can "solve for angle x," for example, because we know something about these abstract concepts which allow us to recognize that the imperfect shapes we draw or construct are imitations of the eternal and perfect forms that we grasp intellectually.

Theory of Forms

Movement away from the visible world and toward the intelligible one takes us to Plato's **Theory of Forms**. In contrast to objects of perception in the visible world, which are physical, those objects of the intelligible world at level (B) are abstract or intangible and immaterial. Whereas perception focuses on concrete particulars, intellection and rational deduction focus on that which is universal.

The objects of perception found in the realm of becoming are in a constant process of Heraclitean flux; on the other hand, the objects of the intellect at the level of being are unchanging, displaying a Parmenidean eternal immutability. Those *concepts* of objects, as opposed to the objects themselves, Plato calls *forms*. Examples of these forms include mathematical and geometrical concepts such as *Circle* and *Triangle*, as well as concepts we name in our everyday vocabulary such as *Flower*, *Chair*, *Leather*.

The word 'concept' may suggest to you a mental feature, but in Platonic theory, the forms are not simply products of anyone's mind. They have an independent existence and are considered more real than material objects. People's general ideas may change; every material thing has a beginning and end; but forms are eternal. The concept or form *Human* does not disappear with any particular person's death. The form *Computer-Game* existed before the first one was invented, or even thought of! Thus, we can perhaps think of forms as pure essences or abstract entities capturing the essential qualities of particular things.

Plato considers the forms to be *perfect*. Physical objects, which in some sense *partake in* or *belong to* forms themselves, are imperfect approximations of them. We saw how this could be so earlier with my geometry lesson about points in space, straight lines, and right-angled triangles. Remember, we can roughly approximate such things physically through drawings, representations, or constructions of some sort, but our visible renderings can never achieve theoretical perfection no matter how hard we try. The best we can produce are imperfect *copies* of the forms of which they partake.

In this context, we can say that knowledge of perfect forms in the intelligible world of being is superior to knowledge of imperfect physical objects in the visible world of becoming. Perfection trumps imperfection, immutability beats uncertain flux. And, just as original objects at level (C) make shadows and images of them possible at level (D), so too, forms at level (B) make it possible for us to know the actual world of things, along with the objects of mathematics, the sciences, and philosophy.

Particular things are *real* only insofar as they measure up to, copy, or partake of the eternal reality and truth of their corresponding forms. Put another way, things are knowable in the visible world only insofar as we can name or identify them by a form, as members of a class of things that share the same form, the same set of defining qualities. Without the form of *Beauty*, for instance, we wouldn't be able to judge a particular person or thing as a good or bad example of it. Without presupposing a concept of (perfect) *Justice*, it would be impossible to justifiably criticize an action as unfair. The fact that we have never seen or experienced perfect justice in the material, physical world does not prevent us from charging that this person is unfair or that that act is unjust. We can recognize just and fair things in the visible world because we intellectually comprehend *Justice* and *Fairness*, even though we have never witnessed perfect (or even any) examples in the visible world.

At level (B) on the divided line, we find lower forms of mathematics and science. Knowledge of such forms at level (B) is still inferior. Even mathematicians must still use visual diagrams of triangles, lines, circles, and squares, etc., in providing geometrical proofs. They cannot prove their own hypothetical or conditional assumptions using first principles that are unconditionally true. With respect to scientists, their studies are often tied to observations of instances, particulars, or examples from the visible world, and if we accept Plato's thinking, we know that absolute certainty cannot be found there.

At the uppermost level of knowledge (A), there is no need for perception, interpretation, or deductive reasoning, for the mind directly apprehends the higher forms. These higher forms are even more basic to thought than mathematical ones. Presupposed in every act of knowing are such fundamental ideas as *Equality*, *Difference*, *Sameness*, *Unity*, and *Diversity*. For example, to *know* how a circle differs from a triangle, the concept of difference must first be grasped. Without an intellectual acquaintance with the form *Difference*, one could not perceive objects as separate and distinguishable from one another or make a judgment about how they are not alike.

THINKING ABOUT YOUR THINKING

Think of a time when you were in the presence of something beautiful. It could have been a scene in nature, a piece of music that you heard, a painting you looked at, or something else. Whatever it is, pick something that you immediately recognized as beautiful as soon as you encountered it. What idea of beauty did you already have in your thoughts that allowed you to recognize the thing as beautiful? Try to describe in words the idea of beauty that you were aware of in that moment. Take care not to describe your reactions to the beautiful thing or the particular details of it. Instead, try to describe beauty itself. Is it difficult to do so? Why do you think that is? Does the difficulty of explaining beauty make its existence any less real?

Simile of the Sun

Of all the higher forms, Plato considers **Goodness** (or *The Good*) as the absolute highest. It is given a privileged status because he claims goodness is what makes reality, truth, and the existence of everything else possible. Like all the other forms (higher and lower), it exists beyond the metaphysical level of becoming, residing at the highest reaches of being.

To help us understand how *The Good* makes all else possible, Plato likens it to the sun. He asks, for instance, what is required for vision. Beyond objects to be seen and eyes to see them, what is still needed is a source of light. Without it, darkness descends and vision becomes impaired. However, with the sun's illumination, figures stand out with vibrant clarity. So, too, with the form *Goodness*. It is a form of intellectual illumination that makes objects knowable by the faculty of knowledge. Without it, reality could not exist. In the excerpt that follows, Plato gives pride of place to the form *Good*.

Plato, Simile of the Sun [5]

Plato's Republic *is comprised of 10 parts or "books." The passage below comes from Book Six in which the characters Socrates and Glaucon discuss the traits of true philosophers. Principal among those traits is knowledge of the most important subject, namely, the good itself. The analogy described in this passage is widely known as the* **simile of the sun***.*

———

[**Socrates**] We say that there are many beautiful things and many good doings, and so on for each kind, and in this way we distinguish them in words.

[**Glaucon**] We do.

[**Socrates**] And what is the main thing, we speak of beauty itself and good itself, and so in the case of all the things that we then set down as many, we turn about and set down in accord with a single form of each, believing that there is but one, and call it "the being" of each.

[**Glaucon**] That's true.

[**Socrates**] And we say that the many beautiful things and the rest are visible but not intelligible, while the forms are intelligible but not visible.

[**Glaucon**] That's completely true.

[**Socrates**] With what part of ourselves do we see visible things?

[**Glaucon**] With our sight.

[**Socrates**] And so audible things are heard by hearing, and with our other senses we perceive all the other perceptible things.

[**Glaucon**] That's right.

[**Socrates**] Have you considered how lavish the maker of our senses was in making the power to see and be seen?

[**Glaucon**] I can't say I have.

[**Socrates**] Well, consider it this way. Do hearing and sound need another kind of thing in order for the former to hear and the latter to be heard, a third thing in whose absence the one won't hear or the other be heard?

[**Glaucon**] No, they need nothing else.

[**Socrates**] And if there are any others that need such a thing, there can't be many of them. Can you think of one?

[**Glaucon**] I can't.

[**Socrates**] You don't realize that sight and the visible have such a need?

[**Glaucon**] How so?

[**Socrates**] Sight may be present in the eyes, and the one who has it may try to use it, and colors may be present in things, but unless a third kind of thing is present, which is naturally adapted for this very purpose, you know that sight will see nothing, and the colors will remain unseen.

[**Glaucon**] What kind of thing do you mean?

[**Socrates**] I mean what you call light.

[**Glaucon**] You're right.

[**Socrates**] Then it isn't an insignificant kind of link that connects the sense of sight and the power to be seen—it is a more valuable link than any other linked things have got, if indeed light is something valuable.

[**Glaucon**] And, of course, it's very valuable.

[**Socrates**] Which of the gods in heaven would you name as the cause and controller of this, the one whose light causes our sight to see in the best way and the visible things to be seen?

[Glaucon] The same one you and others would name. Obviously, the answer to your question is the sun.

[Socrates] And isn't sight by nature related to that god in this way?

[Glaucon] Which way?

[Socrates] Sight isn't the sun, neither sight itself nor that in which it comes to be, namely, the eye.

[Glaucon] No, it certainly isn't.

[Socrates] But I think that it is the most sunlike of the senses.

[Glaucon] Very much so.

[Socrates] And it receives from the sun the power it has, just like an influx from an overflowing treasury.

[Glaucon] Certainly.

[Socrates] The sun is not sight, but isn't it the cause of sight itself and seen by it?

[Glaucon] That's right.

[Socrates] Let's say, then, that this is what I called the offspring of the good, which the good begot as its analogue. What the good itself is in the intelligible realm, in relation to understanding and intelligible things, the sun is in the visible realm, in relation to sight and visible things.

[Glaucon] How? Explain a bit more.

[Socrates] You know that, when we turn our eyes to things whose colors are no longer in the light of day but in the gloom of night, the eyes are dimmed and seem nearly blind, as if clear vision were no longer in them.

[Glaucon] Of course.

[Socrates] Yet whenever one turns them on things illuminated by the sun, they see clearly, and vision appears in those very same eyes?

[Glaucon] Indeed.

[Socrates] Well, understand the soul in the same way: When it focuses on something illuminated by truth and what is, it understands, knows, and apparently possesses understanding, but when it focuses on what is mixed with obscurity, on what comes to be and passes away, it opines and is dimmed, changes its opinions this way and that, and seems bereft of understanding.

[Glaucon] It does seem that way.

[Socrates] So that what gives truth to the things known and the power to know to the knower is the form of the good. And though it is the cause of knowledge and truth, it is also an object of knowledge. Both knowledge and truth are beautiful things, but the good is other and more beautiful than they. In the visible realm, light and sight are rightly considered sunlike, but it is wrong to think that they are the sun, so here it is right to think of knowledge and truth as godlike but wrong to think that either of them is the good—for the good is yet more prized.

[Glaucon] This is an inconceivably beautiful thing you're talking about, if it provides both knowledge and truth and is superior to them in beauty. You surely don't think that a thing like that could be pleasure.

[Socrates] Hush! Let's examine its image in more detail as follows.

[Glaucon] How?

[Socrates] You'll be willing to say, I think, that the sun not only provides visible things with the power to be seen but also with coming to be, growth, and nourishment, although it is not itself coming to be.

[**Glaucon**] How could it be?

[**Socrates**] Therefore, you should also say that not only do the objects of knowledge owe their being known to the good, but their being is also due to it, although the good is not being, but superior to it in rank and power.

READING QUESTIONS

1. How does your study of Plato's *Euthyphro* in Chapter 2 help you to read and understand this passage from Plato's *Republic*? Is there a similar method or theme to Socrates's questions that you recognize? Does this strategy of applying what you learned about another Platonic dialogue make this one easier to understand? How so or why not?

2. Socrates distinguishes between things seen but not known and ideas known but not seen. By his account, what is the role of the sun in seeing things? What is the role of the good in knowing ideas?

Allegory of the Cave

Plato uses the "**Allegory of the Cave**" to tell us more about the ascent from illusion to philosophical illumination and its associated difficulties. Consider the ways in which components of this allegory connect with the earlier ideas of the Divided Line and the Simile of the Sun.

Level of Knowledge	Allegorical Depiction	State of Mind
A (highest)	Looking at real things in the world outside the cave in the surface world	Intelligence
B	Those looking at shadows and reflections in the surface world and the ascent thereto	Reason
C	Those freed prisoners within the cave	Belief
D (lowest)	Prisoners, chained and facing the inner walls of the cave	Illusion

Plato, Allegory of the Cave[6]

The famous imagery contained in this passage occurs at the beginning of Book Seven of The Republic. *It immediately follows Socrates's simile of the sun and his description of a line divided into two sections: the visible and the intelligible.*

———

[Socrates] ... Imagine human beings living in an underground, cavelike dwelling, with an entrance a long way up, which is both open to the light and as wide as the cave itself. They've been there since childhood, fixed in the same place, with their necks and legs fettered, able to see only in front of them, because their bonds prevent them from turning their heads around. Light is provided by a fire burning far above and behind them. Also behind them, but on higher ground, there is a path stretching between them and the fire. Imagine that along this path a low wall has been built, like the screen in front of puppeteers above which they show their puppets.

[Glaucon] I'm imagining it.

[Socrates] Then also imagine that there are people along the wall, carrying all kinds of artifacts that project above it—statues of people and other animals, made out of stone, wood, and every material. And, as you'd expect, some of the carriers are talking, and some are silent.

[Glaucon] It's a strange image you're describing, and strange prisoners.

[Socrates] They're like us. Do you suppose, first of all, that these prisoners see anything of themselves and one another besides the shadows that the fire casts on the wall in front of them?

[Glaucon] How could they, if they have to keep their heads motionless throughout life?

[Socrates] What about the things being carried along the wall? Isn't the same true of them?

[Glaucon] Of course.

[Socrates] And if they could talk to one another, don't you think they'd suppose that the names they used applied to the things they see passing before them?

[Glaucon] They'd have to.

[Socrates] And what if their prison also had an echo from the wall facing them? Don't you think they'd believe that the shadows passing in front of them were talking whenever one of the carriers passing along the wall was doing so?

[Glaucon] I certainly do.

[Socrates] Then the prisoners would in every way believe that the truth is nothing other than the shadows of those artifacts.

[Glaucon] They must surely believe that.

[Socrates] Consider, then, what being released from their bonds and cured of their ignorance would naturally be like if something like this came to pass. When one of them was freed and suddenly compelled to stand up, turn his head, walk, and look up toward the light, he'd be pained and dazzled and unable to see the things whose shadows he'd seen before. What do you think he'd say, if we told him that what he'd seen before was inconsequential, but that now—because he is a bit closer to the things that are and is turned towards things that are more—he sees more correctly? Or, to put it another way, if we pointed to each of the things passing by, asked him what each of them is, and compelled him to answer, don't you think he'd be at a loss and that he'd believe that the things he saw earlier were truer than the ones he was now being shown?

[Glaucon] Much truer.

[Socrates] And if someone compelled him to look at the light itself, wouldn't his eyes hurt, and wouldn't he turn around and flee towards the things he's able to see, believing that they're really clearer than the ones he's being shown?

[**Glaucon**] He would.

[**Socrates**] And if someone dragged him away from there by force, up the rough, steep path, and didn't let him go until he had dragged him into the sunlight, wouldn't he be pained and irritated at being treated that way? And when he came into the light, with the sun filling his eyes, wouldn't he be unable to see a single one of the things now said to be true?

[**Glaucon**] He would be unable to see them, at least at first.

[**Socrates**] I suppose, then, that he'd need time to get adjusted before he could see things in the world above. At first, he'd see shadows most easily, then images of men and other things in water, then the things themselves. Of these, he'd be able to study the things in the sky and the sky itself more easily at night, looking at the light of the stars and the moon, than during the day, looking at the sun and the light of the sun.

[**Glaucon**] Of course.

[**Socrates**] Finally, I suppose, he'd be able to see the sun, not images of it in water or some alien place, but the sun itself in its own place, and be able to study it.

[**Glaucon**] Necessarily so.

[**Socrates**] And at this point he would infer and conclude that the sun provides the seasons and the years, governs everything in the visible world, and is in some way the cause of all the things that he used to see.

[**Glaucon**] It's clear that would be his next step.

[**Socrates**] What about when he reminds himself of his first dwelling place, his fellow prisoners, and what passed for wisdom there? Don't you think that he'd count himself happy for the change and pity the others?

[**Glaucon**] Certainly.

[**Socrates**] And if there had been any honors, praises, or prizes among them for the one who was sharpest at identifying the shadows as they passed by and who best remembered which usually came earlier, which later, and which simultaneously, and who could thus best divine the future, do you think that our man would desire these rewards or envy those among the prisoners who were honored and held power? Instead, wouldn't he feel, with Homer, that he'd much prefer to "work the earth as a serf to another, one without possessions," and go through any sufferings, rather than share their opinions and live as they do?

[**Glaucon**] I suppose he would rather suffer anything than live like that.

[**Socrates**] Consider this too. If this man went down into the cave again and sat down in his same seat, wouldn't his eyes—coming suddenly out of the sun like that—be filled with darkness?

[**Glaucon**] They certainly would.

[**Socrates**] And before his eyes had recovered—and the adjustment would not be quick—while his vision was still dim, if he had to compete again with the perpetual prisoners in recognizing the shadows, wouldn't he invite ridicule? Wouldn't it be said of him that he'd returned from his upward journey with his eyesight ruined and that it isn't worthwhile even to try to travel upward? And, as for anyone who tried to free them and lead them upward, if they could somehow get their hands on him, wouldn't they kill him?

[**Glaucon**] They certainly would.

[**Socrates**] This whole image, Glaucon, must be fitted together with what we said before. The visible realm should be likened to the prison dwelling, and the light of the fire inside it to the power of the sun. And if you interpret the upward journey and the study of things above as the upward journey of the soul to the intelligi-

ble realm, you'll grasp what I hope to convey, since that is what you wanted to hear about. Whether it's true or not, only the god knows. But this is how I see it: In the knowable realm, the form of the good is the last thing to be seen, and it is reached only with difficulty. Once one has seen it, however, one must conclude that it is the cause of all that is correct and beautiful in anything, that it produces both light and its source in the visible realm, and that in the intelligible realm it controls and provides truth and understanding, so that anyone who is to act sensibly in private or public must see it.

READING QUESTIONS

1. Building on your study of Plato's philosophy, consider how the allegory of the cave relates to the simile of the sun passage you read earlier in this chapter. For instance, what is the sun in the allegory of the cave? What is the Good? What still remains difficult to understand in this passage? Why?

2. In Plato's philosophy, knowledge is not sensory. For example, seeing circular shapes does not amount to knowing the essence of what a circle is. That knowledge, like all knowledge, is an idea grasped by the intellect alone, not by sensation. Why do you think, then, that Socrates appeals to a sensory metaphor—involving vision—in order to make his argument? What does his use of sense-based images say about his audience, including us?

3. In general, do you think allegorical arguments, arguments by analogy, or arguments based on metaphor and simile are effective? Or, are they little more than dubious rhetorical devices, things that philosophers should be wary about? Why?

SEEING THROUGH APPEARANCES

The Platonic notion that there exists an eternal and immutable reality behind the transitory and ever-changing world of appearances can be difficult to grasp. How can we penetrate apparent reality and break through to the other side? We have to go back to Plato for guidance on this, but we can still try to simulate the experience of what it must be like to envision a different and higher-order reality in an example of stereogram art.

Unfocus your eyes and hold the image about 12 inches from your face. Look and be patient. Sooner or later the three-dimensional image should reveal itself to you. If you become excited about this new perception, can you imagine what the philosophical illumination of ultimate goodness must be like!

(Don't look now, but in the Image Sources section at the back of the book you are told what is embedded here.)

Plato's influence on the history of philosophy cannot be overstated. From providing the portrait of a philosopher in the character of Socrates to the episte-mological distinctions he made between opinion and knowledge, and between sensible things and intelligible forms, Plato left a lasting legacy.

Let's now move forward into the modern period of philosophy where, two millennia after his death, the philosophy of Plato was still a lively topic of discussion and debate. As you will notice, some of these modern philosophers agree with Plato and some of them disagree with him, but none of them ignore his ideas about knowledge and reality. Consider those points of agreement and disagreement as we proceed.

Up first, we will learn about a philosopher who came to realize that he was like the unenlightened prisoners in Plato's cave, bound by bonds since childhood to accept sensory images as true reality. In response to that realization, this philosopher developed a method for using his own faculty of reason to break free from those chains and exit the cave. You may even already know something about his method for discovering knowledge. Have you ever heard the expression "I think, therefore I am"? Let's meet the philosopher who coined it.

René Descartes

René Descartes is one of the most significant figures of the Western rational tradition and is considered the father of modern* philosophy. Born in 1596 in La Haye, France, at the cusp of the seventeenth century, Descartes entered the Jesuit College of La Flèche around the age of 10 and studied there for about 8 years. He subsequently went on to study law at the University of Poitiers, graduating in 1616 but never actually practicing as a lawyer.

With a sizable family fortune to support him and feeling somewhat restless, Descartes began a series of travels throughout Europe, joining different armies in the process. In 1618, he went to the Netherlands for a year, where he befriended a likeminded intellectual, Isaac Beeckman, who influenced Descartes's work on mathematics and physics. Descartes's self-centeredness and quick temper brought the friendship to an end, but his fondness for the Netherlands endured.

Descartes returned there in 1628 and remained for over 20 years, moving around the countryside and the cities, living a private and independent life. In a 1634 letter to a friend, he shared his motto for how he lived: *bene vixit, bene qui latuit* or *one who lives well, lives well hidden*. Despite his hidden ways, Descartes was a prolific correspondent, and his numerous letters offer tremendously rich insights into the contemplations and convictions of this great thinker.

Descartes's two decades in the Netherlands were remarkable in many ways. He began writing *The World* but abandoned it; he fathered a child, Francine, who died at the age of 5; he published on optics, meteorology, geometry, metaphysics, nature, and the emotions. He also began an intellectually and personally rewarding correspondence with Princess Elisabeth of Bohemia, which lasted until his death. On one occasion he embroiled himself in a heated debate with the rector of Utrecht University that sparked a libel charge against Descartes and a ban on his philosophy in the city.

In 1649 he left the Netherlands and went to Sweden on the invitation of Queen Christina. It was not a rewarding journey for Descartes, who did not take well to the country's severe winter climate and the rigorous early morning schedule imposed by the Queen. Not long after he arrived, he contracted pneumonia and died on February 11, 1650.

Famous in his own time and ever since, Descartes made his mark on philosophy with his ambitious project to develop a system of natural science based on known principles of mathematics and mechanics, as opposed to the mysterious principles of activity and change (based on Aristotle) that he had learned about in school and that were popular in philosophical thinking at the time. With this break from tradition, he inspired many in the seventeenth century, including the philosopher Nicolas Malebranche, who reportedly experienced hyperventilation when he read Descartes's writings for the first time. The teachings, based on Descartes's views, of professor and physician Henricus Regius, had the effect of inciting student riots.

It can be difficult to fully appreciate the influence that Descartes had when we are so unwittingly accustomed to his legacy. As one twentieth-century scholar remarked about Descartes's book *Discourse on the Method*, "Everything that came before it was old; everything that came after it is new."[7] What was new then eventually became his legacy.

Descartes's quest to reform all knowledge with a unifying system based on philosophical principles was inspired by a series of dreams that he had one November night when he was 23 year old. He had spent the day in deep philosophical reflection by a warm stove, shut in

---

* Don't let this word 'modern' confuse you. Historians date the beginning of the "modern era" to when the medieval age left off, perhaps with the advent of the "early modern era" during the sixteenth century. It's often thought that the twentieth century saw the end of the "modern era"— and perhaps the beginning of the "post-modern era."

by the cold. That evening, as if in response to the profound thoughts of the day, he experienced three vivid dreams that provided him with a vision laying out his mission in life.

Descartes had the revelation that he was to find the key to the mysteries of nature in a system of knowledge based on reason. For his emphasis on reason in his philosophical works, Descartes is considered by some to be an "armchair philosopher"—one who thinks instead of looking.* This is false. In fact, Descartes was experienced in scientific observation. For example, he watched dissections and vivisections when he was living in the butcher's quarter in Amsterdam and he used his access to animal parts to study the physiology of bodies. Although he did not publish much in the life sciences, he wrote a great deal about the functions of the human body and declared to one of his correspondents, "the preservation of health has always been the principal end of my studies."[8]

The best-known works by Descartes are *Discourse on Method* and *Meditations on First Philosophy (in which the Existence of God and the Real Distinction between the Soul and the Body of Man Are Demonstrated)*. Other notable works include *Treatise on Man*, *Principles of Philosophy*, and *Passions of the Soul*.

---

* Not uncommon among philosophers. Aristotle, for example, despite having been a keen observer, sometimes derived his beliefs about nature from general rational considerations instead of from experiment and observation. He wrote, for example, that men have more teeth than women, a belief he might easily have corrected by looking into Mrs. Aristotle's mouth.

4.3 René Descartes's Rational Method of Doubt

> *"In our search for the direct road to truth, we should busy ourselves with no object about which we cannot attain a certitude equal to that of the demonstration of arithmetic and geometry."*
>
> RENÉ DESCARTES

Historical Context

In response to the uncertainty and contradictions that he encountered in studies at school, and given his desire for a stable and firm foundation for the sciences, seventeenth-century philosopher **René Descartes** famously presented us with a method of doubt for shedding our reliance on our senses and using our faculty of reason to acquire knowledge of the truth. But before we examine that method and other details of his philosophy, let us focus for a few moments on the historical context out of which Descartes's thinking emerged.

René Descartes lived during a very exciting period in human history. Up until about the end of the sixteenth century, the medieval view of the world was dominant in Europe. It permeated many areas of life, including education. In fact, Descartes was immersed in this medieval worldview throughout his entire Jesuit schooling at the college in La Flèche. As a student, he encountered a number of theological and philosophical beliefs that were perpetuated and justified on the basis of tradition and authority.

He was also aware of the dangerous consequences of challenging such beliefs. For instance, most ancient astronomers, including Aristotle, advanced a **geocentric view** of the universe, which was compatible with Christian church doctrine and divine revelation. In the geocentric view, the Sun and planets revolve around the Earth; an opposing picture, however, was presented by the sixteenth-century Polish astronomer **Mikolaj Kopernik** (1473–1543; this is his Polish name, but you may be more familiar with his Latinized name, 'Nicolaus Copernicus'). Kopernik presented a Sun-centered **heliocentric theory** that the Earth actually revolves on its own axis around the Sun. This "anti-religious" notion, contrary to the biblical teachings of the church, gave rise to the so-called **Copernican Revolution** in human thought. Scientists who were supportive of Kopernik's heliocentric theory were excommunicated from the church; others were burned at the stake (Bruno, 1600; Vanini, 1620). In addition, Galileo—who, through the development of the telescope, observed the satellites of Jupiter, Saturn's rings, and the surface of the moon, and who supported the Copernican doctrine—was forced by the Inquisition to condemn it, to do penance, and to serve a life sentence of imprisonment at his home in Florence.

In spite of church opposition, the new modern science adopted the view that human reason had the power to know the truth of reality, a reality that was neither transcendent nor divine. For modern science, a philosophical worldview based on **medieval scholasticism**[*] was no longer adequate. A new philosophy for the modern age was called for, but it had to be presented in a careful way, to avoid anything like Galileo's fate. Enter René Descartes.

The modern philosophical era begins with Descartes's revolutionary overthrow of all prior belief. Descartes breaks with the medieval world, including the authority of church-controlled scholastic philosophy. In such a philosophy, he finds no certainty. On the subject of his own Jesuit education steeped in philosophical tradition, Descartes writes in his *Discourse on Method*,

> I was nourished on literature from the time of my childhood, and because I was persuaded that through literature one could acquire a clear and assured understanding of everything useful in life, I had an intense desire to take it up. But as soon as I had completed that entire course of study at the end of which one is usually accepted into the rank of scholars, I changed my opinion completely. For I found myself burdened by so many doubts and errors that it seemed to me I had gained nothing by trying to instruct myself, other than having increasingly discovered my own ignorance.[9]

For his method, as well as his conclusions, Descartes is considered the father of modern philosophy and, as such, is typically associated with the start of the historical period in Western philosophy called the *early modern period*. This period runs from roughly the start of the seventeenth century to the end of the eighteenth century. It was a remarkable period of ambitious and revolutionary philosophical projects conducted by a diversity of thinkers in epistemology, metaphysics, and, as we will learn in Chapter 5, ethics.

The Quest for Certainty

Before Descartes, the methods of scholastic philosophy often involved comparing and contrasting the views of recognized authorities. However, weary of textbooks and learning procedures that merely rehashed the tired old ideas of Aristotle and the dogmas of scholasticism, and skeptical of their "truths," especially in view of the findings and developments of modern science, Descartes was determined to accept nothing as true until he himself, as an individual, had established solid grounds for believing it to be true. His iconoclastic, revolutionary overthrow of traditional belief was necessary if **certainty** was to be achieved and if he were to fulfill his visionary dream of establishing a universal science—one that would offer a unified set of principles from which he could deduce all answers to scientific questions.

---

[*] So-called because it was taught in the medieval *schools*. Scholastic thought approached philosophical problems against the backdrop of Christian religious dogma, with a strong influence from Aristotle.

Descartes was very much impressed with Kopernik and Galileo, witnessing how the methods of mathematics could revolutionize the study of astronomy. For Descartes, a mathematically precise method was the only reliable way to discover the truth about the universe. Motivated by a new spirit of scientific inquiry, he adopted mathematical rigor in his re-examination of everything.

In his *Rules for the Direction of the Mind*, Descartes spelled out two mental operations of mathematics by which true knowledge can be attained, namely **intuition** and **deduction**. Self-evident principles are known intuitively and recognized as absolutely true by a faculty he calls the "Light of Nature." The rational mind cannot doubt them. To say that "A straight line is the shortest distance between two points," or that "7 + 5 = 12," is understood intuitively—meaning that such statements are recognized by reason alone as necessary and certain.

As for deduction, Descartes means orderly, logical reasoning or inference-making from solidly established, self-evident propositions, just as geometry is reasoned in strict order by a process of deduction from its self-evident axioms and postulates. The idea behind establishing a proper method is to arrange all facts into a deductive logical structure. *Descartes wanted to use intuition and deduction as building blocks to erect a system of philosophy as certain and imperishable as geometry.*

His initial task, then, was to find a **self-evident principle** that could serve as the basis for his philosophy, for without it, no absolutely certain philosophy could be deduced. To serve as the foundation for his entire philosophy, the principle or axiom would have to be impossible to doubt; its certainty would have to be ultimate and not dependent upon any other belief, and it would have to point to something actually existing, if the existence of other things in the world were to be deduced from it.

Inspired by the methods mathematicians used for achieving certain knowledge in mathematics, Descartes adopted a four-step method for achieving certain knowledge in other areas as well. Indeed, Descartes's ambitions covered a whole system of knowledge, including physics, metaphysics, medicine, and mechanics, but he cautioned that one should start with "very easy and simple questions like those in mathematics" before attempting "to tackle true philosophy in earnest."[10] He presents this method in his *Discourse on Method* as follows:

> The first rule was that I would not accept anything as true which I did not clearly know to be true. That is to say, I would carefully avoid being over-hasty or prejudiced, and I would understand nothing by my judgments beyond what presented itself so clearly and distinctly to my mind that I had no occasion to doubt it.*
>
> The second was to divide each difficulty which I examined into as many parts as possible and necessary to resolve it better.
>
> The third was to conduct my thoughts in an orderly way, beginning with the simplest objects, the ones easiest to know, so that little by little I could gradually climb right up to the knowledge of the most complex, even assuming an order among those

---

* Descartes's *Principia Philosophiae*, 1:45–46, discusses (in Latin) his use of these terms: "I call an idea clear (*claram*) when it is present and manifest to a mind focusing on it, just as we say we perceive something clearly when it is present to the observing eye, and stimulates it sufficiently strongly and fully. I call an idea distinct (*distinctam*) which, while it is clear, is separated and marked off from everything else in such a way that it consists of absolutely nothing which is not clear." Descartes may have in mind the clarity and distinctiveness of geometrical propositions. [Editor's footnote]

things which do not naturally come one after the other.

And the last was to make my calculations throughout so complete and my reviews so general that I would be confident of not omitting anything.[11]

In sum, this is Descartes's method for using reason well. It begins with doubting what is dubitable, then discovering an indubitable principle and building more complex knowledge on that principle, and finally, like any good mathematician, checking one's work. This approach is known as **rationalism**.

Notably, there is nothing special about Descartes's idea of reason that makes knowledge more attainable for him than any of the rest of us. Rather, he believes that all human beings have reason and the ability to use their reason to know the truth. The catch, however, is that most of us do not use our faculty of reason well. We lack knowledge and find ourselves in confusions and contradictions because our rationality has been clouded since childhood with wrong opinions and erroneous preconceptions.

Primary among these falsehoods is the belief that our sense perceptions accurately report how the world really is. For example, we think that if something appears red, that is because it *really is* red, or if it tastes sweet, that is because it *really is* sweet. For Descartes, however, our sensory immersion in the world overwhelmed our thinking as children and, by habit, sensory-based beliefs became established in our thoughts. As a result, we have come to accept appearances as reality.

This belief, however, is not the same as knowledge. According to Descartes's method, knowledge is achieved when we put aside our opinions and preconceptions and use reason to discover the truth. The truth about reality, then, starts with us withdrawing from our reliance on our senses. According to the first step in Descartes's method, the way to do that is with doubt.

Method of Doubt

Ironically, the way Descartes set about to achieve certainty was to begin by doubting absolutely everything. Whatever would serve as the intuitively self-evident basis for the new Cartesian **method of doubt** would have to meet certain conditions. Practically speaking, it would be impossible for Descartes to doubt every single one of his inherited beliefs individually. For this reason, he examined them by groups or classes to see if he could discover one that was impossible to doubt—ultimately true and about something that certainly exists.

Descartes chose to examine first those beliefs based on sense perceptions, concluding in the end that they were unreliable and therefore couldn't lead to certain knowledge. For example, things observed from far away look different up close. Straight sticks can look bent or broken when placed in a glass of water. Our sense perceptions may thus be subject to illusion.

Furthermore, no matter how certain we are about our current sensory perceptions (for example, the fact that we're sitting in a chair or lying in a bed reading), it could also be that we are dreaming. Dreams can seem so real sometimes that when awake we wonder if the events really occurred. How can I know with *absolute certainty* that whatever I see or hear or touch is not just part of some dream I am having? I cannot, for I can question whether or not I am experiencing them as objects in a convincing dream. By this account, the existence of the external objects is cast into doubt, as I could be dreaming or imagining this chair or bed, this book, and even these hands!

"If a man will begin with certainties, he shall end in doubts. But if he will be content to begin with doubts, he shall end in certainties."
FRANCIS BACON

WHEN SCIENCE AND FAITH CONFLICT

The ideas of Kopernik and Galileo were considered by many of their time as anti-religious and a threat to religious authority. Martin Luther, leader of the Protestant Reformation, accused Kopernik of being a heretic in view of his heliocentric views, which allegedly contradicted the teachings of the Bible.

What should a religious believer do when scientific findings run contrary to scripture? Consider, for example, the apparent conflicts between some fossil records and biblical accounts of human origins. Should the fossil records be denied? Should they be interpreted in a way that is factually compatible with scripture? Should the biblical account be interpreted as metaphorical? What must we conclude about dinosaur bones?

What should be the basis for decision-making here? Discuss.

Martin Luther once described Kopernik as "that fool [who would] reverse the entire art of astronomy." Luther accepted the Ptolemaic* conception of the universe, which had the Sun revolve around the Earth—a conception that was consistent with Christian biblical belief. Kopernik's heliocentric perspective challenged the traditional Christian worldview. In this illustration taken from Martin Luther's Bible, we see God as the orderer of the Ptolemaic universe.

* Named for Ptolemy (100 CE–170 CE), Egyptian/Roman scientist, whose work on the Earth-centered view of the solar system was hugely influential for centuries.

There might seem, at first glance, to be at least one sphere of knowledge whose principles and axioms are beyond skeptical doubt: namely, arithmetic and geometry. However, Descartes entertains the possibility—however improbable—that we have been deceived our entire lives by some evil genius or by some all-powerful malevolent being. Perhaps, he says, we have always been mistaken when we have added numbers together; and maybe we have always been wrong to conclude that a square is an enclosed figure containing four equal sides and four right angles. Suppose we've been tricked all along, so to speak, into believing in falsehoods that seem obviously true to us!

In raising such doubts, Descartes is not trying to be ridiculous or difficult. His skepticism is designed to sweep away *all* uncertainty. If any belief can be doubted in the least—however remote the possibility that it is untrue—it must be rejected as quickly and as thoroughly as those beliefs that are patently and obviously false. Descartes is on the hunt for absolute certainty, not relative assurance. Let us now read Descartes so that we might better appreciate his process of methodological doubt.

René Descartes, First Meditation[12]

The following excerpt comes from the first of the six meditations that make up Descartes's Meditations on First Philosophy. *Despite the fact that Descartes wrote the* Meditations *in the first-person, the book is not an autobiography. Instead, treat Descartes's use of "I" as an invitation to be an active and engaged reader who meditates seriously and, in so doing, follows Descartes's method for using one's own reason well.*

———

It is now several years since I noticed how from the time of my early youth I had accepted many false claims as true, how everything I had later constructed on top of those [falsehoods] was doubtful, and thus how at some point in my life I needed to tear everything down completely and begin again from the most basic foundations, if I wished to establish something firm and lasting in the sciences. But this seemed an immense undertaking, and I kept waiting until I would be old enough and sufficiently mature to know that no later period of my life would come [in which I was] better equipped to undertake this disciplined enquiry. This reason made me delay for so long that I would now be at fault if, by [further] deliberation, I used up the time which still remains to carry out that project. And so today, when I have conveniently rid my mind of all worries and have managed to find myself secure leisure in solitary withdrawal, I will at last find the time for an earnest and unfettered general demolition of my [former] opinions.

Now, for this task it will not be necessary to show that every opinion I hold is false, something which I might well be incapable of ever carrying out. But reason now convinces me that I should withhold my assent from opinions which are not entirely certain and indubitable, no less than from those which are plainly false; so if I uncover any reason for doubt in each of them, that will be enough to reject them all. For that I will not need to run through them separately, a task that would take forever, because once the foundations are destroyed, whatever is built above them will collapse on its own. Thus, I shall at once assault the very principles upon which all my earlier beliefs rested.

Up to this point, what I have accepted as true I have derived either from the senses or through the senses. However, sometimes I have discovered that these are mistaken, and it is prudent never to place one's entire trust in things which have deceived us even once.

However, although from time to time the senses deceive us about minuscule things or those further away, it could well be that there are still many other matters about which we cannot entertain the slightest doubt, even though we derive [our knowledge] of them from sense experience—for example, the fact that I am now here, seated by the fire, wearing a winter robe, holding this paper in my hands, and so on. And, in fact, how could I deny that these very hands and this whole body are mine, unless perhaps I were to compare myself with certain insane people whose brains are so troubled by the stubborn vapours of black bile* that they constantly claim that they are kings, when, in fact, they are very poor, or that they are dressed in purple, when they are nude, or that they have earthenware heads, or are complete pumpkins, or made of glass? But these people are mad, and I myself would appear no less demented if I took something from them and applied it to myself as an example.

A brilliant piece of reasoning! But nevertheless I am a person who sleeps at night and experiences in my dreams all the things these [mad] people do when wide awake, sometimes even less probable ones. How often have I had an experience like this: while sleeping at night, I am convinced that I am here, dressed in a robe and seated by the fire, when, in fact, I am lying between the covers with my clothes off! At the moment, my eyes are certainly wide open and I am looking at this piece of paper, this head which I am moving is not asleep, and I am aware of this hand as I move it consciously and purposefully. None of what happens while I am asleep is so distinct. Yes, of course—but nevertheless I recall other times when I have been deceived by similar thoughts in my sleep. As I reflect on this matter carefully, it becomes

---

* One of the four basic bodily fluids then thought to be associated with disease when in imbalance. [Editor's footnote]

completely clear to me that there are no certain indicators which ever enable us to differentiate between being awake and being asleep, and this is astounding; in my confusion I am almost convinced that I may be sleeping.

So then, let us suppose that I am asleep and that these particular details—that my eyes are open, that I am moving my head, that I am stretching out my hand—are not true, and that perhaps I do not even have hands like these or a whole body like this. We must, of course, still concede that the things we see while asleep are like painted images, which could only have been made as representations of real things. And so these general things—these eyes, this head, this hand, and this entire body—at least are not imaginary things but really do exist. For even when painters themselves take great care to form sirens and satyrs with the most unusual shapes, they cannot, in fact, give them natures which are entirely new. Instead, they simply mix up the limbs of various animals or, if they happen to come up with something so new that nothing at all like it has been seen before and thus [what they have made] is completely fictitious and false, nonetheless, at least the colours which make up the picture certainly have to be real. For similar reasons, although these general things—eyes, head, hand, and so on—could also be imaginary, still we are at least forced to concede the reality of certain even simpler and more universal objects, out of which, just as with real colours, all those images of things that are in our thoughts, whether true or false, are formed.

Corporeal nature appears, in general, to belong to this class [of things], as well as its extension,* the shape of extended things, their quantity or their size and number, the place where they exist, the time which measures how long they last, and things like that.

Thus, from these facts perhaps we are not reaching an erroneous conclusion [by claiming] that physics, astronomy, medicine, and all the other disciplines which rely upon a consideration of composite objects are indeed doubtful, but that arithmetic, geometry, and the other [sciences] like them, which deal with only the simplest and most general matters and have little concern whether or not they exist in the nature of things, con-

tain something certain and indubitable. For whether I am awake or asleep, two and three always add up to five, a square does not have more than four sides, and it does not seem possible to suspect that such manifest truths could be false.

Nevertheless, a certain opinion has for a long time been fixed in my mind—that there is an all-powerful God who created me and [made me] just as I am. But how do I know He has not arranged things so that there is no earth at all, no sky, no extended thing, no shape, no magnitude, no place, and yet seen to it that all these things appear to me to exist just as they do now? Besides, given that I sometimes judge that other people make mistakes with the things about which they believe they have the most perfect knowledge, might I not in the same way be wrong every time I add two and three together, or count the sides of a square, or do something simpler, if that can be imagined? Perhaps God is unwilling to deceive me in this way, for He is said to be supremely good. But if it is contrary to the goodness of God to have created me in such a way that I am always deceived, it would also seem foreign to His goodness to allow me to be occasionally deceived. The latter claim, however, is not one that I can make.

Perhaps there may really be some people who prefer to deny [the existence of] such a powerful God, rather than to believe that all other things are uncertain. But let us not seek to refute these people, and [let us concede] that everything [I have said] here about God is a fiction. No matter how they assume I reached where I am now, whether by fate, or chance, or a continuous series of events, or in some other way, given that being deceived and making mistakes would seem to be something of an imperfection, the less power they attribute to the author of my being, the greater the probability that I will be so imperfect that I will always be deceived. I really do not have a reply to these arguments. Instead, I am finally compelled to admit that there is nothing in the beliefs which I formerly held to be true about which one cannot raise doubts. And this is not a reckless or frivolous opinion, but the product of strong and well-considered reasoning. And therefore, if I desire to discover something certain, in future I should also withhold my assent from those former opinions of mine, no less than [I do] from opinions which are obviously false.

---

*   Something's extension is its spatial magnitude—the volume of space it occupies. [Editor's footnote]

But it is not sufficient to have called attention to this point. I must [also] be careful to remember it. For these habitual opinions constantly recur, and I have made use of them for so long and they are so familiar that they have, as it were, acquired the right to seize hold of my belief and subjugate it, even against my wishes, and I will never give up the habit of deferring to and relying on them, as long as I continue to assume that they are what they truly are: opinions which are to some extent doubtful, as I have already pointed out, but still very probable, so that it is much more reasonable to believe them than to deny them. For that reason, I will not go wrong, in my view, if I deliberately turn my inclination into its complete opposite and deceive myself, [by assuming] for a certain period that these earlier opinions are entirely false and imaginary, until I have, as it were, finally brought the weight of both my [old and my new] prejudices into an equal balance, so that corrupting habits will no longer twist my judgment away from the correct perception of things. For I know that doing this will not, for the time being, lead to danger or error and that it is impossible for me to indulge in excessive distrust, since I am not concerned with actions at this point, but only with knowledge.

Therefore, I will assume that it is not God, who is supremely good and the fountain of truth, but some malicious demon, at once omnipotent and supremely cunning, who has been using all the energy he possesses to deceive me. I will suppose that sky, air, earth, colours, shapes, sounds, and all other external things are nothing but the illusions of my dreams, set by this spirit as traps for my credulity. I will think of myself as if I had no hands, no eyes, no flesh, no blood, nor any senses, and yet as if I still falsely believed I had all these things. I shall continue to concentrate resolutely on this meditation, and if, in doing so, I am, in fact, unable to learn anything true, I will at least do what is in my power and with a resolute mind take care not to agree to what is false or to enable the deceiver to impose anything on me, no matter how powerful and cunning [he may be]. But this task is onerous, and laziness brings me back to my customary way of life. I am like a prisoner who in his sleep may happen to enjoy an imaginary liberty and who, when he later begins to suspect that he is asleep, fears to wake up and willingly cooperates with the pleasing illusions [in order to prolong them]. In this way, I unconsciously slip back into my old opinions and am afraid to wake up, in case from now on I would have to spend the period of challenging wakefulness that follows this peaceful relaxation not in the light, but in the inextricable darkness of the difficulties I have just raised.

READING QUESTIONS

1. Are you certain that you are not dreaming right now? If so, what is your certainty based on? If not, what evidence would you need in order to be certain?

2. By the end of the First Meditation, what beliefs has Descartes put into doubt? Can you think of anything he has not put into doubt?

3. Both Descartes and Plato encourage us to do philosophy by first putting aside our opinions and preconceptions. Which method do you find more compelling: Descartes's methodological doubt or Plato's Socratic Method? Why?

Cogito Ergo Sum—I Think, Therefore I Am

Doubting absolutely everything that he ever learned or took for granted before, Descartes appears to have placed himself in an epistemological bind as far as his quest for certainty is concerned. In some ways, he seems worse off now than before he began. However, in the darkness of skeptical obscurity, he finds rational illumination. Descartes discovers the *intuitively self-evident truth* upon which he can base subsequent epistemological deductions in line with his vision of a natural philosophy containing the precision of mathematics. Even if he is deceived in his experience by sensory illusions, dreams, or even by an all-powerful but evil being, the one thing that cannot be denied is that there is an "I" that is being deceived. It is this same "I" that doubts and has doubted the existence of everything that can be put into doubt.

Thus, even if we are confused about what we are, where we are, or the nature of reality that surrounds us, the one thing we cannot deny is that we are a thinking thing—a thing that doubts, understands, conceives, wills, rejects, imagines, and perceives. From the fact that *I think*, one knows with certainty that *I exist*.

In the *Discourse on Method*, Descartes captures this insight with the Latin phrase **cogito ergo sum** (I think, therefore I am). Although famous, that is not how Descartes delivers his first and foundational piece of knowledge in the *Meditations*. In that book he uses the meditative method, not argument, to guide us to our own awareness of the self-evident and simple intuition that it is impossible to think and not to exist. Let us turn now to Descartes's "Second Meditation" to see more clearly how he arrives at the truth of the "*cogito.*"

René Descartes, Second Meditation, featuring the *Cogito*[13]

The second of Descartes's Meditations *begins with his search for an indubitable piece of knowledge that withstands all of the doubts raised in the First Meditation. Soon enough, he discovers just such a piece of knowledge. In the Objections and Replies published along with the first edition of the* Meditations *in 1641, Descartes explains that he does not arrive at that certain truth by formal argumentation but, rather, as "something self-evident by a simple intuition of the mind."*[14]

———

Yesterday's meditation threw me into so many doubts that I can no longer forget them or even see how they might be resolved. Just as if I had suddenly fallen into a deep eddying current, I am hurled into such confusion that I am unable to set my feet on the bottom or swim to the surface. However, I will struggle along and try once again [to follow] the same path I started on yesterday—that is, I will reject everything which admits of the slightest doubt, just as if I had discovered it was completely false, and I will proceed further in this way, until I find something certain, or at least, if I do nothing else, until I know for certain that there is nothing certain. In order to shift the entire earth from its location, Archimedes asked for nothing but a fixed and immovable point. So I, too, ought to hope for great things if I can discover something, no matter how small, which is certain and immovable.

Therefore, I assume that everything I see is false. I believe that none of those things my lying memory represents has ever existed, that I have no senses at all, and that body, shape, extension, motion, and location are chimeras. What, then, will be true? Perhaps this one thing: there is nothing certain.

But how do I know that there exists nothing other than the items I just listed, about which one could not entertain the slightest momentary doubt? Is there not some God, by whatever name I call him, who places these very thoughts inside me? But why would I think this, since I myself could perhaps have produced them? So am I then not at least something? But I have already denied that I have senses and a body. Still, I am puzzled, for what follows from this? Am I so bound up with my body and my senses that I cannot exist without them? But I have convinced myself that there is nothing at all in the universe—no sky, no earth, no minds, no bodies. So then, is it the case that I, too, do not exist? No, not at all: if I persuaded myself of something, then I certainly existed. But there is some kind of deceiver, supremely powerful and supremely cunning, who is constantly and intentionally deceiving me. But then, if he is deceiving me, there again is no doubt that I exist—for that very reason. Let him trick me as much as he can, he will never succeed in making me nothing, as long as I am aware that I am something. And so, after thinking all these things through in great detail, I must finally settle on this proposition: the statement *I am, I exist* is necessarily true every time I say it or conceive of it in my mind.

But I do not yet understand enough about what this *I* is, which now necessarily exists. Thus, I must be careful I do not perhaps unconsciously substitute something else in place of this *I* and in that way make a mistake even here, in the conception which I assert is the most certain and most evident of all. For that reason, I will now reconsider what I once believed myself to be, before I fell into this [present] way of thinking. Then I will remove from that whatever could, in the slightest way, be weakened by the reasoning I have [just] brought to bear, so that, in doing this, by the end I will be left only with what is absolutely certain and immovable.

What then did I believe I was before? Naturally, I thought I was a human being. But what is a human being? Shall I say a *rational animal*? No. For then I would have to ask what an *animal* is and what *rational* means, and thus from a single question I would fall into several greater difficulties. And at the moment I do not have so much leisure time that I wish to squander it with subtleties of this sort. Instead I would prefer here to attend to what used to come into my mind quite naturally and spontaneously in earlier days every time I thought about what I was. The first thought, of course, was that

I had a face, hands, arms, and this entire mechanism of limbs, the kind one sees on a corpse, and this I designated by the name *body*. Then it occurred to me that I ate and drank, walked, felt, and thought. These actions I assigned to the *soul*.

... But what [am I] now, when I assume that there is some extremely powerful and, if I may be permitted to speak like this, malevolent and deceiving being who is deliberately using all his power to trick me? Can I affirm that I possess even the least of all those things which I have just described as pertaining to the nature of body? I direct my attention [to this], think [about it], and turn [the question] over in my mind. Nothing comes to me. It is tedious and useless to go over the same things once again. What, then, of those things I used to attribute to the soul, like eating, drinking, or walking? But given that now I do not possess a body, these are nothing but imaginary figments. What about sense perception? This, too, surely does not occur without the body. And in sleep I have apparently sensed many objects which I later noticed I had not [truly] perceived. What about thinking? Here I discover something: thinking does exist. This is the only thing which cannot be detached from me. *I am, I exist*—that is certain. But for how long? Surely for as long as I am thinking. For it could perhaps be the case that, if I were to abandon thinking altogether, then in that moment I would completely cease to be. At this point I am not agreeing to anything except what is necessarily true. Therefore, strictly speaking, I am merely a thinking thing, that is, a mind or spirit, or understanding, or reason—words whose significance I did not realize before. However, I am something real, and I truly exist. But what kind of thing? As I have said, a thing that thinks....

But what then am I? A thinking thing. What is this? It is surely something that doubts, understands, affirms, denies, is willing, is unwilling, and also imagines and perceives.

This is certainly not an insubstantial list, if all [these] things belong to me. But why should they not? Surely I am the same I who now doubts almost everything, yet understands some things, who affirms that this one thing is true, denies all the rest, desires to know more, does not wish to be deceived, imagines many things, even against its will, and also notices many things which seem to come from the senses? Even if I am always asleep and even if the one who created me is also doing all he can to deceive me, what is there among all these things which is not just as true as the fact that I exist? Is there something there that I could say is separate from me? For it is so evident that I am the one who doubts, understands, and wills, that I cannot think of anything which might explain the matter more clearly. But obviously it is the same I that imagines, for although it may well be case, as I have earlier assumed, that nothing I directly imagine is true, nevertheless, the power of imagining really exists and forms part of my thinking. Finally, it is the same I that feels, or notices corporeal things, apparently through the senses: for example, I now see light, hear noise, and feel heat. But these are false, for I am asleep. Still, I certainly seem to see, hear, and grow warm—and this cannot be false. Strictly speaking, this is what in me is called sense perception and, taken in this precise meaning, it is nothing other than thinking.

READING QUESTIONS

1. At what first certain truth does Descartes arrive? Meditate with Descartes and discover this truth for yourself. Do you know it is true even if you are dreaming? What if a powerful being is deceiving you with false thoughts? Explain how knowledge of this truth is or is not undermined by these doubts.

2. According to Descartes, what is "I"? Eventually in the *Meditations*, Descartes argues that soul and body are distinct substances, but at this early stage, when the doubts of the First Meditation are still in effect, does Descartes know if "I" is a spiritual being or a material being?

3. Descartes is not the first philosopher in this book to plunge into extreme skepticism and find a way out of it. Recall that Chapter 1 contains a passage from *Deliverance from Error* by Abu Hamid al-Ghazali, in which al-Ghazali recounts his own experience with skepticism and his way out of it. In what ways is Descartes's *cogito* similar to al-Ghazali's discovery of certainty? In what ways are they different?

We see then, that the *cogito* represents for Descartes the axiomatic and indubitable truth he needs and uses as the foundation for his new system of philosophy. But how much does that philosophy contain? Remember, Descartes has already called into question the existence of the external world because perception of it is based on doubtful sensory experience. So even though he has achieved a piece of certain knowledge, everything else is still in doubt.

In this state of **solipsism**, that is, of knowing only that he exists as a thinking thing, he does not know if anything else exists or what anything is really like. A lonely state of knowledge, indeed, but this is not the end of Descartes's search for knowledge; it is only the beginning. Now that he has a simple and true piece of knowledge, he can continue along with his method to build his knowledge of more complex truths.

In that search, the *cogito* serves as a model for knowledge, providing the litmus test of "clear and distinct" ideas. Anything else that is as clear and distinct as his own existence as a thinking being would also have to be certain. Notably, Descartes does not mean clear and distinct to his eyes, ears, or any other sense organ. All of those are in doubt. He means clear and distinct in thought alone.

Using the ***clear and distinct* criterion** of truth, Descartes goes on in his meditations to establish beyond doubt that a God exists who would not deceive him. One of several arguments for the existence of God goes like this:

(a) something cannot come from nothing—all effects (including ideas) are caused by something;

(b) the reality of a cause must be as much or more than the reality of its effect;

(c) the idea I have of God as a perfect and infinite being was caused by something;

(d) since I am finite and imperfect, I could not be the cause of this idea;

(e) therefore God, understood as an infinite and perfect being, exists.

Descartes finds, then, within the certainty of the *cogito*, grounds for certainty in the belief that God does in fact exist. One can see clearly and distinctly that *God must exist as a logical prerequisite* for having the idea of a perfect and infinite being.

In God's certain existence and infinite perfection, Descartes also finds certainty in the existence of the external world. A perfect God would not use deception and trick Descartes into believing that an outer reality exists when it does not. What does this mean? It means that not only does the "I" or the *cogito* exist, but so too does God and the physical material world. The existence of all three has been arrived at by building from the first indubitable truth to subsequent truths.

Descartes's mathematically-inspired method has been summed up this way:

> Descartes's doubting methodology is like the axiomatic method in logic and mathematics, in which a theorem whose truth initially seems likely but not *totally* certain [for example, the physical world exists] is demonstrated to be certain by deriving it from basic axioms by means of rules of inference. Descartes's "axiom" is, in effect, "I think, therefore I am," and his "rule of inference" is clear and distinct perception.[15]

THINKING ABOUT YOUR THINKING

How do you know when you know something is true? To guide your thoughts on this question, think of a time when your senses tricked you. How did you figure out that your senses had tricked you and what did you do to correct your thoughts? How do you know now that your realization and correction were, in fact, correct? Is it possible that you were tricked once again?

On the subject of method, you should recall at this juncture that Descartes never appealed to the senses to discover the indubitable first truth on which to base his philosophy. His epistemological approach was purely rational and deductive. To demonstrate the power of reason, not sensory observation, in the quest for certain knowledge, Descartes uses "the wax example." In it, he demonstrates the limitation of the senses and the resources of the mind alone. This demonstration emphasizes Descartes's contention that the knowledge of objects does not come from our sensing them, but rather from thinking.

As you read "the wax example" below, note that it comes at a point in Descartes's meditations when he has not yet proved that anything else beyond himself exists. However, it anticipates what he eventually establishes about the true nature of material things and how he arrives at that knowledge. Contrary to his childhood opinions, he discovers that material objects are not really the way they appear to us. Strip away all of an object's sensible qualities and what remains is something extended and changeable, not something that is, for example, really white, cold, floral-scented, hard, or any other sensible quality. As for how he arrives at that discovery, it is through the use of his intellect alone.

Again, contrary to what we might think as children, that knowledge about the wax's real nature cannot come from the senses. If knowledge were derived from, or based exclusively on, the senses, then changes in the appearance of a melted ball of wax would force us to conclude that the subsequent puddle of wax was not the same wax that we started with—something clearly false. The intellect alone enables us to understand the enduring real properties of the wax, which maintain its identity regardless of superficial changes to its sensory-based qualities and appearances. For Descartes, the intellect alone, not experience, is the ultimate source of knowledge about the world.

René Descartes, Second Meditation, featuring The Wax Example[16]

Descartes's "wax example" occurs in the Second Meditation after his discovery of the cogito. *At this point in his meditations, he acknowledges the difficulty of remaining in a state of doubt, and he allows himself to go back to his habitual ways of trusting his senses. To his surprise, he discovers that he understands things about the wax that are not reported by his senses.*

———

Let us consider those things we commonly believe we understand most distinctly of all, that is, the bodies we touch and see—not, indeed, bodies in general, for those general perceptions tend to be somewhat more confusing, but rather one body in particular. For example, let us take this [piece of] beeswax. It was collected from the hive very recently and has not yet lost all the sweetness of its honey. It [still] retains some of the scent of the flowers from which it was gathered. Its colour, shape, and size are evident. It is hard, cold, and easy to handle. If you strike it with your finger, it will give off a sound. In short, everything we require to be able to recognize a body as distinctly as possible appears to be present. But watch. While I am speaking, I bring the wax over to the fire. What is left of its taste is removed, its smell disappears, its colour changes, its shape is destroyed, its size increases, it turns to liquid, and it gets hot. I can hardly touch it. And now, if you strike it, it emits no sound. After [these changes], is what remains the same wax? We must concede that it is. No one denies this; no one thinks otherwise. What then was in [this piece of wax] that I understood so distinctly? Certainly nothing I apprehended with my senses, since all [those things] associated with taste, odour, vision, touch, and sound have now changed. [But] the wax remains.

Perhaps what I now think is as follows: the wax itself was not really that sweetness of honey, that fragrance of flowers, that white colour, or that shape and sound, but a body which a little earlier was perceptible to me in those forms, but which is now [perceptible] in different ones. But what exactly is it that I am imagining in this way? Let us consider that point and, by removing those things which do not belong to the wax, see what is left over. It is clear that nothing [remains], other than something extended, flexible, and changeable. But what, in fact, do *flexible* and *changeable* mean? Do these words mean that I imagine that this wax can change from a round shape to a square one or from [something square] to something triangular? No, that is not it at all. For I understand that the wax has the capacity for innumerable changes of this kind, and yet I am not able to run through these innumerable changes by using my imagination. Therefore, this conception [I have of the wax] is not produced by the faculty of imagination. What about extension? Is not the extension of the wax also unknown? For it becomes greater when the wax melts, greater [still] when it boils, and once again [even] greater if the heat is increased. And I would not be judging correctly what wax is if I did not believe that it could also be extended in various other ways, more than I could ever grasp in my imagination. Therefore, I am forced to admit that my imagination has no idea at all what this wax is and that I perceive it only with my mind. I am talking about this [piece of] wax in particular, for the point is even clearer about wax in general. But what is this wax which can be perceived only by the mind? It must be the same as the wax I see, touch, and imagine—in short, the same wax I thought it was from the beginning. But we should note that the perception of it is not a matter of sight, or touch, or imagination, and never was, even though that seemed to be the case earlier, but simply of mental inspection, which could be either imperfect and confused as it was before, or clear and distinct as it is now, depending on the lesser or greater degree of attention I bring to bear on those things out of which the wax is composed.

However, now I am amazed at how my mind is [weak and] prone to error. For although I am considering these things silently within myself, without speaking aloud, I still get stuck on the words themselves and am almost deceived by the very nature of the way we speak. For if the wax is there [in front of us], we say that we see the wax itself, not that we judge it to be there from the colour or shape. From that I could immediately conclude that I recognized the wax thanks to the vision in my eyes, and not simply by mental inspection. But by analogy, suppose I happen to glance out of the window at people crossing the street; in normal speech I also say I see the people themselves, just as I do with the wax. But what am I really seeing other than hats and coats, which could be concealing automatons underneath? However, I judge that they are people. And thus what I thought I was seeing with my eyes I understand only with my faculty of judgment, which is in my mind.

But someone who wishes [to elevate] his knowledge above the common level should be ashamed to have based his doubts in the forms of speech which ordinary people use, and so we should move on to consider next whether my perception of what wax is was more perfect and more evident when I first perceived it and believed I knew it by my external senses, or at least by my so-called *common sense*, in other words, by the power of imagination, or whether it is more perfect now, after I have investigated more carefully both what wax is and how it can be known. To entertain doubts about this matter would certainly be silly. For in my first perception of the wax what was distinct? What did I notice there that any animal might not be capable of capturing? But when I distinguish the wax from its external forms and look at it as something naked, as if I had stripped off its clothing, even though there could still be some error in my judgment, it is certain that I could not perceive it in this way without a human mind.

But what am I to say about this mind itself, in other words, about myself? For up to this point I am not admitting there is anything in me except mind. What, I say, is the *I* that seems to perceive this wax so distinctly? Do I not know myself not only much more truly and certainly, but also much more distinctly and clearly than I know the wax? For if I judge that the wax exists from the fact that I see it, then from the very fact that I see the wax it certainly follows much more clearly that I myself also exist. For it could be that what I see is not really wax. It could be the case that I do not have eyes at all with which to see anything. But when I see or think I see (at the moment I am not differentiating between these two), it is completely impossible that I, the one doing the thinking, am not something. For similar reasons, if I judge that the wax exists from the fact that I am touch-

ing it, the same conclusion follows once again, namely, that I exist. The result is clearly the same if [my judgment rests] on the fact that I imagine the wax or on any other reason at all. But these observations I have made about the wax can be applied to all other things located outside of me. Furthermore, if my perception of the wax seemed more distinct after it was drawn to my attention, not merely by sight or touch, but by several [other] causes, I must concede that I now understand myself much more distinctly, since all of those same reasons capable of assisting my perception either of the wax or of any other body whatsoever are even better proofs of the nature of my mind! However, over and above this, there are so many other things in the mind itself which can provide a more distinct conception of its [nature] that it hardly seems worthwhile to review those features of corporeal things which might contribute to it.

And behold—I have all on my own finally returned to the place where I wanted to be. For since I am now aware that bodies themselves are not properly perceived by the senses or by the faculty of imagination, but only by the intellect, and are not perceived because they are touched or seen, but only because they are understood, I realize this obvious point: there is nothing I can perceive more easily or more clearly than my own mind. But because it is impossible to rid oneself so quickly of an opinion one has long been accustomed to hold, I would like to pause here, in order to impress this new knowledge more deeply on my memory with a prolonged meditation.

READING QUESTIONS

1. Apply the details of the wax example to a different material object, such as piece of fruit or a tree leaf. Imagine that object before and after a change in its appearance. According to Descartes, what about that object persists through the changes? Using Descartes's thinking, what kind of change would the object not persist through? What kind of change would destroy it?

2. Before meditating with Descartes about the wax, how did you think that you knew about the world? By your senses? By your teachers and your textbooks? Now that you have meditated with Descartes, do you think any differently about how you can know about the world? How so?

Whereas Descartes used the wax example to wrestle us from our reliance on our senses in the search for truth, the next philosopher whom we will look at, namely John Locke, used sensory observation in experiments much like the wax example in order to draw conclusions about the world. Yet despite their different approaches to knowledge, Descartes and Locke came to some similar conclusions. They fundamentally differed in *how* they explained how we acquire knowledge but not, necessarily, what we know. From them, we can learn a lesson about principled disagreement and identifying the location of philosophical differences.

"What can give us more sure knowledge than our senses? How else can we distinguish between the true and the false?"
LUCRETIUS

4.4 John Locke's Empiricist Theory of Ideas

Like other philosophers before him, John Locke wanted to separate knowledge from mere opinion. Specifically, he set out to remove the *metaphysical rubbish* from philosophical inquiry so that he might achieve his goal, which was "to inquire into the original certainty and extent of human knowledge"[17] for the purpose of advancing the sciences. What Locke considered "rubbish," however, some of those other philosophers—including Plato and Descartes—considered knowledge.

Critical of knowledge claims that go beyond our human capacity for knowledge, Locke observed that scientists and metaphysicians alike made a bad practice of using words such as *space*, *time*, *cause*, *substance*, *self*, and other descriptive terms such as *hard*, *soft, round*, and *white* without accurate accounts of what they were referring to. He reasoned that if claims containing such terms and descriptors were to make any sense at all, they must all correspond to ideas located in the mind. In short, the terms must be meaningful. The first order of business, then, was *not* to investigate the *essence* of things—the nature of reality or other-worldly entities (a preoccupation with metaphysicians)—but to examine the source of our ideas of those things about which we make knowledge claims. That is the project that occupies Locke in *An Essay Concerning Human Understanding*.

What's called an "essay" nowadays is a short piece of writing on a particular topic. Locke's *Essay* is not that. Rather, it is a sizable treatise comprising four "books" covering many topics, including science, language, personal identity, and God.

"It is ambition enough to be employed as an under-laborer in clearing the ground a little and removing some of the rubbish that lies in the way of knowledge."
JOHN LOCKE

John Locke

John Locke was born in 1632 in Somerset, England, into a Puritan home emphasizing the virtues of temperance, simplicity, and aversion to display. Locke received home instruction until 1646, at which time he entered Westminster School to study the classics, Hebrew, and Arabic. Locke then went on to Oxford, earning his bachelor's and master's degrees. He eventually studied medicine, receiving his medical degree in 1674, but never practiced as a physician. He did, however, serve as a medical and political adviser to Lord Ashley, the future Earl of Shaftesbury. After accepting Locke's recommendation to drain an abscess on his liver, Shaftesbury credited Locke with saving his life.[18] Through his affiliation with Shaftesbury, Locke became involved in the civil service, met many significant politicians and scientists, and traveled to Holland and France. Locke's political interests are evidenced by the fact that in 1669 he helped to draft a constitution for the American Carolinas.

A voracious reader with a special interest in French philosophers, Locke had extensive familiarity with Descartes's writings and highly regarded Descartes as the one who liberated him from the philosophy that he had learned in school.[19] Like Descartes, Locke was critical of the suppression of reason by institutionalized authorities and traditional textbooks, and like him wanted to separate real knowledge from mere opinion, especially in the service of advancing science.

Yet despite Locke's similarities with and praise for the Frenchman, he had some significant epistemological disagreements with him as well. Most fundamentally, in contrast to Descartes's method of withdrawing from the senses in order to discover clear and distinct ideas lying innate within the mind, Locke was an **empiricist**; that is, he held that all of our ideas—and, hence, knowledge—originate in sensory experience.

Today, John Locke is especially remembered not only for his epistemology but also for his political theorizing, which centered on the forming of a *social contract* and which attacked the notion of the divine right of kings and the nature of the state as conceived by the English philosopher Thomas Hobbes. In his political writings, Locke argues that we are naturally equal and independent and, therefore, have a natural obligation not to harm the "life, health, liberty, or possessions" of another. Not unrelated, in his writings on education, he emphasizes the development of good citizens who live well with others in liberal society. Major works by Locke include *Two Treatises of Government* (1689), *An Essay Concerning Human Understanding* (1690), and *Some Thoughts on Education* (1693).

Locke died in Oates, England, on October 28, 1704.

Tabula Rasa

In answer to his own question as to the source of our ideas, Locke advances an essentially psychological thesis. He claims that when children are born into the world, their minds are like a blank slate or blank writing tablet—a ***tabula rasa***, to use the Latin expression. There is nothing on that slate that is not put there by experience. At birth, we are ignorant of everything. Locke writes:

> Let us then suppose the mind to be as we say, white paper, void of all characters, without any ideas: How comes it to be furnished? Whence comes it by that vast store which the busy and boundless fancy of man has painted on it with an almost endless variety? Whence has it all the *materials* of reason and knowledge? To this I answer, in one word, from *experience*. In that all our knowledge is founded; and from that it ultimately derives itself.[20]

For Locke, there are actually two forms of experience. The one form is called **sensation**, and it is the type that provides ideas of the external world. The ideas we have of *yellow*, *white*, *hot*, *cold*, *soft*, *hard*, *bitter*, and *sweet* come from external objects and are conveyed to the mind. The second type of experience is called **reflection**, and it comes from "the perception of the operations of our own mind within us, as it is employed about the ideas it has got."[21] Included under reflection are ideas of perception, thinking, doubting, memory, imagination, believing, reasoning, knowing, and willing—all different acts of the mind. From observing ourselves engaged in such processes of mind, we receive distinct sorts of ideas from what we get when external bodies affect our senses. This source of ideas is like an "internal sense"—the ideas it provides "being such only as the mind gets by reflecting on its own operations within itself."[22]

When Locke says, then, that all knowledge is derived from experience, he is referring either to direct sensory experience or the result of the mind combining or reflecting on those experiences. The ideas we get through experience serve as the materials that are used by our mental faculties. To remember, we call up an idea; when we communicate, our intended meanings are conveyed by ideas; when we judge or discriminate, we compare ideas.

The ideas that furnish the mind may be either *simple* or *complex*. **Simple ideas** come from simple sensations like *hard*, *cold*, or *sweet*. **Complex ideas** like *giraffe* or *government* can be broken down and analyzed into simple ones. Though imaginary ideas like *unicorn* or *satyr* may not at first glance seem to come from experience, upon further reflection it becomes clear that they are composed of simple ideas originating in our experience, either in sensation or reflection. Add *horn* to *horse* to produce the idea of *unicorn*. Of course, ideas like *horn* and *horse* can all be broken down further until we arrive at simple ideas.

Criticisms of Innate Ideas

The notion of the mind as a *tabula rasa* is derived from Locke's rejection of innate ideas and contains important epistemological implications that separate Locke the empiricist from rationalists like Descartes who came before him. Although this point was not explicitly made in any detail in the preceding section of this chapter, implicit in what was said is the fact that Descartes did abide by the notion of **innate ideas**. For him, all clear and distinct ideas are inborn. They are implanted in the mind by nature—or, as some say, by God.

Even the idea of God itself is innate. Remember that for Descartes, in order for an imperfect (human) being to have the idea of a perfect being (God), the perfect being must exist and must be the *cause* of that idea implanted in the imperfect being's mind. Imperfect humans cannot themselves generate the idea of perfection. They are placed there by an omniscient and omnipotent God.

And just as the idea of God is innate, so too are the self-evident propositions of logic and mathematics and the clear and distinct ideas we have about things like *cause* and *substance*. An infinite and perfect Cartesian God would never deceive us into believing a world exists when it doesn't, that things exist when they don't, or that 2 + 2 = 5 when the sum is really 4.

In Chapter 1 of Book 1 of *An Essay Concerning Human Understanding*, Locke spells out his objections to the notion of innate ideas. He does not address Descartes directly, but refers to "men of innate principles" whose opinions he wishes to criticize.[23] His initial task is to prepare the empiricist foundations of knowledge by disposing of the theory of innate ideas. According to Locke, defenders of the thesis of innate ideas believe it holds true as evidenced by universal consent. They argue that there are universally agreed upon principles (both practical and speculative) to which all would agree.

In response, Locke argues that even if it were true that all people could agree on certain truths, this in itself would still not prove their innateness. Rather than being inborn, the universal agreement surrounding "innate truths" could be demonstrated to result in different ways. This demonstration is not necessary, however, since there are no principles to which humankind gives its universal consent in the first place.

Locke takes two examples of so-called innate principles to illustrate his point. The first is "Whatsoever is, is" and the second is "It is impossible for the same thing to be and not to be." He quickly points out that young children and "idiots" are unable to understand these principles and therefore cannot give their assent to them. According to Locke, this observation alone is enough to destroy the universal consent notion of innate ideas. Even if we said that infants come to see innate ideas clearly and distinctly once older and sufficiently educated, this implies learning and hence experience—Locke's point.

According to his *tabula rasa* concept, we can assert that the mind, prior to experience, is blank. Experience is the ultimate source of all ideas in the mind and therefore the foundation of all thinking and knowledge.

Primary and Secondary Qualities of Objects

If Locke's *tabula rasa* notion is correct, then, as suggested already, all of us start life with no innate knowledge. We enter a world of myriad sensations, one of virtually infinite sights and sounds, textures, tastes, and smells. Locke claims that from our simple sensations, we form simple ideas, whereas by using our capacity for reflecting on them, we combine our simple ideas into complex ones. For example, the complex idea of a snowball is the result of us combining the simple ideas of 'white', 'cold', 'spherical', and 'hard'. Either way, simple or complex, all of our ideas of the material world ultimately have their origin in sensory experience.

Now, the interesting epistemological question arises as to whether our ideas about the world actually correspond to it. This was a question that occupied Locke's attention and, as we learned already in this chapter, occupied Descartes's attention also. According to Descartes, we naively believe as children that our ideas about the world resemble how the world really is; however, by withdrawing from those old opinions and using reason alone, we discover that is not the case.

Recall that, in Descartes's wax example, even though every sensible quality changed during the time it was melted by the heat, we still were able to understand that it was the same piece of wax—that is, that the same thing endured throughout exhaustive sensible changes. While the color, scent, and solidity of the wax had been transformed, what remained was the same physical substance, something unavailable to the senses. Thus, our childhood opinion that our sense perceptions reflect reality turned out to be wrong.

Locke refines that conclusion with his distinction between primary sensible qualities (which do match reality) and secondary sensible qualities (which do not). Unlike Descartes, however, Locke does not use the intellect alone to draw any of his conclusions or to know what lies beyond all of the sensible qualities of an object.

When faced with an object, ideas of sensation are caused in us by the actions of the material objects on our sense organs. The idea or image that is caused, then, represents the object that caused it. Locke contends that some of the sensations we receive from objects really do resemble the object's qualities, though others do not. The sensations that do resemble the properties of material objects are called **primary qualities**. They include *figure*, *solidity*, *extension*, *motion*, and *number*. Such qualities are "wholly inseparable from [the body] ... and such as in all the alterations and changes it suffers ... it constantly keeps."[24]

By contrast, there are qualities that do not resemble "utterly inseparable" properties of material objects. They are described as **secondary qualities** and include *color*, *taste*, *texture*, *odor*, *smell*, and so forth. Locke writes: "The ideas of primary qualities of bodies are resemblances of them, and their patterns do really exist in the bodies themselves, but the ideas produced in us by these secondary qualities have no resemblance of them at all."[25] To justify his claim that primary qualities are inseparable from material objects—from every particle of matter—he uses the following illustration:

> Take a grain of wheat, divide it into two parts; each part has still solidity, extension, figure and mobility; divide it again, and it retains still the same qualities; and so divide it on, till the parts become insensible; they must retain still each of them all those qualities. For division ... can never take away either solidity, extension, figure, or mobility from any body, but only makes two or more distinct separate masses of matter, of that which was but one before.[26]

From this example, we see that, for Locke, the real primary qualities of objects are those that remain after repeated divisions. He argues that other apparent, secondary qualities of objects (for example, color) disappear as we divide them into smaller and more minute particles. This being the case, they cannot be the *real qualities* of objects.

In contrast with Descartes, however, Locke bases his position on observation, including the powerful observations afforded by the then recently invented microscope. To support his point about how secondary qualities can change and hence cannot constitute the real qualities of objects, Locke writes:

> Had we senses acute enough to discern the minute particles of bodies, and the real constitution on which their sensible qualities depend, I doubt not but they would

produce quite different ideas in us; and that which is now the yellow colour of gold, would then disappear, and instead of it we should see an admirable texture of parts, of a certain size and figure. This microscopes plainly discover to us; for what to our naked eyes produces a certain colour, is, by thus augmenting the acuteness of our senses, discovered to be quite a different thing.[27]

Locke agreed with the scientists of his time who believed that the material world is ultimately made up of tiny imperceptible particles or "corpuscles" that operate according to mechanical laws. Thus, for Locke, the secondary qualities that we perceive as ideas are really minute primary qualities in bodies that are too small for us to see as they actually are.

Because our ideas are produced by our experiences, we cannot have adequate ideas of the real, fundamental constitution of material objects that are too small for us to experience. For example, we cannot be sure of the shape, size, and arrangements of the corpuscles that give a piece of wax its sensible color, temperature, solidity, scent, and taste because we cannot observe those minute particles directly. Nevertheless, we can apply our knowledge of sensible primary qualities to our reasoning about insensible primary qualities, and that, for Locke, is much preferable to introducing any "metaphysical rubbish" into his philosophical system. In his *Essay Concerning Human Understanding*, Locke writes:

> The particular parcel of matter which makes the ring I have on my finger, is forwardly, by most men, supposed to have a real essence, whereby it is *gold*; and from whence those qualities flow, which I find in it, *viz*. its peculiar colour, weight, hardness, fusibility, fixedness, and change of colour upon a slight touch of mercury, *etc*. This essence, from which all these properties flow, when I enquire into it, and search after it, I plainly perceive I cannot discover: the farthest I can go, is only to presume, that it being nothing but body, its real essence, or internal constitution, on which these qualities depend, can be nothing but the figure, size, and connexion of its solid parts; of neither of which, I having any distinct perception at all, I can have no *idea* of its essence, which is the cause that it has that particular shining yellowness; a greater weight than any thing I know of the same build; and a fitness to have its colour changed by the touch of quicksilver.* If any one will say, that the real essence, and the internal constitution, on which these properties depend, is not the figure, size, and arrangement or connexion of its solid parts, but something else, call'd its particular *form*; I am farther from having any *idea* of its real essence, than I was before.[28]

As for what supports the qualities that compose a material object, Locke refers to that as pure substance, or substratum. It is what underlies the qualities of material objects and is, itself, quality-less. For that reason, it is an "I-know-not-what," for we have no idea of it, nor can we. By Locke's theory of ideas, any ideas we have about material objects are produced by the qualities of those objects, and since substratum has no qualities, we have no idea of it. We certainly don't have an innate idea of it, according to Locke. Rather, we suppose the existence of substratum in order to make sense of the world; qualities aren't just floating out there on their own! But supposing substratum exists is not the

---

*　Mercury. It quickly covers a gold object it touches, coloring it silver.

same as having an idea of it. So, unlike Descartes, who used his intellect alone to know that something remains after all the sensible qualities of the wax were stripped away and what that something is like (extended, flexible, changeable), Locke is left to conclude that he doesn't know what lies beyond the sensible qualities we observe (or could observe if our senses were strong enough). In Locke's words,

> [I]f any one will examine himself concerning his notion of pure substance in general, he will find he has no other idea of it at all, but only a supposition of he knows not what support of such qualities, which are capable of producing simple ideas in us ... If any one should be asked, what is the subject wherein colour or weight inheres, he would have nothing to say, but the solid extended parts: and if he were demanded, what is it, that that solidity and extension inhere in, he would not be in a much better case, than the Indian before mentioned; who, saying that the world was supported by a great elephant, is asked, what the elephant rests on; to which his answer was a great tortoise: but being again pressed to know what gave support to the broad-back'd tortoise, replied, something, he knew not what.[29]

Notably, Locke draws the same point about our minds or souls: we only know our thoughts and not the thing that is having those thoughts. The thing that thinks is an "I-know-not what."

Ultimately, then, our knowledge of the material world comes down to suppositions and not certainty. Doubt is not part of Locke's method, as it is for Descartes, but appears to be an outcome. Arguably, that is the cost of doing philosophy without "metaphysical rubbish." Better to know our limits than pretend we know more than we do.

4.5 David Hume's Radical Skepticism

Similar to Descartes and Locke, Hume's philosophical investigations into human cognition were motivated by his dissatisfaction with conventional thinking and the uncertainty that it promulgated. The idea that it's better to know what we do not know, than disagree about what we falsely think we know, is a sentiment shared by these three early modern thinkers. In Hume's case, what we do not know includes many of the metaphysical findings that Descartes and Locke thought we could know, including the existence of the self as a thinking thing, the existence and nature of the material world, and God. So it is in that aspect of David Hume's epistemology where we find the hard-hitting limits to our claims on knowledge.

Hume's thought forms a **radical skepticism**, an instrument of mass theoretical destruction that smashes metaphysics as pretentious nonsense, shattering notions of *God*, *mind*, and the *immaterial self* to smithereens. Into the scrapheap of skepticism are also tossed ideas of *physical substance* and *innate knowledge*, both of which are rendered epistemologically meaningless. Hume even goes so far as to question the philosophical validity of the most revered of all scientific concepts, namely that of *causality* itself, arguing that our use of it cannot be rationally justified either in scientific or in commonsense thinking.

Like so many other philosophers before and after him, Hume upsets conventional thinking and forces us to reexamine our previously accepted beliefs about ourselves and

"When we run over libraries, persuaded of these [empiricist] principles, what havoc must we make? If we take in our hand any volume of divinity or school metaphysics, for instance—let us ask, Does it contain any abstract reasoning concerning quantity or number? No. Does it contain any experimental reasoning concerning matter of fact and existence? No. Commit it then to the flames, for it can contain nothing but sophistry and illusion."
DAVID HUME

about the nature of reality. His writings confront us with several basic questions: "How do we know?" "What is the source of our knowledge?" and lastly, "What are its limits?" In the end, Hume concludes that we have no certain knowledge about the world but only beliefs that we feel are true.

As noted, Hume set out to sort out the disagreements that unsettled the thinking of his time by establishing how it is that we think at all. Despite the remarkable achievements of science in his day, Hume was disturbed by all the disagreements that seemed to pour from the scientific community. In the Introduction to *A Treatise of Human Nature*, he writes:

> Nor is there required such profound knowledge to discover the present imperfect condition of the sciences, but even the rabble outside may judge from the noise and clamour, which they hear, that all goes not well within. There is nothing which is not the subject of debate, and in which men of learning are not of contrary opinions. The most trivial question does not escape our controversy, and in the most momentous we are not able to give any certain decision. Disputes are multiplied, as if everything was uncertain; and these disputes are managed with the greatest warmth, as if everything was certain. Amidst all this bustle it is not reason, which wins the prize, but eloquence; and no man needs ever despair of gaining proselytes to the most extravagant hypothesis, who is artistic enough to represent it in any favourable colours. The victory is not gained by the men at arms, who manage the pike and the sword, but by the trumpeters, drummers, and musicians of the army.[30]

In efforts to establish the proper limits of knowledge and to get us back on a solid epistemological footing, Hume goes back to the beginning, as it were, and asks where our knowledge ultimately comes from. To discover the answer, Hume turns the study of human nature—in particular, human cognition. His rationale for doing so is given in the *Treatise*:

> It is evident, that all the sciences have a relation, greater or less, to human nature; and that however wide any of them may seem to run from it, they still return back by one passage or another. Even *Mathematics*, *Natural Philosophy*, and *Natural Religion*, are in some measure dependent on the science of Man; since they lie under the cognizance of men, and are judged of by their powers and faculties. It is impossible to tell what changes and improvements we might make in these sciences were we thoroughly acquainted with the extent and force of human understanding, and could explain the nature of the ideas we employ, and of the operations we perform in our reasons.[31]

In short, the functioning of human understanding serves as the foundation for all knowledge—scientific and otherwise. By identifying the origins of our ideas, as well as the relations and operations among them, Hume initially set out to lay the foundations for all the sciences. In this regard, Hume's project concerning human knowledge in general, and progress in the sciences in particular, is quite similar to those of Descartes and Locke. As mentioned, however, the results of his efforts turned out to be quite different from theirs.

David Hume

David Hume was born in 1711 in Edinburgh, Scotland, into a Calvinist family of modest economic resources. Described as "uncommonly wake-minded" by his mother, little did she know that her precocious child would grow into a brilliant thinker whose skeptical ideas would devastate much of traditional epistemology and metaphysics.

Hume was still a child when he started attending the University of Edinburgh with his older brother, but he left at the age of 16, without finishing his degree. He subsequently studied law, but eventually abandoned his legal studies as well, finding "insurmountable aversion to everything but the pursuits of philosophy and general learning." Law became "nauseous" to him. Hume confessed that achieving literary fame had become a ruling passion.

In his early twenties, he moved to France, for its affordability, and wrote *A Treatise of Human Nature*—the book that presumably was to give him the celebrity he so much desired. Unfortunately for Hume, it did not garner the attention he had hoped for during his lifetime as it "fell dead-born from the press," to use his words.[32]

In efforts to salvage the book, now a philosophical classic, he rewrote and combined the first two parts of it in a more popular and lively fashion, titling the new, shorter work *An Enquiry concerning Human Understanding* (1748). This time around, however, he included a controversial discussion of miracles that he had cut from the *Treatise*.

In 1751, a revised version of the third part of the *Treatise* was published under the title *An Enquiry Concerning the Principles of Morals*. Surprisingly, perhaps, it was his six-volume *History of England* (1754–62) that finally brought him the recognition he so craved. By 1763, his reputation as historian and man of letters preceded him.

In addition to seeking fame, Hume wished to become a university professor. This dream was never realized, however, as he failed to land a post at both Edinburgh and at the University of Glasgow. It was his deep-rooted skepticism and atheistic contempt for the day's prevailing religious beliefs that probably prevented him from finding employment as an academic. Instead, his jobs included working as a tutor, a librarian, and a diplomat. During the period he spent at the British Embassy in Paris, Hume led the life of a celebrity in leading social circles, hobnobbing with such luminaries as Voltaire and Jean-Jacques Rousseau.

Interestingly, and notwithstanding the hard edges of his skeptical criticism of traditional thought, Hume was a kind and gentle person admired by many. Friends called him St. David, and in remembrance of this fact, the street on which he lived in his final years is still called that today. Hume spent the last years of his life in Edinburgh, only at this point, in contrast to his modest beginnings, he lived a very opulent and contented lifestyle.

David Hume died in 1776 at the age of 65. In anticipation of his death, he had devoted the last year of his life to completing the *Dialogues Concerning Natural Religion*, which he had begun writing over 20 years earlier. Hume entrusted the manuscript to his friend, the economist and fellow Scottish philosopher Adam Smith, but Smith ended up withholding the *Dialogues* from publication. Some speculate this was because Smith was worried about being associated with Hume's controversial religious views.[33] Hume's nephew eventually published the *Dialogues* in 1779. Smith, however, did do his part to have Hume's autobiography, *My Own Life*—which Hume called "a very inoffensive piece"[34]—published in 1777. Hume's essays "Of Suicide" and "Of the Immortality of the Soul" were also published that year.

> *"The most lively thought is still inferior to the dullest sensation."*
> DAVID HUME

On the Origin of Ideas

Hume begins his analysis of human understanding by examining the "perceptions of the mind," things that Locke and Descartes would label "ideas." Through a kind of introspective process, he discovers that "we may divide all the perceptions of the mind into two classes or species, which are distinguished by their different degrees of force and vivacity."[35] Those perceptions containing the greatest force are called **impressions**, whereas those with lesser force and vivacity are dubbed **ideas**.

If, for example, you sustain a multiple fracture while trying to perform a gymnastics maneuver, the experience of pain would likely saturate your consciousness and envelop your entire being. No doubt, you would be *impressed* by the physical discomfort. If, on the other hand, you remember months later, when all is healed and well, how your leg did hurt once upon a time, you are having a thought or idea about the incident. Clearly, *recalling* the break is less painful than actually *experiencing* it at the moment it occurred. The recollection of the fracture can be regarded as a *copy* of the original experience, but different from it in terms of *liveliness* and *strength*. Another example: look at a red apple. Then look away, but recall that experience: it seems you see a red apple "in your mind's eye"; but this "idea" is much less vivid than the "impression"—the experience of seeing the apple itself.

Impressions and ideas apply not only to physical sensations or sensory-based experiences, but also to all other perceptions of the mind, including sentiments and affections such as anger and love. Remember, though, that experiencing anger in the moment is very different from thinking about a past outburst of it. Again, the former has greater *force* and *vivacity*. The latter may be emotionally upsetting as well, but not to the same degree. Hume writes: "When we reflect on our past sentiments and affections, our thought is a faithful mirror and copies its objects truly, but the colors which it employs are faint and dull in comparison of those in which our original perceptions were clothed."[36] Thus, the experience of anger constitutes an impression, but the thought of a previous outburst of anger is an idea. This partly explains the truth of the expression "Time heals." With the passage of time, poignant and unpleasant feelings that are originally experienced seem to fade into the distance.

Important to note at this juncture is that there is a direct, one-to-one correspondence between impressions and ideas. All of our ideas are derived from our initial experiential impressions, no matter how bizarre or fantastic these ideas may seem. For example, Pegasus, the winged horse of Greek mythology, is not purely an invention of the imagination, completely devoid of any sensory impressions, for clearly, the idea of *horse* and the idea of *wings* ultimately come from impressions people have of such things.

Hume uses the example of a golden mountain to make the same point. He contends that when we think of a *golden mountain*, all we really do is join two ideas, *gold* and *mountain*, with which we were formerly acquainted. The mind did not create something in a rational vacuum independent of everything experiential. Hume says that the "creative power of the mind amounts to no more than the faculty of compounding, transposing, augmenting, or diminishing the materials afforded us by the senses and experience."[37]

Rejection of the *Cogito*

Hume's rather simple-sounding distinction between impressions and ideas contains powerful implications that may not be obvious at first glance. Recall Descartes's first and most certain truth, the *cogito*. That indubitable piece of knowledge that *I am, I exist* is the firm and certain foundation for all other knowledge in Descartes's philosophy. As for what *I*, or the *self* is for Descartes, it is a thinking thing, which Descartes reasons is an immaterial substance or soul.

Locke has skeptical leanings when it comes to talk of substances; nevertheless, he cautiously agrees with Descartes that soul exists as the thing that thinks—or at least, Locke affirms, we all suppose that it does. For even though we do not experience the soul itself and Locke famously calls it "an-I-know-not-what," we all, according to Locke, suppose that the operations of the mind that we experience, such as doubting, reasoning, and fearing, do not exist alone in themselves but in a spiritual substance or soul.[38]

The problem for Hume is that the idea of a mind, self, or mental substance cannot be traced back to experience either. Consequently, it is a fiction as much as physical substance is. Whatever we refer to as the "self" is nothing more than a stream of consciousness. In Book One, Part IV, Section 6 of the *Treatise*, Hume has this to say about mind and personal identity:

> For my part, when I enter most intimately into what I call *myself*, I always stumble on some perception or other, of heat or cold, light or shade, love or hatred, pain or pleasure. I never can catch *myself* at any time without a perception, and never can observe anything but the perception. When my perceptions are removed for any time, as by sound sleep; so long am I insensible of *myself*, and may truly be said not to exist. And were all my perceptions removed by death, and could I neither think, nor feel, nor see, nor love, nor hate after the dissolution of my body, I should be entirely annihilated, nor do I conceive what is farther requisite to make me a perfect non-entity. If anyone upon serious unprejudiced reflection, thinks he has a different notion of *himself*, I must confess I can reason no longer with him. All I can allow him is, that he may be in the right as well as I, and that we are essentially different in this particular. He may perhaps perceive something simple and continued, which he calls *himself*; though I am certain there is no such principle in me.... But setting aside some metaphysicians of this kind, I may venture to affirm of the rest of mankind, that they are nothing but a bundle or collection of different perceptions, which succeed each other with an inconceivable rapidity, and are in a perpetual flux and movement.... The mind is a kind of theatre, where several perceptions successively make their appearance; pass, re-pass, glide away, and mingle in an infinite variety of postures and situations. There is properly no *simplicity* in it at one time, nor *identity* in different; whatever natural propensity we may have to imagine that simplicity and identity. The comparison of the theatre must not mislead us. They are the successive perceptions only, that constitute the mind; nor have we the most distant notion of the place, where these senses are represented, or of the materials, of which it is composed.[39]

When Hume turns his attention inwards, he finds thoughts occurring, but he has no impression of a single, simple *thing* that thinks. That is, he perceives a stream of thoughts, but he does not perceive anything like a mind that stays the same as the thoughts flow by. As such, Hume believes that philosophers who talk about the self as a soul or mental substance are engaged in metaphysical nonsense. They use words without any corresponding impression and, hence, without meaning. In a similar way, Hume criticizes religious beliefs. Hume argues that since the idea of God has no basis in sense experience, it too

"[It is] certain we cannot go beyond experience; and any hypothesis, that pretends to discover the ultimate original qualities of human nature, ought at first to be rejected as presumptuous and chimerical."*
DAVID HUME

* The imagining of something non-existent.

is epistemologically meaningless. Because there is no impression to which it can correspond, the idea of God becomes as baseless as 'substance' and 'self.' Also, in view of the fact that all these concepts do not originate in sense experience, they can never direct us toward knowledge of the nature and character of reality. For this reason, Hume concludes that meaningless metaphysics should be abandoned.

Association of Ideas

In further analysis of mental contents and processes, Hume lays out the **laws of association.** He was influenced very much by other thinkers of the eighteenth century who understood experience to be comprised of atomistic units in the same way that physicists saw particles in motion. Following the lead of Newton, who discovered the laws that govern physical particles, Hume saw the task of philosophy as setting out the laws governing mental particles (ideas). He found three patterns of association: **resemblance**, **contiguity**, and **cause and effect**. These patterns would explain for Hume the "bond of union" or "gentle force" that attracts one idea to another as analogous to gravity.

In the case of *resemblance*, think of how the photograph of a friend brings to mind that friend herself. Perhaps you have had the experience of mistaking a stranger for that friend. The reason for thinking of your friend when you look at the picture or the stranger is that ideas that are similar tend to be associated with one another.

"To me there appear to be only three principles of connection among ideas, namely, Resemblance, Contiguity in time or place, and Cause and Effect."
DAVID HUME

The second law of association is captured by Hume with the example of an apartment dwelling. He says, "The mention of one apartment in a building naturally introduces an inquiry or discourse concerning the others."[40] Ideas that appear closely together in time or space are oftentimes connected in thought. This principle is called *contiguity*.

Lastly, when one event follows another in regular fashion, we link them together using the principle of *cause and effect*. The experience of stepping on the gas pedal of a car in gear, for example, is associated with movement. The two events occur together so regularly that we associate them. The former "cause" leads to the latter "effect."

Hume makes the point that the *gentle force* accounting for these principles of association is not reason but **imagination.** The connections made by the imagination, however, are not **necessary connections**, as is the case in mathematics or deductive reasoning. For Hume, patterns of association emerge more from *feeling* or *psychological impulse* than from rationality. We want the universe to be orderly, so we associate events in understandable cause-and-effect relationships. However, Hume argues that *this pattern resides in us and not in the events we observe*.

Critique of Causality

Given that Sir Isaac Newton's scientific advancements were largely predicated on causal laws that could explain the movements of celestial bodies, ocean tides, and apples falling from trees, Hume's suggestion that causality is not found in nature, but in our imaginations, is radical. His critical analysis of causality could be seen as a philosophical wrecking-ball, destroying the very foundations of science. If there is no causal order in the universe, then scientific cause-and-effect explanations are unjustified and ultimately wishful thinking.

Of all three laws concerning the association of ideas, 'cause and effect' is the most important and powerful connection. Inevitably, when we reason about matters of fact, we use causal reasoning, which means we use causal reasoning very frequently.

What Hume calls "matters of fact" are the conclusions about the world that we draw when we reason from our experience, which we do all of the time. There will be more said about matters of fact later in this section on Hume, but, for now, the point to emphasize is that examples of matters of fact are in abundance: reasoning that someone is at your door when you hear the doorbell, that you get angry in embarrassing situations, that when you see smoke you expect to find fire, or that drinking coffee at night can interfere with a good night's sleep, are examples of matters of fact. Note how ordinary and commonplace these examples are. Let's now apply Hume's thinking to them.

Hume points out that when we reason about matters of fact, we reason from cause to effect. "Why did the doorbell ring?" "*Because* someone pressed the button." "Why are you in a foul mood?" "*Because* I was just embarrassed." "Why is there smoke coming out of the building?" "*Because* there is a fire." "Why are you up so late?" "*Because* I drank coffee after dinner." The conjunction "because" introduces the cause in answer to each question. We use causal reasoning so much that we seldom think about it.

Our most important thinking concerning matters of fact is found in scientific reasoning, with its causal laws of nature. Knowledge of those laws can unlock medical cures, technological advances, and answers to the mysteries of the world. We treat the laws of science as universal and necessary. For example, we use them to draw conclusions about prehistoric events by reasoning that the same laws hold for all time. We also use them to predict future events, reasoning that certain effects must follow from certain causes. Recognizing the importance of cause-and-effect explanations to scientific inquiry, as well as commonsense understanding for that matter, Hume set out to analyze the concept of causation, assuming that it must be based on certain relations among objects.

When we consider one event to be the cause of another, there must be **constant conjunction** of those events; that is, they have always, in our experience, happened together. Secondly, there must be **contiguity**. That which is considered the cause must make spatio-temporal contact with its effect in some fashion. If a firecracker exploded in your hand and you immediately felt pain, the two events would be contiguous, and you would likely link them together. If you were at a fireworks display, however, and witnessed an exploding firecracker from a great distance, you would be unlikely to associate the distant explosion with the pain you coincidentally experienced in your hand. The two events would not be spatially contiguous.

Judgments of causality also involve **priority in time**. Causes come before, not after, their effects. If, for instance, you take medication to fight a headache, and minutes later the pain goes away, you probably associate the pain reduction with the ingestion of medicine: taking medication caused reduction of pain. Of course, contiguity can play a role here as well. You likely would not associate the disappearance of headache pain with the medication you took last week or last year, or with medication someone else took. Furthermore, you wouldn't claim that the soda pop you drank immediately *after* the headache went away caused it to do so. This wouldn't make any sense, for even though the two events were contiguous, the event of drinking soda followed the dissipation of pain; because it was not prior in time, we understand that it couldn't have been the cause.*

So far, all of this may appear intuitively clear to you, but Hume claims that ordinary judgments of causal connection depend on an additional criterion: for X to be a cause of Y, the connection of X and Y must be *necessary*: Y would not happen without X. This is what is supposed to make the connection between X and Y more than just a coincidence. When one billiard ball rolls along and hits a second ball, it causes the second to move because (we think) the motion in the second was necessarily connected to the motion of the first; it's not just a coincidence that one ball moves after having been met with by another. Given the contact and force (we think) the causal power of the first ball necessitated the motion of the second ball.

But Hume asks: *What is our idea of necessity?* His answer to this question certainly adds power and force to his wrecking-ball of radical skepticism. Hume argues that we have no idea of such a "necessity." Our experience is of only one thing (or event, or collection of things) contiguous with and preceding another.

Secondly, causality is not found in objects themselves either. Hume says, "From the first appearance of an object we never can conjecture what effect will result from it ... In reality, there is no part of matter that does ever, by its sensible qualities, discover any power or energy, or give us ground to imagine that it could produce anything, or be followed by any object, which we could determine its effect."[41]

Back to the billiard ball example. Though you perceive size, shape, and color in the first ball, nowhere in it do you find the causal power to move another billiard ball. Our ideas of *necessary connection* and *causal power* do not correspond to anything in experience. What do they look like, after all? We don't *see* them. Hume writes:

> It appears, then, that this idea of a necessary connection among events arises from a number of similar instances which occur, of the constant conjunction of these events; nor can that idea ever be suggested by any one of these instances surveyed in all possible lights and positions. But there is nothing in a number of instances, different from every single instance, which is supposed to be exactly similar, except only that after a repetition of similar instances the mind is carried by *habit*, upon the appearance of one event, to expect its usual attendant and to believe that it will exist. This connection, therefore, which we *feel* in the mind, this customary transition of the imagination from one object to its usual attendant, is the sentiment or impression from which we form the idea of power or necessary connection. Nothing further is the case. Contemplate the subjects on all sides, you will never find any other origin of that idea.[42]

If you were dropped on Earth today with no previous experience of billiard balls and knew nothing about their qualities, you would not be able to determine by reason alone if they exploded, melted, or were sweet and intended to be eaten.

---

* Here's one modification of Hume's view that appears appropriate. *Invariable* co-occurrence is not necessary for attributing cause. Smoking causes cancer, though some people smoke and never get cancer. In cases like this, we think that smoking is just one of several *causal factors* for cancer (but an important one). The other causal factors need to be in place too, for the effect to appear. This complicates the Humean view but does not contradict it.

If you witnessed one ball hitting another on a billiard table and then a second one moved, you would regard these two events as *conjoined*, to use Hume's term. Only after repeated instances of watching the hitting of one billiard ball setting another in motion would you conclude that these two events are connected. Hume asks: "What alteration has happened to give rise to this idea of connection?" In answer to his own question, he replies: "Nothing but that [one] now *feels* these events to be *connected* in [one's] *imagination*, and can readily foretell the existence of one from the appearance of the other."[43]

The implications of Hume's conclusion should not be underestimated here. The rigor of scientific inquiry has been seriously undermined. In place of verifiable scientific knowledge, we have only **feelings of compulsion**, that is, a *gentle force* or *mental gravity* that makes us feel that our ideas are connected by cause and effect. The astonishing claim is that scientific laws have their source in feelings, human expectations, and attitudes. They are based upon nothing but sense impressions, which are connected by psychological laws of association and by the feelings of compulsion they exert. There is no sense impression for *necessary connection* itself. On Hume's view, then, the idea that this is one of the criteria for causation is nonsense. The only connection is one between our ideas.

To the extent, then, that causal necessity is a subjective notion emanating from the laws of our own psychology, and to the degree it is not derived from rational self-evidence or from any empirical sense impressions, Hume's *wrecking-ball* appears to destroy the scientific foundations of causal necessity. For him, there are no objective cause-and-effect relationships between things for scientists to observe. There is only a subjective compulsion to relate things by the psychological laws of association. Causal necessity finds no source in our sense impressions, but only in the laws of our own psychology.

"Hume's Fork" and Types of Reasoning

Hume's rejection of metaphysics and his insistence that we know nothing about the world apart from our sensory impressions of it severely restricts the range of legitimate philosophical inquiry. He divides the proper objects of human inquiry into two prongs ("**Hume's Fork**"): they either show the **relations of ideas**, or describe **matters of fact**.

Propositions referring to the relations of ideas are those that belong to geometry, algebra, and arithmetic. Every affirmative statement that comes from these is known with certainty. For example, "That the square of the hypotenuse is equal to the square of the two sides" is a proposition that expresses a relation between these figures. "That three times five is equal to the half of thirty" expresses a relation between these numbers.

These propositions are self-evidently true or true *by definition*. They are known independently of experience and observation; nothing in experience can refute them, and nothing in experience is required to justify them. "Everyone's sister is their sibling" is another proposition that is true by definition. Consider why sense-experience is not necessary to establish this proposition, and couldn't possibly refute it. Knowing this is just knowing what words mean, and is not knowledge about the outside world. It's empty knowledge. Hume thinks that the truths of Euclidian geometry follow from definitions as well: "Though there never were a circle or triangle in nature, the truths demonstrated by Euclid would forever retain their certainty and evidence."[44] Arithmetic truths are in the same boat. It's not easy to see how arithmetic and geometry are just a matter of what follows from definitions, and how they're empty. But arithmetic may be understood as a set of definitions, and what follows from them.

The second prong of Hume's Fork refers to propositions describing matters of fact. Such propositions are designed to tell us about the world, and unlike relations of ideas, they are *not* known with certainty. Hume writes: "The contrary of every matter of fact is still possible, because it can never imply a contradiction and is conceived by the mind with the same facility and distinctness as if ever so conformable to reality. *That the sun will not rise tomorrow* is no less intelligible a proposition and implies no more contradiction than the affirmation *that it will rise*. We should in vain, therefore, attempt to demonstrate its falsehood."[45]

Given that matters of fact are expressed in propositions derived from impressions and ideas, and also, given that no real necessary causal relations can be derived from such impressions and ideas, there can be no certainty achieved in our knowledge claims about the world.

Consequently, not only are universality and necessity in our knowledge of metaphysics and science impossible, but so too in commonsense knowledge of everyday life, to the extent that it is based on causal reasoning. We have no basis for providing explanations or predicting events. We cannot with reason, by universal and necessary laws derived from the events of yesterday, determine what will happen today or tomorrow.

And with this devastating conclusion, we may say that the job of Hume's wrecking-ball is complete. What we know for certain does not tell us about the world. What we "know" about the world is not certain. Moreover, propositions that do not relate to matters of fact or relations of ideas are meaningless and not worth discussing (for example, the thesis that God exists). In view of this, the radical skeptic has undermined metaphysics, science, and commonsense knowledge of the world. Quite possibly, you may now be as badly shaken as Hume was when he wrote the following in the *Treatise*:

> The intense view of these manifold contradictions and imperfections in human reason has so wrought upon me and heated my brain that I am ready to reject all belief and reasoning and can look upon no opinion even as more probable than another. Where am I, or what? From what causes do I derive my existence and to what condition shall I return? I am confounded with all these questions and begin to fancy myself in the most deplorable condition imaginable, surrounded by the deepest darkness and utterly deprived of the use of every part of my body and every ability.[46]

On this somewhat depressing note concerning the limits of human knowledge, let us end this segment of the chapter on Hume by reading a selection from the skeptic himself.

David Hume, *An Enquiry Concerning Human Understanding*[47]

The following excerpt is Part One in Section Four in Hume's An Enquiry Concerning Human Understanding. *First published in 1748, it is a shorter reworking of Book One of Hume's* A Treatise of Human Nature, *which, in Hume's words, "fell dead-born from the press, without reaching such distinction as even to excite a murmur among the zealots"[48] when it was published in 1739. Meanwhile, Immanuel Kant would go on to single out the* Enquiry *as the book that woke him from his "dogmatic slumber."[49]*

PART I

20. All the objects of human reason or enquiry may naturally be divided into two kinds, namely, Relations of Ideas, and Matters of Fact. Of the first kind are the sciences of Geometry, Algebra, and Arithmetic; and in short, every affirmation which is either intuitively or demonstratively certain. That the square of the hypotenuse is equal to the square of the two sides, is a proposition which expresses a relation between these figures. That three times five is equal to the half of thirty, expresses a relation between these numbers. Propositions of this kind are discoverable by the mere operation of thought, without dependence on what is anywhere existent in the universe. Though there never were a circle or triangle in nature, the truths demonstrated by Euclid would forever retain their certainty and evidence.

21. Matters of fact, which are the second objects of human reason, are not ascertained in the same manner; nor is our evidence of their truth, however great, of a similar nature with the first objects. The contrary of every matter of fact is still possible; because it can never imply a contradiction, and is conceived by the mind with the same facility and distinctness, as if ever so conformable to reality. That the sun will not rise tomorrow is no less intelligible a proposition, and implies no more contradiction than the affirmation, that it will rise. We should in vain, therefore, attempt to demonstrate its falsehood. Were it demonstratively false, it would imply a contradiction, and could never be distinctly conceived by the mind.

22. All reasonings concerning matter of fact seem to be founded on the relation of Cause and Effect. By means of that relation alone we can go beyond the evidence of our memory and senses. If you were to ask a man, why he believes any matter of fact, which is absent—for instance, that his friend is in the country, or in France—he would give you a reason; and this reason would be some other fact: e.g., a letter received from him, or the knowledge of his former resolutions and promises. A man finding a watch or any other machine in a desert island, would conclude that there had once been men in that island. All our reasonings concerning fact are of the same nature. And here it is constantly supposed that there is a connection between the present fact and that which is inferred from it. Were there nothing to bind them together, the inference would be entirely precarious. The hearing of an articulate voice and rational discourse in the dark assures us of the presence of some person: Why? Because these are the effects of the human make and fabric, and closely connected with it. If we examine and classify all the other reasonings of this nature, we shall find that they are founded on the relation of cause and effect, and that this relation is either near or remote, direct or indirect. Heat and light are indirect effects of fire, and the one effect may justly be inferred from the other.

23. If we would satisfy ourselves, therefore, concerning the nature of that evidence, which assures us of matters of fact, we must enquire how we arrive at the knowledge of cause and effect.

I shall venture to affirm, as a general proposition, which admits of no exception, that the knowledge of this relation is not, in any instance, attained by reasonings *a priori**; but arises entirely from experience, when we find that any particular objects are constantly con-

---

* *A priori* reasoning is thought that does not use or need any input of sense-information. It is very important in Plato and Descartes. Hume here argues that it can discover the truth of relations-of-ideas propositions, never of matter-of-fact. Much more about this is said in the section on Kant that follows.

joined with each other. Let an object be presented to a man of ever so strong natural reason and abilities; if that object be entirely new to him, he will not be able, by the most accurate examination of its sensible qualities, to discover any of its causes or effects. Adam, though his rational faculties be supposed, at the very first, entirely perfect, could not have inferred from the fluidity and transparency of water that it would suffocate him, or from the light and warmth of fire that it would consume him. Nothing can ever be discovered, on the basis of the qualities which appear to the senses, either the causes which produced anything, or the effects which will arise from it; nor can our reason, unassisted by experience, ever draw any inference concerning real existence and matter of fact.

24. This proposition, that causes and effects are discoverable, not by reason but by experience, will readily be admitted with regard to such objects, as we remember to have once been altogether unknown to us; since we must be conscious of the utter inability, which we then lay under, of foretelling what would arise from them. Present two smooth pieces of marble to a man who has no idea of physics; he will never discover that they will adhere together in such a manner as to require great force to separate them in a direct line, while they make so small a resistance to a lateral pressure. Such events, as bear little analogy to the common course of nature, are also readily confessed to be known only by experience; nor does any man imagine that the explosion of gunpowder, or the attraction of a magnet, could ever be discovered by arguments *a priori*. In like manner, when an effect is supposed to depend upon an intricate machinery or secret structure of parts, we make no difficulty in attributing all our knowledge of it to experience. Who will assert that he can give the ultimate reason, why milk or bread is proper nourishment for a man, not for a lion or a tiger?

But the same truth may not appear, at first sight, to have the same evidence with regard to events, which have become familiar to us from our first appearance in the world, which bear a close analogy to the whole course of nature, and which are supposed to depend on the simple qualities of objects, without any secret structure of parts. We are apt to imagine that we could discover these effects by the mere operation of our reason, without experience. We fancy, that were we brought on a sudden into this world, we could at first have inferred that one billiard-ball would communicate motion to another upon impulse; and that we needed not to have waited for the event, in order to pronounce with certainty concerning it. Such is the influence of custom, that, where it is strongest, it not only covers our natural ignorance, but even conceals itself, and seems not to take place, merely because it is found in the highest degree.

25. But to convince us that all the laws of nature, and all the operations of bodies without exception, are known only by experience, the following reflections may, perhaps, suffice. Were any object presented to us, and were we required to pronounce concerning the effect, which will result from it, without consulting past observation. How, I beg to ask, must the mind proceed in this operation? It must invent or imagine some event, which it ascribes to the object as its effect; and it is plain that this invention must be entirely arbitrary. The mind can never possibly find the effect in the supposed cause, by the most accurate scrutiny and examination. For the effect is totally different from the cause, and consequently can never be discovered in it. Motion in the second billiard-ball is a quite distinct event from motion in the first; nor is there anything in the one to suggest the smallest hint of the other. A stone or piece of metal raised into the air, and left without any support, immediately falls: but to consider the matter *a priori*, is there anything we discover in this situation which can beget the idea of a downward, rather than an upward, or any other motion, in the stone or metal? And as the first imagination or invention of a particular effect, in all natural operations, is arbitrary, when we don't consult experience; so must we also esteem the supposed tie or connection between the cause and effect, which binds them together, and renders it impossible that any other effect could result from the operation of that cause. When I see, for instance, a billiard-ball moving in a straight line towards another; even suppose motion in the second ball should by accident be suggested to me, as the result of their contact or impulse; may I not conceive, that a hundred different events might as well follow from that cause? May not both these balls remain at absolute rest? May not the first ball return in a straight line, or leap off from the second in any line or direction?

All these suppositions are consistent and conceivable. Why then should we give the preference to one, which is no more consistent or conceivable than the rest? All our reasonings *a priori* will never be able to show us any foundation for this preference.

In a word, then, every effect is a distinct event from its cause. It could not, therefore, be discovered in the cause, and the first invention or conception of it, *a priori*, must be entirely arbitrary. And even after it is suggested, the conjunction of it with the cause must appear equally arbitrary; since there are always many other effects, which, to reason, must seem fully as consistent and natural. In vain, therefore, should we pretend to determine any single event, or infer any cause or effect, without the assistance of observation and experience.

26. Hence we may discover the reason why no philosopher, who is rational and modest, has ever pretended to assign the ultimate cause of any natural operation, or to show distinctly the action of that power, which produces any single effect in the universe. It is confessed, that the utmost effort of human reason is to reduce the principles, productive of natural phenomena, to a greater simplicity, and to understand the many particular effects by reference to a few general causes, by means of reasonings from analogy, experience, and observation. But as to the causes of these general causes, we should in vain attempt their discovery; nor shall we ever be able to satisfy ourselves, by any particular explication of them. These ultimate forces and principles are totally shut up from human curiosity and enquiry. Elasticity, gravity, cohesion of parts, communication of motion by impulse; these are probably the ultimate causes and principles which we shall ever discover in nature; and we may esteem ourselves sufficiently happy, if, by accurate enquiry and reasoning, we can trace up the particular phenomena to, or near to, these general principles. The most perfect philosophy of the natural kind only staves off our ignorance a little longer: as perhaps the most perfect philosophy of the moral or metaphysical kind serves only to discover larger portions of it. Thus the observation of human blindness and weakness is the result of all philosophy, and meets us at every turn, in spite of our endeavours to elude or avoid it.

27. Nor is geometry, when taken into the assistance of physics, ever able to remedy this defect, or lead us into the knowledge of ultimate causes, by all that accuracy of reasoning for which it is so justly celebrated. Every part of applied mathematics proceeds upon the supposition that certain laws are established by nature in her operations; and abstract reasonings are employed, either to assist experience in the discovery of these laws, or to determine their influence in particular instances, where it depends upon any precise degree of distance and quantity. Thus, it is a law of motion, discovered by experience, that the momentum of a body in motion is proportional to its mass times its velocity; and consequently, that a small force may remove the greatest obstacle or raise the greatest weight, if, by any contrivance or machinery, we can increase the velocity of that force, so as to make it an overmatch for its antagonist. Geometry assists us in the application of this law, by giving us the correct dimensions of all the parts and figures which can enter into any species of machine; but still the discovery of the law itself is owing merely to experience, and all the abstract reasonings in the world could never lead us one step towards the knowledge of it. When we reason *a priori*, and consider merely any object or cause, as it appears to the mind, independent of all observation, it never could suggest to us the notion of any distinct object, such as its effect; much less, show us the inseparable and inviolable connection between them. A man must be very sagacious who could discover by reasoning that glass is the effect of heat, and ice of cold, without being previously acquainted with the operation of these qualities.

READING QUESTIONS

1. Use Hume's distinction between "relations of ideas" and "matters of fact" to classify these statements: "A triangle has three sides" and "July is the warmest month." If you are having difficulty, try using this feature of Hume's distinction to help you: the denial of a relation of ideas is not possible (because it necessarily is the way it is) but the denial of a matter of fact is (because it is not necessarily the way that it is). Now come up with a pair of examples of your own.

2. How does Hume convince his readers that causal relationships are known only by experience? Does he convince you? Why or why not?

David Hume's Origins and Limits of Knowledge: A Summary

1. What we can possibly know must be limited to our impressions and corresponding ideas derived from experiencc.
2. We have no basis for scientific knowledge, only associations of ideas through habit, psychological expectancy, and compulsion.
3. Metaphysics is impossible. There are no impressions corresponding to metaphysical concepts like God, the Platonic forms, mind, self, or the Cartesian *cogito*.
4. We predict future events on the basis of past experience, but this prediction is never certain knowledge.
5. Common-sense knowledge of everyday events is impossible, as it presupposes cause-and-effect relations.

4.6 Immanuel Kant's Synthesis of Reason and Sensory Experience

"There can be no doubt that all our knowledge begins with experience…. But though all our knowledge begins with experience, it does not follow that it all arises out of experience."
IMMANUEL KANT

Like Descartes's philosophy, Kant's was born from a reaction to what he learned in school. Significantly dissimilarly, however, Kant reacted to an education steeped in reason. In Europe, the early modern period (seventeenth and eighteenth centuries) was a time of exceptional philosophical activity, and less than a century after Descartes endorsed a form of rational meditation as a means to achieving metaphysical truths, Kant became critical of the use of **reason** or pure intellect as a basis for making claims about God and the essences of mind and matter. He argued that philosophers like Descartes could not possibly know what they claimed to know about such things, since direct knowledge of a mind-independent reality goes beyond the capacity of the human intellect to comprehend.

Plato was also a target of Kant's critical project. Recall that it was Plato who revered pure reason in the quest for knowledge. The Greek placed great faith in the powers of the mind to achieve an intellectual acquaintance with the eternal and immutable truths found in the supernatural realm of forms. We'll soon learn why Kant takes issue with this notion that knowledge of supersensible realities is possible.

On this note, you would be correct to associate Kant's project with Hume's criticism of metaphysical claims that exceed human understanding. Kant famously wrote that reading Hume awakened him from his "dogmatic slumber." This awakening caused Kant to become disillusioned with the philosophy of his youth.

From his new enlightened position, Kant concluded that philosophers had failed to critically assess the powers of human reason before engaging in their grand speculations. This is not to suggest that Kant uncritically accepted all of Hume's ideas. He certainly took issue with Humean skepticism in particular. As we proceed through this section, you will come to appreciate how Kant undertook his philosophical thinking with an open yet critical mind, and how he combined ideas from various traditions in the development of his own synthetic epistemology.

Immanuel Kant

Immanuel Kant was born on April 22, 1724, in what was then the East Prussian town of Königsberg (renamed Kaliningrad, it is now in a Russian enclave between Poland and Lithuania). Immanuel was the fourth of nine children, only five of whom survived to adulthood. His parents were Pietist Lutherans who belonged to the lower middle class. Throughout his life, Kant always maintained an honest respect for religion and a deep moral sense, though he eventually abandoned the puritanical pietism that had been a dominating influence in his family.

Kant's life could hardly be described as eventful and is now famous for its routine. He was very much a creature of habit, having a fixed hour for all of his daily activities, whether it was waking, drinking coffee, eating lunch, or going for a stroll. It has been said that people could set their clocks by Kant's afternoon walks at half past three. Each day he would put on his gray coat and, bamboo cane in hand, walk down Lime Tree Avenue (now called "Philosopher's Walk" in honor of Kant).

Though Kant had a good number of friends and associates, he never married, and in contrast to many of his contemporaries who were filled with the spirit of travel, he never ventured more than about 40 miles from Königsberg. This lack of travel apparently did not affect his wandering intellectual genius, however. For more than a dozen years, Kant lectured as a *Privatdozent*, at what was then known as Albertus University, on subjects as varied as mathematics, logic, geography, history, and philosophy. He also worked as a family tutor before finally being appointed professor of philosophy at his *alma mater* in 1770. Apparently Kant had a reputation as an excellent lecturer, full of wit and good nature. A late bloomer of sorts, his first important book was not published until he was 57 years old, a fact that doesn't go entirely unnoticed among aging and frustrated academics today!

Immanuel Kant is considered by many contemporary philosophers as the greatest thinker since Plato and Aristotle. His influence is still strong not only in epistemological circles, but in fields as diverse as cognitive psychology, moral education, ethics, and social/political philosophy. Kant is best known for the following books: *Critique of Pure Reason* (1781), *Prolegomena to Any Future Metaphysics* (1783), *Groundwork of the Metaphysics of Morals* (1785), and *Critique of Judgment* (1790).

Immanuel Kant died on February 12, 1804.

The Role of the Senses in Knowledge

Kant's unique stamp on epistemology can be better understood by initially looking at how each perspective we have discussed viewed the role of the senses in the search for knowledge. For Plato, the senses report the flux and flow of physical objects in the visible world, not the universal, unchanging truth of the intelligible realm. True knowledge of the forms is grasped by the intellect alone, not by the senses. The forms are the true realities of Plato's metaphysics; hence, reality is not the way that it appears to the senses. Reality is not all flux and flow. Likewise, the first step in Descartes's search for certain knowledge was to withdraw from thinking that the senses accurately report reality. Recall how Descartes used the technique of methodological doubt to arrive at the conclusion that the ultimate foundation of knowledge had to be the *cogito*, or *I Think*. All sensory-based **experience** could be doubted as illusory, as an evil deception, or a dream perhaps. What could not be doubted was the existence of the thing having those thoughts. The *wax example* paved the way for building up more knowledge without relying on the senses.

In his *wax example*, Descartes demonstrates that there are things in the mind that did not arrive there from the senses. By eliminating the changing, sensory-based qualities of the wax, he arrives at its essential nature—a nature he does not see, hear, taste, touch, or smell. For Descartes, an overreliance on the senses obscures the truth. The wax is not really a white, hard, and cold thing; those sensible qualities can change and yet we still understand that it is the same wax. For their view that truth is discoverable by reason alone, Descartes and Plato are considered "rationalists."

In sharp contrast, Locke and Hume differed with Descartes, arguing that there is nothing in the mind that did not get there from the senses. For these "empiricists," the source of all knowledge—indeed, all ideas—is found in experience. For Locke, the mind was a *tabula rasa*—a blank slate upon which objects in experience imprinted themselves. In the case of primary qualities, they imprint accurate resemblances of themselves. If an object appears round and heavy, that is because it really is round and heavy. As for the secondary qualities, however, appearances do not resemble the corpuscles that cause us to see colors, smell scents, taste flavors, and so on.

Concerning the activities of the mind, Locke contends that even if we are directing our thoughts inward while reflecting on our thinking, we need to first have sense experiences to have any content to think about. There is no thinking about yourself doubting, remembering, understanding, willing, and so forth if you have no ideas to doubt, remember, understand, or will. There is no thinking without sense experience; there is no knowledge without sense experience.

Hume, as well, posited that all mental ideas, even fantastic ones like ideas of unicorns, ultimately have their source in experience, in sensory impressions. According to him, every idea is derived from a prior impression. Hume describes impressions as vivacious and forceful. We receive them without any activity on our part. From there, we may actively combine, augment, or transpose, or diminish our ideas of them, but we cannot create ideas that have no basis in them. That includes any idea of the self.

In response to empiricists, Kant accepts the notion that knowledge begins with sensory impressions. He calls those impressions **sensible intuitions**.* However, for Kant, there is a second element to knowledge, which comes from the mind itself. According to Kant, the human mind is not a passive entity that simply receives impressions of the world reflecting the way the world really is. Put slightly differently, it does not merely register and record what comes to it from the external world through the senses. Rather, for Kant, the mind is *active*, providing the *forms* into which the contents of experience are poured, shaped, and arranged. We *actively construct* and make sense of the outer world, bringing mental forms to our encounter with objects, making experience possible in the first place.

Reality as we know it is, therefore, not completely independent of ourselves. We actually *do something* to incoming sensory data to produce our experience of the world. This process is instantaneous and pre-reflective, and consequently we are not usually aware that it is happening when it does.

> *"... no form of knowledge, not even perceptual knowledge, constitutes a simple copy of reality, because it always includes a process of assimilation to previous structures."*
> JEAN PIAGET

---

* By 'intuition,' Kant does not mean special insight or any kind of sixth sense. When something is given in intuition, it becomes the object of the mind's direct awareness. Ordinary perception involves intuition.

ACTIVE CONSTRUCTION

In an effort to momentarily slow down this unconscious process of reality construction, the assimilation of sense data into perceptual and cognitive forms furnished by the mind, look at Figure 4.4. What do you see in Box A? Look before reading further…. Do you see a triangle? If so, your mind actively linked the three dots together. Perhaps you saw the 'therefore' symbol used in logic and mathematics. In either case, sensory input provided the raw data, or content, of this perception, while your mind provided the forms of understanding that allowed you to give unity to it and make sense of three otherwise unrelated dots.

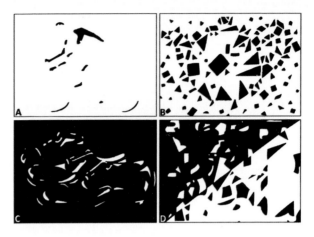

FIGURE 4.5 Abstractions

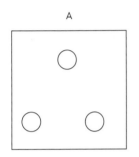 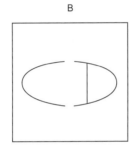

FIGURE 4.4 Kantian shapes

Now look at Box B. What do you see there? Perhaps you see the letters C and D. If so, ask yourself what they mean. What judgment can you make about what you see? If you come from a computer background, the letters may mean *change directory*. If you know something about fashion, they may stand for the designer label *Christian Dior*. If you are a music enthusiast, they could mean *compact disc*. The point is that however Box B is perceived and understood depends on how it fits into the structural forms provided by your mind. (By the way, many people do not see the letters CD at all, but rather a *shoe print*.)[50]

Just in case you are still having trouble understanding how random content is structured by the mind, look now at Figure 4.5. There you have four more frames, only this time, they are a little more complex. What do you see in each frame? (Don't read on until you look for a while at each one.)

As you looked at the frames, did you notice how your *mind's eye* kept trying to assemble or rearrange the shapes in each one to "fit" some idea or concept of what it might be? The perceptual mechanisms of your mind spontaneously tried to *assimilate the sensory data (content, sensible intuition in Kant's terms) of the various frames into pre-existing mental or cognitive forms derived from the understanding.* Perhaps you were readily able to see objects in each frame. If so, the process was spontaneous and automatic. As a result, you might not have appreciated the cognitive process that made the experience possible. If you haven't been able to see anything, let me give you concepts, forms or *conceptual categories* that you can use in each frame to make sense of it.

In Frame A, look for a *person on a bicycle*. In Frame B, look for a *teapot*. In Frame C, look for *three shoes*, and in Frame D, look for a *water faucet*. Now that you have been given these concepts or forms, I suspect you will begin to mentally arrange the sensory impressions to see what is there.

Notice the significant activity involved in the experience of seeing various objects in the above exercise. Perception is not a passive recording but an **active construction**—Kant's point illustrated. However, had you lived in a culture where running tap water did not exist, where faucets were unheard of, where there were no such things as bicycles, where tea was unknown, and where people walked barefoot, it would have been impossible for you to *see* the objects in the manifold sensory data presented to you. You had to *bring something to the experience* itself. Without your contribution of mental concepts, and the *cognitive construction* involved, the content of experience would never have formed identifiable objects. As Kant says in the "Introduction" to his *Critique of Pure Reason*,

"Mind is the law-giver to Nature."
IMMANUEL KANT

There can be no doubt that all our knowledge begins with experience. For how should our faculty of knowledge be awakened into action did not objects affecting our senses partly of themselves produce representations, partly arouse the activity of our understanding to compare these representations, and, by combining or separating them, work up the raw material of the sensible impressions into that knowledge of objects which is entitled experience? In the order of time, therefore, we have no knowledge antecedent to experience and with experience all our knowledge begins.

But though all our knowledge begins with experience, it does not follow that it all arises out of experience. For it may well be that even our empirical knowledge is made up of what our own faculty of knowledge (sensible impressions serving merely as the occasion) supplies from itself. If our faculty of knowledge makes any such addition, it may be that we are not in a position to distinguish it from the raw material, until with long practice of attention we have become skilled in separating it.[51]

The Copernican Revolution in Epistemology

In an earlier reference to Mikolaj Kopernik, the Polish astronomer, we learned how humanity's worldview was changed when he presented the thesis that the Earth revolved around the Sun on its own axis and not the other way around. In effect, Kopernik stripped the Earth of its "God-given" status and position as the center of the universe, transforming it into just one planet among others. Understandably, this led to an upheaval in human and scientific thought.

In a similar fashion, Kantian epistemology represents a Copernican revolution in philosophical thinking. Before Kant, attention was generally focused on the external world. Knowledge meant knowledge of objects or things *out there*. Human understanding had to conform to its objects, which possessed primary and secondary qualities (Locke), or which produced sensory impressions on which mental ideas were ultimately based (Hume). In a Copernican fashion, Kant reverses all of this, asking us to consider the possibility that the mind does not conform to objects but that objects must conform to the mind. Kant writes:

Hitherto it has been assumed that all our knowledge must conform to objects. But all attempts to extend our knowledge of objects by establishing something in regard to them, by means of concepts, have, on this assumption, ended in failure. We must therefore make trial whether we may not have more success in the tasks of metaphysics if we suppose that objects must conform to our knowledge. This would agree better with what is desired, namely, that it should be possible to have knowledge of objects, determining something in regard to them prior to their being given. We should then be proceeding precisely on the lines of Copernicus' primary hypothesis.[52]

In the activity we've just completed, involving the structuring of sense data by conceptual forms, we observed first-hand how our minds play an active role in determining experience. When we see objects (e.g., shoes and faucets) as objects of knowledge, sense data from experience must be arranged and ordered to conform to the structural forms imposed on them by the mind.

The new Kantian way of conceptualizing knowledge constitutes an important turn in philosophy—a turn away from seeing the external world as something possessing an independent nature and a turn toward the inner workings, activities, and powers of the mind. For Kant, the mind's structure holds an important key to what we experience and what we can know. With the external world stripped of its independent status, the object of knowledge becomes always, and in some degree, the creation or construction of the subject. Whatever is experienced or known results in large part as a product of the mind itself, in interaction with sense data (what Kant terms 'sensible intuitions' or 'sensible impressions'). To have knowledge, objects must conform to the concepts by which the mind understands things.

Remember, however, that the mind alone, without external sensations, has nothing to structure, and hence, without sensory intuitions, the rational understanding cannot do the job. Capturing the *interactive* nature of mind and world experience in a nutshell, Kant writes: "Without sensibility no object would be given to us, without understanding no object would be thought. Thoughts without content are empty, intuitions [sense data] without concepts are blind."[53]

A Priori Elements of Knowledge

The perceptual activity involving the faucet, teapot, and other objects (see the Philosophers in Action box above) was helpful with respect to understanding how form and content relate to one another and how the mind interacts with sense data to make experience possible. What could have been a little misleading in the illustration, however, were the concepts to be applied, since they were all *empirical*—that is, derived from a particular cultural experience.

The point was even made that if you were born and raised in a society that had no concept of 'shoes,' 'running water,' 'tea,' or 'two-wheeled transportation' (and assuming you had never been exposed to them before), it would have been impossible for you to have seen such objects in each frame. Granted this, I suppose the empiricist could argue that such concepts are clearly learned through experience, and thus, even if forms do indeed give structure to the content of sensory impressions, the forms are still ultimately empirically derived.

In further clarification of Kant, it should be pointed out that the forms that most concern him are not empirical but *a priori*. Describing the Kantian forms as *a priori* means they are not derived from experience or learned from it; they are *prior* to it in the sense of being *logically presupposed* in it. The Kantian *a priori* categories (forms of intuition and understanding) are universal and necessary. They form the structure of the mind, of any consciousness. Without the *a priori* forms of experience, there could be no knowledge, nor even any experience itself. This requires some explanation.

In a section of the *Critique of Pure Reason* titled "The Transcendental Aesthetic," Kant introduces the *a priori* concepts of **space** and **time**. He calls them **forms of intuition**. Let us take space first. For Kant, space is one of the mind's forms that serves to arrange sensations. Note that it is not itself a sensation. There is no sense impression of space. We do not actually experience space itself, though we experience objects that are spatially structured within it. Kant says, "By means of outer sense, a property of our mind, we represent to ourselves objects as outside us, and all without exception in space."[54] It is in space that objects take on shape, magnitude, and relations to one another (that is, closer or farther apart). Three-dimensional objects take up space and are experienced in space.

Thus, without the category of space already being embedded in the experience of any particular object, the experience of that object would be impossible. Try to remember any experience you've had of a tree or chair or other object that does not occupy space. You cannot. *Space is the form of outer sense structuring the experience of all objects external to us.*

Whereas space is the form of outer sense, *time* is the form of inner sense. Kant says, "Time cannot be outwardly intuited any more than space can be intuited as something in us."[55] The fact that objects appear permanent or at least appear to endure from one moment to the next, and the fact that we can represent to ourselves a number of things existing simultaneously or successively (one after the other) presupposes the *a priori* concept of time. An object is either here now or it is not; an object can come before or after or at the same time. The object in front of us at this moment in time remains the same object in the next moment. We do not experience a new world of ever-changing objects every instant of our lives. To borrow a phrase from cognitive-developmental psychology, we perceive *object permanence* through time.[56]

Like space, time is a *pure form of sensible intuition* necessarily underlying all our sensory experiences of objects. Objects that appear to us must do so in time. As Kant points out, "Appearances may, one and all, vanish; but time (as the universal condition of their possibility) cannot itself be removed."[57] This being said, it becomes clear that for Kant that all our knowledge and experience of objects stemming from sensibility must be organized and arranged by the *a priori* forms of space and time.

Of course, sensations and the forms of intuition do not, in themselves, afford us actual knowledge of objects. If cognitive (mental) functioning involved only the mechanisms of perception, we would have spatially and temporally ordered sensations but not knowledge itself.

In addition to the **faculty of sensibility** from which we get space and time, Kant also formulated a **faculty of understanding**, which houses an entire set of other categories allowing us to connect experiences and make judgments about them. Kant writes: "... there are two stems of human knowledge, namely *sensibility* and *understanding*, which perhaps spring from a common, but to us unknown, root. Through the former, objects are given to us; through the latter, they are thought."[58]

In his examination of the kinds of judgments we can make about objects (found in the "Transcendental Deduction" of the *Critique*), Kant discovers that there are 12 kinds and believes it is possible to logically deduce the categories (*a priori* concepts) required to make them. The 12 categories fall under four headings: *quantity*, *quality*, *relation*, and *modality*.

A complete and detailed coverage of the Kantian *a priori* categories of the understanding would take us far beyond the introductory purposes of this text. What we can do, however, is focus on the specific categories of *substance* and *cause* to better appreciate Kant's disagreements with the empiricists—and Hume in particular. But before we do so, allow me to make a clarifying point by bringing Plato back into the discussion for a moment.

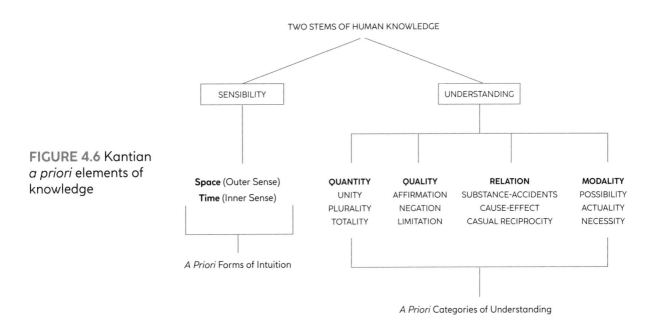

FIGURE 4.6 Kantian *a priori* elements of knowledge

Kantian versus Platonic Forms

Earlier in this chapter, we learned about Plato's Divided Line Theory of Knowledge and his conceptualization of a realm of forms. Plato argued that forms or ideas in this realm exist apart from all minds and physical objects. They represent the ultimate structures of reality that the world of flux copies. As we learned, any particular object participates in its form, which is perfect and ideal. Actual objects themselves are merely transitory and imperfect approximations of what is ultimately real. They belong to the visible world of becoming.

By contrast, Kantian forms are not structures of metaphysical reality but *structures of human consciousness*. They constitute the ordering principles of the mind, which combine with sensations to make experience possible. Unlike Plato, who grants forms their own realm within which to reside, Kant gives them only epistemological significance. He does not imbue them with any special metaphysical or ontological status in the way Plato does. It is important, therefore, for you to distinguish between Kantian and Platonic forms and not to confuse them for purposes of your own understanding of epistemology.

The Categories of *Cause* and *Substance*

While objects are given to us in sensibility through the two forms of intuition—space, and time—we make judgments about them in the understanding, presupposing *a priori* categories like "causality" and "substance." David Hume allowed for no coherent notion of substance, since all ideas must have their origin in impressions. Because there is no impression corresponding to substance, any discussion of it becomes for him pure fantasy.

Hume also pointed out that there is no sense impression of causality. Causes do not exist in objects or substance either. For Hume, when we assign cause-and-effect relationships, the human mind is really just falling prey to habit or custom. After witnessing two separate and isolated events occur contiguously and one always before the other, we erroneously conclude that a "necessary causal connection" exists. A "gentle force" makes us "feel" that the objects are connected by cause and effect. Causal necessity is not a feature of the world but a subjective construct emanating from a habitual association of ideas.

As for Kant, he would agree that there are no impressions, sensory or otherwise, that correspond to substance and causality, yet he does not give in to Humean skepticism. This is not to suggest that Kant believes that substance, for instance, is some kind of mind-independent entity, as Locke and Descartes argued. For Kant, substance constitutes an *a priori* category of the understanding by means of which the mind selectively groups sensations from experience and unifies them into meaningful and coherent units we recognize as objects.

For example, the category of substance is presupposed when we combine the sensations of salty, greasy, crunchy, and yellowy-white into the empirical concept of *potato chip*. Thus, the *a priori* category of substance is not derived from experience but *logically presupposed* in it. Without substance, the experience of objects, *as objects*, would be impossible. Had the category of substance been absent, we couldn't have experienced the potato chip *as a potato chip*.

Kant's thinking on causality is similar to that on substance. He would admit that there is no sense impression that corresponds to causality, and to this extent, he would agree with Hume. Furthermore, remember that, for Hume, causality is not somehow embedded in reality as an ontological or metaphysical fact. Again, Kant would agree here. However, Kant disagrees with Hume, who argued that our belief in causality comes merely from custom and mental habit or from the observation of consistent conjunction. Hume used this claim to reject the necessity of causal connection. What happened yesterday or many times before cannot guarantee what will happen today or tomorrow. Of course, it is precisely upon causality that matters of fact are known and, ultimately, how science is built. Hume's rejection of their legitimacy thus constitutes a skeptical attack on the very foundations of scientific knowledge. Knowledge cannot be universal and necessary when the concepts involved in knowledge claims are not universal and necessary

As a challenge to Humean skepticism, Kant claims that we do, in fact, have knowledge about necessary connections and universally true propositions because we have *a priori* concepts to apply to our experiences. For example, we know that heavy objects cannot float in space under normal gravitational conditions, that they must always fall to the ground necessarily. We know this without having seen every heavy object fall. Furthermore, we say with confidence things like "Every change must have a cause" and we say this though we have not learned it from experience.

In Kantian epistemology, we recognize cause-and-effect relationships in the world of experience because of the way in which we are *cognitively wired* to perceive objects given to us in sensible intuition. The experiences we have are structured and organized through the cognitive filter of causality that our understanding is outfitted with from the start. Like the other forms of sensibility and categories of the understanding, causality is what makes experience possible. Seeing "causal connections" is not something that results only as a product of repeated pairings in experience; these perceived connections presuppose the concept of causality in the first place. So whereas Hume shows us that universal and necessary concepts, such as cause, cannot be *drawn from experience*, Kant contends that universal and necessary concepts are logically prior, as they are *brought to experience* and make experience possible.

Consider again the scenario Hume imagines of being dropped into the world today. According to Kant, with our psychological apparatus being what it is, you could form judgments about substances and causes without any prior experience of bundles of qualities or constantly conjoined events. Those *a priori* categories of the understanding would already be in your understanding to apply to your sensible intuitions. You would not have to build up a body of experiences to extract them *out* of your experiences; you would bring them *to* your experiences. Indeed, you might make incorrect judgments, but you could still apply the concepts from your very first sensory encounter with the world. Universal and necessary knowledge is at least possible.

For Kant, experience will always have a universal and necessary structure. Forms of intuition (space and time) and categories of the understanding (e.g., causality and substance) guarantee that we are not presented with a mere random display of meaningless sensory impressions giving rise to a buzzing, blooming, confusion. When we open our eyes, we consistently see objects that appear external to ourselves and are in some relation to each other. Our minds take impressions from the sensible manifold, unify them, and organize them into objects within a three-dimensional representation of space. Instead of seeing a flat, two-dimensional blur, we see substantial things "out there." The upshot of the Kantian *a priori* categories of thought is that they provide us with knowledge about objects in experience that is both universal and necessary.

Since the forms of intuition and the categories of understanding come into play on the occasion of experience but are not derived from it, they can be described as *a priori*, free of anything empirical. In short, there can be certain knowledge that is not based entirely on sense impressions or ideas stemming from our experience of objects.

"There will always be metaphysics in the world, and what is more, in everyone, especially in every thinking man."
IMMANUEL KANT

Metaphysics and the Regulative Function of Transcendental Ideas

NOUMENA VERSUS PHENOMENA

At this point in our discussion, it should be clear how Kant made efforts to undo the damage done by the Humean wrecking-ball of skepticism. However, it should be clearly noted that Kant does assign limits to knowledge by drawing a distinction between **noumena** and **phenomena**. Remember that, for Kant, knowledge is comprised of two components: the sense data provided by the sensible manifold and the categories of the mind. The implication of this dual contribution is that we cannot know reality as it actually is, but only as it is organized by the human understanding. The world as we experience it can be called *phenomenal reality* and the things and events within it *phenomena*.

By contrast, *noumenal* reality is a reality independent of our perceptions. *Noumena* are **things-in-themselves** that have not been structured by the mind's *a priori* categories. *Noumena*, whatever they are, ultimately cannot be known, for in the cognitive activity of imposing order, the mind transforms things-in-themselves into something that is comprehensible to it. All we can know, then, is what appears to us in experience; we cannot know things as they are in themselves. Ultimate reality, or any transcendental reality of pure essences, is beyond our grasp.

PURE REASON AS THE SOURCE OF TRANSCENDENTAL IDEAS

We find in the *Critique* that Kant posits the existence of a third faculty besides *sensibility* and *understanding*, namely **reason** or **pure reason**, as it is called. Reason is a higher faculty than understanding, in the same way that understanding is a higher faculty than sensibility. By means of its categories, the understanding provides rules for the systematizing and arranging of sensible intuitions. Similarly, through what Kant calls **transcendental ideas**, reason seeks to provide principles for a type of higher-level ordering of concepts and judgments produced by the understanding. The faculty of reason is also what makes logic and syllogistic inference possible.

The transcendental ideas just referred to cannot be used to increase our scientific knowledge of objects. Nor can they give us special knowledge of things-in-themselves and supersensible realities. For Kant, because all genuine knowledge is the product of an interaction between sensibility and understanding, the *noumenal* realities, imperceptible substances, things in themselves, and so on—to the extent they exist at all—fall beyond the scope of human knowledge. For this reason, Kant regards traditional speculative metaphysics as illusory. Describing the features of deities or the essence of things is beyond the human capacity to know. What is beyond experience is beyond human knowledge. Nonetheless, Kant does allow for certain revised metaphysical notions to constitute part of his thinking.

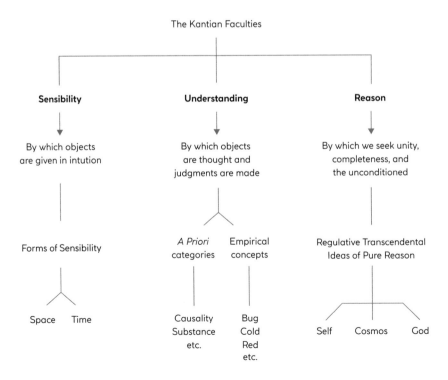

FIGURE 4.7 The Kantian faculties

In Kant's view, the impulse to metaphysics is an inescapable impulse in the human mind. The problem with this natural instinct toward metaphysical speculation is that the faculty of pure reason tends sometimes to fly beyond experience and to illegitimately draw conclusions about the *noumenal* realm that only lead to paradoxes and illusions. Nonetheless, for Kant, the faculty of reason generates several transcendental ideas that properly perform a positive **regulative function**, even though they do not expand our knowledge. These regulative ideas include the notions of *self*, the *cosmos*, and *God*.

Self

Logically presupposed in any experience of the world or in any knowledge of objects is the knower or **self** who experiences. The reference here is not to an **empirical self**, defined by some particular individual's physical and psychological characteristics, but to the **I Think** which accompanies anyone's thoughts and mental representations. This *I Think* or **logical self** is labeled by Kant as the *original synthetic* or **transcendental unity of apperception**.[59] Given its transcendental nature, we do not experience this self directly. It is logically implied in view of the fact that our actual experience displays a coherence and unity.

For example, we speak of thoughts or memories as *belonging to me* or being *mine*. It has to be the same self that senses the objects, remembers them, and imposes upon them forms of space and time, as well as categories like substance. If there were not this transcendental unity of apperception (to apprehend = to perceive or take cognizance of), then the sensible manifold could never be combined into a structured and organized whole within one unified self. Sensible intuitions would be scattered and not cohere as objects. All temporal sequence would be lost in experience.

Like the *a priori* categories of thought, the transcendental "I" is void of content. All we can say about it is that it is "an expression of the necessary unity of consciousness, a unity that manifests itself in the fact that all that is said, thought, and represented must necessarily always be able to be combined with an 'I.' To speak about pure apperception or the pure 'I' is not to speak about an act, a process, or a thing but about the fundamental logical condition of having concepts like 'judgment,' 'assertion,' and 'consciousness.'"[60]

Pure reason's generation of the transcendental "I" thus serves a useful regulative function by synthesizing experience on a grander scale than the faculty of understanding alone would allow. The many judgments made by the understanding are unified by the *I Think*. Always remember, though, that the "I" is not a person in the ordinary sense. Rather, it is a transcendental or logically necessary idea without empirical content.

Cosmos

A second regulative idea produced by pure reason is the notion of **cosmos**. It refers to the totality of all phenomena. By means of it, reason attempts to create a synthesis of the many events in experience by forming the concept of the world. Put another way, the idea of cosmos takes us from considering experiences singly to considering experience as a whole—that is, as *the collective unity or absolute totality of all possible experience*.

When you ponder life, ask why things happen, or wonder about your place in the universe—what your role and significance might be—you are posing cosmological questions and implicitly attempting to form a metaphysical cosmology. Of course, when you do so, you may allow yourself to take reason beyond its proper limits, as Kant charges philosophers have done before.

In the *Critique*, Kant tries to show how reason becomes entangled by a number of inconsistencies when it proceeds to draw conclusions about ultimate (*noumenal*) realities, beyond the realm of human experience. He labels these inconsistencies **antinomies** and attributes each side of the apparent logical inconsistencies to either rationalism or empiricism. Kant points out that it is possible to argue, in an equally cogent fashion, for opposing metaphysical claims about the universe that clearly contradict each other.

For example, one could argue equally well for the thesis that: (a) *The world had a beginning in time and is limited in space*; and (b) *The world had no beginning and is infinite in time and space*. The rational cogency of each contradictory position illustrates for Kant that reasoning about such topics leads to metaphysical nonsense, and that reason has overstepped its proper boundaries of application.

Whatever the cosmos is, it cannot be experienced as a phenomenon, nor can it be made an object of knowledge. Metaphysical talk about the specific nature of the cosmos is therefore illusory. Like the transcendental idea of the self or "I," *cosmos* serves an overarching regulative and unifying function that brings separate experiences together. *Cosmos* itself is without empirical content.

God

God is the third concept produced by pure reason, and like *self* and *cosmos* is without empirical content. Like them, as well, it performs a regulative function serving to give completeness and finality. According to Kant, the idea of God is not an arbitrary invention, but for any being that reasons, it is an absolutely unavoidable concept. Kant's reasoning here is rather obscure, but perhaps we can get an idea of what it is.

Our ordinary concepts are indeterminate in some respects. For example, suppose you feel like eating a sandwich, though you don't have any particular one in mind. The sandwich you have a concept of is neither toasted nor non-toasted, and neither with or without mayonnaise; thus it is not fully realized—in a sense, not fully real. But indeterminate conceptualization logically presupposes a concept of a particular thing that *is* fully determinate: that is, which has all possible characteristics—that is, positive characteristics, ones that do not involve limitation or deficiency. This would be a concept, a creation of the intellect only, of the being with the fullest reality—one that makes all those other "less real" beings possible, since the concept of any ordinary thing falls short of this fully determinate concept. This being—the foundation for the possibility of a partially determinate nature of all other things—we call God.

Kant explicitly rejects the soundness of the usual "proofs" of God's existence, and his reasoning here is not intended to be such a proof. What he intends to show is not that a God exists who is the source of all being, but rather, that the idea of such a God is presupposed by any bit of thought about the world. Given that the idea of God is produced by reason without the aid of sensible intuitions, it cannot provide us with knowledge of what God is, understood as a *noumenal* reality or thing-in-itself. By refusing to overstep the boundaries of human knowledge in order to make dogmatic and illusory claims about the nature of God, Kant does not advance atheism but leaves room for faith.[61] Worth noting, however, is that what Kant attempts to justify here is far from the belief in the personal God as conceived and understood by Christian believers, for example. Prayer to God, worship, trust, and so on, seem irrelevant, given Kant's rarified view.

Immanuel Kant, *Prolegomena to Any Future Metaphysics*[62]

The Prolegomena to Any Future Metaphysics *was published in 1783, two years after Kant's* Critique of Pure Reason. *It was intended to make the* Critique *more accessible in view of its initial disappointing reception in 1781. In this selection from the* Prolegomena, *Kant critically addresses the thinking of David Hume in his efforts to answer the question as to whether metaphysics, understood as a science, is possible at all.*

————

My intention is to convince all of those who find it worthwhile to occupy themselves with metaphysics that it is unavoidably necessary to suspend their work for the present, to consider all that has happened until now as if it had not happened, and before all else to pose the question: "whether such a thing as metaphysics is even possible at all."

If metaphysics is a science, why is it that it cannot, as other sciences, attain universal and lasting acclaim? If it is not, how does it happen that, under the pretense of a science it incessantly shows off, and strings along the human understanding with hopes that never dim but are never fulfilled? Whether, therefore, we demonstrate our knowledge or our ignorance, for once we must arrive at something certain concerning the nature of this self-proclaimed science, for things cannot possibly remain on their present footing. It seems almost laughable that, while every other science makes continuous progress, metaphysics, which desires to be wisdom itself, and which everyone consults as an oracle, perpetually turns round on the same spot without coming a step further. Further, it has lost a great many of its adherents, and one does not find that those who feel strong enough to shine in other sciences wish to risk their reputations in this one, where anyone, usually ignorant in all other things, lays claim to a decisive opinion, since in this region there are in fact still no reliable weights and measures with which to distinguish profundity from shallow babble.

It is, after all, not completely unheard of, after long cultivation of a science, that in considering with wonder how much progress has been made someone should finally allow the question to arise: whether and how such a science is possible at all. For human reason is so keen on building that more than once it has erected a tower, and has afterwards torn it down again in order to see how well constituted its foundation may have been. It is never too late to grow reasonable and wise; but if the insight comes late, it is always harder to bring it into play.

To ask whether a science might in fact be possible assumes a doubt about its actuality. Such a doubt, though, offends everyone whose entire belongings may perhaps consist in this supposed jewel; hence he who allows this doubt to develop had better prepare for opposition from all sides. Some, with their metaphysical compendia in hand, will look down on him with scorn, in proud consciousness of their ancient, and hence ostensibly legitimate, possession; others, who nowhere see anything that is not similar to something they have seen somewhere else before, will not understand him, and for a time everything will remain as if nothing at all had happened that might yield fear or hope of an impending change.

Nevertheless I venture to predict that the reader of these prolegomena who thinks for himself will not only come to doubt his previous science, but subsequently will be fully convinced that there can be no such science unless the requirements expressed here, on which its possibility rests, are met, and, as this has never yet been done, that there is as yet no metaphysics at all. Since, however, the demand for it can never be exhausted, because the interest of human reason in general is much too intimately interwoven with it, the reader will admit that a complete reform or rather a rebirth of metaphysics, according to a plan completely unknown before now, is inevitably approaching, however much it may be resisted in the meantime.

Since the Essays of *Locke* and *Leibniz*, or rather since the rise of metaphysics as far as the history of it reaches, no event has occurred that could have been more decisive with respect to the fate of this science than the attack made upon it by *David Hume*. He brought no light to this kind of knowledge, but he certainly struck a spark from which a light could well have been kindled, if it had hit some welcoming tinder whose glow was carefully kept going and made to grow.

Hume started mainly from a single but important concept in metaphysics, namely, that of the *connection of cause and effect* (and also its derivative concepts, of force and action, etc.), and called upon reason, which pretends to have generated this concept in her womb, to give him an account of by what right she thinks: that something could be so constituted that, if it is posited, something else necessarily must thereby also be posited; for that is what the concept of cause says. He indisputably proved that it is wholly impossible for reason to think such a connection a priori and from concepts, because this connection contains necessity; and it is simply not to be seen how it could be, that because something is, something else necessarily must also be, and therefore how the concept of such a connection could be introduced a priori. From this he concluded that reason completely and fully deceives herself with this concept, falsely taking it for her own child, when it is really nothing but a bastard of the imagination, which, impregnated by experience, and having brought certain representations under the law of association, passes off the resulting subjective necessity (i.e., habit) for an objective necessity (from insight). From which he concluded that reason has no power at all to think such connections, not even merely in general, because its concepts would then be bare fictions, and all of its cognitions allegedly established a priori would be nothing but falsely marked ordinary experiences; which is so much as to say that there is no metaphysics at all, and cannot be any.

As premature and erroneous as his conclusion was, nevertheless it was at least founded on inquiry, and this inquiry was of sufficient value, that the best minds of his time might have come together to solve (more happily if possible) the problem in the sense in which he presented it, from which a complete reform of the science must soon have arisen....

I freely admit that the remembrance of *David Hume* was the very thing that many years ago first interrupted my dogmatic slumber and gave a completely different direction to my researches in the field of speculative philosophy. I was very far from listening to him with respect to his conclusions, which arose solely because he did not completely set out his problem, but only touched on a part of it, which, without the whole being taken into account, can provide no enlightenment. If we begin from a well-grounded though undeveloped thought that another bequeaths us, then we can well hope, by continued reflection, to take it further than could the sagacious man whom one has to thank for the first spark of this light.

So I tried first whether *Hume*'s objection might not be presented in a general manner, and I soon found that the concept of the connection of cause and effect is far from being the only concept through which the understanding thinks connections of things a priori; rather, metaphysics consists wholly of such concepts. I sought to ascertain their number, and as I had successfully attained this in the way I wished, namely from a single principle, I proceeded to the deduction of these concepts, from which I henceforth became assured that they were not, as *Hume* had feared, derived from experience, but had arisen from the pure understanding. This deduction, which appeared impossible to my sagacious predecessor, and which had never even occurred to anyone but him, even though everyone confidently made use of these concepts without asking what their objective validity is based on—this deduction, I say, was the most difficult thing that could ever be undertaken on behalf of metaphysics, and the worst thing about it is that metaphysics, as much of it as might be present anywhere at all, could not give me even the slightest help with this, because this very deduction must first settle the possibility of a metaphysics. As I had now succeeded in the solution of the Humean problem not only in a single case but with respect to the entire faculty of pure reason, I could therefore take sure, if still always slow, steps toward finally determining, completely and according to universal principles, the entire extent of pure reason with regard to its boundaries as well as its content, which was indeed the very thing that metaphysics requires in order to build its system according to a sure plan.

We have long been accustomed to seeing old, threadbare cognitions newly trimmed by being taken from their previous connections and fitted out by someone in a systematic garb of his own preferred cut, but under new titles; and most readers will beforehand expect nothing else even from this critique. Yet these *Prolegomena* will bring them to understand that there exists a completely new science, of which no one had previously formed merely the thought, of which even the bare idea was unknown and for which nothing from all that has been provided before now could be used except the hint that *Hume*'s doubts had been able to give; Hume also foresaw nothing of any such possible formal science, but deposited his ship on the beach (of skepticism) for safekeeping, where it could then lie and rot, whereas it is important to me to give it a pilot, who, provided with complete sea-charts and a compass, might safely navigate the ship wherever seems good to him, following sound principles of the helmsman's art drawn from a knowledge of the globe....

READING QUESTIONS

1. Kant calls for a pause on metaphysics until a certain question about metaphysics is answered. What is that question? Why does Kant ask the question? Kant suggests a reason why other people have not asked the question. What is that reason?

2. Kant's relationship with Hume is complicated; he both praises Hume and criticizes him. According to Kant, what did Hume get right? According to Kant, what did Hume fail to notice?

4.7 Critiques of Traditional Western Approaches to Epistemology and Metaphysics

In their epistemological research and writings, Plato, Descartes, Locke, Hume, and Kant investigated how we know and what we can know, i.e., the nature and conditions of knowledge. Their collective efforts constitute a story that subjects human cognition to objective study and universal standards. Especially with the early moderns, their investigations involved isolating thought as its own object of study and drawing generalizations from their findings.

The readings that follow challenge that historical treatment by revealing and questioning the truth of the assumptions that (1) human cognition can be an isolated object of study and (2) that human cognition can be generalized to all from the introspections of oneself and observations of others like oneself.

Among other things, these critiques serve to draw attention to some of the possible prejudices that we have inherited from philosophers who themselves were railing against prejudicial opinions!

Standpoint Epistemology

Descartes famously withdrew into a meditative study in order to shed his false opinions and discover objective truths about the world and what it is really like. One of those truths—the first among them—was the discovery of the *cogito*: I exist as a thing that thinks. This discovery dispels the insulting opinion that some people are vacuously "empty-headed," "airheads" not equipped to think. According to Descartes, we would not exist as the very things that we are—namely, thinking things—if we did not *think*. Thinking is essential to our being. Furthermore, Descartes believed that we all have the same capacity to think. Disorders of the body or distractions of daily life may inhibit our thinking but, fundamentally, all thinking things—all minds, according to Descartes—have reason and the ability to reason well. As Descartes wrote in the opening of his *Discourse on Method*,

> The most widely shared thing in the world is good sense ... the power of judging well and distinguishing what is true from what is false, which is really what we call good sense or reason, is naturally equal in all people, and thus the diversity of our opinions does not arise because some people are more reasonable than others, but only because we conduct our thoughts by different routes and do not consider the same things.[63]

THINKING ABOUT YOUR THINKING

According to Kant, philosophers struggled to answer metaphysical questions because they had not yet asked the right question about metaphysics. Can you think of a time when you struggled to answer a question because there was an issue with the question, not your ability to answer it?

Alternatively, can you think of a time when someone else struggled to answer a question you asked because there was a problem with your question? Chances are that at least one of those two scenarios has happened to you, and if it has happened more than once, pick one such experience to focus on. What did the experience teach you about formulating questions?

If Descartes is correct, then we all have reason and, if we were to use our reason well, each of us would be able to correctly distinguish between truths and falsehoods. On the one hand, the message is empowering: knowledge is not exclusive to some; it is available to all. On the other hand, the message is exclusionary: knowledge is available only to those who think in the *right way*, namely a way that is solitary, impersonal, unemotional, and detached from bodily experiences.

Is that the right way to reason? Is pure reason the right way to achieve knowledge? According to **standpoint epistemology** theorists, knowledge is socially situated and, thus, research should take account of our lived experiences rather than assume an impartial stance stripped of all context. In particular, research should begin with the lived experiences of those who are marginalized in order to shed light on the distorted viewpoints of the unmarginalized. The author of the next original source text, Patricia Hill Collins, is a standpoint theorist. Among other things, her thoughts challenge the ideals of **epistemological objectivity** and universality that Descartes and so many others have espoused, drawing attention to the biases embedded in that method and the epistemological viewpoints that it ignores.

Patricia Hill Collins, *Black Feminist Thought*[64]

*Patricia Hill Collins (b. 1948) is a sociologist whose re-search on the experiences of African American women calls into question sociology's tradition of **positivism**. One of the tenets of that tradition is that we can obtain objectivity by detaching ourselves from our emotions and values and by employing reason and observation alone. This excerpt comes from her chapter "Black Feminist Epistemology" in her book* Black Feminist Thought.

———

Positivist approaches aim to create scientific descriptions of reality by producing objective generalizations. Because researchers have widely differing values, experiences, and emotions, genuine science is thought to be unattainable unless all human characteristics except rationality are eliminated from the research process. By following strict methodological rules, scientists aim to distance themselves from the values, vested interests, and emotions generated by their class, race, sex, or unique situation. By decontextualizing themselves, they allegedly become detached observers and manipulators of nature. Moreover, this researcher de-contextualization is paralleled by comparable efforts to remove the objects of study from their contexts. The result of this entire process is often the separation of information from meaning.

Several requirements typify positivist methodological approaches. First, research methods generally require a distancing of the researcher from her or his "object" of study by defining the researcher as a "subject" with full human subjectivity and by objectifying the "object" of study. A second requirement is the absence of emotions from the research process. Third, ethics and values are deemed inappropriate in the research process, either as the reason for scientific inquiry or as part of the research process itself. Finally, adversarial debates, whether written or oral, become the preferred method of ascertaining truth: the arguments that can withstand the greatest assault and survive intact become the strongest truths.

Such criteria ask African-American women to objectify ourselves, devalue our emotional life, displace our motivations for furthering knowledge about Black women, and confront in an adversarial relationship those with more social, economic, and professional power. It therefore seems unlikely that Black women would use a positivist epistemological stance in rearticulating a Black women's standpoint. Black women are more likely to choose an alternative epistemology for assessing knowledge claims, one using different standards that are consistent with Black women's criteria for substantiated knowledge and with our criteria for methodological adequacy. If such an epistemology exists, what are its contours? ...

Because Black women have access to both the Afrocentric and the feminist standpoints, an alternative epistemology used to rearticulate a Black women's standpoint should reflect elements of both traditions ... While an Afrocentric feminist epistemology reflects elements of epistemologies used by African-Americans and women as groups, it also paradoxically demonstrates features that may be unique to Black women. On certain dimensions Black women may most closely resemble Black men; on others, white women; and on still others Black women may stand apart from both groups. Black women's both/and conceptual orientation, the act of being simultaneously a member of a group and yet standing apart from it, forms an integral part of Black women's consciousness....

Rather than emphasizing how a Black women's standpoint and its accompanying epistemology are different from those in Afrocentric and feminist analysis, I use Black women's experiences to examine points of contact between the two. Viewing an Afrocentric feminist epistemology in this way challenges additive analyses of oppression claiming that Black women have a more accurate view of oppression than do other groups. Such approaches suggest that oppression can be quantified and compared and that adding layers of oppression produces a potentially clearer standpoint. One implication of standpoint approaches is that the more subordinated the group, the purer the vision of the oppressed group. This is an outcome of the origins of standpoint approaches in Marxist social theory, itself an analysis of social structure rooted in Western either/or dichotomous thinking. Ironically, by quantifying and ranking human oppressions, standpoint theorists invoke criteria for methodological adequacy characteristic of positivism. Although it is tempting to claim that Black women are more oppressed than everyone else and therefore have the best standpoint from which to understand the mechanisms, processes, and effects of oppression, this simply may not be the case....

For most African-American women those individuals who have lived through the experiences about which they claim to be experts are more believable and credible than those who have merely read or thought about such experiences. Thus concrete experience as a criterion for credibility frequently is invoked by Black women when making knowledge claims. For instance, Hannah Nelson describes the importance personal experience has for her: "Our speech is most directly personal, and every black person assumes that every other black person has a right to a personal opinion. In speaking of grave matters, your personal experience is considered very good evidence. With us, distant statistics are certainly not as important as the actual experience of a sober person." Similarly, Ruth Shays uses her concrete experiences to challenge the idea that formal education is the only route to knowledge: "I am the kind of person who doesn't have a lot of education, but both my mother and my father had good common sense. Now, I think that's all you need. I might not know how to use thirty-four words where three would do, but that does not mean that I don't know what I'm talking about.... I know what I'm talking about because I'm talking about myself. I'm talking about what I've lived through." Implicit in Ms. Shays's self-assessment is a critique of the type of knowledge that obscures the truth, the "thirty-four words" that cover up a truth that can be expressed in three.

Even after substantial mastery of white masculinist epistemologies, many Black women scholars invoke our own concrete experiences and those of other African-American women in selecting topics for investigation and methodologies used....

Experience as a criterion of meaning with practical images as its symbolic vehicle is a fundamental epistemological tenet in African-American thought systems ... In valuing the concrete, African-American women invoke not only an Afrocentric tradition but a women's tradition as well....

"Dialogue implies talk between two subjects, not the speech of subject and object. It is a humanizing speech, one that challenges and resists domination," asserts bell hooks. For Black women new knowledge claims are rarely worked out in isolation from other individuals and are usually developed through dialogues with other members of a community. A primary epistemological assumption underlying the use of dialogue in assessing knowledge claims is that connectedness rather than separation is an essential component of the knowledge validation process.... Not to be confused with adversarial debate, the use of dialogue has deep roots in an African-based oral tradition and in African-American culture.

READING QUESTIONS

1. What is the positivist approach to research? Why do researchers adopt that approach? What requirements are typical of it?

2. Collins criticizes the positivist approach. What are her reasons for her position? Does her position challenge your assumptions about science, research, and what counts as knowledge? If so, how? Where did your as-

sumptions about science, research, and knowledge come from?

3. Collins describes an African American feminist epistemology that uses "different standards" for assessing knowledge claims. Provide at least two examples of Afrocentric and feminist standards for assessing knowledge that Collins uses in her writing.

4. Consider the historical and social contexts of the philosophers discussed earlier in this chapter. It was emphasized that many of their ideas were constructed in response to the prevailing intellectual movements of their time (for example, Descartes's ideas reacted to the medieval scholastic philosophy that was prominent in early modern Europe). In light of this, is there reason to worry that our ideas about knowledge and reality are biased, or that they may not be compatible with the experiences of people from other cultures and backgrounds? Why or why not?

Mind-Body Metaphysics

Descartes's *cogito* confirms the existence of the self as a thing that thinks. Subsequently, Descartes argues that the *thing* doing the thinking is an immaterial substance or mind and not a material substance or body. On that point, Descartes famously held that minds and bodies are entirely separate substances. Minds are thinking substances that have ideas and form judgments about those ideas, and bodies are corporeal substances with properties of size, shape, and motion. As two substances, minds and bodies do not and cannot share any properties in common; they are completely different from one another. This metaphysical distinction between minds and bodies is a common variety of dualism.

One feature of this theory is that brains, strictly speaking, do not think. Instead, minds think, and, what is more, they can think in the absence of a body altogether. That idea of the mind's independence from the body has a long history and is found in Plato's *Phaedo*. In that dialogue, Socrates makes the provocative claim that "those who practice philosophy in the right way are in training for dying and they fear death least of all men."[65] He reasons that death is the separation of soul and body and that, after death, the soul is freed from the distractions of pleasures and pains caused by the body and can fully engage in the philosophical search for pure knowledge. Until then, philosophers "train to live in a state as close to death as possible,"[66] just like Descartes does when he meditates and withdraws from his body and into the thoughts of his mind alone. What underscores this prevalent view that the body is merely an obstacle of deception and distraction that can and should be removed from the philosopher's path to knowledge is the theory of mind-body substance dualism.

The next original source text, by Yasuo Yuasa, challenges the conclusion that we should strive for the separation of soul and body—and not their union—by questioning the assumption that mind and body are distinct substances that can separate. At the same time, the text also draws our attention to the role that culture has in shaping our basic assumptions about the world as well as the value that cross-cultural exchange has in questioning those assumptions.

Yasuo Yuasa, *Toward an Eastern Mind-Body Theory*[67]

In his book The Body: Toward an Eastern Mind-Body Theory, *Japanese philosopher* **Yasuo Yuasa** *(1925–2005) explores the relationship of the mind and body—an interest that developed out of his study of the concept of self. Critical of the Cartesian theory of dualism that treats the mind and body as separate entities, Yuasa draws upon historical Asian philosophies about the body to inform his treatment of mind and body as whole. In this selection, he discusses several Asian concepts that bear on the issues of mind and body, including* **shinjin ichinyo**, **shugyō**, *and* **tainin/taitoku**.

———

In broadest terms, what might be the distinguishing features of an Eastern theory of the body? In the East, there is an ancient term, "the oneness of body-mind" (*shinjin ichinyo*). This phrase was first used by the famous medieval Japanese Zen master, Eisai, to express the elevated inner experience of Zen meditation. This phrase is also often used in Japanese theatrical arts (the Nō drama, for example) as well as in martial arts (Jūdō and Kendo, for instance). To put it differently, the oneness of the body-mind is an ideal for inward meditation as well as for outward activities.

How can the essence of meditation and activity be the same? This unity of mind and body as a goal is probably understandable, to a degree, to the modern Westerner. For example, well-trained athletes can move the various parts of their bodies as their minds command. Ordinarily, though, one cannot do this; usually, the mind and body function separately. We can gradually approach the inseparability of the body-mind only by a long, accumulative training. According to the view held in modern sports, however, the training and enhancement of the body's capacity has nothing to do with the enhancement of one's moral personality, that is, the training of one's mind. In contrast, in the East, physical training that is not accompanied by the training of the mind as well is regarded an aberration, for

the mind and body cannot be essentially separated. Consequently, the Eastern martial arts have been regarded since ancient times as an outward-moving form of meditation.

In the traditional Western views of the body, there is a strong tendency to distinguish analytically the mental from the somatic mode. The Cartesian mind-body dualism, the starting point for modern philosophy, typifies this. If the historical source of this conceptual attitude can be traced back to the Christian spirit-flesh dualism, we have found a long-standing divergence between the intellectual histories of East and West.

Obviously, it is self-evident and common sense that the mind and body are inseparable, and Western thinkers do not lack such common sense. Modern philosophy since Descartes has taken up the question of how to overcome this dualism. For example, the philosophy of Merleau-Ponty attempts to elucidate the ambiguous mode of being a body—the oneness of the body, shall we say, embracing a dual tension. So it is incorrect to assert baldly that the oneness of mind and body has been grasped only in the Eastern traditions. Going one step further, we must ask in what sense, or according to what kind of thinking, the inseparability between mind and body can be maintained. Our inquiry starts here.

In my opinion, it would seem that the theory of body not only pertains to the philosophical investigation of the mind-body relationship; it also opens the way to a wider set of problems. Inquiring what the body is, or what the relationship between the mind and body is, relates to the nature of being human. In this respect, we might say that the theory of body takes us into metaphysics. As is evident by the fact that the Cartesian dualism served as a starting point for modern epistemology, and that Merleau-Ponty's theory of body is closely interrelated with problems in ontology, the theory of body leads into a broader realm of philosophical problems.

At this point in our comparison between the intellectual East and West, we discover a fundamental difference in their philosophies and metaphysics. In other words, there is a marked difference in the methodological foundations of the theoretical organization of Eastern and Western philosophy. Unless we examine this point, we cannot grasp the uniqueness of the Eastern theory of body....

What might we discover to be the philosophical uniqueness of Eastern thought? One revealing characteristic is that personal "cultivation" (*shugyō*) is presupposed in the philosophical foundation of the Eastern theories. To put it simply, true knowledge cannot be obtained simply by means of theoretical thinking, but only through "bodily recognition or realization" (*tainin* or *taitoku*), that is, through the utilization of one's total mind and body. Simply stated, this is to "learn with the body," not the brain. Cultivation is a practice that attempts, so to speak, to achieve knowledge by means of one's total mind and body.

READING QUESTIONS

1. According to Yuasa, are the mind and body fully unified by default? If not, what does one have to do to unite them?

2. Based on what Yuasa presents in this text, what are some advantages of uniting mind and body?

4.8 Proofs for the Existence of God

Discussions of reality and metaphysics easily segue into considerations of God, an important matter for us to consider. If you think about it, very much hinges, personally and philosophically, on the existence or nonexistence of God. If, for example, there is such a thing as a Creator-God, a supreme being as conceived by the Abrahamic religions of Judaism, Christianity, and Islam, then it makes sense to talk about a spiritual soul, an afterlife, and a reality beyond that of the physical world. If, on the other hand, there is no God in heaven, then perhaps moral concepts of right and wrong need to be reinterpreted. (For a discussion of this, see Chapter 5, Section 5.6, pertaining to Friedrich Nietzsche's moral philosophy.) Maybe what has given us spiritual direction and meaning in the past is completely misguided, a symptom of psychological neurosis? Further, if there is no God, then what happens to political and legal systems based on *natural law*—a perspective that presupposes God establishes order in the moral universe in the same way that He establishes the laws of nature in the physical universe?

Appreciating how important the metaphysical issue of God is for all of us, let us now examine several proofs for His existence provided by St. Anselm and St. Thomas Aquinas. Given what you know about sound and cogent reasoning from Chapter 2, try to analyze and philosophically evaluate the arguments that are presented.

"The fool has said in his heart, 'There is no God.'"
PSALM 14:1

"I do not seek to understand that I may believe; no, I believe so that I may understand."
ST. ANSELM

St. Anselm

St. Anselm was a Christian philosopher, theologian, and church leader who attempted to prove the existence of God by the use of reason. His now-famous **ontological argument** is still debated today, centuries after its initial statement, and so establishes Anselm as one of philosophy's intellectual immortals.

Anselm was born of a noble family in 1033 in Aosta, a Burgundian town in the Italian Alps on the frontier with Lombardy. Though we have little information about his early life, we do know that he rejected the political career for which his father had prepared him. He apparently left home at the age of 23 upon the death of his mother, feeling rebellious toward his father.

For several years, he wandered about Burgundy and France and eventually ended up in Normandy in 1059. It was there that Anselm's interest was captured by the Benedictine abbey at Bec, whose reputable school was directed by Lanfranc, the abbey's prior (a monk next in dignity to an abbot). Lanfranc was a famous scholar and teacher under whose leadership the school at Bec had become an important center of learning, especially for dialectics. (Dialectics is that branch of logic that teaches the rules and modes of reasoning.) In 1060, Anselm entered the abbey as a novice, and as a result of his great intellect and obvious spiritual gifts, he was elected to succeed Lanfranc as prior when the latter was appointed abbot of Caen in 1063. When Herluin, the founder and first abbot of Bec, died, Anselm was elected abbot in 1098.

Though busy with teaching, administration, and extensive correspondence as an adviser and consultant to dignitaries, Anselm still managed to further the reputation of Bec as an important intellectual center by writing several philosophical and theological works, including the *Monologion* (1076), a soliloquy in which, reflecting on the influence of St. Augustine, Anselm wrote of God as the highest being, and investigated God's attributes. In the meditative *Proslogion* (1077–78), meaning 'discourse,' (1077–78) we find the original statement of the ontological argument. Anselm also wrote four philosophical dialogues: *De grammatico*, *De veritate*, *De libertate arbitrii* (1080–85), and *De casu diaboli* (1085–90).

Anselm continued to follow his master Lanfranc when, in 1093, he was installed Archbishop of Canterbury. Then King, William Rufus, kept the position vacant so that he could plunder the archiepiscopal revenues. William was hostile toward the Church, intending to impose royal authority over ecclesiastical affairs. To demonstrate this power, William did not allow Anselm to return after he visited Rome in 1097 without the King's permission. After William was killed in 1100, Henry I, his successor, invited Anselm to return to his see (i.e., diocese). However, Henry was much like William insofar as he wanted to maintain royal jurisdiction over the Church, and soon Anselm found himself exiled again from 1103 to 1107.

Anselm continued to write at a great rate before and during exile and following his installation. Having been a simple monk for three years, prior for 15, abbot for 15, and archbishop for 16, Anselm died on April 21, 1109, at age 76. He was canonized a saint by the Catholic Church in 1494 and named a Doctor of the Church in 1720.

St. Anselm's Ontological Proof

For centuries, human beings have wrestled with the question: Does God exist? For some of us, this question only takes on a special urgency on our deathbed or when facing the very real possibility of death. Philosophers and non-philosophers alike have recognized the importance of arriving at an answer to this fundamental question for, as I mentioned earlier, so much hinges on it.

In the eleventh century CE, St. Anselm tried to provide a proof for the existence of God by formulating what has come to be known as the *ontological argument*. The argument, found in Anselm's *Proslogion*, was branded with the descriptive label of "ontological" by one of its critics, Immanuel Kant, in the eighteenth century. (The term *ontological* comes from the Greek word for "being.") Anselm's argument does not begin empirically from facts about the world but goes directly from the idea of God to a conclusion about His actual existence (or being).

Anselm's proof addresses the skeptical disbelief of the atheist. He tries to demonstrate on purely logical grounds that such disbelief is unjustified and irrational. Referring to Psalm 14:1, he tells us that, "The fool has said in his heart, 'There is no God.'" Anselm's proof is a response to the psalmist's fool and an effort to convince the disbeliever that he is wrong. For philosophical beginners, Anselm's argument may at first glance appear overly subtle and complex, but in truth is rather simple. His ontological proof, as found in Chapter 2 of the *Proslogion*, may be summarized as follows:

1. Contained within my understanding is some notion or idea of God.
2. God can be understood as "something-than-which-nothing-greater-can-be-thought."
3. Even the psalmist's "fool" understands what is meant by the concept or idea of God when he hears it.
4. Something (or any being) is greater if it exists in reality than if it exists only in the understanding.
5. If God (the greatest conceivable Being), "something-than-which-nothing-greater-can-be-thought," exists only in the understanding, then it is possible for a greater being to be conceived, that is, one that also exists in reality.
6. However, premise 5 must be contradictory, for it allows us to conceive a greater being than the greatest conceivable being. (Anselm's assumption here is that actually existing in reality is "greater than" existing only in the understanding.)
7. So, if I have an idea of the greatest conceivable being, such a being must exist both in my understanding and in reality.
8. Given premise 7, God must therefore exist in reality.[68]

In brief, Anselm asks us to accept again the notion that we have an idea of God, and that this idea is of the greatest conceivable being or "something-than-which-nothing-greater-can-be-thought." A being that exists in reality is greater than one that does not exist (or that exists only in the understanding but not in reality). And therefore, since God is by definition the greatest, He must exist.

St. Thomas Aquinas

St. Thomas Aquinas is recognized today as one of the greatest philosopher theologians within the Roman Catholic tradition. He was born the youngest son to Teodora and Landulph, Count of Aquino, in the castle of Rocca Secca about halfway between Naples and Rome. Thomas's parents planned to groom their beloved son for a career of service in the church. Their ambitions were not entirely honorable, however. They hoped he would climb to a position of ecclesiastical authority, thereby achieving political influence and wealth. Unfortunately for Thomas's parents, things did not turn out as they planned.

By the age of five, Thomas began his elementary studies under the Benedictine monks at nearby Monte Cassino. It was there that he received his basic religious instruction, while developing his academic skills and good study habits. The Benedictines were well-known for their modest lifestyles, which involved much physical labor and spiritual discipline.

In about the year 1236, Thomas was sent to the Imperial University of Naples, where he studied the liberal arts. The Abbot of Monte Cassino wrote to Thomas's father that a boy with such talents should not be left in obscurity and so should move on. This was perhaps not surprising, since a holy hermit had made a prediction to Teodora before the birth of her son that his learning and sanctity would be so great that no one would ever be found to equal him.

While at the University of Naples, Thomas befriended a number of Dominican monks whose order was dedicated to education and preaching to common folk. Members of the Dominican order were also obliged to take vows of poverty, chastity, and obedience. Obviously influenced by his newfound friends, Thomas entered the Order of St. Dominic sometime between 1240 and 1243.

It was a bit surprising, perhaps, that such a noble young man should join a mendicant (begging) order and don the garb of a poor Dominican friar. Obviously, Thomas's decision was not in line with his parents' aspirations for him. After learning about Thomas's decision to become a Dominican, his mother, Teodora, rushed to Naples to visit her son. The Dominicans feared that she would take him away, so they sent him to Rome, en route to his ultimate destination of Paris or Cologne. Thomas's brothers, who were soldiers serving under Emperor Frederick, captured Thomas near Aquapendente and confined him for nearly two years in the fortress of San Giovanni at Rocca Secca. His family endeavored by various means—possibly even using a temptress, as one story goes—to destroy his vocation, but to no avail. Eventually, his family became convinced of Thomas's commitment and finally released him.

Once freed, Thomas went to Cologne, where he studied for a number of years with Albert the Great (Albertus Magnus), whose major contribution to the Church was the realization of the need to ground Christian faith in philosophy and science. Thomas was very much influenced by Albert's breadth of knowledge, his familiarity with Christian, Muslim, and Jewish writers, and his efforts to make Aristotle accessible by paraphrasing many of his works. In the end, Thomas went far beyond his teacher's efforts by building a rational theology of his own.

In 1245, Albert was sent to Paris, and Thomas accompanied him as a student. Both returned in 1248, when Albert was appointed regent of the new *studium generale*, a variety of medieval university, where Thomas was to teach under him. In 1250 Thomas entered the priesthood and began to preach the Word of God in Germany, France, and Italy. In 1251 or 1252, Thomas was sent back to Paris by the master general of the order to fill the office of Bachelor (subregent) in the Dominican *studium*. This appointment launched his public career, attracting the attention of both students and professors alike. At the University of Paris, Thomas earned the degree of Doctor in Theology in October 1257.

On a personal note, it might be mentioned that, given his heavy-set frame, quiet and humble rural manners, and inclination to slow response in class, Thomas earned the nickname "the Dumb Ox," soon after his arrival as a student in Paris. However, when Albert heard of Thomas's brilliant defense of a difficult thesis, he explained: "We call this young man a dumb ox, but his bellowing in doctrine will one day resound throughout the world."

Thomas Aquinas was a prolific writer, having produced more than 60 works in a lifespan of less than 50 years. His works may be classified as either philosophical, theological, scriptural, or apologetic, though these categories may not always hold up under closer scrutiny. Two of his better-known major works are a multi-volume series titled the *Summa Theologica* (Summary of Theology) and *Summa Contra Gentiles* (Summary on the Truth of the Catholic Faith against the Gentiles*).

On December 6, 1273, the prolific Thomas laid down his pen for good and wrote nothing more. While

---

* 'Gentile' nowadays means someone who is not Jewish; but earlier, and in the case of this book's title, it meant someone who is not a Christian.

saying Mass, he experienced a mystical revelation of God, subsequent to which he concluded, "All that I have written seems to me like straw compared to what has now been revealed to me." Consequently, the *Summa Theologica* was never finished, having been completed only as far as the nineteenth question of the third part.

In 1274, Thomas set out on foot from Italy for Lyons, France, to attend a general council meeting invoked by Pope Gregory X. Unfortunately, Thomas's health failed, and he fell to the ground near Terracina. He received care there until the end by the Cistercian monks of *Fossa Nuova*, dying on March 7, 1274 at age 49.

In 1323, less than 50 years after his death, Thomas Aquinas was canonized a saint. In 1879, Pope Leo XIII recommended that Thomism—that is, the philosophy of Thomas Aquinas—become the model for Catholic thought. His rational, metaphysical basis for Christian theology remains the dominant intellectual influence on the Church today.

St. Thomas Aquinas's "Five Ways": Proofs for the Existence of God

To better appreciate Aquinas's five ways for proving the existence of God, it is helpful to begin by reviewing some historical context. Before and during Aquinas's lifetime, the complete works of Aristotle, the Greek philosopher, became available to Christian scholars. Aristotle's works were very persuasive and systematic, notwithstanding the fact that some of his teachings appeared to contradict church doctrine. For instance, Aristotle's view of the world as eternal and uncreated opposed Christianity's notion of a Creator-God. Furthermore, a number of ideas and assumptions embedded in neo-Platonic philosophy had already influenced the minds of Christian thinkers for so long that, by contrast, Aristotle's empirical and naturalistic leanings appeared dangerously alien.

No doubt influenced by his mentor Albert the Great, Aquinas tried, as he did, to apply Aristotelian insights to the Christian tradition. Aquinas believed that Platonic Christianity, with its concentrated focus on the eternal and its otherworldly notion of the spiritual realm, was ill-equipped to keep pace with the social changes and scientific achievements of the day. Aquinas believed that by merging Aristotle with Christianity, he could gain an understanding of things like culture, science, and politics that would display philosophical rigor while at the same time remaining theologically acceptable.

In his attempted reconciliation between Christianity and Aristotelianism, Aquinas carefully discriminated between what "natural reason" can do and what must be learned from scripture. He certainly had respect for philosophers, who were lovers of wisdom, but he felt that they lacked the fullness of wisdom as revealed only in Christ.

Unlike St. Augustine (and Protestant reformers to come in later centuries), however, who felt that the natural light of reason is distorted in sinful, unbelieving minds, Aquinas

"The divine rights of grace do not abolish the human rights of natural reason."
THOMAS AQUINAS

maintained that sinful minds may obscure the truth, but that on its own, human reason can do much. He held that spiritual revelation builds upon reason but does not destroy it. As Aquinas says: "The truth of the Christian faith ... surpasses the capacity of reason, nevertheless that truth that the human reason is naturally endowed to know can not be opposed to the truth of the Christian faith."[69] In this statement, Aquinas would have us separate theology from philosophy, believing that the former supplements, but appreciates, the value of the latter. Theology provides knowledge through faith and revelation, whereas philosophy provides knowledge through the natural powers of reason available to all.

The distinction between theology and philosophy led Aquinas to divide the field of human knowledge into two areas. In the first, truths are given in revelation and known in faith. In the second, truths are revealed in nature and known by reasoning through experience. But revelation can sometimes overlap philosophical knowledge; the same truth can be grasped either by faith *or* by reason.

For example, the existence of God or the presence of a soul can be revealed by faith or proven using rational means. Where faith and reason overlap like this, we have *natural* theology*. In this region of inquiry, philosophy and theology cannot contradict one another because both reveal those truths which ultimately originate in the Source of All Truth. It is here that reason serves as the loyal servant of faith. Aquinas's depiction of the relationship between philosophy (reason) and theology (faith) is captured in Figure 4.8.

The well-known *Summa Theologica* contains a brilliant example of Aquinas's method of natural theology using what is now known as the *scholastic* form of presentation. Essentially, it comprises the following steps:

1. First, the question at issue is stated.
2. Second, answers to the question are listed. These answers, called "objections," represent positions that Aquinas aims to refute.
3. The third step begins with, "On the contrary." At this step of the reasoning process, Aquinas's answer to the question is provided—one that contradicts the previous answers but supports his own views.
4. The fourth step begins with, "I answer that." Here Aquinas develops his own position and provides arguments to defend it.
5. The last step details the separate replies to each of the objections originally offered against his own position.

In the *Summa Theologica*, Aquinas rejects Anselm's ontological argument for God's existence. He does not accept Anselm's idea that the proposition "God exists" is self-evident. Clearly, if it were, then all people would believe this as an *a priori* truth, but this is not the case.

Furthermore, Aquinas doesn't think we can know God's nature through reason, for such truths must be revealed by the *light of faith*, not human intelligence. As Frederick Copleston puts it, "... the intellect has no a priori knowledge of God's nature. In other words, owing to the weakness of the human intellect, we cannot discern a priori the positive possibility of the supremely perfect Being, the Being the essence of which is existence, and we come to a knowledge of the fact that such a being exists not through an analysis or consideration of the idea of such a Being, but through arguments from its effects, *a posteriori*."[†70]

---

*   'Natural' here meaning *from observable facts (of nature)*, contrasted with *from revelation*.
†   The phrase *a posteriori* contrasts with *a priori* and means *knowable only after, and on the basis of, sense experience*.

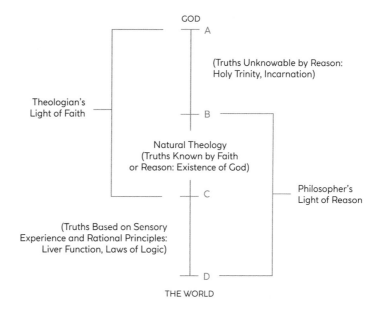

FIGURE 4.8 Truths captured by faith and reason

GOD

A

(Truths Unknowable by Reason:
Holy Trinity, Incarnation)

Theologian's
Light of Faith

B

Natural Theology
(Truths Known by Faith
or Reason: Existence of God)

C

Philosopher's
Light of Reason

(Truths Based on Sensory
Experience and Rational Principles:
Liver Function, Laws of Logic)

D

THE WORLD

Line Key   A to B = Truths Known Only by Revelation and Faith

B to C = Truths Permitting Overlap between Revelation (Faith) and Philosophical Knowledge (Reason)

C to D = Truths Belonging to Sensory Observation and Logic That Cannot Be Known by Divine Revelation

Natural Theology = A Branch of Philosophical Inquiry Seeking to Prove Conclusions about God Based on
Natural Reason and Experience

Let us now look at Aquinas's five ways for proving the existence of God using logical argumentation.

THE FIRST WAY: ARGUMENT FROM MOTION

A quick look around reveals the indisputable fact that things in the world are constantly in motion. Think of motion here not only in terms of movement from one location to another, but also in terms of change or transformation from one (potential) state to another (actual) state.

A rack of billiard balls may be sitting stationary one moment on a pool table, only to be dispersed in all directions when hit by the cue ball in the opening break. Marshmallows, which are potentially hot, can become actually hot when toasted over a campfire; what was cool, white, and spongy becomes hot, toasty, and gooey. In both cases, however, neither the billiard balls nor the marshmallows can move or transform themselves. In fact, *nothing in nature can move itself*.

Thus, for an object to be in motion, *it must have a mover*. In the case of the pool table, the rack is set in motion only after being hit by a cue ball directed at it. The cue ball, once motionless itself, is set into motion after being struck by a cue stick. And that stick was without motion until someone picked it up and took a shot, causing the tip of the cue stick to strike the cue ball. The player in this case was initially set into motion at conception, or what we describe as the time of "quickening" during pregnancy, when the baby's first movements can be detected.

This kind of causal explanation is intuitively obvious, but it indirectly poses the problem of *infinite regress*. Couldn't we go back forever, finding a cause for every preceding cause? The problem with infinite regress is that we cannot account for the fact that objects are actually in motion now. The conclusion that follows is that there must be a first mover that is not itself moved; this is known as the **argument from motion.** "First Mover" is another way of saying "God."

THE SECOND WAY: ARGUMENT FROM CAUSE

Even if you agree with Aquinas's depiction of motion in the first argument, you might still remain unconvinced about the existence of God. What, after all, could account for the very existence of things like marshmallows and cue balls in the first place? To answer this question, Aquinas offered a second *cosmological argument* built on the Aristotelian concept of efficient cause.*

In essence, it states that because it is impossible for natural things to be the complete and sufficient sources of their own existence, there must be an *uncaused cause* capable of imparting existence to all other things. Let's see why.

To begin with, I could not be the source of my own existence. For that to be the case, I would have had to exist before I existed, and this is logically absurd. Your biological parents existed and they conceived you. In like fashion, your parents had their own biological parents—your grandparents—who, in turn, had their own parents, namely, your great grandparents.

This **argument from cause** appears at first glance to be liable to infinite regress, just as with the first argument from motion. If everything that exists requires a cause for its own existence, a cause which itself was brought into existence as an effect by a more distant "caused cause," then at no time would there be a first cause, and hence, nothing in existence at all, since nothing in nature can be the cause of itself. Yet the fact is that people and things do exist.

The conclusion follows, therefore, that there must be an *Uncaused Cause*—a Cause that is the complete and sufficient source of its own existence, a Cause that imparts existence to all else. Because everything "in nature" has a cause, this Uncaused Cause must be outside nature—supernatural. That Uncaused Cause is God. Without God, no effect would have ever occurred, so nothing in the natural world would exist today.

THE THIRD WAY: ARGUMENT FROM NECESSITY

Aquinas's **argument from necessity** begins with the distinction between *possibility* and *contingency*. Contingent things in the world have no necessity to their existence; they might or might not exist at any particular point in time. What is true about contingent things is that they will eventually cease to exist. My cat Sigmund or your dog Fido does not exist out of necessity. There was a time before they existed, and a time will unfortunately come in the future when they will cease to exist again.

The important point to note about possible or contingent things in nature is that it is impossible for them to *always* exist. Now, if it is possible for everything not to exist, then at one time there could have been nothing at all in existence. But if there was a time when nothing was in existence, then nothing could have begun to exist, and nothing would exist, since that which does not exist only begins to exist by something else already existing.

Again, a brief look around confirms the fact that things actually do exist in the world. Hence, there must exist a *necessary* being, one that must always have existed and will never cease to exist. This *Necessary Being* causes all possible things to come into existence and

---

* An "efficient cause" is the "triggering" action or motion that begins the thing.

caused the first thing to exist at a time when nothing else existed. This Necessary Being must be the cause of itself, requiring no other cause outside of itself. This being is God.

THE FOURTH WAY: ARGUMENT FROM PERFECTION AND DEGREE

The **argument from perfection and degree** begins with the observation that the things we experience in the world do not all have the same value. We find some things that are better, truer, or more noble than others. When we make comparative evaluations about better and worse, we assume that there is something that is best—not just better than everything else, but the best possible.

To underscore the point, Aquinas argues that things possessing degrees of goodness, truth, nobility, and so on, depend on a superlative for their very being. Without the superlative or perfect exemplar, the imperfect approximations could not exist. In other words, if there were not in existence a superlative degree of goodness, then the existence of any lesser degree of goodness would be impossible and inexplicable.

The notion here sounds very Platonic and is reminiscent of Plato's Divided Line Theory, which separates being and becoming. Remember how, for him, physical objects are lesser, imperfect approximations of the supernatural (timeless/spaceless) forms they reflect or in which they participate. One could say their transitory, imperfect existence derives from, or is contingent upon, perfect forms of Being. For Aquinas, in order for lower degrees of anything to exist, the maximum must also really exist. "The maximum is what explains the fact that we observe all these degrees of goodness in things: It is their cause. This maximum best of all things, Aquinas concludes, is what we call God.

THE FIFTH WAY: ARGUMENT FROM INTELLIGENT DESIGN

Beginning again empirically with the observation of earthly realities, Aquinas notices that the natural world displays order, purpose, and design. For example, in the northern hemisphere, birds migrate south for the winter and return northward for the summer, thereby ensuring their survival. The seasons always change in predictable sequence, so that frigid winters do not immediately follow spring times by skipping summers and autumns. Boulders fall down mountainsides; they do not float upwards into the sky.

That the natural world displays order is what makes it possible for us to do physics and to articulate scientific laws. "Things happen for a reason," as we often say. Given that order and natural design imply purpose, plan, or conscious intent, and given that inanimate objects lack both consciousness and intentionality, it follows logically for Aquinas that there must be a Grand Designer or Master Intelligence governing the world. As Aquinas himself says in the fifth proof,

> Now whatever lacks intelligence cannot move towards an end, unless it be directed by some being endowed with knowledge and intelligence; as the arrow is shot to its mark by the archer. Therefore some intelligent being exists by whom all natural things are directed to their end; and this being we call God.[71]

Falling boulders do not determine their own movement and direction, nor does the Earth establish its own seasons. Inanimate, unconscious entities cannot act intentionally with purpose or design in mind. This is why there must be a God, according to the **argument from intelligent design**.

St. Thomas Aquinas, Whether God Exists[72]

Thomas Aquinas (1225–1274) wrote his unfinished yet best-known work The Summa Theologica (Summary of Theology) *between 1265 and 1274. Within the three parts of the* Summa, *the "five ways" or five proofs of the existence of God occur in the Third Article of the Second Question of the First Part. Aquinas presents his proofs of God's existence in response to two objections, both of which are arguments that God does not exist. After his five proofs, he returns to the objections to refute them.*

———

Objection 1. It seems that *God* does not exist; because if one of two contraries be infinite, the other would be altogether destroyed. But the word "God" means that He is infinite goodness. If, therefore, *God* existed, there would be no evil discoverable; but there is evil in the world. Therefore *God* does not exist.

Objection 2. Further, it is superfluous to suppose that what can be accounted for by a few principles has been produced by many. But it seems that everything we see in the world can be accounted for by other principles, supposing *God* did not exist. For all natural things can be reduced to one principle which is nature; and all voluntary things can be reduced to one principle which is human reason, or will. Therefore there is no need to suppose *God 's existence*.

On the contrary, it is said in the person of *God*: "I am Who am." (Exodus 3:14)

I answer that, The *existence of God* can be proved in five ways.

The first and more manifest way is the argument from motion. It is certain, and evident to our senses, that in the world some things are in motion. Now whatever is in motion is put in motion by another, for nothing can be in motion except it is in potentiality to that towards which it is in motion; whereas a thing moves inasmuch as it is in act. For motion is nothing else than the reduction of something from potentiality to actu-ality. But nothing can be reduced from potentiality to actuality, except by something in a state of actuality. Thus that which is actually hot, as fire, makes wood, which is potentially hot, to be actually hot, and thereby moves and changes it. Now it is not possible that the same thing should be at once in actuality and potentiality in the same respect, but only in different respects. For what is actually hot cannot simultaneously be potentially hot; but it is simultaneously potentially cold. It is therefore impossible that in the same respect and in the same way a thing should be both mover and moved, i.e. that it should move itself. Therefore, whatever is in motion must be put in motion by another. If that by which it is put in motion be itself put in motion, then this also must needs be put in motion by another, and that by another again. But this cannot go on to infinity, because then there would be no first mover, and, conse-quently, no other mover, seeing that subsequent movers move only inasmuch as they are put in motion by the first mover, as the staff moves only because it is put in motion by the hand. Therefore it is necessary to arrive at a first mover, put in motion by no other, and this ev-eryone understands to be *God*.

The second way is from the nature of the efficient cause. In the world of sense we find there is an order of efficient causes. There is no case known (neither is it, indeed, possible) in which a thing is found to be the efficient cause of itself; for so it would be prior to it-self, which is impossible. Now in efficient causes it is not possible to go on to infinity, because in all efficient causes following in order, the first is the cause of the intermediate cause, and the intermediate is the cause of the ultimate cause, whether the intermediate cause be several, or only one. Now to take away the cause is to take away the effect. Therefore, if there be no first cause among efficient causes, there will be no ultimate, nor any intermediate cause. But if in efficient causes it is possible to go on to infinity, there will be no first effi-cient cause, neither will there be an ultimate effect, nor any intermediate efficient causes; all of which is plainly false. Therefore it is necessary to admit a first efficient cause, to which everyone gives the name of *God*.

The third way is taken from possibility and necessity, and runs thus. We find in nature things that are possible to be and not to be, since they are found to be generated, and to corrupt, and consequently, they are possible to be and not to be. But it is impossible for these always to exist, for that which is possible not to be at some time is not. Therefore, if everything is possible not to be, then at one time there could have been nothing in existence. Now if this were true, even now there would be nothing in existence, because that which does not exist only begins to exist by something already existing. Therefore, if at one time nothing was in existence, it would have been impossible for anything to have begun to exist; and thus even now nothing would be in existence—which is absurd. Therefore, not all beings are merely possible, but there must exist something the existence of which is necessary. But every necessary thing either has its necessity caused by another, or not. Now it is impossible to go on to infinity in necessary things which have their necessity caused by another, as has been already proved in regard to efficient causes. Therefore we cannot but postulate the existence of some being having of itself its own necessity, and not receiving it from another, but rather causing in others their necessity. This all men speak of as *God*.

The fourth way is taken from the gradation to be found in things. Among beings there are some more and some less good, true, noble and the like. But "more" and "less" are predicated of different things, according as they resemble in their different ways something which is the maximum, as a thing is said to be hotter according as it more nearly resembles that which is hottest; so that there is something which is truest, something best, something noblest and, consequently, something which is uttermost being; for those things that are greatest in truth are greatest in being, as it is written in Metaph. ii. Now the maximum in any genus is the cause of all in that genus; as fire, which is the maximum heat, is the cause of all hot things. Therefore there must also be something which is to all beings the cause of their being, goodness, and every other perfection; and this we call *God*.

The fifth way is taken from the governance of the world. We see that things which lack intelligence, such as natural bodies, act for an end, and this is evident from their acting always, or nearly always, in the same way, so as to obtain the best result. Hence it is plain that not fortuitously, but designedly, do they achieve their end. Now whatever lacks intelligence cannot move towards an end, unless it be directed by some being endowed with knowledge and intelligence; as the arrow is shot to its mark by the archer. Therefore some intelligent being exists by whom all natural things are directed to their end; and this being we call *God*.

Reply to Objection 1. As *Augustine* says (Enchiridion xi): "Since *God* is the *highest good*, He would not allow any evil to exist in His works, unless His omnipotence and goodness were such as to bring good even out of evil." This is part of the infinite goodness of *God*, that He should allow evil to exist, and out of it produce good.

Reply to Objection 2. Since nature works for a determinate end under the direction of a higher agent, whatever is done by nature must needs be traced back to *God*, as to its first cause. So also whatever is done voluntarily must also be traced back to some higher cause other than human reason or will, since these can change or fail; for all things that are changeable and capable of defect must be traced back to an immovable and self-necessary first principle, as was shown in the body of the Article.

READING QUESTIONS

1. Reconstruct the argument in Objection One. Is Aquinas's reply to Objection One a compelling defense of God's existence and goodness? Why or why not? Can you think of other ways to refute Objection One? Explain what you have in mind.

2. Select any one of Aquinas's Five Ways and reconstruct the reasoning. As you do so, pay attention to the claims and the logical inferences that lead to the conclusion. As well, pay attention to the conclusion: what exactly does it assert about God? Do you think there are any problems with the reasoning? Explain.

3. Compare and contrast the philosophical method of Aquinas's *Summa Theologica* with Plato's dialogue *Euthyphro* and Descartes's *Meditations*. What are the advantages and disadvantages of each approach to philosophical reasoning? How could each approach be integrated into the day-to-day living of a philosophical life?

INSTRUCTIONS: Fill in the blanks with the appropriate responses listed below. (Answers at back of book.)

becoming	mind	socially situated	causality
goodness	primary qualities	pure reason	categories
deduction	rationalist	epistemology	lived experience
wax example	impressions	simple ideas	synthesis
tabula rasa	self	secondary qualities	innate ideas
sensibility	wrecking-ball	Aristotle	active construction
ontological argument	allegory of the cave	opinion	natural theology
cogito ergo sum	John Locke	Copernican revolution	
complex idea	being	body	
metaphysics	methodological doubt	thoughts	

1. The term meaning the theory or study of knowledge is   .

2. The branch of philosophy that studies ultimate and transcendent reality is called   .

3. What changes, and is characterized by impermanence, belongs to Plato's metaphysical realm of   .

4. According to Plato's Divided Line Theory, perception and imagination belong to the level of knowledge called   .

5. For Plato, the lower and higher forms belong to the intelligible world of   .

6. The highest Platonic form compared to the illumination of the Sun is   .

7. The   captures the fact that most of us confuse transitory appearances with ultimate reality.

8. The most influential   of the seventeenth century is René Descartes.

9. The   replaced the geocentric view of the world with the heliocentric theory, which states that the Earth revolves around the Sun, not vice versa.

10. For Descartes, knowledge is to be achieved through the combined mental operations of intuition and   .

11. Descartes discovered the self-evident principle upon which to base his philosophy using a process of   .

12. The intuitive first principle that Descartes uses to deduce all other epistemological conclusions can be stated as   .

13. Descartes's   proves to him that the senses cannot provide the certainty he seeks.

14.   said he wished to clear the "metaphysical rubbish" from philosophical inquiry.

15. The   notion of the mind presents it as passive and receptive.

16. According to John Locke, a   like *unicorn* can be built upon   stemming from sensory experience.

17. Locke rejects the notion of   .

18. For Locke, _____ are found in the object, whereas _____ are located in the subject perceiving them.

19. David Hume's radical skepticism has been described as a _____.

20. For Hume, those perceptions of the mind with the greatest force and vivacity are called _____, while those with lesser force and vivacity are called _____ or ideas.

21. According to Hume, what we call the _____ is nothing more than a steady stream of consciousness.

22. In Humean epistemology, there is no sense impression that corresponds to _____; we arrive at the notion from habit and the perception of constant conjunction.

23. Kant's epistemology can be seen as a _____ between rationalism and empiricism.

24. For Kant, knowledge of experience is not a passive recording, but an _____.

25. Space and time are *a priori* forms of _____ or intuition, according to Kant.

26. In Kant's view, the understanding allows us to make judgments about objects through *a priori* _____ of thought.

27. Kant claims that the transcendental ideas of self, cosmos, and God serve a regulative function and are generated by _____.

28. According to standpoint epistemology, knowledge is _____ and should start with _____.

29. Yasuo Yuasa rejects Descartes's dualism, arguing for a unity of _____ and _____.

30. St. Anselm provided an _____ for the existence of God.

31. St. Thomas Aquinas was heavily influenced in his thinking by the Greek philosopher _____.

32. Aquinas claims that with respect to _____, reason and faith cannot contradict each other.

Key Terms

epistemology: the theory or study of knowledge   220

metaphysics: the study of ultimate reality   220

Plato's Metaphysical Epistemology

Allegory of the Cave: used to explain our ascent from illusion to philosophical illumination   230

becoming: the realm perceived by the senses; always changing and impermanent   222

being: the realm of the intelligible world and knowledge   222, 226

Divided Line Theory: a visual representation of Plato's view of the universe with both its permanent and impermanent features   222

Doctrine of Recollection: the thesis that all learning is recollection; the idea that the soul already contains knowledge, and the right questions help us to discover it   223

Goodness: highest form; found at the highest reaches of Being   227

Heraclitus of Ephesus: best known for his doctrines that things are constantly changing (universal flux), that opposites coincide (unity of opposites), and that fire is the basic material of the world   222

imagination: the lowest level of belief in Plato's Divided Line Theory, the level of opinions and illusions   224

intelligible world: the realm known through direct intellectual acquaintance, without the necessity of sensory perception   226

knowledge: "true" knowledge is belief deriving from the intelligible world of the forms; this includes deductive reasoning and direct intellectual apprehension   226

monist: a philosopher whose view is that everything constitutes a unity, has the same nature. A variety of monism holds that (1) Being is singular, eternal, indi-

visible, perfect, complete, and whole; (2) reality never changes in any way   221

opinions: what knowers are limited to at the level of imagination, illusions   224

Parmenides of Elea: a monist philosopher and influence on Plato   221

perception: one level of belief up from imagination on Plato's Divided Line Theory; beliefs based on the senses   224

Plato: Greek philosopher and founder of the Academy; student of Socrates and teacher of Aristotle   221

Simile of the Sun: about the nature of reality and how we come to know it; similar in explanatory purpose to the Divided Line Theory   228

Theory of Forms: idea that the perceived physical world is only a shadow or reflection of true reality found in the realm of forms   223, 226

visible world: belongs to Plato's realm of becoming   225

René Descartes's Rational Method of Doubt

certainty: the complete absence of doubt   227

clear and distinct criterion: a Cartesian standard of certainty and truth that must be met before moving on to making rational inferences   247

cogito ergo sum: Latin for "I think, therefore I am"   244

Copernican revolution: a revolution in cosmological thinking contrary to biblical teachings   236

deduction: see 'intuition'   238

geocentric view: the view that the Sun and planets revolve around the Earth   236

heliocentric theory: the view that the Earth revolves in an orbit around the Sun   236

intuition: one of two mental operations of mathematics by which true knowledge can be attained   238

medieval scholasticism: the medieval school of philosophy having a Latin Catholic theistic basis; it dominated teaching in the medieval universities in Europe   237

method of doubt: Descartes's technique for discovering his desired 'self-evident principle'   239

Mikolaj Kopernik: better known as Copernicus; Polish astronomer who advanced a heliocentric theory of the universe; initiator of the scientific revolution   236

rationalism: an epistemological theory that maintains that reason is the ultimate source of knowledge   239

René Descartes: seventeenth-century French rationalist philosopher, known as the "father of modern philosophy"   236

self-evident principle: the basis for Descartes's mathematical philosophy   238

solipsism: the idea that one's self and its mental contents is all that one can know to exist   247

John Locke's Empiricist Theory of Ideas

complex ideas: ideas made out of a combination of simple sensations; e.g., *apple, clock, unicorn*   253

empiricism: the view that all of our ideas—and hence, knowledge—originate in sensory experience   252

innate ideas: ideas that are stamped on the mind from its beginning, not gained by sense-experience along the way   253

John Locke: Seventeenth-century British philosopher best known for his empiricist epistemology and metaphysics, as well as his defenses of liberty and property rights   252

primary qualities: inseparable properties of material objects; e.g., figure, solidity, extension, etc.   255

reflection: a second type of experience dealing with the acts or operations of the mind   253

secondary qualities: properties separable from material objects; e.g., color, taste, texture, smell   255

sensation: one form of experience; provides ideas of the external world   253

simple ideas: originate in simple sensations like 'hard,' 'cold,' and 'sweet'   253

***tabula rasa*:** Latin for "blank or clean slate"; nature of the mind before experience imprints itself on it   253

David Hume's Radical Skepticism

cause and effect: the notion that a prior event constantly close in time or space to a following one necessitated the second   262

constant conjunction: definition of that which occurs when two events are repeatedly conjoined or constantly come together   263

contiguity: ideas that come closely together in space and time   262, 263

David Hume: eighteenth-century British empiricist whose philosophy presents a radical skepticism   259

feelings of compulsion: a "gentle force" or "mental gravity"   265

Hume's Fork: concept used to divide proper objects of human inquiry   265

ideas: perceptions of the mind having less force or vivacity compared with impressions; for Hume, every idea is a copy of an initially experienced impression   260

imagination: the faculty of the mind that generates the belief in causal relations   262

impressions: perceptions containing the greatest force and vivacity   260

laws of association: laws governing combinations and comparisons of perceptions; e.g., resemblance, contiguity, cause and effect   262

matters of fact: the other element of Hume's Fork; e.g., ideas about the physical, material, experiential world   265

necessary connection: the bond between cause and effect that supposedly forces the effect to occur without exception 262

priority in time: a cause must come before an effect in time 263

radical skepticism: Hume's challenge to the Age of Enlightenment, the scientific achievements of Newton, as well as religion and beliefs in God 257

relations of ideas: one element of Hume's Fork; e.g., ideas of geometry and mathematics 265

resemblance: law of association; one stimulus can bring to mind other resembling stimuli; e.g., a picture of a person can bring to mind the person or some experience of that person 262

Immanuel Kant's Synthesis of Reason and Sensory Experience

active construction: what is necessary for the perception of objects, as objects 274

antinomies: inconsistencies that arise when trying to draw conclusions about noumenal realities 282

cosmos: a regulative idea produced by reason; allows us to take experience as a whole 281

empirical self: the physical and psychological notion of person or personal self 281

experience: the source of knowledge for empiricist philosophers 271

faculty of sensibility: that which orders spatial and temporal sensations 276

faculty of understanding: houses concepts or categories (e.g., 'cause,' 'object,' 'number') which allow us to make judgments 276

forms of intuition: space and time; make experience and rational thought about it possible 276

God: for Kant: a regulative concept produced by pure reason allowing an understanding of the partial determinateness of ideas 282

"I Think": Descartes's *cogito* 281

Immanuel Kant: Eighteenth-century Prussian philosopher known for his synthesis of rationalist and empiricist metaphysics as well as his deontological ethical theory 271

logical self: that which gives our experience coherence and unity; cannot be experienced directly; logically inferred; a logical requirement for the possibility of experience 281

noumena: things-in-themselves; ultimately unknowable 279

phenomena: things as they appear; knowledge by the conditions of experience 279

(pure) reason: a faculty higher than understanding; provides higher-level ordering of concepts and judgments produced by the faculty of understanding 280

reason: the source of knowledge for rationalist philosophers 270

regulative function: gives unity and coherence to knowledge and experience 281

self: the entity which has experiences and structures knowledge 281

sensible intuitions: sensory impressions coming from experience 280

space: form of sensible intuition allowing objects to be seen as objects 276

things-in-themselves: not structured by the sensible forms and categories of the mind 279

time: form of sensible intuition allowing objects to be seen as enduring objects 276

transcendental ideas: ideas of *self*, *the cosmos*, and *God*; generated by faculty of reason; perform regulative function 280

transcendental unity of apperception: the coherence and unity of that which is experienced 281

Critiques of Traditional Western Approaches to Epistemology and Metaphysics

epistemological objectivity: a rational ideal requiring that all biases and contaminating influences in thinking be removed   286

Patricia Hill Collins: sociologist specialized in issues of race, gender, and inequality, especially with regard to African Americans   287

positivism: rational method aiming to produce objective conclusions devoid of values, interests, and emotions generated by class, race, sex, or context   287

shinjin ichinyo: the oneness of body-mind   290

shugyō: personal "cultivation"; presupposed in the philosophical foundations of Eastern theories   290

standpoint epistemology: theoretical view that knowledge is socially situated and, thus research should begin with lived experiences as opposed to striving for an objective position stripped of all context   286

tainin/taitoku: the idea that knowledge cannot be obtained simply by means of theoretical thinking, but only through "bodily recognition or realization," that is, through the utilization of one's total mind and body; to learn with the body, not the brain   290

Yasuo Yuasa: twentieth century Japanese philosopher who wrote about theories of the body in the East and the West   290

Proofs for the Existence of God

argument from cause: argument that God is the only uncaused cause   298

argument from intelligent design: the argument that because the natural world displays order, purpose, and design, there must be some sort of grand designer of the universe, i.e., God   297

argument from motion: argument that because everything that moves is moved by something else, there must therefore exist an unmoved mover to avoid infinite regress   298

argument from necessity: proof for the existence of God based on the notion of contingency   298

argument from perfection and degree: argument for the existence of God using notions of 'degree' and 'superlatives'   299

ontological argument: argument for God's existence using only reason and *a priori* principles   292

St. Anselm: medieval Christian philosopher who developed the ontological argument for God's existence   292

St. Thomas Aquinas: thirteenth century Christian philosopher who profoundly influenced Catholic thought   294

Summary of Major Points

1. What are the definitions of epistemology and metaphysics?

▸ *Epistemology*: The theory of knowledge—the study of its origins, nature, and justification.

▸ *Metaphysics*: The field of philosophy addressing itself to issues beyond nature and the realm of the physical; the study of being, the universe, ultimate reality; the critical examination of the underlying assumptions employed by our system of knowledge.

2. What is Plato's metaphysical conception of the universe?

▸ The universe containing objects of knowledge is divided into the intelligible world of being and the visible world of becoming.

▸ Lower and higher forms belong to the world of being; physical things and their shadows or reflections belong to the visible world of becoming.

▸ Knowledge is belief founded on the intelligible world; opinion is belief founded on the visible world.

3. What are the four levels of knowledge discussed in Plato's Divided Line Theory?

▸ Direct intellectual apprehension

▸ Deductive reasoning

▸ Perception

▸ Imagination

4. How does Plato conceptualize the forms?

The forms are perfect, eternal, and immutable. Objects in actual experience partake of the forms; the forms are "more real" than the things we perceive. Physical objects are merely rough approximations of the forms; forms have an independent ontological status beyond any individual mind.

5. Of what significance is the "Simile of the Sun"?

Plato uses the simile to capture the nature of Goodness—the highest of all the forms. The sun is used to illustrate how Goodness is absolutely essential to our experience of reality and our understanding of all things.

6. How is the Allegory of the Cave used?

Plato uses it to describe the ascent from illusion to philosophical illumination. The cave dwellers erroneously take the shadows in the cave as ultimate reality, whereas those who escape the darkness of the cave to gaze at the Sun represent the enlightened ones.

7. What is Descartes's method of doubt? For what is it used?

The French rationalist René Descartes used the method of doubt as a way to achieve certainty. By establishing a first principle that was indubitably certain, Descartes's intention was to deduce other conclusions about reality.

8. What became Descartes's first principle of certainty?

"*Cogito ergo sum*" (I think, therefore I am) became Descartes's self-evident foundation for all future deductions.

9. In what ways is Descartes's Wax Example important to rationalistic philosophy?

The Wax Example illustrates how knowledge cannot ultimately be based on sensory experience.

10. Who was John Locke? What was his philosophical mission?

John Locke is considered the founder of British empiricism. He launched an attack against the continental rationalists with the aim of removing the "metaphysical rubbish" from philosophical inquiry.

11. How did Locke conceive of the human mind?

The human mind is a *tabula rasa* (blank slate); it is passive and receptive. The mind is furnished by experience. All ideas (simple and complex) are derived from experience.

12. How does Locke conceptualize the subject-object relation?

Primary qualities (such as solidity) are found in objects; secondary qualities (such as color) are found in subjects.

13. How is David Hume's theory the equivalent of a philosophical wrecking-ball?

Hume's thought forms a radical skepticism; it smashes to bits causal scientific explanation; it reduces metaphysics to pretentious nonsense; "God" and "self" are reduced to illusions.

14. From where do ideas originate according to Hume?

All ideas are derived from our initial experiential impressions. Even ideas of fantasy (e.g., unicorns) are ultimately combinations of sensory-based impressions.

15. In what ways can ideas be associated for Hume?

Patterns of association include resemblance, contiguity, and cause and effect.

16. What are the essential features of so-called "causes"?

▸ *Contiguity*: spatially or temporally close
▸ *Priority in time*: causes precede effects
▸ *Necessary connection*: an effect is always preceded by the same thing or event if it is to be considered the cause

17. What is Hume's view of causality?

The perception of causality is an act of the imagination. Causes are not found in objects, but from a perception of constant conjunction and the development of habit and custom. We feel (by gentle force) that one thing will lead to another, as we have always seen. There is no sense impression of "necessary connection."

18. What is "Hume's Fork"?

Epistemological statements either refer to "relations of ideas" or "matters of fact"—the two prongs of the "fork." Anything between (any statement that does not fit into one of these categories) is meaningless.

19. In general terms, how could one describe Kant's epistemology?

It could be described as a synthesis of rationalism and empiricism. It is certainly a response to Humean skepticism.

20. How does Kant conceptualize knowledge?

Knowledge is an active construction. It results as the product of an interaction between reason and experience. From experience, sense data are given; from reason, forms of sensibility and understanding are imposed.

21. To what does the *Copernican revolution* of Kantian philosophy refer?

Instead of having the mind conform to objects of knowledge, Kant turned things around and had objects conform to the mind.

22. What are the *a priori* elements of knowledge?

A priori forms of sensibility include space and time. *A priori* categories of understanding include causality and substance, etc. Whatever is a priori is "pure"—empty of all empirical content and derivation.

23. How are Kantian and Platonic forms different?

Platonic forms are metaphysical realities (more real than actual objects); they have an independent ontological status. Kantian forms originate in the human faculties; they are not located "somewhere out there," but in the mind of the knower.

24. What is Kant's response to Hume?

Kant agrees with Hume that no impressions directly correspond to causality and substance, for example. For Kant, however, a concept like substance is already logically presupposed in experience. Without the concept already assumed, we could not perceive objects as objects. Causal connections are also made logically possible by being presupposed in our perceptions; they are not derived from them, as Hume would say, through the experience of "constant conjunction." For Kant, certain and reliable knowledge is possible when limited to experience, given its universal and necessary structure, as defined by the *a priori* forms and categories of understanding.

25. What metaphysical ideas does Kant discuss? What is their origin? How do they function?

God, *self*, and *cosmos* are three metaphysical ideas covered by Kant in the context of the distinction between *noumena* and *phenomena*. These three so-called "transcendental ideas" find their origin in the faculty of pure reason. These transcendental ideas serve a regulative function giving unity and completeness to our experience.

26. What is positivist epistemology?

It is a theory of knowledge using rational methods to produce objective conclusions devoid of values, interests, and emotions generated by class, race, sex, or context.

27. What is standpoint epistemology?

It is a Black feminist theory and approach to the study of knowledge. It does not discount the value of gender, race, or context in its investigations and thus is critical of positivist epistemology.

28. How is Eastern philosophy different from Cartesianism?

From an Eastern perspective, knowledge is not achieved through purely rational reflection or simply by means of theoretical thinking—the type that Descartes engaged in—but as Yasuo Yuasa puts it, only through "bodily recognition or realization," that is, through the utilization of one's total mind *and* body. Hence, Descartes's mind-body dualism is rejected.

29. How did St. Anselm try to prove the existence of God?

Anselm did not try to prove God exists by any empirical means; rather, he proceeded from the idea of God to the conclusion about His actual existence. His proof was labeled by Immanuel Kant as the "ontological argument." Supporting premises lead to the following conclusion: So, if I have an idea of the greatest conceivable being, such a being must exist both in my understanding and in reality.

30. What arguments did St. Thomas Aquinas use to prove that God exists?

He used the following arguments: 1. Argument from motion; 2. Argument from cause; 3. Argument from necessity; 4. Argument from perfection and degree; and 5. Argument from intelligent design.

Additional Resources

For interactive quizzes, stories, supplements, and other materials for study and review, visit:

sites.broadviewpress.com/experiencing-philosophy/chapter4
Passcode: w4822kj

Or scan the following QR code:

CHAPTER 5

Ethics and Moral Decision Making

Take It Personally 314

Know Thyself: The Ethical Perspective Indicator 319

5.1 Plato's Character Ethics 322
Plato's Teleology 323
Vision of the Soul 323
Moral Balance and Plato's Functional Explanation of Morality 324
ORIGINAL SOURCE: Plato, Virtue, and Justice in the Individual and in the State 325
Know Thyself: Platonic Character Type Index (PCTI) 329
Plato's Character Types 331

5.2 Aristotle's Virtue Ethics 338
Aristotle's Teleology 338
Happiness (*Eudaimonia*) and the Ends of Human Life 339
Kinds of Lifestyles 342
Virtue and the Virtuous Lifestyle 345
ORIGINAL SOURCE: Aristotle, *Nicomachean Ethics* 350

5.3 Jeremy Bentham's Utilitarian Ethics 353
The Principle of Utility 354
Is-Ought Fallacy 355
The Hedonic Calculus 356
The Theory of Sanctions 360
ORIGINAL SOURCE: Jeremy Bentham, *An Introduction to the Principles of Morals and Legislation* 362

5.4 Immanuel Kant's Deontological Ethics 365
The Rational Basis of Morality 365
Concept of the Good Will 366
Notion of Duty 367
Maxims and Moral Behavior 370
The Categorical Imperative 371
Autonomy versus Heteronomy of the Will 373

ORIGINAL SOURCE: Immanuel Kant, On Pure Moral Philosophy 375
The Impermissibility of Lying: Maria von Herbert's Correspondence with Kant 377

5.5 Carol Gilligan's and Nel Noddings's Care Ethics—Two Critiques of Male Moral Bias 379
Gilligan on Male Bias in Moral Research 379
Gilligan's Ethic of Care 384
Nel Noddings and Care Ethics 386
ORIGINAL SOURCE: Nel Noddings, *Caring: A Feminine Approach to Ethics and Moral Education* 391

5.6 Friedrich Nietzsche's Will to Power 394
God Is Dead 394
Will to Power 395
ORIGINAL SOURCE: Friedrich Wilhelm Nietzsche, *The Gay Science* 398
Master versus Slave Morality 399
Traditional (Herd) Morality and the Revaluation of All Values 401
Evaluating Values 402
The Superman/*Übermensch* 403

5.7 Religion and Ethics: Islamic, Hindu, and Christian Perspectives 405
Islamic Ethics 405
ORIGINAL SOURCE: Riffat Hassan, "Islamic View of Peace" 408
Hindu Ethics 410
ORIGINAL SOURCE: Ashok Kumar Malhotra, *Transcreation of the Bhagavad Gita* 412
Christian Ethics 414
ORIGINAL SOURCE: Brian Berry, Roman Catholic Ethics: Three Approaches 416

Progress Check 420

Study Guide 422
Key Terms 422
Summary of Major Points 426

LEARNING OUTCOMES

After successfully completing this chapter, you will be able to

▸ Explain the teleological nature of Plato's ethics in terms of his tripartite division of the soul

▸ Offer Plato's functional explanation of morality

▸ Provide a descriptive outline for each of Plato's character types

▸ Apply an understanding of Platonic character types to yourself and others

▸ Explain what role happiness plays in the ethics of Aristotle

▸ Describe various Aristotelian lifestyles, giving reasons why some are limited or deficient

▸ Understand Aristotle's rationale as to why, for him, the contemplative life is best

▸ Grasp the nature of virtue and reflect on how virtuous you are at this time

▸ Show how sanctions are involved in moral action

▸ Apply the criteria of Jeremy Bentham's hedonic calculus to a practical decision

▸ Give Immanuel Kant's justification for why reason should be the basis of morality

▸ Explain how moral duty relates to rational principle

▸ Offer insight into self-referring and other-referring duties

▸ Elucidate the relationship between moral maxims and formal principles

▸ Distinguish between moral and non-moral imperatives

▸ Appreciate the importance of personal autonomy in the context of morality

▸ Explain Gilligan's argument regarding psychological bias in moral reasoning research

▸ Describe Gilligan and Nodding's respective accounts of care-based ethics

▸ Understand how "care" and "relation" have roles to play in moral judgment and action

▸ Explain the meaning and relevance of the Nietzschean notion that "God is dead"

▸ Elucidate how and why the *will to power* serves as the basis of Nietzsche's morality

▸ Distinguish among master, slave, and herd moralities

▸ Define what is meant by the concept of *Übermensch* (Superman)

▸ Express how religion can inform moral and ethical judgment

▸ Spell out the positive account of peace that is central in the religio-moral worldview of Islam

▸ Gain insight into the role that duty plays in Hindu ethics

▸ Apply Christian ethics from the vantage point of three different Catholic perspectives

FOCUS QUESTIONS

1. On what kinds of things have philosophers tried to base morality? To what have they given priority?

2. What is the place of the "I," or the individual, or the "ego-self" in the various approaches to morality?

3. What are the advantages and disadvantages of purely rational, and non-rational, ethical viewpoints?

4. Does gender make a difference to moral thinking and theorizing? If so, how?

5. What relevance do notions of freedom, autonomy, and liberation have for the moralists discussed here?

6. Do virtue and character have any relevance to morality? If so, how?

7. Is religion relevant to ethics? How so?

8. What insights into moral and ethical thinking do religions provide?

9. What roles do peace, duty, and rationality play in religious ethics?

10. What are some of the most provocative and challenging ideas presented in this chapter?

Take It Personally

Of all the sub-disciplines of philosophy outlined in Chapter 1, the study of ethics is perhaps the most strikingly relevant and practical, especially given that so much of our life is awash in morality. For example, after the death of George Floyd on May 25, 2020,* some called for blood vengeance, others for reform, and still others for calm adherence to the rule of law. There were those who wanted immediate criminal prosecution, while many advocated complete defunding of police departments. When events like these occur, people are stunned into a new ethical awareness, frequently characterized by confusion and moral self-doubt. Questions are asked: "What *should* we do?" "What is the *right* response?"

Not only in such extreme cases as George Floyd's death, but also with respect to world events in general, a moral response is demanded from all of us. In plain view of poverty, hunger, global injustice or the inequitable treatment of minorities, for example, we may choose as moral agents to accept responsibility and take action. Quite possibly, however, we may do nothing by ignoring the problem, defensively rationalizing our noninvolvement, or blaming the victims who suffer. One should note, though, that even choosing not to respond is itself a moral response needing justification.

When it comes to the mistreatment and abuse suffered by racialized minorities, for instance, many concerned citizens have protested, yelling, "Silence is violence!" Doing nothing or standing on the sidelines while injustices are being perpetrated is tantamount to collusion or at least tacit approval, in the estimation of many people. So, even if neutrality is an ethical position that has consequences and requires justification, it would appear that there is, in fact, no escaping moral responsibility. What is more, an examined life—a life *worth living*—cannot be lived in a moral vacuum.

Given this, let's apply here in this context a metaphor used in Chapter 2: Recall the notion that we can either stay afloat in our *philosophical lifeboats*, by making ongoing repairs to our damaged and leaking *moral planks*, or we can break apart and capsize in a whirlpool of moral confusion and indecision. If we don't wish to be uncontrollably pushed this way and that by the turbulent waters of life, and if we wish to steer properly and maintain the integrity of our existential vessels with any success, morality is not something that should be left unattended. Our own safe travels on life's journey depend upon our having a working moral compass. We all need to know when to make proper directional adjustments in and during the course of our lives.

In view of the fact that morality is unavoidable and so important, the question arises as to why so many people still try to sidestep it. Part of the reason, perhaps, is because of morality's serious, difficult, and sometimes overwhelming nature. Morality often deals with the *big issues* of life, things like war, capital punishment, and euthanasia—favorite topics covered in many applied ethics textbooks.

Because most of us are not in the military, on death row, or dying from a terminal illness, however, these enormously important moral issues and others like them can sometimes appear like distant hypothetical concerns, things we needn't worry about while commuting to school in rush hour traffic or stocking the shelves at work. Nevertheless,

---

* George Floyd was an African American who was killed by a police officer in Minneapolis. The officer, Derek Chauvin, knelt on Floyd's neck for over nine minutes while Floyd was lying face down and handcuffed. Chauvin was sentenced to 22.5 years in prison.

let me suggest that morality is not all *out there*, nor is it always too daunting or too huge to be handled by us as individuals. A great deal of morality is an *inside job* dealing with personal issues and practical decision-making—especially where principles or rules of conduct are concerned. One could even argue that morality is part of human consciousness—that who we are as persons is a reflection of our morality. Indeed, the originator of psychoanalysis, Sigmund Freud, observed this himself when developing his concept of the *superego*.

According to Freud, the psychodynamics of the personality cannot be properly understood without appreciating the roles played by *moral conscience* and our *ego-ideals*. The internalization of moral standards—stemming from parental, religious, social, and educational influences, for example—helps to define for us what is acceptable and non-acceptable behavior. Violation of these standards is what leads to guilt feelings, moral anxiety, and, in extreme cases, to what Freud diagnosed as *neurosis*.

When, for instance, biological instincts like aggression and sexuality, arising out of the Freudian *id*, seek expression, superego moral prohibitions may dictate that we leave those instincts unexpressed, as this would constitute some sort of violation against societal norms or personal standards of morality. Consequently, the ego structure of the personality is left either to "sublimate" those instincts in socially acceptable ways, that is, to displace them onto less morally objectionable objects, deny that they exist, or repress them in the unconscious.

When what the biological *id* desires is deemed by the *superego* (moral conscience) to be morally wrong, it becomes the rational *ego*'s task to diffuse the tension between those two opposing psychic structures. Without a proper resolution to the moral conflict involved, we are left with a disturbed and conflicted mind.

The Freudian depiction of moral conflict is in fact predated by the Christian New Testament. The conflict here is placed in the context of the flesh (*id*) opposing the spirit (moral conscience). It is written: "For the flesh lusteth against the Spirit and the Spirit against the flesh: and these are contrary the one to the other: so that ye cannot do the things that ye would" (St. Paul to the Galatians, 5:17).

Though many of the biologically deterministic and sexual components of Freudian theory are considered dubious in light of contemporary psychological research, the notion that moral conscience can lead to mental disturbance is one insight most of us can intuitively grasp and hence more easily accept.

Shakespeare's *Hamlet* brilliantly illustrates the psychological torment that a conflicted moral conscience can cause. The basic moral dilemma that Hamlet faces is whether he should accept stoically the events that affect his life or take action against them. You may recall that Hamlet's uncle kills his father and then marries his mother. Hamlet feels compelled to avenge his father's death, but to do so requires an act of murder. Hamlet's moral indecision gives rise to his famous soliloquy in Act 3, Scene 1, beginning with the words "To be, or not to be, that is the question: / Whether 'tis nobler in the mind to suffer the slings and arrows of outrageous fortune, / Or to take arms against a sea of troubles / And by opposing end them."

For a slightly less dramatic illustration, suppose you were taught as a youngster to value honesty, loyalty, and friendship, but you are now troubled because you have been subpoenaed to testify in court against your best buddies, who have been charged with a crime you know they did, in fact, commit. If you're honest and tell the truth, you'll

"I wrestled with my conscience— and I won."

probably lose friends who'll resent you for sending them to jail. If you stand by your friends out of loyalty and lie to the authorities, you're committing the crime of perjury—an immoral and illegal act. This difficult situation can obviously cause indecision and a lot of worry, guilt, and fear. Being able to decide what is the right thing to do certainly does have real-life practical value; your psychological well-being may depend upon it!

On this note, I'm reminded of the time when a former student of mine raised his hand in class. He was obviously very agitated and upset. We had been discussing the ethics of abortion that day when he suddenly blurted out: "C'mon Tony, you've been studying this ethics stuff for years. You're the expert. Let's stop all of this arguing. It's driving me crazy. Just tell me, will you, is abortion right or wrong?"

Thinking back to this painful experience of my student, I cannot help but become a little disturbed myself by the mental torment he was suffering.

He was apparently experiencing considerable anxiety in his efforts to make the correct moral value judgment on the controversial issue of abortion. He knew that abortion was a serious matter and that it was important for him to take the right moral position on it; yet he was uncertain about how to decide for himself. He wanted me to decide for him.

Like this student, you too may experience mental anguish when making important moral or ethical decisions. Values must be championed, people must be confronted, principles must be defended, and sometimes difficult or unpleasant actions must be carried out. When there is much uncertainty or diversity of opinion, psychological tension can result. Moral doubt can be a significant source of stress in modern life.

In desperate efforts to cope with the moral suffering of the mind, some people like my tormented student look to experts and gurus for answers. By placing their faith in the judgment of others, people try to relieve themselves of the burden of having to decide for themselves. By granting moral authority to an ethics professor, a religious leader, a politician, or a military officer, some people attempt to escape from the personal responsibility of making moral decisions as independent agents. If any wrongdoing or bad judgment arises as a result of someone else's decision, the moral authorities are to blame, not the would-be moral escape artists.

It is possible, then, that in some cases, deferring to moral authority is little more than a veiled attempt to get off the moral hook of life. Perhaps the most obvious example of this was found in the war crimes trials that followed World War II. At that time, a number of senior German officers pleaded innocent to war crimes charges on the grounds that they were "just obeying orders" from the *Führer*. In their minds, they were not responsible. World opinion would suggest otherwise.*

Another psychological strategy to relieve morally induced mental stress is to quit thinking and simply conclude that all values are a matter of personal preference. Once this stance is adopted, there is no real need to agonize over moral matters. After all, no one person has the *right* to make a value judgment on the actions or character of another.

---

* Admittedly, this example is not really so straightforward. These officers would have been executed had they refused to obey orders. What should they have done? A saint would have died rather than done such evil, but can we expect people to be saints?

As the saying goes, *different strokes for different folks*. People just have different feelings and opinions about what is morally acceptable in any situation or given set of circumstances.

Although this **relativism** is a position that some might wish to defend, and though it offers a degree of psychological solace, it is fraught with difficulties. If, for example, everybody is right and nobody is wrong because rightness and wrongness are relative to the person, culture, or generation, then opposite and conflicting moral positions could both be right at the same time—a proposition that does not make very much logical sense.

Furthermore, if there were no objective way to decide matters of right and wrong or good and bad, then there would be no ethical basis for criticizing social policies or for improving society. We'd even be forced to concede that, from the "terrorists' perspective," the 9/11 attack in New York was justified, and further, we would have no *objective* basis for concluding otherwise. So, too, in cases like slavery, child abuse, or discrimination against women; we would have to accept them on the grounds that, morally speaking, it is all a matter of personal opinion and how people feel at the time.

If we are not to abandon morality in our lives and the possibility of social progress, if we do not wish to wash our hands of moral responsibility or to escape from it by becoming mindless followers and sheep, we must look for adequate ways to make moral decisions for ourselves.

Fortunately for us, a great many thinkers have grappled for centuries with the problems of moral and ethical decision-making. We need not bow down and worship these thinkers; nor do we have to accept unconditionally all of what they say to us. This would be mindless following again. As thoughtful and mature adults, equipped with some of the basics of logic and higher-order thinking useful for critical analysis, what we can do is begin to consider intelligently the insights the thinkers have to offer and evaluate their moral philosophies from a rational, objective perspective. We can decide which ideas have worth, which ones need alteration, and which ones must be rejected altogether. We can do all this if we choose to be free and independent thinkers ourselves, and if we assume at the outset that when it comes to moral matters, debate is meaningful and there are better and worse decisions to be made.

With this assumption in mind, we move into the realm of moral theory. Of course, in an introductory text such as this, it would be impossible to cover all of the significant moral thinkers from ancient times to the present. What is manageable is a brief sampling, so to speak, of different and widely varying ethical perspectives presented by major figures in the field. The sampling can help you to appreciate the complexity of moral thought, as well as its many useful insights for responsible and enlightened living. It can also serve as an invitation for you to continue your ethical explorations independently beyond the boundaries of what is presented here.

Our moral trek in this chapter will start off with Plato's character ethics. This ancient Greek perspective will facilitate moral self-reflection and consideration of the type of person we would like to become. Next, we will turn to Aristotle, Plato's student. One could describe Aristotle as a *virtue ethicist*, one who has much to say about alternative lifestyles and which one is most befitting of humankind.

After completing our study of Greek character and virtue ethics, we leap forward to Jeremy Bentham, a representative of British utilitarianism. Bentham would help us very much with our moral decision-making by providing us with a *hedonic calculus*—a tool we can use to arrive at our moral conclusions in a *spirit of scientific objectivity*. Immanuel

Kant also tries to provide us with a solid and secure foundation for ethical choice by presenting us with the *categorical imperative*—what he believes to be a purely rational, universally prescriptive principle we can use to derive all other moral maxims and ethical rules of conduct.

In stark contrast to Kant, we then move on to consider the work of two contemporary American women: Nel Noddings and Carol Gilligan. They offer us modern alternatives to (allegedly) male-biased approaches like Kant's and its derivatives.

After the discussion of Noddings and Gilligan's theories, we will then enter the dangerous territory of another European, namely Friedrich Wilhelm Nietzsche. Nietzsche explodes our complacency based on moral tradition and authority. He advocates a moral perspective that transcends rationality and what he regards as dishonesty cloaked in a mantel of altruism and community-mindedness. Nietzsche rejects reason as the basis of morality, making the *will to power* the foundation of his ethical thinking.

Lastly, we will briefly examine religious ethics—specifically, Islamic ethics, Hindu duty-based morality as presented in the *Bhagavad Gita*, and Christian ethics as interpreted from a modern-day Roman Catholic perspective.

But before we begin our study of moral theories, I invite you, as has become custom by now, to engage in a bit of self-examination by completing the *Know Thyself* diagnostic that follows. It will help you to identify your ethical assumptions and presuppositions before we start covering some others. You no doubt hold many ethical views already, but you may not yet have articulated them, either to yourself or others. Now is the time to make them explicit and to become clearer about exactly what it is that you value in life. Knowing what your values are is a logical prerequisite for appraising their justifiability and worth.

The Ethical Perspective Indicator

AIM

The purpose of this measure is to enable you to identify your moral value beliefs, assumptions, and presuppositions by finding which moral perspective covered in this chapter most closely resembles your own.

(Note: The diverse religious ethical perspectives found in Section 5.7 of this chapter will not be included in this self-diagnostic. The significant differences among them make it difficult to produce one coherent category of "Religious Ethics." If you are a religious person, it can still be interesting to discover which general philosophical ethical perspective you prefer. As well, it's an opportunity to *know thyself* in the light of ethical theories you perhaps haven't thought of or known about before.)

INSTRUCTIONS

Each statement that follows reflects a particular moral perspective. Your task is to indicate your level of agreement or disagreement with each one using the scale provided.

1 = strongly disagree
2 = disagree somewhat
3 = agree somewhat
4 = strongly agree

1. _____ At its core, morality is about character and finding psychological balance.

2. _____ Morality should be based on happiness and the desire for pleasure.

3. _____ Human reason should serve as the basis of morality.

4. _____ Morality should be understood in terms of care and maintaining human relationships rather than in terms of rights, principles, duties, and the pursuit of personal happiness.

5. _____ Morality cannot have a religious basis, for there is no creator-God.

6. _____ The purpose of morality is to help us live the good life, a life of moderation.

7. _____ A moral person is one whose personality functions with integrity.

8. _____ Humans are biologically determined to seek pleasure and avoid pain. Hence, actions that maximize pleasure or reduce pain are good.

9. _____ Morality is basically about duty—doing your duty for the sake of duty.

10. _____ Moral decisions must be made by individuals in context. It is misguided to think that general principles of morality can be applied unconditionally across situations.

11. _____ Morality should affirm and celebrate self-will.

12. _____ Functioning in accordance with our human nature is the ultimate end of life.

13. _____ People become morally corrupt when their appetites and desires take over their lives.

14. _____ No actions are inherently right or wrong in themselves. Whether an action is right or wrong depends on its consequences.

15. _____ A person is moral when he or she is motivated to do the right thing for the right reason.

16. _____ Philosophers throughout history appear to have romanticized rationality, giving it far too much importance. The right thing to do is not always the purely rational thing to do.

17. _____ Traditional religious moralities are nihilistic, or life-denying, condemning those values and instincts that belong to "natural man."

18. _____ Things like money and pleasure are just a means to something more worthwhile.

19. _____ Morality is largely about the virtues of courage, temperance, and wisdom.

20. _____ When making moral decisions, it's best to engage in a kind of cost-benefit analysis. Those actions producing the greatest benefits relative to cost should be preferred.

21. _____ When people do the right thing (their moral duty) for the wrong reason (exclusively for self-interest), their action does not belong to the moral domain. It has no moral worth.

22. _____ Exceptions to purely rational principles of morality are almost always inevitable, making them less sound than they appear at first.

23. _____ Some forms of morality are dishonest, serving only the interests of the weak and fearful.

24. _____ Virtue is its own reward.

25. _____ The faculty of reason should harness both appetite and passion in the human character.

26. _____ Punishment should be used only as a practical deterrent, not for retribution or revenge.

27. _____ Moral duties—whether to ourselves or others—are unconditional and prescriptive for all.

28. _____ Principles and duties should sometimes be overridden in order to maintain caring relationships.

29. _____ People are not equal. Some characters are higher or nobler than others.

30. _____ Happiness is found in a way of living, not in material possessions or fame.

31. _____ People do wrong not because they are inherently evil, but because they are ignorant.

32. _____ It's possible to make moral judgments in a spirit of scientific objectivity using mathematics-like calculations.

33. _____ In order for a principle to be considered morally justifiable, it must be rationally consistent and universally applicable regardless of person, place, or time.

34. _____ It's not dour obligation that moves us to moral action, but joy and desire to exercise the virtue of goodness by fulfilling ourselves in others.

35. _____ The best way to live is to see yourself as an artist and life as a work of art. You're the artistic creator, free and unbridled, painting the masterpiece in any way you choose.

36. _____ A life of rational contemplation is the most sublime of all alternative lifestyles.

SCORING

Record your scaled answers next to the question numbers listed in the columns below.

Character Moralist	Utilitarian	Deonto- logist	Care Ethicist	Existential Atheist	Virtue Ethicist
1:	2:	3:	4:	5:	6:
7:	8:	9:	10:	11:	12:
13:	14:	15:	16:	17:	18:
19:	20:	21:	22:	23:	24:
25:	26:	27:	28:	29:	30:
31:	32:	33:	34:	35:	36:

TOTALS:

INTERPRETATION OF RESULTS

Compare the totals. The highest total suggests that your current values, ideals, and moral beliefs are most consistent with the particular ethical theory identified by the descriptive label.

According to my highest score, my present views on morality and ethics are most closely aligned with the ▨▨▨▨▨▨▨▨▨.

Character Moralist

Those adopting this perspective see morality largely in terms of character development. They ask with Plato, "What sort of person should I strive to become?" and "What constitutes the good life?" Perhaps another way of putting it is "How should I live?" (with emphasis on the "I"). Character moralists fitting the Platonic mold seek to balance various elements of what he calls the *soul*, or human character structure, but appreciate the special importance of *reason* when it comes to harnessing one's appetites and unruly passions. Platonic character moralists see the highest level of moral development in the "philosopher king or ruler," one who displays virtues like temperance, wisdom, and courage. Misguided lives result from character imbalances arising from ignorance.

Virtue Ethicist

The virtue ethicist conceptualizes morality in terms of human function, like Aristotle does. Our unique function as human beings is rational in nature and so our ultimate goal or end in life is to perform that function well, with excellence. While it is recognized that things like pleasure, money, honor, and appetite gratification are all worthwhile ends, they are subordinate to the ultimate end in life, which is flourishing—something achieved by living a rationally ordered life of wisdom and virtuous moderation. The contemplative life is regarded as the ideal or highest form of human existence, something almost divine. Success is not about wealth and status or physical enjoyment, but rather about fulfilling our distinctive function as human beings.

Utilitarian

The utilitarian moralist bases ethical decision making on the principle of utility. The morally right thing to do in any situation is that which produces the greatest utility, i.e., happiness for everyone affected. Thus, the consequences of actions determine their moral worth. No actions are necessarily right or wrong in themselves. For a utilitarian like Bentham, the moral value of actions can be determined by a kind of cost-benefit analysis known as the *hedonic calculus*. Actions producing the greatest net value of utility are those we're obligated to perform. The idea is that the only thing good in itself is utility or happiness and the only thing bad in itself is disutility or unhappiness. On this account, the ends justify the means.

Deontologist

The Kantian deontologist is a rational, principled, duty-based moralist. The right thing to do is to act for the sake of duty alone. Acting in accordance with duty but not out of respect for duty, however, is insufficient for moral correctness. Dutiful acts are regarded as intentional human behaviors based on rules or maxims derived from the moral law as opposed to inclinations and desires. Given their basis in moral law, morally justified actions are those whose underlying maxims are logically consistent, universally prescriptive, unconditional, impartial, and rationally objective. Formal principles of rational thought serve, therefore, as the criteria determining whether actions are moral and morally justified. The thrust here is to act in accordance with rational, duty-based principles, not to maximize utility or promote happiness. Here, the ends do *not* justify the means. Morality is *not* about the outcomes of actions; it's about the state of the agent who performs the actions. Someone who recognizes, and acts on, the moral law has a good will and does a good deed, not for personal gain but for objective principles. In Kantian ethics, the highest moral law is the categorical imperative: *"Act only according to that maxim by which you can at the same time will that it should become a universal law."*

Care Ethicist

Care ethicists, like Carol Gilligan and Nel Noddings, take issue with the whole notion of a principle-based morality, arguing that exceptions to rules are inevitable and that strict and unyielding adherence to principles often undermines the very human relationships they are intended to strengthen and protect. They argue that morality should be based on *care* and the *human affective response*. The emphasis of morality should foster interdependence and responsibility for others, not the exertion of self-interest or the defense of individual rights (though these are important as well). For the care ethicist, emotional detachment is not a virtue but an unrecognized bias resulting from a history of males idolizing abstract principles. It is not the rational subject (Descartes's *cogito*) that is fundamental; rather *the relationship with others* that is ontologically basic. Morality doesn't arise from the *a priori* structure of reason (Kant), but rather from the *interpersonal dynamic of persons in relation*.

Existential Atheist

The existential atheism covered in this chapter, namely Friedrich Nietzsche's, begins with the premise that there is no creator-God. Furthermore, morality is not somehow embedded in nature, to be discovered by the rational mind. Human beings do not need redemption, as they are *not* born stained with original sin. Human beings are ultimately free and self-determining. By exercising their instinctual will to power, they become legislators of morality themselves. The ideal for Nietzschean moralists is to live as nobles (those able to master themselves), overcome obstacles, and unhesitatingly display strength, courage, and pride. By sublimating the power of passion into creative acts of self-will, individuals can become "supermen," making life an aesthetic phenomenon.

5.1 Plato's Character Ethics

As we enter the moral domain, let us take what guidance we can from the immortal wisdom of **Plato**. In his writings, Plato addressed such perennial questions as "What constitutes the good life?" and "What sort of person should I endeavor to become?" To answer such questions, Plato paid particular attention to the soul. He believed that, like the body, the soul could enjoy health or could suffer from dysfunction. If the soul is to become and to remain healthy, then, for Plato, a certain harmonious balance of psychic elements must be established within the self. Physical, emotional, and intellectual components of the personality must be coordinated to work smoothly together. A smoothly functioning psyche constitutes a healthy, well-ordered soul, whereas an imbalanced psyche makes for a disordered one.

The insight that we gain from this thinking is that if one wishes to live a life of virtue, then certain inner adjustments may be required. Morality is, as we suggested earlier, an *inside job*. To understand precisely what is meant by this suggestion, it is necessary to examine Plato's notion of teleology and how it fits into his concept of the soul.

Plato's Teleology

According to Plato's doctrine of **teleology**, everything in the universe has a *proper function* to perform within a harmonious hierarchy of purposes. This means that the development of anything follows from the fulfillment of the purpose for which it was designed. For us to evaluate something as good or bad, we must, therefore, examine and appraise it in light of its proper function. Does it perform well what it was designed to do?

Take a pen, for example. A pen performs well if it writes smoothly and without blotting. This is what a pen is designed to do. Given the function of a pen, we should not expect it to perform well as an eating utensil or as a weapon of self-defense. Our evaluation of a pen's good or bad performance depends on its designated purpose.

As for humans, we too have a function. In view of Plato's teleological explanation of morality, *we live the morally good life insofar as we perform our distinctively human function well*. Being less efficient than a robot on a factory assembly line, for instance, does not make us bad or morally deficient. We are not designed by nature to be mindless machines. What we are designed to do and how we are supposed to function, according to Plato, can best be understood by turning to his explanation of the structure and workings of the human soul.

Vision of the Soul

Plato conceptualizes human nature in terms of a three-part division of the soul. When reading about Plato's concept here, try not to invest 'soul' with any religious significance. Understand that for Plato, the **soul** is the principle of life and movement, the repository of *motives* or *impulses to action*. Since the bodily self is inanimate, it must be moved by something and, for Plato, that something is the soul. While Plato's discussion of the soul is not intended as a scientific analysis of the mind, seeing the soul as something akin to self or personality structure is helpful for analytical purposes.

Plato's soul is made up of **appetite**, **spirit**, and **reason**, each aiming at different things. Take appetite first. Appetite, or *desire* as it is sometimes called, seeks to satisfy our biological, instinctive urges. It looks after the physical side of our lives. We all wish to eat, drink, sleep, satisfy our sexual urges, minimize pain, experience pleasure, acquire a certain number of possessions, and live comfortably. When we diet, date, shop, or work out, for example, we are being driven by appetite—the physical side of our selves.

The second structural element of the human soul is spirit, that which drives us toward action. Sometimes referred to as *passion*, it includes our self-assertive tendencies. Spirit targets things like glory, honor, reputation, and the establishment of a good name. It also provides the impetus or force behind all ambitious pursuits, competitive struggles, and feelings of moral outrage and indignation. It is also the seat of human enterprise and pugnacity. As the emotional element of the psyche, spirit manifests itself in our need to love and be loved. It is present when we wish to make an impression, to be accepted and admired by others, or when we work hard to be liked.

Reason is the third element of the soul, representing what might be called the intellect. Reason can be described as the faculty that calculates, measures, and decides. It seeks knowledge and understanding, affording us insight and the ability to anticipate the future with foresight. By means of reason we are able to think and to make up our minds before we act. We can weigh options, follow rules, compare alternatives, suppress dangerous urges, and make reasonable choices. Whenever we are curious, trying to make

"Character is fate."
HERACLITUS

sense of things, or whenever we display an inquiring mind in our search for knowledge and meaning, reason is that which moves us.

Moral Balance and Plato's Functional Explanation of Morality

"Zeal without knowledge is a runaway horse."
PROVERB

Having outlined the parts of the soul, let us go back to Plato's **functional explanation of morality**. Remember that, for Plato, anything is good to the extent that it performs its function well. So the question now becomes: How is the human soul supposed to function? How are we supposed to care for our souls to make them function well?

In answer to this, Plato suggests that the soul that is functioning properly is doing so in a kind of harmonious **moral balance**. When the faculty of reason governs both appetite and spirit—that is, our physical desires as well as our passions and emotions—then an orderly and well-balanced moral character results. People who are living the morally good life maintain a rational, biological, and emotional equilibrium with reason in charge.

Control of inner harmony by reason is not easy to achieve. We all experience turmoil and psychological conflict. It is as if there were warring factions within the soul that cause tension and upheaval. This internal conflict is not necessarily abnormal or psychopathological; it is part of the human condition. Inner struggle is part of life.

To help us better appreciate this struggle, Plato describes it metaphorically, using the illustrative example of a charioteer with two horses in rein. The charioteer symbolizes the faculty of reason; the horses represent appetite and spirit. One horse (appetite) "needs no touch of the whip, but is guided by word and admonition only." The other horse (spirit) is unruly, "the mate of insolence and pride ... hardly yielding to whip and spur." While the charioteer (reason) has a clear vision of the destination and the good horse is on track, the bad horse "plunges and runs away, giving all manner of trouble to his companion and charioteer."[1]

In the scenario presented to us by Plato, we have two horses pulling in different directions, while a charioteer watches his commands go unheeded. The charioteer's job is to guide and control the horses. What is clear is that the chariot cannot go anywhere unless the driver can work together with the two horses and bring them under control. So too it is with life. Just as both horses are necessary to achieve the charioteer's goal, appetite and spirit are indispensable to reason. Reason identifies the goal, harnessing the power of appetite and spirit as it proceeds toward its chosen destination. Appetite and spirit cannot be disposed of, since they are essential to the well-ordered functioning of the human soul.

When reason is in control and the soul is functioning in a harmonious balance, we can say that it is functioning as it should. For Plato, fulfillment of our function as human beings is equivalent to the attainment of **moral virtue**. When we are unhappy or when we have lost our sense of well-being, disharmony of the soul is the problem. If the "wild horses" of passion and desire are running rampant in our lives, then we fall into disorder manifesting itself in ignorance. We begin to confuse **appearance** with **reality**. We mistake apparent goods for real goods. We pursue things we think will make us happy when, in fact, they will not. We make wrong choices and do wrong things out of false knowledge. As poor misguided souls, we fall prey to moral evil and corruption.

Only by allowing reason to regain control of our lives can we enjoy peace of mind, inner harmony, and lasting happiness. Reason can offer us true knowledge of what is ultimately good, and only reason can properly guide us in what we should do with our lives. It is reason that yields the knowledge necessary for moral virtue; ignorance can produce only evil and misdirection.

Plato, Virtue, and Justice in the Individual and in the State[2]

Book IV of Plato's Republic *begins with a discussion about the ideal city-state. It can be described as "just," meaning: the structural organization of the producers, guardians, and rulers is in order, and each group does its own work and does it well. The following excerpt picks up later in Book IV where Socrates, in conversation with Glaucon, compares the just state (called here the "city"*) with the just individual. Justice in each involves harmony or inner balance, with one element taking on a dominant role.*

———

[**Socrates**] … We are pretty much agreed that the same number and the same kinds of classes as are in the city are also in the soul of each individual.

[**Glaucon**] That's true.

[**Socrates**] Therefore, it necessarily follows that the individual is wise in the same way and in the same part of himself as the city.

[**Glaucon**] That's right.

[**Socrates**] And isn't the individual courageous in the same way and in the same part of himself as the city? And isn't everything else that has to do with virtue the same in both?

[**Glaucon**] Necessarily.

[**Socrates**] Moreover, Glaucon, I suppose we'll say that a man is just in the same way as a city.

[**Glaucon**] That too is entirely necessary.

[**Socrates**] And we surely haven't forgotten that the city was just because each of the three classes in it was doing its own work.

[**Glaucon**] I don't think we could forget that.

[**Socrates**] Then we must also remember that each one of us in whom each part is doing its own work will himself be just and do his own.

[**Glaucon**] Of course, we must.

[**Socrates**] Therefore, isn't it appropriate for the rational part to rule, since it is really wise and exercises foresight on behalf of the whole soul, and for the spirited part to obey it and be its ally?

[**Glaucon**] It certainly is.

[**Socrates**] And isn't it, as we were saying, a mixture of music and poetry, on the one hand, and physical training, on the other, that makes the two parts harmonious, stretching and nurturing the rational part with fine words and learning, relaxing the other part through soothing stories, and making it gentle by means of harmony and rhythm?

[**Glaucon**] That's precisely it.

[**Socrates**] And these two, having been nurtured in this way, and having truly learned their own roles and been educated in them, will govern the appetitive part, which is the largest part in each person's soul and is by nature most insatiable for money. They'll watch over it to see that it isn't filled with the so-called pleasures of the body and that it doesn't become so big and strong that it no longer does its own work but attempts to enslave and rule over the classes it isn't fitted to rule, thereby overturning everyone's whole life.

---

* Plato was talking about what we sometimes call 'city-states,' independent sovereign cities acting as centers of political, economic, and cultural life over a specific territory. Athens was the largest example.

[Glaucon] That's right.

[Socrates] Then, wouldn't these two parts also do the finest job of guarding the whole soul and body against external enemies—reason by planning, spirit by fighting, following its leader, and carrying out the leader's decisions through its courage?

[Glaucon] Yes, that's true.

[Socrates] And it is because of the spirited part, I suppose, that we call a single individual courageous, namely, when it preserves through pains and pleasures the declarations of reason about what is to be feared and what isn't.

[Glaucon] That's right.

[Socrates] And we'll call him wise because of that small part of himself that rules in him and makes those declarations and has within it the knowledge of what is advantageous for each part and for the whole soul, which is the community of all three parts.

[Glaucon] Absolutely.

[Socrates] And isn't he moderate because of the friendly and harmonious relations between these same parts, namely, when the ruler and the ruled believe in common that the rational part should rule and don't engage in civil war against it?

[Glaucon] Moderation is surely nothing other than that, both in the city and in the individual.

[Socrates] And, of course, a person will be just because of what we've so often mentioned, and in that way.

[Glaucon] Necessarily.

[Socrates] Well, then, is the justice in us at all indistinct? Does it seem to be something different from what we found in the city?

[Glaucon] It doesn't seem so to me.

[Socrates] If there are still any doubts in our soul about this, we could dispel them altogether by appealing to ordinary cases.

[Glaucon] Which ones?

[Socrates] For example, if we had to come to an agreement about whether someone similar in nature and training to our city had embezzled a deposit of gold or silver that he had accepted, who do you think would consider him to have done it rather than someone who isn't like him?

[Glaucon] No one.

[Socrates] And would he have anything to do with temple robberies, thefts, betrayals of friends in private life or of cities in public life?

[Glaucon] No, nothing.

[Socrates] And he'd be in no way untrustworthy in keeping an oath or other agreement.

[Glaucon] How could he be?

[Socrates] And adultery, disrespect for parents, and neglect of the gods would be more in keeping with every other kind of character than his.

[Glaucon] With every one.

[Socrates] And isn't the cause of all this that every part within him does its own work, whether it's ruling or being ruled?

[Glaucon] Yes, that and nothing else.

[Socrates] Then, are you still looking for justice to be something other than this power, the one that produces men and cities of the sort we've described?

[Glaucon] No, I certainly am not.

[Socrates] Then the dream we had has been completely fulfilled—our suspicion that, with the help of some god, we had hit upon the origin and pattern of justice right at the beginning in founding our city.

[Glaucon] Absolutely.

[Socrates] Indeed, Glaucon, the principle that it is right for someone who is by nature a cobbler to practice cobblery and nothing else, for the carpenter to practice carpentry, and the same for the others is a sort of image of justice—that's why it's beneficial.

[Glaucon] Apparently.

[Socrates] And in truth justice is, it seems, something of this sort. However, it isn't concerned with someone's doing his own externally, but with what is inside him, with what is truly himself and his own. One who is just does not allow any part of himself to do the work of another part or allow the various classes within him to meddle with each other. He regulates well what is really his own and rules himself. He puts himself in order, is his own friend, and harmonizes the three parts of himself like three limiting notes in a musical scale—high, low, and middle. He binds together those parts and any others there may be in between, and from having been many things he becomes entirely one, moderate and harmonious. Only then does he act. And when he does anything, whether acquiring wealth, taking care of his body, engaging in politics, or in private contracts—in all of these, he believes that the action is just and fine that preserves this inner harmony and helps achieve it, and calls it so, and regards as wisdom the knowledge that oversees such actions. And he believes that the action that destroys this harmony is unjust, and calls it so, and regards the belief that oversees it as ignorance.

[Glaucon] That's absolutely true, Socrates.

[Socrates] Well, then, if we claim to have found the just man, the just city, and what the justice is that is in them, I don't suppose that we'll seem to be telling a complete falsehood.

[Glaucon] No, we certainly won't.

[Socrates] Shall we claim it, then?

[Glaucon] We shall.

[Socrates] So be it. Now, I suppose we must look for injustice.

[Glaucon] Clearly.

[Socrates] Surely, it must be a kind of civil war between the three parts, a meddling and doing of another's work, a rebellion by some part against the whole soul in order to rule it inappropriately. The rebellious part is by nature suited to be a slave, while the other part is not a slave but belongs to the ruling class. We'll say something like that, I suppose, and that the turmoil and straying of these parts are injustice, licentiousness, cowardice, ignorance, and, in a word, the whole of vice.

[Glaucon] That's what they are.

[Socrates] So, if justice and injustice are really clear enough to us, then acting justly, acting unjustly, and doing injustice are also clear.

[Glaucon] How so?

[Socrates] Because just and unjust actions are no different for the soul than healthy and unhealthy doings are for the body.

[Glaucon] In what way?

[Socrates] Healthy things produce health, unhealthy ones disease.

[Glaucon] Yes.

[Socrates] And don't just actions produce justice in the soul and unjust ones injustice?

[Glaucon] Necessarily.

[Socrates] To produce health is to establish the components of the body in a natural relation of control and being controlled, one by another, while to produce disease is to establish a relation of ruling and being ruled contrary to nature.

[Glaucon] That's right.

[Socrates] Then, isn't to produce justice to establish the parts of the soul in a natural relation of control, one by another, while to produce injustice is to establish a relation of ruling and being ruled contrary to nature?

[Glaucon] Precisely.

[Socrates] Virtue seems, then, to be a kind of health, fine condition, and well-being of the soul, while vice is disease, shameful condition, and weakness.

[Glaucon] That's true.

[Socrates] And don't fine ways of living lead one to the possession of virtue, shameful ones to vice?

[Glaucon] Necessarily.

[Socrates] So it now remains, it seems, to enquire whether it is more profitable to act justly, live in a fine way, and be just, whether one is known to be so or not, or to act unjustly and be unjust, provided that one doesn't pay the penalty and become better as a result of punishment.

[Glaucon] But, Socrates, this inquiry looks ridiculous to me now that justice and injustice have been shown to be as we have described. Even if one has every kind of food and drink, lots of money, and every sort of power to rule, life is thought to be not worth living when the body's nature is ruined. So even if someone can do whatever he wishes, except what will free him from vice and injustice and make him acquire justice and virtue, how can it be worth living when his soul—the very thing by which he lives—is ruined and in turmoil?

[Socrates] Yes, it is ridiculous....

READING QUESTIONS

1. Bad analogies are like bad windshield wipers—in trying to make things clearer, they make things opaque or more difficult to see. Good analogies, however, are like finely-crafted and well-oiled machines. They are done with precise purpose and fulfill their functions flawlessly. (Please judge those analogies as you see fit!) Based on your understanding of this passage, why do you think Plato has the character of Socrates make the analogy between the individual and the city-state? Is it an effective comparison for getting the ideas across? Explain why or why not.

2. Socrates describes justice as a harmonious condition of an individual's soul. What are the three parts of an individual's soul? What function is associated with each of the three parts? Correspondingly, what virtue is associated with each of the three parts? Create and describe a scenario in which the three parts are in harmony.

3. Use the text to explain the following statement: "It is better to live a just life that goes unnoticed than an unjust life that goes unpunished."

Platonic Character Type Index (PCTI)[3]

AIM

The PCTI is an informal tool of self-analysis that can help you begin identifying which part of your psyche or soul is dominant at this time in your life. Knowledge of this fact can help you to better understand the internal workings of your "Platonic character type." Such information can also suggest paths for future character development and healthy personality maintenance.

Your results are not intended to be scientifically valid, but rather suggestive. (I am not sure the soul lends itself very well to empirical, scientific investigation!) Furthermore, Plato's account of character types is highly contentious, and you shouldn't worry about whether your results fit well with Plato's ideals. The accuracy of the results ultimately will be determined by your own honest introspective self-reflections—a kind of "philosophical psychoanalysis," bringing to conscious awareness what was only subconscious before.

INSTRUCTIONS

Next to each phrase below, indicate how reflective of you the item, action, or activity is.

How accurate would it be to say that you …

1 = not at all reflective of me
2 = hardly reflective of me
3 = very reflective of me
4 = exactly reflective of me

1. _____ seek truth

2. _____ wish to become famous

3. _____ want to make large sums of money

4. _____ enjoy being carefree

5. _____ experience pleasure through artificial or chemical means

6. _____ trust thinking more than sensory perception

7. _____ are competitive

8. _____ wish strongly to live a materially comfortable lifestyle

9. _____ avoid restrictions and restraints

10. _____ look out for number one

11. _____ pursue knowledge (as opposed to mere data and information)

12. _____ have difficulty dealing with subordinates (those lower in rank)

13. _____ do not waste time on activities that have little financial payoff

14. _____ treat all of your wants and desires as equal

15. _____ do what you want regardless of the consequences for other people

16. _____ control your physical urges and biological appetites most of the time

17. _____ want to be liked by others

18. _____ value being frugal and economical

19. _____ live in the moment and for the moment

20. _____ deceive people to get what you want

21. _____ do what is right, putting aside personal feelings and wants

22. _____ value achievement (fame or recognition) over money

23. _____ avoid financial disaster

24. _____ enjoy equally all the pleasures of life

25. _____ fall prey to manias or compulsions

26. _____ like intellectual thought

27. _____ try to look successful to others

28. _____ seize opportunities to better yourself economically

29. _____ take life a day at a time

30. _____ tell people whatever is necessary to get what you want

31. _____ display temperance (moderation)

32. _____ assume an attitude of superiority

33. _____ work hard to ensure the basic necessities of life

34. _____ do what feels good

35. _____ take by force, if necessary

36. _____ regulate personal habits

37. _____ enjoy exhibitions of courage and strength

38. _____ live consistently with the principle: *Money first, then morality.*

39. _____ frequently change your mind about what you want

40. _____ display addictive behavior

SCORING

Next to each of the question numbers below, fill in the corresponding numerical value you provided above. Add the total scores for each column to determine the highest. That highest score best reflects your character at this time understood in Platonic terms.

Philosopher King	Timarchic Character	Oligarchic Character	Democratic Character	Tyrannical Character
1:	2:	3:	4:	5:
6:	7:	8:	9:	10:
11:	12:	13:	14:	15:
16:	17:	18:	19:	20:
21:	22:	23:	24:	25:
26:	27:	28:	29:	30:
31:	32:	33:	34:	35:
36:	37:	38:	39:	40:

TOTALS:

INTERPRETATION OF RESULTS

To learn what your results mean, refer to the abbreviated descriptions that follow. Further information on each character type is found in the more detailed main text descriptions. Note that you probably have a mixture of different character elements making up your personality. It is unlikely that anybody is purely one type. Nonetheless, the character type with the highest score may be most reflective of what you are like as an individual right now. Your responsibility is to decide for yourself. After reading the descriptions of the character types, you may be favorably impressed or you may feel the need to change as a result. The moral decision is yours!

Timarchic Character
Driven by spirit, energetic, competitive, self-assertive, can also be insecure, jealous, vain and self-inflating, fearful of falling behind

Democratic Character
Versatile, easy-going, treats all passions and desires equally, but is frequently aimless, without principle, torn apart inside

Philosopher King/Ruler
Enlightened, internally balanced, morally virtuous, i.e., temperate, courageous, wise, just, ruled by reason, careful to distinguish between appearance and reality

Oligarchic Character
Driven by appetite, frugal, hardworking, materialistic and oftentimes money-hungry, dissatisfied, internally disturbed, dirty and wretched opportunist

Tyrannical Character
Possessed by master passion, criminal personality, totally undisciplined, least self-sufficient, anxiety ridden

Plato's Character Types

In *The Republic*, differently functioning souls are described using Plato's notion of **character types**. The philosopher king or ruler exemplifies the ideal character. Corrupt, imperfect types are given the following labels: *timarchic, oligarchic, democratic,* and *tyrannical.* You will note that all of these types are political-sounding. The reason for this, according to Plato, is that in each kind of societal structure there is a corresponding individual who is admired within it, so that in an oligarchy, for instance, the values and attributes of the oligarchic character are praised. Likewise, in a timarchic society, the qualities you find in the timarchic person would be extolled as virtues there.

Understand, however, that not every individual in a particular society necessarily displays the corresponding character type. Oligarchs can be found in democracies, virtuous

THINKING ABOUT YOUR THINKING

Think about the last time your appetites, feelings, or passions directed your behavior. What did you do? If reason had directed your behavior, what would you have done differently and why? Would you have been better off in the short term if reason had been in charge? Would you have been better off in the long term? What does "better off" mean to you in this context?

people can be found in tyrannies, and so on. The point is that dominant individuals give rise to societies that, in turn, praise the qualities possessed by those individuals.

An interesting parallel between individuals and societies can also be seen by looking at the class system proposed by Plato for the *just society*—the system that functions in harmonious balance. In the ideal or just society, there would emerge three classes of people corresponding to the three parts of the soul. Each class would serve different, but complementary, roles.

First, there would be those whose lives would be driven primarily by the appetites. These would be the craftsmen, artisans, and traders. In modern times, we might see these people as the producers, workers, consumers, and business class. Second, there would be the auxiliaries, motivated in their lives mostly by spirit. They would serve to protect and preserve internal order under the guidance of rulers. Examples of this class in today's world would include the police, militia, and civil servants. Third, individuals would be selected from the auxiliaries to become the most highly trained and educated members of an elite **guardian class**, namely the philosopher kings/rulers.

Membership in any class would not be determined by birth or inheritance; rather, children would be moved from class to class according to merit and capability. Only those who passed the most rigorous tests and who would be best suited to work for the good of the community would become philosopher rulers. In the just society, the lower classes would not gain undue influence, or else internal anarchy would result, just as it does when appetite or spirit overrule reason in the individual. Reason must rule, as must those whose lives are governed by reason, not by greed (appetite) or self-assertion (spirit).

Let us now look at the character of the philosopher king and examine in more detail the corrupt character types located at lower levels of society. Though the notion that an elite ruling class should govern society may not be popular today, Plato argued that "the human race will not be free of evils until either the stock of those who rightly and truly follow philosophy acquire political authority, or the class who have power in the cities be led by some dispensation of providence to become real philosophers."[4] To paraphrase: rulers must become philosophers or philosophers must become rulers if we wish to establish the ideal social system. Just as reason must rule the soul, so too must philosophers rule the social order if the just society is ever to become a reality.[5]

"Know thyself."
THE ORACLE AT DELPHI

PHILOSOPHER KINGS/RULERS

According to Plato, the just society is a form of **aristocracy.*** In an aristocracy, **philosopher kings** who belong to the *guardian class* become the rulers. (Note that no gender discrimination is intended by the use of the label "kings." Plato was clear that qualified women also would be selected to serve as rulers in his ideal city.)

Philosopher kings (or rulers) are morally virtuous individuals. They are *temperate*, allowing no physical appetites or material desires to enslave them. Virtuous souls regulate their appetites by reason. Plato says, "It is because of the spirited part, I suppose, that we

---

* For us, this word designates the "highest" class, often the hereditary nobility. In its original meaning, and for Plato, an aristocracy was a state ruled by the *best*, by those—the "aristocrats"—whose nature made them most suitable to rule.

call a single individual courageous, namely, when it preserves through pains and pleasures the declarations of reason about what is to be feared and what isn't."[6] Plato thinks that philosophers, more than others, manifest courage.

The morally virtuous person is also *wise*, knowing what is best for each part of the soul. Plato said that one is wise "because of that small part of himself that rules in him and makes those declarations and has within it the knowledge of what is advantageous for each part and for the whole soul, which is the community of all three parts."[7] In addition, philosopher rulers are *just*. With respect to character, remember that *just* means balanced and *functioning harmoniously*. In the just character of the philosopher king, reason, emotion, and physical nature work well together, with reason in charge, of course. It is the faculty of reason that prevents inner rebellion and disorder of the soul. It establishes an internal constitution based on peaceful coexistence.

Besides being truly virtuous, another distinguishing characteristic of philosopher kings is that they have *special knowledge*. By an elaborate process of education, philosopher kings learn how to distinguish between appearance and reality. They learn how to acquaint themselves intellectually with the eternal and immutable **realm of forms**. The "forms" can be known only by reason and, according to Plato, are more real than the transitory things that we see, hear, taste, touch, and feel. Sensory experience can yield only imperfect approximations of the ideal forms.

For example, it is rational acquaintance with the form *justice* that allows us to describe any act as fair or unfair, just or unjust. Even though we have never seen complete fairness or universal justice in the world, we still know what it is, and we recognize imperfect examples in the everyday world by comparison to the form. Reason offers us perfect knowledge in an imperfect world. It shows us what the eyes have not seen. (To learn more about the perfect Platonic forms found in the realm of being, read about the Divided Line Theory in Section 4.2 of this text, paying attention to Figures 4.2 and 4.3 as you do so.)

Those who fall prey to the imperfect knowledge offered by the senses, and those who become morally sidetracked by physical appetites and emotions, end up living disordered lives of unhappy ignorance. Philosopher rulers make no such mistake. They are not lured away from the truth and moral goodness by misleading appearances, by the *bee's honey* or the *power monger's prestige and influence*. Philosopher kings appreciate how such things can only end in disillusionment and moral bankruptcy. Philosopher kings are enlightened souls who are not entrapped by fantasies and temptations, but are guided on the right path by the light of true moral goodness.

Now, before you foolishly bow down in humble worship of your philosophy teacher, understand that being a philosopher king today has nothing to do with occupation, but everything to do with character and disposition. A philosophy professor may teach all the right things, but for selfish and vainglorious motives to which he or she will not admit. Joe or Jill Average, on the other hand, may display many, or all, of the philosopher king's virtues without ever teaching the subject itself. Be aware, then, that anybody, even the student sitting beside you in class, could be a "closet philosopher." Maybe it is time for you to come out of the "king's closet" yourself and continue your character training as one of society's future guardians? Will you accept the call?

If a philosopher king or ruler were put in power today, what sources of injustice would he or she be able to identify in the current class system—what some might describe as our contemporary stratified society?

What changes do you think that philosopher king or ruler would need to make in order to achieve a balanced harmony across the class system? In other words, what would that ruler have to do to achieve justice as Plato conceived of it?

Alternatively, would justice be better served if the philosopher king or ruler abolished the class system entirely? Why or why not? Consider whether justice is consistent with a class system of any type, or specifically one ruled by the wise and intellectually elite?

TIMARCHIC CHARACTER

The dominant part of the soul that drives the **timarchic character** is *spirit*. People with timarchic characters are distinguished, in large part, by their energy, competitiveness, and the urge to dominate. For example, do you know anyone whose life seems to be based on constant "one-upmanship"? Does that person seemingly try to better you at anything and everything, no matter what? Do all of your accomplishments seem to pale in comparison to that other individual? Is whatever you do unfavorably compared or belittled by your timarchic friend's (alleged) superior performance? In short, does it seem that being with this person is like being engulfed in a continual struggle, an athletic contest, or a battle of wills? If so, then you can appreciate what this character type brings to the table of life.

Timarchic characters are self-assertive individuals, liking to be *out there* and trying to make an impression on other people. No matter how favorable the impression made or how successful the person is, they still retain a nagging insecurity, however. Reputations must be maintained; people must continue to be impressed; nobody else must be allowed to dominate, control, or look better. Life at the top of the ladder of success is very precarious. Once at the top, there is only one way to go—down—down in the estimation of others and, hence, down in one's own estimation.

The ambitious pride characterizing timarchic persons can thus create only a very thin veneer of confidence. Below the surface, these people fear that they will fall behind, lose, be humiliated and embarrassed, or that approval from others will be withdrawn at any time. These fears will manifest themselves in jealousy, as timarchic persons begrudge or diminish the successes of others.

The pitfalls of the timarchic character can be observed in the misguided athlete. Investing years of one's life in hopes of winning an Olympic gold medal in the shot-put event, for example, may leave a person wasted and could result in financial ruin. Finishing twelfth after years of self-financed training—out of the medals and out of the record books, with no fame, no endorsements, and possibly no perceived future—could also leave the person embittered and insecure. Failed efforts at vainglorious pursuits are not always pretty to witness.

With or without success, the timarchic character is destined to a life of underlying fears, jealousies, and insecurities. Ignorant of the fact that vanity and self-inflation cannot ultimately lead to a tranquil and balanced soul, timarchic characters will never achieve true and lasting happiness. At best, they will achieve only an artificial and transitory semblance of it.

OLIGARCHIC CHARACTER

In a society where wealth dominates and the wealthy are in control (arguably, our own), the qualities of the **oligarchic character** are revered. In the oligarch, we discover a character transformation from the ambitious, competitive type of person to the money-loving business person. Suggesting that our own society is a form of oligarchy is arguably a fairly accurate assessment. After all, is it not true that many people in North American society judge the worth of an individual by what that person owns? "How much are they worth?" we ask. Is it not a widespread belief that you are a *somebody* because you own many expensive things? Is it not the case that some people think having a lot of cash makes them more important than the rest of us? When people say they want to better themselves, is it not the case that they usually mean acquire more wealth or material possessions?

Of course, not everybody in contemporary society displays an oligarchic character. Those who do are simply the ones who are recognized and rewarded. They are the ones on the cover of *Fortune* magazine or featured in the *Wall Street Journal*. The oligarch's main objective in life is to make money. In the oligarchic character, appetite rules and dominates the rest of the soul by a desire for riches. When reason is called upon, it is called upon only in the service of making more money. Spirit, by contrast, isn't allowed to "have any ambition other than the acquisition of wealth or whatever might contribute to getting it."[8]

Plato's oligarch is frugal, economical, and hardworking, wasting as little as possible on nonessentials, so that no opportunity for wealth is wasted. Hard effort is spent on trying to satisfy only necessary wants. Unnecessary wants and desires, which do not function to accumulate greater wealth, are regarded as pointless and, therefore, supressed. A stingy oligarch today might not want to spend all of that hard-earned money on a flashy new automobile, for instance, as it is little more than a depreciating asset—a bad financial investment. Better to lease it and write it off as a business expense.

The character imperfections of the oligarch are, perhaps, most plainly evident in the huckster, peddler, or hawker on late-night television infomercials. Plato says the oligarch possesses a squalid (dirty and wretched) character "always on the make and putting something by" others. The person who can get you to buy more than you wanted, or persuade you to purchase what you really do not need, is the one who becomes rich, famous, and admired.

In the oligarch, there is a dramatic movement from ambition to avarice. For the oligarch, there is no advantage to having a good name and a moral reputation if there are no financial rewards. Because money and profit are the basic driving forces behind the oligarchic character, this person will be dishonest whenever doing so is advantageous. The only deterrent is fear of punishment; there is certainly no moral conviction or taming of desire by reason.

Plato described oligarchs as having dual personalities. They usually manage to maintain a certain degree of respectability as, on the whole, better desires master the worse. Nonetheless, good and bad desires engage in a battle for dominance within the psyche of the oligarch. The unfortunate result is that oligarchic individuals are never really at peace within themselves. When the worse desires are subdued, the oligarch is "more respectable than many, but the true virtue of a single-minded and harmonious soul far escapes him."[9]

Lastly, though oligarchs can achieve some degree of social respectability, they will usually make little significant contribution to public life where money and profit may

> *"… and the higher the prestige of wealth and the wealthy, the lower that of goodness and good men will be."*
> PLATO

have to be sacrificed. An oligarch might ask, "Why be a politician when there is so little financial reward?" Did you know that the lowest paid rookie in the National Basketball Association earns more money than the President of the United States, the leader of 330 million people? Oligarchs would probably say, "Rightly so!"

When it comes to the worth of a man or woman, oligarchs would most likely let the market decide. Given the thinking of oligarchs, their achievements and ambitions in public life are not likely to amount to much, but then again, they are also not likely to sustain large financial losses in pursuing vain ambitions of power or political glory.

DEMOCRATIC CHARACTER

In contrast to the oligarchic character, who distinguishes between necessary and unnecessary desires, the **democratic character** does not. All desires and appetites are treated equally. Democrats are charming but aimless individuals, spending as much money, time, and effort on necessary wants and desires as on unnecessary ones. For the democratic personality, no pleasure is underprivileged; each gets its fair share of encouragement. This type of character lives from day to day, indulging in any momentary pleasure that presents itself. The pleasures are varied. About the democratic person, Plato writes:

> He lives on, yielding day by day to the desire at hand. Sometimes he drinks heavily while listening to the flute; at other times, he drinks only water and is on a diet; sometimes he goes in for physical training; at other times, he's idle and neglects everything; and sometimes he even occupies himself with what he takes to be philosophy. He often engages in politics, leaping up from his seat and saying and doing whatever comes into his mind. If he happens to admire soldiers, he's carried in that direction, if money-makers, in that one. There's neither order nor necessity in his life, but he calls it pleasant, free, and blessedly happy, and he follows it for as long as he lives.[10]

People displaying a democratic character are versatile because they lack principles. The problem is that if people do not live a rational, principled life, then diverse and incompatible pleasures, appetites, and passions can pull them in different directions, all at the same time. When this happens, their personalities are consequently not integrated and functioning harmoniously. Individuals with a democratic character become torn apart inside. As Plato says, there is no order or restraint, but rather, disorder and lack of control. (Plato calls this the "democratic" character because he has a similar analysis and criticism of political democracy. But we'll consider this in the next chapter.)

Persons obsessively pursuing different and sometimes conflicting pleasures cannot avoid becoming disorganized and fragmented. Their lives exhibit a definite lack of rational coherence and direction. Democrats are like children in a candy store. They are excited but torn apart inside because they want everything in the store at the same time, and this is impossible.

Plato speculates as to how the democratic character is formed. He believes that children who are raised in a strict oligarchic household, where unnecessary pleasures have been denied, eventually become lured by those outside the family who regularly enjoy them. A basic diet, for instance, becomes unsatisfactory as their desire grows for exotic food. Simple tastes are replaced by sophisticated ones. Unnecessary desires, immediate pleasures, and extravagant tastes eventually transform the oligarchic person into a democratic character. Plato writes:

> [**Socrates**] Let's go back, then, and explain how the democratic man develops out of the oligarchic one. It seems to me as though it mostly happens as follows.

> [**Glaucon**] How?

> [**Socrates**] When a young man, who is reared in the miserly and uneducated manner we described, tastes the honey of the drones and associates with wild and dangerous creatures who can provide every variety of multicolored pleasure in every sort of way, this, as you might suppose, is the beginning of his transformation from having an oligarchic constitution within him to having a democratic one.[11]

TYRANNICAL CHARACTER

According to Plato, the **tyrannical character** is the worst, being the most unhappy and undesirable. The tyrant personifies the criminal personality. People with a tyrannical character suffer from a kind of mania. Maniacs possess one master passion that controls all other desires. This master passion becomes so powerful that it runs wild, causing madness in the individual. The object of this passion may be sex, alcohol, or drugs, for example.

In the tyrannical personality's pursuit of pleasure, there is no shame or guilt, as all discipline is swept away and usurped by madness. Tyrannical people are thus the least self-sufficient of all individuals. Their satisfaction depends entirely on external things and objects of maniacal desire.

Those with a tyrannical personality are full of anxiety and constantly trying to fulfill their unrelenting appetite for more. They will do anything to satisfy themselves, even if they must perform terrible deeds and become hated in the process. Tyrants' lives are lawless and disgusting. Though all of us have aggressive, bestial, and erotic urges—evidenced especially in dreams—most of us are able to control them; the tyrant, however, cannot.

If they have spent all of their money indulging their master passion, tyrants will start borrowing to satisfy it. When they are no longer able to borrow, they may rob, commit fraud, or engage in acts of violence. Tyrannical characters become thieves, pickpockets, kidnappers, church robbers, and murderers to satisfy their manias. From this fact alone, it should be clear why tyrants are the most morally corrupt of all the character types.

Select a well-known historical figure or notorious individual from contemporary society. The person could be an actor, sports celebrity, villain, businessperson, literary figure, or fictional character from any book, movie, or television show. Examine and appraise that person's actions, intentions, and motivations. What Platonic character type does that individual display? Give support for your answer.

5.2 Aristotle's Virtue Ethics

Aristotle's Teleology

Aristotle begins his *Nicomachean Ethics* with the following words: "Every art and every investigation, and similarly every action and pursuit, is considered to aim at some good. Hence the Good has been rightly defined as 'that at which all things aim.'"[12] He points out, for example, that health is the end of medicine, a ship is the end of shipbuilding, victory is the end of military leadership, and wealth is the end of economics or household management. This focus on the ends of human activity is what makes Aristotle a **teleologist**. For him, all human action has a *purpose* or *end* to achieve.

Like his mentor Plato, Aristotle incorporated within his teleological framework a *functional explanation of morality*—in this case, a kind of **self-realization ethic**. In his efforts to understand what constitutes the ultimate good or end of life, Aristotle examined human activity in terms of its function. He said:

> This might perhaps be achieved by grasping what is the function of man. If we take a flautist or a sculptor or any artist—or in general any class of men who have a specific function or activity—his goodness and proficiency is considered to lie in the performance of that function; and the same will be true of man, assuming that man has a function.[13]

If, on this functional account, a good flautist, say, is one who plays well, then a good life is one that is well lived and good persons are those who perform their distinctively human functions well or with excellence. To better appreciate how the good life is tied to function, let us consider very briefly Aristotle's notion of **entelechy**.

Aristotle maintained that every living thing in nature possesses an *entelechy* or *inner urge* to become its unique self—to self-actualize as it were. There is potential and drive toward self-actualization in whatever that "self" consists. For instance, an acorn has the potential, marked by an inner urge, to become an oak tree. If conditions are right—namely if there is enough good soil, sun, rain, and space to flourish—then the acorn will actualize its potentialities and become an oak tree. Similarly, a newborn child has something within itself that naturally unfolds and ultimately manifests into an adult, assuming no terminal disease or fatal accident causing premature death, of course.

Now, if each and every living thing has an end within itself to achieve, i.e., its *entelechy*, then things do not just happen randomly, but develop according to their natural aim or purpose. When things go normally, they will develop into their full potential. So, because things do not always go normally, we, as humans, can fail to actualize our inner potentialities and consequently fail to completely or properly express our nature. We can fall short, miss the mark, or follow paths that take us away from our highest function. In other words, we can *malfunction* and become less than what we were meant to become by natural purpose. Aristotle's notions of happiness and the ends of human life help us to discover how and why we often fall short.

Happiness (*Eudaimonia*) and the Ends of Human Life

Though Plato and Aristotle were both teleologists who offered us functional explanations of morality, their similarities abruptly end, however, when it comes to efforts to locate the source of true goodness in life. Plato maintained that knowledge of the Good had to be discovered separate from the concrete world of everyday experience. One had to go beyond the tangible world, where things are imperfect and transitory, to a world of unchanging and immutable forms. Knowledge of Goodness required, for Plato, a rational acquaintance with a nonmaterial realm. By contrast, Aristotle worked from experience and people's beliefs to identify what the ultimate good of humankind could consist in.

"To enjoy the things we ought, and to hate the things we ought, has the greatest bearing on excellence of character."
ARISTOTLE

Grounding his reasoning on experience, common sense, and human observation, Aristotle concluded that, no matter who you are or where you live, **happiness** is the ultimate end of life. As he points out, people from all walks of life believe that it is happiness toward which all of human behavior is ultimately aimed. Given this, let us now look a little more closely at how Aristotle conceptualizes ends, ultimate and otherwise.

TYPES OF ENDS

In the *Nicomachean Ethics*, Aristotle discusses a hierarchy of goods corresponding to a hierarchy of ends. Ends can be *instrumental*, *intrinsic*, and/or *ultimate*. When we pursue a good corresponding to an **instrumental end**, we want to achieve that end because we think it will lead to something else we value. For instance, your goal next summer may be to get a job picking tomatoes. This would be, with little doubt, not an end in itself, but a means to a further end, say, earning a paycheck. While earning a paycheck is a pretty good end, the paycheck itself is a means to a further end, perhaps the purchase of a new car. You may be dreaming about buying a flashy new automobile so that you can impress your friends; yet, on closer inspection, even this turns out to be only a means. One could ask why it is that you want to impress your friends. Whatever answer you give to this question points to a still more distant end. Instrumental ends are never for themselves, but for the sake of something else.

Intrinsic ends are qualitatively different from instrumental ends. Acts performed for their intrinsic worth are performed *for their own sake*. They are valued in themselves, not because of what they produce or whatever else they might lead to. Wars, for example, do not have intrinsic value; they are fought to achieve such things as liberty and justice. Even victory in war is not an end in itself, according to Aristotle, for it is simply a means to create the conditions by which people, as human beings, can fulfill their purpose.

But to ask why someone wants liberty, justice, or fulfillment of purpose would be somewhat bewildering because it is generally accepted that such things have intrinsic value, that they are good in themselves. In today's world, notions like 'liberty' and 'justice', are often used to defend and justify political actions and governmental policies; they are not objects of justification and defense themselves. They are usually regarded as intrinsically valuable.

Recognizing that there are many "goods" relating to different kinds of ends (instrumental and intrinsic), Aristotle discusses what captures the highest good or **ultimate end of life**. For him, it is "happiness" or to use the appropriate Greek term: *eudaimonia*.

Aristotle[14]

Aristotle (384–322 BCE) was born in Stagira. He was the son of a physician who lived and worked at the royal court of Amyntas II, king of Macedonia. At the age of 17, Aristotle went to Athens to enroll at Plato's Academy. For 20 years he worked and studied under Plato, for whom he had great respect as a philosopher and good feelings as a friend. Upon the death of Plato, Aristotle left Athens and spent a number of years in Asia Minor, eventually returning to Macedonia in order to become tutor to Alexander, the heir to the throne, who later became known as Alexander the Great.

After an eight-year stay in Macedonia, he left again for Athens, where he established a new school called the *Lyceum*. It was patterned after Plato's Academy insofar as community life, friendliness, and dialogue were emphasized. As many of Aristotle's dialogues with students were conducted while strolling down a garden path (*peripatos*), his followers came to be known as "*peripatetics*."

In 323 BCE, Alexander the Great died suddenly. The Athenians, who were under the yoke of Alexander, regarded his death as an opportunity to rid themselves of Macedonian control. Aware of his Macedonian ties, and fearing the prospect of having to stand trial for impiety (as had Socrates), Aristotle fled Athens. He died in exile one year later.

Aristotle wrote on subjects as varied as logic, ethics, aesthetics, metaphysics, biology, physics, psychology, and politics. He had a profound influence on medieval Hebrew, Arabic, and Christian philosophers, most notably St. Thomas Aquinas and his later scholastic followers who helped to formulate the official moral theology of the Catholic Church. Works by Aristotle include *Categories*, *Prior* and *Posterior Analytics*, *Physics*, *On the Heavens*, *On the Soul*, *Metaphysics*, *Politics*, *Rhetoric*, and two books on ethics: *Eudemian Ethics* and *Nicomachean Ethics*.

HAPPINESS AS THE ULTIMATE END

Understanding **happiness** or ***eudaimonia*** as the ultimate end of human conduct means that no matter what else we want—be it a job picking tomatoes, an automobile, victory in war, liberty, justice, or peace in the land—when all is said and done, the reason we want it is really because we want to be happy. Material things like cars, furniture, or sports memorabilia, for example, are instrumental goods pointing to something beyond. No reasonable person would argue that the good life should be based on a pursuit of such things having such minor value. Thus, they cannot serve as the absolutely final end of life and hence do not represent ultimate goodness.

Aristotle is also careful to distinguish happiness as the ultimate end from other things like physical pleasure and amusement. For Aristotle, happiness is serious business that takes us beyond mere fun and the satisfaction of bodily appetites. Although such things are pleasurable and have their rightful place in human experience, they cannot serve as the ultimate basis for living *The Good Life*. Their value is instrumental. Even something as noble sounding as moral virtue cannot, for Aristotle, capture ultimate goodness. Why so?

Many would agree that moral virtue has intrinsic value. As the saying goes: *Virtue is its own reward*. While seemingly true, it is possible that we could live a virtuous life in misery and pain, seriously undermining anything that could be properly described as a happy or good life. As the down-to-earth practical philosopher Aristotle points out, courageous and just people can still suffer illnesses and misfortunes that make their lives something far less than happy. Further, the exercise of virtue may often require the involvement of others or the possession of material necessities for their expression. It's difficult to be generous, for example, if you have nothing to give or share. Thus, while moral virtue can be an intrinsic end, it is nonetheless incomplete in itself.

The fact that moral virtue is incomplete means that it, too, cannot serve as the ultimate basis of the good life. Make no mistake about the fact that morality is a good for Aristotle. Acting virtuously can even become pleasurable with proper character training—it can certainly be rewarding. For Aristotle, however, all of our actions and traits are subordinate to something higher: our ultimate purpose.

FEATURES OF THE ULTIMATE END

Aristotle argues that the ultimate end of life must fulfill three conditions. First, the ultimate end must be **self-sufficient**, in a way that moral virtue alone is not. It must make life desirable and lack nothing. Second, this end must be **final**. It must be desirable in itself. In this sense, the ultimate good is intrinsically, not instrumentally, valuable. While some ends like patience, honor or knowledge, for instance, can have both intrinsic and instrumental value, this is not the case with the ultimate end. It is always intrinsically valuable and represents the end of the road, so to speak. Third, this end must be **attainable** or achievable by action. A goal that cannot be achieved in principle may lead to such things as frustration and despair. For Aristotle, the only end that is final, self-sufficient, and attainable is happiness.

Now, if the final end—happiness—is not solely about virtue, pleasure, money, appetite satisfaction or amusement, then the question still remains, "What is it?"

In his remarks on Aristotle's *Nicomachean Ethics*, Aristotle scholar Jonathan Barnes elaborates upon *eudaimonia* to help us understand what Aristotle meant by it. He points out, for example, that Aristotle was not a **hedonist**. Happiness or *eudaimonia* is not about feeling pleasure, something with which many of us equate it. Although pleasure contributes to a complete and enjoyable life, it is not about having a constant succession of pleasurable experiences.

The Greek concept of *eudaimonia*, Jonathan Barnes tells us, should be understood as "well-living" and "well-acting." Happiness is a normative or value-related concept, not an emotional or psychological one. Happiness is not a feeling, but a *mode of living*. In particular, the mode of living in which one is *flourishing*. To express it otherwise, happiness for Aristotle is not a **state**, but an **activity**. Barnes goes on to suggest, "The notion of *eudaimonia* is closely tied, in a way in which the English common-sense notion of happiness is not, to **success**: the *eudaimon* is the person who makes a success of his life and actions, who realizes his aims and ambitions as a man, who fulfills himself."[15]

Barnes's close reading of Aristotle leads him to the conclusion that in the *Nicomachean Ethics* we are not directly being told how to be morally good people or even how to be "humanly happy." For Barnes, Aristotle is in fact trying to explain to us how to live successful human lives and how to fulfill ourselves as human beings. To the extent this is true, the *Nicomachean Ethics* is arguably more about character development than about rules of morality and principles of moral behavior. We live the good life by performing

"... we regard something as self-sufficient when all by itself it makes a life choiceworthy and lacking nothing; and that is what we think happiness does."
ARISTOTLE

Using Aristotelian insights, explore the relationship between achievement and successful living. Are the two notions roughly equivalent? Why or why not? Is it possible to achieve one's goals and yet be unsuccessful in life at the same time? Explain.

our distinctive function well, not by correctly applying principles of action or by living in accordance with moral maxims. So, what is our distinctive function and how do we fulfill it?

THE GOOD LIFE AS A FULFILLMENT OF OUR DISTINCTIVE FUNCTION

Aristotle's search for our **distinctive function** as humans begins with a comparison between plants and human beings. Plants and humans, he points out, share life in common; that is, they are both living organisms. They both grow, develop, and take in nourishment in the process of realizing their *biological capacities*. Aristotle thus concludes that mere existence based on nutrition and growth, is not peculiar to human beings. We share these aspects of life with plants.

Aristotle next compares us with animals. Humans share with animals a *sensory capacity* to feel and experience the world. In this respect, sense perception makes us no different than a horse, an ox, or any other animal. A life committed to sensation and physical appetite gratification is, therefore, not befitting of humans; it is the life of cattle as well.

Aristotle's thinking here is common in mainstream culture. People who overindulge their physical or sexual appetites are often unkindly referred to today as "pigs." Others, whose lives are largely devoted to doing nothing but lazing around all day, are said to be "vegging-out" or are called "couch-potatoes."

On a more serious note, we even sometimes consider terminating the lives of so-called "vegetables"—people in a vegetative state whose bodies manage to survive on life support systems, but who have no brain activity. Some argue that such a life is not worth living. In some people's minds, being human involves conscious awareness, choice, reaction, communication, and intentional activity beyond mere existence—that which entails more than just beating hearts and respiration.

In Aristotle's account, the good life—understood as the fulfillment of our distinctively human function—involves the exercise of our **rational capacities**. He says: "The function of man is a certain form of life, and that form of life is defined as the exercise of the soul's faculties and activities in association with rational principle."[16] Shortly, we will look at why the rational lifestyle is most befitting of humans, but before we do, let us examine some lifestyles that fall short of the human ideal of the good life. Once we know what the good life is not, we will be better able to appreciate what it is.

Kinds of Lifestyles

THE LIFESTYLE OF PLEASURE AND APPETITE GRATIFICATION

As already pointed out, there are individuals who believe that happiness and the good life are found in the **lifestyle of pleasure** and **appetite gratification**. This lifestyle can be enhanced by the accumulation of large sums of money. Money allows people to buy things in order to satisfy their physical and material desires, thereby helping them to experience lots of pleasure. Yet, money has only instrumental worth. Coins and bank notes have no intrinsic value. They are simply used to acquire other things beyond themselves. Money is merely a means. As such, it cannot be our ultimate end as defined by Aristotle.

As for pleasure, though it is considered very valuable and an important part of life for Aristotle, remember: he is not a hedonist. For Aristotle, to see life primarily or exclusively as the pursuit of pleasure would be to advocate for people an existence suitable for pigs and cattle. While pleasure has a certain intrinsic worth according to Aristotle, it must be a lesser good because, as mentioned, it also serves as an instrumental end. We pursue pleasure because we believe it will make us happy. If we did not believe this, then we would not seek it.

"How much money does it take to make a man happy? Just one more dollar."
JOHN D. ROCKEFELLER

THE STATESMAN'S LIFESTYLE

There are some people who see a certain vulgarity in a life devoted to the endless pursuit of money, pleasure, and material acquisition, so they pursue what, in their minds, is a higher or a more noble good. They choose to live a life of public service or **the statesman's lifestyle** of action, where honor is paramount.

As with the pursuit of pleasure, Aristotle rejects this lifestyle as our highest good. Such a life depends too much on the fickle opinions of others. Others bestow honor; honor is not something internally generated or something over which any individual has independent control. A person may work for a long time to gain people's praise and approval—things that can be withdrawn at any time.

Even if other virtues, besides the ambition related to honor, are regarded as the end of political life, problems still exist. Virtuous people can suffer terrible misfortunes. Their life circumstances may prevent them from acting or from expressing their virtues publicly. Lack of resources, for instance, may stop them from doing what they want to do or what they believe ought to be done in the public interest. Changing circumstances and other contingencies can seriously interfere with the statesman's well-being.

Furthermore, as with pleasure, the goods of the statesman are subordinate goods because they remain instrumentally valuable. People seek honor, for example, because they believe that it will make them happy. If honor did not make them happy and if misery were its result, then it would cease to be sought as an end. Happiness is *not* sought for the sake of honor; honor is sought for the sake of happiness. Honor is, therefore, something lower in the hierarchy of human goods.

THE CONTEMPLATIVE LIFESTYLE AS THE HIGHEST FORM OF HUMAN FUNCTIONING

Aristotle underscores the fact that it is in the *exercise of our rational capacities* that we distinguish ourselves from plant and animal life. It is reason that makes us unique and it is in rational activity that we express our highest level of functioning—our *entelechy*. In view of this, Aristotle defines **the good life** in rational terms. He explains: "For man ... the best and most pleasant life is the life of the intellect, since the intellect is in the fullest sense the man. So this life will also be the happiest."[17]

In Book I of the *Nicomachean Ethics*, Aristotle defines the eudaimonistic life of the intellect in the following terms: "An activity of the soul in accordance with virtue."[18]

Unlike being intelligent, which is *having* a power, being happy is *using* a power. Happiness is not a passive emotional or psychological *state*, but a rational *activity*.

As in translations of Plato, the word '**soul**' can be misleading here. It has no religious significance in Aristotle. It is the "thing" common to all living organisms. Its activities are things organisms do by nature's design; plants grow; animals move and have sensation. The highest unique part of the human soul involves the activity of reasoning.

Now, if the good thing is that which performs its function well, then for Aristotle the teleologist, the good person, is one who reasons well—like a virtuoso, we might say. To reason *in accordance with virtue* is not to display some kind of saintliness. To reason in accordance with virtue means that one reasons in an excellent way, i.e., that one performs the rational function well.

But some forms of intellectual life are better than others; Aristotle argues that **the contemplative lifestyle** is our highest good because, first, it is most *self-sufficient*. A lifestyle based on pleasure and enjoyment or political honor, for example, requires intellectual activity, but it also requires numerous externals and accessories. By contrast, people can practice contemplation alone, without much else, certainly with less than other lifestyles require.

Second, contemplation is *intrinsically choice-worthy*. "Nothing is gained from it except the act of contemplation, whereas from practical activities we expect to gain something more or less over and above the action."[19]

Third, contemplation, understood as the highest end that is *achievable* by human beings, provides the purest pleasure with the greatest permanence and enduring qualities. The contemplative lifestyle offers us the most leisure and as much freedom from fatigue as is humanly possible. Pursuing politics or warfare, by contrast, gives little time for rest.

Aristotle even goes so far as to suggest that the contemplative life transcends mere mortal existence and becomes something god-like. When we engage in rational activity, he says, we express that which is **divine** in us. All other practical activities are merely human and hence lower in the hierarchy of goods.

As an eminently common-sense philosopher, Aristotle recognizes the obstacles and difficulties that can easily prevent the attainment of happiness. On this note, Aristotle argues that happiness must be seen in the context of a complete life. People cannot be said to have lived happy lives by virtue of some momentary state or life event. Unlike pleasure or ecstasy, the flourishing of happiness is a long-term matter. The good life is one lived over an extended period of successful functioning as a human being.

Now, although riches cannot guarantee happiness (witness all the unhappy millionaires), Aristotle recognizes how, practically speaking, things like money and wealth can help out a lot. It is easier to be happy if you are rich than if you are penniless and living on the streets. Sure, having a good mental attitude and proper disposition are important to happiness, but so too is physical health. Aristotle would say that you cannot be happy in the fullest sense if, for example, you are grotesquely ugly, lonely, or childless.[20] Put simply, things can get in the way of anyone's personal happiness. A certain amount of luck is required; so too are the basic necessities of life.

But the good life is not about totally uninterrupted and continuous contemplation. It involves a kind of **balancing process**, in which intellectual, social, and physical needs are balanced. This balance can be achieved by a rational ordering of one's priorities, and

People often say that winning the lottery would make them happy or that buying new clothes or a new car would make them happy or that having sex with an attractive partner would make them happy. How would Aristotle reply? What do you think would make you happy? If Aristotle were alive today, how would he respond to you? How would you respond to Aristotle?

moderation in all pursuits. The key ideas here are *moderation* and *rational ordering*. These features mark how well a life is lived and whether it is virtuously lived with excellence.

Think of the unbalanced and driven workaholic businessperson striving to become rich and successful. That person could earn a lot of money and achieve a high degree of status and power, but still miss much in life. Unethical actions might have to be taken to push agendas or maximize quarterly profits. Possessed by things like ego, ambition, and greed, the individual might seldom slow down enough to actually enjoy life, feel gratitude, or appreciate one's blessings.

In the context of this immoderate frenzied lifestyle, friends might also be ignored because one is too busy; other people may need to be used for personal gain, personal hygiene could suffer, and stress-related illnesses could result from overwork. Obsessive efforts to make money or achieve success could easily result in conflicting priorities and responsibilities—thus making a pleasant, rationally ordered life extremely difficult to live.

Ironically, then, the obsessive success-seeker wishing to find happiness in wealth, pleasure, appetite gratification, and material acquisition may indeed become the architect of his or her own problems and dissatisfactions with life. And, on top of that, remember that pleasure and appetite gratification are sought for the sake of happiness, not the other way around. Such things are instrumentally, not intrinsically valuable.

Overly ambitious and frenzied money-hungry pleasure-seekers are not the only ones falling short of the Aristotelian ideal. As was discussed earlier, people who are disenchanted with the vulgar pursuit of pleasure and money often try to find happiness in public life. The problem is that such a life could be equally unbalanced as compared with the materialistic pleasure seeker. Personal sacrifice and time away from family and friends are frequently necessary. (Think of politicians in the nation's capital forced to move away from family and home to do their jobs.)

Also, since famous and powerful people may easily fall out of favor, political life will often be experienced as insecure. Still further, people devoted to public life typically need many so-called 'accessories'—security guards for protection, or perhaps advisors and a whole entourage of people for personal support. People in public life can thus lack not only balance, but also an *independent self-sufficiency* that is provided by the contemplative lifestyle.

Virtue and the Virtuous Lifestyle

The point has already been made that the life of unbroken contemplation is something god-like or divine for Aristotle. The *Eudaimon*'s complete and balanced life would of course include morality, practical wisdom, and the proper dispositions associated with moral virtue. It is in the exercise of both intellectual virtue as well as moral virtue that we fully realize our potentialities and function as human beings.

As something less than gods, however, most of us can aspire to live the contemplative life of intellectual virtue for only brief periods at a time. In fact, many of us cannot hope realistically to live it at all because of our life circumstances, temperaments, or character dispositions. Therefore, virtually all people for some of the time, and many people for most or all of the time, must be contented with the performance of the second-best of human activities: the exercise of moral virtue.

While a divinely gifted few may perhaps be capable of constant rational contemplation of knowledge and the truth, happiness for most of us mere mortals will consist in the practice of **virtue** and living an upright life. This being the case, let us examine Aristotle's understanding of virtue and the virtuous lifestyle so we can place happiness within reach of ordinary individuals. Though we should not discourage efforts to achieve ultimate happiness found through rational contemplation, we should recognize our personal and practical limitations and work toward *secondary happiness* as necessary.

> "So it is a matter of no little importance what sort of habits we form from the earliest age—it makes a vast difference, or rather all the difference in the world."
> ARISTOTLE

KINDS OF VIRTUE: INTELLECTUAL AND MORAL

For Aristotle, there are two kinds of virtue: **intellectual** and **moral**. Intellectual virtues are the virtues of intellectual activity. These virtues involve wisdom, for example, and they are acquired chiefly through instruction. Moral virtue, by contrast, includes things like temperance and courage and results as a product of **habit**. When we speak of individuals as morally good persons, we are not so much referring to their intellectual activities as to their dispositions, feelings and actions—the elements of moral virtue. As such, moral virtues are the virtues of character. Of course, reason and judgment are involved in virtuous conduct; deciding what to do entails practical wisdom and decision-making, though the target objects and processes of deliberation in each type of virtue (intellectual versus moral) are different.

According to Aristotle's **virtue ethics**, we can say that we are constituted by nature to have the *potential* for moral virtue, but that its *actualization* can occur only through practice. People become generous by giving generously, brave by doing brave acts, or just by performing just acts. But we could just as well become selfish, cowardly, or unjust. Unlike a stone's tendency to drop down to earth under normal gravitational conditions, a crystal vase's tendency to break, or even our tendency to grow from infants to adults, we are not naturally disposed to behave in this way or that. How we tend to perform actions is a matter of habit, and habits need to be formed—and they need to be formed well if they are to become virtuous dispositions. By comparison, anyone can become a builder by building, but one becomes an excellent builder only by building well. According to Aristotle, early habit formation is critical to the virtue of our character and, hence, our happiness. If we practice virtue in our actions and feelings, then we will eventually develop the character traits of a morally virtuous person. With that, we will conduct ourselves well in the world or, in more teleological terms, function well in our practical lives.

DOCTRINE OF THE MEAN

If we are to develop states of character that will ultimately enable us to fulfill our proper function as rational beings, or at least to find secondary happiness in the moral life, then we must try to live our lives in moderation or according to what is often called Aristotle's **Doctrine of the Mean**.

Moral virtue, for Aristotle, is a "purposive disposition, lying in a mean* that is relative to us and determined by a rational principle, and by that which a prudent man would use to determine it. It is a mean between two kinds of vice, one of excess and the other of deficiency."[21] Right conduct, then, is incompatible with excess or deficiency. You can talk about your accomplishments too much (boastfulness) or too little (understatement); you can rush into scary situations (rashness) or hide from anything that makes you afraid (cowardice). If something doesn't go your way, you can get extremely upset (irascibility) or you can be unmoved (lack of spirit). To live morally, we must find a midpoint or happy balance between two extremes. For example, you can talk about your accomplishments with *truthfulness*, face scary situations with *courage*, and be *patient* when things don't go your way. Put simply, the morally virtuous life can and must be lived in **moderation**.

In arithmetic and geometry, the 'mean' has a precise calculable value; but in Aristotle's application of this notion to virtue, figuring out what the mean is between two extremes is not a simple straightforward matter of calculation. It's clear, for example, that boastfulness is too much and understatement is too little, but we can't just do some kind of mathematical calculation to determine what's right exactly. And even where there are numbers involved, they don't necessarily yield the answer either. Suppose, for example, you're wondering about how much to spend on a wedding gift. Let's say $1000 is clearly too much (prodigality) and $10 is clearly too little (reflecting stinginess or what Aristotle calls illiberality); that doesn't mean that the right amount (displaying generosity/liberality) is exactly the midway point between the two opposite figures if calculated thus: ($1000 + $10) ÷ 2, or $505. Of course, you may want to be generous, but Aristotle's idea gives no confident guidance about what this mean might be, even with such a calculation. He would agree that the right amount for you to spend, as a college student with a part-time job, say, would be stinginess for a someone among the top 1% of wage-earners, and prodigality for someone with no income. He says that when deciding what constitutes moderation, we must determine the mean from our individual perspectives. To further illustrate the point: For a tiny person, a double veggie-burger may be an excessive amount of food, but it may not be enough food for a professional football player. Nutritional needs vary according to physical size, and considerations of moderation must take this into account.

The fact that Aristotle's views don't guide us with any universality or precision has resulted in some criticism. But Aristotle suggests that *we should not demand more precision from an inquiry than the inquiry itself permits*. The study of moral virtue, or at least the practice of moral virtue, is not an exact science. What Aristotle's views are designed for is to give you a rather loose framework for thought about what actions are virtuous, given your circumstances. Thinking about what's too much, and what's too little, may help you think about the virtuous mean.

The performance of a virtuous act is no guarantee that one is actually virtuous. A soldier may run into battle because the commanding officer may be more frightening than the enemy. Such an act would not be indicative of courage, though running into battle is something the courageous person would do. Likewise, an individual may avoid stealing because he or she fears punishment, not because of any virtuous trait such as honesty. For Aristotle, the virtuous person must choose to be virtuous, enjoy the virtuous act, and perform it without regret. Virtue becomes its own reward. Charitable behavior is

---

*   A mean is a middle point, equally distant from two extremes.

thus displayed knowingly, cheerfully and joyfully, not under pressure, with resentment or with bitter reluctance. In the context of physical pleasure, Aristotle writes:

> A man who abstains from bodily pleasures and enjoys the very fact of so doing is temperate; if he finds it irksome he is licentious. Again, the man who faces danger gladly, or at least without distress, is brave; the one who feels distressed is a coward. For it is with pleasures and pains that moral goodness is concerned. Pleasure induces us to behave badly, and pain to shrink from fine actions. Hence the importance (as Plato says) of having been trained in some way from infancy to feel joy and grief at the right things: true education is precisely this.[22]

Besides the necessity of being performed gladly, without pain or regret, if actions are to be considered virtuous, they must also fulfill certain other conditions. Individuals must know what they are doing; they must consciously and deliberately choose to perform virtuous acts; virtue is not a matter of whim. Also, they must perform them for their own sake. Worthy of note too is the fact that the action performed must not be an isolated incident, but rather a manifestation of an enduring state of character. According to Aristotle, one donation does not a charitable person make. Nor is giving only to enhance one's reputation or to reduce one's taxable income a virtue. The act of giving must be performed for itself.

THINKING ABOUT YOUR THINKING

Think about the last time you posted something on social media. What did you post? Why did you post what you did? What character traits of yours factored into the posting? Would you say those traits are habitual tendencies of yours? If so, are they habitual tendencies that are making your life go well or would you be better off if you increased or diminished these character traits so that you acted with more or fewer or them?

For non-users of social media: If you don't use social media, why not? What character traits factor into your decision not to use it? Do these traits undermine or contribute to your personal flourishing? Why or why not?

For further thought: If you wanted to, what would you have to do in order to modify your character traits?

Also important to note is that virtue does not apply to all activities—a proper mean does not exist for some types of behavior. Although one may drink or eat in moderation, one cannot murder, steal or commit adultery in moderation; nor can one establish a virtuous level of hatred, envy, or spite. These attitudes, feelings, and related behaviors are bad in themselves. Since these things are always wrong, it is absurd to look for deficiency, moderation, or excess where they are concerned.

In his *Nicomachean Ethics*, Aristotle mentions a number of virtues capturing the means between various vices of excess and deficiency. Courage, for instance, is the mean between rashness and cowardice, while modesty is the mean between shyness and shamelessness. These are common and easily appreciated virtues.

As you read Aristotle's discussion of virtues, take time to reflect on where you would place yourself on the scale between excess and deficiency for each virtuous trait. Such a self-reflection might offer you some direction for future character development.

TABLE 5.1 Aristotle's Table of Virtues and Vices[23]

Sphere of Action or Feeling	Excess	Mean	Deficiency
Fear and Confidence	Rashness	Courage	Cowardice
Pleasure and Pain	Licentiousness / Self-indulgence	Temperance	Insensibility
Getting and Spending (minor)	Prodigality	Liberality	Illiberality / Meanness
Getting and Spending (major)	Vulgarity / Tastelessness	Magnificence	Pettiness / Stinginess
Honor and Dishonor (major)	Vanity	Magnanimity	Pusillanimity
Honor and Dishonor (minor)	Ambition / Empty vanity	Proper ambition / Pride	Unambitiousness / Undue humility
Anger	Irascibility	Patience / Good temper	Lack of spirit / Unirascibility
Self-expression	Boastfulness	Truthfulness	Understatement / Mock modesty
Conversation	Buffoonery	Wittiness	Boorishness
Social Conduct	Obsequiousness	Friendliness	Cantankerousness
Shame	Shyness	Modesty	Shamelessness
Indignation	Envy	Righteous indignation	Malicious enjoyment / Spitefulness

Aristotle, *Nicomachean Ethics*[24]

The Nicomachean Ethics *is the title given to Aristotle's best-known treatise on ethics and, arguably, the first treatise distinctively on ethics. "Nicomachean" is presumably in reference to Aristotle's son, Nicomachus, who may have edited the work or to whom Aristotle may have dedicated the work. In the ten parts or "books" that comprise the* Nicomachean Ethics, *Aristotle offers his account of happiness and a systematic study of virtue that includes his philosophical examinations of justice, pleasure, and friendship. The following selection comes from chapters 6 to 9 in Book 2. The virtue of character is the main topic of that Book.*

——

A PROVISIONAL DEFINITION OF VIRTUE

So virtue is a purposive disposition, lying in a mean that is relative to us and determined by a rational principle, and by that which a prudent man would use to determine it. It is a mean between two kinds of vice, one of excess and the other of deficiency; and also for this reason, that whereas these vices fall short of or exceed the right measure in both feelings and actions, virtue discovers the mean and chooses it. Thus from the point of view of its essence and the definition of its real nature, virtue is a mean; but in respect of what is right and best, it is an extreme.

BUT THE RULE OF CHOOSING THE MEAN CANNOT BE APPLIED TO SOME ACTIONS AND FEELINGS, WHICH ARE ESSENTIALLY EVIL

But not every action or feeling admits of a mean; because some have names that directly connote depravity, such as malice, shamelessness and envy, and among actions adultery, theft and murder. All these, and more like them, are so called as being evil in themselves; it is not the excess or deficiency of them that is evil. In their case, then, it is impossible to act rightly; one is always wrong. Nor does acting rightly or wrongly in such cases depend upon circumstances—whether a man commits adultery with the right woman or at the right time or in the right way, because to do anything of that kind is simply wrong. One might as well claim that there is a mean and excess and deficiency even in unjust or cowardly or intemperate actions. On that basis there must be a mean of excess, a mean of deficiency, an excess of excess and a deficiency of deficiency. But just as in temperance and courage there can be no mean or excess or deficiency, because the mean is in a sense an extreme, so there can be no mean or excess or deficiency in the vices that we mentioned; however done, they are wrong. For in general neither excess nor deficiency admits of a mean, nor does a mean admit of excess and deficiency.

THE DOCTRINE OF THE MEAN APPLIED TO PARTICULAR VIRTUES

But a generalization of this kind is not enough; we must apply it to particular cases. When we are discussing actions, although general statements have a wider application, particular statements are closer to the truth. This is because actions are concerned with particular facts, and theories must be brought into harmony with these. Let us, then, take these instances from the diagram.*

In the field of Fear and Confidence the mean is Courage; and of those who go to extremes the man who exceeds in fearlessness has no name to describe him (there are many nameless cases), the one who exceeds in confidence is called Rash, and the one who shows an excess of fear and a deficiency of confidence is called Cowardly. In the field of Pleasures and Pains—not in all, especially not in all pains—the mean is Temperance, the excess Licentiousness; cases of defective response to pleasures scarcely occur, and therefore people of this sort too have no name to describe them, but let us class them as Insensible. In the field of Giving and Receiving Money the mean is Liberality, the excess and deficiency are Prodigality and Illiberality; but these show excess and deficiency in contrary ways to one another: the prodigal man goes too far in spending and not far enough in getting, while the illiberal man goes too far in getting money and not far enough in spending it. This present

---

*   Aristotle presented his works as lectures to his students. At this point he must have shown a diagram very much like the reconstructed one, just above.

account is in outline and summary, which is all that we need at this stage; we shall give a more accurate analysis later.

But there are other dispositions too that are concerned with money. There is a mean called Magnificence* (because the magnificent is not the same as the liberal man: the one deals in large and the other in small outlays); the excess is Tastelessness and Vulgarity, the deficiency Pettiness. These are different from the extremes between which liberality lies; how they differ will be discussed later. In the field of Public Honor and Dishonor the mean is Magnanimity, the excess is called a sort of Vanity, and the deficiency Pusillanimity. And just as liberality differs, as we said, from magnificence in being concerned with small outlays, so there is a state related to Magnanimity in the same way, being concerned with small honors, while magnanimity is concerned with great ones; because it is possible to aspire to [small] honors in the right way, or to a greater or less degree than is right. The man who goes too far in his aspirations is called Ambitious, the one who falls short, Unambitious; the one who is a mean between them has no name. This is true also of the corresponding dispositions, except that the ambitious man's is called Ambitiousness. This is why the extremes lay claim to the intermediate territory. We ourselves sometimes call the intermediate man ambitious and sometimes unambitious; that is, we sometimes commend the ambitious and sometimes the unambitious. Why it is that we do this will be explained in our later remarks. Meanwhile let us continue our discussion of the remaining virtues and vices, following the method already laid down.

In the field of Anger, too, there is excess, deficiency and the mean. They do not really possess names, but we may call the intermediate man Patient and the mean Patience; and of the extremes the one who exceeds can be Irascible and his vice Irascibility, while the one who is deficient can be Spiritless and the deficiency Lack of Spirit.

There are also three other means which, though different, somewhat resemble each other. They are all concerned with what we do and say in social intercourse, but they differ in this respect, that one is concerned with truthfulness in such intercourse, the other two with pleasantness—one with pleasantness in entertainment, the other with pleasantness in every department of life. We must therefore say something about these too, in order that we may better discern that in all things the mean is to be commended, while the extremes are neither commendable nor right, but reprehensible. Most of these too have no names; but, as in the other cases, we must try to coin names for them in the interest of clarity and to make it easy to follow the argument.

Well, then, as regards Truth the intermediate man may be called Truthful and the mean Truthfulness; pretension that goes too far may be Boastfulness and the man who is disposed to it a Boaster, while that which is deficient may be called Irony and its exponent Ironical. As for Pleasantness in Social Entertainment, the intermediate man is Witty, and the disposition Wit; the excess is Buffoonery and the indulger in it a Buffoon; the man who is deficient is a kind of Boor and his disposition Boorishness. In the rest of the sphere of the Pleasant—life in general—the person who is pleasant in the right way is Friendly and the mean is Friendliness; the person who goes too far, if he has no motive, is Obsequious; if his motive is self-interest, he is a Flatterer. The man who is deficient and is unpleasant in all circumstances is Cantankerous and Ill-tempered.

There are mean states also in the sphere of feelings and emotions. Modesty is not a virtue, but the modest man too is praised. Here too one person is called intermediate and another excessive—like the Shy man who is overawed at anything. The man who feels too little shame or none at all is Shameless, and the intermediate man is Modest. Righteous Indignation is a mean between Envy and Spite, and they are all concerned with feelings of pain or pleasure at the experiences of our neighbors. The man who feels righteous indignation is distressed at instances of undeserved good fortune, but the envious man goes further and is distressed at *any* good fortune, while the spiteful man is so far from feeling distress that he actually rejoices.† ...

---

* The Greek word here may also be translated as 'great bounty' or 'munificence.' It means spending large amounts freely, but not ostentatiously.

† It's not exactly clear what's meant here. Some authorities feel that the Greek text we have is missing some words at this point, or that Aristotle later amended here.

THE MEAN IS OFTEN NEARER TO ONE EXTREME THAN TO THE OTHER, OR SEEMS NEARER BECAUSE OF OUR NATURAL TENDENCIES

Thus there are three dispositions, two of them vicious (one by way of excess, the other of deficiency), and one good, the mean. They are all in some way opposed to one another: the extremes are contrary both to the mean and to each other, and the mean to the extremes. For just as the equal is greater compared with the less, and less compared with the greater, so the mean states (in both feelings and actions) are excessive compared with the deficient and deficient compared with the excessive. A brave man appears rash compared with a coward, and cowardly compared with a rash man; similarly a temperate man appears licentious compared with an insensible one and insensible compared with a licentious one, and a liberal man prodigal compared with an illiberal one and illiberal compared with a prodigal one. This is the reason why each extreme type tries to push the mean nearer to the other: the coward calls the brave man rash, the rash man calls him a coward; and similarly in all other cases. But while all these dispositions are opposed to one another in this way, the greatest degree of contrariety is that which is found between the two extremes. For they are separated by a greater interval from one another than from the mean, just as the great is further from the small, and the small from the great, than either is from the equal. Again, some extremes seem to bear a resemblance to a mean; e.g. rashness seems like courage, and prodigality like liberality; but between the extremes there is always the maximum dissimilarity. Now contraries are by definition as far distant as possible from one another; hence the further apart things are, the more contrary they will be. In some cases it is the deficiency, in others the excess, that is more opposed to the mean; for instance, the more direct opposite of courage is not the excess, rashness, but the deficiency, cowardice; and that of temperance is not the deficiency, insensibility, but the excess, licentiousness. This result is due to two causes. One lies in the nature of the thing itself. When one extreme has a closer affinity and resemblance to the mean, we tend to oppose to the mean not that extreme but the other. For instance, since rashness is held to be nearer to courage and more like it than cowardice is, it is

cowardice that we tend to oppose to courage, because the extremes that are further from the mean are thought to be more opposed to it. This is one cause, the one that lies in the *thing*. The other lies in ourselves. It is the things towards which we have the stronger natural inclination that seem to us more opposed to the mean. For example, we are naturally more inclined towards pleasures, and this makes us more prone towards licentiousness than towards temperance; so we describe as more contrary to the mean those things towards which we have the stronger tendency. This is why licentiousness, the excess, is more contrary to temperance.

SUMMING UP OF THE FOREGOING DISCUSSION, TOGETHER WITH THREE PRACTICAL RULES FOR GOOD CONDUCT

We have now said enough to show that moral virtue is a mean, and in what sense it is so: that it is a mean between two vices, one of excess and the other of deficiency, and that it is such because it aims at hitting the mean point in feelings and actions. For this reason it is a difficult business to be good; because in any given case it is difficult to find the mid-point—for instance, not everyone can find the center of a circle; only the man who knows how. So too it is easy to get angry—anyone can do that—or to give and spend money; but to feel or act towards the right person to the right extent at the right time for the right reason in the right way—that is not easy, and it is not everyone that can do it. Hence to do these things well is a rare, laudable and fine achievement.

For this reason anyone who is aiming at the mean should (1) keep away from that extreme which is more contrary to the mean, just as Calypso advises:

Far from this surf and surge keep thou thy ship.*

For one of the extremes is always more erroneous than the other; and since it is extremely difficult to hit the mean, we must take the next best course, as they say, and choose the lesser of the evils; and this will be most

---

* In Homer's *Odyssey* (12.219), Calypso was a minor deity who took Odysseus prisoner for seven years. But Aristotle is mistaken: these words are said by Odysseus, conveying to his steersman Circe's advice to avoid the whirlpool of Charybdis which will engulf them all and steer nearer to the monster Scylla who will devour only some of them.

readily done in the way that we are suggesting. (2) We must notice the errors into which we ourselves are liable to fall (because we all have different natural tendencies—we shall find out what ours are from the pleasure and pain that they give us), and we must drag ourselves in the contrary direction; for we shall arrive at the mean by pressing well away from our failing—just like somebody straightening a warped piece of wood. (3) In every situation one must guard especially against pleasure and pleasant things, because we are not impartial judges of pleasure. So we should adopt the same attitude towards it as the Trojan elders did towards Helen,* and constantly repeat their pronouncement; because if in this way we relieve ourselves of the attraction, we shall be less likely to go wrong.

---

* In Homer's *Iliad* (3.156–60), Helen, the most beautiful woman in the world, is kidnapped by the Trojans, leading to the Trojan War. Peace is promised if she is returned to the Greeks, but the Trojans love her for her beauty. Troy's elders, realizing that this love would result in disaster, against their own affections urge that Helen go.

READING QUESTIONS

1. According to Aristotle, why is it "a difficult business to be good"? He claims that virtue is a mean, so why is it not as easy as finding a mathematical mean?

2. To illustrate the differences between virtue and vice, describe a case in which two people perform the same type of action, but one person acts with virtue and the other person does not.

3. Would Aristotle agree with the following statement: It is possible to be virtuous and live a good life by luck alone? Why or why not.

4. Plato was influential in Aristotle's thinking. Using what you have learned in this chapter, consider the way(s) Plato's ethical theory and Aristotle's ethical theory are similar. In what way(s) are their ethical theories different? To help you answer those questions, consider what you would need to know in order to put their respective theories into action and how you would know it.

5.3 Jeremy Bentham's Utilitarian Ethics

In the world of moral philosophy, when the subject of **utilitarianism** is raised, the name **Jeremy Bentham** is one of the first to come to mind. For many, his name is virtually synonymous with this ethical theory. It should be noted, however, that Bentham was not the sole inventor of this theoretical perspective, nor its sole proponent. Elements of utilitarianism are found in the writings of such thinkers as Thomas Hobbes, John Locke, and John Stuart Mill, who influentially refined the theory to defend it against criticisms to which Bentham's version was subject. Bentham's significant contribution comes from his efforts to connect and apply utilitarianism's basic principles to the problems of his time. He sought to provide nineteenth-century English society with philosophical foundations for moral thought and practical social reform.

Bentham believed that ethical questions could be answered in a **spirit of scientific objectivity**. He rejected such things as tradition, aristocratic privilege, and religious faith as legitimate bases for moral evaluation. He believed that such things too easily serve the interests of the dominant ruling classes and that they lead to the continued mistreatment of the poor and disenfranchised.

Rather than appeal to religious, political, or cultural authorities, Bentham chose to adopt a much more commonsense empirical approach to the improvement of society. He argued that people's actions and those of government could, and should, be evaluated according to how much good they produce. For Bentham, *no action is necessarily right or wrong in itself*. The ethical value of anything is determined by its real-life results. Utilitarianism is, therefore, a form of **consequentialism**. It is the consequences—the *effects*—of an action or rule that establish its moral worth. The action or rule that generates the most **utility**, or minimizes the most disutility, is the morally right action. Thus, morality requires of us that we perform that action or accept that rule.

The Principle of Utility

In his most famous work, *An Introduction to the Principles of Morals and Legislation* (1789), Bentham outlines his objective basis for morality. He calls it the **principle of utility**. Bentham writes:

> By the principle of utility is meant that principle which approves of every action whatsoever, according to the tendency which it appears to have to augment or diminish the happiness of the party whose interest is in question: or, what is the same thing in other words, to promote or to oppose that happiness. I say of every action whatsoever; and therefore not only of every action of a private individual, but of every measure of government.[25]

The term *utility* is one you might not use in everyday conversation. Think of it as the same thing as *benefit, advantage, pleasure, happiness,* and *goodness*. Whatever prevents mischief, pain, evil, suffering, or unhappiness also has utility or utilitarian value for Bentham. In essence, utility means pleasure and the absence of pain.

Bentham's utilitarianism is based on the principle that it is human nature for us to seek pleasure and to avoid pain. To quote Bentham: "Nature has placed mankind under the governance of two sovereign masters, pain and pleasure. It is for them alone to point out what we ought to do, as well as to determine what we shall do."[26]

If this were all Bentham were saying, that we are motivated by pleasure and pain alone, then he would be making nothing other than a psychological claim about human behavior that we could try to verify empirically. To assert that humans are motivated by a self-interested pursuit of pleasure would simply make Bentham a *psychological hedonist*. However, in making a connection between moral or ethical *oughts* and *pleasure*, Bentham is suggesting that right and wrong, or good and bad, cannot properly be understood in any other way than by hedonist value. It is only pleasure and the avoidance of pain that give actions any real value, so the right or good thing to do (the thing we ought to do) is to maximize overall pleasure, and, conversely, the wrong or bad thing (the thing we ought not to do) is to reduce or minimize the amount of pleasure. It is also wrong—and the only wrong—to produce pain, misery, and suffering.

Bentham's focus on pleasure is reminiscent of Aristippus, the Hedonist we learned about in Chapter 3. To differentiate Bentham from Aristippus, it's important to note that, for Bentham, the *intensity of pleasure produced* is not the only way to judge the relative worth between actions, as it was for Aristippus. As we'll see in a moment, Bentham allows for pleasures to be compared in terms of their *purity*, for example, in a way that Aristippus didn't. Also, in contrast to Aristippus, Bentham held that potential pleasures in the future can sometimes outweigh *actual pleasures* in the present. Bentham's "hedonic calculus" also

Jeremy Bentham

Jeremy Bentham was born in London in 1748. An intellectually precocious child, he was already studying Latin grammar by the age of 4, and at age of 12 he enrolled at Queen's College, Oxford. In 1763 Bentham earned a Bachelor of Arts degree and thereupon began legal studies at Lincoln's Inn. In that same year, he returned to Oxford for what turned out to be one of the most decisive experiences of his intellectual life.

Bentham attended a number of lectures on law given by Sir William Blackstone, who presented his legal theory based on *natural rights*. Regarding this theory as little more than rhetorical nonsense, Bentham began setting the stage for the development of his own utilitarian conception of law, justice, and society.

Bentham earned his Master of Arts degree in 1766 and then proceeded to London. Having never really developed a fondness for the legal profession, he decided against becoming a practicing lawyer. Instead, he embarked on a literary career, the basic object of which was to bring order and moral defensibility into what he perceived as the deplorable state of the law and the social realities it made possible in his day.

Jeremy Bentham can thus be regarded as a social reformer. He undertook the task of trying to modernize British political and social institutions. There is little doubt that it was due, at least in part, to his influence that an historical landmark was established, the Reform Bill of 1832, which transformed the nature of British politics. To simplify a complex process: the control of Britain's Parliament was taken away from the landed aristocracy and placed into the hands of the urban bourgeoisie.

On a personal note, Jeremy Bentham was the godfather of John Stuart Mill, who went on to become a famous philosopher, social reformer, and author of the book *Utilitarianism*. Mill, in his old age, became the godfather of Bertrand Russell, profiled in Chapter 1 of this book. Starting with Bentham, therefore, a philosophical lineage evolved that had political activism as an essential element.

suggests that judgments about pleasure are not purely a matter of individual preference or choice, as they were for Aristippus; rather, that they can be made *objectively* using a kind of mathematical computation.

Is-Ought Fallacy

Now, returning to Bentham's leap from psychological hedonism to the principle of utility, it might make good intuitive sense to you. From a purely logical perspective, however, it falls prey to what, in logic, is called the "**is-ought fallacy**." When this fallacy is committed, the reasoner tries unjustifiably to derive a moral *ought* from an *is* of experience. To illustrate, just because it is factually true that people lie, kill, cheat, and steal, we cannot conclude solely on that basis that they morally *should* or *ought* to do so. The reason is that the moral content of the conclusion isn't found elsewhere in the premise, which is silent on morality and merely states a fact. It is a problem of logic whenever brand-new information appears in the conclusion of an argument because it means that the reasons don't actually support that conclusion. Further reasons are required. In this case, reasons with moral content are required for a conclusion about morality. Those moral reasons and the moral conclusion that they support might even lead to the determination that the "is" of how people behave is what "ought" to be repressed, mitigated, and somehow extinguished. As we can see, then, arguing from what is true to what ought to be is a problematic step in Bentham's reasoning.

Bentham did not deal at length with the is-ought problem inherent in his utilitarianism. What he did was to suggest that all other moral theories were either vague and inconsistent, or else reducible to pleasure and the principle of utility in the end. Furthermore, providing no substantial defense or justification of the principle of utility as the basis of morality, he simply concluded that "that which is used to prove everything else, cannot itself be proved: a chain of proofs must have their commencement somewhere. To give such proof is as impossible as it is needless."[27]

The Hedonic Calculus

To help individuals, as well as lawmakers and legislators, decide what ought to be done in any given set of circumstances, Bentham developed what has come to be known as the **hedonic calculus**. As the term suggests, the hedonic calculus involves the calculation of pleasure or *hedonistic* consequences. Remember that Bentham wanted to conduct moral inquiry in a spirit of scientific objectivity. By using the hedonic calculus to determine the pleasures and pains produced by any particular action or policy, say, he thought we could decide empirically on what is the right or good thing to do.

The hedonic calculus might be more understandable if you see it as a kind of *cost-benefit analysis*. In moral and ethical decision-making, Bentham recommends that *the bottom line should be the maximization of pleasure and the minimization or elimination of pain*. Actions producing the greatest happiness for the individual or group concerned are actions we morally ought to perform.

The hedonic calculus gives us seven criteria by which to measure the pleasure and pain produced by any particular action:

Intensity:	Ask how strong the pleasure or emotional satisfaction is.
Duration:	Ask how long the pleasure will last. Will it be short-lived or long-lasting?
Certainty:	Ask how likely or unlikely it is that pleasure will actually result. What is the probability of the result?
Propinquity:	Ask how soon the pleasure will occur. How near are the consequences?
Fecundity:	Ask how likely it is that the action will produce more pleasure in the future. What will the results be down the road?
Purity:	Ask if there will be any pain accompanying the action (some pleasurable acts are accompanied by painful elements). Is there some bad you have to take with the good?
Extent:	Ask how many people will be affected by the considered action.

Suppose you have to decide between doing *A* and not-doing *A*. Which action should you choose from a utilitarian perspective? First, look at *A* in regard to its intensity, duration, and other elements of the hedonic calculus. How much pleasure and how much pain is produced? On balance, is there more pleasure or more pain? Now, consider not-doing

Do you agree with Bentham's description of human nature? Do you think that pleasure and pain are the only things that motivate us? Would it be wise to accept an *unnatural* morality, one that requires us to work against our natural urges and inclinations? Is it even possible to go against our natural urges and inclinations? Discuss.

A. Again, calculate the quantities of pain and pleasure, using the criteria of the hedonic calculus. Once the calculations are done for each alternative action—doing *A* versus not doing *A*—compare them. The alternative action producing the most pleasure is the morally preferable one. If both alternatives produce a net balance of pain, then the alternative producing the least pain is preferable.

If the implications of the considered action go beyond the individual to include others, then Bentham recommends that we repeat the hedonic calculus taking their interests into account as well. What is the net balance of pleasure and pain for others if alternative *A* is performed? What are the hedonic consequences for them if *A* is not performed? Note that *Bentham was interested not only in maximizing the happiness of the individual but also in maximizing the happiness of the broader community*. Thus, if our actions have an impact on others, then we must account for them in our hedonic calculation.

Bentham was not unrealistic. For him, "It is not to be expected that this [hedonic calculation] process should be strictly pursued previously to every moral judgment, or to every legislative or judicial operation."[28] To do a formal hedonic calculation every time we were about to act would be highly impractical. Yet according to Bentham, each of us goes through some semblance of this process on a commonsense intuitive level, only we may do it so quickly that we are virtually unconscious that we have done it. We may not wittingly go through all of the criteria outlined by Bentham, but in general terms, we probably go through some kind of weighing and balancing process, considering pros and cons before we act.

A Hedonic Calculation

When making a moral or ethical decision, Bentham suggests you attach numerical values to each of the elements listed above. You can use any scale you like. For our purposes, let us use a scale ranging from -100 to +100. Negative values indicate pain; positive values indicate pleasure. Thus, -100 means high pain, -50 means moderate pain, and -10 means low pain. Similarly, +100 stands for high pleasure, +50 stands for moderate pleasure, and +10 stands for low pleasure. Once the scale is determined, you can then perform a pain-pleasure calculation of alternative courses of action.

The hedonic calculus can be made more understandable by working out an actual example. Let us say that you are back in high school and that you are thinking about going on to a college or university in a distant city. The school you have in mind has the best program in your chosen field, and for years you have longed to attend it. The problem is that you have become involved in a serious relationship with someone who prefers that you stay in your hometown and find employment at the local manufacturing plant. You two have discussed the possibility of marriage, though no firm commitments have been made either way. Your dilemma involves choosing between (A) staying at home to work and continuing to develop your personal relationship with your special someone; and (B) going away to school and pursuing your career and academic dreams. What is the best thing to do? Let's find out using the hedonic calculus.

Note that a complete calculation would entail not only a consideration of your interests but also a consideration of the interests of the other party involved. For brevity's sake, we will do a partial calculation based only on your interests. The values given to each part of the decision would likely vary in real life from person to person. For demonstration purposes, I will take the liberty here of reading your mind and feeling your emotions. Afterwards, you will be prompted to use Bentham's hedonic calculus to think through a decision on your own.

ALTERNATIVE A—STAY AT HOME AND WORK IN THE LOCAL PLANT

1. Intensity: If I choose to stay at home, I will probably experience intense feelings of disappointment. I may also become regretful and may possibly resent how another person has frustrated the pursuit of my personal dream. Some of the resentment and anger I feel will be diminished by the loving feelings I have for my partner and by the love I feel for my family. **(-50)**

2. Duration: Any acute feelings of anger and resentment are likely to subside in a relatively short period of time. Nagging doubts, however, may remain for years, causing unpleasantness and insecurity. Time may heal, but the emotional scars may remain. **(-25)**

3. Certainty: Who knows? What people want often changes. I might change my mind about working at the plant. It is possible that I will learn to like it there, though I really believe I will not. **(-10)**

4. Propinquity: The frustration and disappointment will result fairly soon. It is now July and classes start in September. The mental pain is not that far down the road. **(-50)**

5. Fecundity: If I stay at home, I can save a lot of money. Mom and Dad will not accept rent from me, so I will be able to save almost everything I earn. I also will not have to pay ridiculously high tuition fees that I cannot afford. I will be able to invest the money I earn in the stock market. I do not think I could ever recoup what I would lose in wages, residence fees, and tuition by going off to school. **(+100)**

6. Purity: Sure, there will be financial gains if I stay at home, but I will experience considerable pain due to possible missed opportunities. There will be things I never learn and people I never meet because I opt for the financially preferable course of action. **(-25)**

7. Extent: Other people will be affected by my decision. Mom and Dad do not value formal education, so they would prefer that I stay home. My partner also prefers that I stay home. I get the feeling that people in the neighborhood would also like me to stay. They say they would miss me if I went away. **(+100)**

Utilitarian Value of Alternative A		
	Utility	**Disutility**
Intensity:		-50
Duration:		-25
Certainty:		-10
Propinquity:		-50
Fecundity:	+100	
Purity:		-25
Extent:	+100	
Total	**+200**	**-160**
Result:	Alternative A would produce +40 net units of pleasure	

ALTERNATIVE B—GO AWAY TO SCHOOL

1. Intensity: If I choose to go away to school, the excitement will be wonderful. I will be enthusiastic, energized, and optimistic about going to a new place, meeting new people, and learning new things. **(+75)**

2. Duration: I know my positive feelings will tend to subside in time. Reality sinks in during exams. I am likely to miss my family and special loved one. I know I can sometimes easily become bored. Nonetheless, I think the experience will be great and I will like it. **(+25)**

3. Certainty: Well, if I go, I am pretty certain of having fun and enjoying myself. I have been accepted both at the school and at the residence, so I know that there are no practical obstacles preventing me from going. I guess it is possible my roommate and I will be incompatible, but I will hope for the best. **(+75)**

4. Propinquity: The good times will start soon. We are just weeks away from homecoming, pub-crawls, intermural sports—you name it. If I choose to go to school, I will not have to wait long to enjoy myself. **(+75)**

5. Fecundity: I know that by going to school, I am going to cultivate my mind and possibly open up new horizons I never dreamed of before. I do not know of anyone who has ever been hurt by gaining more knowledge and understanding. On the downside, I do stand to lose a lot of money over the next four years. Getting a job at the plant would have paid well, and I could have invested my earnings. No doubt about it, I will lose in the immediate future, but I hope to make it up over my lifetime. **(+25)**

6. Purity: I know that going off to school is not all fun and games, at least if I want to pass. Studying is hard and so are exams. You cannot party when you are doing an all-nighter mastering Plato. Furthermore, I am likely to encounter professors and courses I do not like very much. I guess school has its good and bad sides, just like everything else. **(+10)**

7. Extent: I know the people around me will be sorry to see me go. They will be saddened and possibly lonely. I hope my partner does not take my decision personally. I do not mean to hurt, but I cannot help but think that hurt feelings will result anyway. **(-50)**

Utilitarian Value of Alternative B		
	Utility	**Disutility**
Intensity:	+75	
Duration:	+25	
Certainty:	+75	
Propinquity:	+75	
Fecundity:	+25	
Purity:	+10	
Extent:		-50
Total	**+285**	**-50**
Result:	Alternative B would produce +235 net units of pleasure	

Comparing Alternatives		
	A	**B**
	Staying at home	*Going to school*
Intensity:	-50	+75
Duration:	-25	+25
Certainty:	-10	+75
Propinquity:	-50	+75
Fecundity:	+100	+25
Purity:	-25	+10
Extent:	+100	-50
Total	**+40**	**+235**
Result:	Alternative B would produce +235 net units of pleasure	

Findings: Alternative B produces greater pleasure than Alternative A.

Conclusion: Alternative B is the right thing to do.

The Theory of Sanctions

If, as Bentham claims, pleasure and the avoidance of pain is what motivates people to behave as they do, then what is preventing them from doing anything they want at any time they want, even if this entails diminishing the pleasure or increasing the displeasure of others? For Bentham, the answer is found in the notion of **sanctions**. Think of a sanction as a source of pleasure and pain that acts to give *binding force* to any law or rule of conduct. Sanctions can also be seen as rewards and punishments or as causal and determining factors influencing our behavior.

According to Bentham, we, as individuals, respond egoistically to sanctions, trying to maximize our own pleasure and minimize our own pain. We generally avoid behaving in ways that lead to pain and other negative sanctions for ourselves, preferring instead to act in ways that lead to pleasure, happiness, personal benefit, or satisfaction for ourselves. Sanctions govern what we do, perhaps more than we sometimes realize.

Sanctions come in a variety of types. *Physical sanctions* are not administered by any human or divine source. They are what bind us to the laws of nature. For example, you cannot jump off the CN Tower in Toronto or off a mountain peak in Washington State without suffering the consequences. The law of gravity in this case will produce "grave" consequences for you—no pun intended. Because we recognize the physical sanctions associated with certain kinds of dangerous acts like these, virtually all of us refrain from them.

Moral sanctions arise in our informal relationships with others. If you have ever experienced peer pressure, you can probably appreciate the power, influence, and control that public opinion can have. To spare ourselves mental pain, or embarrassment and loneliness, we often go along with the crowd and conform to the expectations of others. Other people actually contribute to the governance of our behavior in ways we are not always consciously aware of. For instance, if your friends start avoiding you because you constantly lie to them, you may be dissuaded from continuing the practice. The underlying fear of ostracism is often enough to prompt a change in behavior.

In addition to physical and moral sanctions, our behavior can also be regulated by *religious sanctions*, that is, if we believe in a rewarding and punishing Supreme Being. People may do what is right according to their religion, church, or holy book in hope of entering the gates of heaven or because they fear the hell-fire of eternal damnation. Religious sanctions affecting the afterlife can have an impact on behavior in the here and now.

Lastly, Bentham writes of *political sanctions*. These sanctions are issued formally by judges and magistrates on behalf of the state. Punishments issuing from the state (province, county, municipality, federal court) include things like fines, penalties, and jail terms. Fear of such punishment is what deters people from breaking the law and violating the rights of other citizens. On a positive note, things like peace and good order, which result from abiding by the law, are what people find rewarding. Such things create the conditions most conducive to our pursuit of pleasure.

Of all sanctions, Bentham was most interested in the political type. As a reformer, he wished to change the laws of English society such that the general welfare would be promoted by each individual pursuing his or her own advantage. Political sanctions embodied by the rewards and punishments issued by a carefully crafted legal system

For this exercise, your task is to perform a hedonic calculation for the following situation:

> You've been offered a job at a company that you believe engages in discriminatory and environmentally harmful practices. You think you might be able to influence their practices in a positive direction if you take the position, but you worry that you might instead end up contributing to the company's success and making things worse. The job pays well, and you could donate some of your earnings to charity if you take it.

What should you do? Decide using Bentham's hedonic calculus. Do you agree with Bentham about what you should do? Why or why not?

would promote the greatest happiness for the greatest number. Thus, for Bentham, laws should serve utilitarian ideals. Laws are not necessarily right or wrong in themselves, but they are acceptable only to the extent that they further human happiness. State or governmental laws may sometimes require individuals to sacrifice what is in their immediate egoistic self-interest or what has the most personal utility for them, but in a way that, in the long run, benefits society and the individuals constituting it.

Jeremy Bentham, *An Introduction to the Principles of Morals and Legislation*[29]

The following excerpt opens Chapter 1 in Jeremy Bentham's An Introduction to the Principles of Morals and Legislation. *Originally printed in 1780 and then revised by Bentham in 1789,* An Introduction to the Principles of Morals and Legislation *was the first major book on the theory of utilitarianism. True to Bentham's interest in social reform, the book builds from the principle of utility to an analysis of the purpose and role of law and punishment.*

OF THE PRINCIPLE OF UTILITY

I. Nature has placed mankind under the governance of two sovereign masters, pain and pleasure. It is for them alone to point out what we ought to do, as well as to determine what we shall do. On the one hand the standard of right and wrong, on the other the chain of causes and effects, are fastened to their throne. They govern us in all we do, in all we say, in all we think: every effort we can make to throw off our subjection, will serve but to demonstrate and confirm it. In words a man may pretend to renounce their control: but in reality he will remain subject to it all the while. The principle of utility recognizes this subjection, and assumes it for the foundation of that system, the object of which is to increase happiness through the use of reason and of law. Systems which attempt to question it, deal in sounds instead of sense, in caprice instead of reason, in darkness instead of light.

But enough of metaphor and declamation: it is not by such means that moral science is to be improved.

II. The principle of utility is the foundation of the present work: it will be proper therefore at the outset to give an explicit and determinate account of what is meant by it. By the principle of utility is meant that principle which approves or disapproves of every action whatsoever, according to the tendency which it appears to have to augment or diminish the happiness of the party whose interest is in question: or, what is the same thing in other words, to promote or to oppose that happiness. I say of every action whatsoever; and therefore not only of every action of a private individual, but of every measure of government.

III. By 'utility' is meant that property in any object, whereby it tends to produce benefit, advantage, pleasure, good, or happiness, (all this in the present case comes to the same thing) or (what comes again to the same thing) to prevent the happening of harm, injury, pain, evil, or unhappiness to the party whose interest is relevant: if that party is the community in general, then the happiness of the community is what is to be considered: if a particular individual, then the happiness of that individual is what is to be considered.

IV. The 'interest of the community' is one of the most general expressions that can occur in the vocabulary of moral talk; no wonder that its meaning is often lost. When it has meaning, it is this. The community is a fictitious body, composed of the individual persons who are considered as constituting its members. The interest of the community then is, what?—the sum of the interests of the several members who compose it.

V. It is vain to talk of the interest of the community, without understanding what is the interest of the individual. A thing is said to promote the interest, or to be for the interest, of an individual, when it tends to add to the sum total of his pleasures: or, what comes to the same thing, to diminish the sum total of his pains.

VI. An action then may be said to be in agreement with the principle of utility, or, for shortness sake, to utility, (meaning with respect to the community at large) when the tendency it has to increase the happiness of the community is greater than any it has to diminish it.

VII. A measure of government (which is but a particular kind of action, performed by a particular person or persons) may be said to be in agreement with, or dictated by, the principle of utility, when in like manner the tendency which it has to increase the happiness of the community is greater than any which it has to diminish it.

VIII. When an action, or in particular a measure of government, is supposed by a man to be in agreement with the principle of utility, it may be convenient, for the purposes of considering it, to imagine a kind of law or dictate, called a law or dictate of utility: and to speak of the action in question, as being conformable to such law or dictate.

IX. People may be said to be supporters of the principle of utility, when the approval or disapproval they feel to any action, or to any measure, is determined by and in proportion to the tendency which it has to increase or reduce the happiness of the community: or in other words, to its agreement or disagreement with the laws or dictates of utility.

X. Of an action that is in agreement with the principle of utility one may always say either that it is one that ought to be done, or at least that it is not one that ought not to be done. One may say also, that it is right it should be done; at least that it is not wrong it should be done: that it is a right action; at least that it is not a wrong action. When thus interpreted, the words ought, and right and wrong, and others like them, have meaning: when otherwise, they have none.

XI. Has the correctness of this principle been ever formally contested? It should seem that it had, by those who have not known what they meant to do. Is it susceptible of any direct proof? It should seem not: for that which is used to prove everything else, cannot itself be proved: a chain of proofs must have their commencement somewhere. To give such proof is as impossible as it is needless.

XII. Not that there is or ever has been that human creature breathing, however stupid or perverse, who has not on many, perhaps on most occasions of his life, deferred to it. It is human nature to rely without thinking about it on this principle: if not to control their own actions, then at least to evaluate them, as well as the actions of other men. There have been people who accept it purely and without reserve, although perhaps not many people, perhaps not even a large proportion of the most intelligent. Many argue against it, either because they don't understand how to apply it, or because of some prejudice or other which they were afraid to examine, or could not bear to part with. For such is the stuff that man is made of: in principle and in practice, on the right track and off it, the rarest of all human qualities is consistency.

XIII. When a man attempts to argue against the principle of utility, he uses reasons drawn from that very principle, without being aware of it. His arguments, if they prove anything, prove not that the principle is wrong, but that, according to the applications he supposes to be made of it, it is misapplied. Is it possible for a man to move the earth? Yes; but he must first find another earth to stand on.

XIV. It is impossible to disprove the correctness of this principle by argument. However, a man might happen to be disposed not to relish it, for the reasons mentioned above, or because he has a confused or incomplete idea of it. Where this is the case, if he thinks the adjustment and firm establishment of their opinions on such a subject are worth the trouble, let him take the following steps, and at length, he may come to accept the principle.

1. Let him figure out whether he wants to discard this principle altogether; if so, let him consider what it is that all his reasoning (in matters of politics especially) can amount to?

2. Let him settle with himself whether he would rather judge and act without any principle, or whether there is any other principle he would judge and act by?

3. If there is, let him examine and satisfy himself whether the principle he thinks he has found is really any separate intelligible principle; or whether it is a mere principle in words, a kind of phrase, which at bottom expresses nothing more than his own unfounded sentiments; that is, what in another person he might be apt to call an arbitrary whim?

4. If he is inclined to think that his own approval or disapproval of an act without any regard to its consequences, is a sufficient foundation for him to base his judgement of the act, let him ask himself whether this sentiment is supposed to be a standard of right and wrong for everyone, or whether everyone's sentiment has the same privilege of being a standard?

5. In the first case, let him ask himself whether his principle is tyrannical, and hostile to all the rest of the human race?

6. In the second case, whether it is anarchic, and whether that would mean that there are just as many standards of right and wrong as there are people? and whether on this view, something which is right today, might (without the least change in its nature) be wrong tomorrow? and whether the same thing is not right and wrong in the same place at the same time? and in either case, whether all argument is not at an end? and whether, when two men have said, "I like this," and "I don't like it," they can (given this view) have anything more to say?

7. If they say no, because the sentiment which is proposed as a standard must be grounded on reflective thought, let him say what particular facts the reflective thought is based on? If it's based on particulars related to the utility of the act, then this is deserting his own principle, and borrowing assistance from the very principal that is opposed. If not on those particular facts, then on which others?

8. If he prefers a more complex theory, adopting his own principle in part, and the principle of utility in part, we should know what the details of this mix are.

9. If the part that utility plays in this new theory is settled, why not simply adopt utility as the whole theory? Why modify it, and how much?

10. Admitting any other principle than the principle of utility to be a right principle, a principle that it is right for anyone to pursue; admitting (what is not true) that the word 'right' can have a meaning without reference to utility, let him say whether there is any such thing as a motive that anyone could have to pursue the dictates of rightness: if there is, what is that motive? How it is to be distinguished from those which enforce the dictates of utility. If there is no motive, then what is this other principle good for?

READING QUESTIONS

1. When Bentham claims that, "Nature has put mankind under the governance of two sovereign masters, pain and pleasure. It is for them alone to point out what we ought to do, as well as to determine what we shall do," what sort of claim is he making: a factual statement or a value judgment? What would it take to prove the claim is false? Should we accept the claim as true? Why or why not?

2. What is the "principle of utility"? Find Bentham's statement of it in the text. In the absence of a direct proof of the principle of utility, Bentham lays out a series of ten sets of questions. Do Bentham's questions convince you to accept the principle of utility? Why or why not?

In concluding this discussion, it is interesting to note that one of the implications of Bentham's utilitarianism is that the same action can have a different moral value in different circumstances. Take the example of lying. Lying to your friend in order to make him or her feel better could have positive utility, whereas lying under oath could have negative utility (if you are caught with the lie, that is!). The point is, you told a lie in both instances, but the consequences and, hence, the moral value of the action differ on an act-by-act basis. This use of the principle of utility *to determine the moral value of individual actions* by their *unique outcomes*, in particular circumstances, is known as **act utilitarianism**.

By contrast, some utilitarians apply the hedonic calculus to *rules of action* rather than specific actions themselves. For example, if, as a rule, everyone told lies, it would result in more disutility than utility. The chaos and disorder would be very unpleasant and all the lies would create a lot of suffering. Eventually, nobody would believe anybody. Therefore, *as a rule*, telling lies is wrong.

According to this version of utilitarianism, known as **rule utilitarianism**, the right thing to do is to follow that rule as determined by the question which produces the best consequences. The question is, "What would the consequences be if everyone acted this way?" The circumstances and the outcome of a single action do not matter, morally speaking. What matters is the outcome of everyone behaving in accordance with, or in violation of, the rule upon which the action is based.

Perhaps you are thinking at this point that moral *duties and obligations* are not variable in the way act-utilitarianism argues. Maybe you think they are somehow absolute and universal, and that what you morally ought to do in the next minute, day, or decade does *not* depend on results or changing conditions. After all, how are you supposed to know what the right thing to do is if you cannot be *certain* about what will happen when you do it! Rule utilitarianism goes some way toward addressing this concern, as compared with act-utilitarianism. Nevertheless, you might still object on the grounds that morally right action should not depend on consequences at all—either those flowing from individual acts or general rules of conduct. You could live a perfectly happy life under the illusion of one big lie, for example, but it is still wrong to be lied to and manipulated by that lie. What makes people happy is one thing; what is moral may be something completely different.

For a philosophical position that develops these kinds of thoughts into a theory of absolute and universal rules, read on.

5.4 Immanuel Kant's Deontological Ethics

So far in our treatment of ethical theories, we have learned how thinkers throughout the ages have sought the philosophical foundations of morality in different places and in different things. As we just learned, Bentham argued that the morality of particular actions could be founded on psychological hedonism. For him, an action was good to the extent that it produced pleasure, bad to the extent that it caused pain. Aristotle based his ethics on the nature of the human being. Good human beings were human beings who flourished by means of developing virtues. As for Plato, remember how he too sought the basis of morality in his philosophical investigations. He eventually located moral goodness in a harmoniously functioning soul. As we turn now to **Immanuel Kant**'s **deontological ethics**, we will see how he uses *reason* and *rationality* to provide morality with a solid and secure foundation.

"Two things fill the mind with ever new and increasing admiration and awe ... the starry heavens above and the moral law within."
IMMANUEL KANT

The Rational Basis of Morality

To begin, note that Kant does not think that morality is dependent on circumstances or on cultural, historical, or social factors. Although it is undeniably true that people are different and often choose to differ with one another on moral matters, that fact alone does not, for him, make morality a matter of opinion. Kant would admit it is also certainly true that cultural practices vary throughout the world, and that different values are more or less important to different societies, groups, or nationalities. Moreover, it cannot be denied that values undergo changes and transformations over time. Compare today's attitudes toward sexuality, for example, with those of the conservative 1950s or the puritanism of Queen Victoria's era (1837 to 1901).

In recognition of human diversity, and the fact that what people actually do, say, experience, believe, think, feel, and value varies, Kant concludes that no **moral certainty** can be found there. If morality is to make any sense, and if it is to be considered valid and binding for everybody, then moral certainty must be found somewhere apart from the transitory and diverse world of everyday experience. For Kant, it is to be found in the *structure of reason* itself. The ultimate basis of morality must be purely rational, or **a priori**, not in any way derived from experience or dependent upon it. Only then can morality be binding, universal and necessary.

For example, rational moralists would no doubt condemn the torturing of innocent children, regardless of whether anybody actually engages in this practice or whether any society condones it. The moral judgment in this instance is not derived from experience or observation of people's behavior. Such knowledge is *a priori*—that is, independent of what people actually do and the experiences that they have. For Kant, it is up to the human sciences (e.g., anthropology, psychology, sociology) to inform us about human behavior and the differences we find among people; it is philosophy's task to use reason to help us determine what is right and wrong.

In support of Kant, one could argue that despite the apparent diversity easily observable among people throughout the world, the faculty of reason is one common and unchanging universal element shared by all human beings. Explaining why reason must be the basis of morality, Kant writes:

> Is it not of the utmost necessity to construct a pure moral philosophy which is completely freed from everything which may be only empirical and thus belong to anthropology? That there must be such a philosophy is self-evident from the common idea of duty and moral laws. Everyone must admit that a law, if it is to hold morally, i.e., as a ground of obligation, must imply absolute necessity; he must admit that the command, "Thou shalt not lie" does not apply to men only, as if other rational beings had no need to observe it. The same is true for all other moral laws properly so called. He must concede that the ground of obligation here must not be sought in the nature of man or in the circumstances in which he is placed, but sought *a priori* solely in the concepts of pure reason, and that every other precept which rests on principles of mere existence, even a precept which is in certain respects universal, so far as it leans in the least on empirical grounds (perhaps only in regard to the motive involved), be called a practical rule but never a moral law.[30]

Concept of the Good Will

In the First Section of the *Groundwork for the Metaphysics of Morals*,* Kant asserts that moral goodness is not something psychological or external to the moral agent. He recognizes that *talents of the mind* (intelligence, judgment, wit), *qualities of temperament* (courage, resoluteness, perseverance), and *gifts of fortune* (power, riches, honor, contentment), which contribute to happiness, may in many respects be good and desirable. He underscores, however, the fact that such things are not unconditionally good. Power, for instance, could lead to pride or corruption if not corrected by reason and good will. The cool courage of a

---

* Sometimes this title is translated as *Foundations for* (or *Fundamental Principles of*) *the Metaphysics of Morals*.

In an effort to appreciate moral diversity,

First, try to identify some norms, values, or beliefs that differ from one individual or culture to the next. Such things could be personal, social, political, or religious, for example.

Second, once you have identified these different and possibly conflicting values, norms, or beliefs, ask yourself whether all sides are on an equal footing. Are there any specific values, norms, or beliefs that you think are better than the alternatives?

Third, ask: Would you necessarily be bigoted, biased, chauvinistic, or discriminatory if you held the opinion that some values, beliefs, or norms were better or worse than others? Why or why not?

Fourth, does tolerance of moral diversity mean that you are obligated to accept everyone's values no matter what? Does tolerance of moral diversity mean that you are obligated to accept someone else's intolerance of moral diversity?

For further thought and discussion: Is there something that makes people reluctant to criticize the values, behaviors, or lifestyle choices of others? If so, what? Do we have any social responsibility to ensure that people make the right choices in their lives? Explain and justify. If you were willing to criticize any particular value or norm as unacceptable, what would be the basis of your moral disagreement?

villain is not morally praiseworthy in itself, and the actions following from such a virtue are more likely to cause harm than lead to ethically acceptable behavior.

The good will as Kant thinks of it, is the desire to do something simply because it is the right thing to do, not because of any other motive. It is good even if it is prevented from achieving its end in any particular situation. The goodness of the good will is established solely by virtue of its willing. The motive to do the right thing for the right reason is enough to make the good will good. Kant says, "The good will is not good because of what it effects or accomplishes or because of its adequacy to achieve some proposed end; it is good only because of its willing, i.e., it is good of itself."[31]

In view of this, people who are motivated and make efforts to do the right thing, but fail in their attempts, can still be seen to be acting morally. By contrast, people who somehow manage to achieve their ends or enjoy uninterrupted happiness in life, but without the influence of good will motivating their behavior, are not, in Kant's opinion, even worthy of being happy. Right things can be done for the wrong reasons. Good things like pleasure and happiness can result from bad acts or moral injustices—a fact that calls into question the value of such things. This is why only a good will is unconditionally good.

Individuals, then, are morally good or behave in a morally good fashion when they will to do the right thing simply because it is their **duty**—*simply for the sake of duty alone*. The morally virtuous person is not concerned with maximizing people's happiness or cultivating moderation in their lifestyle, but with doing what is required by *practical reason* (reason in its applications to morality). *The moral quality of an act is, therefore, established by the rational principle to which the good will assents*.

Notion of Duty

Kant gives us some insight into what he means by *duty*, a basic building block of his ethical thinking. For Kant, "Duty is the necessity of an action executed from respect for [moral] law."[32] He goes on to say, "An action performed from duty does not have its moral worth in the purpose which is to be achieved through it but in the **maxim** [rule of conduct] by which it is determined."[33] We will examine the formal characteristics of moral maxims in a moment, but first let us look at a couple of important distinctions Kant makes with respect to the notion of duty.

IN ACCORDANCE WITH DUTY, BUT NOT FOR DUTY'S SAKE

Kant observes that while some actions accord with duty, they are not performed for the sake of duty. In other words, people can act consistently with what duty requires, but still not act for the sake of duty or in recognition of the moral law. For example, maybe you have stopped yourself from stealing in the past, not because of any rational choice to do your moral duty, but because you feared getting caught and going to jail. If so, then doing the right thing out of fear or self-interest did not give your action any moral worth.

Actions performed in accordance with duty but not for duty's sake do not belong to the moral domain. It's not that they are immoral; they are just not relevant to morality, having no moral status. For Kant, this example of refraining from stealing would be an instance of **prudence**, not morality. Doing what is in your self-interest because of self-interest alone is non-moral behavior. In *Groundwork for the Metaphysics of Morals*, Kant offers his own illustration to support the point that *not all actions in accordance with moral duty possess moral worth.*

> It is in fact in accordance with duty that a dealer should not overcharge an inexperienced customer, and wherever there is much business the prudent merchant does not do so, having a fixed price for everyone, so that a child may buy of him as cheaply as any other. Thus, the customer is honestly served. But this is far from sufficient to justify the belief that the merchant has behaved in this way from duty and principle or honesty. His own advantage required this behavior, but it cannot be assumed that over and above that he had a direct inclination to the purchaser and that, out of love, as it were, he gave none an advantage in price over another. Therefore, the action was done neither from duty nor from direct inclination, but only for a selfish purpose.[34]

The merchant might lose customers if it was discovered that he charged different prices to different people for the same thing. Being honest is the right thing to do, but the merchant's action is not morally praiseworthy, because it was done out of prudence, not morality. It wasn't that the action was wrong, or that there was something wrong with the merchant's reason. It simply was not moral. It is worth noting, then, that actions can be *moral* (morally relevant and right), *non-moral* (not morally relevant), or *immoral* (morally relevant and wrong). To argue, as Kant does, that the merchant has acted prudently (for his own advantage) is not to condemn him; nor is it to praise him morally.

IN ACCORDANCE WITH DUTY, BUT OUT OF INCLINATION

To further clarify the nature of (moral) duty, Kant also distinguishes between actions performed out of **inclination** and those performed out of recognition of duty. He argues that only the latter are genuinely moral. Suppose, for example, that you are the kind of person who is generally predisposed by temperament to act kindly toward others. Perhaps you simply like being nice to people. In fact, being nice to others is *what comes naturally* to you. If this were so, Kant would say that, as nice as you are, there is still no moral worth to your actions. It is not that you are morally corrupt or that you are doing anything wrong; it is just that the naturally-inclined actions you perform have no moral status or value.

If this seems counterintuitive, it will help to look at another example. Suppose two romantic partners are completely in love and they both have no inclination to cheat on each other (that is, each one is inclined to be faithful); should we praise their fidelity? From a Kantian perspective, fidelity is good (because it conforms to the moral law), but nonetheless, the couple's mutual fidelity here turns out to be *morally neutral* since each one's faithful behavior came naturally or spontaneously, because of feelings, not for the sake of duty or out of any sense of obligation. Had either person's inclinations been different, however—had either of them been tempted to cheat but resisted out of a sense of duty to the other—the act (of faithful resistance) would indeed be morally praiseworthy. But, doing what one feels like doing without thought or recognition of moral duty gives one's action no moral worth. The *motive* or *willful intent* behind the action determines its moral status. Distinguishing between inclination and duty, using kindness as an example, Kant writes:

> To be kind where one can is duty, and there are, moreover, many persons so sympathetically constituted that without any motive of vanity or selfishness they find an inner satisfaction in spreading joy, and rejoice in the contentment of others which they have made possible. But I say that, however dutiful and amiable it may be, that kind of action has no true moral worth.[35]

IN ACCORDANCE WITH DUTY, AND FOR THE SAKE OF DUTY

Well, if morality is not about natural inclination or prudence, then we are left needing further clarification. For Kant, a morally praiseworthy action must not only accord with duty (be consistent with it) but it must also be performed by the agent *for the sake of duty*.

To illustrate the moral priority of duty over inclination, Kant asks us to imagine a person whose life has been entirely clouded by sorrow. This person is miserable, and to a very large extent, any sympathetic feelings he might have had toward others have been extinguished. The person still possesses the means to help others and to improve their situations, but his deadened sensibility leaves him untouched by their unfortunate plight.

Now, as Kant suggests, if this individual, who is too miserable to have any feelings for others, or inclination to help them, tears himself away from his own preoccupations to assist another distressed person because of a recognition of duty, then his action assumes moral worth. The individual does what should be done, not out of inclination, but for the sake of duty only. You could say, then, that a test of moral character is to discover whether one is strong enough to follow duty in spite of one's inclination not to do so.

MORAL DUTIES TO ONESELF AND TO OTHERS

In *Lectures on Ethics*, Kant points out that moral duties include not only those obligations we have toward others, but also those we have toward ourselves.[36] In other words, Kant allows for both personal and social dimensions of morality. This is not to suggest that personal morality is private and subjective, or that duties to oneself are somehow conditional, relativistic, and not applicable to others. For Kant, all moral duties are universal. We *all* have the same moral duties toward ourselves just as we *all* have the same moral duties toward other people.

"Suicide is not an abomination because God has forbidden it; it is forbidden by God because it is abominable."
IMMANUEL KANT

Although it goes almost without saying that morality involves relations and duties to others, Kant contends that individual morality should not be considered an afterthought to ethical inquiry. Too often moral discussions are restricted to social issues and interpersonal conflicts. Kant insists, however, that, "our duties towards ourselves are of primary importance and should have pride of place."[37] Arguing that we can expect nothing from a person who dishonors his own person, he maintains that "a prior condition of our **duties to others** is our **duty to ourselves**; we can fulfill the former only insofar as we first fulfill the latter."[38]

To illustrate and support his point, Kant asks us to consider alcoholics. Such people may do no harm to others, and provided their physical constitutions are strong, they may not even harm themselves. Nonetheless, Kant claims that alcoholics become, for us, objects of moral contempt. Such individuals degrade themselves and damage their personal dignity. They lose their inner worth as moral subjects. Kant writes:

> Only if our worth as human beings is intact can we perform our other duties; for it is the foundation stone of all other duties. A man who has destroyed and cast away his personality, has no intrinsic worth, and can no longer perform any manner of duty.[39]

In *Lectures on Ethics*, Kant enumerates and explains a number of *self-regarding* and *other-regarding duties*. In reference to the former, we have duties of *proper self-respect*, *self-mastery*, *duties concerning the body*, and *duties concerning how we occupy ourselves in work and in play*. With respect to the latter, we have *duties to show respect for all persons* and *to honor their inherent worth and dignity as human beings*.

Maxims and Moral Behavior

According to Kant, we are morally responsible for the actions we perform voluntarily, not by external pressure or manipulation. Moral assessment lies with the agent—specifically the will of the agent, not factors beyond the agent's control. To be even more specific, *moral agents are responsible for the particular maxims they choose to will into action*.

As Kant sees it, anytime you act voluntarily, you operate under some kind of *maxim*, *rule*, or *directive*. For instance, if in situation A, you choose to do B, then you are acting on the maxim "In situation A, do B." This kind of thinking is what has led some people to describe humans as *rule-governed* animals. Unlike lower-level organisms, which are mostly reactive to external stimuli or responsive to instinctual impulses and other determining factors, we, as human beings, can act freely and rationally on the basis of self-generated rules or laws of conduct.

If this seems a bit vague, imagine yourself lying to your course instructor about the reasons why you missed a term test. You might say that you were ill, when, in fact, you slept in because you were up very late the night before partying with friends. In this case, the personal maxim or rule of conduct underlying your behavior could be expressed something like

THINKING ABOUT YOUR THINKING

Our maxims are often implicit, but thinking about our thinking can make them explicit. To that end, think about a time when you performed an action that you were morally proud of. Maybe you volunteered somewhere, helped someone, protested for social reform, made a charitable donation, or simply made someone's day a little better with a friendly note.

Now think about why you performed that action. What was the principle of your action in that moment? Don't rewrite history; be honest! Now that you've identified your maxim, reassess your action. This time, instead of morally assessing the action itself, assess that maxim you acted on. Are you still morally proud of what you did? Why or why not?

this: "When in trouble, lie your way out of it" or "If caught doing something wrong, then lie" or "Lie to get what you want."

To say maxims underlie our intentional behavior does not mean to suggest that we always abide by them. For example, on most occasions when you are caught doing something wrong, you might *fess up*; however, at other times, you might lie, as in the preceding illustration. You should also note that people are not always or usually aware of the maxims that they use to govern their behavior. Implicit maxims are most likely to come to people's attention and to be made explicit when they are asked to justify their behaviors to others or when conscience forces them to justify their actions to themselves. Aware of them or not, maxims are embedded in our actions and in the way we behave.

The Categorical Imperative

To explain which maxims of behavior are distinctively moral and morally acceptable and which are not, Kant formulated **the categorical imperative**. This supreme and absolute moral imperative can be expressed in a number of different ways, but the best-known formulation is the following: *Act as if the maxim of your action were to become, by your will, a universal law of nature*.[40] According to this formulation, a moral maxim is one that can, *without contradiction*, be *prescribed* to be a rule of conduct for everyone—in other words, the maxim can logically be *universalized*. If the maxim can't be universalized, that doesn't necessarily mean the action is immoral: it might be simply without moral significance.

The categorical imperative implies that the essence of morality lies in acting on the basis of an impersonal principle that is *valid for every person*, including oneself. In other words, it is wrong to make an exception of yourself.

Of course, Kant is not a consequentialist, so universalization is not determined by outcomes. Rather, it is determined by reason. For example, the maxim "Never help others, but always accept help from them" might appear personally advantageous; however, it cannot be accepted as a valid moral rule of conduct because of its *logical* implications. It does not make sense even to talk about accepting help from others if the maxim were universalized and acted upon, because if it were valid for all people—if everyone used this as a rule for action—then nobody would ever try to help others, and thus, there would never be any help to be accepted. This maxim tells people never to do an action whose description would make no sense. From this illustration, we see how the categorical imperative's *formal requirement of universal consistency* allows us to evaluate the moral acceptability of particular maxims and rules of conduct. The categorical imperative can serve as a test of morality or an ultimate standard for moral evaluation. Note carefully that Kant is not talking about whether the *results* of the maxim's being a universal law would be good or bad. He's talking about whether that universal status is logically possible.

Compare this with the rule-utilitarians' theory, which made a different type of universalizability the test of the morality of an action. Rule-utilitarians would say: if an action would have *bad consequences* if everybody performed it, then that action is wrong. One might think of this standard or principle of evaluation as the *universal consequences test* in order to distinguish it from Kant's purely logical understanding of universalizability.

A second formulation of the categorical imperative draws attention to its social implications. It states: *Act so that you treat humanity, whether in your own person or in that of another, always as an end and never as a means only*.[41] According to this statement, we should show respect for all human beings *unconditionally* and avoid exploiting anyone.

The moral duties not to manipulate, not to steal, not to purposely mislead, not to objectify, and not to enslave, all highlight the point at the core of this formulation. When we exploit others, abuse or disrespect them in these ways, we treat them merely as *objects* or as a *means to our own ends*. We use them as instruments to achieving our personal goals. In doing so, we fail to respect others as rational beings whose existence has absolute worth in itself.

Of course, to some extent, we all use one another. For instance, you may use your neighbor as a babysitter for your child, or your neighbors may use you to cut their grass. These *voluntary* relationships are not what Kant is talking about when he talks about violations of the second formulation of the categorical imperative. In many practical and moral ways, we all "use" one another in cooperative living. It is when we violate others, abuse or mistreat them, or use them *merely* as a means to achieve our own ends that we dishonor their dignity as persons.

From Kant's perspective, the dignity and worth of any person are not conditional on any goals or benefits they could be used for, say in the way your pen is valuable to you until it runs out of ink. The value of persons is unconditional, full stop. As such, it is wrong for you to use people against their will and to exploit them or treat them only as objects or merely as a means to achieve your own ends. As Kant reminds us, that includes how we treat ourselves.

Although Kant offers different formulations of the categorical imperative, they are all formulations of the supreme moral law and, thus, they all share certain features in common. For one thing, *universality* is a requirement of morality. The moral law holds for all people, at all times, in all places, without exception. An act must be acceptable *objectively*, regardless of whether the individual is at the giving or the receiving end of an action.

The criterion of *universality* points to the idea that moral maxims must also display *impartiality*; that is, the rightness or wrongness of actions, and the moral adequacy of their underlying maxims, must have nothing to do with *who* happens to be in a favored or disadvantaged position regarding the actions. Certain acts are right or wrong in themselves, regardless of whose interests are served and regardless of the favorable or unfavorable consequences to oneself or anyone else for that matter.

The categorical imperative is an abstract principle that requires that empirical content particulars be removed as much as possible from the ethical appraisal and justification process. Because morality must have a *purely rational a priori* basis, particulars of content referring to specific persons, places, times, interests, desires, inclinations, and so forth must be removed when the moral acceptability of maxims is being determined. Recall that, for Kant, morality cannot have an empirical basis, for this would not provide him with the solid and secure ethical foundation that he seeks. Only reason can provide the *certainty* and *necessity* required for a universal, binding morality.

Another element contained in the categorical imperative is the notion of *prescriptivity*. One cannot simply opt out of morality if one chooses, for the requirements of morality are *unconditionally binding* on all rational beings. One cannot justifiably argue that morality applies to everyone else *but me*, or that everyone else should always tell the truth *but me*. Ethically speaking, you cannot make yourself the exception to the rule. To do so is to use two standards of morality, one for others and a different one for yourself. For Kant, there is only one morality that applies to both you *and* others. There is not one for thee, but another for me!

"*Sexual love makes of the loved person an object of appetite: as soon as that appetite has been stilled, the person is cast aside as one casts aside a lemon which has been sucked dry.*"
IMMANUEL KANT

In order to understand the categorical imperative in action, consider the following case of a duty to others that Kant offers in the *Groundwork for the Metaphysics of Morals*:

A man in need finds himself forced to borrow money. He knows well that he won't be able to repay it, but he sees also that he will not get any loan unless he firmly promises to repay it within a fixed time. He wants to make such a promise, but he still has conscience enough to ask himself whether it is not permissible and is contrary to duty to get out of difficulty this way. Suppose, however, that he decides to do so. The maxim of his action would then be expressed as follows: *When I believe myself to be in need of money, I will borrow money and promise to pay it back, although I know that I can never do so*. Now this principle of self-love or personal advantage may be quite compatible with one's entire future welfare, but the question is now whether it is right.[42]

In pairs, or in two separate groups, use the first two formulations of the categorical imperative presented in this chapter to answer the question of whether it is right to act on the proposed maxim stated in Kant's example.

One person or group applies the first formulation of the categorical imperative by answering the following

questions: What is the proposed action? What is the proposed maxim for that action? Is that maxim universalizable? In other words, could it be a universal law? Why so? If not, why not? (Hint: Remember, Kant is not a consequentialist.)

The other person or group applies the second formulation of the categorical imperative by answering the following questions: What is the proposed action? What is the proposed maxim supporting it? Does that maxim respect the dignity of human beings? Does it avoid treating other people as a mere means? Why so? If not, why not?

For further thought and discussion: Individuals or groups are invited to compare their answers to Kant's question about the case: "Is it right?" Since both parties are working with two formulations of the same moral law, they should arrive at the same answer with different explanations.

Pairs or groups can also work together to formulate a maxim for the proposed action that would be morally right. That is, they can make efforts to formulate a maxim for borrowing money that does not violate either of the first two formulations of the categorical imperative.

If the practice of making personal exceptions were universalized, then nobody would be required to adhere to the moral law, and any objective morality would become impossible. You cannot, therefore, be freed of moral obligation simply because you do not feel like living up to the moral law or because making an exception in your case is likely to further your own interests or promote greater personal happiness. Distinctively moral maxims and principles of ethical conduct apply to everyone unconditionally, whether people like them or not. Thinking that they don't apply to you leaves you free to exploit others. That's where the obligation to treat others with the dignity they deserve comes in.

Autonomy versus Heteronomy of the Will

In closing this discussion of Kantian ethics, a brief mention should be made of the role played by **autonomy** in morality, for without personal autonomy, morality becomes an impossibility. When people act morally, they act freely and willfully out of respect or reverence for the moral law. They willingly obey the moral law for the sake of the moral law alone. To go back to a point made earlier, moral agents do their duty for duty's sake, not because of external incentives or coercive influence. When outside determining forces are not present, then we can speak of autonomy of the will.

Heteronomy of the will, by contrast, is evident when the will obeys laws, rules, or injunctions from any other source besides reason. Obeying the law because you fear incarceration or doing your duty only under threat of physical force does not reflect autonomous moral action. Rather, it is more like protecting your hindside.

Lastly, when as autonomous and rational moral agents, we base our actions on universally valid laws that we have laid down for ourselves, we participate in something Kant calls the **kingdom of ends**—a kind of ideal moral universe in which we respect the intrinsic worth and dignity of all persons. In this kingdom, we never treat people solely as means to our ends, but as ends in themselves.

Immanuel Kant, On Pure Moral Philosophy[43]

In the Preface to the Groundwork for the Metaphysics of Morals *(1785), Kant outlines his system of philosophy and the place that moral philosophy has in it. In his systematizing, Kant separates out the metaphysics of morals from practical anthropology to indicate that his treatment of morality is cleansed of all things empirical. As such, moral philosophy is based on* a priori *principles of pure reason, not experience and circumstance. Only then, for Kant, can the answer to the question "What ought I to do?" be universal and necessary.*

——

PREFACE

Ancient Greek philosophy was divided into three sciences: physics, ethics, and logic. This division is perfectly suitable to the nature of the thing; and the only improvement that can be made in it is to add the principle on which it is based, so that we may both satisfy ourselves of its completeness, and also be able to determine correctly the necessary subdivisions.

All rational knowledge is either material or formal: the former considers some object, the latter is concerned only with the form of the understanding and of the reason itself, and with the universal laws of thought in general without distinction of its objects. Formal philosophy is called logic. Material philosophy, however, has to do with determinate objects and the laws to which they are subject, is again twofold; for these laws are either laws of nature or of freedom. The science of the former is physics, that of the latter, ethics; they are also called natural philosophy and moral philosophy respectively.

Logic cannot have any empirical part; that is, a part in which the universal and necessary laws of thought should rest on grounds taken from experience; otherwise it would not be logic, i.e., a canon for the understanding or the reason, valid for all thought, and capable of demonstration. Natural and moral philosophy, on the contrary, can each have their empirical part, since the former has to determine the laws of nature as an object of experience; the latter the laws of the human will, so far as it is affected by nature: the former, however, being laws according to which everything does happen; the latter, laws according to which everything ought to happen. Ethics, however, must also consider the conditions under which what ought to happen frequently does not.

We may call all philosophy empirical, so far as it is based on grounds of experience: on the other hand, that which delivers its doctrines from *a priori* principles alone we may call pure philosophy. When the latter is merely formal it is logic; if it is restricted to definite objects of the understanding it is metaphysics.

In this way there arises the idea of a twofold metaphysic—a metaphysic of nature and a metaphysic of morals. Physics will thus have an empirical and also a rational part. It is the same with Ethics; but here the empirical part might have the special name of practical anthropology, the name morality being appropriated to the rational part.

All trades, arts, and handiworks have gained by division of labour, namely, when, instead of one man doing everything, each confines himself to a certain kind of work distinct from others in the treatment it requires, so as to be able to perform it with greater facility and in the greatest perfection. Where the different kinds of work are not distinguished and divided, where everyone is a jack-of-all-trades, there manufactures remain still in the greatest barbarism. It might deserve to be considered whether pure philosophy in all its parts does not require a man specially devoted to it, and whether it would not be better for the whole business of science if those who, to please the tastes of the public, are accustomed to blend the rational and empirical elements together, mixed in all sorts of proportions unknown to themselves, and who call themselves independent thinkers, giving the name of minute philosophers to those who apply themselves to the rational part only—if these, I say, were warned not to carry on two employments together which differ widely in the treatment they demand, for each of which perhaps a special talent is required, and the combination of which in one person only produces bunglers. But I only ask here whether the nature of science does not require that we should always carefully separate the empirical from the rational part, and prefix to Physics proper (or empirical physics) a metaphysic of nature, and to practical anthropology a metaphysic of morals, which must be carefully cleared of everything empirical, so that we may know much can be accomplished by pure reason in both cases, and from what sources it draws this its *a priori* teaching, and that whether the latter inquiry is conducted by all moralists (and there are many), or only by some who feel a calling thereto.

As my concern here is with moral philosophy, I limit the question suggested to this: Whether it is not of the utmost necessity to construct a pure moral philosophy which is completely freed from everything which may be only empirical and which belongs to anthropology? for that such a philosophy must be possible is evident from the common idea of duty and of the moral laws. Everyone must admit that if a law is to have moral force, i.e., to be the basis of an obligation, it must carry with it absolute necessity; that, for example, the precept, "Thou shalt not lie," is not valid for men alone, as if other rational beings had no need to observe it; and so with all the other moral laws properly so called; that, therefore, the basis of obligation must not be sought in the nature of man, or in the circumstances in the world in which he is placed, but *a priori* simply in the conception of pure reason; and although any other precept which is founded on principles of mere experience may be in certain respects universal, yet in as far as it rests even in the least degree on an empirical basis, perhaps only as to a motive, such a precept, while it may be a practical rule, can never be called a moral law.

Thus not only are moral laws with their principles essentially distinguished from every other kind of practical knowledge in which there is anything empirical, but all moral philosophy rests wholly on its pure part. When applied to man, it does not borrow the least thing from the knowledge of man himself (anthropology), but gives laws *a priori* to him as a rational being. No doubt these laws require a judgement sharpened by experience, in order on the one hand to distinguish in what cases they are applicable, and on the other to procure for them access to the will of the man and effectual influence on conduct; since man is acted on by so many inclinations that, though capable of the idea of a practical pure reason, he is not so easily able to make it effective in concrete situations in his life.

A metaphysic of morals is therefore indispensably necessary, not merely for speculative reasons, in order to investigate the sources of the practical principles which are to be found *a priori* in our reason, but also because

morals themselves are liable to all sorts of corruption, as long as we are without that clue and supreme canon by which to estimate them correctly. For in order that an action should be morally good, it is not enough that it conform to the moral law, but it must also be done for the sake of the law, otherwise that conformity is only very contingent and uncertain; since a principle which is not moral, although it may now and then produce actions conformable to the law, will also often produce actions which contradict it. Now it is only in a pure philosophy that we can look for the moral law in its purity and genuineness (and, in a practical matter, this is of the utmost consequence): we must, therefore, begin with pure philosophy (metaphysic), and without it there cannot be any moral philosophy at all. That which mingles these pure principles with the empirical does not deserve the name of philosophy (for what distinguishes philosophy from common rational knowledge is that it treats in separate sciences what the latter only comprehends confusedly); much less does it deserve that of moral philosophy, since by this confusion it even spoils the purity of morals themselves, and counteracts its own end.

READING QUESTIONS

1. How does your study of Kant's epistemology and metaphysics in Chapter 4 help you to understand this passage concerning his moral philosophy?

2. According to Kant, why is it necessary to construct a pure moral philosophy?

3. Based on your reading of the text, give a Kantian assessment of the morality of the following scenario:

In an effort to attract customers who want to spend their money responsibly, a shopkeeper decides to only stock products made by companies that pay fair wages to their employees. Her plan is successful. The new customers are happy to buy products that make them feel good about how they spend their money, and the shopkeeper is happy to have the increased business.

The Impermissibility of Lying: Maria von Herbert's Correspondence with Kant

Kant's deontological ethics is not without its critics. One common criticism is that his conception of the moral law as a categorical imperative is too severe. There are many forms that this criticism has taken over the centuries, but the general thread to them is that a moral philosophy consisting of universal and necessary duties is too strict in its applications, particularly given the complex and muddy circumstances of human life. Sometimes, so the criticism goes, exceptions to the rules are in order. Sometimes the moral thing to do is not what the moral law demands.

Critics need go no further than Kant's writings to illustrate their concerns over the strictness and rigidity of his moral philosophy. First up for your consideration is a short piece Kant wrote titled, "On a Supposed Right to Lie Because of Philanthropic Concerns." In it, Kant considers the scenario of an inquiring murderer who shows up at your doorstep in pursuit of your friend and asks you whether or not your friend is in your house. Do you have a duty to tell the truth to the person who intends to murder your friend?

According to Kant, yes. You are morally obliged to tell the truth because it is your duty to tell the truth. The moral law demands that all human beings have a duty to tell the truth no matter what consequences may follow from doing so. In Kant's words, "Truthfulness in statements that cannot be avoided is the formal duty of man to everyone, however great the disadvantage that may arise therefrom for him or for any other."[44] So as well-intentioned it may be to lie in order to save your friend's life, duty requires you to tell the truth. Duty does not admit of exceptions.

Kant took a similar hard line on truthfulness in his correspondence with **Maria von Herbert** (1769–1803), an Austrian woman and a devoted follower of Kant's philosophy. In 1791, when she had just entered her twenties, Herbert wrote to the philosopher she admired so much in search of his guidance in a profoundly troubling personal matter. She had lost the affection of the man she loved after disclosing the truth about "a long drawn out lie" she had told him.[45]

Suffering from wrenching heartbreak, she was on the brink of suicide, but her study and understanding of Kant's philosophy and the Kantian duty not to kill oneself held her back. Desperate for direction on how to go on living, she wrote to Kant, telling him that she did not see a way to do that in accordance with the principles of the moral law: "Now put yourself in my place, and either damn me or comfort me. I've read the metaphysic of morals, and the categorical imperative, and it doesn't help a bit. My reason abandons me just when I need it. Answer me, I implore you—or you won't be acting in accordance with your own imperative."[46]

Kant responded with what he called a "pure moral sedative" but warned Herbert that she had "sought counsel from a physician who is no flatterer."[47] With no dose of comfort in his letter to Herbert, Kant defended the "justified indignation" of a man whose love she had lost.[48] When she lied to her beloved, Kant told her, she violated a moral duty. She deceived him; thus, she denied him the respect that he deserved as a rational human being. What is more, he added, she would be further removed from morality if she regretted telling him the truth because of the consequences as opposed to the duty to truthfulness. He didn't refer at all to her mention of suicide.

As both of these examples from Kant's writing demonstrate, Kant thought that it is always wrong to lie. No matter the relationships involved or the consequences of the action, it is categorically, absolutely, without exception, always wrong to lie. It is this sort of strictness that can raise the concern that Kant's moral philosophy is too severe.

One way to take that position is to argue that circumstances should matter in morality or that life is too multi-faceted for hard and fast rules. For example, in the case of the inquiring murderer, one could draw attention to the detail that the intended victim is your friend and argue that you owe protection to a friend more than honesty to a murderous stranger.

In the case of Maria von Herbert's lost love, contemporary Kantian scholar Rae Langton offers an especially illuminating version of the criticism that Kant's ethics is too rigid. In her article titled "Duty and Desolation," Langton analyzes the correspondence between Kant and Herbert. In doing so, she draws attention to the details of Herbert's situation—specifically, her situation as a *woman* in eighteenth-century Europe.

Herbert was a woman of many privileges, as her education in Kant's philosophy indicates; nevertheless, she was a woman in a social context that denied women the ability to make choices equal to those of men. Instead, Langton explains, Herbert would have had to make choices against the backdrop of social institutions that did not respect her as a person but, rather, treated her as a thing. Langton writes,

> Central among the institutions she must encounter in her life is that of the sexual marketplace, where human beings are viewed as having a *price*, and not a dignity, and where the price of women is fixed in a particular way. Women, as things, as items in the sexual marketplace, have a market value that depends in part on whether they have been used. Virgins fetch a higher price than second hand goods. Such are the background circumstances in which Herbert finds herself. They are, I suggest, evil circumstances.[49]

Considering Herbert's life circumstance in this way reveals a serious challenge to the strictness of Kant's moral philosophy. The world is often evil and, as Langton points out, in an evil circumstance like Herbert's, the consequences of obeying the moral duty to tell the truth jeopardizes the Kantian moral ideal of a kingdom of ends wherein persons are able to receive the dignity and respect they deserve. Herbert is justified in her despair. In a situation where she is a standing target of disrespect, her way to be respected is to disrespect someone she loves. Strategizing for the sake of the kingdom of ends—that is, lying for the sake of her friendship with her beloved—should be permitted, argues Langton.

> "On the day when it will be possible for woman to love not in her weakness but in strength, not to escape herself but to find herself, not to abase herself but to assert herself—on that day love will become for her, as for man, a source of life and not of mortal danger."
> SIMONE DE BEAUVOIR

Maria Von Herbert[50]

Maria von Herbert was born on September 6, 1769 in Klagenfurt, Austria, to a well-off family headed by an industrialist father. In 1781, her brother, Franz Paul von Herbert, took over the family factory, but in 1789, he left that position to pursue a philosophical education. He spent two years in Weimar and Jena learning about Immanuel Kant's philosophy from a number of Kant's intellectual contemporaries, who were also significant philosophers in their own rights, such as Karl Leonhard Reinhold and Friedrich Schiller. When Maria's brother returned to Austria, he was armed with great admiration of the East Prussian philosopher and eager to spread word of his philosophy, which he did. Soon enough, the von Herbert household became a hotbed for study and debate about Kantian morality.

Maria von Herbert shared her brother's enthusiasm for Kant's philosophy, which inspired her to reach out

to the philosopher himself. In 1791, at the age of 22, Maria von Herbert sent the above-described letter to Kant, then 67 years old. At the beginning of 1793 and in then in 1794, von Herbert sent him two more letters, but Kant did not reply to either of them.

Maria von Herbert's letters demonstrate that she was an informed and serious student of Kant's writings as well as an impassioned critical thinker. She also divulges her struggle to reconcile Kant's teachings and her conduct, and her letters raise serious challenges to Kantian ethics.

Maria von Herbert died in 1803. After hosting a party at her home, she disappeared and drowned herself in the Drau River. Her body was never recovered. Her words, however, survive in her correspondence with Kant.

5.5 Carol Gilligan's and Nel Noddings's Care Ethics—Two Critiques of Male Moral Bias

Gilligan on Male Bias in Moral Research

Carol Gilligan and Nel Noddings are two contemporary scholars who have delved deeply into issues of bias in moral theory and have offered us fresh new insights challenging traditional male-oriented ethical viewpoints. While their criticisms of these viewpoints differ somewhat, and their theories take them in different directions, they still share a number of commonalities. This will become apparent as we proceed. We'll get to Nodding's work shortly, but before we do, let's first have a look at Gilligan's.

Gilligan argues that there has been an inherent **psychological bias** contained in the assumptions underlying a lot of the research on moral reasoning development—a bias that devalues the female perspective and considers it less developed and less adequate as compared to forms of ethical thinking preferred by males and more likely to be exhibited by them.[51]

Though a prolonged historical absence of women's voices in the standard canon of moral theorizing should have been a clue for modern ethicists that "something was up," so to speak, it was in the field of developmental psychology and moral education that allegations of male bias in ethics were perhaps most loudly voiced. Let's now briefly examine that developmental moral psychology that Gilligan finds so problematic. Later, we'll explore her concerns and reactions to it.

LAWRENCE KOHLBERG'S STAGES OF MORAL DEVELOPMENT

In his now-classic studies of **moral reasoning development**, Harvard researcher Lawrence Kohlberg claimed to have discovered the universal sequence of moral development for all human beings. This sequence was based on moral reasoning abilities, and was said to involve three basic levels of moral progression, each consisting of two sub-stages, making six stages in all. Kohlberg labeled these levels *pre-conventional*, *conventional*, and *post-conventional*. (See Figure 5.1.)

At pre-conventional Level One, children are responsive to cultural rules and labels of good and bad, right and wrong. These labels are interpreted either in terms of their physical-hedonistic consequences (punishment, reward, exchange of favor) or in terms of the physical power of those who state the rules and apply the labels.

Stage One of this level is called the "Punishment and Obedience Orientation." At this stage, avoiding punishment and adhering unquestioningly to power are valued in their own right—not because one is cognizant of any underlying moral order. *Might makes right*, as it were, as those with power and authority dictate what is, and is not, acceptable.

At Stage Two—"The Instrumental-Relativist Orientation"—right actions are those which instrumentally satisfy one's own needs and occasionally the needs of others. Human relations are viewed as marketplace exchanges. Moral reciprocity at this stage can be translated as, "I'll scratch your back if you scratch mine." Fairness and equal sharing are present but are always interpreted in a physical or pragmatic way. Reciprocity, here, has nothing to do with loyalty, gratitude, or justice.

At the conventional level, perceptions of morality change, as does thinking about it. What becomes important are the expectations of one's family, group, or nation. These are valued in their own right, regardless of immediate, obvious consequences. Individuals at the conventional level of morality conform to personal expectations and the requirements of maintaining social order. They act out of loyalty to it, actively supporting and justifying the order and identifying with the persons or group involved in it.

At Stage Three of the conventional level, what Kohlberg calls "The Interpersonal Concordance or 'Good Boy-Nice Girl' Orientation," good behavior is that which helps others and is approved by them. People's actions are judged by the *intentions* behind them. The idea that *the person meant well* becomes important for the first time. At Stage Three, one is able to earn approval by being *nice*.

As we move to Stage Four, "The Law and Order Orientation," the focus turns to fixed rules, authority, and the preservation of the social order. The right thing to do is one's duty. This shows respect for authority and *maintaining the social order for its own sake*. The law must be obeyed, for *a law is a law!*

At the post-conventional level of morality, we find clear efforts to define moral values and ethical principles that have validity and application aside from the authority of the groups or persons holding these principles and distinct from the moral agent's own identification with these persons and groups. Post-conventional morality is therefore the most *autonomous* of all three levels. Like the others, it contains two sub-stages.

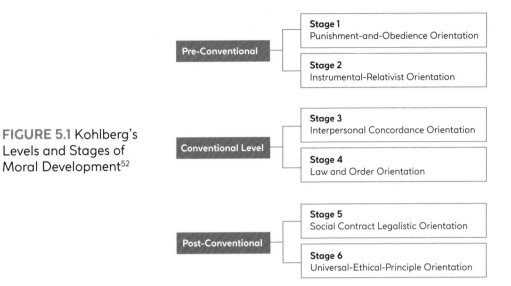

FIGURE 5.1 Kohlberg's Levels and Stages of Moral Development[52]

We discover at Stage Five, "The Social-Contract Legalistic Orientation," that there are utilitarian overtones. What is right is defined with respect to generally agreed upon individual rights and in terms of standards that have been critically examined, evaluated, and agreed upon by the whole society—not just some subgroup within it. At this stage, people emphasize the legal point of view but accept the possibility that the law might have to be changed in view of rational considerations of social utility (in contrast to strictly upholding the law in terms of Stage Four law and order, where *a law is a law*). Here, free and contractual agreement becomes the binding element of obligation. Kohlberg sees Stage Five morality as the *official morality* of the U.S. government and Constitution.

Finally, at Stage Six, "The Universal-Ethical-Principle Orientation," what is right is established in accordance with self-chosen ethical principles—ones appealing to *logical comprehensiveness, universality, and consistency*. Principles at Stage Six are *formal* and *abstract*. Examples would include The Golden Rule and Kant's categorical imperative. It's been said that, "[a]t heart, these are universal principles of justice, of the reciprocity and equality of human rights, and of respect for the dignity of human beings as individual persons."[53]

In the context of the transition from one stage or level to the next, Kohlberg argues on the basis of empirical study that movement is *invariant* and *sequential*, and furthermore, that it is *culturally universal*. In stage development, people are cognitively attracted to reasoning one step above their own. Movement is effected when *psychological disequilibrium* is created; that is, when individuals discover that their current thinking is somehow inadequate to deal with the moral problem at issue. *Moral thinking progresses and gains in adequacy by becoming less concrete and more morally abstract.*

To explain: At the pre-conventional level, moral goodness is determined by tangible and physical consequences; at the conventional level, by group wishes and the maintenance of social order for its own sake; and lastly, at the post-conventional level, by adherence to abstract universal principles of justice, which transcend any individual or group.

The post-conventional level represents, for Kohlberg, the most adequate, developed, and ethically sound form of moral reasoning.

Kohlberg's Stage Six morality sits squarely in line with Kant's categorical imperative.[54] For Kohlberg, Stage Six principled morality is superior by virtue of its being the preferred choice of *rational self-interested persons* finding themselves in what the Kantian-influenced political philosopher John Rawls describes as *the original position* in his important treatise, *A Theory of Justice*.[55]

Using the original position, Rawls provides us with a modern interpretation of justice consistent with a number of Kantian principles and supported by Kohlbergian research. Like Kant, Rawls tries to remove empirical factors as much as possible from the initial establishment of principles that would guide moral decision-making in the context of conflict resolution. To this end, potentially conflicting parties, i.e., rationally self-interested individuals, are hypothetically placed behind a *veil of ignorance*, something that prevents them from knowing who they are, and what is to their advantage when deciding what to do. Without such personal knowledge, rational parties must formulate, *in advance*, mutually acceptable principles they can use to adjudicate conflicts if and when they arise in the future. The results of such adjudication would be *objectively fair* and *just*.

Since no personal reference can be made to favor any one party behind the veil of ignorance, the resulting principles turn out to be purely rational, formal, and abstract. Thus, to argue that moral principles must be *objective*, *rational*, *consistent*, *impartial*, and *reversible* is not to dictate any specific content-laden prescriptions about precisely what must be done or avoided by any one person in any one specific situation. Acceptable principles must simply display these formal characteristics.

To illustrate: if a moral principle is to be deemed impartial and objectively justified, it must be acceptable to the person or persons most disadvantaged by its application, given that the person or persons advancing it don't know whether they are on the *receiving end* of that principle. If self-interested conflicting parties are both or all prepared, in advance, to be the individual or individuals most adversely affected by the application of the principle in question, then it meets the *reversibility criterion*. If no personal factors are allowed to skew or bias the moral principle proposed, fairness is ensured, since no favor or disfavor is built into it. If the principle is non-contradictory, then it is rationally consistent. Note again that no substantive matters are at issue here, just formal ones.

GILLIGAN'S CRITIQUE

In response to Kohlberg's theory and empirical findings, Gilligan points out that his original research was limited to an all-male sample of subjects. For 15 years, Kohlberg studied the development of moral reasoning and judgment by following the same group of 75 boys at three-year intervals from early adolescence through young adulthood. The boys/men were presented with **hypothetical moral dilemmas**, their responses to related questions recorded. It was on the basis of these *exclusively male responses to hypothetical dilemmas* that Kohlberg initially formulated his theory of moral development.

Gilligan takes exception to the fact that Kohlberg's dilemmas were used with an all-male sample, likely skewing the empirical results of his study. It's problematic to state firm general conclusions about moral reasoning development when you leave women out of your study—a fact Gilligan strongly underscores.

"I've learned that whenever I decide something with an open heart, I usually make the right decision."
MAYA ANGELOU

Furthermore, Gilligan takes exception to the fact that the dilemmas that were addressed by research subjects were *canned*, or prepared in advance without any input from those responding to them. Moral problems were *presented, not constructed* by the subjects themselves. They were *hypothetical*, *abstract*, and *artificial*. This is important for Gilligan, since she claims, on the basis of her own research, that *women tend to view morality more personally in concrete terms*, rather than impersonally and abstractly—the ideal for Kohlberg. Women also tend, according to Gilligan, to operate more naturally from a *position of moral care and relationship* and less from a *position of rational principle and impersonal justice*, ideas with which adjudications of interpersonal conflicts work most easily.

On this note, one should be reminded that Gilligan conceptualizes the differences between masculine and feminine morality more by theme than by gender itself.[56] Although it is empirically true that more women tend to operate from a perspective of feminine morality, nothing prevents them from displaying masculine moral preferences. Likewise, men can function morally from both perspectives as well, only they tend to prefer a more detached rational objectivity, often presupposing that it is more adequate or superior in some fashion.

This is true, in fact, for Kohlberg. Women, who often do not "reach" Stage Six in his conceptual framework, come out as less developed and less mature in their moral reasoning abilities. What Gilligan would describe as an **ethic of care** fits into Kohlberg's scheme at the conventional level—a less adequate form of moral thinking as compared with the more autonomous, impersonal, and detached forms of morality found at Stages Five and Six of the post-conventional level.

On this basis, Gilligan argues that Kohlberg's studies of morality fail to do justice to women's moral experience. Women are not less developed morally, as some of the empirical studies might suggest; rather, for Gilligan, there has been a failure by theorists to produce models of human growth that acknowledge and respect male-female differences. The universal and prescriptive paradigm of Kantian-Rawlsian morality, supported by Kohlberg's cognitive-developmental studies, is arguably not more adequate or more justified—just more male.

THINKING ABOUT YOUR THINKING

First, think about the following scenario: Imagine you are a lawyer hired to defend a client who has been accused of a serious crime. There is a flaw in the prosecution's case that you could use to argue that the charges be dropped. Your argument would most likely be successful, and your client would walk free. On the other hand, your client has admitted guilt to you. Furthermore, it is very likely your client would commit the same serious crime again. What should you do?

Second, have you ever cared about someone but thought that person made morally bad decisions? Think about a scenario from your own life when your personal commitments to a friend or family member have been in conflict with your beliefs about the morality of their actions. If you were in that situation again, what should you do?

Third, compare your thinking in these two situations. What kinds of considerations came up as you thought through both of them? Did you base your two decisions on different moral principles or give different kinds of reasons for your decisions? If there were any differences in your moral thinking, what do you think explains those differences?

"... the logic underlying an ethic of care is a psychological logic of relationship, which contrasts with the formal logic of fairness that informs the justice approach."
CAROL GILLIGAN

Carol Gilligan

Although Carol Gilligan (b. 1936) is an American psychologist, the scope and variety of her work challenges that simple label. Gilligan earned a Ph.D. in social psychology from Harvard University and taught in the Graduate School of Education there before visiting as a fellow in the Faculty of Social and Political Sciences at the University of Cambridge in England. She also held a Gender Studies Chair upon her return to Harvard and was its first Gender Studies professor. In addition, Gilligan has been a professor at New York University's Faculty of Law, and since the spring of 2021 has been Professor of Humanities and Applied Psychology there. Her lifetime of theorizing and research has had an enormous impact on thinkers in the fields of education, psychology, moral philosophy, and beyond.

During her time at Harvard in the 1960s, Gilligan worked as a research assistant on Lawrence Kohlberg's studies of moral reasoning development. That is when she came to her realization that the scholarship on moral development ignored the moral voices of women and the emphasis on care that is common (although not necessarily exclusive) to the moral perspectives of women.

In her own work on the topic, Gilligan criticizes long-held assumptions about moral development, specifically those contained in cognitive-developmental theories based on rational, universalistic assumptions that she believes contain a male bias. Such theories, argues Gilligan, devalue the caring relational nature of feminine moral experience, relegating women's moral thinking to a position of inferior and less adequate moral reasoning development. Gilligan calls into question the ultimate authority of reason as the basis of morality and, because of this, is relevant to philosophical inquiry.

Gilligan's book, *In a Different Voice: Psychological Theory and Women's Development* (1982), had a groundbreaking influence in the areas of psychology and education and inspired the ethics of care movement in philosophy. The book is, however, not without its critics or controversy, including criticism that it reinforced stereotypes about women and was not based on adequately rigorous research. Regardless, the discussion about women's voices that she created has had a lasting impact.

In 1996, Gilligan was named one of *Time* magazine's 25 Most Influential People and in 2019 the *New York Times* profiled the so-described *Feminist Rock Star* in an article titled "Carefully Smash the Patriarchy." In addition to being a prolific academic writer, Gilligan is also a playwright and novelist.

Gilligan's Ethic of Care

The different voice of morality to which Gilligan would have us listen may very well have its roots in individual **identity formation**. Gilligan cites the research of Nancy Chodorow to explain how men and women come to experience and conceptualize morality differently. As Gilligan says, *female identity formation occurs in a context of ongoing relationships*. Mothers have a tendency to experience their daughters as more like them, as extensions of themselves. Correspondingly, daughters, in their self-identifications as females, experience themselves as similar to their mothers. Thus, the experience of attachment is fused with the process of identity formation.

By contrast, as boys develop, they tend to separate their mothers from themselves and thereby curtail their primary love object and sense of empathetic tie. Chodorow concludes that male development entails a "more emphatic individuation and a more defensive firming of experienced ego boundaries."[57] The ultimate result of this that "girls emerge from this period with a basis for 'empathy' built into their primary definition of self in a way that boys do not."[58] Furthermore, "Girls emerge with a stronger basis for experiencing another's needs or feelings as [their] own."[59] They experience themselves as less differentiated than boys and as more continuous with, and related to, others.

Given the differences between boys' and girls' psychological attachments and individuation patterns, male gender identity is threatened by **intimacy**, while female gender identity is threatened by **separation**, according to Chodorow. If so, it becomes more easily understandable how *rational detachment* becomes a virtue from a masculine moral perspective, whereas *relation and care* become hallmarks of feminine morality.

Commenting on Kohlberg and the alleged historical male bias in moral theorizing, Gilligan writes:

> The quality of embeddedness in social interaction and personal relationships that characterizes women's lives in contrast to men's, however, becomes not only a descriptive difference but also a developmental liability when the milestones of childhood and adolescent development in the psychological literature are markers of increasing separation. Women's failure to separate then becomes by definition a failure to develop.[60]

Of course, Gilligan sees nothing wrong with women's experience of morality, but does point to serious flaws in models of morality (like Kohlberg's) that fail to capture it properly. An ethic of care is only less developed and less adequate when viewed through the lens of masculine values and male identity formation.

In her own developmental research, Gilligan did not present subjects with abstract, hypothetical dilemmas for resolution. Instead, she asked people (1) how they defined moral problems themselves and (2) what experiences they construed as moral conflicts in their lives. In an *abortion decision* study, her sample of 29 women, ages 15 to 33 years, looked at the relation between experience and thought and the role of conflict in development. The women in the study were initially interviewed in the first trimester of their pregnancies, at a time when they were contemplating having abortions. Most of the women were interviewed again at the end of the year following their choice. Complete interview data were available for 24 of them.

In a second "rights and responsibility" study, a sample of males and females were matched for age, intelligence, education, occupation, and social class at nine points across the life cycle. Data were collected on conceptions of self and morality, experiences of moral conflict and choice, and judgments on hypothetical moral dilemmas.

Gilligan's findings from her studies suggest we should broaden our understanding of human (moral) development. Women apparently tend to display perspectives different from men when it comes to (1) images of humankind, (2) the human condition, (3) human development, and (4) what is of value in life. In brief, moral development for women involves a progressive change in the understanding of responsibility and relationships. For men—or at least for Kohlberg—morality, seen as justice, ties development to the logic of equality and reciprocity.

In her book, *In a Different Voice: Psychological Theory and Women's Development*, Gilligan spells out for us the developmental sequence for the ethics of care. At Stage One, the individual is most concerned with *caring for herself* to ensure survival. In time, this life position and the judgments flowing from it come to be criticized as selfish.

"... as long as the categories by which development is assessed are derived from research on men, divergence from the masculine standard can be seen only as a failure of development. As a result, the thinking of women is often classified with that of children."
CAROL GILLIGAN

A transitional phase emerges whereby a new understanding of connection between oneself and others is articulated. Here, at Stage Two, good is essentially equated with *caring for others*. A type of maternal morality develops that seeks to ensure care for the dependent and unequal. Stage Two eventually opens the door to the next transitional phase. When only others are allowed to be the recipients of the woman's care—when she cannot care for herself without being selfish—this exclusion of herself gives rise to problems in relationships and thereby creates disequilibrium.

At the third and final stage of development, care is understood not in a dichotomous fashion (caring only for me *or* only for others) but as an interconnection between oneself *and* others. This third stage highlights the *dynamics of relationships* whereby we see a reduction in the tension between selfishness and responsibility. As Gilligan puts it:

> Care becomes the self-chosen principle of a judgment that remains psychological in its concern with relationships and response but becomes universal in its condemnation of exploitation and hurt. Thus a progressively more adequate understanding of the psychology of human relationships—an increasing differentiation of self and other and a growing comprehension of the dynamics of social interaction—informs the development of an ethic of care. This ethic, which reflects a cumulative knowledge of human relationships, evolves around a central insight, that self and other are interdependent.[61]

Clearly, we can appreciate now how Gilligan's ethic of care, characterized by *interdependence and responsibility for others*, stands in stark contrast to the Kantian-Rawlsian-Kohlbergian model of morality, defined by autonomy, impartiality, and other such formal abstract principles. As philosophers, we might ask: Is one moral perspective necessarily better or more adequate than the other? Should an ethic of care overrule an ethic of justice, or are both perspectives limited viewpoints of something perhaps much broader in scope? Maybe we need to *reason more with care, and care more about reason*?

Nel Noddings and Care Ethics

"Indeed, one who attempts to ignore or to climb above the human affect at the heart of ethicality may well be guilty of romantic rationalism."
NEL NODDINGS

In her book, *Caring: A Feminine Approach to Ethics and Moral Education*,[62] **Nel Noddings** presents an ethic of care that diverges from Carol Gilligan's work in some significant ways, but, as mentioned before, bears a noticeable resemblance to it. She provides slightly different criticisms of rational morality, as compared with Gilligan, but shares the view, for example, that the male-dominated philosophical community has been guilty of bias insofar as it has concentrated its studies of morality largely on rational principles, in contrast to basing it on *emotion* or the *human affective response*. She also accepts, like Gilligan, the notion that there are at least two basic approaches to morality, which tend to be either more masculine or more feminine in orientation.

Both Noddings and Gilligan would also likely agree that an ethic like Kant's, for instance, which is characterized by *rational consistency*, *detachment*, *objectivity*, and the *universal prescriptive application of principles*, is an ethic guided by the "masculine spirit." Specifically for Noddings, the problem with this is that this presentation of ethics gives it a mathematical appearance, as if it were governed by the same kind of logical necessity characteristic of geometry. There is another alternative capturing the "feminine spirit," Noddings claims, one which is a less abstract approach to morality. It is rooted in *care*, or what can be called the *receptive rationality of caring*, and is known as *care ethics*.

Nel Noddings

Nel Noddings (1929–2022) is an American educator and philosopher. Among her friends and family, she was also known as a gardener, lover of animals, mentor, cook, and mother (of 10 children).

Noddings completed her Bachelor of Arts degree in mathematics and physical science at Montclair State College before going on to do her Master's degree in mathematics at Rutgers and her Ph.D. degree in Educational Philosophy and Theory at Stanford University (1973). She taught at all levels of education, from elementary school to university. In her positions at various American universities, she directed courses in educational philosophy, moral education, and contemporary social and ethical philosophy. After her retirement in 1998, she became the Lee L. Jacks Professor of Education, *Emerita*, at Stanford University.

In addition to *Caring: A Feminine Approach to Ethics and Moral Education* (1984), Noddings produced numerous other publications, including *Women and Evil* (1989), *Philosophy of Education* (1995), and more than 200 articles and book chapters. She served as president for the Philosophy of Education Society and the John Dewey Society. Noddings was the recipient of many awards and distinctions, including the Medal for Distinguished Service given by the Teacher's College of Columbia University.

ROMANTICIZING PRINCIPLES

Noddings draws our attention to some of the limitations inherent in an approach grounded in abstract principles. She alleges that such a morality is ambiguous and unstable. In her view, whenever you have a principle, exceptions are almost always implied. The general principle "Never kill," for instance, could easily be followed by "except in self-defense" or "except in defense of an innocent other," and so on. Her point is that general principles of conduct are not as solid and reassuring as some would like to think.

Noddings claims another drawback to principled morality is that principles can often separate people and alienate them from one another. For example, have you ever stubbornly refused to budge *on principle*? Have you ever terminated a relationship for the same reason? Have principles ever pushed you farther away from others, instead of bringing you closer to them? If so, then you can appreciate how principled thought and action could be counterproductive as far as bringing people together and having them live harmoniously are concerned. As Noddings expresses it, "We may become dangerously self-righteous when we perceive ourselves as holding a precious principle not held by the other. The other may then be devalued and treated 'differently.' Our ethic of caring will not permit this to happen."[63]

Noddings's rejection of principled morality leads her to reject the rational concept of **universalizability**. From our coverage of Immanuel Kant's theory, you may remember that, for Kant, any maxim or principle of behavior had to be *universalizable*, or *universally prescriptive*, in order for it to belong to morality and to be morally justifiable. Maxims or

principles of conduct that could not be universally prescribed were deemed to be either non-moral (e.g., prudential) or immoral. With respect to morality, if under condition *X*, you are morally required to do *A*, then under sufficiently similar conditions, I too am required to do *A*, along with everyone else. The moral obligation applies to everybody universally and unconditionally.

Noddings rejects this line of moral thinking because, in her estimation, it fails to recognize and preserve the *uniqueness of human encounters*. Due to the highly personal, idiosyncratic, and subjective experience of those involved in particular moral or ethical relations, conditions are *seldom sufficiently similar* for anyone to declare what we must do in our situation or what anyone else should do in their situation.

So, for Noddings, the universalizability criterion doesn't work, as principles of moral conduct simply cannot be properly universalized. *Efforts to abstract universal principles from concrete situations, or attempts to apply such principles from on high, cause us to lose sight of the unique features and personal variables that gave rise to the moral questions or dilemmas in the first place.* Though two situations may appear somewhat similar from a detached observer's perspective, they are likely not sufficiently similar when viewed from *within the situation*. Consequently, the detached application of a universal principle from one situation to another is not appropriate.

Given Noddings's rejection of the universalizability criterion and her criticism of principled morality, it is interesting to refer back for a moment to Lawrence Kohlberg's theory of moral development. Remember that, for him, the most highly developed and most adequate morality is the one that is the most abstract and universal. That which is concrete or person-specific is less developed and less mature, labeled as conventional or pre-conventional.

However, insofar as Noddings's criticisms are justified, we should reexamine the assumptions underlying a principle-based "masculine" morality. As Noddings says, "Women can and do give reasons for their acts, but the *reasons often point to feelings, needs, impressions, and a sense of personal ideal rather than to universal principles and their application.* We shall see that, as a result of this 'odd' approach, women have often been judged inferior to men in the moral domain."[64] The point here is that women who operate from the vantage point of feminine ethics do not proceed from principles superimposed on situations. In response to Kohlberg's dilemmas, women would seek to fill out those hypothetical situations in a "defensible move toward concretization."[65]

In the case of administering punishment, say, for one who is guilty of committing a crime, the traditional approach asks about the principle under which this case falls, so that it may be applied. Care ethics, by contrast, asks us to consider the feelings involved and the personal history of the wrongdoer. When the situation is *concretized* by such things as feelings and personal histories, what is appropriate punishment or what is the appropriate resolution to the conflict may change.

For Noddings, *there is no virtue in abstraction, where thinking can occur in a logical vacuum, apart from the complicating factors of particular persons, places, and circumstances.*[66] These *complicating factors* are what make the moral situation *real*. The move toward logical abstraction, which admittedly unclutters the complexity of any moral dilemma, in the end undermines itself with artificiality and the prospect of destroying interpersonal relationships—the very thing morality is meant to preserve and protect.

RELATION AS ONTOLOGICALLY BASIC

In articulating her conception of morality, Noddings clearly does not begin with abstract principles. Furthermore, in contrast to John Rawls, who conceptualizes the moral agent as rational, self-interested, autonomous, and independent of others, Noddings takes the caring **relation** as ethically basic. To be human is to be in relation to others. We do not stand alone, isolated and apart from others, either psychologically or existentially. Human existence is relational. Morality comes not from the *a priori* structure of reason itself like Kant claims, but rather from the interpersonal human dynamic of persons in relation. It is affect and connection that should serve as the basis of morality, not abstract principles.

In her book, Noddings spells out the details of her care-based ethic, and for a fuller appreciation of what's at issue, you are invited to read it in full. For our purposes here, we'll just touch on a few of the general features characterizing this moral perspective and follow that with an excerpt from her writing.

BRIEF OUTLINE OF NODDINGS'S CARE-BASED ETHIC

To say that the caring relation is ontologically basic is to say that there is the **one caring** and the **one cared for**, to use Noddings's terminology, and that this is the basic fact behind ethical thinking. The conception of morality she has in mind establishes an ethical ideal of what it means to be the one caring for others. It involves reaching out to others and growing in response to others. Interpreting morality in terms of persons in relation is different from relying on an emotionally sterile conception of rationally self-interested individuals seeking to further their own goals and cooperating only when it is mutually advantageous. Ethical caring emerges from **natural caring**—a condition toward which we long and strive.

In our infancies, we begin to develop memories of *caring* and *being cared for*. The resulting caring attitude provides the motivation to be moral, and because it is so basic and natural, it is universally accessible. The relation of natural caring represents moral goodness. When we remain in a concrete caring relation and enhance the ideal of ourselves as ones caring, we do the morally good thing. Everything hinges on the nature and strength of this ideal. There are no absolutes to guide us.

This does not mean, for Noddings, that morality disintegrates into relativity, however, since the natural caring attitude supporting ethical caring is a universal phenomenon. Universality, understood as a foundational basis of morality, is not rational but relational for Noddings. *Moral Obligation is therefore not a matter of acting in ways consistent with abstract-formal principles (regardless of who's involved) but a response to commitments and to the maintenance of relationships.* Noddings writes: "The source of my obligation is the value I place

THINKING ABOUT YOUR THINKING

Imagine if someone you loved could not live independently anymore and you were in charge of the decision on where that person should be moved: to an assisted living home, in with family, or elsewhere. If you were to make that decision using Kantian principles of morality, what considerations would you have to think about in order to determine what you should to do? In contrast, if you acted out of care rather than by strict adherence to Kantian principles, what considerations would you have to think about in order to decide what to do? Which manner of thinking about morality is preferable to you in this scenario: Kantian ethics or care ethics thinking? Why?

As a follow up to your analysis above, it might be interesting and insightful to compare applications of utilitarian ethics with care-based ethics as well. Which moral approach best deals with the issues raised by the question or dilemma as presented? Why so? What do you learn about your own moral thinking in arriving at your personal conclusions?

on the relatedness of caring. This value itself arises as a product of actual caring and being cared-for and my reflection on the goodness of these concrete caring situations."[67]

In short, the ethical ideal of maintaining the caring relation should, for Noddings, be placed above abstract principles as a guide to moral action. In this, we find a basic difference between Noddings's care ethics and the approaches represented by thinkers like Kant, Kohlberg, and Rawls.

The last point to be made here refers to the basic human affect grounding morality. Unlike suffering existentialists, who recognize their unique subjectivity as aloneness in the world, and who consequentially experience anguish, Noddings considers *joy as the fundamental human emotion rooted in relation*. She states that it is our recognition of, and longing for, relatedness that forms the foundation of care ethics. "[T]he joy that accompanies fulfillment of our caring enhances our commitment to the ethical ideal that sustains us as one-caring."[68] It's not dour obligation that moves us to moral action, then, nor capricious subjectivity, but rather the joy and desire to exercise the virtue of goodness by fulfilling ourselves in the other. Responsiveness and receptivity are key, not detachment, nor cold rational aloofness.

In this moral attitude or psychological posture, we find a fundamental difference between care ethics and the approaches discussed earlier in this chapter. And in the discussion of this difference, we discover many fresh new insights that challenge the male-dominated historical assumptions about morality.

Nel Noddings, *Caring: A Feminine Approach to Ethics and Moral Education*[69]

The following excerpt comes from the Introduction in Nel Noddings's Caring: A Feminine Approach to Ethics and Moral Education. *First published in 1984, the book is based on the recognition that many people who live moral lives do not approach moral problems with principles and arguments but, rather, from a position of caring. That caring viewpoint involves seeing another's reality as a possibility for oneself.*

―――

INTRODUCTION

Ethics, the philosophical study of morality, has concentrated for the most part on moral reasoning. Much current work, for example, focuses on the status of moral predicates and, in education, the dominant model presents a hierarchical picture of moral reasoning. This emphasis gives ethics a contemporary, mathematical appearance, but it also moves discussion beyond the sphere of actual human activity and the feeling that pervades such activity. Even though careful philosophers have recognized the difference between "pure" or logical reason and "practical" or moral reason, ethical argumentation has frequently proceeded as if it were governed by the logical necessity characteristic of geometry. It has concentrated on the establishment of principles and that which can be logically derived from them. One might say that ethics has been discussed largely in the language of the father: in principles and propositions, in terms such as justification, fairness, justice. The mother's voice has been silent. Human caring and the memory of caring and being cared for, which I shall argue form the foundation of ethical response, have not received attention except as outcomes of ethical behavior. One is tempted to say that ethics has so far been guided by Logos, the masculine spirit, whereas the more natural and, perhaps, stronger approach would be through Eros, the feminine spirit. I hesitate to give way to this temptation, in part because the terms carry with them a Jungian baggage that I am unwilling to claim in its totality. In one sense, "Eros" does capture the flavor and spirit of what I am attempting here; the notion of psychic relatedness lies at the heart of the ethic I shall propose. In another sense, however, even "Eros" is masculine in its roots and fails to capture the receptive rationality of caring that is characteristic of the feminine approach.

When we look clear-eyed at the world today, we see it wracked with fighting, killing, vandalism, and psychic pain of all sorts. One of the saddest features of this picture of violence is that the deeds are so often done in the name of principle. When we establish a principle forbidding killing, we also establish principles describing the exceptions to the first principle. Supposing, then, that we are moral (we are principled, are we not?), we may tear into others whose beliefs or behaviors differ from ours with the promise of ultimate vindication.

This approach through law and principle is not, I suggest, the approach of the mother. It is the approach of the detached one, of the father. The view to be expressed here is a feminine view. This does not imply that all women will accept it or that men will reject it; indeed, there is no reason why men should not embrace it. It is feminine in the deep classical sense—rooted in receptivity, relatedness, and responsiveness. It does not imply either that logic is to be discarded or that logic is alien to women. It represents an alternative to present views, one that begins with the moral attitude or longing for goodness and not with moral reasoning. It may indeed be the case that such an approach is more typical of women than of men, but this is an empirical question I shall not attempt to answer....

Women, in general, face a ... problem when they enter the practical domain of moral action. They enter the domain through a different door, so to speak. It is not the case, certainly, that women cannot arrange principles hierarchically and derive conclusions logically. It is more likely that we see this process as peripheral to, or even alien to, many problems of moral action. Faced with a hypothetical moral dilemma, women often ask for more information. We want to know more, I think, in order to form a picture more nearly resembling real moral situations. Ideally, we need to talk to the participants, to see their eyes and facial expressions, to receive what they are feeling. Moral decisions are, after all, made in real situations; they are qualitatively different from the solution of geometry problems. Women can and do give reasons for their acts, but the reasons often point to feelings, needs, impressions, and a sense of personal ideal rather than to universal principles and their application. We shall see that, as a result of this "odd" approach, women have often been judged inferior to men in the moral domain.

Because I am entering the domain through a linguistic back door of sorts, much of what I say cannot be labeled "empirical" or "logical." (Some of it, of course, can be so labeled.) Well, what is it then? It is language that attempts to capture what Wittgenstein advised we "must pass over in silence." But if our language is extended to the expressive—and, after all, it is beautifully capable of such extension—perhaps we can say something in the realm of ethical feeling, and that something may at least achieve the status of conceptual aid or tool if not that of conceptual truth. We may present a coherent and enlightening picture without *proving* anything and, indeed, without claiming to present or to seek moral *knowledge* or moral *truth*. The hand that steadied us as we learned to ride our first bicycle did not provide propositional knowledge, but it guided and supported us all the same, and we finished up "knowing how."

This is an essay in practical ethics from the feminine view. It is very different from the utilitarian practical ethics of, say, Peter Singer.* While both of us would treat animals kindly and sensitively, for example, we give very different reasons for our consideration. I must resist his charge that we are guilty of "speciesism" in our failure to accord rights to animals, because I shall locate the very wellspring of ethical behavior in human affective response. Throughout our discussion of ethicality we shall remain in touch with the affect that gives rise to it. This does not mean that our discussion will bog down in sentiment, but it is necessary to give appropriate attention and credit to the affective foundation of existence.

Indeed, one who attempts to ignore or to climb above the human affect at the heart of ethicality may well be guilty of romantic rationalism. What is recommended in such a framework simply cannot be broadly applied in the actual world.

I shall begin with a discussion of caring. What does it mean to care and to be cared for? The analysis will occupy us at length, since relation will be taken as ontologically basic and the caring relation as ethically basic. For our purposes, "relation" may be thought of as a set of ordered pairs generated by some rule that describes the affect—or subjective experience—of the members.

In order to establish a firm conceptual foundation that will be free of equivocation, I have given names to the two parties of the relation: the first member is the "one-caring" and the second is the "cared-for." Regular readers of "existentialist" literature will recognize the need for such terminology—bothersome as it is. One may recall Sartre's use of for-itself and in-itself, Heidegger's being-in-the-world, and Buber's I-Thou and I-It. There are at least two good reasons for invoking this mechanism. First, it allows us to speak about our basic entities without explaining the entire conceptual apparatus repeatedly; second, it prevents us from smuggling in meanings through the use of synonyms. Hence, even though hyphenated entities offend the stylist, they represent in this case an attempt to achieve both economy and rigor. Another matter of style in connection with "one-caring" and "cared-for" should be mentioned here. In order to maintain balance and avoid confusion, I have consistently associated the generic "one-caring" with the universal feminine, "she," and "cared-for" with the masculine, "he." Clearly, however, when actual persons are substituted for "one-caring" and "cared-for" in the basic relation, they may be both male, both female, female-male, or male-female. Taking *relation* as ontologically basic simply means that we recognize human encounter and affective response as a basic fact of human existence. As we examine what it means to care and to be cared for, we shall see that both parties contribute to the relation; my caring must be somehow completed in the other if the relation is to be described as caring.

This suggests that the ethic to be developed is one of reciprocity, but our view of reciprocity will be different from that of "contract" theorists such as Plato and John

---

* Singer (b. 1946), currently at Princeton, is a philosopher very well-known for his advocacy of animal rights and vegetarianism, based on utilitarian theory. [A.F.'s footnote.]

Rawls. What the cared-for gives to the caring relation is not a promise to behave as the one-caring does, nor is it a form of "consideration." The problem of reciprocity will be, possibly, the most important problem we shall discuss, and facets of the problem will appear in a spiral design throughout the book. When we see what it is that the cared-for contributes to the relation, we shall find it possible to separate human infants from nonhuman animals (a great problem for those who insist on some form of rationality in those we should treat ethically), and we shall do this without recourse to notions of God or some other external source of "sanctity" in human life.

The focus of our attention will be upon how to meet the other morally. Ethical caring, the relation in which we do meet the other morally, will be described as arising out of natural caring—that relation in which we respond as one-caring out of love or natural inclination. The relation of natural caring will be identified as the human condition that we, consciously or unconsciously, perceive as "good." It is that condition toward which we long and strive, and it is our longing for caring—to be in that special relation—that provides the motivation for us to be moral. We want to be *moral* in order to remain in the caring relation and to enhance the ideal of ourselves as one-caring.

It is this ethical ideal, this realistic picture of ourselves as one-caring, that guides us as we strive to meet the other morally. Everything depends upon the nature and strength of this ideal, for we shall not have absolute principles to guide us. Indeed, I shall reject ethics of principle as ambiguous and unstable. Wherever there is a principle, there is implied its exception and, too often, principles function to separate us from each other. We may become dangerously self-righteous when we perceive ourselves as holding a precious principle not held by the other. The other may then be devalued and treated "differently." Our ethic of caring will not permit this to happen. We recognize that in fear, anger, or hatred we will treat the other differently, but this treatment is never conducted ethically. Hence, when we must use violence or strategies on the other, we are already diminished ethically. Our efforts must, then, be directed to the maintenance of conditions that will permit caring to flourish. Along with the rejection of principles and rules as the major guide to ethical behavior, I shall also reject the notion of universalizability. Many of those writing and thinking about ethics insist that any ethical judgment—by virtue of its *being* an ethical judgment—must be universalizable; that is, it must be the case that, if under conditions X you are required to do A, then under sufficiently similar conditions, I too am required to do A. I shall reject this emphatically. First, my attention is not on judgment and not on the particular acts we perform but on how we meet the other morally. Second, in recognition of the feminine approach to meeting the other morally—our insistence on caring for the other—I shall want to preserve the uniqueness of human encounters. Since so much depends on the subjective experience of those involved in ethical encounters, conditions are rarely "sufficiently similar" for me to declare that you must do what I must do. There is, however, a fundamental universality in our ethic, as there must be to escape relativism. The caring attitude, that attitude which expresses our earliest memories of being cared for and our growing store of memories of both caring and being cared for, is universally accessible. Since caring and the commitment to sustain it form the universal heart of the ethic, we must establish a convincing and comprehensive picture of caring at the outset.

READING QUESTIONS

1. What does it mean for Noddings to take a "feminine view" of ethics as opposed to a "masculine view"? What "risk" is Noddings taking with her "feminine view" of ethics?

2. What does Noddings mean when she claims that "relation" is ontologically basic? What conditions must be met in order for a relation to be caring?

3. Ethical principles are action-guiding. For example, think of how a utilitarian uses the principle of utility to decide what to do. Noddings rejects ethical principles. Why? Furthermore, without principles, what guides our actions in Noddings's ethic of care?

Developmental theory would appear to force us as philosophers to revisit the idea that "the more objective and less emotional, the better." Could it be that a large part of Western philosophy is biased by the fact that so much of it was historically written by men? Discuss.

5.6 Friedrich Nietzsche's Will to Power

In the history of philosophy, perhaps no other thinker explodes our moral complacency as much as **Friedrich Nietzsche**. He is truly a disturber of the peace, our peace of mind. With his bombastic writing style and iconoclastic outpourings, he produces outrage in the hearts of the religiously devout, and of conventional thinkers and traditionalists who unquestioningly accept their ancestors' ethical prescriptions about how life ought to be lived.

So be forewarned, our explorations here take us ashore and will require travel over some rocky and dangerous terrain. Along the way, you may suffer a number of psycho-spiritual bumps and bruises, if not deep lacerations to the psyche severing you from some of your most cherished beliefs. This part of our exploratory journey into ethics is not for the faint of heart. It is for bold, courageous individuals who are not afraid to affirm life and take responsibility for themselves. Proceed with caution, then. The future of your life is at stake here! (How's that for a little Nietzschean bombast?)

God Is Dead

Many moralists throughout history have sought direction and solace in a belief in God. If there exists a God, then all is secure. God, understood as the grand architect of the universe, establishes order, structure, and predictability. As our creator, God determines human nature, defining who we are and prescribing the purpose for which we were born. For those belonging to one of the **Abrahamic religious traditions** (Christianity, Islam, and Judaism), for instance, the task of life is to do God's will and obey His commandments. Although it is difficult sometimes to abide by the rules, at least there are rules for personal moral guidance.

In a world created by God, "essence precedes existence," to use existentialist phraseology (see Section 3.2). We do not have the freedom to determine our natures, but we do have the freedom of choice to realize our God-given potentialities as His servants. We cannot determine the future, only respond to it with humble acceptance of God's will. What we don't understand or what makes no apparent sense is simply beyond human comprehension. As the saying goes, *God works in mysterious ways*. Who are we to judge? In a world created by God, morality is objective, absolute, and universally binding. All that happens does so for the best as part of the divine plan. In this we find safety and moral certainty.

In *The Gay Science*,* Nietzsche became a prophet for the twentieth century. He predicted with some accuracy that with the growing secularism in European society, a new

---

* Nietzsche did not mean 'gay' in the sense that word is most often used today, and he did not exactly mean 'science' in its modern sense either. The original German title of this work, *Die fröhliche Wissenschaft*, was often translated into English as *The Joyful Wisdom*, until the popularity of a modern edition made its current title, *The Gay Science*, more common.

psychological and cultural phenomenon would take place in which people would no longer find relevance in the notion of God. Notwithstanding the fact that theism had played a significant part in the development of Western civilization, he boldly proclaimed that the age of belief was over. In his typically bombastic and dramatic way, Nietzsche made his proclamation through the ravings of a madman entering a town square.

Rather than get depressed about the death of God or worry that the world is going to hell in a handbasket, we should celebrate, according to Nietzsche. We are no longer bound by supernatural superstitions and invented moral restraints; nor need we any longer be prisoners chained by projections of our own fears onto a man-made idol called God. We are free, free at last! In celebration of the death of God, Nietzsche writes:

> Indeed, we philosophers and 'free spirits' feel, when we hear the news that 'the old god is dead,' as if a new dawn shone on us; our heart overflows with gratitude, amazement, premonition, expectation. At long last the horizon appears free to us again, even if it should not be bright; at long last our ships may venture out again, venture out to face any danger; all the daring of the lover of knowledge is permitted again; the sea, *our* sea, lies open again; perhaps there has never yet been such an 'open sea.'[70]

Although, personally, you may resist the notion that God is dead, and perhaps be confused or terrorized by such a proposition, for Nietzsche, "His death" should be viewed in a positive light. Since God and religion are both hostile to life, the destruction of a belief in God makes it possible for man's creative energies to develop fully. We no longer have to hate our sinful natures or discount the value or our flesh and blood lives. No longer must we engage in purgative, pious rituals and humiliating confessions of self-loathing. No more need we direct our gaze toward some unreal supernatural realm formed by our desperate imaginations. Rather than dream of other nonexistent worlds, we can live in this one. Instead of feebly hoping that a phantom God will tell us what to do, we can take the place of God as legislators ourselves, creating our own values. *Oh, glory to humankind!*

Will to Power

If belief in God should not properly serve as the basis of morality, then the question arises: What should become the moral foundation for life? Nietzsche has a life-affirming answer for us: the **will to power**. For Nietzsche, the will to power is a fundamental psychological force.

At first glance, it may seem that Nietzsche is advancing some kind of Darwinian universe governed by the principle of survival of the fittest. In truth, Nietzsche does agree with Charles Darwin that nature is a brutal arena of struggle and war. However, in contrast to Darwin, Nietzsche does not regard survival as the absolute end. Some people will, in fact, risk their self-preservation in order to expand their power. People often do dangerous things at great risk to achieve dominance or position. As human beings, we continually press onward, trying to exceed limits and constraints to achieve greatness or some type of distinction. Seldom are we content with where we are, incessantly striving to go beyond what we have accomplished and to become more than we have become.

Friedrich Nietzsche

A brief excursion through the philosophy section of any major North American bookstore is likely to reveal a disproportionate number of books written by a particular author, namely, Friedrich Wilhelm Nietzsche. Though not recognized as such for almost his entire lifetime, Nietzsche has now come to be celebrated as a *philosophical superstar* of sorts—one of the most provocative and influential thinkers of the nineteenth century. Serious philosophers and lay people alike have responded intellectually and in a deeply emotional fashion to his bombastic style and disturbing allegations regarding the moral corruption of religious and conventional moralists. Agree or disagree with Nietzsche's philosophy, there can be little doubt that exposure to it leaves one wondering about previously unquestioned assumptions and beliefs.

Nietzsche was born on October 15, 1844, in Prussian Saxony. Given that he was born on the birthday of the reigning King of Prussia, and also given that his father was a great admirer of the monarch, young Nietzsche was named after him, Friedrich Wilhelm.

Friedrich was raised in a family with a long religious tradition. His father and both grandfathers were Lutheran ministers, and for the first five and a half years of his life he was raised in a parsonage (a home for members of the clergy). In 1849, Nietzsche's father passed away. This left him to be raised by his mother, sister, grandmother, and two aunts in Naumburg. From 1854 to 1858, young "Fritz" studied at the local *gymnasium* before moving on to a celebrated boarding school at Pforta (1858–64).

After completing his studies there, he distinguished himself at the Universities of Bonn and Leipzig, where he studied classical philology (the study of languages in connection with the moral and intellectual tradition of the peoples using them). Although religiously devout in his younger years—examples of his devotional poetry exist—Nietzsche became acquainted with the work of Arthur Schopenhauer and eventually departed from his earlier piety.

By his early twenties, he had espoused a hard-hitting atheism, which was later to rock the very foundations of traditional religion itself. A brilliant scholar, in 1869 at the age of 25 he was appointed as professor of classical philology at the University of Basel, even before he had earned his doctorate. Unfortunately, chronic ill health with symptoms of nausea, bad eyesight, and migraine headaches led him to retire from his academic post in 1878. He spent much of his time after that traveling from one resort to another throughout Switzerland and Italy in efforts to regain his health.

From 1880 to 1890, Nietzsche published the books for which he is best known. They include *The Gay Science* (1882); *Thus Spoke Zarathustra* (1883–85); *Beyond Good and Evil* (1886); *On the Genealogy of Morals* (1887); and *Twilight of the Idols* and *The Antichrist* (both in 1889).

In January 1889, Nietzsche collapsed in the street while protecting a horse from being beaten by its owner. Following that breakdown, and for the remaining years of his life, he was tragically disabled and mentally ill. After failed efforts to treat him in clinical settings, he was taken home and cared for by his mother and later by his sister. Nearing the end of his life, when his writings were receiving a great deal of notice, he was unfortunately not lucid enough to enjoy his celebrity. Nietzsche died on August 25, 1900.

A parting note: it is understandable how some have regarded Nietzsche as the prototypical Nazi. His notions of the *Übermensch* (loosely translated as the "superman" or "overman") and *master morality* have been linked to Hitler's notions of the master race. He was also Hitler's favorite philosopher. But it may indeed be that some Nazi propagandists, including Nietzsche's sister, twisted his ideas for their own purposes. Many contemporary

Nietzsche scholars, however, agree that his views are not very compatible with Nazism and that his expressed resentment of German ethnic nationalism illustrates that he would have strongly opposed the Nazi movement.

Nietzsche lived by a romanticized myth, namely that he was descended from Polish nobility—which is highly unlikely. In a letter to the noted Danish critic Georg Brandes, he writes: "My ancestors were Polish noblemen (Nietzky); the type seems to have been well preserved despite three generations of German mothers." R.J. Hollingdale, a commentator on Nietzsche, suggests that Nietzsche did not so much wish to be thought of as aristocratic but rather as Polish. He believes Nietzsche's propagation of the legend was part of his campaign against (a decadent) Germany. Given that Hitler considered Slavs one of the inferior races, it is ironic, then, that a proud (albeit mistaken) self-professed Slav should be seen as the prototypical Nazi.

When you are tired and completely exhausted as a rock climber, for instance, but drag yourself up to the next plateau before mounting upward again to reach the summit, the will to power is what drives you. When you study all night in order to get the highest grade needed to win the scholarship, the will to power is active again. Freed from religious fears of vanity, selfishness, and the sin of pride (metaphysical inventions), you can now self-assertively attempt to climb your mountains, win your prizes, and realize your ambitions without unnatural guilt induced by otherworldly sources. You are free to make of yourself what you will. "Let *Thy* will be done" now transforms into, "Let *my* will be done!"

The will to power aims not at mere survival, but at a particular way of surviving or *being in the world*. As we can see ourselves from everyday experience, many people do not wish to live a paltry mediocre existence. Simply trying to survive or just get by is not enough. They exhibit a strong will to overcome obstacles and make something of themselves. Here, the goal of power is manifested by **self-overcoming** and **self-mastery**. People seek to overcome their fears and rise above their limitations. They strive constantly to get beyond themselves and to achieve some sort of excellence. Trying to go beyond your comfort zone is, it seems, helpful for the realization of your ambitions.

The will to power may sometimes emerge in tyrannical rulers who wish to dominate others. However, it should be noted that domination here is really instrumental—a means to an end. Ultimately, the goal is to increase power and to gain mastery over oneself. Striving for power, then, is not necessarily military, political, or economic, though it can be. In expressing the will to power, we seek to create ourselves by surmounting those obstacles that would block our self-realization.

In the will to power, we find the instinctual urge to express our freedom. When we express that freedom in the act of self-creation, we build a monument to our own glory. We become masters in our own home. We perfect ourselves and thereby distinguish ourselves by our very uniqueness as human beings. Even when the saint engages in rituals of fasting and meditation, the true goal is self-transcendence, achieving an ecstatic experience of the holy beyond oneself. When the artist fights against poverty and criticism to impose his vision upon reality, again the will to power is at work. Or when the engineer constructs a dam and diverts the surging river in a direction of her own bidding, we witness yet another manifestation of this same will. The will to power is natural and life-affirming. As the vital life force, it should, and must, be the basis of any honest morality. Not all moralities are "honest," as you will now learn.

"I am no man, I am dynamite."
FRIEDRICH NIETZSCHE

Friedrich Wilhelm Nietzsche, *The Gay Science*[71]

Nietzsche's book The Gay Science *is comprised of "A Prelude in German Rhymes," an appendix of "Songs of Prince Vogelfrei," and 383 "aphorisms" (short fragments of philosophical thought) organized into five "books" or parts. A curiously playful book that deals with important ideas, the title* The Gay Science *conveys Nietzsche's challenge to the conventional idea that serious thinking has to be stodgy or heavy. The following aphorism is number 125 and occurs in the third part.*

———

The madman.—Have you not heard of that madman who lit a lantern in the bright morning hours, ran to the market place, and cried incessantly: "I seek God! I seek God!"—As many of those who did not believe in God were standing around just then, he provoked much laughter. Has he got lost? asked one. Did he lose his way like a child? asked another. Or is he hiding? Is he afraid of us? Has he gone on a voyage? emigrated?—Thus they yelled and laughed.

The madman jumped into their midst and pierced them with his eyes. "Whither is God?" he cried; "I will tell you. *We have killed him*—you and I. All of us are his murderers. But how did we do this? How could we drink up the sea? Who gave us the sponge to wipe away the entire horizon? What were we doing when we unchained this earth from its sun? Whither is it moving now? Whither are we moving? Away from all suns? Are we not plunging continually? Backward, sideward, forward, in all directions? Is there still any up or down? Are we not straying as through an infinite nothing? Do we not feel the breath of empty space? Has it not become colder? Is not night continually closing in on us? Do we not need to light lanterns in the morning? Do we hear nothing as yet of the noise of the gravediggers who are burying God? Do we smell nothing as yet of the divine decomposition? Gods, too, decompose. God is dead. God remains dead. And we have killed him.

"How shall we comfort ourselves, the murderers of all murderers? What was holiest and mightiest of all that the world has yet owned has bled to death under our knives: who will wipe this blood off us? What water is there for us to clean ourselves? What festivals of atonement, what sacred games shall we have to invent? Is not the greatness of this deed too great for us? Must we ourselves not become gods simply to appear worthy of it? There has never been a greater deed; and whoever is born after us—for the sake of this deed he will belong to a higher history than all history hitherto."

Here the madman fell silent and looked again at his listeners; and they, too, were silent and stared at him in astonishment. At last he threw his lantern on the ground, and it broke into pieces and went out. "I have come too early," he said then: "my time is not yet. This tremendous event is still on its way, still wandering; it has not yet reached the ears of men. Lightning and thunder require time; the light of the stars requires time; deeds, though done, still require time to be seen and heard. This deed is still more distant from them than the most distant stars—*and yet they have done it themselves.*"

It has been related further that on the same day the madman forced his way into several churches and there struck up his *requiem aeternam deo* [eternal rest to God]. Led out and called to account, he is said always to have replied nothing but: "What after all are these churches now if they are not the tombs and sepulchers of God?"

READING QUESTIONS

1. What allegation does Nietzsche's madman make? What is the significance of his question "How shall we comfort ourselves?" Are we supposed to think that he is truly mad? On what in the text do you base your answers to these questions?

2. How do the other people in the story respond to the madman? Does reflecting on their responses help you make better sense of the meaning of the story? Explain.

Master versus Slave Morality

Nietzsche asserts that the will to power manifests itself in two basic ethical orientations, which he labels **master morality** and **slave morality**. These moralities are displayed by individuals and more generally by societies. Nietzsche makes the point that they are not necessarily mutually exclusive. Within any given individual or cultural group, there can be mixtures of both moralities, resulting, however, in confusion and misunderstanding.

Regardless of the extent to which we exhibit master and slave moralities—either individually in our personal lives or collectively as a society—we all nonetheless possess the drive to overcome and perfect ourselves. This is what the will to power impels us to do. What Nietzsche claims is that not all people are equal with respect to their strength of will. Not all of us can gain power over ourselves to become creators of our own values. Those of us who do and are able to chart our own course and determine our own values live by a master morality. By contrast, those of us who lack the strength to stand alone must satisfy our will to power in another fashion. For instance, we may obey and follow the dictates of a powerful commander. It is possible to find strength in numbers and obedience to authority.

Though the labels "master morality" and "slave morality" might quickly predispose you to regard one as better than the other, Nietzsche tries to establish the value of each by examining its origins, including the political and psychological conditions under which the moral value orientation was devised.[72] It is here that we enter murky waters, however. In his book *On the Genealogy of Morals*, we find the subtitle *A Polemic*. This raises the question of whether Nietzsche's moral genealogy (study of the line of development) should be taken as an actual historical explanation, or whether it is his way of clarifying and justifying his own conception of human excellence and the moral significance of the moralities that either enhance or diminish it. Historian Peter Berkowitz writes:

> For Nietzsche's genealogy is not gray. Inasmuch as Nietzsche reduces the whole complex and multifarious moral past of mankind to two competing moralities, it is closer to the truth to say that in practice his genealogy is painted in black and white. Nor is Nietzsche's genealogy meticulous. Inasmuch as he names no names, dates no events, and shows scant concern for details, variations, and anomalies, it would be more accurate to call his genealogy inspired guesswork, suggestive speculation, or a likely tale. And Nietzsche's genealogy, strikingly devoid of empirical evidence or scholarly apparatus, is anything but patiently documentary.[73]

Given what Berkowitz says, it may be that Nietzsche is a lousy historian, but we should not, as a consequence, summarily reject his views. Berkowitz goes on to say:

> While he plainly intends the *Genealogy* to at least roughly approximate the actual unfolding of history, in execution his genealogy constitutes the creation of an illustrative myth or poem.... Nietzsche poeticizes history the better to bring out the truth about the origins and thereby the nature, of our moral prejudices.[74]

One thing we can say for Nietzsche, his two basic moralities do have at least loose historical ties to actual master-slave relationships—particularly to the Romans and early Christians, as well as to the Ancient Egyptians and the Jews. For Nietzsche, emerging out of such historical master-slave relations were essentially two ideal types of personality. We will look at these two personality types in a moment. For now, it should be stressed that one needn't literally be a "slave" to live a slave-like existence. By Nietzsche's time, much had been done to abolish slavery, yet Nietzsche regarded nineteenth-century European morality as slavish, in need of re-evaluation.

On the other hand, one could live in a highly conventional slave-like conformist society and yet rise above it as a master, noble type. I suppose it could be said that while the origins of master and slave moralities are historical and sociopolitical, their expressions are psychological, reflecting the values and qualities of individual character. Let us examine the features that typify master and slave moralists.

Master moralists are psychologically powerful, strong-willed individuals. They affirm life, equating "good" with that which leads to self-fulfillment and the exercise of personal power. Master moralists are **nobles**, displaying strength, courage, and pride. They are people of higher caliber. Noble types do not live their lives constantly looking over their shoulders in fear and insecurity. They are never at the mercy of the approval of others.

What we describe as peer pressure would be lost on noble types. The only self-referring value judgments they accept are the ones that they themselves pass on to their own person. Nobles are not interested in conforming to social conventions, fitting in, or finding solace in metaphysical revelations. They regard themselves as creators and moral legislators, determiners of their own values.

Noble types worship power in all of its forms and venues of expression, be it in the arts, politics, philosophy, or war. They show reverence for all that is severe and hard. They like to conquer obstacles and distinguish themselves. Thus, whatever restricts growth and accomplishment is bad; so too is anything born of weakness and timidity. Nobles value toughness and rigor.

Though these values and attitudes of the nobles might make them sound a bit cruel or harsh, this is not necessarily so. Nobles can be kind and helpful to the unfortunate, but never out of pity or utilitarian consideration. When nobles help the unfortunate, they do so out of a generosity of spirit and strength, not pathetic empathy.

What is refreshing about noble types is their **psychological honesty**. They express the will to power openly, without deception, excuse, or guilt. Morality, for them, is an *exercise in self-glorification*. Noble types are often feared because they do not veil their self-assertive tendencies. Nobles are explorers, inventors, and experimenters; their courage and audacity serve to remind the weak exactly how pathetic they really are. What the nobles detest and consider bad are those things that are vulgar and base, plebeian, common, banal, petty, cowardly, timid, or humble. Such things diminish us; they do not glorify and uplift us. Interesting, isn't it, how many of us take pride in being the *average Joe*. The desire to be normal is anything but praiseworthy for Nietzsche's master moralists.

In the *slave moralist* we find a very different kind of individual. Slave moralists, like master moralists, are driven by the will to power, but they are hesitant to express this instinct directly. They do so in a dishonest fashion, using a kind of sour-grapes psychology, condemning the virtues and attributes of the master moralist—those noble traits beyond their reach. In this way slave moralists can feel better about their own weaknesses and inadequacies.

Slave moralists see life in terms of **reaction** and **negation**, as opposed to noble affirmation. They resent the excellence, achievement, unbridled individuality, and power that the master moralists so freely and easily express. Out of their **resentment**, slave moralists negate what is truly great and make it sound evil. Slave moralists thus do not express an authentic self-generated morality, but one created as a *reaction against the values of the powerful*—those whom they fear. In other words, the slave moralist first develops a conception of what is negative or evil and then constructs a framework of morality to support it. It is saturated with suspicion, fear, and resentment, but not much that is positive and life-affirming.

According to Nietzsche's historical genealogical account, variations of slave morality took root among the oppressed peoples of the world. These oppressed people constituted the lowest elements of society. The oppressed were the abused and uncertain. They were the exploited and the enslaved.

Nietzsche describes the early Christians and Jews as two social groups living by a slave morality. He also contends that more modern derivations of Judeo-Christian morality, found in democratic and socialist societies, are also slave-like. It was when the Roman emperor Constantine converted to Christianity that the slave moralists really began to take control. Outnumbered by the slaves and out-maneuvered by their skillful dishonesty, the strong came to accept slave morality. They started to feel guilty about their own power and excellence. Apologetic shamefulness replaced willful self-assertion.

Unfortunately, according to Nietzsche, Western civilization (Europe in particular) accepted the grotesque notion of equality. The values of the mediocre were glorified over the achievements and creative power of the individual. A negative psychic attitude was developed toward the most natural drives of man. Slave morality compounded its moral degeneracy by its inconsistency. The weak ganged together in order to grab the very power they condemned as evil in the master moralist. Their unannounced and surreptitious purpose was to render the nobles harmless so they would no longer constitute a threat to their paltry lives. The slaves would be in control.

What the slave moralists value and consider good, therefore, are those qualities that enable sufferers to endure their life situation. For the weak and powerless, character traits such as patience and humility, submissiveness, friendliness, and compassion are applauded. It is good to resign oneself to a difficult life and to pity others who, like yourself, suffer.

What you notice in the slave moralist is a lack of vitality and a seeking for ease and contentment. Needless to say, perhaps, but such a life is pathetic according to Nietzsche. It reeks of mediocrity, dishonesty, and self-denial. Slave morality is not life-affirming, but life-denying. On the subject of Christian-slave morality, Nietzsche writes: "I regard Christianity as the most fatal seductive lie that has yet existed, as the great unholy lie."[75] Disgusted that the morality of paltry people has been made the measure of all things, he thought that subjecting Europe to the morality produced by a small group of wretched Jesus-followers constituted "the most disgusting degeneration culture has yet exhibited."[76] (I guess you've noticed by now that Nietzsche has no penchant for understatement!)

Traditional (Herd) Morality and the Revaluation of All Values

Clearly, Nietzsche regards slave morality as degenerate in its negativity, dishonesty, inconsistency, and reactivity. And, of course, as just mentioned, he regards Christianity as the prime example of this degeneracy. There is yet another form of inferior morality, which may appear slave-like on the surface, but which contains several subtle differences that Nietzsche does not always clearly explain. This other inferior type can be called **traditional**, **customary**, or **herd morality**.

"The man of faith, the believer is necessarily a small type of man. Hence 'freedom of spirit,' i.e., unbelief as an instinct, is a precondition of greatness."
FRIEDRICH NIETZSCHE

Herd morality teaches behavior in accord with custom. Tradition becomes the higher moral authority we must obey if we are to do the right thing. One can obey tradition as mindlessly as one can obey God or the Pope. The point is that following the prescriptions and demands of tradition requires that we give up our rationality and individual autonomy. Traditional morality suppresses thinking and requires people to surrender their power and freedom for the sake of the collective herd. There is a *payoff* for individuals, of course, or else they likely would not conform to the dictates of traditional authority. The weak can protect themselves from the strong and thereby achieve power.

On the flip side, there is a cost associated with mindless conformity to the herd. As Nietzsche puts it, "All society makes one somehow, somewhere, or sometime—'commonplace.'"[77] Traditional herd morality does not enrich or advance humankind. Those belonging to the communal group will be of average strength and vitality, average confidence and courage, average health, and so on.

In contrast to slave morality, which is reactive to the master moralists, traditional (herd) morality is not. It is produced in *conditions of contentment*, not resentment; its principal function is not revenge or control, but to maintain the life of the herd. Thus, herd moralists simply wish to preserve their situation, whereas slave moralists wish to change theirs.

Another feature of herd morality is expressed by its *mediocrity*. It opposes all rankings of people (higher versus lower). It makes efforts to produce a type of person as close as possible to the herd average. Since the herd is quite content, it has a positive orientation toward life, not like the slaves who are negative and bitter toward the nobles.

Evaluating Values

Because, for Nietzsche, all value orientations are products of human beings, their ultimate worth can and should be determined by the characteristics of their producers. A system of moral values produced by the strong and healthy is thus better than the value system produced by the weak and ailing. We cannot evaluate moral actions in themselves or examine the logical features of moral language to determine right from wrong. The underlying rationale and justification for any morality must be based on the producers of that morality and cannot be properly and fully understood in isolation from them.

Embedded in Nietzsche's thinking is also an extension of the idea just mentioned, namely, that those moralities that serve to produce stronger and healthier types are better than those that produce weaker and sicklier types. A system of morality that, by design, produces moral degenerates is not as good as one that produces moral heroes.

Another criterion Nietzsche uses to evaluate moralities is tied to the notion of human freedom. Systems of value that are generated in conditions of **autonomy** are preferable to systems generated in situations of constraint. In other words, those moralities that are conducive to autonomous and creative self-expression are better than those that call for limits and self-repression. When it comes to evaluating any system of morality, Nietzsche would have us first look at its origins and producers, at its intended and actual function, as well as at its ability to respect and enhance individual autonomy.

In light of these evaluative criteria, Nietzsche concluded that we must reject traditional morality in the name of honesty. In the same way that Christianity was a revaluation of all the values of antiquity, so now the dominant traditional morality of the day must be rejected and refigured in favor of humankind's original and deepest nature. If

Is educational excellence possible in a value system that treats all students as equals? When your professor teaches to the *class average*, is human greatness achieved? How should students be ranked, if at all? How should teaching methods be varied to suit the ranks, if at all? Why?

Are your responses to these questions reflective of your basic moral beliefs? Are you a master, slave, or herd moralist? In view of Nietzsche's hierarchical ordering of moralities, how would he describe you? How would you respond to Nietzsche?

we engage in a critical, historical analysis of modern humankind's ideals, we will find that so-called "moral truth," as we understand it now, is really a perversion.

Nietzsche thought that, once the sources of false moralities were uncovered, true values will emerge—ones based on the internal will to power, using and exploiting the environment for pleasure and satisfaction. By overcoming or going beyond traditional values we, as humans, can fully express the will to power and thereby realize ourselves.

Furthermore, Nietzsche would have us go beyond blind observance to tradition since no set of ready-made rules can be used to apply in every situation. The suggestion is *not* that we become totally selfish and self-centered and that we no longer do for others. However, *what we must do in our revaluation is get beyond the view that unegoistic and selfless actions are morally good*. The fact is that egoism and selfishness are not only unavoidable aspects of human nature, but that their presence is necessary if we would achieve our best.

Nietzsche would have us integrate all aspects of our human nature. This would be life-affirming. Christianity, by contrast, is life-denying insofar as it deprecates the body, condemns instinctual impulse, passion, aesthetic values, as well as the free and untrammeled exercise of the mind. It is motivated by fear based on consciousness of weakness.

The Superman/*Übermensch*

Readers of Nietzsche are sometimes inclined to think that his philosophy subjects us to a gloomy **nihilism**. At first glance, it might appear that life in the Nietzschean universe is meaningless and without value. After all, for him, God is dead, no objective morality exists, slave morality lacks honesty and integrity, and traditional herd morality is a collective cop-out for a pig's life of contentment.

But for Nietzsche, it is slave moralities that are nihilistic. As mentioned, Christianity, for him, is life-denying. According to Christian belief, we are born stained with original sin. We are corrupt or damaged goods at birth. We need to die to the flesh in order to be reborn in the spirit. We must suffer on earth in order to enjoy our rewards in heaven. Our natural cravings and desires are sinful. We must be redeemed and saved from ourselves. We must never display self-will, for this is pride, and we are taught by religionists that *pride cometh before the fall*. We simply cannot be human without guilt, fear, and shame. We are told that while we live *in* this world, we should not be *of* this world.

For Nietzsche, all of this clearly points to nihilism. The Christian promise of spiritual salvation is really an attack on the values of life. He would think he has done the world a great favor by annihilating the nihilism of Christianity.

Nietzsche does indeed provide us with an ideal for humanity—the image of the *Übermensch* (translated into English as **superman** or **overman**). One should not confuse the Nietzschean superman with any television figure or comic book character. The superman is not any particular individual, but a *type of person*. The superman is not produced through biological evolution or any process of eugenics. Neither is he a tyrant, one who has a maniacal need to dominate.

The superman, for Nietzsche, constitutes a "union of spiritual superiority with well-being and an excess of strength."[78] The kind of person Nietzsche has in mind here would combine "the Roman Caesar with Christ's Soul."[79] To put it another way, the superman represents the highest level of development and expression of physical, intellectual, and emotional strength. Nothing would be forbidden to the superman except what interferes with the will to power.

Of course, the superman will be rare. It is only when superior types muster the courage to revalue all values and respond with freedom to their internal will to power that the next stage of human development can be reached. In this context, Nietzsche was impressed by the Greek poet Homer and his accounts of **Apollo** (Greek god of the sun and light, of rational thinking, logic, and order) and **Dionysus** (Greek god of wine and dance, of emotions, instincts, irrationality, and chaos). Nietzsche used these figures as symbols in order to capture two powerful elements in human nature and to illustrate how they could be combined as a *balanced unity* in the superman or superior individual. This harmony could help us, in turn, to understand how life could be lived as an **aesthetic phenomenon**.

Dionysus symbolizes the power of passion. He represents the dynamic stream of life, which knows no restraining barriers. The Dionysian element in us is that which defies all limitations. It is potentially dangerous, serving as the reservoir for the negative, dark, and destructive powers of the soul. We express the Dionysian mood most obviously when boundaries of separation between us and the world are broken down, and as we lapse into drunken frenzies or immerse ourselves in feelings of abandonment in music. Without controls, the Dionysian element would turn us into savage beasts, disgusting individuals capable of great cruelty and voluptuousness.

Fortunately, there is a rational Apollonian element in us as well. Apollo serves as the symbol representing the power to control and restrain the dynamic forces of life. The Apollonian dimension can harness destructive energies and sublimate or transform them into creative acts. Dionysus captures the instinctual drives that are tamed and harnessed by Apollo to produce controlled individual characters.

It should be emphasized that the Dionysian element is not intrinsically evil or diseased. It is not something we wish to get rid of. It is detrimental only when unharnessed and uncontrolled. Without it, life would lack vital energy. The Dionysian element serves as the stimulus for achievement, self-overcoming, and artistic expression in whatever form it might take. What some may describe as the *beast within* is not to be purged or destroyed, but transmuted into an aesthetic phenomenon, a work of art.

Nietzsche's aesthetic ideal or *aesthetic mode of existence* is concerned more with style than with content. What is important is fitting one's traits into "an artistic plan, until every one of them appears as art and reason and even the weaknesses delight the eye."[80] You might wish to think of your "self" as a personal creation—a masterpiece you are in the process of creating throughout your entire lifetime. You could also choose to think of your life as a story, in which the objective is to mold your life's events into a coherent narrative within which you assume the identity that you've created for yourself. The aim here is *not* to realize your essence or pre-given potential, but to blend everything that you have done, are doing, and will do in the future into a perfectly coherent whole. The task, for Nietzsche, is to fully embrace one's existence and to affirm all that one is. This is how you follow Nietzsche's injunction to "Become who you are." This is the meaning of your life and this is what you must do.

For those who wish to learn more about religious morality before deciding whether or not to reject it as Nietzsche did, it is useful to examine religious ethics in some greater detail. We'll do exactly that right now by considering the moral and ethical ideas of Islam, Hinduism, and Christianity in the section that follows.

While reading, give some thought to the notion that religion is *slave-like* and *life denying*. Was Nietzsche right or wrong? In addition to helping you to appreciate Nietzsche more, such a consideration should help you to better understand the nature of both secular and religious ethics and how they compare with one another. It will also provide you with a better appreciation of traditional Eastern, Middle Eastern, and Western perspectives. Still further, try to examine the following ideas in the context of your personal life philosophy. What additions, changes, or deletions will you need to make, if any, as a product of broadening your intellectual perspective on matters of ethics and morality?

5.7 Religion and Ethics: Islamic, Hindu, and Christian Perspectives

For many people in the world today, ethical questions pertain not only to matters of character, duty, fairness, or the protection and preservation of a well-ordered society, but also to considerations of the divine, an afterlife, or one's position within the cosmological order of the universe. For the religious, ethical conduct and decision making are not always seen purely in terms of rational considerations; nor are they necessarily viewed exclusively in terms of hedonic, utilitarian outcomes.

The fact is that for many individuals, morality and religion are often conceived as tightly interwoven, with one sewn right into the fabric of the other. Take the Christian moralist, for example; not only is murder morally wrong for that person, but the moral prohibition against taking innocent human life is sanctioned by God. God's will, as revealed by the Ten Commandments, proscribes murder by stating "Thou shalt not kill." In this case, divinity provides the ultimate foundation for the Christian's system of ethical conduct. In the sections that follow, we will begin to better appreciate the links between religion and morality by briefly examining Eastern, Middle Eastern, and Western perspectives.

Islamic Ethics

Islam is one of the youngest of the world's major religions, belonging to a family of monotheistic faiths that includes Judaism and Christianity. Followers of Islam—Muslims—make up the majority of many countries in the Middle East, Africa, and Asia. In addition, substantial increases in Muslim populations have been recorded during the last quarter-century in the Americas, Europe, and Australia.

In view of this proliferation, it's somewhat amazing to think how little about Islam is actually known in the West, especially given that it is one of the fastest growing religions, boasting one billion adherents, or one-sixth of the world's population. Indeed, you might be surprised to learn that, according to the Pew Research Center, three to four million Muslims now make the United States their home.[81] A study of American culture reveals that Islam has certainly had an impact on the lives of Americans in all walks of life, be they social activists, rappers, politicians, artists, athletes, academics, or just plain folk.

Islam began as a religion over 1,400 years ago when a man named **Muhammad**, sitting in a cave just outside of Mecca, was struck by a brilliant flash of light and commanded by God (whom Muslims refer to as **Allah**) to "Read." This became the first word of a twenty-three-year revelation received from the divine Creator, but largely delivered by the archangel Gabriel. Other sources of inspiration were dreams, instantaneous heart-felt revelations, and a kind of inner-voice dictation.

Muhammad's initial instruction from Allah to "read" is the source from which we get the name **Qur'an**,* literally meaning "reading" or "recital." Because Muhammad was illiterate, the *Qur'an* was given orally to him, and he dictated its verses to others to be written down. In the end, the *Qur'an*, became an inspired holy book consisting of 114 chapters, called *Surahs*, covering a wide variety of moral, spiritual, and social topics. Muslims believe that the ultimate arrangement of all the chapters and verses of the *Qur'an* came under the direction of the archangel Gabriel.

From the vantage point of the practicing Muslim, morality is ultimately dependent on Allah—the absolute sovereign. The supreme good is considered to be faith in the one God and submission to Him. *Islam* means "submission" in Arabic. By showing obedience to Allah and by possessing faith in the truth of the *Qur'an*, Muslims discover not only a religion, but also a way of life or philosophy of living that can be referred to on a daily basis. Islam provides answers to existential, moral, and metaphysical questions such as "Why are we here?" "Who is God?" "What sort of life should a person lead?" and "What happens to us after we die?"

In its answers to these questions, Islam provides a program for opening the heart, developing the mind, and cultivating spiritual strength. For devotees of Islam, a daily regimen of prayer, supplication (humble petition), and good works constitutes a strong commitment to faith and enables Muslims to live in harmony with others and the world around them.

The moral norms and assumptions characterizing Islamic belief and action find their inspiration in two foundational sources. Not surprisingly, the first one is scriptural—embodying the message revealed by Allah to the Prophet Muhammad. The second source of inspiration is the exemplification of the *Qur'an*'s message in the model of the Prophet's words and deeds. This recorded testament of Muhammad's life is called the *Sunnah*. One writer says, "Muslims regard the *Qur'an* as the ultimate closure in a series of revelations to humankind from God, and the *Sunnah* as the historical projection of a divinely inspired and guided human life in the person of the Prophet Muhammad, who is also believed to be the last in a series of Messengers from God [following Moses and Jesus]."[82] In the same way, then, that Jesus became the moral model for Christians, so too Muhammad became the model for hundreds of millions of Muslims throughout the world.

Just as we find different sects or denominations within Christianity, we also find divisions within the Islamic community. The *Sunnis* comprise approximately 90 percent of the world's Muslim population, while the *Shi'as* make up most of the rest.

---

* This spelling is more acceptable to scholars than the more common one, 'Koran'.

A Sunni follows the tradition and example of the Prophet and his companions. For a Sunni, any righteous Muslim can be elected to the position of *Caliph*, or chief civil and religious ruler. Shi'as contend, however, that there is no need for elections, since birthright provides enough legitimacy to rule. For Shi'as, only a descendant of the Prophet Muhammad has the right to assume religious authority.

Within both major branches of the Islamic population are *Sufis*. Sufis, those belonging to Sufism, place a very esoteric, spiritual emphasis on the practice of Islam. They make efforts to experience faith at a deep, heartfelt level in order to achieve a *state of inner ecstasy*. Concerned about Islam's digression from the Prophet's example of frugality and self-denial, and worried about Islam's movement toward opulence and pageantry, the Sufis began to renounce the world and to live simple lives. The name 'Sufi' is derived from the Arabic word for wool, the preferred cloth for these humble believers who shunned silk and other fineries. Earlier reference to the Sufis was made in Chapter 1, where the *Sign of the Presence of God* symbol was mentioned. Some Sufis use this spiritual tool to gain personal wisdom, insight, and understanding.

As well as following the *Qur'an* and the *Hadiths* (those sayings, actions, or things to which Muhammad gave silent approval and which formed the basis of the *Sunnah*), members of Sufism also place great value on the teachings of their great Sufi masters. These teachings consist of poems and wisdom stories possessing important hidden meanings. Sufi practices for achieving enlightenment include chanting in praise of Allah, fasting and meditation in remote natural places, prolonged prayer at night, and pilgrimages to the shrines of past Sufi masters known as saints.

Jalaluddin Rumi (1207–73), is a famed Sufi scholar and poet appreciated today by Sufis and non-Sufis alike. Here's a sample of his efforts to bring ecstasy and joy into the experience of faith: "What God said to the rose and caused it to laugh in full-blown beauty, He said to my heart and made it a hundred times more beautiful."[83] Other important Muslim thinkers include Ibn Sina (970–1037), who combined strands of ancient Greek philosophical and scientific thinking into Islam, and Ibn Rushd (1126–98), known for his commentaries on Aristotle and for emphasizing the importance of philosophy in the religion.

Unfortunately, time and space limitations do not allow for a detailed treatment of these thinkers and the important world religion they represent. What we can do, however, is read the following short excerpt from Riffat Hassan's article, "Islamic View of Peace." Hassan is a feminist Muslim thinker born in Pakistan, educated in England, and now professor *emerita* of religious studies at the University of Louisville in the United States.

The goal of her article is to distinguish between the actual Islamic code of ethics embodied by the *Qur'an* and the prevalent stereotypes and distortions of Islamic belief held by many and perpetuated sometimes by the media. While some of her interpretations of Islamic teachings may not be accepted by all followers of the faith, she supports her claims with references to holy scripture.

Riffat Hassan, "Islamic View of Peace"[84]

Riffat Hassan (b. 1943) is a professor of religious studies, human rights activist, and acclaimed Islamic scholar of the Qur'an. In this reading, she challenges the negative stereotypes of Islam by presenting a positive account of peace that is central to the theological worldview of Islam.

———

... It is profoundly ironic that stereotypes identify Islam with war and militancy, whereas the very term '*islām*' is derived from a root, one of whose basic meanings is "peace." Not only is the idea of peace of pivotal significance in the theological worldview of Islam, it also permeates the daily lives of Muslims. Each time two Muslims greet each other, they say *salam alaikum*, "peace be on you," and reply *alaikum assalam*, "peace be on you (too)." The regularity and fervor with which this greeting is exchanged shows that it is not a mechanical reiteration of words that have little or no meaning but a religious ritual of great importance. The ideal of being at peace with oneself, one's fellow human beings, the world of nature, and God, is deeply cherished by Muslims in general. But if that is the case, why is there such manifest lack of peace, and so much talk of violence, in the present-day world of Islam? In order to answer this question it is necessary to understand what "peace" means according to the perspective of "normative" Islam.

Many, including some who are committed to the ideal of peacemaking, tend, unfortunately, to define peace negatively, as "absence of war" (just as some tend to define "health" as "absence of sickness"). But, in quranic terms, peace is much more than mere absence of war. It is a positive state of safety or security in which one is free from anxiety or fear. It is this state that characterizes both *islām*,[85] self-surrender to God, and *īmān*,[86] true faith in God, and reference is made to it, directly or indirectly, on every page of the Qur'ān through the many derivatives of the roots "s-l-m" and "a-m-n" from which *islām* and *īmān* are derived, respectively. Peace is an integral part not only of the terms used for a believer, "muslim" (i.e., one who professes *islām*) and *mo'min* (i.e., one who

possesses *īmān*), but also of God's names *As-Salām* and *Al-Mo'min* mentioned in the Qur'ān:

> He is Allāh, beside whom there is no God; the King, the Holy, the Author of Peace [As-Salām], the Granter of Security [Al-Mo'min], Guardian over all, the Mighty, the Supreme, the Possessor of greatness [Surah 59.23].[87]

As pointed out by G. A. Parwez, *As-Salām* is the Being who is the source of peace and concord and who assures peaceful existence to all beings. *Al-Mo'min* is the Being who shelters and protects all and bestows peace in every sphere of life.[88]

That God "invites" humanity to *dār as-salām* (i.e., the abode of peace) is stated by the Qur'ān (Surah 10.25), which also promises the reward of peace to those who live in accordance with God's will:

> God guides such as follow His pleasure into the ways of peace, and brings them out of darkness into light by His will, and guides them to the right path [Surah 5.16].[89]

... In other words, peace on earth (which is a precondition of peace in heaven) is the result of living in accordance with God's will and pleasure. Here it is important to note that Islam conceives of God as *Rabb Al-'Alamīn*: Creator and Sustainer of all the peoples and universes, whose purpose in creating (as stated in Surah 51.56) is that all creatures should engage in God's *'ibādat*. This term, which is commonly understood as "worship," in fact has a much broader meaning and refers to "doing what God approves."[90] In Islam "doing what God approves" is not conceived in terms of seeking salvation from the burden of original sin through belief in redemption or a redeemer (none of these ideas/concepts being present in the Qur'ān) or through renunciation of the world (monasticism not being required by God, according to the Qur'ān).[91] Rather, it is conceived in terms of the fulfillment of *Haquq Allāh* (rights of God) and *Haquq al-'ibād* (rights of God's servants—namely, human beings). The Qur'ān considers the two kinds of "rights" to be inseparable as indicated by the constant conjunction of *salāt* (signifying remembrance of, and devotion to, God) and *zakāt* (signifying the sharing of one's possessions with those in need). In fact, as Surah 107 shows, the Qur'ān is severe in its criticism of those who offer their prayers to God but are deficient in performing acts of kindness to those in need:

> Hast thou ever considered [the kind of person] who gives the lie to all moral law?
>
> Behold, it is this [kind of person] who thrusts the orphan away,
>
> and feels no urge to feed the needy.
>
> Woe, then, unto those praying ones whose hearts from their prayers are remote—
>
> those who want only to be seen and praised,
>
> and, withal, deny all assistance [to their fellows].[92]

In Quranic terms, then, peace is obtained in any human society when human beings, conscious of their duty to God, fulfill their duty to other human beings. In fulfilling this duty, they honor what I call the "human rights" of others. These rights are those that all human beings *ought* to possess because they are rooted so deeply in our humanness that their denial or violation is tantamount to negation or degradation of that which makes us human. These rights came into existence when we did; they were created, as we were, by God in order that our human potential could be actualized. These rights not only provide us with an opportunity to develop all our inner resources, but they also hold before us a vision of what God would like us to be: what God wants us to strive for and live for and die for. Rights given by God are rights that ought to be exercised, because everything that God does is for "a just purpose" (Surah 15.85; 16.3; 44.39; 45.22; 46.3)....

READING QUESTIONS

1. What is Riffat Hassan's intention in this reading? What is her method or strategy for achieving that intention? Think about the goal and means of this reading when you answer these questions.

2. In Quranic terms of peace, what is the relationship between freedom from fear, God's approval, and a duty to other human beings?

3. To which ethical perspective is Islamic morality most closely related: utilitarianism, existentialism, natural law theory, or Greek virtue ethics? Explain.

4. In view of what's presented in the reading, would Nietzsche consider Islam to be as life-denying as he does Christianity? Why or why not?

Hindu Ethics

Hinduism is one of the world's major religions, reflecting the beliefs and values of an estimated one billion people. Originating in India sometime around 1500 BCE, it continues to be the dominant religious influence for most of that country's inhabitants today. Because of Indian migration patterns in the past, a significant Hindu presence can also be felt in East and South Africa, Southeast Asia, the East Indies, and England.

A simple and uncomplicated description of Hinduism is very difficult owing to its rich diversity and ancient roots. Not only has Hinduism influenced many other religious traditions during its lengthy, unbroken history, but it too has tended to assimilate elements from other traditions that cannot always be easily integrated and, at times, may even be irreconcilable. In fact, it's been suggested that Hinduism is not something unitary or monolithic, but merely a convenient Western term for the many diverse ideas and practices found in India.

The interesting diversity within Hinduism is perhaps best captured by a study of its major sacred texts, which include the *Vedas*, the *Upanishads*, the **Bhagavad Gita**, and the *Vedanta*. The contemporary Hindu commentator S. Abhayananda tries to help Westerners better understand these texts by classifying the *Vedas* as something akin to the "Old Testament," while referring to the *Upanishads* and the *Bhagavad Gita* as the "New Testament." As for the *Vedanta*, it means "the end of the *Veda*."

The *Vedanta* was originally intended to signify the collection of writings called the *Upanishads*, which were written nearly three thousand years ago by some anonymous Indian sages and appended to earlier *Vedas* as their final portion. Given that the word *Veda* means "knowledge" or "wisdom," the *Vedanta* is therefore regarded by many as the "end of knowledge" or "the ultimate wisdom." One should understand, however, that *Vedanta*, as used today, refers not only to the *Upanishads*, but also includes an entire corpus of writings that explains, elaborates, and comments on the Upanishadic teachings from their conception to the present. The *Vedanta* is equivalent to what is sometimes called "the perennial philosophy," that universal knowledge of unity possessed by all the mystics and sages throughout history. It is the final philosophy discovered time and again by seekers of Truth in every age.[93]

Notwithstanding the fact that the *Vedanta* represents some sort of culmination of Hindu wisdom, the *Bhagavad Gita* provides us with arguably the clearest and most direct treatment of the "ethics of duty." The *Bhagavad Gita*, composed around the fourth century BCE in India, is the most translated book after the Bible.

Scholars have said that in order to appreciate the Hindu mind, one must understand the essence of the *Gita*. This little book contains philosophical, religious, and moral relevance. It begins by discussing human nature and the nature of the world, then depicts the human spirit, the cosmic form of God, and mystical experience.

The *Gita*, in itself, is a relatively short poem that was originally passed down through time by oral tradition. Eventually, it found its way into a Hindu epic poem called the *Mahabharata*, which is the longest poem ever written. In the *Gita*, we find a struggle between the forces of good and evil, with good represented by the Pandavas and evil by the Kauravas, two related royal families torn apart by conflict due to a rivalry over choosing an heir-apparent to the throne.

As we read in the *Gita*, Arjuna arrives on the scene of an imminent battle, instructing his charioteer Krishna to bring their chariot between the two conflicting families.

Arjuna is a member of the Pandavas, while Krishna is actually an avatar, or incarnation of God, who advises Arjuna on the battlefield. Arjuna is caught on the horns of an ethical dilemma. On the one hand, he is moved by the sight of his friends and relatives and has a personal duty to protect family and relatives from physical harm. On the other hand, he is a member of the warrior caste and, therefore, it is his duty to safeguard the kingdom from internal and external dangers—in this case, the evil Kauravas. Arjuna becomes besieged by doubt and indecision as a result of this dilemma. He challenges the morality of war by raising the following questions: Why is he fighting this war? What will be gained? What is the goal of victory? Is killing moral? And is war ever justified?

In response to Arjuna's moral indecision, Krishna offers a number of arguments to explain to Arjuna how he is justified in going to war. Arjuna is not convinced by Krishna's logic, so when reasoning doesn't work, Krishna reveals himself to be God, creator of the universe and all human beings. He tells Arjuna that his assigned task on this earth is to eradicate the evil represented by the Kaurava brothers.

In the end, Arjuna is ready to fight the war as directed by Krishna. Arjuna learns that as long as wars are not fought for personal gain or power, but for a justifiable cause, the mind will not be clouded, allowing the soul to find peace. Krishna teaches Arjuna that doing one's godly ordained duty is the way to true spiritual happiness. Other pleasures pass and eventually end in despair. Arjuna needn't worry too much about killing others, for this involves extinguishing other empirical selves, which are limited and transitory anyway. The transcendental self that Krishna says makes all human beings identical cannot be hurt.

The dialogue between Krishna and Arjuna actually takes place over eighteen chapters, wherein the complete religio-philosophical system of Hinduism is laid out. In what follows, we limit ourselves to the first chapter: *Arjuna's Moral Dilemma*. Later, in what is not included here, Krishna informs Arjuna that there are two paths to salvation, depending on the kind of person one is. The wise take the path of knowledge, whereas the path of action is for "doers," as it were. Because nobody ever achieves perfection through inaction or renunciation, and because Arjuna is a man of action, he should fight the war.

Ashok Kumar Malhotra, *Transcreation of the Bhagavad Gita*[94]

The following comes from the first chapter, 'Arjuna's Moral Dilemma', in Ashok Kumar Malhotra's modernized Transcreation of the Bhagavad Gita. *Whereas a translation is a literal rendering of an original text, a transcreation takes creative license in order to capture the tone, style, and effect of the original text. This creatively-sensitive approach to adapting a text is fitting in the case of the* Bhagavad Gita, *a 700-verse poem whose title means "The Song of God."*

————

ARJUNA'S MORAL DILEMMA

Principal Characters

ARJUNA One of the Pandava princes. He is the great warrior who questions the reasons for fighting the war. His name means "silver white."

BHIMA One of the Pandava princes and brother of Arjuna. His name means "enormous" or "dreadful."

BHISHMA He is the grand uncle of the Pandavas. He has reluctantly chosen to fight the war. His name means "fearsome" or "shocking."

DHRITARASHTRA The blind king whose children (the Kauravas) and nephews (the Pandavas) have gathered together to fight the war. His name means "he who controls the kingdom."

DURYODHANA Chief of the Kaurava princes. His name means "dirty fighter."

DRONA The great teacher who taught both the Kauravas and the Pandavas the art of war.

KRISHNA The god-incarnate. Also, Arjuna's charioteer, who offers a metaphysical discourse which constitutes the text of the *Bhagavad Gita*.

KAURAVAS The 100 sons of the blind king Dhritarashtra. They represent the forces of evil.

PANDAVAS The five Pandava brothers: Yudhisthira, Bhima, Arjuna, Nakula, and Sahdeva. They represent the forces of good.

SANJAYA He is the minister of King Dhristarashtra. Sanjaya is given the divine sight by the sage Vyasa, through which he describes the battle to the blind king.

Summary

The armies of Kauravas and Pandavas have assembled to fight a war. The blind king Dhritarashtra asks his minister, Sanjaya, to describe the battle and the dialogue between Arjuna, the Pandava warrior, and Krishna, the God incarnate, who is Arjuna's charioteer. Arjuna's chariot is brought between the two armies and he sees brothers, cousins, and relatives on both sides. He becomes unsure of fighting this war: to do his caste duty, he must fight his relatives; but to do his family duty, he must not kill them. He undergoes an ethical dilemma and refuses to fight.

Text

Dhritarashtra asked Sanjaya:

Tell me about my children and Pandava's children, who have assembled in the field of righteousness to fight a battle.

Sanjaya replied:

After scrutinizing the army of the Pandavas, Duryodhana came closer to his teacher, Drona, and said:
"Behold the Pandavas' huge army arranged by the intelligent son of Drupada.
In *their* army there are great archers like Arjuna, Bhima, Yayudhana, Virata, and the mighty charioteer Drupada.

Dhrishtaketu, Cekitana, and the mighty king of Varanasi; Purujit, Kuntibhoja, and Saibya, who are the best among men.

The performer of great deeds, Yudhamanyu, the bold Uttamauja, Abhimanyu, and Draupadi's sons, are all great charioteers.

O Drona, great among the brahmins! Now I will tell you the names of *our* mighty soldiers and commanders.

Your revered self, Bhishma, Karna, the victorious Kripa, Ashvatthama, Vikarna, and the son of Somadatta.

Not only are they skilled in weaponry and in the art of warfare, but they are also ready to sacrifice their lives for me.

Bhishma is the defender of our limitless and undefeatable army, whereas Bhima is the defender of the limited and defeatable army of the Pandavas."

Then Duryodhana commanded his army, "All of you take your posts and cautiously safeguard our commander-in-chief Bhishma."

To make Duryodhana happy, Bhishma blew his mighty conch hard, like a lion's roar.

The conches, kettledrums, horns, and tabors resounded together producing a horrifying sound.

While sitting in their chariot with white horses, Krishna and Arjuna of the other army blew their godly conches.

Krishna blew *pancajanya* (acquired from a demon), Arjuna, *devadatta* (bestowed by the gods), and Bhima, *paundra* (powerful conch).

King Yudhisthira, the son of Kunti, blew *ananta-vijaya* (eternal victory), while Nukula and Sahdeva blew *sughosa* (sweet tone) and *manipuspaka* (jewel flower).

The skillful archer, the king of Varanasi, the mighty charioteer-fighter Shikhandin, Dhrishtadyumna, Virata, and the undefeatable Satyaki.

The King Drupada, Draupadi's five sons, and the strong-armed Abhimanyu, blew their conches one by one.

The thunderous sound of the conches shook the earth, the sky, and the confidence of Dhritarashtra's army.

Sanjaya continued his explanation:

Just when the battle was about to start and Dhritarashtra's children were ready to fight, Arjuna picked up his bow and turned to Krishna.

Arjuna said, "Bring my chariot in between the two armies!

I wish to see the ones who are desirous of this war. I want to look at all of those who are supporting the misguided Duryodhana."

As directed by Arjuna, Krishna brought the shining chariot in the middle of the two armies.

Glancing directly toward Bhishma, Drona, and the powerful kings, Krishna said, "Arjuna, look at the Kauravas with your own eyes."

Arjuna saw his uncles, grandfathers, teachers, brothers, sons, grandsons, and friends in the two armies.

Seeing his fathers-in-laws, friends, and relatives assembled for war, Arjuna was overcome with great compassion and said to Krishna:

"On seeing my relatives who are desirous of fighting this war, my limbs have become numb, my throat has turned dry, my body is trembling, and my hair is standing on end.

My skin is burning, my mind is confused, I can't stand up straight, and the mighty bow is falling out of my sweaty hands.

I see unholy omens. This fight seems illogical and unnecessary. Nothing good will come out of killing my own relatives.

Glory, happiness, or victory are no use to me. I do not desire a kingdom, pleasures, or life.

Those who seek a kingdom, pleasures, and enjoyments are assembled here to fight a battle for which they have put their lives and property at stake.

There are teachers, fathers, sons, grandfathers, maternal uncles, fathers-in-laws, grandsons, brothers-in-laws, and other relatives all fighting against each other.

The kingdom of the earth and the three worlds is not worth killing them. I would rather let them take my life instead.

What is the benefit of killing the sons of Dhritarashtra? By slaughtering our ignoble kin, we can only accumulate sin.

For this reason, I shall not kill my relatives. It is below me to kill my kinsmen because there is no happiness in this kind of act.

Blinded by greed, these people do not see any sin in the destruction of their own clan or in the hatred of their friends.

Those of us who have the clarity of mind to discern right from wrong ought to stay away from the destruction of our family.

With the destruction of the family, the ancient traditions would perish, and when tradition is destroyed lawlessness will increase.

With the growth of lawlessness, the women of the family will be corrupted; and if they go astray, the caste system will get mixed up.

The mixing of castes sounds a death knell for all families because therein respect for the ancestors is lost.

Through their wrongdoings, the corrupters of the family would create caste confusion and thus both the caste duties and the traditional laws of the family would be destroyed.

O Krishna, it is common knowledge that when family tradition disappears, the relatives secure their place in hell.

I was ready to kill my own relatives and covet the kingdom, and through that, I was going to perform a terrible deed.

If the sons of Dhritarashtra, armed with weapons, kill me while I am unarmed and unresisting in the field of battle, I will happily find my salvation."

Overwhelmed by grief, Arjuna placed aside his bow and arrows and sat down in the chariot.

READING QUESTIONS

1. What precisely is the moral dilemma that Arjuna faces? Is Arjuna's refusal to fight the same as a refusal to make a moral decision about the moral dilemma? Further to that, consider this: By doing nothing in the face of a moral dilemma, can one avoid moral blame?

2. To which ethical perspective is Arjuna's reasoning most closely related: Greek virtue ethics, deontology, or utilitarianism? Explain your answer.

Christian Ethics

Christianity claims a total membership of 2.3 billion people, more than any other religious group, found in every continent in the globe. Understood as a tradition of belief, Christianity does not constitute a systematic philosophy, as one finds in Platonism or in Aristotle's thinking. In contrast to Platonism (discussed in Chapter 4), which begins with a number of philosophical concepts and principles, Christianity begins with certain significant revelatory historical events and a variety of texts. In the testimonies of the biblical prophets and apostles, we find no grand theoretical formulations of doctrine or abstract metaphysical speculations, but rather descriptions of intense religious experience.

Given the magnitude and geographic breadth of Christianity, it is perhaps not surprising that different sects and denominations have arisen within it. There are really too many to mention individually here, but most Christians could be said to belong either to the Roman Catholic Church, the Eastern Orthodox Church, or one of the Protestant denominations, such as the Episcopalian Church or the Southern Baptist Convention. Notwithstanding all of their differences with respect to ritual, practice, and doctrinal emphasis, a number of core Christian beliefs can still be identified: *the reality of God, the divine creation of the universe, the Holy Trinity, human sinfulness, divine incarnation in the person of Jesus, Christ's reconciliation of man to God through his death and resurrection, the founding of the Christian church, the continuing operation of the Spirit within it, the eventual end to human history, and the fulfillment of God's purpose for his creations.*

These core beliefs and central teachings of the Christian church provide its adherents with moral guidance for the time that they live on this earth. Central to this guidance is the person of **Jesus Christ**. Christians are instructed that His example should be followed and that Christ's teachings about life and fellowship should serve as the basis of all human relations. The ethical message of Jesus is succinctly captured when he responds to the Pharisee who asks what is the greatest commandment in [Jewish/moral] law. Jesus replies: "You shall love the Lord your God with all your heart, and with all your soul, and with all your mind. / This is the great and foremost commandment. / And a second is like it, 'You shall love your neighbor as yourself.' / On these two commandments depend the whole Law and the Prophets" (Matthew 22:36–40). With respect to the second commandment, a variation of it is often referred to as The Golden Rule: "Do unto others as you would have others do unto you."

As simple and straightforward as Jesus's words might seem to you, real life experience reveals that there is much dispute about how these commandments should be applied. This can be easily illustrated, for example, by the fact that some Christians regard the drinking of alcoholic beverages as sinful, while others do not. Some churches may countenance divorce, whereas others will allow no other to "put asunder what God has joined together" in holy matrimony, only with very rare exceptions and under very extraordinary circumstances.

Whatever the contemporary moral issue, Christians can be found on the far right and on the far left, as well as in the middle. There are strict conservatives, moderates, and liberal interpreters of Christ's message. Some take the message of the Bible as literally true and historically accurate, while others regard the truth of the Bible as allegorical and interpretive in nature. Nonetheless, it is still reasonable to speak generally of a "Christian way of life" informed by the call to service and discipleship.

Morally speaking, several basic commitments that all Christians would likely accept involve the following: that every person, created in the likeness of God, has inherent worth; that life is sacred, and that one must strive for justice. Living according to this ethic of love under conditions of existence continues to be difficult, however. Never has there been a "golden age" of universal agreement in which it was otherwise.

On this note, we find a convenient segue for drawing our attention to the article that follows. In it, Brian Berry appreciates the diversity of approach and emphasis within the Christian church. In fact, he observes that even within one major tradition, **Roman Catholicism**, there is a plurality of approaches to ethical thinking, which can potentially give rise to chaos and confusion. Berry contends that the future of Roman Catholic moral theology (and of Christian ethics in general) lies in the dialogue that must occur among these existing approaches, each of which has its basis in the thought of St. Thomas Aquinas (see Section 4.8, where Aquinas is discussed). In the following article, Berry outlines these approaches and thereby gives us a better appreciation of Christian morality viewed from three contrasting Roman Catholic perspectives. As you read this article, compare it with what you've already learned about Immanuel Kant, Thomas Aquinas, and Plato. Get a sense of how philosophers of one epoch can influence the thinking and lives of those at a later time.

THINKING ABOUT YOUR THINKING

Our journey into the moral domain has been a long one. We have taken in the view from various religious and philosophical perspectives. Fortunately, our efforts have been rewarded with wisdom given to us by some of history's intellectual immortals. Like children who take stock of their candy after a night of Halloween trick-or-treating, let us now take inventory and reflect on what we have accumulated during this part of our philosophical quest. What, specifically, impressed you most from the philosophers discussed in this chapter? What impact will they have on your life from now on? What questions remain unanswered for you? What do you still need to know? Comment.

Brian Berry, Roman Catholic Ethics: Three Approaches[95]

Brian Berry, who passed away in 2021, was a professor of religious studies and moral theology. This article he wrote on the three main approaches of Roman Catholic moral theology refers to moral theories that you have learned about in this chapter. It serves as a good reminder that one theory can occur in many versions. Indeed, part of the study of philosophy is learning to catch and understand the often-subtle differences across various versions of the same general concept.

———

One of the evident features of contemporary reflection on ethical issues by Roman Catholic theologians is its plurality. Moral theologians today write about a range of concrete moral issues, such as homosexuality, physician-assisted suicide, and affirmative action. They also specialize in a variety of subdisciplines within moral theology, including sexual ethics, bioethics, social ethics, and environmental ethics. But, most importantly, they approach their reflection from within a variety of moral systems or schools of ethical thought, which have different perspectives on what ethics is and how it should proceed. All of this leads to not only an overwhelming amount of data, but a confusing cacophony of diverse moral positions within the one community of faith. Some even suggest that it has left the discipline of moral theology in a state of "disarray."

This article attempts to bring some order to the seeming chaos that exists in Roman Catholic moral theology today. I suggest that developments in the discipline since the Second Vatican Council can be grouped under three main approaches to ethical reflection, what I describe as deontology, revisionism, and virtue ethics. Each of these approaches has distinct views about what ought to be the subject matter of ethics and its method of moral deliberation. In what follows, I will outline the main features of these three approaches using the thought of representative theologians, showing how their theories shape the position they take on the issue of abortion, a complex moral problem that is of special concern to the Roman Catholic community.

DEONTOLOGY

One of the main approaches to Roman Catholic moral theology since Vatican II* is "deontology." This approach places strong emphasis on human actions. It seeks to evaluate human behavior by asking, "What is my duty?" and appeals to moral laws, norms, principles, and rules that are then applied to particular situations. According to deontological ethics, a behavior is moral if the act in itself is right and it is done with the right motive or intention. The consequences of the act are irrelevant for evaluating its moral status.

A key representative of the deontological approach to Roman Catholic ethics is [French-American philosopher] Germain Grisez [1929–2018]. Taking the formal principle "do good and avoid evil" as his starting point, Grisez argues that knowledge of the good is "self-evident" to human beings. By this he means that human beings, on the basis of their experience of desiring those things towards which all persons are naturally inclined, can know that certain human goods are "basic" or desirable in and of themselves. Grisez identifies eight such basic human goods: life, play, aesthetic experience, speculative knowledge, integrity, practical reasonableness, friendship, and religion. No one of these is more important than any other, and the ideal of integral human fulfillment means the enjoyment of all eight of these basic goods.

How are individual actions to be evaluated from a deontological perspective? Grisez argues that a human action is moral only if it is aimed in some way at securing one or more of the basic human goods. We cannot aim at all eight of the basic goods at all times, but we must act in a way which remains open to those basic goods that we do not actively pursue in any given action. A behavior which aims at one basic good, while arbitrarily slighting another, is immoral to the extent that it turns from a basic good without adequate reason.

This last point is especially important for Grisez. He interprets it to mean that some kinds of actions

---

* The Second Vatican Council, or "Vatican II," was a series of meetings held in Rome from 1962 to 1965 with the aim of modernizing some practices of the Roman Catholic Church. [Editor's footnote]

are never morally permissible. In other words, certain human behaviors are "intrinsically evil," that is, always and everywhere wrong, regardless of the circumstances. Specifically, he insists that any kind of action that involves a direct attack on a basic human good, for example, direct homicide, deliberate contraception, or lying, can never be morally justified.

What are the implications of this interpretation for evaluating the morality of abortion?

Grisez insists that direct abortion is always wrong, since it involves a direct attack on the basic good of human life. However, under certain circumstances, indirect abortion can be morally justified. An abortion is indirect if a good effect is intended, for example, saving the life of the mother, and the bad effect, namely, the killing of the fetus, is not. Classic cases of indirect abortion are those performed in cases of an ectopic pregnancy or cancerous uterus, providing these are done before late second trimester. These are referred to as indirect abortions because the intention is not to kill the innocent life of the fetus, but to remove the pathological condition that will otherwise kill both the mother and the fetus.

While the deontological approach to ethics has traditionally been more typical of Protestant theologians, it exercised a considerable influence on Roman Catholic ethics in the twentieth century, particularly before the Second Vatican Council. The deontological approach of Grisez in particular has also shaped the moral teaching of Pope John Paul II, especially his recent encyclical, Veritatis Splendor [1993].

REVISIONISM

A second main approach to Roman Catholic ethics since the Council is "revisionism" or "proportionalism." Like deontology, this approach places great emphasis on human actions. However, it seeks to evaluate human behavior not deontologically but teleologically by asking "What is my goal?" Viewing the ultimate goal or end of human life as union with God, it then tries to determine which actions are most conducive to achieving the values and goods that will lead to this ultimate end.

Revisionism, while working within the above framework, has a deeper appreciation of the range of goods and evils that might result from a given action than more traditional teleological approaches tended to

acknowledge. Like the deontological approach, it considers the act in itself as well as the intention, but it also takes account of the likely consequences of an action on the human relationships that are involved. It then asks, "Which alternative course of action would not intend wrong and would result in a proportionately greater amount of good over evil?"

A major figure representing the revisionist approach to Roman Catholic ethics is [American Jesuit theologian] Richard McCormick [1922–2000]. McCormick accepts much of Grisez's analysis of basic human goods, and agrees that an action that aims at one basic good, while arbitrarily slighting another without adequate reason, is immoral. Where he differs from Grisez, however, are in his claims that there are no "intrinsically evil" acts, and that directly turning against a basic human good is not always morally wrong. McCormick insists that a direct attack on a basic human good is only a "pre-moral"— rather than a moral—evil if there is a proportionate reason for doing the act. "Premoral" evil here refers to the inconvenience, limitations, and harm that are inevitably a part of all human efforts to do good, since human beings are historical, social and live in a sinful world.

When is there a proportionate reason for doing an action that contains premoral evil? McCormick explains that a "proportionate reason" exists when (a) there is a value at stake at least equal to the value being sacrificed; (b) there is no less harmful way of protecting the value at present; and (c) the manner of protecting it under the circumstances will not actually undermine it. Admittedly, determining whether such conditions exist is a difficult one. It means weighing the likely consequences of an action, but also asking if it would be good if everyone in similar circumstances did this, asking whether one is operating out of cultural bias, paying attention to the wisdom of past experience embodied in moral norms, consulting broadly to avoid personal bias, and allowing the full force of one's religious beliefs to be brought to bear on one's judgment. A correct judgment that a proportionate reason exists would mean that the good intended by a given action outweighs the evil results, and that forming the act would be morally permissible.

What are the implications of this approach for evaluating the morality of abortion?

In a [1989] lecture ... entitled "Abortion: A Middle Ground," McCormick argued that, while there is a moral presumption against abortion since it involves the killing of human life, abortion to save the life of the mother is morally acceptable. By this he would have meant not only that indirect abortions are permissible, such as in cases of an ectopic pregnancy or cancerous uterus, but that direct abortions are sometimes morally justified. In other of his writings, he has suggested that a proportionate reason for abortion may exist in the case of a mother whose life is threatened by pregnancy because she has a bad heart, or in the case of [an] anencephalic fetus.

VIRTUE ETHICS

A third major approach to Roman Catholic ethics since the Council is "virtue ethics." Unlike deontology and revisionism, this approach does not focus on human actions, but on being a certain kind of person. In fact, virtue ethics criticizes deontology and revisionism for focusing on actions and neglecting the importance of moral character. It argues that morality is as much about who we are as about what we do. Who we are extends into what we do and do not do, and what we do and do not do shapes the kind of persons we become.

At the same time, virtue ethics is similar to revisionism inasmuch as it seeks to evaluate moral character teleologically by asking, "What is my goal?" Viewing the ultimate goal or end of human life as union with God, it attempts to determine which virtues ought to be cultivated, both by individuals and communities, to achieve this ultimate end. "Virtues" refer to habits or practiced patterns of doing good and living life well, as opposed to "vices" or habits of doing evil and living life badly. Virtues traditionally have been "theological," such as faith, hope, and love, as well as "moral," such as prudence, justice, temperance, and fortitude.

A major representative of the "virtue ethics" approach in Roman Catholicism today is [American Jesuit theologian and bioethicist] James Keenan. Keenan argues that the focus of ethics should not be on acts, but on who we are, who we are to become, and how we are to get there. The specific tasks of virtue ethics are to help us understand ourselves as the people we are, to set goals for the type of people we ought to become, and to suggest what are the significant steps we should

take to achieve these ends. In other words, for Keenan, the virtues inform us both about who we are to be and about what we are to do. And like revisionism, Keenan sees human relationships as the context within which the moral life is practiced and evaluated.

What implications does this approach have for evaluating the morality of abortion?

Rather than examining the question of whether abortion is ever morally licit, Keenan criticizes aspects of American culture that have led to us having the most liberal abortion policy in the developed world. Rather than pitting the rights of the woman against those of the fetus, and leaving the woman to make her own private decision, Keenan advocates that we rediscover a concern for the common good, address ourselves to why so many pregnancies in our society are unwanted, and ask how we are the way we are and how can we become better. At present, we seem incapable as a society of making ourselves into the kind of people we would or could want to become in our relationships with the unborn.

In this article, I have outlined three main approaches to ethics that typify the thought of Roman Catholic moral theologians writing today. The moral systems of deontology and revisionism are primarily interested in the moral evaluation of particular human actions, the deontologists arguing that only indirect attacks on a basic human good may be justified, the revisionists insisting that even direct attacks may be permissible if there is a proportionate reason. Virtue ethics, however, is more interested in the moral character of persons, inviting us to focus on the good habits we need to cultivate if we are to live a genuinely moral life.

The future of Roman Catholic moral theology, it seems to me, lies in the dialogue between these three existing approaches, each of which have their basis in the thought of Thomas Aquinas. Deontology and revisionism have some specific moral guidance to offer those concerned with such "big-life" moral dilemmas as whether or not to have or provide an abortion, and do so with varying degrees of appreciation of the regrettable and often tragic dimension of much of human existence. At the same time, virtue ethics gives much needed attention to the commonplace, to such things as bettering one's relationships, doing one's job better, taking better care of one's health, and becoming more conscious of one's neighbor, all with a view to helping people become the best persons they can be.

READING QUESTIONS

1. What similarities are there between Immanuel Kant's moral philosophy and the deontological approach to Roman Catholic moral theology? Are there any differences?

2. How does the virtue ethics approach differ from the deontological and revisionist approaches?

3. According to Brian Berry, these three approaches are different but not incompatible. What is his explanation for their compatibility? Is it a compelling explanation or do you think that these three approaches demonstrate irreconcilable rifts in Roman Catholic moral theology? Explain.

INSTRUCTIONS: Fill in the blanks with the appropriate responses listed below. (Answers at back of book.)

philosopher kings/rulers	teleology	sanction	Doctrine of the Mean
Allah	care	deontology	revisionism
utility	*eudaimonia*	similar	slave morality
habit	categorical imperative	will to power	Jesus Christ
sacred texts	Muhammad	Krishna	nature
is-ought	character	rational	good will
relation	rationality	post-conventional	hedonic calculus
God	virtue ethics	revaluation	life of the intellect
Arjuna	ethical bias	soul	
maxims	superman/*Übermensch*	democratic characters	

1. According to the doctrine of _____, everything in the universe has a proper function to perform within a harmonious hierarchy of purposes.

2. For Plato, the _____ is comprised of appetite, spirit, and reason.

3. In Plato's view, the timarchic, oligarchic, democratic, and tyrannical are all corrupt _____ types.

4. Plato argues that the _____ should govern society since they are not corrupted by greed and vanity.

5. _____ are flexible and versatile, but suffer because they lack stable principles by which to govern their lives, according to Plato.

6. The Greek word for happiness is _____.

7. For Aristotle, the _____ is the highest form of human functioning.

8. The _____ would have us choose behaviors between excess and deficiency.

9. Aristotle maintained that moral virtue is formed largely by _____.

10. The concept of _____ serves as the basis of Bentham's moral theory.

11. For Bentham, _____ has placed humankind under the control of two sovereign masters—pain and pleasure.

12. A _____ is a source of pleasure or pain that serves to give binding force to any law or rule of conduct.

13. From the utilitarian perspective, moral decisions can be made in a spirit of scientific objectivity using the _____.

14. One commits the _____ fallacy when one concludes that we should do something because it's simply the way things are.

15. According to Immanuel Kant, morality must have a _____ basis.

16. For Kant, the only thing that is unconditionally good is the _____.

17. From the vantage point of deontological ethics, our moral duties are based on _____ of behavior that can be prescribed universally.

18. The _____ states that we should never use people solely as a means to an end, but always respect them as ends in themselves.

19. According to feminist thinkers such as Gilligan and Noddings, there has been gender-based ⎯⎯⎯⎯⎯ in moral thinking throughout the ages and in contemporary moral development research.

20. According to Lawrence Kohlberg, the highest form of moral reasoning development is captured by ⎯⎯⎯⎯⎯ thinking, which is characterized by impartial, detached, and rational features.

21. Carol Gilligan contends that women interpret morality more from the perspective of ⎯⎯⎯⎯⎯, whereas men are more likely to view moral situations from the vantage point of impersonal justice.

22. Nel Noddings believes that a male-dominated field of philosophical inquiry has tended to romanticize ⎯⎯⎯⎯⎯, failing at the same time to recognize its dangers and limitations.

23. Nodding claims that any two situations are seldom, if ever sufficiently ⎯⎯⎯⎯⎯ in morally relevant respects to allow for proper blanket application of impersonal, abstract principles.

24. For Noddings, the human ⎯⎯⎯⎯⎯ is ontologically basic, not the isolated individual or Cartesian *cogito* (the I Think).

25. It was Nietzsche who declared that "⎯⎯⎯⎯⎯ is dead."

26. According to Nietzsche, morality should not be based on reason, tradition, or authority, but rather on the ⎯⎯⎯⎯⎯.

27. Nietzsche argues that Christianity and Judaism are examples of ⎯⎯⎯⎯⎯.

28. The ⎯⎯⎯⎯⎯ lives by master morality, according to Nietzsche.

29. For Nietzsche, traditional morality requires ⎯⎯⎯⎯⎯ for master morality to emerge.

30. The Prophet ⎯⎯⎯⎯⎯ received the orally dictated message we find in the Qur'an.

31. For practicing Muslims, morality is ultimately dependent on ⎯⎯⎯⎯⎯.

32. The *Vedas*, the *Upanishads*, the *Bhagavad Gita*, and the *Vedanta* comprise the major ⎯⎯⎯⎯⎯ of Hinduism.

33. In the "Gita," the one experiencing the moral dilemma is ⎯⎯⎯⎯⎯.

34. The charioteer in the "Gita" is ⎯⎯⎯⎯⎯.

35. In the context of Christianity, adherents are expected to follow the example and teachings of ⎯⎯⎯⎯⎯.

36. There are at least three approaches to Christian ethics in the context of Roman Catholicism. They are ⎯⎯⎯⎯⎯, ⎯⎯⎯⎯⎯, and ⎯⎯⎯⎯⎯.

Key Terms

relativism: one who sees morality in terms of personal opinions and/or prevailing cultural norms; one who does not believe in moral absolutes   317

Plato's Character Ethics

appearance: the way things appear to the senses   324

appetite: desire, which includes instinctive urges   323

aristocracy: a just society in Plato's view   332

character types: different kinds of functioning souls   331

democratic character: egalitarian in approach to life; aimless   336

desire: see appetite   323

functional explanation of morality: explanation of how 'soul' should function   324

guardian class: ruling class of Plato's aristocracy   332

moral balance: a harmony achieved by a properly functioning soul   324

moral virtue: equivalent to the fulfillment of our function as human beings   324

oligarchic character: desires wealth and money; greedy   335

passion: see spirit   323

philosopher kings: belong to guardian class; they rule in an aristocracy   332

Plato: Greek philosopher and founder of the Academy; student of Socrates and teacher of Aristotle.   322

reality: the way things really are   324

realm of forms: the unchanging and eternal dimension of reality   333

reason: the intellect; faculty that calculates, measures, and decides; knowledge seeking, curious; rational   323

soul: the principle of life and movement   323

spirit: sometimes called 'passion'; our self-assertive tendencies; source of ambition and competitiveness   323

teleology: notion that everything has a proper function within a hierarchy of purposes   323

timarchic character: spirited soul; energetic and competitive; self-assertive; domineering   334

tyrannical character: driven by master passion; most out of control, most corrupt   337

Aristotle's Virtue Ethics

activity: action necessary for the fulfillment of one's function   341

appetite gratification: satisfying a desire; want satisfaction   342

attainable: within reach; achievable; one criterion of Aristotle's ultimate end   341

balancing process: what the good life involves—moderation   344

the contemplative lifestyle: the highest form of human functioning; the life of the intellect   344

distinctive function (for humans): that which separates us from plant life and animals   342

divine: god-like; supernatural   344

Doctrine of the Mean: the principle that we ought to choose the mid-way point between excess and deficiency, something individually defined   346

entelechy: an inner urge to realize potentialities   338

eudaimonia: Greek word for happiness; successful living   340

final: the absolute end   341

the good life: a virtuous life of rational contemplation   343

habit: behaviors that with practice become automatic; the basis for developing moral virtue 346

happiness: the ultimate end of life 339, 340

hedonist: one who pursues pleasure for its own sake 341

instrumental end: an end that is really a means to a further end 339

intrinsic (end): an end that has value in itself 339

lifestyle of pleasure: priorities are money, wealth, material gain, and physical satisfaction 342

moderation: the avoidance of excess and deficiency 347

rational capacities: soul's activities that express reason 342

self-realization ethic: a description of Aristotle's functional account of morality 338

self-sufficient: lacking nothing 341

soul: that which animates living beings 344

state: a more or less stable condition 341

the statesman's lifestyle: way of living focusing on honor and public service 343

success: tied to the human notion of happiness understood as successful living 341

teleologist: one who holds that all pursuits and actions aim at some good and have a purpose 338

ultimate end of life: an end that is self-sufficient, final, attainable, intrinsically valuable 339

virtue: refers to excellence; two basic types: intellectual and moral 346

> **intellectual:** virtue that aims at wisdom 346

> **moral:** virtue that deals with moderation and results from habit 346

virtue ethics: an ancient Greek approach to ethics focusing on virtues such as courage, temperance, and wisdom 346

Jeremy Bentham's Utilitarian Ethics

act utilitarianism: determines the moral value of individual actions by their specific, unique outcomes in a particular situation 364

consequentialism: a theory that determines the morality of an action on the basis of its consequences 354

hedonic calculus: Bentham's mathematical tool used to determine which action is right on the basis of its pleasurable and painful consequences 356

is-ought fallacy: informal fallacy making the inference that because something 'is' the case, it 'ought' to be the case 355

Jeremy Bentham: British philosopher and social reformer who advocated utilitarianism 353

principle of utility: the notion that whatever action maximizes the net amount of pleasure and/or reduces the greatest amount of pain is the morally correct action to take; an approximate calculation is possible, according to Bentham 354

rule utilitarianism: determines the moral value of a rule by the consequences of its general application 365

sanctions: consequences, punishments or rewards that govern behavior 360

spirit of scientific objectivity: evidenced by rational, detached, mathematical, or evidence-based thinking void of personal bias or favor 353

utilitarianism: a form of consequentialist moral theory 353

utility: usefulness, benefit, or advantage 354

Immanuel Kant's Deontological Ethics

a priori: purely rational; not derived from or based on experience 366

autonomy: for Kant, acting willfully out of respect for the moral law 373

the categorical imperative: Kant's rational principle for the foundation of morality; prescriptive and universal in its various statements   371

deontological ethics: normative moral theory focusing on duty, rules, and principles of obligation rather than consequences   365

duties to others: obligations we have toward others   370

duties to ourselves: self-referring obligations   370

duty: obligation; that to which the good will consciously assents   367

the good will: a person's free will motivated purely by reason   367

heteronomy of the will: acting out of fear, coercion, or anything else beside respect for the moral law   374

Immanuel Kant: Eighteenth-century Prussian philosopher known for his synthesis of rationalist and empiricist metaphysics as well as his deontological ethical theory   365

inclination: temperamental predisposition   368

kingdom of ends: an ideal moral universe   374

Maria von Herbert: eighteenth century Austrian thinker who corresponded with Immanuel Kant   377

maxim: rule of conduct   367

moral certainty: having no doubt about what's morally required; for Kant, found in reason   366

prudence: the exercise of caution; doing what's in one's own self-interest   368

Carol Gilligan's and Nel Noddings's Care Ethics—Two Critiques of Male Moral Bias

Carol Gilligan: American psychologist known for developing the ethics of care   379

ethics of care: normative theory emphasizing identity formation and interconnectedness over rational detachment   383

hypothetical moral dilemmas: made-up situations containing conflicts that require difficult moral choices between two or more alternatives (e.g., telling the truth and being honest versus lying and thereby remaining loyal to a friend)   382

identity formation: the process of developing a psychological sense of self   384

intimacy: deep sense of interpersonal and emotional connectedness   385

moral reasoning development: the progression in thinking about morality from a lower stage to a higher stage   380

natural caring: early condition providing the attitude and motivation to be moral   389

Nel Noddings: American philosopher who advocated a care-based ethic grounded in interpersonal relations   386

one cared for: the one receiving the care in a caring relationship   389

one caring: the one doing the caring in a caring relationship   389

psychological bias: cognitive tendency to focus on or emphasize some things while missing, ignoring, or de-emphasizing other pertinent things central to the matter at hand   379

relation: something ontologically basic (Nel Noddings)   389

separation: the state of difference; distance from someone or something; emotionally disconnected   385

universalizability: the idea that a moral or ethical principle must apply to everyone unconditionally if it is to be considered both 'moral' and 'acceptable'   387

Friedrich Nietzsche's Will to Power

Abrahamic religious tradition: a religious descriptor that identifies points of theological, historical, and ethical commonality among the world's largest monotheistic religious traditions of Judaism, Islam, and Christianity   394

aesthetic phenomenon: how life should be lived for Nietzsche   404

Apollo: Greek figure symbolizing the power to control and restrain the dynamic forces of life   404

autonomy: conducive to and necessary for master morality   402

Dionysus: Greek figure symbolizing the power of passion   404

Friedrich Nietzsche: provocative nineteenth-century German philologist and philosopher   394

master morality: the noble moral stance of psychologically powerful, strong-willed individuals   399

negation: a feature of slave morality; the rejection of unbridled individuality   400

nihilism: the rejection of all moral and ethical standards or principles; the notion that life is meaningless   403

nobles: master moralists who display strength, courage and pride   400

psychological honesty: approach to life without deception or excuse   400

reaction: a feature of slave morality   400

resentment: slave moralists reaction to those individuals expressing the will to power   400

self-mastery: self-control   397

self-overcoming: the urge to overcome one's fears and to rise above one's limitations   397

slave morality: a dishonest moral perspective based on reaction, negation, and resentment   399

traditional/customary/herd morality: a morality that aims at safety and security, wherein the right thing to do is to obey customs and traditions and conform to the herd   401

Übermensch/**superman/overman:** one who displays a union of spiritual superiority with well-being and an excess of strength   403

will to power: a fundamental psychological force   395

Religion and Ethics: Islamic, Hindu, and Christian Perspectives

Allah: the Muslim name for God   406

Bhagavad Gita: sacred Hindu text containing an ethics of duty   410

Christianity: a major world religion based on the teachings and example of Jesus Christ   414

Hinduism: major world religion originating in India   410

Islam: the name of the faith practiced by Muslims; means "submission" in Arabic   406

Jesus Christ: considered to be the son of God by Christians   415

Muhammad: religious leader and prophet who founded Islam and received the oral dictation of the *Qur'an*   406

Qur'an: inspired Muslim Holy Book offering moral, spiritual, and social guidance for living   406

Roman Catholicism: one major sect of Christianity, among others   415

Summary of Major Points

1. What ethical perspectives are dealt with in this chapter?

Plato's character ethics, Aristotle's virtue ethics, Jeremy Bentham's utilitarian ethics, Immanuel Kant's deontological ethics, Gilligan's and Noddings's care ethics, Nietzsche's ethics based on the will to power, and religious ethics.

2. From the vantage point of Plato's theory, how are characters corrupted?

Ideally, reason should be the controlling faculty of the soul. When appetite or passion assume control, then either timarchic, oligarchic, democratic, or tyrannical character types result. All are corrupt and inferior relative to the philosopher king, who is ruled by reason.

3. What kind of life does Aristotle consider to be the best? Why?

The best kind of life is the life of rational contemplation. It reflects our highest function as human beings. A life of rational contemplation is self-sufficient, intrinsically valuable, and able to provide the purest and most enduring pleasure. Contemplation is god-like or divine.

4. What tool does Jeremy Bentham provide to help us make moral decisions in a spirit of scientific objectivity?

Bentham offers us the "hedonic calculus" based on the principle of utility to facilitate moral decision-making.

5. What is the foundational principle of Kant's deontological ethics? How is ethical theory formalistic?

The categorical imperative serves as the basis of Kantian ethics. Moral duty can be expressed in maxims or rules of conduct adhering to the following formalistic criteria: they must be rational, *a priori*, impersonal, universalizable, prescriptive, unconditional, impartial, objective, and logically consistent.

6. How do gender considerations bear on traditional moral theories?

Carol Gilligan and Nel Noddings have identified what they claim is a male bias in traditional theories of morality. They argue that male perspectives tend to romanticize rationality and inappropriately abstract from concrete human relationships within which moral concerns arise. Matters of care, relation, and the human affective response can either enrich limited male perspectives or replace them altogether.

7. What are some of the most provocative challenges to traditional morality raised by Friedrich Nietzsche?

Nietzsche rejects God as a basis for morality, arguing that "God is dead." For him, a life-affirming morality must be based on the will to power, not equality or altruism or self-denial. There are higher and lower forms of morality, the latter being inferior and meant for slavish, mediocre types. People are not equal by virtue of the quantum of power they possess; some are weak-willed, others are strong. Religious morality is dishonest and a veiled attempt to grab the power religionists themselves condemn in master moralists. Religious morality is nihilistic, that is, life-denying, anti-human. We should adopt the aesthetic form of life, not the life of reason or religious piety.

8. What are three major religious ethical perspectives? How can they help to inform moral judgment?

Islam, Hinduism, and Christianity are three major religions that help to inform one's morality and ethical decision-making. We find in Hinduism, for example, an ethic of duty as addressed in the *Bhagavad Gita*. Christianity offers different interpretations of scripture, which, in terms of Roman Catholicism, can be seen from the vantage point of deontological ethics, virtue ethics, and revisionism—a kind of teleological ethic whose purpose is union with God. Islam provides moral and ethical direction in personal conduct and social relations using the Prophet Muhammad and the Qur'an as inspirational sources and foundations of moral authority.

STUDY GUIDE

Additional Resources

For interactive quizzes, stories, supplements, and other materials for study and review, visit:

sites.broadviewpress.com/experiencing-philosophy/chapter5
Passcode: w4822kj

Or scan the following QR code:

CHAPTER 6

Political Philosophy

Take It Personally 430

Know Thyself: My Political Outlook 432

6.1 Political Philosophy versus Politics and Political Science 436

6.2 Plato's *Republic* 439
The Individual and the State 440
Plato's Class System 442
Imperfect Societies 445
Women, Marriage, and Family in the Republic 446
ORIGINAL SOURCE: Plato, The Nature of Woman 448

6.3 Thomas Hobbes's and John Locke's Social Contract Theories 453
Thomas Hobbes 453
ORIGINAL SOURCE: Thomas Hobbes, "Of the Causes, Generation, and Definition of a Commonwealth" 461
John Locke 463
ORIGINAL SOURCE: John Locke, "Of the Ends of Political Society and Government" 472

6.4 Karl Marx's Socialism 474
Marx's Metaphysics and Dialectical Materialism 478
Class Conflict 479
Alienation as a Byproduct of Capitalism 482
Idolatry/Fetishism of Commodities 485
Division of Labor 486
After Capitalism 489
ORIGINAL SOURCE: Karl Marx, *Economic and Philosophic Manuscripts* 490

6.5 Martin Luther King Jr.'s Philosophy of Nonviolence 492
Influences on King 492
Logic of Nonviolence 496
ORIGINAL SOURCE: Martin Luther King Jr.'s, "I Have a Dream" Speech 497
ORIGINAL SOURCE: Martin Luther King Jr., *Where Do We Go from Here?* 504

Progress Check 511

Study Guide 513
Key Terms 513
Summary of Major Points 517

LEARNING OUTCOMES

After successfully completing this chapter, you will be able to

▸ Define the field of political philosophy, distinguishing it from politics and political science

▸ Describe Plato's *Republic* and its class system, relating each class to a corresponding element of the soul

▸ Identify the flaws inherent in various types of imperfect societies, according to Plato

▸ Present in summary fashion Hobbes's grim state of nature and the commonwealth *Leviathan* proposed to deal with it

▸ Compare Locke's understanding of natural law and the state of nature with Hobbes's understanding

▸ Explain the importance Locke gives to property rights in any constitutional structure formed by a social compact

▸ Explain the limits John Locke places on government

▸ Discuss Marx's metaphysics, the influences upon his thought, and the notion of dialectical materialism

▸ Appreciate how capitalistic modes of production can foster alienation, idolatry, and oppression

▸ Identify the philosophical influences that had an impact upon Martin Luther King Jr.'s thought

▸ Detail how King's philosophy accepts and rejects elements of both capitalism and communism

▸ Articulate King's logic of nonviolence in the context of equality, structure, direct action, and the relationship between justice and love

FOCUS QUESTIONS

1. How are Plato's views of the state different from those of social contractarians and modern-day libertarians?

2. In what ways can societies be corrupted or flawed, according to the philosophers studied?

3. How does Plato view the role of women in society?

4. What are the theoretical similarities and differences between Hobbes and Locke, both of whom are social contractarians?

5. Which philosopher's conception of the state of nature rings true: Hobbes's or Locke's? Why?

6. How is Marxist theory a challenge to the American dream?

7. What basic components comprise King's logic of nonviolence?

8. Is King's thinking relevant today? How so?

Take It Personally

In a society like ours, preoccupied with economic prosperity, leisure, entertainment, and fun, political philosophy is not likely to be on the minds of most people for much of the time. Sure, in recent years, there have been many social and political activists who have addressed issues like Indigenous rights and movements like Black Lives Matter—certainly not everybody is disengaged. Concerns around such things as income inequality, police and immigration reform, and the idea of reparations for historical injustices are growing as well.

Nonetheless, etiquette usually dictates that we never discuss politics—or religion for that matter—in polite company. Such topics typically evoke strong negative feelings that often give rise to fruitless arguments and interpersonal discord. Presumably, it is better to discuss last night's game or a new recipe, for example, than to debate something as serious as health care reform, systemic racism, the morality of capitalism, police brutality, discrimination against marginalized communities, or the philosophical basis of democracy. Such weighty issues are usually considered far too serious as topics of conversation and, hence, are to be avoided.

For others, even to suggest the possibility that our political system is flawed or that other forms of government have advantages over our own could constitute an act of subversion, especially during wartime or periods of international tension. To criticize the economic or social basis of your society can be regarded as treasonous or unpatriotic.

Of course, a national pastime can be made of presidential scandals and acts of corruption by government officials. Think of the Lewinsky-Clinton affair, for example. (Former US President Bill Clinton was found to have lied about an affair he had with Monica Lewinsky, a White House intern. This lie eventually led to his impeachment proceedings.) In such cases, public interest may not be genuinely philosophical, however, but rather salacious and puerile—something you would expect from immature, gossiping schoolchildren.

In this chapter, we will not enter the minefield of politics; that is, we will not engage in partisan debates on local, national, or international issues. We will leave that to the politicians hoping to win the next election. We also have no intention here of performing any kind of character assassination or challenging the patriotism of those who hold dissenting views. These tasks can be completed, for better or worse, by campaign spin doctors and radio talk show hosts. Instead, what we will do is focus on a few historically important political theorists and their philosophies, examining their underlying assumptions about human nature, morality, and the ideal system of social organization.

To personalize the relevance of political philosophy, it might be useful to think back for a moment to what the Existentialists told us about human existence in Section 3.2. Remember how, according to them, we all simply find ourselves thrown into the world at birth. We could add to this the fact that we tend to be unreflective at early ages, merely responding in spontaneous or instinctive ways to objects, people, and events. Sadly, one could argue, a sizable number of individuals choose to remain largely unreflective throughout their entire lives, living *inauthentically*, as the Existentialists would say, by *mindlessly accepting* the social order into which they were born. Indeed, for some thoughtless, ethnocentric people, the status quo of society may even take on the appearance of being *natural*, unquestionably the best, or as God planned it.

In this chapter, we'll have the opportunity to think about political matters and the socioeconomic structures into which we have been born, and by which we have been raised and educated. If psychology is the study of the obvious, as some have suggested, then perhaps political philosophy might be seen, in part at least, as an inquiry into what seems obvious—or what is accepted when it comes to things like government, social structure, individual rights, and the role of the state.

Though it's apparent, for example, that governments do, in fact, exist, have you ever wondered *why* we need governments in the first place? Anarchists and paramilitary groups are often suspicious of governments and have even taken up arms to protect themselves against what they regard as coercive state powers. For example, the Oklahoma City bombing by domestic terrorist Timothy McVeigh and the postal service anthrax-related deaths across the US following the events of September 11, 2001, point to the fact that some citizens, even *within* the United States, have chosen to wage war against the federal government. You and I, by contrast, might just sit idly by accepting governmental authority with relative complacency.

Are the anarchists and revolutionary paramilitary groups simply crazy conspiracy theorists, or are *we* hopelessly naive and unsuspecting? Is government simply bad in itself, a necessary evil, or something to be minimized? Could it be, on the other hand, that government should be seen as a good and noble institution, a protector of the people whose involvement should be encouraged? Isn't it government that makes the good life possible for all of its citizens? Wouldn't life be horribly insecure without government protection and control?

What would happen, for example, to aging, sick, and unemployed people without some kind of governmental social safety net? What would the COVID-19 pandemic situation have looked like without the economic and medical support provided by national and state governments? Was government intervention needed? Was it helpful? What could have happened without it? Could we not ask those who are critical of national or local agencies the following questions: Are government programs *always* a waste? Should individuals *always* be left *completely on their own* to fend for themselves, regardless of circumstances? Is government assistance really nothing more than a symptom of a dangerous creeping socialism? Or, is it a sign of progressive social evolution?

If you're interested in the role of government in people's lives, then reading about Thomas Hobbes's *Leviathan*, John Locke's *Social Contract*, and Plato's utopian *Republic* should prove helpful. They all provide alternative visions of how societies should properly organize themselves. The treatment of Karl Marx's theory of dialectical materialism should also give you pause to reconsider the moral and philosophical merits of capitalism and Western liberal democracy as it functions today in the context of a global market economy.

In view of the continuing struggle for justice fought by so many minority and marginalized groups today, Martin Luther King Jr.'s action-oriented philosophy of nonviolence, also discussed in this chapter, will have particular relevance. King's words during the US civil rights movement in the middle of the last century are as applicable now as they were then.

Before we get down to work, however, let us first identify your personal sociopolitical values and presuppositions by completing the *Know Thyself* diagnostic that follows.

My Political Outlook

AIM

In this self-diagnostic, you'll begin to identify some of your political values, ideals, and beliefs, however clear or unclear they are at this time. As with the other measures found in this text, the results obtained are not intended to be scientific or conclusive in any way but only suggestive, affording you an opportunity to reflect on your political outlook on life. Of course, reading and thinking about ideas in this chapter may change some of your views, but at least with this diagnostic, you'll have a basis for comparative analysis and evaluation.

INSTRUCTIONS

Indicate your level of agreement or disagreement with each of the following statements using this scale:

1 = strongly disagree
2 = disagree somewhat
3 = agree somewhat
4 = strongly agree

1. _____ Not everybody is suited to govern, so not everybody should have the opportunity.

2. _____ It is naive to think that altruism is a natural emotion and that humans are, by nature, social animals.

3. _____ God has created natural laws governing not only the physical universe, but the moral universe as well.

4. _____ Societies develop and progress as a product of class struggle.

5. _____ The quest for social justice can be spurred on by spiritual motives.

6. _____ Democracies are flawed because the "ignorant masses" are too easily swayed by demagogues (unprincipled orators pandering to the prejudices of the population).

7. _____ Human beings are primarily motivated by egoistic desires to survive and experience pleasure.

8. _____ Reason can be used to discern God's natural laws of morality, which then can serve as the basis of a democratic society.

9. _____ There are no God-created natural laws of morality in the universe. The material interests of the dominant ruling classes ultimately determine right and wrong, good and evil, and social values in general.

10. _____ Majority rule can sometimes be tyrannical.

11. _____ The state is not a necessary evil, but rather an institution enabling individuals to realize themselves and live the good life.

12. _____ In the original state of nature, where no governments ruled, the human condition was a condition of warring enemies, involving distrust, fear, and competition for resources.

13. _____ The right to own property is a *natural right* basic to a democratic society.

14. _____ The highly mechanized and technologically sophisticated modes of production we find in a capitalistic economy cause alienation at work as well as among members of society.

15. _____ Equal rights and equal opportunities are part and parcel of social justice.

16. _____ In an orderly society, people should know their place and not interfere with the responsibilities of others.

17. _____ Without the state, there is no morality, only chaos, disorder, and opposition.

18. _____ Government authority should not be absolute. It too should be subject to the rule of law.

19. _____ A society should be based on the following principle: "We should take from each according to his ability, and give to each according to his need."

20. _____ Social injustice can be structural in nature.

21. _____ Not everyone has the ability to be a good leader; the business of politics should be left to a class of experts who possess the skills, training, and aptitude for it.

22. _____ The best way to protect ourselves and preserve the public order is by everyone relinquishing their rights to the state and allowing state control. Multiple wills are thereby transformed into a single will representing the best interests of all the citizens.

23. _____ Governments cannot be imposed; they must arise from consent, either tacit or direct.

24. _____ A market economy degrades human beings by forcing people to sell themselves in order to procure employment and feed their families.

25. _____ Contemporary operating notions of justice call for a revaluation of values.

26. _____ The people least equipped to govern society are those belonging to the business class.

27. _____ The sovereign body of the state should not be challenged, for then we return to a condition of chaos and disunity.

28. _____ Governments established by public consent should be subject to majority rule.

29. _____ The technology we create as a convenience often becomes our master, dictating what we must know and do in order to survive.

30. _____ Free market systems tend to impede true economic democracy.

31. _____ Corrupt societies produce corrupt individuals who are praised for exhibiting the vices and faults of those societies.

32. _____ The primary function of the state should be the protection of its citizens.

33. _____ Citizens have the right to dissolve governments if governments begin to exert power in capricious and tyrannical ways.

34. _____ Laws of social evolution point to the day when a classless society will eventually emerge, one in which the exploited and their exploiters no longer exist as enemies, for all will be free and equal, working toward the common good of the state.

35. _____ True and lasting change comes not from powerful leaders, but from grass-roots organizations and bottom-up social activism.

SCORING

The statements you just responded to are listed numerically below. Next to each statement number, write down the value you gave it indicating your level of agreement or disagreement. Then add the totals separately.

Plato's Aristocracy	Hobbes's Common- wealth	Locke's Consensual Democracy	Marx's Communism	King's Philosophy of Nonviolence
1:	2:	3:	4:	5:
6:	7:	8:	9:	10:
11:	12:	13:	14:	15:
16:	17:	18:	19:	20:
21:	22:	23:	24:	25:
26:	27:	28:	29:	30:
31:	32:	33:	34:	35:
TOTALS:				

INTERPRETATION OF RESULTS

The column with the highest score suggests that your political philosophy at this time is most in line with that perspective indicated by the heading. The various philosophies in the diagnostic are described briefly below.

My political philosophy is most consistent with

_____.

Plato's Aristocracy*

Plato believed in *rule by the best*. Democracy as we know it in North America, where one person gets one vote, is abandoned in favor of an expert aristocratic elite of guardians who have been properly trained and have proven themselves worthy of political authority. Social harmony is maintained by members of each social class accepting their roles and functioning at their best in those roles. This form of government is based on *meritocracy*. One must earn the right to govern through appropriate character education. Among the guardian elite, women are treated as equals and share in all responsibilities.

Hobbes's Commonwealth

Hobbes assumed that the state of nature is a state of war among men who are essentially desirous of the same things. To have peace and order, people are required in the commonwealth to give up their rights to the great "Leviathan"—a coercive power compelling individuals to live by their covenant or social contract. This strong sanctioning body is like a Mortal God. The Leviathan (sovereign power or assembly of men) is not really divine, but rather a human creation brought into existence to enable individuals achieve their egoistic goals. The agreement is to receive individual protection by everyone forfeiting their rights to the great Leviathan.

---

* As mentioned in an earlier chapter, the word 'aristocracy' is being used here in a somewhat outdated sense, but one in accord with its ancient Greek usage, not to refer to the privileged classes, but to the rule by the best people.

Locke's Consensual Democracy

This political system is based on *natural law*, which sets limits on the individual exercise of human freedom. It dictates, for example, that no one ought to harm the life, liberty, or possessions of another. Natural law, created by God, endows all individuals with rights to self-preservation, self-defense, and personal liberty. The most important of all rights in Locke's political system are property rights as they precede society, and because the primary function of government is to protect them. By establishing government, disputes can be adjudicated by impartial judges who can mete out punishments for wrong-doing when necessary. The government is a servant of the people. By operating according to principles of natural law, it provides a strong philosophical foundation for individualism. Governments assume their authority by consent of all the people and accept decisions by democratic rule.

Marx's Communism

This political philosophy reflects an atheistic materialism. The communistic state represents a classless society and is the final stage of a long evolutionary history of social class struggle between oppressor and oppressed. The moral basis of communism can be so expressed: "From each according to his ability; to each according to his needs." In a classless communistic state, market forces and competition (like those in capitalism) are largely absent, with the consequence that workers enjoy greater dignity. Because wealth cannot become concentrated in the hands of the rich minority, greater numbers of people can enjoy the fruits of their productivity. Also, because the "dog-eat-dog" world of the competitive marketplace is abolished, people can also learn to cooperate, work for the good of the state, and feel less alienated toward their neighbors who, in a capitalist system, are their competitive adversaries.

Martin Luther King Jr.'s Philosophy of Nonviolence

King's philosophy seeks to bring greater justice and dignity to minority peoples in the United States, especially African Americans, through reforming a number of structural inequalities imbedded in the American system. Using a logic of nonviolence and an ethic of love, efforts are designed to eliminate the "quiet terrorism of collective domination—a tyranny of the majority." This philosophy places the concept of 'equality' front and center, as opposed to individual rights and freedoms—things that can sometimes perpetuate discrimination against oppressed, marginalized, or racialized groups. To eradicate structural inequalities, a revaluation of values is required: King's approach would have us become more person-oriented than thing-oriented, more committed to the peace race than the arms race. Such things are to be achieved by means of nonviolent direct action. King seeks *not* to destroy American democracy, but to make it work with specific structural modifications and philosophical reforms.

It's the End of the World as We Know It... Again

A Brief History of Socialist Plots to End the American Way of Life

| PUBLIC SCHOOLS? SOCIALISM!! | PUBLIC WATER SYSTEM? SOCIALISM!! | PUBLIC HIGHWAYS? SOCIALISM!! | PUBLIC PARKS? SOCIALISM!! | PUBLIC HEALTH CARE? SOCIALISM!! |

1790   1808   1842   1905   2009

M. WUERKER POLITICO

6.1 Political Philosophy versus Politics and Political Science

"Those who can make you believe absurdities can make you commit atrocities."

VOLTAIRE

If we wish to make sense of **political philosophy**, then maybe we ought to be precise in our terminology, noting that it is not equivalent to **politics**. The term *politics* is usually used in the context of elections and political campaigns. However, it has also come to be negatively associated with *inflated egos, arm-twisting, name-calling, secret back-room deals, deceptive half-truths, distorted statistics, self-serving lobby groups, dark money, questionable campaign contributions, broken promises, stonewalling, and filibustering.* Little wonder, then, that politics has been given such a bad name and that so many avoid it like the plague. Politics sometimes appears to operate from a perversely *partisan logic of power*, not from a more morally acceptable *logic of impartial reason*. Perhaps if our politicians were swayed less by the desire for power and control, and more by the force of honest rationality, a greater degree of integrity would enter into the political arena, and we could get on with the nation's business.

As dirty as the business of politics can sometimes be, politicians generally hold, implicitly at least, theoretical views that coalesce to form more or less coherent political philosophies and ideological perspectives. In other words, politics takes place against a backdrop of political theory. When unarmed Chinese students are confronted by tanks in Tiananmen Square, when the National Guard shoots protesting students at Kent State

University, when free-trade agreements result in a greater degree of economic globalization, or when nation-states try to protect their cultural industries from foreign domination—in all of these situations, certain philosophical visions of nationhood, legitimate government authority, and individual rights play a role.

Of course, it is not necessarily the case that politicians, protestors, or even voters fully understand their own political presuppositions. Though people often self-identify as Left or Right, Liberal or Conservative, Marxist or Monarchist, a partisan of this party or that, they do not always appreciate the implications of such identifications. Individuals sometimes adopt political views because of family loyalties, social conditioning, indoctrination, peer pressure, or because of other non-rational considerations. In short, we do not always understand the philosophies that support differing political outlooks and their derivative policies, which are passed into legislation and sanctioned by law.

If, then, we wish to become more responsible and enlightened citizens, able to provide good reasons for the stands we take on particular sociopolitical issues, it would behoove us to gain a better appreciation of some differing political theories and their philosophical underpinnings. People are not really politically free to choose until they have alternative options to choose from; and to the extent that true freedom necessitates intelligent and informed choice, an understanding of political theory would seem to be indispensable. This points again to the practical value of philosophy, which helps us to develop this understanding.

So far in our efforts to grasp the nature of political philosophy, we have distinguished it from politics. Remember, political philosophy forms the *theoretical basis* for political action. Another distinction needs to be made for purposes of clarity: that between political philosophy and **political science**. Though the two are related in some ways, they are certainly different.

Political science, as a study of various types of governments and social organizations, is essentially *descriptive* and *empirical*. It explains to us how past and existing social structures function. Political science is a type of *factual inquiry* regarding the structure and workings of political institutions, such as the state and its constitutive parts: the legislative, executive, and judicial. More recently, influenced by psychology and sociology, political scientists have started to focus on the political behaviors of individuals and groups in their investigations.

By contrast to political science, political philosophy tends to be *normative*, prescribing actions, making value judgments, offering justifications, and putting forward suggestions for how society *ought* to be structured and regulated. With its focus on normative considerations, political philosophy is often categorized as a branch of **axiology**—that division of philosophical inquiry dealing with matters of value. Indeed, political philosophy's preoccupation with values sometimes makes it difficult to distinguish it from ethical inquiry. It could be argued that politics is continuous with morality and that many of our political duties and obligations are tantamount to our moral duties and obligations. The individual's civil rights as a member of society are often defended, for example, by reference to the individual's moral rights as a human being. In such instances, the overlap between ethics and political philosophy is undeniable. The claim that one has the civil right to vote, for example, may be based on moral notions of 'freedom' and 'equality.'

Notwithstanding their similarities, however, political philosophy and ethics do diverge from each other at certain points. In general terms, morality is more concerned

THINKING ABOUT YOUR THINKING

Think about a government decision you disagree with. It could be at the local level of government or at the state, provincial, or federal level. It could have to do with education, healthcare, taxes, policing, licensing, traffic laws, public transit, etc. It's likely that you do not have to go far back in your memory to come up with an example. Just think of the last time you had critical thoughts about a policy or procedure made by the government, which probably wasn't that long ago!

Now think about why you disagree with that government decision. If you are thinking about particulars, such as specific people, places, times, and events, try to broaden your thinking to cover what you disagree with *in principle*. In other words, what concepts are at the root of your criticism? Fairness? Justice? Rights? Whatever concepts you are thinking of, what do those concepts mean to you? Finally, sum up your criticism in one sentence that uses concept terms.

with relations between particular individuals and with matters of personal conscience, whereas political philosophy is more concerned with social institutions, governments, and with large and impersonal groups. Morality also directs its attention to the cultivation of virtue and character development, which no doubt have indirect implications for the functioning of a good society, but are not the main focus of political theory.

On this last note, it might be worth adding here that 'political philosophy' and 'political theory' are sometimes used synonymously in the same way that 'ethics' and 'morality' are. We can speak of classical political theories and modern political theories as representing different philosophical ideas and approaches. Classical theories tend to offer advice and prescriptions for achieving an ideal or utopian society. Modern theories, on the other hand, tend to approach the subject matter of political philosophy from a more conceptual-analytical viewpoint. This is done in efforts to clarify the meaning of the advice given in classical theories for the purpose of rendering more intelligible the concepts and terms we use in political discussions.

A political philosopher adopting an analytical approach would ask questions such as "When does an area's people constitute a 'state'?" and "What do we mean when talking about 'human rights'?" By analyzing technical terms and concepts such as 'the state' and 'human rights,' political philosophy separates itself as a specialized discipline that cannot be reduced entirely to ethics or to the empirical social sciences.

Lastly, to grasp the nature and scope of political philosophy, it might be helpful to enumerate some more of the basic questions that theorists in the field have posed. Historically speaking, political philosophers have been preoccupied with definitions of justice, as well as with the attitudes and arrangements that ought to create and perpetuate it. They have also discussed a variety of ideas concerning the organization of human beings into collectivities. A sampling of basic questions asked by political philosophers include the following:

1. What is the ultimate justification for the existence of any form of government?
2. What should be the proper limits of government over the members of society?
3. Why should anyone obey the law?
4. Why should anyone pay taxes?
5. How do we harmonize governmental authority with human rights and individual freedoms?
6. Under what conditions is it legitimate to replace those who currently rule?
7. Should we allow political power to be concentrated in the hands of a few leaders, or should it be widely distributed among the members of society at large?
8. Should politicians vote according to personal conscience or represent the wishes of their constituents?

9. How should inequities—whether at the level of individuals or of social and racial groups—be addressed?

Now that we have a better idea of what political philosophy is all about, let us turn to several historically important representatives in the field, starting with Plato.

6.2 Plato's *Republic*

In **Plato**'s *Republic*, we find not only an epistemology, metaphysics, and theory of character ethics, as we have already learned, but also an example of a classical political theory offering us a vision of the ideal, utopian society. This vision was developed against a backdrop of small but numerous Greek city-states with their own autonomous governments. History reveals that these states were in constant warfare with each other, and also that most suffered from a great deal of internal strife. The result was that life for the average citizen was precarious indeed.

In view of this situation, Plato's aim was to create the blueprint for a society that would be able to achieve its objectives, defend itself against its external enemies, and free itself from defects giving rise to internal disturbances. The general question was posed: "What would the ideal society be like if it were brought into existence?

Note that Plato was not engaged in political science. He was not interested in the empirical study of actual states, but rather, his aim was to present a vision of what states *should* be like, even if they were not as he envisioned. Plato's Republic represents the ideal pattern to which every state ought to conform, in so far as it could. So much the worse for states that fall short of his expressed ideal.

In what follows, we will examine more closely the particulars of Plato's utopian blueprint. Suffice it to say at this juncture that the ideal society constitutes a type of **aristocracy**, a term derived from the Greek roots *ariston* and *krato*, suggesting "rule by the best." This presentation of Plato's utopian ideal will surely give us occasion to reflect upon our own political presuppositions and perhaps reason to modify or even reject them altogether. Just as David Hume awoke Kant from his dogmatic slumbers, maybe Plato (and those who follow) will awaken us to our many accepted, but unexamined, political beliefs regarding justice, autonomy, the rights of individuals, and their proper place in the state. Pardon any discomfort that might ensue. *Becoming woke* (to use the vernacular), or waking from one's deep dogmatic sleep-state, is not usually a pleasant affair, but necessary for rational enlightened living.

The possibility of a rude awakening arises because Plato had only contempt for democracy, as he knew it in his time, and quite possibly, he would heap scorn on contemporary forms of it, which allow the general masses, including those who are ignorant and unwise, selfish and greedy, as well as those who are vain and undisciplined, to seize the reins of power. Also, in democracies, demagogues can too easily manipulate the ignorant masses. In contrast to our modern liberal-democratic state, one in which we allow one person one vote, Plato would prefer governance by an expert elite.

The Individual and the State

"We are bound to admit that the elements and traits that belong to the state must also exist in the individuals who compose it. There is nowhere else for them to come from."
PLATO

As we begin our trek into this, the third decade of the new millennium, it would appear that **individualism** still reigns supreme in North American society. Certainly, group work and team building are collective activities emphasized in contemporary learning and business environments, but usually for instrumental purposes. One learns to function cooperatively in groups and to become a team player within the corporation, for example, for personal advancement and individual gain. Groups are good because of what they get you; they are not necessarily good in themselves. Indeed, even in government, efforts are continuously made to reduce the influence of politicians and legislators in the daily affairs of private citizens. "Reduce government red-tape and interference!" and "Too much government regulation!" are rallying calls for libertarians, business people, and hard-core individualists.

From the individualistic perspective, the less government intervention and control in the lives of private citizens, the better. What is sought is greater independence and liberty for all. Sacrificing the rights and interests of the individual to the welfare of the state or to any collectivity within it smacks of creeping socialism or even worse, totalitarian repression.

Now, as far as Plato is concerned, the state is neither inherently evil nor obstructionist with respect to the attainment of individual goals. State control is not something that must unquestionably be reduced, minimized, and dispensed with whenever possible, though our prevailing value system would sometimes seem to lead us confidently to this conclusion.

The city-state ideal that Plato refers to in his writings would be small.* One could imagine that it would be like a small town where most people know their neighbors. The state governance Plato had in mind would certainly not resemble the Kremlin in Russia or the multilayered impersonal bureaucracy in Washington, DC, both overseeing millions.

In defense of the state and its proper jurisdiction, Plato offers the observation that human beings, as individuals, are not entirely self-sufficient. The reason societies formed in the first place was to establish systems of cooperation that would enable members to achieve the necessities of life that would be more difficult, if not sometimes impossible, to obtain alone.

In large part, the state arose to serve the economic interests of its citizens. Thus, the state is not evil, but potentially very good, satisfying the natural desires of human beings. In fact, for Plato, who regards human beings as social animals, *the good life* cannot be lived apart from active participation in state affairs. The **city-state or *polis*** (to use the Greek equivalent) provides the natural setting for the life of any individual. Since we all have a natural desire to live in communities, cities and their governments are just as natural as human beings are. The good life for the individual is possible only within the good state.

In *The Republic*, Plato explains how the good state is supposed to operate if it is to function properly. His depiction of the properly functioning ideal society interestingly combines principles of psychology and political science. For Plato, the **soul** of the individual—what we would call today the self or personality—is actually a miniature version of the structure of society. Plato believes we can more easily gain insight into the workings of the human soul by examining society first; after all, it is larger and hence easier to see. Conveniently for us, we have already studied the structure and workings of the soul in our earlier moral discussion on Plato (in Section 5.1).

---

* In his time, the existing city-states were mostly quite small—population close to 10,000. There were over 1,000 of them.

The parallels between the individual and the state, as well as the similarities between psychology and political science, can be observed in the correspondence between the three elements of the soul and the three types or classes of people within society that Plato identifies. Just as each part of the soul has its proper target objects and specific role to play in the harmonious functioning of the individual's psyche, so too does each kind of person have his or her special job to perform within society.

For Plato, the ideal state is built around a **division of labor**. We find differences in people's aptitudes, making different people better at different things. Thus, it is most beneficial for all that individuals concentrate on developing their particular talents. If we all do what we're good or best at, or what's suitable for us, then we all win in the end. A society that nurtures the development of individual aptitudes by means of its laws and regulations promotes a pattern of natural growth. Just as there can be an organic harmonious balance within the individual soul, so too can such a balance exist within the state, displayed by a *harmonious hierarchy of purposes among its citizens*.

So far, you might be inclined to side with Plato regarding his conception of the ideal state. After all, who would complain about a state designed to help you develop your natural gifts? Sounds pretty good, doesn't it? Before you get too excited, however, recall what Plato said about the soul in the context of morality and character development. For him, the soul comprises three elements: appetite, spirit, and reason. Also, remember that not all parts of the soul were to have equal influence on the functioning of the personality. Appetite and spirit were seen as *wild horses* to be reined in by the controlling faculty of reason. With authority handed over to reason, *psychological equality* did not exist in the well-functioning personality.

Similarly, for Plato, the harmoniously balanced functional state is *not* based on any notion of *democratic equality*. The business of politics should be left to a class of experts who possess the skills, training, and aptitude for it. Not everyone has the ability to be a good leader, and hence, not just anybody should be given the right to assume leadership positions in society.

This notion appears to be in direct opposition to the American ideal that, in principle, any person should be able to run for public office and even become the president of the United States. This would not be so in Plato's aristocracy. How could the esteemed Plato put forward a conception that is so counterintuitive, even hostile, to the cherished values embodied in a system of government such as the one found in the Western democracies?

Essentially, Plato defends his position by analogy. He argues that just as we should yield to the advice of medical experts when we are concerned about the health of the body, so too, when concerned about the health of the state, we should seek out the advice of experts possessing the necessary wisdom to govern properly. The masses simply lack the knowledge and intelligence needed for proper governance.

Just imagine how silly, even dangerous, it would be when seriously ill to ask every stranger you met on the street for advice. Would you really want to treat your ailment based on the health recommendations of any simpleminded celebrity with a social media account? Surely you wouldn't take a democratic vote among your friends to diagnose your condition or establish the preferred course of treatment. Yet, when it comes to the problems of the *body politic*, affecting the health of the state, we proudly seek the advice of the ignorant masses through such vehicles as elections, polls, referenda, and town hall meetings. Plato asks why it is that,

"He who is unable to live in society, or who has no need of it because he is sufficient unto himself, must be either a beast or a god."
ARISTOTLE

When we Athenians are met together in the assembly, and the matter in hand relates to building, the builders are summoned as advisers; when the question is one of ship-building, then the shipwrights.... But when the question is an affair of state, then everybody is free to have a say—carpenter, tinker, cobbler, merchant, sea captain, rich and poor, high and low—anyone who likes gets up, and no one reproaches him, as in the former case, with not having learned ... and yet giving advice.[1]

Plato's Class System

Given that people possess different aptitudes, not all people are the same, intellectually and morally speaking. While it is true that we all share the same basic elements of the soul and are alike in this respect, we nonetheless find that these elements, taken individually, exert varying degrees of influence or psychological force on different individuals. Spirit dominates some individuals; appetite does so for others. For a few, reason is the dominant influence in life. This fact gives rise to the idea of three different classes in society. For each class a particular element of the soul is dominant. This dominating element motivates members of its corresponding class to value certain types of objects and to display particular kinds of virtues that make them best suited to perform specific kinds of social functions (see Table 6.1).

TABLE 6.1

Parts of the Soul	Classes in Society
Appetite	Artisans/Business Class
Spirit	Auxiliaries/Soldier Class
Reason	Philosopher Kings/Rulers

------ Guardian Class

ARTISANS

Driven primarily by the psychological faculty of appetite are the **artisans** or what we might call today the **business class**. Under this generic heading, we can include merchants and shopkeepers. We can also place workers, traders, and farm producers under this category, as well as those *born to shop*, namely those we would describe as avid consumers. Members of this class value wealth, material possessions, and appetite satisfaction.

Even though this class is regarded as inferior and subordinate to the guardians, it enjoys the most freedom and physical comforts. People in this class are allowed to pursue their material dreams as long as they live within the boundaries of the law, and as long as unacceptable poverty does not develop as a result of an overconcentration of wealth in the hands of too few people. The job of the artisan producer-worker class is to generate trade, commerce, and other economic activities, providing the material necessities of the community.

Members of the artisan class are permitted to marry whomever they wish and to raise their own children—rights not afforded the other two classes.* Using the prevailing

---

* Plato says relatively little about the artisans/business class in *The Republic*. We assume from what he says and doesn't say that the artisans live under normal arrangements by comparison to the guardians, for whom family life and private property is prohibited. See Frederick Copleston, *A History of Philosophy*, vol. 1 (New York: Doubleday, 1993), 107.

values of contemporary North American society as a standard, some might suggest that those in this *lowest class* are the ones best off.

Virtue is manifested in this class through *obedience*, *moderation*, and **self-discipline**. Appetites within the individual are to be controlled and kept temperate. Socially, the artisans are to display moderation and self-discipline by showing due obedience to those who govern and those who carry out the orders of the highest ruling class. In fact, "moderation spreads throughout the whole. It makes the weakest, the strongest, and those in between ... all sing the same song together. And this unanimity, this agreement between the naturally worse and the naturally better as to which of the two is to rule both in the city and in each one, is rightly called moderation."[2]

AUXILIARIES

In the ideal society Plato envisions, not only is it necessary to produce the material necessities of life, but also to maintain *internal order* and *defense against external enemies*. These tasks are allotted to the **auxiliaries**, who comprise the professional soldier class and police, as well as those we would call in today's world government officials, federal agents, and state administrators—civil servants in general. Auxiliaries are actually a subordinate subgroup of a larger **guardian class**, which includes the **philosopher rulers**—those ultimately charged with the authority and control over the city-state.

Auxiliaries have more in common with this aristocratic ruling class than with the workers, merchants, and artisans below them. In fact, the commonalities are so great, that one might be tempted to conclude that Plato's three classes are really only two, one of which is further subdivided.[3] These commonalities are quite apparent in view of the fact that both philosopher rulers and auxiliaries live a life of austere simplicity. Because Plato believed that material possessions constituted the major temptation leading people to sacrifice the public good for personal gain, he required that both auxiliaries and philosopher rulers possess no private property beyond the barest essentials.

Plato believed that Guardians (both auxiliaries and philosopher rulers) were to live and eat communally. Guardians were not allowed to own their own homes or live independently in their own quarters. Basically, they were to live like soldiers in a camp. Guardians were even forbidden to handle gold and silver, being taught that *heavenly* gold and silver had been infused into their very beings by the gods and that it would be "impious for them to defile this divine possession by any admixture of such gold, because many impious deeds have been done that involve the currency used by ordinary people, while their own is pure."[4] This "noble act of deception" (sometimes translated as "noble lie" or "magnificent myth") on the part of the rulers was to be propagated like a folkloric tale in order to build commitment to one's designated societal function and to maintain social order.*

In contrast to the appetite-driven artisan class, naturally infused with bronze, *silver-infused* auxiliaries are motivated by the **spirit** element of the soul. In defense of the state and in the maintenance of its internal order, they must exhibit **courage**, the distinguishing virtue of this class. Of course, courage is required if one is to perform one's duty, because such responsibility can oftentimes be dangerous or aversive in some fashion. Yet the

---

*   I thank professor Tom Robinson at the University of Toronto for clarifying why the translated expression "noble act of deception" is to be preferred over the common translations "noble lie" and "magnificent myth." One issue here is whether Plato is countenancing the use of propaganda against one's own people; he denounces propaganda elsewhere on moral grounds.

auxiliaries must manage somehow to muster the requisite fortitude if they are to achieve the honor that accompanies the dutiful protection of the state and the implementation of the philosopher rulers' decisions.

PHILOSOPHER KINGS/RULERS

The third class envisioned by Plato in his utopian Republic comprises the **philosopher kings** or **rulers** (we will use "rulers" to avoid any suggestion of gender bias). This *gold class* represents the highest social echelon charged with the responsibility of establishing laws and policies within society. The philosopher rulers are not voted into office, but rather earn the right to govern as an aristocracy after a long period of training and moral character development.

The philosopher rulers are truly wise, enlightened leaders, possessing a higher kind of knowledge that comes from an intellectual acquaintance with *Goodness*, something which ultimately resides in a supersensible, timeless, spaceless realm of forms. Rulers having this special knowledge are able to exercise the virtue of wisdom, knowing what is best for all the classes. Because they have demonstrated through tests of moral character that they are not corrupted by greed (appetite) and vanity (spirit), they have the best fit to rule, and so they should. They are the ones who always place care of the state above their own interests. More accurately, they identify the interests of the state as their own.

Historical experience tells us what happens when corrupt and morally unfit people are allowed to assume power. Think of Russia's Joseph Stalin, for instance, who killed millions of Ukrainians through systematic starvation during the 1930s in the *Holodomor*, also known as the 'Terror-Famine' or 'Harvest of Despair.'[5] Maybe Plato was correct when he concluded that rulers must become philosophers or that philosophers must become rulers if the ideal society is ever to be achieved.

THE JUST STATE

So far in our discussion of the ideal state, we have learned that its class members display the virtues of moderation, courage, and wisdom. In this vein, we should recognize that the utopian republic is also characterized by the virtue of **justice**. The just state is one wherein everyone attends to his or her own business without interfering with anyone else's. People know their station in life and perform their function to the best of their ability.

It would be presumptuous and misguided, for example, for artisans to think their wealth and business savvy qualified them to govern as guardians. In the just state, they are required to exhibit obedience to authority, namely the auxiliaries and ultimately to the philosopher rulers above them. When all the citizens of the state exhibit self-discipline, and do what they are qualified to do, keeping their noses out of other people's business, so to speak, then harmony results in the state as it does in the soul when there is a stable balance and governance by reason (see Table 6.2). As Plato puts it,

> Justice, is doing one's own work and not meddling with what isn't one's own.... Meddling and exchange between these three classes, then, is the greatest harm that can happen to the city and would rightly be called the worst thing someone could do to it.... Then, that exchange and meddling is injustice. Or to put it the other way around: For the money-making, auxiliary, and guardian classes each to do its own work in the city, is the opposite. That's justice, isn't it, and makes the city just?[6]

TABLE 6.2 Social Classes, Their Functions, and Values Corresponding to Each Part of the Soul

Dominant Part of the Soul	Social Class	Valued Objects	Societal Functions
Appetite	Artisans/ Business class: Includes merchants, manufacturers, producers, traders, consumers *Symbolic Metal*: Bronze *Virtue*: Moderation, obedience and self-discipline	Wealth, appetite satisfaction, material acquisition, property	Generate economic activity, provide the material and economic necessities of the community
Spirit	Auxiliaries: Soldier class, government officials, civil servants administrators, federal agents *Symbolic Metal*: Silver *Virtue*: Courage	Community service, honor, duty, competition	Soldiering, protection of state interests, assist rulers and enforce their decisions
Reason	Philosopher Kings/Rulers: Elite sub-class of guardians *Symbolic Metal*: Gold *Virtue*: Wisdom	Enlightened understanding of true goodness, acquaintance with the forms	Establish laws and policies within society; govern as aristocracy

Imperfect Societies

In *The Republic*, Plato discusses various forms of **imperfect societies** which directly parallel the corrupt character types described in Chapter 5. They include the **timocracy**, the **oligarchic state**, the **democracy**, and the **tyrannical society**.[7] Along with his descriptions of various character types and explanations of their gradual descent into maniacal immorality, Plato also provides a corresponding outline of how societies can progressively degenerate from a utopian aristocracy (Plato's Republic) to the worst state of all, that is, a tyranny. On his account, which is presumably not to be taken as an accurate historical depiction, democracies mirror the democratic character; oligarchies reflect the oligarchic type, and so on. And just as imperfect character types are ruled by something other than reason, so too are imperfect societies governed by classes driven by spirit and appetite.

In all of the degenerate societies identified by Plato, philosophers lose their place as controlling guardians of the state. Classes best suited to obey and produce goods take on inappropriate roles that they are not properly qualified to play. Values of relatively lesser importance become highly esteemed, while virtue and goodness are dethroned and subordinated in status.

For Plato, the harmonious balance of the healthy functioning aristocracy is disturbed as divisions and conflicts are allowed to arise between rich and poor. The internal security and protection of the state are jeopardized; individuals start interfering with the proper functioning of others; principles of order and good taste are trampled under foot; a disregard for laws and disrespect for authority emerges; and as social relations become inverted—with subjects acting as rulers and rulers acting as subjects—excessive freedom erupts, leading to anarchy and eventually to tyranny—the worst form of unjust state that can exist.

Plato's prescription to end all of this injustice is, of course, to establish an aristocracy where carefully trained and selected philosophers become rulers. Only in such a hierarchal meritocracy can we find enlightened leadership providing order, stability, and proper direction (see Table 6.3).

Women, Marriage, and Family in the Republic

Discussions of women in contemporary society often raise issues of discrimination, gender bias, inequality, and political oppression. Indeed, it goes without saying that women have generally not been treated equally or with complete respect throughout human history. These days, fair-minded people of both sexes have certainly applauded the writings and past efforts of political activists such as Susan B. Anthony, Simone de Beauvoir, Germaine Greer, Gloria Steinem, Nellie McClung, and countless others who, in the second half of the twentieth century, helped to raise our collective consciousness regarding the treatment of women in society.

In view of centuries-old sexism and the relatively recent emergence of the women's movement in the West, it is interesting to note that Plato was arguably an ancient **feminist** of sorts. For Plato, guardian women, at least, were not expected simply to stay at home and mind the baby. While Plato did recognize that men and women are in some ways not alike, especially where reproduction is concerned, he did not regard these biological differences as relevant when it comes to playing leadership roles in society.

In recognition of women's intellectual and moral equality, they were to be given the same education as men. Women, like men were to receive instruction in music, gymnastics, military discipline, astronomy, mathematics, and so forth. As with men, the best of the women, who passed the same moral tests of character and intellectual bars of admission, would be further trained as guardians of the state. The best of the best, of course, would then be selected as elite philosopher rulers. The remaining ones would become part of the auxiliary class. Plato's Republic thus allows for women to be admitted to all social pursuits, even war. Both men and women share the same natural capacities for guardianship, and where physical strength is an issue, women are simply to be given a lighter load.

Women in contemporary society are often torn apart inside trying to achieve a balance between the responsibilities of work and family, or between career and spousal commitments. In Plato's Republic, women in leadership roles are liberated (so to speak) from these responsibilities, but at the cost of being prevented from marrying and having families, things afforded to the artisan class.*

Plato's aim in ridding guardians of distracting loyalties, self-interests, and affectional ties associated with the family system was to ensure that they focused on service to the community. Instead of couple arrangements and nuclear families, then, the guardians would constitute, and belong to, one large extended family—the guardian herd. To ensure

---

*   Plato has been criticized for omitting discussion in *The Republic* of the role of women in the artisan class. What he says elsewhere sometimes encourages the speculation that he would deny artisan women equal treatment. He also says nothing about whether slavery is included in his ideal state. Commentators sometimes are of the opinion that he just takes their presence for granted.

TABLE 6.3 States and Their Corresponding Character Types

States	Social Features	Corresponding Character Types	Psychological Profiles
Aristocracy (*Ideal State*)	Governed by guardian elite, Hierarchical meritocracy, Division of labor, Harmoniously functioning	Philosopher ruler	Virtuous: Wise, courageous, disciplined, just, Enlightened, Dedicated to state's welfare
Timocracy	Military aristocracy, Devoted to war, Overvaluation of physical, Enslaved population, Internal strife	Timarchic	Ambitious, energetic, athletic, Egoistic, self-assertive, insecure, conflicted, spirit-driven
Oligarchy	Wealthy in control, Poor despised, Drone class of criminals emerges, Rampant crime	Oligarchic	Money-hungry, hard-working, squalid character, No moral conviction, appetite-driven

that guardians were not sidetracked by long-term love relations and by contaminating family loyalties, men and women were allowed multiple mating opportunities (with the resulting offspring placed in state-run nurseries). Be clear, however, that this was no system of free love. Contrived lotteries, run by the philosopher rulers, rigged things so that only the bravest and the best of the guardians would be allowed to mate and conceive, and only during scheduled marriage festivals. Plato believed that the offspring of the best and the bravest would most likely produce the desirable traits of their guardian parents.

What Plato had in mind was a systematic program of **eugenics**, bearing great similarity to animal breeding. Plato recognized, or course, that breeding practices cannot always guarantee the best progeny; occasionally a child would be born into the wrong class, and the guardians would be alert to this possibility, and would remove them from their parents, and subject them to the appropriate education and training for their proper class. Class placement was therefore not a birthright, since in Plato's **meritocracy** one was required to display certain natural talents and abilities. Such things would be further nurtured and developed in preparation for assuming future guardian roles.

In closing, it's important to recognize that with marriage abolished for the guardians and with state-run nurseries charged with the responsibility of raising guardian-produced children, women rulers and auxiliaries were thus given freedom and access to the same leadership opportunities as men. Again, for Plato this same level of equality does not seem to have applied to the artisan class. Even in his discussion of the guardians, Plato's assumptions about ability are undeniably sexist by today's standards. Nonetheless, in the context of ancient Greece (and, indeed, of much of Western history), Plato's argument that women should be members of the ruling class is surprisingly modern.

"We have to look and ensure that we're paying attention to what we're doing, so that we don't reflexively institute processes and procedures that exclude people without thought."
SONIA SOTOMAYOR

Plato, The Nature of Woman[8]

The main topic of discussion in Plato's Republic *is virtue. At the start of Book V, however, that discussion is interrupted by characters in the dialogue who want Socrates to explain a curious remark about wives and children that he made earlier in the discussion. At that time, he had stated, "Friends possess everything in common" (424a). Now, in response to the request from his interlocutors for an explanation of that statement, Socrates proposes that women with the same natural ability as men should receive the same education and training to do the same kind of work. As for the "silly" concern that the inclusion of women in training would seem "ridiculous" in the current culture, Socrates states that fear of jokes should not prevent change for the good. The good is a serious matter, and it should not fall prey to the concerns of unserious people.*

———

[Socrates] Do we think that the wives of our guardian watchdogs should guard what the males guard, hunt with them, and do everything else in common with them? Or should we keep the women at home, as incapable of doing this, since they must bear and rear the puppies, while the males work and have the entire care of the flock?

[Glaucon] Everything should be in common, except that the females are weaker and the males stronger.

[Socrates] And is it possible to use any animals for the same things if you don't give them the same upbringing and education?

[Glaucon] No, it isn't.

[Socrates] Therefore, if we use the women for the same things as the men, they must also be taught the same things.

[Glaucon] Yes.

[Socrates] Now, we gave the men music and poetry and physical training.

[Glaucon] Yes.

[Socrates] Then we must give these two crafts, as well as those having to do with warfare, to the women also to use in the same way as the men use them.

[Glaucon] That seems to follow from what you say.

[Socrates] But perhaps much of what we are saying, since it is contrary to custom, would incite ridicule if it were carried out in practice as we've described.

[Glaucon] It certainly would.

[Socrates] What is the most ridiculous thing that you see in it? Isn't it obviously the women exercising naked in the palestras with the men? And not just the young women, but the older ones too—like old men in gymnasiums who, even though their bodies are wrinkled and not pleasant to look at, still love to do physical training.

[Glaucon] Yes, that would look really ridiculous as things stand at present.

[Socrates] But surely, now that we've started to speak about this, we mustn't fear the various jokes that wits will make about this land of change in music and poetry, physical training, and—last but not least—in bearing arms and riding horses.

[Glaucon] You're right.

[Socrates] And now that we've begun to speak about this, we must move on to the tougher part of the law, begging these people not to be silly (though that is their own work) but to take the matter seriously. They should remember that it wasn't very long ago that the Greeks themselves thought it shameful and ridiculous (as the majority of the barbarians still do) for even men to be seen naked and that when the Cretans and then the Lacedaemonians began the gymnasiums, the wits of those times could also have ridiculed it all. Or don't you think so?

[**Glaucon**] I do.

[**Socrates**] But I think that, after it was found in practice to be better to strip than to cover up all those parts, then what was ridiculous to the eyes faded away in the face of what argument showed to be the best. This makes it clear that it's foolish to think that anything besides the bad is ridiculous or to try to raise a laugh at the sight of anything besides what's stupid or bad or (putting it the other way around) it's foolish to take seriously any standard of what is fine and beautiful other than the good.

[**Glaucon**] That's absolutely certain.

[**Socrates**] However, mustn't we first agree about whether our proposals are possible or not? And mustn't we give to anyone who wishes the opportunity to question us—whether in jest or in earnest—about whether female human nature can share all the tasks of that of the male, or none of them, or some but not others, and to ask in which class the waging of war belongs? Wouldn't this, as the best beginning, also be likely to result in the best conclusion?

[**Glaucon**] Of course.

[**Socrates**] Shall we give the argument against ourselves, then, on behalf of those who share these reservations, so that their side of the question doesn't fall by default?

[**Glaucon**] There's no reason not to.

[**Socrates**] Then let's say this on their behalf: "Socrates and Glaucon, there's no need for others to argue with you, for you yourselves, when you began to found your city, agreed that each must do his own work in accordance with his nature."

[**Glaucon**] And I think we certainly did agree to that.

[**Socrates**] "Can you deny that a woman is by nature very different from a man?"

[**Glaucon**] Of course not.

[**Socrates**] "And isn't it appropriate to assign different work to each in accordance with its nature?"

[**Glaucon**] Certainly.

[**Socrates**] "How is it, then, that you aren't mistaken and contradicting yourselves when you say that men and women must do the same things, when their natures are so completely separate and distinct?" Do you have any defense against that attack?

[**Glaucon**] It isn't easy to think of one on the spur of the moment, so I'll ask you to explain the argument on our side as well, whatever it is.

[**Socrates**] This and many other such things, Glaucon, which I foresaw earlier, were what I was afraid of, so that I hesitated to tackle the law concerning the possession and upbringing of women and children.

[**Glaucon**] By god, it doesn't seem to be an easy topic.

[**Socrates**] It isn't. But the fact is that whether someone falls into a small diving pool or into the middle of the biggest ocean, he must swim all the same.

[**Glaucon**] He certainly must.

[**Socrates**] Then we must swim too, and try to save ourselves from the sea of argument, hoping that a dolphin will pick us up or that we'll be rescued by some other desperate means.

[**Glaucon**] It seems so.

[**Socrates**] Come, then. Let's see if we can find a way out. We've agreed that different natures must follow different ways of life and that the natures of men and women are different. But now we say that those different natures must follow the same way of life. Isn't that the accusation brought against us?

[**Glaucon**] That's it exactly.

[**Socrates**] Ah! Glaucon, great is the power of the craft of disputation.

[**Glaucon**] Why is that?

[**Socrates**] Because many fall into it against their wills. They think they are having not a quarrel but a conversation, because they are unable to examine what has been said by dividing it up according to forms. Hence, they pursue mere verbal contradictions of what has been said and have a quarrel rather than a conversation.

[**Glaucon**] That does happen to lots of people, but it isn't happening to us at the moment, is it?

[**Socrates**] It most certainly is, for it looks to me, at any rate, as though we are falling into disputation against our will.

[**Glaucon**] How?

[**Socrates**] We're bravely, but in a quarrelsome and merely verbal fashion, pursuing the principle that natures that aren't the same must follow different ways of life. But when we assigned different ways of life to different natures and the same ones to the same, we didn't at all examine the form of natural difference and sameness we had in mind or in what regard we were distinguishing them.

[**Glaucon**] No, we didn't look into that.

[**Socrates**] Therefore, we might just as well, it seems, ask ourselves whether the natures of bald and long-haired men are the same or opposite. And, when we agree that they are opposite, then, if the bald ones are cobblers, we ought to forbid the long-haired ones to be cobblers, and if the long-haired ones are cobblers, we ought to forbid this to the bald ones.

[**Glaucon**] That would indeed be ridiculous.

[**Socrates**] And aren't we in this ridiculous position because at that time we did not introduce every form of difference and sameness in nature, but focused on the one form of sameness and difference that was relevant to the particular ways of life themselves? We meant, for example, that a male and female doctor have souls of the same nature. Or don't you think so?

[**Glaucon**] I do.

[**Socrates**] But a doctor and a carpenter have different ones?

[**Glaucon**] Completely different, surely.

[**Socrates**] Therefore, if the male sex is seen to be different from the female with regard to a particular craft or way of life, we'll say that the relevant one must be assigned to it. But if it's apparent that they differ only in this respect, that the females bear children while the males beget them, we'll say that there has been no kind of proof that women are different from men with respect to what we're talking about, and we'll continue to believe that our guardians and their wives must have the same way of life.

[**Glaucon**] And rightly so.

[**Socrates**] Next, we'll tell anyone who holds the opposite view to instruct us in this: With regard to what craft or way of life involved in the constitution of the city are the natures of men and women not the same but different?

[**Glaucon**] That's a fair question, at any rate.

[**Socrates**] And perhaps he'd say, just as you did a moment ago, that it isn't easy to give an immediate answer, but with enough consideration it should not be difficult.

[**Glaucon**] Yes, he might say that.

[**Socrates**] Shall we ask the one who raises this objection to follow us and see whether we can show him that no way of life concerned with the management of the city is peculiar to women?

[Glaucon] Of course.

[Socrates] "Come, now," we'll say to him, "give us an answer: Is this what you meant by one person being naturally well suited for something and another being naturally unsuited? That the one learned it easily, the other with difficulty; that the one, after only a brief period of instruction, was able to find out things for himself, while the other, after much instruction, couldn't even remember what he'd learned; that the body of the one adequately served his thought, while the body of the other opposed his. Are there any other things besides these by which you distinguished those who are naturally well suited for anything from those who are not?"

[Glaucon] No one will claim that there are any others.

[Socrates] Do you know of anything practiced by human beings in which the male sex isn't superior to the female in all these ways? Or must we make a long story of it by mentioning weaving, baking cakes, and cooking vegetables, in which the female sex is believed to excel and in which it is most ridiculous of all for it to be inferior?

[Glaucon] It's true that one sex is much superior to the other in pretty well everything, although many women are better than many men in many things. But on the whole it is as you say.

[Socrates] Then there is no way of life concerned with the management of the city that belongs to a woman because she's a woman or to a man because he's a man, but the various natures are distributed in the same way in both creatures. Women share by nature in every way of life just as men do, but in all of them women are weaker than men.

[Glaucon] Certainly.

[Socrates] Then shall we assign all of them to men and none to women?

[Glaucon] How can we?

[Socrates] We'll say, I suppose, that one woman is a doctor, another not, and that one is musical by nature, another not.

[Glaucon] Of course.

[Socrates] And, therefore, won't one be athletic or warlike, while another is unwarlike and no lover of physical training?

[Glaucon] I suppose so.

[Socrates] So one woman may have a guardian nature and another not, for wasn't it qualities of this sort that we looked for in the natures of the men we selected as guardians?

[Glaucon] Certainly.

[Socrates] Therefore, men and women are by nature the same with respect to guarding the city, except to the extent that one is weaker and the other stronger.

[Glaucon] Apparently.

[Socrates] Then women of this sort must be chosen along with men of the same sort to live with them and share their guardianship, seeing that they are adequate for the task and akin to the men in nature.

[Glaucon] Certainly.

[Socrates] And mustn't we assign the same way of life to the same natures?

[Glaucon] We must.

[Socrates] We've come round, then, to what we said before and have agreed that it isn't against nature to assign an education in music, poetry, and physical training to the wives of the guardians.

[Glaucon] Absolutely.

[Socrates] Then we're not legislating impossibilities or indulging in mere wishful thinking, since the law we established is in accord with nature. It's rather the way things are at present that seems to be against nature.

[Glaucon] So it seems.

[Socrates] Now, weren't we trying to determine whether our proposals were both possible and optimal?

[Glaucon] Yes, we were.

[Socrates] And haven't we now agreed that they're possible?

[Glaucon] Yes.

[Socrates] Then mustn't we next reach agreement about whether or not they're optimal?

[Glaucon] Clearly.

[Socrates] Should we have one kind of education to produce women guardians, then, and another to produce men, especially as they have the same natures to begin with?

[Glaucon] No.

[Socrates] Then, what do you think about this?

[Glaucon] What?

[Socrates] About one man being better and another worse. Or do you think they're all alike?

[Glaucon] Certainly not.

[Socrates] In the city we're establishing, who do you think will prove to be better men, the guardians, who receive the education we've described, or the cobblers, who are educated in cobblery?

[Glaucon] Your question is ridiculous.

[Socrates] I understand. Indeed, aren't the guardians the best of the citizens?

[Glaucon] By far.

[Socrates] And what about the female guardians? Aren't they the best of the women?

[Glaucon] They're by far the best.

[Socrates] Is there anything better for a city than having the best possible men and women as its citizens?

[Glaucon] There isn't.

[Socrates] And isn't it music and poetry and physical training, lending their support in the way we described, that bring this about?

[Glaucon] Of course.

[Socrates] Then the law we've established isn't only possible; it is also optimal for a city?

[Glaucon] Yes.

[Socrates] Then the guardian women must strip for physical training, since they'll wear virtue or excellence instead of clothes. They must share in war and the other guardians' duties in the city and do nothing else. But the lighter parts must be assigned to them because of the weakness of their sex. And the man who laughs at naked women doing physical training for the sake of what is best is "plucking the unripe fruit" of laughter and doesn't know, it seems, what he's laughing at or what he's doing, for it is and always will be the finest saying that the beneficial is beautiful, while the harmful is ugly.

[Glaucon] Absolutely.

1. Socrates imagines an adversary's argument opposed to the position taken in conversation with Glaucon. What is the structure of this imagined argument? See if you can summarize it in outline form or present it diagrammatically. What accusation does the adversary make against Socrates? What accusation does Socrates make against the adversary in reply?

2. Use the text to explain this puzzling statement: Different natures can have the same natures.

3. Imagine that Socrates is giving advice to someone who is trying to figure out what to study at school and what kind of career to pursue. What advice would you expect Socrates to give to that person? Would it be good advice? Why or why not?

6.3 Thomas Hobbes's and John Locke's Social Contract Theories

Having considered how Plato would have organized his ideal Greek city-state, let us now leap centuries forward to learn about **social contract theory** and its conception of society. 'Social contract theory' does not refer to the work of a singular theorist or to some sort of singular approach, but is a label assigned to a group of political thinkers whose ideas overlap one another. Social contract theorists give *primacy of place* to the individual in discussions of the state. The collectivity, however conceived, represents the product of an *agreement*, *covenant*, or *contract* among the individuals who constitute it.

By means of a social contract, individuals are brought together in society to form some sort of formal governmental structure upon which they can all agree. The particular parties who contract in society can be individuals or groups. In whatever way contracts are established, we generally find that *individual rights* are recognized and that *consent* is used as the basis for the formation of government.

Thomas Hobbes

Let us now turn to the first social contractarian to be discussed in this chapter, **Thomas Hobbes**, often regarded as the founder of the social contract tradition. Later, we will examine the work of John Locke.

STATE OF NATURE

Thomas Hobbes's political philosophy differs significantly from that of Plato. Living through a period of civil war in England, during which time his own security was threatened, and witnessing the brutality of the Thirty Years' War on the European continent (1618–48), Hobbes certainly did not share the Greek view of the human condition. He considered it unrealistic to assume that people are naturally capable of virtue or would choose to be virtuous for its own sake.

Hobbes would take issue with Aristotle's contention, for example, that humans are, by nature, social animals. He believed that without social conditioning, we have no genetically innate, built-in affinity or sympathy for other members of our own species. Altruism is therefore not a natural emotion. We are simply driven by our egoistic desires to survive and gain pleasure, and nothing guarantees any sort of harmony between the motives of one person and another.

One could ask if slaves and barbarian serfs would gladly and without struggle give up their own desires to serve the needs of the Aristotelian middle class, as would be expected in Aristotle's constitution of the city-state.[9] Would you? Furthermore, is it reasonable to believe that Plato's artisan class would take orders from above and happily perform their inferior functions in service to the Republic's greater good? You can be the judge of that.

According to Hobbes, all human beings are equal by nature with respect to their bodily and mental capacities. He does not suggest that all people possess exactly the same level of physical strength or quickness of mind; rather, he points out that individuals who are deficient or weaker in one respect can make up for this in other ways. For example, those who are physically weak can overcome the physically strong by cunning, craft, or conspiracy.

For Hobbes, the **natural equality** among human beings gives all persons equal hope of satisfying their needs and wants. What we want most generally, according to Hobbes, is the power to acquire the objects of our desires. The problem with this **state of nature**, however, wherein everybody is more or less naturally equal in power and desirous of the same things, is that competition and mistrust of others grow. Add to this the fact that individuals want others to value them as much as they value themselves, so are quick to resent every slight and all signs of contempt. What arises is a *condition of war*. Hobbes writes:

> Hereby it is manifest that during the time men live without a common power to keep them all in awe, they are in that condition which is called war; and such a war, as is of every man against every man.[10]

Commenting on the reasons for conflict among humans, he states:

> So that in the nature of man, we find three principal causes of quarrel. First, competition; secondly, diffidence [mistrust]; thirdly, glory. The first makes men invade for gain; the second, for safety; and the third, for reputation. The first use violence to make themselves masters of other mens' persons, wives, children and chattel [possessions]; the second, to defend them; the third, for trifles, as a word, a smile, a different opinion, and any other sign of undervalue, either direct in their persons, or by reflection in their kindred, their friends, their nation, their profession, or their name.[11]

By positing that the human condition is a condition of warring enemies, Hobbes is not suggesting that everyone around the world is currently, or was during his time, engaged in armed conflict. The natural state of war is a hypothetical condition in which civilization and all its benefits are absent; it is not a historical condition, though Hobbes does remark that the state of nature did exist in many places, such as America, where "savages live at this day in that brutish manner."* For all others, the state of nature is a characterization resulting from a thought experiment, imagining what things would be like without organized society and sanctioned law.

---

* In truth, "Indigenous peoples practiced their own forms of government for thousands of years before the arrival of European and other settlers ..."[12]

In the natural state of war, there are no moral distinctions between right and wrong, good and bad. There is no justice or injustice, only chaos, disorder, and opposition. Of course, today we have governments, constitutions, and ruling bodies supported by law; however, if the veneer of civilization were suddenly stripped of such things, we would revert back to the warring condition Hobbes describes as the state of nature. This does not necessarily imply that war would break out immediately and everywhere, or nonstop for all eternity. For Hobbes, the nature of war consists not just in actual fighting, but in the known disposition to fight while there is no assurance of peace. It is a state of readiness to fight at any moment in order to protect one's interests. Explaining this by analogy to weather, he writes:

> For war consists not in battle only, or the act of fighting, but in a tract of time, wherein the will to contend by battle is sufficiently known: and therefore the notion of time is to be considered in the nature of war, as it is in the nature of weather. For as the nature of foul weather lies not in a shower or two of rain but in an inclination thereto of many days together, so the nature of war consists not in actual fighting but in the known disposition thereto, during all the time there is no assurance to the contrary.[13]

In the state of nature, there is no place for industry, hard work, or distribution of labor, since the fruits of one's efforts are always at risk of invasion or destruction by others. Living in continual fear and in danger of violent death, much of what we take to be included in our conception of a civilized society becomes impossible or at least seriously threatened—things like culture, travel (navigation), construction, the pursuit of knowledge, literature, the arts, and so on. As Hobbes put it, "The life of man [becomes] solitary, poor, nasty, brutish, and short."[14]

Hobbes arrives at the conclusion that life in the natural state is characterized by competitive struggle, fear, and distrust based on a consideration of man's passions and natural inclinations. He also provides examples from everyday experience, drawing our attention, for example, to the fact that people going on trips (in his day) arm themselves for protection. When going to sleep at night, they lock the doors. Even when at home, they lock their valuables away, knowing that there are laws and armed officers to protect them and prosecute those who would harm them or violate them in any way. Rhetorically, Hobbes asks, aren't such protective measures and security officers in truth accusations? Addressing the individual who takes precautions against his fellow men, Hobbes writes:

> ... what opinion he has of his fellow subjects, when he rides armed, of his fellow citizens when he locks his doors; and of his children, and servants, when he locks his chests. Does he not there as much accuse mankind by his actions, as I do by my words?[15]

Thomas Hobbes

Thomas Hobbes was born prematurely on April 5, 1588, during a period of international turbulence and family turmoil. Legend, if not truth, has it that his early arrival was induced by his mother's anxiety about the threatening invasion by an approaching Spanish armada. This belief led Hobbes to conclude the following about himself: "Fear and I were born twins."

Things were no more secure on the family front. Hobbes's father was a quarrelsome and uneducated vicar of Westport, near Malmesbury, Wiltshire, England. Not only did his unruly father destroy his career by engaging in fisticuffs with another clergyman at the front door of his own church, he then fled to London, abandoning his family altogether. Rescued financially by a wealthy relative, Hobbes was lucky enough to receive a good education in spite of his family's unfortunate plight. He eventually earned a Bachelor's degree at Oxford University's Magdalen Hall.

While at Oxford, Hobbes received a traditional Scholastic education, consisting mainly of studies in logic and the philosophy of Aristotle. Though he developed a number of serious disagreements with Aristotelian philosophy, he must have been influenced by Aristotle to some extent, since he was the first major political theorist since Aristotle to separate politics from theology, lending greater weight to the adage that "Our enemies help define us."

After graduating from Oxford, Hobbes accepted an appointment as tutor to the son of William Cavendish, the first Earl of Devonshire. This began a life-long relationship with three generations of the Cavendish clan as tutor, scholar, and companion. As a wonderful result of his long-term affiliation with the wealthy Cavendishes, Hobbes was given many opportunities to travel and to meet some of the most prominent figures of the day, including Sir Francis Bacon and, in Italy, Galileo. Hobbes interacted with René Descartes as well, providing a set of objections to accompany Descartes's *Meditations*.

In 1640, Hobbes was forced to leave England and seek refuge in France because of his support for the monarchy. He lived during an unsettled time in English history highlighted by civil war between defenders of the throne and the antiroyalists. After an eleven-year period of self-imposed exile for prudential reasons, Hobbes ironically had to escape back to England when he found himself in danger of assassination by his political foes. Upon his return home, he discovered that his writings were now considered subversive. In 1662, he was ordered upon threat of imprisonment to refrain from publishing any further works on social and political matters.

Hobbes died in Hardwick, Derbyshire, in 1679 at the age of 91. He is best known for his book *Leviathan*. Lesser known works include *The Elements of Law, Natural and Political*, and *A Short Tract on First Principles*. Hobbes's initial publication was actually a translation of Thucydides's *History of the Peloponnesian War*.

On a final note, the melancholy Hobbes was nicknamed "the Crow" in his youth. As his namesake might suggest, this political bird presents us with a dark and ominous conception of human nature and a vision of political organization founded upon the fear of death.

The *rule* of a potluck party is that everyone brings enough servings of a food dish to share with the other partygoers. The *reality* of a potluck is that there is always more than enough food and it goes to waste at the end of the party. With this in mind, imagine that you have been invited to a potluck next weekend. Do you put in the time and money required to bring food to share or, instead, do you show up empty-handed, sparing yourself the effort and enjoying the spread of food provided by those who followed the potluck rules? Suppose that the party will be so busy that no one there will know what you do either way.

First, answer the question on your own. Next, compare your answer with the answers of your classmates. If your class comprised the list of invitees to this imaginary potluck, what would the food situation at the party be? Would there be a lot of food, some food, or no food? What does this exercise reveal about human nature? Furthermore, what does it reveal about the conditions under which we do (and don't) follow rules? Discuss with your classmates.

LAWS OF NATURE

In the preceding section, we learned how Hobbes arrived at his conception of a natural state of war based on the nature of humanity and our passions. Note too that for him, in the state of nature, no desires or passions could be considered right or wrong in themselves, as there is no objective morality. And where there is no objective morality and no law, there is no injustice. The only "**right of nature**," so-called by Hobbes, that we all share is *the freedom to use our power in any way we wish for purposes of self-preservation*, even if this entails attacking another's body. In a lawless condition of natural equality, wherein everyone has the right to anything and everything that one desires, there can be no security for anybody.

Fortunately, the same natural passions that lead to war can also lead to peace. According to Hobbes, fear of death, a desire to acquire and hold on to things that are necessary to "commodious" (comfortable and convenient) living, and hope of achieving such things through personal effort are passions that incline us all to seek peace. What reason dictates is that we get out of a condition of war and into a position of personal security—that which Hobbes calls a **law of nature**.

Think of a law of nature as a kind of *duty to oneself*. All people strive for security and self-preservation. We are not merely creatures of instinct and blind impulse, genetically determined to behave in this way or that. There is something one might refer to as *rational self-preservation*. The laws of nature state the conditions of this rational self-preservation. On this topic, Hobbes says, "A Law of Nature (*Lex Naturalis*) is a precept or general rule, found out by reason, by which a man is forbidden to do that which is destructive of his life, or takes away the means of preserving the same, and to omit that by which he thinks it may be best preserved."[16]

In *Leviathan*, Hobbes enumerates nineteen laws of nature in all. We will restrict ourselves here to the three most important ones. The first precept, or natural law of reason, is stated so: "That every man ought to endeavor peace, as far as he has hope of obtaining it; and when he cannot obtain it, that he may seek and use all helps and advantages of war."[17] The first part of this precept tells us to seek peace and follow it; the second part

"Where there is no common power, there is no law; where no law, no injustice. Force and fraud are in war the two cardinal virtues."
THOMAS HOBBES

underscores our natural right to defend ourselves, when peace is impossible, by all means possible.

From the first fundamental law of nature follows the second, which ensures our survival. It prescribes: "That a man be willing, when others are so too, as far forth as for peace and defence of himself he shall think it necessary, to lay down this right to all things, and be contented with so much liberty against other men as he would allow other men against himself."[18] Expressed in more contemporary English: We should give up our individual rights to take by force whatever we want, provided that everyone else does too, in order to preserve the peace. Like the first law of nature, this one also constitutes an **egoistic rule of prudence**—something like a *selfish golden rule*. By denying our rights to ourselves (on the condition that others do too), we are not being altruistic or self-sacrificial; we are doing what is in our own best interest. We are all, individually, better off when everyone does it, than we would be if nobody does it.

Closely related to the second precept is the third law of nature, namely: "That men perform their covenants made: without which covenants are in vain, and but empty words; and the right of all men to all things remaining, we are still in the condition of war."[19] To establish a covenant—an agreement, contract, or deal—but not live by its terms, is to accomplish nothing and to secure nothing. We go back to where we started—in a condition where everyone is enemy to everyone else.

THE COMMONWEALTH—HOBBES'S LEVIATHAN

On the assumption that human beings are vain and greedy egoists, who are likely to violate each other when it is in their self-interest to do so, Hobbes concludes that "there must be some coercive power, to compel men equally to the performance of their covenants, by the terror of some punishment greater than the benefit they expect by the breach of their covenant."[20] In other words, there must be some sort of strong sanctioning body, which, by threat of severe retribution, forces people to live by their promises and agreements with others.

For Hobbes, the only way for people to ensure that covenants are not broken is "to confer all their power and strength upon one man, or upon one assembly of men, that may reduce all their wills, by plurality of voices, unto one will."[21] This "man" or "assembly of men" Hobbes calls the "great **Leviathan**," literally a sea monster of immense size; Hobbes uses the term figuratively (to mean something large and formidable). He even refers to it as that "*Mortal God*, to which we owe under the *Immortal God*, our peace and defence."[22]

Ultimately, the sovereign power of the Leviathan is based on people's fear of the "war" that would otherwise take place. It is that fear that transforms multiple self-serving individuals to agree that a sovereign's will and judgment represent the will and judgment of all the citizens. No attempt is made by Hobbes to derive the legitimacy of sovereign power either from theological or metaphysical principles.

Though a royalist himself (see his Philosopher Profile), he does not give kings or queens any divine right to govern. Governments are not instituted by God. Rather, they are purely human creations brought into existence in order to enable individuals to achieve their egoistic goals. The covenant among individuals could, in principle, establish any one of a variety of governmental structures besides a monarchy, including, say, a democracy or aristocracy. Whatever form of governance the Leviathan assumes, self-interest will lie at the basis of it.

Frontispiece for Hobbes's *Leviathan*

This intriguing frontispiece offers a symbolic overview of the core themes in Hobbes's *Leviathan*. Located at the bottom half center, we find the title of Hobbes's work. On the left and right sides of the title we see symbols representing balanced, but sometimes competing, powers. The emblems on the left represent earthly powers and those on the right symbolize the ecclesiastical powers of the Church. Thus we find the following juxtapositions: "... castle to church, crown to mitre [ceremonial headgear worn by Church officials], cannon to excommunication, weapons to logic, and the battlefield to the religious courts."[23]

As for the main figure at the top center, he holds in his hands the symbols of both these powers, representing the union of the secular and the spiritual in the Sovereign King. His body looks a bit like chainmail, but is actually composed of individual figures, those who comprise the total citizenry. It is difficult to discern, perhaps, but these citizens—consenting to the social contract—face away from the viewer and towards the Sovereign King. This symbolizes how citizens must subject their individual wills to the will of the great Leviathan, if there would be peace and security for all.

THE SOCIAL CONTRACT

The ability of the Leviathan or sovereign body to secure the safety, security, and peace of all its citizens depends on a **social contract**. This contract should not be taken literally as a historical artifact, as in an actual document signed by lawyers representing warring enemies; rather, it is a notion that stipulates what is ultimately required by the laws of nature that direct us toward peaceful coexistence. In order to survive peacefully, we must implicitly, or explicitly, all agree to transfer our rights to one ruler or assembly. According to Hobbes, the agreement could be expressed as follows:

> I authorize and give up my right of governing my self, to this man, or to this assembly of men, on this condition: that you give up your right to him, and authorize all his actions in like manner.[24]

When the multitude of citizens is so united in one person or governing body, we have what Hobbes calls a "Common-Wealth." The **commonwealth** (to use the contemporary spelling) is instituted for a very specific purpose, namely, for the peaceful security of those who are a party to the social covenant. Its purpose is therefore utilitarian. Hobbes firmly believed that if one centralized authority in the person of the sovereign, then the evil Hobbes dreaded—namely, civil chaos—could be avoided.

Whatever form it takes (e.g., monarchy), the sovereign body has to be indivisible and absolute. If one tried to divide or limit sovereignty, one would risk anarchy. Furthermore, limiting sovereignty would be illogical, since it would then create opposing and warring parties—something over which the sovereign was to have absolute authority. Absolutism thus becomes a logical consequence of government by consent.

The subjects belonging to a commonwealth cannot change the form of government or repudiate the authority of the sovereign, as this would only serve to return isolated individuals to a disunited and chaotic multitude. The sovereignty of the great Leviathan cannot be taken away by the people. No sovereign can justly be executed or punished in any way by his subjects. If the sovereign is guilty of iniquitous actions, then the matter becomes one between the sovereign and God, not between the citizens and the sovereign. The sovereign is created by the contract, but not subject to it.

CONDITIONS ON THE SOVEREIGN

There are some conditions that can be placed on the sovereign in the commonwealth notwithstanding his absolute authority. Subjects are absolved of their duty to obey the sovereign if (1) he relinquishes his sovereignty; (2) the commonwealth is torn apart internally and the sovereign no longer has effective power, at which time the subjects go back to the state of nature requiring a new sovereign; and (3) the sovereign is conquered in war, and surrenders to the victor, in which case the citizens become subjects to the latter.

Let us now read some Hobbes to get a better appreciation of his work as it pertains to his notion of commonwealth and the role of the Leviathan within it.

Thomas Hobbes, "Of the Causes, Generation, and Definition of a Commonwealth"[25]

Thomas Hobbes's Leviathan *is a substantial book comprising forty-seven chapters organized into four parts: "Of Man," "Of Common-Wealth," "Of a Christian Common-Wealth," and "Of the Kingdome of Darkness." The following selection comes from the beginning of Chapter XVII, "Of the Causes, Generation, and Definition of a Common-Wealth," which opens Part II. Earlier, in Part I, Hobbes had presented his account of human nature and the "solitary, poor, nasty, brutish, and short" life in the state of nature, reasoning that a Sovereign is required to enforce the laws that would allow peace to prevail. Starting here at the beginning of Part II, Hobbes lays out the rights and authorities of that Sovereign.*

———

The final cause, end, or design of men, who naturally love liberty and dominion over others, in the introduction of that restraint upon themselves in which we see them live in commonwealths is the foresight of their own preservation, and of a more contented life thereby—that is to say, of getting themselves out from that miserable condition of war which is necessarily consequent, as has been shown to the natural passions of men when there is no visible power to keep them in awe and tie them by fear of punishment to the performance of their covenants and observation of those laws of nature set down....

For the laws of nature—as *justice*, *equity*, *modesty*, *mercy*, and, in sum, *doing to others as we would be done to*—of themselves, without the terror of some power to cause them to be observed, are contrary to our natural passions, that carry us to partiality, pride, revenge, and the like. And covenants without the sword are but words, and of no strength to secure a man at all. Therefore, notwithstanding the laws of nature (which everyone has then kept when he has the will to keep them, when he can do it safely), if there be no power erected, or not great enough for our security, every man will—and may lawfully—rely on his own strength and art for caution [as a precaution] against all other men. And in all places where men have lived by small families, to rob and spoil one another has been a trade, and so far from being reputed against the law of nature that the greater spoils they gained, the greater was their honor; and men observed no other laws therein but the laws of honor—that is, to abstain from cruelty, leaving to men their lives and instruments of husbandry [household and farming]. And as small families did then, so now do cities and kingdoms, which are but greater families, for their own security enlarge their dominions upon all pretenses of danger and fear of invasion or assistance that may be given to invaders, and endeavor as much as they can to subdue or weaken their neighbors by open force and secret arts, for want of other caution, justly; and are remembered for it in after ages with honor.

Nor is it the joining together of a small number of men that gives them this security, because in small numbers small additions on the one side or the other make the advantage of strength so great as is sufficient to carry the victory, and therefore gives encouragement to an invasion. The multitude sufficient to confide [trust] in for our security is not determined by any certain number, but by comparison with the enemy we fear, and is then sufficient when the odds of the enemy is not of so visible and conspicuous moment [outstanding in significance] to determine the event [outcome] of war as to move him to attempt.

And be there never so great a multitude, yet if their actions be directed according to their particular judgments and particular appetites, they can expect thereby no defense nor protection, neither against a common enemy nor against the injuries of one another. For being distracted in opinions concerning the best use and application of their strength, they do not help but hinder one another, and reduce their strength by mutual opposition to nothing; whereby they are easily not only subdued by a very few that agree together, but also, when there is no common enemy, they make war upon each other for their particular interest. For if we could suppose a great multitude of men to consent in the observation of justice and other laws of nature without a common power to keep them all in awe, we might as well suppose all mankind to do the same; and then there neither would be, nor need to be, any civil government or commonwealth at all, because there would be peace without subjection.

Nor is it enough for the security which men desire should last all the time of their life that they be governed and directed by one judgment for a limited time, as in one battle or one war. For though they obtain a victory by their unanimous endeavor against a foreign enemy, yet afterwards, when either they have no common enemy or he that by one part is held for an enemy is by another part held for a friend, they must needs, by [because of] the difference of their interests, dissolve and fall again into a war among themselves.

It is true that certain living creatures, as bees and ants, live sociably one with another—which are therefore by Aristotle numbered among political creatures—and yet have no other direction than their particular judgments and appetites, nor speech whereby one of them can signify to another what he thinks expedient for the common benefit; and therefore some man may perhaps desire to know why mankind cannot do the same. To which I answer:

First, that men are continually in competition for honor and dignity, which these creatures are not; and consequently among men there arises on that ground envy and hatred and finally war, but among these not so.

Secondly, that among these creatures the common good differs not from the private; and being by nature inclined to their private, they procure thereby the common benefit. But man, whose joy consists in comparing himself with other men, can relish nothing but what is eminent [conspicuous].

Thirdly, that these creatures—having not, as man, the use of reason—do not see nor think they see any fault in the administration of their common business; whereas among men there are very many that think themselves wiser and abler to govern the public better than the rest, and these strive to reform and innovate, one this way, another that way, and thereby bring it into distraction and civil war.

Fourthly, that these creatures, though they have some use of voice in making known to one another their desires and other affections, yet they want [lack] that art of words by which some men can represent to others that which is good in the likeness of evil, and evil in the likeness of good, and augment or diminish the apparent greatness of good and evil, discontenting men and troubling their peace at their pleasure.

Fifthly, irrational creatures cannot distinguish between *injury* and *damage*, and therefore, as long as they be at ease, they are not offended with their fellows; whereas man is then most troublesome when he is most at ease, for then it is that he loves to show his wisdom and control the actions of them that govern the commonwealth.

Lastly, the agreement of these creatures is natural, that of men is by covenant only, which is artificial; and therefore it is no wonder if there be somewhat else required besides covenant to make their agreement constant and lasting, which is a common power to keep them in awe and to direct their actions to the common benefit.

The only way to erect such a common power as may be able to defend them from the invasion of foreigners and the injuries of one another, and thereby to secure them in such sort as that by their own industry and by the fruits of the earth they may nourish themselves and live contentedly, is to confer all their power and strength upon one man, or upon one assembly of men that may reduce all their wills, by plurality of voices, unto one will; which is as much as to say, to appoint one man or assembly of men to bear their person, and everyone to own and acknowledge himself to be author of whatsoever he that so bears their person shall act or cause to be acted in those things which concern the common peace and safety, and therein to submit their wills every one to his will, and their judgments to his judgment. This is more than consent or concord; it is a real unity of them all in one and the same person, made by covenant of every man with every man, in such manner as if every man should say to every man, *I authorize and give up my right of governing myself to this man, or to this assembly of men, on this condition, that you give up your right to him and authorize all his actions in like manner.* This done, the multitude so united in one person is called a COMMONWEALTH, in Latin CIVITAS. This is the generation of that great LEVIATHAN (or rather, to speak more reverently, of that *mortal god*) to which we owe, under the *immortal God*, our peace and defense. For by this authority, given him by every particular man in the commonwealth, he has the use of so much power and strength conferred on him that, by terror thereof, he is enabled to form the wills of them all to peace at home and mutual aid against their enemies abroad. And in him consists the essence of the commonwealth, which, to define it, is *one person, of whose acts a great multitude, by mutual covenants one with another, have made themselves every one the author, to the end he may use the strength and means of them all as he shall think expedient for their peace and common defense.* And he that carries this person is called SOVEREIGN and said to have *sovereign power*; and everyone besides, his SUBJECT.

The attaining to this sovereign power is by two ways. One, by natural force, as when a man makes his children to submit themselves and their children to his government, as being able to destroy them if they refuse, or by war subdues his enemies to his will, giving them their lives on that condition. The other is when men agree among themselves to submit to some man or assembly of men voluntarily, on confidence to be protected by him against all others. This latter may be called a political commonwealth, or commonwealth by *institution*, and the former a commonwealth by *acquisition*. And first I shall speak of a commonwealth by institution.

READING QUESTIONS

1. How does Hobbes envision the state of nature without government? Given what he describes, would you want to live in that state? Why or why not? What freedoms would you be willing to give up in order to leave that state in order to live in a society with rules and order?

2. According to Hobbes, human beings are reasonable. So why, according to Hobbes, is it reasonable for human beings to subject themselves voluntarily to the "fear of punishment" and "terror of power" by a sovereign? What is the role of the sovereign?

3. "But that's not fair!" By Hobbes's account, what is the difference between accusing someone of being unfair to you in the state of nature without government versus in a commonwealth? What does the answer to that question reveal about the nature of fairness and other moral concepts for Hobbes?

4. What is the point of the list of six items that Hobbes makes in this selection from *Leviathan*? Does he give adequate support for all six items? Explain and illustrate.

John Locke

John Locke is a political philosopher whose ideas have been interwoven into the very fabric of American society. We could describe him as one of the theoretical architects of democracy in the Western world. He certainly exerted a profound influence on the formation of the political philosophies underlying the American and French republics. His thinking is said to have served as a main source of the ideas supporting the American Revolution of 1776. (For more on Locke's biography, see his Philosophical Profile in Section 4.4.)

The observation has been made that a good deal of the language contained in the **Declaration of Independence**, and the later **American Constitution**, was taken from Locke's **Second Treatise of Government**. (Locke's *First Treatise* was an attack on divine right monarchy, while his second was written in opposition to Hobbesian absolutism, though Hobbes is never mentioned explicitly.) Some have even accused Thomas Jefferson of copying the *Second Treatise*. Though such a charge may be somewhat overstated, there are indeed some interesting similarities of expression between Locke and Jefferson that are worth noting. What is certain is that Locke's writings provide an impressive framework for refining Western democratic and political ideas relating to concepts of property, individual rights, and the ultimate sovereignty of the citizen population.

> *"The end [goal] of government is the good of mankind."*
> JOHN LOCKE

Like Hobbes, Locke belongs to the social contract and natural law tradition of political thought, and like Hobbes as well, he allows a central role to be played by considerations of self-preservation. Despite these broad similarities, however, there are profound differences between these two political philosophers that need to be explained. Perhaps the best place to start is with how each conceptualizes the state of nature.

LOCKE'S STATE OF NATURE AND THE NATURAL LAW

As we've already learned, Hobbes presented us with a rather grim picture of life before the establishment of sovereign-controlled society. Recall how the natural state, for Hobbes, was a state of war in which every person was at war with every other person. Motivated by competitiveness, mistrust, and egoistic pride, humans were portrayed as nasty, antisocial brutes, both greedy and selfish. In the Hobbesian state of nature, there is no objective morality or altruistic tendencies. The only natural right anyone has is freedom based on power—more specifically, the right to do anything necessary for survival—and we are all equal in this. There is no goodness or justice and no power to keep things in check. Clearly, the Hobbesian state of nature is not a very hospitable setting.

Like Hobbes, Locke also bases his political philosophy on an interpretation of human nature, but he comes to radically different conclusions about it. He says, "We must consider what state all men are naturally in, and that is a state of perfect freedom to order their actions and dispose of their possessions and persons as they think fit, within the bounds of the law of nature, without asking leave or depending upon the will of any other man."[26]

> *"We hold these truths to be self-evident, that all men are created equal, that they are endowed by their Creator with certain unalienable Rights, that among these are Life, Liberty, and the pursuit of Happiness—That to secure these rights, Governments are instituted among Men, deriving their just powers from the consent of the governed."*
> AMERICAN DECLARATION OF INDEPENDENCE

The key phrase in the preceding statement is "within the bounds of the law of nature." In the state of nature, humans have *freedom but not license* to do absolutely anything they wish. Locke says, "The **state of nature** has a law of nature to govern it, which obliges every one; and reason, which is that law, teaches all mankind who will but consult it that, being all equal and independent, no one ought to harm another in his life, health, liberty or possessions."[27]

This **natural law**, like human beings, is "the workmanship of one omnipotent and infinitely wise Maker"[28]—namely, God. Thus, even prior to organized society, people can distinguish between right and wrong by reference to the moral law. **God** created human beings as rational creatures, acquainting them with the law of nature, which enjoins them to be helpful and well-disposed toward one another. Given that we are all free and equal, then, and cognizant of the fact that freedom is not tantamount to license, the natural law would have us seek peace and the preservation of all humankind, not just our own personal gain and survival.

In contrast to Hobbes, for whom natural law meant the law of power, force, and fraud, for Locke it means "a universally obligatory moral law promulgated by human reason as it reflects on God and His rights, on man's relation to God and on the fundamental equality of all men as rational creatures."[29] Viewing natural law in this way, Locke grants human beings **natural rights** independently of any state and its legislation. All individuals have the right to self-preservation, self-defense, and personal liberty.[30]

From here, we can see that Locke's state of nature is *pre-political*, but not *pre-social*. The law of nature, by which their rights and responsibilities are determined, guides individuals living together. There is a significant amount of peace, good will, and mutual assistance, quite unlike Hobbes's natural state of enmity, malice, violence, and mutual destruction.

Capturing the pre-political condition of humankind, Locke writes: "Men living together according to reason, without a common superior on earth with authority to judge between them, is properly the state of nature."[31] Even with an earthly superior, however, remember that human rationality can be counted upon to produce a fair amount of order and stability, for human nature being what it is, we are so inclined to want such things.

Of course, human beings are not perfect. The relatively peaceful state of nature can become like a state of war whenever anyone threatens the self-preservation of another. Threats can be direct or indirect. Direct threats endanger the life or person of another; indirect threats represent an attack on the person's property. Locke regards attacks upon an individual's property as essentially an attack upon the individual, the reason being that property is necessary to preserve life. Also, by virtue of mingling their labors with things and objects, such things and objects belong to the person and become part of them. To attack a person's property is, therefore, the same thing as declaring an intention to do with the person what one pleases, including the taking of that person's life.

If you've ever been the victim of robbery or vandalism yourself, then you probably know intimately the experience of feeling violated. The act of theft or destruction of your property is like an attack on yourself. We take up the business of property rights in more detail in the next section. For now, the point should be stressed that in the event of any transgressions against one's person or property, "every man has a right to punish the offender and be executioner of the law of nature."[32] Natural law requires that retribution be proportionate to the transgression, governed by calm reason and conscience, and serve only for purposes of reparation and restraint, "for these two are the only reasons why one man may lawfully do harm to another."[33]

PROPERTY RIGHTS

So far, we have identified a number of rights stemming from natural law: the right to self-preservation, the right to personal liberty, and the right to punish those who violate the law of nature. It is important to repeat that the rights we have are not bestowed upon us by some sort of social authority; rather, they follow from an objective rule and measure emanating from God and discernable by human reason. The law of nature, which gives rise to natural rights, provides a test or criterion by which political institutions and behaviors can be limited and judged.

Of all the rights embedded in natural law, Locke pays most attention to **property rights**. In his coverage of them in the *Second Treatise*, we find again some very substantial differences between himself and his predecessor Hobbes. For Hobbes, before society exists, there is *no thine or mine*. Individuals own what they take by force; they have no natural or earned entitlements. To quote Hobbes, "every man has a right to everything, even to one another's body."[34]

At first glance, it might appear by his use of terminology that at least one pre-societal right does exist, namely, the "right to everything." However, if we all have a right to

THINKING ABOUT YOUR THINKING

When philosophers like Hobbes and Locke prompt you to think about human beings in a state of nature, what comes to your mind? Is the state of nature just an imaginary fiction concocted by philosophers or is there an actual state of nature that you can—and do—think of while reading about these social contract theories?

Furthermore, when philosophers like Hobbes and Locke make claims about what human beings are like in the state of nature, what kinds of evidence could, or should, be used to determine the truth of those claims? What, if any, claims about human beings in the state of nature do you find compelling and why? If you don't find any such claims compelling, why not?

everything, including the bodies of others, then in effect we own nothing. If what we have can be forcefully taken by others without moral repercussions, and if it is not inherently "wrong" to steal what is not yours because you have the power to take what you want, then the whole notion of property rights flies in the face of anyone who holds a conventional understanding of ownership. According to Hobbes, individuals own what they can hold by force. They have no inherent or natural "right" to anything that others have a duty to respect. "Property," as such, is a creation of society, and rights to it must be sanctioned by sovereign authority.

Locke, on the other hand, regarded property as a natural right that precedes society and is not created by it. In fact, Locke regards the protection of property or one's property rights as the primary function of government. He states: "The great and chief end, therefore, of man's uniting into commonwealths and putting themselves under government is the preservation of their property."[35]

By "property," Locke means one's "life, liberty, and estate."[36] He says: "By property I must be understood here, as in other places, to mean that property which men have in their persons as well as goods."[37] The notion of property rights is closely tied, for Locke, to the **right of self-preservation**. Just as individuals have the right (and correlative duty) to self-preservation, so too do they have a right to those things which are necessary for it. Locke's assumption is that God has given the earth to humankind, and all that is contained within it is for their support and well-being.

Furthermore, reason reveals that, though the earth was not originally partitioned off with property fences, and objects did not have the stamp of possession upon them, it is consistent with God's will that there should be private property. The reference here is not only with respect to the fruits of the earth and the things upon it, but also with respect to the earth itself. Given that the earth was not created with boundaries demarcating what is *thine or mine*, the question arises as to what constitutes the primary title to private property? Simply, what makes something "mine"?

Locke would concede that initially, in the state of nature, the earth and all its fruits are common to all. To use the metaphor of fruits literally, let us say that there is an apple tree in a distant field. The tree belongs to no one; nor does its bountiful fruit. However, if someone takes the time and trouble to pick a basket of apples from the tree, the fruit would suddenly belong to the individual. How so? According to Locke, there is *property* in an individual's labor: *I own my work* or *My work is mine*. When I perform an action upon a thing or object, in this case by picking apples from a tree, I mix my labor (so to speak) with those fruits, making them objects of my possession. Similarly, shells and stones at the seaside are there for everyone's pleasure and interest, but once I gather some and place them in my collection, they belong to me. I have labored over these natural curiosities, giving me property rights over them.

Limits accompany natural property rights. The right to land acquisition is not unbounded. With respect to land, Locke says: "As much land as a man tills, plants, improves, cultivates, and can use the product of, so much is his property. He by his labor does, as it were, enclose it from the common."[38] Individuals are entitled to as much property as they can use without spoilage. Taking more than necessary or more than one can work with is wrong. Also, any appropriations of property that would leave others without "enough, and as good"[39] would be similarly unacceptable.

POLITICAL SOCIETY AND GOVERNMENT

If all human beings are born free and equal, endowed with natural rights and subordinate to nobody, then the question arises as to why anybody would allow themselves to be subjected to the control of any other power. As alluded to earlier, the primary reason is for the preservation of property. In the state of nature, there is no sanctioning body or public law that has been established and promulgated as a measure of right and wrong. There is no formal procedure to identify rights violations or to settle interpersonal property disputes. Furthermore, "though the law of nature be plain and intelligible to all rational creatures, yet men, being biased by their interest as well as ignorant for want [lack] of studying it, are not apt to allow of it as a law binding on them in the application of it to their particular cases."[40] In short, the civil law does not exist in nature, and the natural law that does exist is either unknown, ignored, or twisted in one's favor.

Given this, it is to one's advantage to establish a **political society** so that *impartial judges* can be installed in positions of authority. Judges can be responsible for resolving disputes in a rational and disinterested fashion. To use Locke's descriptive term, judges can be "indifferent," that is, unbiased. The problem with allowing individuals in the state of nature to be both judge and executioner of the natural law is that "passion and revenge is very apt to carry them too far and with too much heat,"[41] especially when prosecuting others guilty of offense. Still further, partiality toward oneself, as well as "negligence and unconcernedness,"[42] are likely to make one remiss in prosecuting cases of wrongdoing involving other people's rights. Simply, people tend to decide in their own favor and neglect the interests of others. Impartial and disinterested judges can remedy this, as they are in the best position to reasonably adjudicate conflicts and issue punishments.

Locke describes the partial and negligent tendencies inherent in people's efforts to punish wrongdoers as "inconveniencies." He writes the following about human beings in the natural state:

> The inconveniencies [misfortunes, injuries] that they are therein exposed to by the irregular and uncertain exercise of the power every man has of punishing the transgressions of others make them take sanctuary under the established laws of government and therein seek the preservation of their property. It is this makes them so willingly give up every one his single power of punishing, to be exercised by such alone as shall be appointed to it amongst them; and by such rules as the community, or those authorized by them to that purpose, shall agree on. And in this we have the original right of both the legislative and executive power, as well as of the governments and societies themselves.[43]

By entering a civil society, human beings do not transfer all of their natural rights to any judge or sovereign body. Morality continues to precede civil society, and civil society can still be judged in terms of morality. By entering into society, individuals give up only the power of punishment to an **executive** whom they appoint. This is very different from Hobbes, whose absolute monarchy required all rights (power) to be given up to the monarch so that the sovereign could govern by decree.

For Locke, the rule of law—not force—becomes the basis of society. Without law, a government becomes tyrannical, operating arbitrarily by whim and caprice, much like Hobbes's brutish egoist. Locke's political society, by contrast, must create laws consistent with the law of nature and enforce them for the good of all. The ultimate end of law making and law enforcement is the "peace, safety, and public good of the people."[44]

Understanding civil society in this way, the government is entrusted with the welfare of its citizens and serves only a **fiduciary role**. That is, its authority is not unconditional or absolute; the government is a servant to the people, not the other way around. Individuals do not work for the benefit of the state; the state works for the benefit of citizens. Indeed, Locke's conception of civil society and his reformulation of natural law provide us with a strong philosophical foundation for **individualism**. Precepts issuing from the law of nature, which buttress civil society, are concerned mostly with individual rights, rather than with individual responsibilities to society. It would appear, then, that many of the seeds of contemporary individualism were sewn by John Locke generations ago.

SOCIAL COMPACT

It has been said that in order to protect their property rights, to establish non-discriminatory public laws, to have impartial judges, and also to be protected by a power that can enforce the law by executing the sentences of judges, human beings are led into a commonwealth through the formation of a political society. Specifically, for Locke, this is done through the creation of a **social compact**, i.e., a social agreement.

Locke's social compact uses **consent** as its rational foundation. Since all individuals are free, equal, and independent in the state of nature, nobody can be subjected to the political power of another without his or her permission. Such permission or *consent* must, of course, be freely given without coercion of any kind. Individuals who do not wish to belong to civil society are permitted to go elsewhere or to remain in the state of nature.

In Locke's day, it was no doubt easier to find unsettled territories and wilderness lands where one could actually live independently in relative isolation. However, immigration laws, national boundaries, increases in world population, state-owned lands, and other such factors create limitations that would obviously make "free-range" living in the state of nature much more problematic today. In any case, for those who participate in a Lockean civil society, the choice to do so must be unanimous. The contract or agreement here is not between the sovereign state, or ruling monarch and the individual citizens, but rather among the citizens themselves.

The issue of consent raises an historical problem. Did a state of nature ever actually exist, and was a social compact ever entered into in the creation of political society? In answer, Locke says yes. Regarding the state of nature, he cites Josephus Acosta, who reported that in many parts of America, for example, there was no government at all, presumably leaving it in a state of nature.* Locke goes on to name Rome and Venice as two places where, "by the uniting together of several men free and independent of one another, amongst whom there was no natural superiority or subjection,"[45] a political society was formed.

Though these and other examples used by Locke may represent questionable facts contributing to some shoddy history, Locke appears unconcerned. Actual historical

---

* Just one among the many false beliefs about Indigenous peoples held by Europeans in those days. An example of their confederacies is *The Haudenosaunee* (People of the Longhouse), commonly referred to as *The Iroquois League* or *League of Five Nations* in New York state, first assembled in 1200 CE. Because the American Indigenous people were thought of by Europeans as being in a state of nature, their lives were falsely assumed to be the way this state was described variously by Hobbes, or by Locke, or by Rousseau (who thought of this state as idyllic).

documentation of social contracts being signed or agreed to are mostly impossible to locate, since

> Government is everywhere antecedent to records, and letters seldom come in amongst a people till a long continuation of civil society has, by other more necessary arts, provided for their safety, ease, and plenty; and then they begin to look after the history of their founders and search into their original, where they have outlived the memory of it; for it is with commonwealths as with particular persons—they are commonly ignorant of their own births and infancies; and if they know anything of their original, they are beholden for it to the accidental records others have kept of it. And those that we have of the beginning of any politics in the world, excepting that of the Jews, where God himself immediately interposed, and which favors not at all paternal dominion, are all either plain instances of such a beginning as I have mentioned, or at least have manifest footsteps of it.[46]

Even if we grant Locke the historical proposition that individuals were once in the state of nature and entered into a social compact to form society, we could still ask whether any individual today must abide by its terms, since that individual was not present at the time of the original agreement. Locke's answer is this: there are two types of consent. The first is *direct*, the second is *tacit* (meaning *silent*, *unspoken*). We give **tacit consent** to the social compact which preceded us by enjoying all the privileges of citizenship; that is, by owning and exchanging property, relying on the police and the courts for protection, and so on. When we accept the benefits of civil society, we tacitly give consent to our participation, which entails certain responsibilities of citizenship. And like other citizens, we give up certain things (the right to punish violators of the law of nature). The fact that we stay in a particular country or state, when we could just as easily leave, confirms our consent.

Tacit consent is not an extraordinary notion. Imagine that you join in an existing poker game. Nobody asks you whether you agree to the basic rules of the game (e.g., no grabbing extra cards from the deck, no looking at other players' hands); you understand rules like this and by your joining you tacitly, without saying anything, agree to them.

LIMITS ON GOVERNMENT
Whether our consent is direct and overt or tacit and implied, we do not, of course, automatically agree to just any law or any decision of the state. There are certain limitations. The laws, which are made and enforced, must confirm those inalienable rights that people have by virtue of nature—underscoring again the fact that *morality precedes civil government*, that *natural law overrides civil law*.

Consent, as Locke understands it, also involves acceptance of **majority rule**. He writes:

> And thus every man, by consenting with others to make one body politic under one government, puts himself under an obligation to every one of that society to submit to the determination of the majority and to be concluded [bound] by it; or else this original compact, whereby he with others incorporates into one society, would signify nothing, and be no compact, if he be left free and under no other ties than he was in before in the state of nature.[47]

The myriad daily decisions taken by an established civic community cannot depend upon unanimity or consensus. Such a requirement would be highly impractical. Though the social compact must be agreed to unanimously, Locke was reasonable enough to assume that the majority would rule once the social compact became a *done deal*. This is not to suggest that minorities could be abused by the tyranny of the majority, or that the majority could pass any and all legislation at will. Laws would still have to be properly promulgated and applied equally to all groups and classes. Furthermore, another limitation on government would be its inability to raise taxes without the consent of the people or their deputies.

Compare all of this with Hobbes. For Hobbes, the sovereign power is absolute. Whatever the monarch or governing assembly dictates goes. The authority of the legislative body cannot be questioned on moral grounds, since that body creates justice and goodness by its own proclamations. Allowing the Leviathan to be attacked places us all back in what Hobbes described as the condition of war. Presumably, either the Leviathan has absolute power, or we are all back to anarchy.

As for Locke, while he regards the legislative government as the "supreme" body, he does not accept Hobbes's idea that it is "absolute"—unquestionable in its authority. The point was made earlier that, for Locke, the legislative is entrusted by the citizen population to govern in favor of its own interests, giving the legislative power only a *fiduciary role*. As a result, "there remains still in the people a supreme power to remove or alter the legislative when they find the legislative act contrary to the trust reposed in them."[48]

DIVISIONS OF POWER

To ensure that the state does not assume greater power than justified, and that it does not violate its own laws with impunity, Locke envisioned *a system of checks and balances* involving different levels of government, each wielding its own power. He labeled them the *legislative*, *executive*, and *federative*. Intuitively, we can probably all appreciate how it would be undesirable for lawmakers to be responsible for executing the laws they create for us. Locke says: "they may exempt themselves from obedience to the laws they make, and suit the law, both in its making and execution, to their own private advantage, and thereby come to have a distinct interest from the rest of the community contrary to the end of society and government."[49]

Locke concludes, therefore, that the executive branch of government should be distinct from the legislative. The executive does not have the authority to make laws like the legislative branch, but it has judicial powers to make sure the laws are followed. The third branch, envisioned by Locke, called the federative, was given the power to make war and peace, alliances, and treaties with other nations, and to conduct, "all the transactions with all persons and communities without [outside of] the commonwealth."[50]

In the *Second Treatise*, Locke addresses the notion of **prerogative power** and how it may be given to the executive when the legislative is not in session. Worried about too much executive control, Locke underscores the fact that it has no authority of its own and cannot claim the right of obedience except when it is enforcing the law of society. Members of the executive can be removed from office if the legislative or the people believe that they have violated the limits of power assigned to them. With the legislative branch of government making sure the executive does not go too far in executing its dictates, and with the executive branch ensuring that the legislative live according to the laws of the state, we can see a clear example of how government power is regulated by a system of checks and balances.

THE DISSOLUTION OF GOVERNMENT

Governments are not absolute and eternal entities. They can be dissolved from "within" or "without." In the latter case, the cause is generally war. Putting it quite graphically, Locke writes: "Conquerors' swords often cut up governments by the roots and mangle societies to pieces, separating the subdued or scattered multitude from the protection of and dependence on that society which ought to have preserved them from violence."[51] Dissolution from within can occur from rebellion against authority, for example, when the citizenry is subjected to the arbitrary caprice of tyrannical power. Let's say a prince in a constitutional monarchy changes the methods of elections or alters the legislative branch without the people's consent and in violation of their trust. Let's assume further that this tyrant then goes on to claim dominion over people's lives, liberties, and property. In such a case, overthrow of the government would be justified.

Unlike Hobbes, Locke allows government rule to be questioned and, if necessary, replaced without assuming that the dissolution of governmental authority necessarily leads us back to a state of chaos and jungle warfare. Society and government are not synonymous for Locke. While it is true that when societies are dissolved, governments must necessarily disappear, the converse is not so; governments can be dissolved, leaving societies with the task of establishing new governmental structures.

John Locke, "Of the Ends of Political Society and Government"[52]

The following sections come from the ninth chapter, titled "Of the Ends of Political Society and Government," in John Locke's Second Treatise of Government. *Although the* Second Treatise *is, as its title indicates, the second of the two treatises that comprise Locke's* Two Treatises of Government, *it is anything but second in status. In it, Locke presents what are now classic theories of human nature, limited government, property rights, and the right of revolution. Locke published the* Two Treatises *anonymously in 1689, the same year he returned to England after six years of exile on account of his political views. In the Preface, he states that his purpose in writing it was to justify the outcome of the Glorious Revolution (1688), which saw William III take the English throne, and "to justify to the world the people of England, whose love of their just and natural rights, with their resolution to preserve them, saved the nation when it was on the very brink of slavery and ruin."[53]*

———

Sec. 123. If man in the state of nature be so free, as has been said; if he be absolute lord of his own person and possessions, equal to the greatest, and subject to nobody, why will he part with his freedom, why will he give up this empire, and subject himself to the dominion and control of any other power? To which it is obvious to answer, that though in the state of nature he has such a right, yet the enjoyment of it is very uncertain, and constantly exposed to the invasion of others: for all being kings as much as he, every man his equal, and [since] the greater part [are] no strict observers of equity and justice, the enjoyment of the property he has in this state is very unsafe, very unsecure. This makes him willing to quit a condition, which, however free, is full of fears and continual dangers: and it is not without reason, that he seeks out, and is willing to join in society with others, who are already united, or have a mind to unite, for the mutual preservation of their lives, liberties and estates, which I call by the general name, property.

Sec. 124. The great and chief end, therefore, of men's uniting into commonwealths, and putting themselves under government, is the preservation of their property. To which in the state of nature there are many things wanting [lacking and needed]. First, there wants an established, settled, known law, received and allowed by common consent to be the standard of right and wrong, and the common measure to decide all controversies between them: for though the law of nature be plain and intelligible to all rational creatures; yet men being biased by their interest, as well as ignorant for want of study of it, are not apt to allow of it as a law binding to them in the application of it to their particular cases.

Sec. 125. Secondly, In the state of nature there wants a known and indifferent judge, with authority to determine all differences according to the established law: for everyone in that state being both judge and executioner of the law of nature, men being partial to themselves, passion and revenge is very apt to carry them too far, and with too much heat, in their own cases; as well as negligence, and unconcernedness, to make them too remiss in other men's.

Sec. 126. Thirdly, In the state of nature there often wants power to back and support the sentence when right, and to give it due execution. They who by any injustice offended, will seldom fail, where they are able, by force to make good their injustice; such resistance many times makes the punishment dangerous, and frequently destructive, to those who attempt it.

Sec. 127. Thus mankind, notwithstanding all the privileges of the state of nature, being but in an ill condition, while they remain in it, are quickly driven into society. Hence it comes to pass, that we seldom find any number of men live any time together in this state. The inconveniencies that they are therein exposed to, by the irregular and uncertain exercise of the power every man has of punishing the transgressions of others, make them take sanctuary under the established laws of government, and therein seek the preservation of their property. It is this [that] makes them so willingly give up, every one, his single power of punishing, to be exercised by such alone, as shall be appointed to it amongst them; and by such rules as the community, or those authorized by them to that purpose, shall agree on. And in this we have the original right and rise [source] of both the legislative and executive power, as well as of the governments and societies themselves.

Sec. 128. For in the state of nature, to omit the liberty he has of innocent delights, a man has two powers.

The first is to do whatsoever he thinks fit for the preservation of himself, and others within the permission of the law of nature: by which law, common to them all, he and all the rest of mankind are one community, make up one society, distinct from all other creatures. And were it not for the corruption and viciousness of degenerate men, there would be no need of any other; no necessity that men should separate from this great and natural community, and by positive agreements combine into smaller and divided associations.

The other power a man has in the state of nature, is the power to punish the crimes committed against that law. Both these he gives up, when he joins in a private, if I may so call it, or particular politic society, and incorporates into any common-wealth, separate from the rest of mankind.

Sec. 129. The first power, viz. of doing whatsoever he thought for the preservation of himself, and the rest of mankind, he gives up to be regulated by laws made by the society, so far forth as the preservation of himself, and the rest of that society shall require; which laws of the society in many things confine the liberty he had by the law of nature.

Sec. 130. Secondly, The power of punishing he wholly gives up, and engages his natural force, (which he might before employ in the execution of the law of nature, by his own single authority, as he thought fit) to assist the executive power of the society, as the law thereof shall require: for being now in a new state, wherein he is to enjoy many conveniences [advantages], from the labour, assistance, and society of others in the same community, as well as protection from its whole strength; he is to part also with as much of his natural liberty, in providing for himself, as the good, prosperity, and safety of the society shall require; which is not only necessary, but just, since the other members of the society do the like.

Sec. 131. But though men, when they enter into society, give up the equality, liberty, and executive power they had in the state of nature, into the hands of the society, to be so far disposed of by the legislative, as the good of the society shall require; yet it being only with an intention in every one the better to preserve himself, his liberty and property; (for no rational creature can be supposed to change his condition with an intention to be worse) the power of the society, or legislative constituted by them, can never be supposed to extend farther, than the common good; but is obliged to secure every one's property, by providing against those three defects above mentioned, that made the state of nature so unsafe and uneasy. And so whoever has the legislative or supreme power of any common-wealth, is bound to govern by established standing laws, promulgated and known to the people, and not by extemporary [makeshift, arising at the moment] decrees; by indifferent and upright judges, who are to decide controversies by those laws; and to employ the force of the community at home, only in the execution of such laws, or abroad to prevent or redress foreign injuries, and secure the community from inroads and invasion. And all this to be directed to no other end, but the peace, safety, and public good of the people.

READING QUESTIONS

1. How does your study of Hobbes's philosophy earlier in this chapter help you read and understand this passage from Locke's *Second Treatise*? Are there similarities in the two philosophers' ideas that you recognize? Are there differences? Does this strategy of applying what you learned about Hobbes's social contract theory make understanding Locke's social contract theory easier? What still remains difficult to understand in this selection?

2. According to Locke, what powers do people give up when they enter into society? For what reasons do they give those powers up willingly? Locke lists three reasons. Explain them using examples of your own creation to illustrate the ideas.

6.4 Karl Marx's Socialism

Though dead for well over a century, the mere mention of **Karl Marx** is still able to conjure up a number of different and sometimes frightening images in the minds of people acquainted with his work. Many Christians, for example, regard this atheist as the embodiment of the anti-Christ, a threat to all that is good and holy in the world. Marxism and the communistic system of government that glorified it were identified during the Cold War period (1950–91) as powerful threats to America. President Ronald Regan described the Marxist-Leninist-based Soviet Union, before its collapse, as the "evil empire."[54] Communism had to be stamped out for love of God and country.

On this note, I can remember, for example, when former Canadian prime minister Pierre Elliott Trudeau was not allowed into the United States for a time for fear that he was a socialist who had communist ties around the world (Trudeau once visited Fidel Castro in Cuba). A 1960s rock-and-roll song titled "Share the Land," by the rock band The Guess Who, was also banned on many US radio stations due to its collectivist insinuations.

Combine these facts with the political witch-hunts carried out during the Joseph McCarthy era (1950–54), when efforts were made to investigate supposedly subversive communist activities in the United States. The result was to destroy the reputation, careers, and lives of a large number of people either associated closely, very distantly, or not at all in fact, with Marxist groups. This fact demonstrates how anything Marxist had been demonized. In addition, fears escalated, and by the end of 1950, the Chinese communists had seized power in China, the Soviet Union (Russia and its satellite states) had developed the atomic bomb, and North Korea had invaded democratic South Korea. As a reaction, a wave of anticommunist hysteria washed over the United States.

With respect to Cold War sentiments, German philosopher and Marxist Erich Fromm wrote the following in 1961:

> The world is torn today between two rival ideologies—that of "Marxism" and that of "Capitalism." While in the United States "Socialism" [read Marxism-Communism] is a word on the Devil's tongue and not one that recommends itself, the opposite is true in the rest of the world. Not only do Russia and China use the term "socialism" to make their systems attractive, but most Asian and African countries are deeply attracted to the ideas of Marxist socialism. To them socialism and Marxism are appealing not only because of the economic achievements of Russia and China, but because of the spiritual elements of justice, equality and universality which are inherent in Marxist socialism (rooted in the Western spiritual tradition).[55]

With the dissolution of the Soviet Union in 1991, the Cold War fizzled out to a large extent. Trade and treaty agreements began to be negotiated between liberal democracies and communist governments. Nevertheless, an objective analysis of Karl Marx's ideas is still made difficult today by a *Cold War hangover*, so to speak. Many people still make associations or implicit identifications between Marx and the oppressive political regimes of communist states. However, it should be noted that opposing the political actions taken by *so-called* communist countries under the banner of Marxism is not the same as opposing Marx himself. On this note, Fromm writes:

I am convinced that only if we understand the real meaning of Marxist thought, and hence can differentiate it from Russian and Chinese pseudo-Marxism, will we be able to understand the realities of the present-day world and be prepared to deal realistically and constructively with their challenge. I hope [to] … contribute not only to a greater understanding of Marx's humanist philosophy, but also … to diminish the irrational and paranoid attitude that sees in Marx a devil and in socialism a realm of the devil.[56]

Put simply, Marxism *as practiced* is not Marxism as Karl Marx envisioned it. In fact, Marx once declared that he was not a Marxist himself. I suspect this statement is related to his reactions regarding what people were doing with his ideas. After Marx, we should note that neither Stalinist oppression, Maoist conformity, Vladimir Putin's authoritarianism, nor any other type of military dictatorship, such as North Korea's, embodies the basic principles of Marxist thought. To condemn Marx for others' perversions of his ideas is neither fair, nor rational.

Interestingly, Marx never intended to profess any political ideology at all. He believed that his work was *scientific*, in the sense that he was uncovering the *structural dynamics underlying social-historical change*. The predicted communist revolution was *not an ideal* but a *developmental necessity*. Marx was not setting himself up as a hero but rather as a historian doing political science. He writes: "It is the ultimate aim of this work [*Das Kapital*] to lay bare the economic law of motion of modern society."[57] He thought that a scientific understanding of human nature and the physical universe could solve the most significant of our social problems.

If there is any group that rightfully should be terrorized by Marxist thought, perhaps it should be philosophers themselves. Indeed, Marx could be dubbed the *anti-philosopher*. He reviled philosophy as a symptom of social malaise that would disappear once the inevitable communist revolution placed society on a healthier foundation.[58] After the revolution, philosophy would become unnecessary, as men and women would be brought back to the study of *the real world*. The *idealistic phantoms* of 'reason,' 'justice,' and 'liberty' that philosophers consoled themselves with in a sick society would finally be exorcized.[59]

Traditionally, philosophers have often taken for granted the notion that intellectual ideas are the causes of historically significant changes in the social order. By contrast, Marx maintained that, "it is not the consciousness of men that determines their being but their social being that determines their consciousness."[60] For Marx, gone is the belief that philosophers can objectively stand back in a detached fashion to rationally discuss *eternal forms*, *natural laws*, *human essences*, and the like. Rational objectivity and its fruits are themselves the products of social conditioning whose determining influences are manifest in historical circumstances and the society's prevailing mode of production.

Philosophy, for Marx, is thus stripped of its independent, exalted status as the queen of all the sciences. It is seen merely as the product of social forces. In view of this, it is not surprising that Marx is sometimes regarded as the father of sociology and not the champion of philosophical inquiry. The irony of all this is that since Marx's death, his anti-philosophy, and the theory of historical/dialectical materialism on which it is based, have blossomed into a veritable philosophical doctrine itself. The anti-philosopher has become a prime subject of philosophical study.

"Religion is the sigh of the oppressed creature, the heart of a heartless world, just as it is the spirit of spiritless conditions. It is the opium of the people."
KARL MARX

Karl Marx

Karl Marx was born on May 5, 1818, in Trier, a small Prussian town in what is now Germany. A descendant of a long line of rabbis, his secularly-educated, middle-class lawyer father converted from Judaism to Lutheranism in order to avoid anti-Semitic complications that might have interfered with retaining his legal position in the Prussian civil service. At the time, new laws were passed preventing Jews from occupying governmental positions. What might have turned out to be religiously confusing for the young Marx (who, along with his six siblings, was baptized into the Lutheran Church) became inconsequential in one respect, since in later life he became a rabid atheist, declaring that religion was nothing more than a stupefying opium for the masses.

After receiving a liberal education as a child, Marx began his first year of university education in 1835 at Bonn, where he studied law. His days there were limited but not entirely uneventful. On one occasion he was arrested for drunkenness, and on another he sustained a wound from dueling. That episode left him with a lasting scar. Displeased with events at Bonn, Marx's father sent Karl to continue his studies more seriously at the University of Berlin. There, the young Marx turned his attention away from his previous legal studies and toward philosophy and history. He became familiar with the work of the great Georg Wilhelm Friedrich Hegel (1770–1831) and associated himself with one particular branch of politically minded Hegelianism known as the *Young Hegelians* or *Hegelians of the Left*.

In 1841, Marx submitted his dissertation and received his doctorate from the University of Jena, though he never studied there formally. The dissertation was titled *On the Difference Between the Democritean and Epicurean Philosophies of Nature*.

While becoming a university professor after graduation seemed to be the obvious option for Marx, that option abruptly became unavailable when the Prussian Ministry of Education condemned the Young Hegelians with whom Marx had become associated. His reputation as a militant atheist didn't help either. Unlike his father, who once gave a mild speech for social reform and then recanted when the Prussian authorities showed up at his doorstep, Karl was not one to back down or compromise morally for personal advantage. Summarizing Marx's personality, the German-American statesman Carl Schurz wrote:

I have never seen a man whose bearing was so provoking and intolerable. To no opinion, which differed from his, he accorded the honor of even a condescending consideration. Everyone who contradicted him he treated with abject contempt; every argument that he did not like he answered either with biting scorn at the unfathomable ignorance that had prompted it, or with opprobrious aspersions upon the motives of him who had advanced it.[61]

For an alternative portrayal of Marx's personality, Erich Fromm claims that Marx was in fact a highly productive individual, with a great capacity for love and friendship judging by his relationships with Friedrich Engels and members of his family. His apparent arrogance purportedly stemmed from his inability to tolerate sham, deception, and dishonest rationalization.[62]

In retrospect, it would appear that Karl Marx's exclusion from academia was just a prelude to the turbulent times to come. After drifting for about a year following his graduation, Marx entered the field of journalism and became the editor of a liberal newspaper in Cologne, the *Rheinische Zeitung*. After moving the paper politically to the left, he resigned in a futile effort to forestall its eventual banning in 1843. In that same year, he and Jenny Westphalen—the daughter of neighbor Baron von Westphalen who had befriended Marx in his youth— were married, and despite opposition from both sides of the family, they moved to Paris.

During his stay in Paris, Marx encountered a number of important radical intellectuals including the poet Heinrich Heine, the anarchist Mikhail Bakunin, and the socialist Pierre-Joseph Proudhon. Of all his new acquaintances, the most significant for Marx was another German, Friedrich Engels. Together they formed one of the most important literary partnerships in western intellectual history. During this time, Marx also sketched out his *Economic and Philosophic Manuscripts of 1844*, containing an insightfully original view of human society that integrated elements of French socialism, English economics, and German philosophy. As Marx continued his struggle against Prussian aristocracy, he began what was to become a lifelong exile.

In 1845, after Marx and Engels collaborated on a book of social criticism, *The Holy Family*, Marx was forced to leave Paris at the behest of the French government. Banished again, he settled in Brussels, Belgium, where he became affiliated with a working-class association, *The League of the Just*, which was in the midst of reestablishing itself as the *Communist League*.

Marx and Engels were given the task of producing a written statement of the party's purpose and principles. The result was a little book that would become the gospel for millions around the world: *Manifesto of the Communist Party* (referred to more simply as *The Communist Manifesto*). The book was published in London in 1848, just a few weeks before the first of a number of European revolutions that took place at that time. Unfortunately for Marx, in the midst of the upheaval of 1848, the Belgian authorities expelled him from Brussels, even though the *Manifesto* likely played no part in contributing to any uprisings.

After going back first to Paris, Marx then returned to Cologne, where a democratic government had been elected. He edited the *Neue Rheinische Zeitung* during a brief and ultimately suppressed experiment in parliamentary democracy. Once things crumbled, Marx was arrested, tried for sedition, acquitted, and then expelled in 1849. Again in exile, he lived the rest of his life in London, supported financially by Friedrich Engels, who worked for his father's textile company.

Marx never did have a full-time, regular job in England. He did earn an income as a journalist writing articles for the *New York Tribune*, but only until his political differences with the newspaper's editorial board caused him to end that relationship. Most of the time, however, he spent in the British Museum, gathering research material for his monumental historical analysis of capitalism, *Das Kapital* (1867), only the first volume of which he was ever to publish. (Engels put together volumes 2 and 3 from posthumous papers.) Marx's only political activity during this period in England was personal involvement in the International Working Men's Association. It was formed in 1864 and then scuttled by Marx in 1872 after prolonged internal conflict.

Marx left quite a legacy. His life was dedicated to political revolution and to the passionate quest for a synthetic view of history and culture. No truly educated person can ignore the ideas and influence of this intellectual immortal.

In closing, it could be said that Marx did not enjoy an easy life. In addition to repeated banishments forcing him from country to country, Marx suffered from poverty, chronic illness, and the early deaths of three of his children (three daughters survived). He also suffered from obscurity and intellectual isolation, surely stinging conditions for a genius that so moved the world.

Marx's wife, Jenny, died in 1882; Karl died the following year. At the burial site in Highgate Cemetery, his lifelong friend, Friedrich Engels, began Marx's eulogy with the following words: "On the 14th day of March, at a quarter to three in the afternoon, the greatest living thinker ceased to think."[63]

Marx's Metaphysics and Dialectical Materialism

Underlying Marx's political thought is a metaphysics, which he borrowed from German philosopher **Georg Wilhelm Friedrich Hegel** (1770–1831), but then modified under the influence of another German philosopher Ludwig Feuerbach (1804–1872). The slogan often associated with the Hegelian worldview, known as **absolute idealism**, is "The real is the rational and the rational is the real."[64]

Contained in this rather cryptic statement is the notion that reality displays the characteristics of mind. It reflects *Absolute Mind* or *Spirit*, what some have argued is just a euphemism for God. This Absolute Mind reveals itself in all areas of human experience and knowledge, from history and politics, to art, religion, and philosophy. God, who is total reality and truth, reveals Himself to our limited minds in every aspect of life. The task of metaphysics for Hegel thus becomes one of showing the diversity of components comprising reality, their limits, and their interconnections in a unified whole.

Like other nineteenth-century philosophers, Hegel was seeking the so-called *philosopher's stone* in some form of universal wisdom.* Unlike his predecessors who were baffled by the ephemeral nature of things—apparently the stone was a little too slippery to hold on to—Hegel made *change* the core concept of his world-system. Change, for him, resulted as a product of conflicting ideas.

The process of change can be explained in the following fashion. First of all, an idea (captured, say, by a principle) presents itself as the *thesis.* This idea is then challenged by its opposite, called the *antithesis.* Neither side wins in the conflict, for out of the tension between them emerges the *synthesis*—a combination of both. In time, this synthesized idea becomes its own thesis, to be challenged again by a new antithesis. Out of this second conflict emerges a second synthesis, only to be challenged by still another antithesis, and so on and so on.

Hegel believed that this **dialectical process** of thesis-antithesis-synthesis moves ever forward, gradually revealing **Absolute Mind** or Spirit (as it is sometimes translated). Eventually this dialectic would reach its term, and the ideal would be achieved.

Important to note is that the dialectical process is not just about the contents of minds. It's imbedded in the basic structure of external reality. Thus, the "dialectic" that is described here is not just a reasoning process or conceptual scheme in somebody's consciousness, but the structure of historical human change, and other changes in the universe as well.

Regardless of type, all of these changes in the dialectical process move toward perfection. At first, Hegel thought the dialectical ideal of history had been reached with Napoleon. Later he believed it had been discovered in the Prussian state, which presumably represented the perfect society.[65] This dialectical process is captured graphically in Figure 6.1.

From Hegel, Marx borrowed the notion of dialectic as a template for explaining historical evolution and change, but influenced by the materialist philosopher Ludwig Feuerbach (1804–1872), he concluded that the entities involved in historical change were not ideas in the human or metaphysical sense; but were the material conditions of

---

* Medieval alchemists believed that the philosopher's stone was a substance that could change other metals to gold, cure all diseases, etc., and finding this was their chief goal; then and now it is spoken of figuratively, as a key to perfect unified knowledge and living. Hegel thought of his eventual views as the philosopher's stone, a key opening the door to the mysteries of the universe.

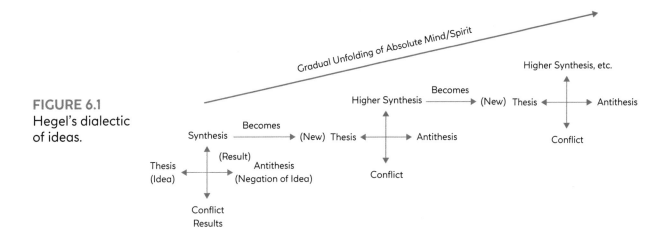

FIGURE 6.1
Hegel's dialectic of ideas.

human societies: social organizations and their sources in how people "make their living." Human ideas and concepts spring from such factors—their conflicts are thus the effect, not the cause, of real change. The source of conflict was in the *material world* itself. Ideas spring from conflict; they do not in themselves cause it.

For Marx, the only demonstrable reality became matter, not some fuzzy conception of history as Absolute Mind revealing itself in an interplay of ideas. Marx found Hegelianism standing on its head, so to speak, and he intended to put it right side up. He argued that any meaningful thought-system must first start with real, existing individuals and with the actual concrete conditions in which they live, not with abstract ideas. By giving primacy to matter over mind, and by injecting Hegelianism with a good dose of concrete reality, Marx replaced Hegel's dialectical idealism with **dialectical materialism** (sometimes called 'historical materialism'). In *The German Ideology*, Marx wrote:

> In direct contrast to German philosophy [esp. Hegel] which descends from heaven to earth, here we ascend from earth to heaven.... We set out from real, active men, and on the basis of their real-life process we demonstrate the development of the ideological reflexes and echoes of this life process.[66]

Class Conflict

While in Paris, Marx encountered the Comte de Saint-Simon (1760–1825), another radical thinker who concluded that economic conditions determine history. Specifically, he argued that historical change is the product of **class conflict**. Those who control the means of production are in a never-ending struggle with those who do not. Accepting this insight, and integrating it with Feuerbach's materialism as well as Hegel's dialectic,

Marx produced his own unique theory of historical development. Class conflict, which was used to explain historical change, was given an economic, material foundation and interpreted in the context of a Hegelian dialectical framework. The importance of class conflict to historical progression is addressed by Marx and Engels, who wrote the following in *The Communist Manifesto*:

> The history of all hitherto existing society is the history of class struggles.... Freeman and slave, patrician and plebeian, lord and serf, guild-master and journeyman, in a word, oppressor and oppressed, stood in constant opposition to one another, carried on an uninterrupted, now hidden, now open fight, a fight that each time ended, either in a revolutionary re-constitution of society at large, or in the common ruin of the contending classes.[67]

On the Marxist account, history, in essence, is the ongoing result of constant tensions or struggles arising between dominant and subordinate classes, between upper classes of rulers and lower classes of those who are controlled and exploited. Marx's point is that conflicts between the classes are essentially economic, and that out of the class-conflict struggle between different and opposing economic interests there emerge brand new economic structures.

The five stages of historical development or "**epochs of history**" identified by Marx and Engels as having structurally different modes of economic production are:

1. Primitive/communal
2. Slave
3. Feudal
4. Capitalist
5. Socialist/Communist

Details of Marx's explanation for how the actual historical process unfolds are very sketchy for epochs prior to feudalism and the emergence of capitalism. He postulated that there must have been a first epoch of history in which the mode of production was a primitive type of communism, without division of labor and without exploiters and the exploited. Presumably, all succeeding epochs display the economic laws of motion characterizing dialectical materialism.

According to Marx, from an initial situation where people lived cooperatively together, a slave economy was born due to the need for more labor, arising from increasingly sophisticated tools and techniques of production. In the slave economy, slave-owners owned the means of production—the slaves themselves—and the products of their labor, resulting in the inevitable conflict between these two classes.

In time, production skills and techniques continued to improve, along with the greater accumulation of information. The result was that people began to gather around towns, making possible the emergence of craft guilds. Craft guilds, in turn, made specialization possible. Fewer people were required to work at meeting basic agricultural needs, thereby allowing craftsmen the opportunity to further develop their expert talents. With this economic development, slaves needed more freedom than they had earlier been given, and labor needed to become even more concentrated.

Marx predicted that as the rich get richer and the poor get poorer in a capitalistic society, the proletariat would eventually overthrow the political system in violent revolution, ushering in the new communist state. Do you think his prediction has, or will ever, come true? Explain and illustrate why. What factors today make the revolution more or less likely to occur?

In response to these needs, the feudal system arose. In this economic arrangement, the lords owned the land, while the serfs leased portions of it, giving in lease payment most of what they produced. Feudal society represented a period of comparative semi-freedom—a time when the majority of the population resided in semi-rural or small but growing towns. But again there were two classes with opposing interests. The lords owned much of the means of production (land, buildings, etc.) and much of the results of production, while the serfs owned virtually nothing except their labor.

"The most radical revolutionary will become a conservative the day after the revolution."
HANNAH ARENDT

As craft guilds further refined their specialized manufacturing techniques, increasing numbers and varieties of goods became available. The growing demand for these goods increased trade and barter, paving the way for **capitalism**. With trade and barter, money became increasingly important, as did the need for financial brokers. Once steam-powered manufacturing techniques came into use, feudalism was doomed because of its inefficiency and inability to satisfy the wants of an emerging capitalist middle class.

The industrial age gave birth to great centers that provided the power and transportation services necessary for mass production. Goods became less expensive, their numbers and varieties continued to grow, while the demand for them accelerated. The consequence of all this activity was that a new class of middlemen (speculators, entrepreneurs) who neither owned the means of production, nor produced anything themselves, grew in power. They worked at investing and acquiring greater and greater sums of capital. Again, this created the conditions for the continuation of class conflict. How so?

Marx predicted in his day that the inequalities in wealth between the **bourgeois capitalists** (speculators and those owning the modes of production) and the **proletariat** (wage-earning workers) would continue to increase. Putting it simply, the reason for this is that a worker's pay to make one object would be too little to buy that object, because of the additions to its price to cover pay and profit for the other class. The rich (thesis element in society) would get richer, and the poor (antithesis element in society) would get poorer. The bourgeois capitalists would earn their money on the backs of a larger exploited proletarian class. Eventually, discontent would become so deep and widespread that workers would rise up in violent revolution. On this, Marx writes in *The Communist Manifesto*: "What the bourgeoisie, therefore, produces, above all, is its own grave-diggers. Its fall and the victory of the proletariat are equally inevitable."[68]

The final synthesis of historical development culminating in **communism** would require the abolition of private property, transferring the ownership of the means of production to everyone. Basic needs would be met, enabling all people to live a dignified, meaningful life. Rather than trying to outdo one another in the competitive marketplace jungle, people would live harmoniously, actively engaged in creative, satisfying work that would benefit not only themselves, but also the rest of society. Since all classes would be abolished, so too would all class conflict.

Once capitalism became an obsolete and defunct economic system, a stage of transition would actually be required before reaching the end of the dialectical process. The transitional state would require the *dictatorship of the proletariat*—a necessarily unhappy time when the proletariat would use their political power to stamp out the last vestiges of capitalism. A socialist intermediary state would arise wherein the state would take over the means of production. Eventually, the socialist phase would give way to the final stage of communism wherein the people would control political decision-making as well as the economic life of the country. This would constitute a utopian ideal based on the moral dictum, "From each according to his ability, to each according to his needs."[69]

Alienation as a Byproduct of Capitalism

Before leaving Marxist theory, it is important to clear up a serious misunderstanding often associated with it. Many people believe that Marx's central criticism of capitalism pertains to the injustice in the distribution of wealth within society. Surely Marx did object to the growing disparities in income between rich and poor, and insisted that they would only precipitate what, for him, was the inevitable communist revolution. Nonetheless, the problem with capitalism goes far deeper than the size of one's paycheck. Marx says: "An enforced *increase in wages* ... would be nothing more than a *better remuneration of slaves*, and would not restore, either to the worker or to the work, their human significance and worth."[70]

Especially in the *Economic and Philosophic Manuscripts*, but in other places as well, Marx addresses the problem of *alienated labor* and how it is a direct result of the capitalist mode of production. He says that the capitalist system degrades workers, alienates them, and reduces them to saleable commodities in the workplace.

Generally speaking, **alienation** is a feeling of *separation*, *difference*, or *estrangement*. When people feel alienated, they do not experience themselves as freely and actively engaged in the world. There is a *disconnect* or *disengagement*, creating a perception that one is not comfortably immersed in reality, but that objects and people in it stand over and against oneself. Such perceptions and feelings are not necessary. For Marx, they are the products of a capitalist system. For a vivid illustration of how the assembly line, as a capitalist mode of production, can be humanly degrading and thereby alienating, read the first news article that follows.

Almost two decades after this article about General Motors was published, it appears that some employers still haven't figured out how the human body works. See the second article below, about the experience of a journalistic investigator who worked at an Amazon warehouse in the United Kingdom.

As someone who has worked both in a shipping warehouse and on an assembly line in a manufacturing plant producing air conditioners, I recall only too clearly how the capitalist mode of production regulated my biological functions, including when I ate and slept. Thinking back to my factory experience, I remember that, hungry or not, I was forced to eat lunch from 12:00 to 12:30 p.m. Need it or not, my rest breaks were at 9:30 a.m. and 2:15 p.m. If I was moved to the night shift—without my consent I might add—then I had to sleep unnaturally during the daylight hours. If I was overheated and perspiring profusely in a poorly ventilated workspace during the summer months, I was given salt tablets to cope. By contrast, the factory owners and executives on the other side of the plant wall enjoyed air-conditioned comfort; this while their cooling

GM Suspends Worker for Going to Bathroom[71]

Foreman Orders Ailing Man to Stay at His Post On Line
June 21, 2000
Tony Van Alphen, Business Reporter

General Motors of Canada Ltd. suspended a worker last week because he left his work station to go to the bathroom.

Greg Taylor, a veteran assembler at GM's Number 2 car plant in Oshawa, lost more than $800 in net pay when he decided to answer nature's call instead of following a direct order to remain on the production line.

"I simply had to go but they (management) kept ordering me to stay," Taylor said yesterday. "They never showed me any dignity. Obviously none of them believed I had a condition."

Taylor, 39, suffers from irritable bowel syndrome, which sometimes forces frequent trips to the bathroom.

His union, the Canadian Auto Workers, has filed a grievance to recover the five days of lost pay.

"The whole situation is appalling," said Doug Sanders, a union committee man at the plant.

"I think it's very unjust that people are not allowed to go to the bathroom. GM is more concerned about efficiency than letting people go wee-wee."

Stew Low, GM's director of public relations, said the company would not discuss details of the incident because it is a private matter between an employee and management.

"There is a formalized grievance process to ensure both sides have a fair hearing on the issue," Low said.

Under company rules, employees must provide documentation of physical conditions that may warrant special accommodation in the workplace. Taylor said he didn't think the rule applied to his situation.

He said that when he showed his foreman an intestinal relaxant he uses to help control his problem, the foreman said he needed a doctor's note to justify leaving his work station frequently for bathroom trips.

The next day, on June 7—before he had a chance to see his doctor—Taylor said he felt a serious urge to go to the bathroom. He sought a relief employee to continue his work of bolting engines to chassis.

His work team leader arrived but the foreman insisted Taylor stay on the job. Taylor refused and walked off to the bathroom.

Taylor, who has worked for GM for 15 years, said the foreman asked him repeatedly if he understood the order.

"I told him, 'I don't understand and excuse me, I'm going to the bathroom,'" Taylor said.

GM, the country's biggest auto maker, put Taylor on notice for refusing a job order and leaving his work area.

units spewed forth hot-air exhaust onto the factory shop floor. If this wasn't insulting enough, assembly line workers were required to ask for *permission* to get a drink of water before break.

On the subject of permission, if replacement workers were not available for my particular workstation to be momentarily vacated, then permission was usually denied by the production foreman. *The line* simply could not be stopped. It was not as if I, or anyone else for that matter, had a job that nobody else could do. My task was simply to affix the lid of an air conditioner with screws. Every 30 seconds or so, another air conditioner confronted me like an unwanted enemy, sucking the enthusiasm and life-blood from my body.

I grew to hate air conditioners, and like other longtime employees, dubbed *lifers*, I was sometimes tempted to sabotage the assembly line so that the relentless thing would finally stop and give everyone a rest. I couldn't even afford to buy one of the air conditioning

Under Pressure, Afraid to Take Bathroom Breaks? Inside Amazon's Fast-Paced Warehouse World[72]

July 2, 2018
Nina Shapiro, The Seattle Times

Working at an Amazon warehouse in the U.K., James Bloodworth, an investigative journalist, came across a bottle of straw-colored liquid on a shelf. It looked like pee....

As he tells it, urinating into a bottle is the kind of desperation Amazon forces its warehouse workers into as they try to avoid accusations of "idling" and failing to meet impossibly high productivity targets—ones they are continually measured against by Big Brother-ish type surveillance....

Bloodworth's grim picture of Amazon's blue-collar workplaces—he compares the warehouse he worked in, alternately, to a prison and a totalitarian state—is bringing new attention to the company's treatment of its workers....

Adding to the oppressive atmosphere, in Bloodworth's telling: Amazon's security measures to prevent theft, ... entailed having workers go through airport-style metal detectors.

The author summed up his experience: "You were not seen as a human being. You were seen as a robot."

units I produced with my own hands—only *rich* people could, not a poor student like me. Talk about feeling alienated from the fruits of my labors! In view of my own experience, it is perhaps easier to understand what Marx meant when he wrote:

> Within the capitalist system all methods for raising the social productiveness of labor are brought about at the cost of the individual laborer; all means for the development of production transform themselves into means of domination over, and exploitation of, the producer; they mutilate the laborer into a fragment of a man, degrade him to the level of an appendage of a machine, destroy every remnant of charm in his work and turn it into a hated toil; they estrange from him the intellectual potentialities of the labor process in the same proportion as science is incorporated in it as an independent power.[73]

In response to Marx, one might argue that working conditions have improved and are improving all the time, making his comments much less relevant today. For instance, an NBC news report informs us that

> A California bill aims to change working conditions for warehouse workers who have come under increased productivity pressure from major retailers that track their every move.... The bill ... aims to ensure that workers are not penalized for time spent on personal hygiene, such as hand washing or using the restroom. Many workers say automated monitoring systems warn management if they spend too much time "off task." ... The bill would apply to warehouse workers for Amazon, Walmart, Target and other large retailers across California.[74]

In defense of capitalism, one might also say the greater wealth afforded to a much larger middle class no longer makes alienation the problem it once was. Witness all the sport utility vehicles on the highways, expensive clothes, summer and winter vacation packages, electronic gadgets, and so on. None of this affluence points to an exploited proletariat, dominated and oppressed by the industrial factory owner. Maybe it is only the blue-collar industrial working class that needs liberation. In response to such a suggestion, Erich Fromm answers for Karl Marx:

> If anything, the clerk, the salesman, the executive, are even more alienated today than the skilled manual worker. The latter's functioning still depends on the expression of certain personal qualities like skill, reliability, etc., and he is not forced to sell his "personality," his smile, his opinions in the bargain; the symbol manipulators are hired not only for their skill, but for all those personality qualities which make them "attractive personality packages," easy to handle and manipulate. They are true "organization men"—more so than the skilled laborer—their idol being the corporation.[75]

Fromm's point in supporting Marx is that just because one enjoys greater wealth or wears a white collar instead of a blue one at work does not mean that one is any less alienated under a capitalist system. Selling your smile or your dignity as a "symbol manipulator" (image consultant, advertiser, corporate executive, or social media influencer) is no less demeaning than being forced to sell your muscle power as an appendage to a machine in order to survive and earn a living for yourself and your family.

Idolatry/Fetishism of Commodities

Marx claims that people can be alienated* from a number of things—from nature, themselves, from what he calls their "species-being," and from other people. All of these forms of alienation are associated with economic forces embodied in the predominant societal mode of production. As already stated, Marx contends that capitalism greatly contributes to alienation. It does so by giving rise to a kind of **idolatry** or **fetishism of commodities** whereby lifeless material things are endowed with power over the living subjects who should be their master.

For example, we talk about the *almighty dollar* when we make money our god. Also, take the computer. Once thought to be a convenient calculator or a rapid information processor that would make our collective lives easier and more efficient, this technological device now lords it over us. How much pressure is placed on you, or any prospective employee, to have "the right" social media presence? How disadvantaged are you in the job market without computer skills? Clearly, in today's world, many doors of opportunity are closed to people who cannot make use of computer technology. The servant has become the master, dictating what we must know and be able to do if we wish to work and feed ourselves.

This idolatry or fetishism of commodities also exhibits itself in capitalistic consumerism. For instance, we often attribute human qualities to man-made objects, describing vehicles as *sexy* and compressed carbon crystals (diamonds) as symbols of love, without which commitment is questioned. How many times have you felt frustrated, insecure, or

---

*   *Separation, estrangement*, in this word's central sense.

inadequate because you could not afford to buy some status symbol or article of clothing that would make you feel good, enhance your self-esteem, or place you higher up in the social pecking order?

Remember what the image consultants tell us: "Clothes make the man," or "You never get a second chance to make a first impression." Have you ever believed that by eating at trendy restaurants in trendy clothes you are *a special somebody*, but that by drinking convenience store coffee, while wearing generic box-store jeans and warehouse outlet runners, you amount to *an insignificant nothing* or *nobody*? Have you ever felt ennobled by the pursuit of a particular photo-worthy meal or designer label? Has a carefully *curated* menu or fashion style become your obsession? Have you ever had to relate to the "haves" as one of the "have-nots"? How do you think the "haves" perceived you? Were you bestowed with dignity, brought into more intimate relations, or alienated further by envy, jealousy, and egoistic pride? If capitalistic consumerism makes people so happy, then why are so many so lonely and sad?

Division of Labor

From our increasing knowledge, and out of the more sophisticated techniques of production, characterizing the various historical epochs, what emerged was the information-based technological age of today. Throughout this historical development, we have witnessed ever-increasing specialization in the workplace. This tendency toward specialization, which was clearly present in Marx's time, required a **division of labor**, another contributing factor to alienation.

To help you understand in plain terms what is meant by this, let's imagine ourselves going back to simpler days before computerized robotics, assembly lines, global markets, world exports, and electronic information highways and social media platforms. As someone in the primitive communal epoch, you hunted and gathered in the morning, built huts in the afternoon, made and worked with tools in the early evening, and spent time together with other members of the community in ritualistic celebration at night. You did many different things and played many different roles (hunter, builder, storyteller, protector). Things were done in community with a common purpose—the most obvious of which was survival. Relations were close and interests were common.

Now, let us fast-forward to the feudal era. Imagine yourself as a cobbler centuries ago, living in a small village where everybody knew of your reputation for making fine sandals. You took great pride in going to neighbors' farms to purchase the finest hides you could find, magically treating the leathers in your patented way. You creatively designed your sandals and then painstakingly cut out the patterns before you stitched them up. You enjoyed the expert workmanship you put into the sandal and felt a sense of pride as you stamped your initials into the sole. You also took pleasure greeting prospective buyers of your footwear, talking to them about their families and future plans.

In this quaint recreation of the past, you can begin to appreciate how the cobbler was very active and certainly in control of their life, attached to the products of their labor and the creative process that went into the fabrication of the sandal. There was no foreman or factory owner dictating the pace, stifling the cobbler's creativity for mass-market consumption, or requiring quotas of production.

Suggesting that the alienation of work in capitalistic modes of production is much greater than during earlier times, when production was by **handicraft** and **manufacture** (making articles from raw material), Marx says:

> In handicrafts and manufacture, the workman makes use of a tool; in the factory the machine makes use of him. There the movement of the instrument of labor proceeded from him; here it is the movement of the machines that he must follow. In manufacture, the workmen are parts of a living mechanism; in the factory we have a lifeless mechanism, independent of the workman, who become its mere living appendage.[76]

He says further:

> This fact expresses merely that the object which labor produces—labor's product—confronts it as *something alien*, as a *power independent* of the producer. The product of labor is labor which has been embodied in an object, which has become material: it is the *objectification* of labor. Labor's realization is its objectification. Under these economic conditions this realization of labor appears as *loss of realization* for the workers; objectification as *loss of the object and bondage to it*; appropriation as *estrangement*, as *alienation*.
>
> So much does labor's realization appear as loss of realization that the worker loses realization to the point of starving to death. So much does objectification appear as loss of the object that the worker is robbed of the objects most necessary not only for his life but for his work. Indeed, labor itself becomes an object which he can obtain only with the greatest effort and with the most irregular interruptions. So much does the appropriation of the object appear as estrangement that the more objects the worker produces the less he can possess and the more he falls under the sway of his product, capital.[77]

What Marx is saying here is that in the capitalist economy, products of labor (belonging to the employer) become alien objects. Labor, in fact, itself becomes a commodity. The more the worker produces, the less he or she is worth. The individual, as a person, is transformed into cheap labor, earning a wage that is less than the worth of the products produced. The **surplus value** constituting the profit can then be used for further investment. The worker is left to pray that markets do not evaporate and that sales continue for fear of lay-off or plant-closures.

In a capitalistic market economy, the future is in the hands of uncontrollable market forces and subject to the whims of factory owners, shareholders, and corporate presidents. If company profits can be maximized by shutting down operations in a particular location and moving them to China or Mexico, say, then they often are without much concern about the displaced and now unemployed workers. That's business, after all. Don't take it personally!

It doesn't require much psychological insight to grasp how doing mindless, repetitive work in an insecure market environment, which could cost workers their jobs at any moment, undermines human dignity. Workers are robbed of their freedom and the opportunity for creative self-fulfillment. They are prevented from expressing their own nature or "species-being," as they are enslaved by uncontrollable economic forces. They are alienated from the objects of their labor and placed in competitive struggles with other people for scarce jobs. Marx says:

> An immediate consequence of the fact that man is estranged from the product of his labor, from his life activity, from his species-being, is the *estrangement of man* from *man*. When man confronts himself, he confronts the *other* man. What applies to a man's relation to his work, to the product of his labor and to himself, also holds of a man's relation to the other man, and to the other man's labor and object of labor.[78]

In such a dreadfully alienated state,

> The worker therefore only feels himself outside his work, and in his work feels outside himself. He feels at home when he is not working, and when he is working he does not feel at home. His labor is therefore not voluntary, but coerced; it is *forced labor*. It is therefore not the satisfaction of a need; it is merely a *means* to satisfy needs external to it. Its alien character emerges clearly in the fact that as soon as no physical or other compulsion exists, labor is shunned like the plague.[79]

One could argue that as testimony to the truth of Marx's insight here, a person only needs to point to the abundance of diversion and escape that we've created. We spend millions, if not billions, on sports and entertainment, all with the painful subconscious realization that we have to go to work tomorrow morning.

The film *American Beauty* exquisitely captures what Marx might describe as the alienating moral bankruptcy of capitalism. In it, we find an exploration of alienation in the character of Lester Burnham, a middle-aged man "trapped in a marriage that he no longer takes any pleasure in, father of a daughter who seems to hate him, and worker at a job that he finds totally boring and morally compromising, and from which he expects to be removed for the sake of efficiency."[80] *American Beauty* masterfully portrays the emptiness of the American Dream. Though Burnham has achieved the good life by capitalistic standards—a well-paying job, attractive wife, intelligent daughter, and fine home in the suburbs—he's trapped in a world of sham and inauthenticity.

His wife, who so desperately clings to appearances and "idols of success," is so alienated from herself that she cannot experience genuine feelings any longer. In one attempt to reconnect passionately with his wife, Carolyn, Lester fails because she cannot release her vain and neurotic attention to her home's appearance long enough to be swept up by the tide of physical desire that is about to pour over her. As film reviewer Thomas Wartenberg observes,

> "Once it has staked out the alienation of the American male as its subject ... *American Beauty* seems eager to contain the possibility that there is something rotten at the core of the American Dream.... Faced with the possibility that Burnham's discovery of the emptiness of his own life will lead to a more general condemnation of America's lust for more, the film proposes an aesthetic stance to life as the solution to Burnham's *angst*."[81]

This "solution" reflects the inevitable **dehumanization of capitalism** according to Marx. On the subject of retreating to the "aesthetic stance of life," Marx writes:

> As a result, therefore, man (the worker) only feels himself freely active in his animal functions—eating, drinking, procreating, or at most in his dwelling and in dressing-up, etc.; and in his human functions he no longer feels himself to be anything but an animal. What is animal becomes human and what is human becomes animal. Certainly eating, drinking, procreating, etc., are also genuinely human functions. But taken abstractly, separated from the sphere of all other human activity and turned into sole and ultimate ends, they are animal functions.[82]

After Capitalism

Time and space limitations do not allow detailed discussion of Marx's socialist-communist utopia, which will follow after the fall of capitalism. Briefly, what can be said is that the basic mode of production within society will not be competitive, but cooperative and by association. Production will be brought under the control of workers in a rational and unalienated way. Socialism will provide a system that allows for the actualizing of human potentiality at its best, by overcoming alienation. A socialist-communist state will create the conditions necessary for living in a truly free, active, rational, and independent fashion. It will aim at the destruction of idols and at the satisfaction of the true needs of mankind, not the gratification of synthetic, artificially produced needs created by capitalistic hucksters. Who *really* needs satellite TV, for example, and why should anyone be made to feel deprived because they don't have it? For Marx, a system like capitalism, hellbent on producing artificial needs, is necessarily destined to produce a class of alienated individuals.

Karl Marx, *Economic and Philosophic Manuscripts*[83]

Published posthumously in 1932, the Economic and Philosophic Manuscripts *of 1844 is a collection of writings that Marx composed between April and August 1844 while he was living in Paris. The title refers to the three unfinished manuscripts contained in the collection. These "notes" of sorts offer insight into a young Marx's criticisms of the political economy and economic system of "the bourgeoisie." In this, a selection from the first and earliest of the manuscripts, Marx examines the "alienation of labor" in a capitalist system. In this translation, alienated labor is often called estranged labor. Whenever 'estranged' is used, one could read 'alienated.'*

———

What, then, constitutes the alienation of labor?

First, the fact that labor is *external* to the worker, i.e., it does not belong to his intrinsic nature; that in his work, therefore, he does not affirm himself but denies himself, does not feel content but unhappy, does not develop freely his physical and mental energy but mortifies his body and ruins his mind. The worker therefore only feels himself outside his work, and in his work feels outside himself. He feels at home when he is not working, and when he is working he does not feel at home. His labor is therefore not voluntary, but coerced; it is *forced labor*. It is therefore not the satisfaction of a need; it is merely a *means* to satisfy needs external to it. Its alien character emerges clearly in the fact that as soon as no physical or other compulsion exists, labor is shunned like the plague. External labor, labor in which man alienates himself, is a labor of self-sacrifice, of mortification. Lastly, the external character of labor for the worker appears in the fact that it is not his own, but someone else's, that it does not belong to him, that in it he belongs, not to himself, but to another. Just as in religion the spontaneous activity of the human imagination, of the human brain and the human heart, operates on the individual independently of him—that is, operates as an alien, divine or diabolical activity—so is the worker's activity not his spontaneous activity. It belongs to another; it is the loss of his self.

As a result, therefore, man (the worker) only feels himself freely active in his animal functions—eating, drinking, procreating, or at most in his dwelling and in dressing-up, etc.; and in his human functions he no longer feels himself to be anything but an animal. What is animal becomes human and what is human becomes animal.

Certainly eating, drinking, procreating, etc., are also genuinely human functions. But taken abstractly, separated from the sphere of all other human activity and turned into sole and ultimate ends, they are animal functions.

We have considered the act of estranging practical human activity, labor, in two of its aspects. (1) The relation of the worker to the *product of labor* as an alien object exercising power over him. This relation is at the same time the relation to the sensuous external world, to the objects of nature, as an alien world inimically opposed to him. (2) The relation of labor to the *act of production* within the *labor* process. This relation is the relation of the worker to his own activity as an alien activity not belonging to him; it is activity as suffering, strength as weakness, begetting as emasculating, the worker's *own* physical and mental energy, his personal life—for what is life but activity?—as an activity which is turned against him, independent of him and not belonging to him. Here we have *self-estrangement*, as previously we had the estrangement of the *thing*.

We have still a third aspect of *estranged labor* to deduce from the two already considered.

Man is a species-being, not only because in practice and in theory he adopts the species (his own as well as those of other things) as his object, but—and this is only another way of expressing it—also because he treats himself as the actual, living species; because he treats himself as a *universal* and therefore a free being.

The life of the species, both in man and in animals, consists physically in the fact that man (like the animal) lives on organic nature; and the more universal man (or the animal) is, the more universal is the sphere of inorganic nature on which he lives. Just as plants, animals, stones, air, light, etc., constitute theoretically a part of human consciousness, partly as objects of natural science, partly as objects of art—his spiritual inorganic nature, spiritual nourishment which he must first prepare to make palatable and digestible—so also in the realm of practice they constitute a part of human life and human activity. Physically man lives only on these products of nature, whether they appear in the form of food, heating, clothes, a dwelling, etc. The universality of man appears in practice precisely in the universality which makes all nature his *inorganic* body—both inasmuch as nature is (1) his direct means of life, and (2) the material, the object, and the instrument of his life activity. Nature is man's *inorganic body*—nature, that is, insofar as it is not itself human body. Man *lives* on nature—means that nature is his *body*, with which he must remain in continuous interchange if he is not to die. That man's physical and spiritual life is linked to nature means simply that nature is linked to itself, for man is a part of nature.

In estranging from man (1) nature, and (2) himself, his own active functions, his life activity, estranged labor estranges the *species* from man. It changes for him the *life of the species* into a means of individual life. First it estranges the life of the species and individual life, and secondly it makes individual life in its abstract form the purpose of the life of the species, likewise in its abstract and estranged form.

For labor, *life activity, productive life* itself, appears to man in the first place merely as a *means* of satisfying a need—the need to maintain physical existence. Yet the productive life is the life of the species. It is life-engendering life. The whole character of a species, its species-character, is contained in the character of its life activity; and free, conscious activity is man's species-character. Life itself appears only as a *means to life*.

The animal is immediately one with its life activity. It does not distinguish itself from it. It is *its life activity*. Man makes his life activity itself the object of his will and of his consciousness. He has conscious life activity. It is not a determination with which he directly merges. Conscious life activity distinguishes man immediately from animal life activity. It is just because of this that he is a species-being. Or it is only because he is a species-being that he is a conscious being, i.e., that his own life is an object for him. Only because of that is his activity free activity. Estranged labor reverses the relationship, so that it is just because man is a conscious being that he

makes his life activity, his *essential being*, a mere means to his *existence*.

In creating a *world of objects* by his personal activity, in his *work upon* inorganic nature, man proves himself a conscious species-being, i.e., as a being that treats the species as his own essential being, or that treats itself as a species-being. Admittedly animals also produce. They build themselves nests, dwellings, like the bees, beavers, ants, etc. But an animal only produces what it immediately needs for itself or its young. It produces one-sidedly, whilst man produces universally. It produces only under the dominion of immediate physical need, whilst man produces even when he is free from physical need and only truly produces in freedom therefrom. An animal produces only itself, whilst man reproduces the whole of nature. An animal's product belongs immediately to its physical body, whilst man freely confronts his product. An animal forms only in accordance with the standard and the need of the species to which it belongs, whilst man knows how to produce in accordance with the standard of every species, and knows how to apply everywhere the inherent standard to the object. Man therefore also forms objects in accordance with the laws of beauty.

It is just in his work upon the objective world, therefore, that man really proves himself to be a *species-being*. This production is his active species-life. Through this production, nature appears as *his* work and his reality. The object of labor is, therefore, the *objectification of man's species-life*: for he duplicates himself not only, as in consciousness, intellectually, but also actively, in reality, and therefore he sees himself in a world that he has created. In tearing away from man the object of his production, therefore, estranged labor tears from him his *species-life*, his real objectivity as a member of the species and transforms his advantage over animals into the disadvantage that his inorganic body, nature, is taken from him.

Similarly, in degrading spontaneous, free activity to a means, estranged labor makes man's species-life a means to his physical existence.

The consciousness which man has of his species is thus transformed by estrangement in such a way that species [-life] becomes for him a means.

Estranged labor turns thus:

(3) *Man's species-being*, both nature and his spiritual species-property, into a being *alien* to him, into a *means*

of his *individual existence*. It estranges from man his own body, as well as external nature and his spiritual aspect, his *human* aspect.

(4) An immediate consequence of the fact that man is estranged from the product of his labor, from his life activity, from his species-being, is the *estrangement of man* from *man*. When man confronts himself, he confronts the *other* man. What applies to a man's relation to his work, to the product of his labor and to himself, also holds of a man's relation to the other man, and to the other man's labor and object of labor.

In fact, the proposition that man's species-nature is estranged from him means that one man is estranged from the other, as each of them is from man's essential nature.

The estrangement of man, and in fact every relationship in which man [stands] to himself, is realized and expressed only in the relationship in which a man stands to other men.

READING QUESTIONS

1. What does Marx mean when he claims that the "alienation of labor" is constituted by labor that is "external to the worker"? According to Marx, what result does that kind of labor have on our relationships with ourselves? How does it affect our relationships with other human beings? Can you provide any personal examples from your own work experience?

2. How could the advocate of capitalist economics answer Marx's charge that corporate industry is alienating and disenfranchising for the laborer? How would you evaluate this possible response?

6.5 Martin Luther King Jr.'s Philosophy of Nonviolence

Most people familiar with the life and times of **Martin Luther King Jr.** tend to think of him as a preacher and extraordinary orator or as a civil rights leader who heroically led protests for racial equality in the United States during the 1950s and 1960s. What fewer people are likely to appreciate is the political philosophy which gave form to his moving speeches and which served as a theoretical platform of support for his activist endeavors. This is perhaps because King aimed at arousing people to action, rather than at explaining and defending a political philosophy, and also because he wrote no extended philosophical works.[84]

Influences on King

As an advocate of social change, Martin Luther King Jr. bears some similarity to Karl Marx and indeed even acknowledges Marx's influence on him. King found something compelling about Marx's discussion of workers and their struggles against the oppressive ruling classes. A number of insights in Marx's writings would leave a lasting impression on King the thinker. He writes:

I was deeply concerned from my early teen days about the gulf between superfluous wealth and abject poverty, and my reading of Marx made me even more conscious of this gulf. Moreover Marx had revealed the danger of the profit motive as the sole basis of an economic system: capitalism is always in danger of inspiring men to be more concerned about making a living than making a life. Thus capitalism can lead to a practical materialism that is as pernicious as the materialism taught by communism.[85]

King was influenced by Marx but was not a Marxist, as is evident from his religious motivations and his attachment to nonviolence. He took some of what is valuable from Marx and developed it along different lines but without all of the ideological baggage which, especially during the Cold War era, became the focal point of dispute between capitalists and their communist adversaries.

Like Marx, King sought to promote the aspirations of the oppressed masses, but at the same time he was careful to preserve peaceful options. The violent overthrow of the existing social order was neither necessary nor desirable. King's prescription for change, through nonviolent **mass action**, thus reveals itself as something quite different from the proletarian revolution envisioned by Marx. From King's vantage point, Marx's historical class analysis, which makes revolution inevitable, reflects a dogmatism that King would not embrace.

Furthermore, the unique features of the black struggle could not, for King, be fully or accurately captured by the Marxist notion of class conflict, though King does acknowledge that the two are connected. King would admit, for example, that there are structural problems embedded within the capitalist system, problems which have led to the suffering of black people. However, unlike Marx, who sees a preferred political structure in communism, King chooses to advance change under conditions of a modern industrial democracy, as he knew it in his day. In other words, he wanted to transform what he saw as the **structure of racist imperialism** from within, believing that abuses related to poverty, racism, and war could not all be understood entirely in terms of class conflict. And on the subject of evil, he rejected Marxist ideology because, at bottom, it too was for him morally corrupt. Communism adopts metaphysical materialism and ethical relativism, both of which were anathema to King's Christian beliefs. The actual practice of communism in the world has also given rise to totalitarianism, something King could not accept.

A second important influence on King was Mohandas K. Gandhi (1869–1948), the famed Indian nationalist leader who helped gain his country's freedom through nonviolent revolution. Trained as a lawyer in England, Gandhi practiced in South Africa, where he found himself treated as a second-class citizen due to his race. Inspired by the teachings of Jesus, as well as by Russian novelist Leo Tolstoy and American transcendentalist Henry David Thoreau (especially Thoreau's essay, "Civil Disobedience"), Gandhi began to teach a policy of passive resistance to—and non-cooperation with—South African authorities, with some success. He later abandoned the term 'passive resistance' to use a Sanskrit alternative, "*satyagraha*," meaning *truth-force*.[86]

Returning to British-controlled India, Gandhi became the leader of a campaign for home rule, becoming the international symbol of a free India. He practiced a spiritual and ascetic life of prayer, fasting, and meditation, depriving himself sexual pleasure and wearing the garb typical of members of the lowest Indian caste.

After a series of tumultuous events, including, frustrated outbreaks of violence and revolt (which went against Gandhi's principles), the outbreak of World War II, and a sequence of repeated jailings for Gandhi, the British government finally agreed to Indian

"You can't separate peace from freedom because no one can be at peace unless he has his freedom."
MALCOLM X

"Happiness is when what you think, what you say, and what you do are in harmony."
MAHATMA GANDHI

Dr. Martin Luther King Jr. stands next to a portrait of Mahatma Gandhi in his office in 1966.

"Stand for something or you will fall for anything. Today's mighty oak is yesterday's nut that held its ground."

ROSA PARKS

independence on the condition that two contending nationalist groups—the Muslim League and the Indian National Congress—resolve their differences. Gandhi, who opposed the partition of a free India, pleaded with Hindus (represented by the Congress) and Muslims to co-exist peacefully. However, their differences proved irreconcilable, and in 1947 the British divided the Indian subcontinent into India (primarily Hindu) and Pakistan (primarily Muslim).

On January 30, 1948, just days after ending yet another fast to quell the violence following the country's partition, Gandhi was assassinated by Nathuram Godse, a Hindu fanatic, while on his way to an evening prayer meeting.

Martin Luther King Jr. was so impressed by Gandhi's pacifism and so vocal in his admiration of him, that he was once asked by fellow Christians to tone down his public praise of the non-Christian Hindu. King said, "It is ironic, yet inescapably true, that the greatest Christian of the modern world was a man who never embraced Christianity."[87]

Martin Luther King Jr.

Martin Luther King Jr. is a man whose name is immortalized in the annals of American history. A preacher and prominent civil rights leader in the United States during the 1950s and 1960s, he is probably best remembered today more for his social activism and eloquent speeches, than for the political philosophy he promulgated in support of his struggles against poverty and racial discrimination. However, King's activism did not take place in a theoretical vacuum; in fact, King articulates a coherent and systematic philosophy that combines ideas reminiscent of Marx's admonition that philosophers change the world with Mohandas Gandhi's prescription that political change proceed peacefully. The result is a philosophical logic of nonviolence that takes us beyond Cold War antagonisms and lukewarm liberal commitments to social justice, which for King only serve to perpetuate an unacceptable status quo.

Martin Luther King Jr. was born on January 15, 1929, at the family home in Atlanta, Georgia. He was the first son and second child of Reverend Martin Luther King Sr. and Alberta Williams King. As a young man, King married Coretta Scott, with whom he had four children.

King was obviously a very bright and precocious student, as he advanced to Morehouse College at the age of 15 before graduating high school and after skipping both the ninth and twelfth grades. After graduating from Morehouse with a Bachelor's degree in sociology, King was ordained as a Christian minister in 1948 at the age 19. In 1951, he entered Crozer Theological Seminary in Pennsylvania, where he graduated in only three years with a Bachelor's degree in divinity. He then completed his Ph.D. at the Boston University School of Theology, with a dissertation titled "A Comparison of the Conception of God in the Thinking of Paul Tillich and Henry Nelson Wieman." From 1954 to 1959, King served as Pastor of Dexter Avenue Baptist Church, leaving to become more politically involved.

Throughout his life, King received several hundred awards for leadership in the civil rights movement. He was listed in "Who's Who in America" in 1957, named as the "Man of the Year" by *Time* magazine in 1963, and in 1964 was honored with the Nobel Peace Prize. Dr. King

was the youngest man, the second American, and the third black person to be given this prestigious award.

Martin Luther King lived during a turbulent time of great social upheaval in America. Two events in particular set the stage for his rise as a great civil rights leader. On May 17, 1954, in the *Linda Brown et al. v. Board of Education of Topeka* case, the US Supreme Court ordered the desegregation of all public schools. This ruling sent shock waves across the country. As a result, white racist and separatist groups such as the Ku Klux Klan and the White Citizens' Council began an escalating series of violent attacks on black people.

In a second event, which occurred on December 1, 1955, Rosa Parks, a 42-year-old black seamstress in Montgomery, Alabama, defied the law by refusing to give up her seat on a bus to a white man when ordered to do so by the driver. Her arrest attracted national attention, and in response to the Parks situation, King led black followers in a 381-day nonviolent boycott of the Montgomery public transportation system.

The boycotters demanded an end to segregated seating, protesting the insulting treatment that black people were forced to endure at the hands of whites. They also wanted black bus drivers to be hired for bus lines serving predominantly black neighborhoods. It was during this boycott that four black churches were bombed, along with the homes of King and another protesting black minister, Reverend Ralph Abernathy. A year and a half after the *Brown* decision, Reverend George W. Lee was lynched in Belzoni, Mississippi, after he tried to register as a voter in Humphreys County. Lamar Smith and fourteen-year-old Emmett Till were also lynched in that state as the South erupted in murderous racial violence.

Notwithstanding the lynching, bombings, arson, and intimidation tactics employed by racist whites, the civil rights movement continued. In 1957, King founded the Southern Christian Leadership Conference, an organization which, despite its name, had a national mandate to improve the situation of black people in America. King was in Memphis, Tennessee, to help lead sanitation workers in a protest against low wages and intolerable working conditions, when he was shot dead on April 4, 1968.

During his lifetime, King published six books: two collections of sermons, *The Measure of a Man* (1959) and *Strength to Love* (1963); a collection of radio addresses, *The Trumpet of Conscience* (1968); and three so-called "movement books": *Stride Toward Freedom* (1958), *Why We Can't Wait* (1964), and *Where Do We Go from Here: Chaos or Community?* (1967). These last three works contain a great deal of King's philosophical thinking.

Logic of Nonviolence

"Where justice is denied, where poverty is enforced, where ignorance prevails, and where any one class is made to feel that society is in an organized conspiracy to oppress, rob, and degrade them, neither persons nor property will be safe."
FREDERICK DOUGLASS

Some interpretations of King's philosophy make him out to be a kind of rationalist who deduces his whole system of thought from first principles. Cast in this light, King appears to emerge out of the classical western tradition in philosophy, especially the Christian traditions that influenced him so much. However, alternative analyses suggest that a proper understanding of King's work requires that we focus attention on its relation to the contemporary conditions and experiences that motivated King.

Seen from this perspective, King's thinking combines his own experience with a lineage of black activism and thought, for example in the works of Frederick Douglass, W.E.B. Du Bois, A. Philip Randolph, Ralph J. Bunche, and Howard Thurman. This liberation philosophy denounces Marxist metaphysics but also criticizes American capitalism because of its materialistic and divisive nature.

Embedded within King's philosophical system are several interrelated concepts: *equality*, *structure*, *nonviolent direct action*, *justice*, and *love*. Using these key concepts, King is able to establish the groundwork for a new age of social-political philosophy. Although he tries to reawaken the deepest spiritual motives to be found in the enduring human quest for justice, that reawakening is not about liberal sentimentalism or good intentions.

The reawakening King has in mind is pragmatic, action-oriented, and designed to purge violence from our social relations in order to eliminate social oppression. At bottom, the logic of nonviolence is founded on a compelling **ethic of love**, one that incorporates justice as part of its definition. It aims at nothing less than a "revolution of conscience"—a liberation from fear, anger, and hatred.

Martin Luther King Jr.'s "I Have a Dream" Speech[88]

On August 28, 1963, as part of the March on Washington for Jobs and Freedom, Martin Luther King Jr. delivered his so-called "I Have a Dream" speech at the Lincoln Memorial in Washington, DC, to a crowd of over 250,000 people. Widely regarded as one of the most iconic speeches in history, it holds an especially significant place in the history of the civil rights movement in America.

———

…

I have a dream that one day this nation will rise up and live out the true meaning of its creed: "We hold these truths to be self-evident, that all men are created equal."

I have a dream that one day on the red hills of Georgia, the sons of former slaves and the sons of former slave owners will be able to sit down together at the table of brotherhood.

I have a dream that one day even the state of Mississippi, a state sweltering with the heat of injustice, sweltering with the heat of oppression, will be transformed into an oasis of freedom and justice.

I have a dream that my four little children will one day live in a nation where they will not be judged by the color of their skin but by the content of their character.

I have a *dream* today!

I have a dream that one day, down in Alabama, with its vicious racists, with its governor having his lips dripping with the words of "interposition" and "nullification"—one day right there in Alabama little black boys and black girls will be able to join hands with little white boys and white girls as sisters and brothers.

I have a *dream* today!

I have a dream that one day every valley shall be exalted, and every hill and mountain shall be made low, the rough places will be made plain, and the crooked places will be made straight; "and the glory of the Lord shall be revealed and all flesh shall see it together."

This is our hope, and this is the faith that I go back to the South with.

With this faith, we will be able to hew out of the mountain of despair a stone of hope. With this faith, we will be able to transform the jangling discords of our nation into a beautiful symphony of brotherhood. With this faith, we will be able to work together, to pray together, to struggle together, to go to jail together, to stand up for freedom together, knowing that we will be free one day.

And this will be the day—this will be the day when all of God's children will be able to sing with new meaning:

My country 'tis of thee, sweet land of liberty, of thee I sing. Land where my fathers died, land of the Pilgrim's pride, from every mountainside, let freedom ring!

And if America is to be a great nation, this must become true.

And so let freedom ring from the prodigious hilltops of New Hampshire.

Let freedom ring from the mighty mountains of New York.

Let freedom ring from the heightening Alleghenies of Pennsylvania.

Let freedom ring from the snow-capped Rockies of Colorado.

Let freedom ring from the curvaceous slopes of California.

But not only that:

Let freedom ring from Stone Mountain of Georgia.

Let freedom ring from Lookout Mountain of Tennessee.

Let freedom ring from every hill and molehill of Mississippi.

From every mountainside, let freedom ring.

And when this happens, and when we allow freedom to ring, when we let it ring from every village and every hamlet, from every state and every city, we will be able to speed up that day when *all* of God's children, black men and white men, Jews and Gentiles, Protestants and Catholics, will be able to join hands and sing in the words of the old Negro spiritual:

Free at last! Free at last!

Thank God Almighty, we are free at last!

1. Sometimes we dream of possibilities and sometimes we dream of fantasies. What kind of dream do you think King's dream is? Try to use evidence from the text to explain your interpretation of King's choice word.

2. What would have to be the case for King's dream to become real? Consider that decades before King wrote and spoke the eloquent words above, slavery was abolished in the United States, and soon after King delivered this speech, the Civil Rights Act of 1964 officially banned segregation in the United States. Were those acts enough to turn the dream into reality? If not, what else is needed to achieve the equality and freedom King dreams of?

"I have a dream that ... little children will one day live in a nation where they will not be judged by the color of their skin but by the content of their character."

MARTIN LUTHER KING JR.

"Liberty and justice consist in restoring all that belongs to another ..."

OLYMPE DE GOUGES

King's philosophy of nonviolence confronts both obvious oppression as well as the more subtle quiet terrorism of collective domination: a *tyranny of the majority*. If it were possible for King to address Friedrich Nietzsche (see Section 5.6) today, he would probably be quick to point out that the ethic underlying his philosophy of nonviolence is not some sort of "slave morality," to be taken literally or, as Nietzsche defined it, as some form of perverted inversion of weakness. It is not one dishonestly translated into a glorified victimology whereby some people embrace their abuse and endless subjugation as a virtue to be rewarded in heaven.

Rather, King regards nonviolence as the high road to true **power**, rejecting the viewpoint that assumes violence is a sign of strength. Power is sought within a disciplined framework that views violence as essentially shortsighted. King does not accept the assumption that we are violent by nature or that we are the nasty egoistic brutes Hobbes envisions us to be.

The change King seeks does not require that we use the method (i.e., violence) that we hope to destroy. This would be illogical and, in the end, provide other perpetrators of violence with further weak rationalizations for engaging in vengeful and destructive acts. The elimination of violence cannot be achieved through violence itself, but only through others features of our being. Showing sympathy for the other, for instance, when the other is the terrorizing authority of segregation, exploitation, and callous indifference, can be frighteningly redemptive.

King's philosophy appeals to the motivating influences of a **principled conscience**. Such a philosophy is forged upon the anvil of American popular culture and fashioned to generate active creative tension, not romantic quietism or slave-like passivity.[89] Despite its national origins, this philosophy, born of the American experience, speaks to oppressed peoples throughout the world and offers them a theoretical framework of action and a method of liberation. This constitutes King's lasting philosophical contribution to humanity, and especially to those suffering under the yoke of injustice. Pointing to the broader relevance and application of his efforts, King writes:

> The hard cold facts today indicate that the hope of the people of color in the world may rest on the American Negro and his ability to reform the structure of racist imperialism from within and thereby turn the technology and wealth of the West to the task of liberating the world from want.[90]

King's dream of a just society places the concept of **equality** front and center. It serves as the pre-eminent value for his logic of nonviolence. King does not get bogged down in semantics or in formal definitions of equality, refusing to engage in theoretical squabbles over the meaning of the term. In his estimation, such squabbles only serve to delay change and perpetuate an unacceptable status quo, one in which real people suffer indignities and cruel injustices on a daily basis.

"The fight is not just being able to keep breathing. The fight is actually to be able to walk down the street with your head held high—and feel like I belong here, or I deserve to be here, or I just have [a] right to have a level of dignity."
ALICIA GARZA

Analytical debates over precise definitions constitute a luxury afforded only to intellectuals and the privileged dominant classes. Such debates are largely pointless to the hungry, disadvantaged, and unemployed, and represent simply another method of postponing engagement with reality. To use an expression that is stinging to the ears of those occupying the ivory tower, debates over precise definitions are "purely academic" (meaning useless and irrelevant). With change as a priority, King thus accepts a conventional, common sense understanding of equality as his starting point.

With equality front and center, this notion assumes a privileged position once held by the concept of **freedom** in traditional discussions of political philosophy. By opting for equality over freedom, King relinquishes, in effect, an individualistic term in favor of a more *relational concept*. You can only be equal in relation to someone else, and that someone else can be equal, or not equal, only in relation to you and others. Rather than conceptualizing society in terms of free, autonomous, and rationally self-interested individuals who are constantly conflicting with one another in a situation of chaos and competing interests, King frames it in terms of a **community of harmonizing equals**.

The emphasis here is not on the protection of individual rights or on the adjudication of competing claims, but on cooperative effort and alliance building. Though King is very much in favor of the principle of equality, he is scathing in his attack on interpretations of it from many white Americans, which he holds to be self-serving and discriminatory in application. To illustrate his point, he directs our attention to the cultural experience of America. He claims that, historically speaking, there has been a grave contradiction between *creeds* and *deeds*.

While the high-sounding principles of the Declaration of Independence, for instance, provide worthy goals for social progress, their application clearly reflects a double standard. When Thomas Jefferson wrote that "all men are created equal," he found the expression handy as a revolutionary slogan against British colonialism. However, when the same expression posed an ethical, philosophical dilemma with respect to slavery, "equality got short shrift under the guise that blacks were not really 'men'," as King scholar Greg Moses puts it.[91] And let us not forget that Thomas Jefferson was himself a slave-owner.

Even though equality has not always been honored in practice, it is still a shared value legitimized by America's cultural heritage and one that King makes his foundational cornerstone. However, for King, liberal ideals of "equal opportunity and equal treatment of people according to their individual merits" are "old concepts" in need of re-evaluation.[92] Equality is also a term that does not confine itself to relations between races, but also extends to involve relations between those belonging to the so-classed dominant race. In other words, King's philosophy is not just for black people.

STRUCTURE

King examines the inequality prevalent in the United States in terms of **structure**. Building upon the notion of "**the color line**" borrowed from W.E.B. Du Bois, he argues that the "visibly invisible" barrier, which prevents black people from participating as full and equal members of society, can more properly be called the **structural evil of racism**. King recognizes the harsh fact of **racism** and that there are individual racists who would deny black people their equality; nonetheless, he does not seek out guilty parties or assign individual blame or culpability. The realities of racism go far beyond any single person. In King's words, the struggle for civil rights led black people to see the "deeper causes for the crudity and cruelty that governed white society's responses to their needs. They discovered that their plight was not a consequence of superficial prejudice but was systemic."[93]

Two other structural evils combine with racism to form an unholy trinity of injustice: **poverty** and **war**. As King said,

> Somehow these three evils are tied together. The triple evils of racism, economic exploitation, and militarism.... Oh my friends, it's good for us to fight for integrated lunch counters, and for integrated schools. And I'm going to continue to do that. But wouldn't it be absurd to be talking about integrated schools without being concerned about the survival of a world in which to be integrated.[94]

The link between racism and poverty is perhaps most apparent when one looks at the **structural inequalities** embedded in the US capitalist system. King argues that the economic foundation of America demands that some workers never rise from servitude. Underscoring King's point, Greg Moses states that "without menial labor, wealth has no platform to stand upon."[95] In support of his structural account, King writes the following:

> Depressed living standards for Negroes are not simply the consequence of neglect. Nor can they be explained by the myth of the Negro's innate capacities, or by the more sophisticated rationalization of his acquired infirmities (family disorganization, poor education, etc.). They are a structural part of the economic system in the United States. Certain industries and enterprises are based upon a supply of low-paid, underskilled and immobile nonwhite labor. Hand assembly factories, hospitals, service industries, housework, agricultural operations using itinerant labor would suffer economic trauma, if not disaster, with a rise in wage scales.[96]

In addition to suffering materially from the gulf created by the structural economic inequalities of capitalism, black Americans also experience a psychological torment that results from discrimination endemic to those inequalities. In 1968, King reported polls revealing that 88% of white Americans would object to their teenage child dating a black person, almost 80% would be troubled if a close friend or relative married a black person, and 50% would not want a black person as a neighbor.[97] Addressing the black person's pain stemming from systematic racism and discrimination, King wrote the following:

> I guess it is easy for those who have never felt the stinging darts of segregation to say, "Wait." But when you have seen vicious mobs lynch your mothers and fathers at will and drown your sisters and brothers at whim; when you have seen hate-filled

policeman curse, kick, brutalize and even kill your black brothers and sisters with impunity; when you see the vast majority of your twenty million Negro brothers smothering in an airtight cage of poverty in the midst of an affluent society; when you suddenly find your tongue twisted and your speech stammering as you seek to explain to your six-year-old daughter why she can't go to the public amusement park that has just been advertised on television, and see tears welling up in her little eyes when she is told that Funtown is closed to colored children, and see the depressing clouds of inferiority begin to form in her little mental sky, and see her begin to distort her little personality by unconsciously developing a bitterness toward white people; when you have to concoct an answer for a five-year-old son asking in agonizing pathos: "Daddy, why do white people treat colored people so mean?"; when you take a cross-country drive and find it necessary to sleep night after night in the uncomfortable corner of your automobile because no motel will accept you; when you are humiliated day in and day out by nagging signs reading "white" and "colored"; when your first name becomes "nigger" and your middle name becomes "boy" (however old you are) and your last name becomes "John," and when your wife and mother are never given the respected title "Mrs."; when you are harried by day and haunted by night by the fact that you are a Negro, living constantly at tiptoe stance never quite knowing what to expect next, and plagued with inner fears and outer resentments; when you are forever fighting a degenerating sense of "nobodiness"; then you will understand why we find it difficult to wait [for change and the end of discrimination].[98]

To eradicate structural inequalities, King asserts that a "revaluation of values" is required, one that has global implications and repercussions for militaristic engagement abroad. He states that "our loyalties must be ecumenical rather than sectional. This call for world-wide fellowship that lifts neighborly concern beyond one's tribe, race, class and nation is in reality a call for an all-embracing and unconditional love for all men."[99] What we should do is shift from an "arms race" to a "peace race."

Intellectual genius and material resources should be used for the purpose of making "peace and prosperity a reality for all the nations of the world."[100] This requires action, not merely a passive, morally complacent denunciation of war. It also necessitates that we become a "person-oriented" society rather than a "thing-oriented" society. As King states, "When machines and computers, profit motives and property rights are considered more important than people, the giant triplets of racism, materialism and militarism are incapable of being conquered."[101] A capitalist perspective sees markets to dominate, cheap labor in foreign lands to exploit, and international threats to American interests, which must be attacked. By contrast, writes King:

A true revolution of values will soon look uneasily on the glaring contrast of poverty and wealth. With righteous indignation, it will look at thousands of working people displaced from their jobs with reduced incomes as a result of automation while the profits of the employers remain intact, and say: "This is not just." It will look across the oceans and see individual capitalists of the West investing huge sums of money in Asia, Africa and South America, only to take the profits out with no concern for the social betterment of the countries, and say: "This is not just." It will look at our alliance with the landed gentry of Latin America and say: "This is not just." The Western arrogance of feeling that it has everything to teach others and nothing to learn from them is not just. A true revolution of values will lay hands on the world order and say of war: "This way of settling differences is not just." This business of burning human beings with napalm, of filling our nation's homes with orphans and widows, of injecting poisonous drugs of hate into the veins of peoples normally humane, of sending men home from dark and bloody battlefields physically handicapped and psychologically deranged, cannot be reconciled with wisdom, justice and love. A nation that continues year after year to spend more money on military defense than on programs of social uplift is approaching spiritual death.[102]

NONVIOLENT DIRECT ACTION

To rectify the injustices that are structurally embedded within capitalist liberal democracy, a program of **nonviolent direct action** is needed. King came out from behind the preacher's pulpit and down from the academic's ivory tower to bring justice to the streets of America with the long-range plan of helping to liberate oppressed peoples around the world. His protest demonstrations were carefully thought out and strategized in hopes of establishing true economic democracy, something he believed was being suppressed in the name of popular free-market ideologies.

King constructed his theory of action using principles suggested by the theologian and civil rights activist Howard Thurman (1899–1981), who served as his mentor and advisor. From Thurman, King accepted the principles of *truth-telling*, *love*, and *courage* which provided the ethical criteria of his philosophy of action. These same principles were used to order protests, demonstrations, boycotts, and other collective manifestations of will designed to transform corrupt structures of injustice.

Even under conditions of desperate struggle, then, the ends and means of justice were not to be separated. The connection to Gandhi could not be more evident here, given what Gandhi once said: "If we take care of the means, we are bound to reach the end sooner or later. When once we have grasped this point, final victory is beyond question."[103]

JUSTICE AND LOVE

Justice and **love** occupy an interesting place within King's logic of nonviolence. Traditionally, these two concepts have received separate treatments and have been recognized as more or less different from each another. For instance, I have often heard Christians, rightly or wrongly, contrast their faith with Judaism, suggesting that the "law of Moses" has been superseded by the "love of Jesus" and that a morality of love is to be preferred to the justice considerations embedded in legalistic Judaic morality.

In nonreligious contexts, others are quick to point out that the law cannot require that we "love" others, but that it can force us not to harm them by threat of legal sanction. In such examples, love and justice would seem to be different and unrelated. By contrast, King places justice and love in much closer and inextricably linked connection. In cases where conceptions of justice fail to meet the test of love, King offers criticism and reconstruction. All inquiries into justice are thus regulated by love.[104] This should be explained.

To begin with, there is a psychological, emotional connection between the two concepts. The general idea is that love awakens one's perceptions to injustices.[105] Without love, there remains a good chance of more bad-faith apologies and rationalizations of good intent. Love is necessary to invigorate the quest for equality.

King suggests that "true economic democracy" is suppressed by free-market ideologies. What precisely do you think is meant by this? Are any myths or half-truths associated with these ideologies? If so, what are they? Is the concept of the "American Dream" somehow related? Again, if so, explain.

If people do not "care" and callously look upon the suffering of others as disinterested observers, no real change to the status quo is possible. By means of nonviolent direct action, human suffering is presented as an extraordinary plea for compassion. Efforts are made to open the heart and awaken the spirit to the plight of others burdened by poverty and injustice.

The aim to minimize economic differences between social groups may sound laudable. However, as Greg Moses puts it, "we do not honor the principle of respect for all persons so long as we define justice in terms that would merely minimize social disparities. When love serves as the arbiter of justice, inequalities are not minimized—they are abolished. Thus, the principle of equality does not fall from the sky but rather proceeds directly from the heart."[106]

In order to awaken the spirit and open the heart, King uses methods of nonviolence to confront injustice. By refusing to use violent force, King does not believe he is giving up power. Rather, what he says is the following: "What is needed is a realization that power without love is reckless and abusive and that love without power is sentimental and anemic.... It is precisely this collision of *immoral power* with *powerless morality* which constitutes the major crisis of our times."[107]

"One's life has value so long as one attributes value to the life of others, by means of love, friendship, and compassion."
SIMONE DE BEAUVOIR

Not only does Martin Luther King Jr. offer a sublime message of hope, telling us that in the end love will conquer evil and injustice, but as we've seen he also provides a practical six-step means to ensure love's victory in the name of justice. As an interesting aside for those who still believe that a morality of love is little more than a sentimental rationalization for the weak (Nietzsche), or that the expression of power is an evil and sinful manifestation of human nature (religious moralists), King says the following:

One of the greatest problems of history is that the concepts of love and power are usually contrasted as polar opposites. Love is identified with a resignation of power and power with a denial of love. It was this misinterpretation that caused Nietzsche, the philosopher of the "will to power," to reject the Christian concept of love. It was this same misinterpretation which induced Christian theologians to reject Nietzsche's philosophy of the "will to power" in the name of the Christian idea of love. Power at its best is love implementing the demands of justice. Justice at its best is love correcting everything that stands against love.[108]

THINKING ABOUT YOUR THINKING

In this chapter, you have had the opportunity to examine a wide range of ideas belonging to the sub-discipline of political philosophy. Now that you have reached the end of this chapter—and book!—review those ideas in your thoughts before we end our explorations into the philosophical domain. What ideas did you find most interesting, shocking, or enlightening? What principles or concepts really caused you to stop and reflect on your current value system? Is there anything in particular that you found most enriching or disturbing? What and why?

Martin Luther King Jr., *Where Do We Go from Here?*[109]

Dr. Martin Luther King Jr. delivered this address at the Eleventh Annual Southern Leadership Conference in Atlanta, Georgia, on August 16, 1967. That same year, King published Where Do We Go from Here: Chaos or Community? *The question central to both works reflects King's thinking after more than a decade of public involvement in the human rights movement.*

Despite achievements in the form of political reforms, King anticipated the next decade would introduce new struggles for the movement, noting in his book that "The persistence of racism in depth and the dawning awareness that Negro demands will necessitate structural changes in society have generated a new phase of white resistance."[110] In the words of one scholar, King "had become increasingly aware that economic inequality and injustice would prove harder to combat than formal segregation and discrimination."[111] In the Foreword to Where Do We Go from Here?, *King's wife, Coretta Scott King, writes these optimistic words of hope: "The solutions that he [King] offered can still save our society from self-destruction."[112]*

In this reading, the parenthetical words indicate the audience's responses during King's presentation of the speech.

———

Now, in order to answer the question, "Where do we go from here?" which is our theme, we must first honestly recognize where we are now. When the Constitution was written, a strange formula to determine taxes and representation declared that the Negro was sixty percent of a person. Today another curious formula seems to declare he is fifty percent of a person. Of the good things in life, the Negro has approximately one half those of whites. Of the bad things of life, he has twice those of whites. Thus, half of all Negroes live in substandard housing. And Negroes have half the income of whites. When we turn to the negative experiences of life, the Negro has a double share: There are twice as many unemployed; the rate of infant mortality among Negroes is double that of whites; and there are twice as many Negroes dying in Vietnam as whites in proportion to their size in the population. (*Yes*) [*applause*]

In other spheres, the figures are equally alarming. In elementary schools, Negroes lag one to three years behind whites, and their segregated schools (*Yeah*) receive substantially less money per student than the white schools. (*Those schools*) One-twentieth as many Negroes as whites attend college. Of employed Negroes, seventy-five percent hold menial jobs. This is where we are.

Where do we go from here? First, we must massively assert our dignity and worth. We must stand up amid a system that still oppresses us and develop an unassailable and majestic sense of values. We must no longer be ashamed of being black. (*All right*) The job of arousing manhood within a people that have been taught for so many centuries that they are nobody is not easy.

Even semantics have conspired to make that which is black seem ugly and degrading. (*Yes*) In Roget's *Thesaurus* there are some 120 synonyms for blackness and at least sixty of them are offensive, such words as blot, soot, grim, devil, and foul. And there are some 134 synonyms for whiteness and all are favorable, expressed in such words as purity, cleanliness, chastity, and innocence. A white lie is better than a black lie. (*Yes*) The most degenerate member of a family is the "black sheep." (*Yes*) Ossie Davis has suggested that maybe the English language should be reconstructed so that teachers will not be forced to teach the Negro child sixty ways to despise himself, and thereby perpetuate his false sense of inferiority, and the white child 134 ways to adore himself, and thereby perpetuate his false sense of superiority. [*applause*] The tendency to ignore the Negro's contribution to American life and strip him of his personhood is as old as the earliest history books and as contemporary as the morning's newspaper. (*Yes*)

To offset this cultural homicide, the Negro must rise up with an affirmation of his own Olympian manhood. (*Yes*) Any movement for the Negro's freedom that overlooks this necessity is only waiting to be buried. (*Yes*) As long as the mind is enslaved, the body can never be free. (*Yes*) Psychological freedom, a firm sense of self-esteem, is the most powerful weapon against the long night of physical slavery. No Lincolnian Emancipation Proclamation, no Johnsonian civil rights bill can totally bring this kind of freedom. The Negro will only be free when he reaches down to the inner depths of his own being and signs with the pen and ink of assertive manhood his own emancipation proclamation. And with a spirit straining toward true self-esteem, the Negro must boldly throw off the manacles of self-abnegation and say to himself and to the world, "I am somebody. (*Oh yeah*) I am a person. I am a man with dignity and honor. (*Go ahead*) I have a rich and noble history, however painful and exploited that history has been. Yes, I was a slave through my foreparents (*That's right*), and now I'm not ashamed of that. I'm ashamed of the people who were so sinful to make me a slave." (*Yes sir*) Yes [*applause*], yes, we must stand up and say, "I'm black (*Yes sir*), but I'm black and beautiful." (*Yes*) This [*applause*], this self-affirmation is the black man's need, made compelling (*All right*) by the white man's crimes against him. (*Yes*)

Now another basic challenge is to discover how to organize our strength into economic and political power. Now no one can deny that the Negro is in dire need of this kind of legitimate power. Indeed, one of the great problems that the Negro confronts is his lack of power. From the old plantations of the South to the newer ghettos of the North, the Negro has been confined to a life of voicelessness (*That's true*) and powerlessness. (*So true*) Stripped of the right to make decisions concerning his life and destiny, he has been subject to the authoritarian and sometimes whimsical decisions of the white power structure. The plantation and the ghetto were created by those who had power, both to confine those who had no power and to perpetuate their powerlessness. Now the problem of transforming the ghetto, therefore, is a problem of power, a confrontation between the forces of power demanding change and the forces of power dedicated to the preserving of the status quo. Now, power properly understood is nothing but the ability to achieve purpose. It is the strength required to bring about social, political, and economic change. Walter Reuther defined power one day. He said, "Power is the ability of a labor union like [the] UAW [United Auto Workers] to make the most powerful corporation in the world, General Motors, say, 'Yes' when it wants to say 'No.' That's power." [*applause*]

Now a lot of us are preachers, and all of us have our moral convictions and concerns, and so often we have problems with power. But there is nothing wrong with power if power is used correctly.

You see, what happened is that some of our philosophers got off base. And one of the great problems of history is that the concepts of love and power have usually been contrasted as opposites, polar opposites, so that love is identified with a resignation of power, and power with a denial of love. It was this misinterpretation that caused the philosopher Nietzsche, who was a philosopher of the will to power, to reject the Christian concept of love. It was this same misinterpretation which induced Christian theologians to reject Nietzsche's philosophy of the will to power in the name of the Christian idea of love.

Now, we got to get this thing right. What is needed is a realization that power without love is reckless and abusive, and that love without power is sentimental and anemic. (*Yes*) Power at its best [*applause*], power at its best is love (*Yes*) implementing the demands of justice, and justice at its best is love correcting everything that stands against love. (*Speak*) And this is what we must see as we move on.

Now what has happened is that we've had it wrong and mixed up in our country, and this has led Negro Americans in the past to seek their goals through love and moral suasion devoid of power, and white Americans to seek their goals through power devoid of love and conscience. It is leading a few extremists today to advocate for Negroes the same destructive and conscienceless power that they have justly abhorred in whites. It is precisely this collision of immoral power with powerless morality which constitutes the major crisis of our times. (*Yes*)

Now we must develop progress, or rather, a program—and I can't stay on this long—that will drive the nation to a guaranteed annual income. Now, early in the century this proposal would have been greeted with ridicule and denunciation as destructive of initiative and responsibility. At that time economic status was considered the measure of the individual's abilities and talents. And in the thinking of that day, the absence of worldly goods indicated a want of industrious habits and moral fiber. We've come a long way in our understanding of human motivation and of the blind operation of our economic system. Now we realize that dislocations in the market operation of our economy and the prevalence of discrimination thrust people into idleness and bind them in constant or frequent unemployment against their will. The poor are less often dismissed, I hope, from our conscience today by being branded as inferior and incompetent. We also know that no matter how dynamically the economy develops and expands, it does not eliminate all poverty.

The problem indicates that our emphasis must be twofold: We must create full employment, or we must create incomes. People must be made consumers by one method or the other. Once they are placed in this position, we need to be concerned that the potential of the individual is not wasted. New forms of work that enhance the social good will have to be devised for those for whom traditional jobs are not available. In 1879 Henry George anticipated this state of affairs when he wrote in *Progress and Poverty*:

> The fact is that the work which improves the condition of mankind, the work which extends knowledge and increases power and enriches literature and elevates thought, is not done to secure a living. It is not the work of slaves driven to their tasks either by ... a taskmaster or by animal necessities. It is the work of men who somehow find a form of work that brings a security for its own sake and a state of society where want is abolished.

Work of this sort could be enormously increased, and we are likely to find that the problem of housing, education, instead of preceding the elimination of poverty, will themselves be affected if poverty is first abolished. The poor, transformed into purchasers will do a great deal on their own to alter housing decay. Negroes, who have a double disability, will have a greater effect on discrimination when they have the additional weapon of cash to use in their struggle.

Beyond these advantages, a host of positive psychological changes inevitably will result from widespread economic security. The dignity of the individual will flourish when the decisions concerning his life are in his own hands, when he has the assurance that his income is stable and certain, and when he knows that he has the means to seek self-improvement. Personal conflicts between husband, wife, and children will diminish when the unjust measurement of human worth on a scale of dollars is eliminated.

Now, our country can do this. John Kenneth Galbraith said that a guaranteed annual income could be done for about twenty billion dollars a year. And I say to you today, that if our nation can spend thirty-five billion dollars a year to fight an unjust, evil war in Vietnam, and twenty billion dollars to put a man on the moon, it can spend billions of dollars to put God's children on their own two feet right here on earth. [*applause*]

Now, let me rush on to say we must reaffirm our commitment to nonviolence. And I want to stress this. The futility of violence in the struggle for racial justice has been tragically etched in all the recent Negro riots. Now, yesterday, I tried to analyze the riots and deal with the causes for them. Today I want to give the other side. There is something painfully sad about a riot. One sees screaming youngsters and angry adults fighting hopelessly and aimlessly against impossible odds. (*Yeah*) And deep down within them, you perceive a desire for self-destruction, a kind of suicidal longing. (*Yes*)

Occasionally, Negroes contend that the 1965 Watts riot [in Los Angeles] and the other riots in various cities represented effective civil rights action. But those who express this view always end up with stumbling words when asked what concrete gains have been won as a result. At best, the riots have produced a little additional anti-poverty money allotted by frightened government officials and a few water sprinklers to cool the children of the ghettos. It is something like improving the food in the prison while the people remain securely incarcerated behind bars. (*That's right*) Nowhere have the riots won any concrete improvement such as have the organized protest demonstrations.

And when one tries to pin down advocates of violence as to what acts would be effective, the answers are blatantly illogical. Sometimes they talk of overthrowing racist state and local governments and they talk about guerrilla warfare. They fail to see that no internal revolution has ever succeeded in overthrowing a government by violence unless the government had already lost the allegiance and effective control of its armed forces. Anyone in his right mind knows that this will not happen in the United States. In a violent racial situation, the power structure has the local police, the state troopers, the National Guard, and finally, the army to call on, all of which are predominantly white. (*Yes*) Furthermore, few, if any, violent revolutions have been successful unless the violent minority had the sympathy and support of the non-resisting majority. Castro may have had only a few Cubans actually fighting with him and up in the hills (*Yes*), but he would have never overthrown the Batista regime unless he had had the sympathy of the vast majority of Cuban people. It is perfectly clear that a violent revolution on the part of American black would find no sympathy and support from the white population and very little from the majority of the Negroes themselves.

This is no time for romantic illusions and empty philosophical debates about freedom. This is a time for action. (*All right*) What is needed is a strategy for change, a tactical program that will bring the Negro into the mainstream of American life as quickly as possible. So far, this has only been offered by the nonviolent movement. Without recognizing this we will end up with solutions that don't solve, answers that don't answer, and explanations that don't explain. [*applause*]

And so I say to you today that I still stand by nonviolence. (*Yes*) And I am still convinced [*applause*], and I'm still convinced that it is the most potent weapon available to the Negro in his struggle for justice in this country.

And the other thing is, I'm concerned about a better world. I'm concerned about justice; I'm concerned about brotherhood; I'm concerned about truth. (*That's right*) And when one is concerned about that, he can never advocate violence. For through violence you may murder a murderer, but you can't murder murder. (*Yes*) Through violence you may murder a liar, but you can't establish truth. (*That's right*) Through violence you may murder a hater, but you can't murder hate through violence. (*All right, That's right*) Darkness cannot put out darkness; only light can do that. [*applause*]

And I say to you, I have also decided to stick with love, for I know that love is ultimately the only answer to mankind's problems. (*Yes*) And I'm going to talk about it everywhere I go. I know it isn't popular to talk about it in some circles today. (*No*) And I'm not talking about emotional bosh when I talk about love; I'm talking about a strong, demanding love. (*Yes*) For I have seen too much hate. (*Yes*) I've seen too much hate on the faces of sheriffs in the South. (*Yeah*) I've seen hate on the faces of too many Klansmen and too many White Citizens' Councilors in the South to want to hate, myself, because every time I see it, I know that it does something to their faces and their personalities, and I say to myself that hate is too great a burden to bear. (*Yes, That's right*) I have decided to love. [*applause*] If you are seeking the highest good, I think you can find it through love. And the beautiful thing is that we aren't moving wrong when we do it, because John was right, God is love. (*Yes*) He who hates does not know God, but he who loves has the key that unlocks the door to the meaning of ultimate reality.

And so I say to you today, my friends, that you may be able to speak with the tongues of men and angels (*All right*); you may have the eloquence of articulate speech; but if you have not love, it means nothing. (*That's right*) Yes, you may have the gift of prophecy; you may have the gift of scientific prediction (*Yes sir*) and understand the behavior of molecules (*All right*); you may break into the storehouse of nature (*Yes sir*) and bring forth many new insights; yes, you may ascend to the heights of academic achievement (*Yes sir*) so that you have all knowledge (*Yes sir, Yes*); and you may boast of your great institutions of learning and the boundless extent of your degrees; but if you have not love, all of these mean absolutely nothing. (*Yes*) You may even give your goods to feed the poor (*Yes sir*); you may bestow great gifts to charity (*Speak*); and you may tower high in philanthropy; but if you have not love, your charity means nothing. (*Yes sir*) You may even give your body to be burned and die the death of a martyr, and your spilt blood may be a symbol of honor for generations yet unborn, and thousands may praise you as one of history's greatest heroes; but if you have not love (*Yes, All right*), your blood was spilt in vain. What I'm trying to get you to see this morning is that a man may be self-centered in his self-denial and self-righteous in his self-sacrifice. His generosity may feed his ego, and his piety may feed his pride. (*Speak*) So without love, benevolence becomes egotism, and martyrdom becomes spiritual pride.

I want to say to you as I move to my conclusion, as we talk about "Where do we go from here?" that we must honestly face the fact that the movement must address itself to the question of restructuring the whole of American society. (*Yes*) There are forty million poor people here, and one day we must ask the question, "Why are there forty million poor people in America?" And when you begin to ask that question, you are raising a question about the economic system, about a broader distribution of wealth. When you ask that question, you begin to question the capitalistic economy. (*Yes*) And I'm simply saying that more and more, we've got to begin to ask questions about the whole society. We are called upon to help the discouraged beggars in life's marketplace. (*Yes*) But one day we must come to see that an edifice which produces beggars needs restructuring. (*All right*) It means that questions must be raised. And you see, my friends, when you deal with this you begin to ask the question, "Who owns the oil?" (*Yes*) You begin to ask the question, "Who owns the iron ore?" (*Yes*) You begin to ask the question, "Why is it that people have to pay water bills in a world that's two-thirds water?" (*All right*) These are words that must be said. (*All right*)

Now, don't think you have me in a bind today. I'm not talking about communism. What I'm talking about is far beyond communism. (*Yeah*) My inspiration didn't come from Karl Marx (*Speak*); my inspiration didn't come from Engels; my inspiration didn't come from Trotsky; my inspiration didn't come from Lenin. Yes, I read *Communist Manifesto* and *Das Kapital* a long time ago (*Well*), and I saw that maybe Marx didn't follow Hegel enough. (*All right*) He took his dialectics, but he left out his idealism and his spiritualism. And he went over to a German philosopher by the name of Feuerbach, and took his materialism and made it into a system that he called "dialectical materialism." (*Speak*) I have to reject that.

What I'm saying to you this morning is communism forgets that life is individual. (*Yes*) Capitalism forgets that life is social. (*Yes, Go ahead*) And the kingdom of brotherhood is found neither in the thesis of communism nor the antithesis of capitalism, but in a higher synthesis. (*Speak*) [*applause*] It is found in a higher synthesis (*Come on*) that combines the truths of both. (*Yes*) Now, when I say questioning the whole society, it means ultimately coming to see that the problem of racism, the problem of economic exploitation, and the problem of war are all tied together. (*All right*) These are the triple evils that are interrelated.

And if you will let me be a preacher just a little bit. (*Speak*) One day [*applause*], one night, a juror came to Jesus (*Yes sir*) and he wanted to know what he could do to be saved. (*Yeah*) Jesus didn't get bogged down on the kind of isolated approach of what you shouldn't do. Jesus didn't say, "Now Nicodemus, you must stop lying." (*Oh yeah*) He didn't say, "Nicodemus, now you must not commit adultery." He didn't say, "Now Nicodemus, you must stop cheating if you are doing that." He didn't say, "Nicodemus, you must stop drinking liquor if you are doing that excessively." He said something altogether different, because Jesus realized something basic (*Yes*): that if a man will lie, he will steal. (*Yes*) And if a man will steal, he will kill. (*Yes*) So instead of just getting bogged down on one thing, Jesus looked at him and said, "Nicodemus, you must be born again." [*applause*]

In other words, "Your whole structure (*Yes*) must be changed." [*applause*] A nation that will keep people in slavery for 244 years will "thingify" them and make them things. (*Speak*) And therefore, they will exploit them and poor people generally economically. (*Yes*) And a nation that will exploit economically will have to have foreign investments and everything else, and it will have to use its military might to protect them. All of these problems are tied together. (*Yes*) [*applause*]

What I'm saying today is that we must go from this convention and say, "America, you must be born again!" [*applause*] (*Oh yes*)

And so, I conclude by saying today that we have a task, and let us go out with a divine dissatisfaction. (*Yes*)

Let us be dissatisfied until America will no longer have a high blood pressure of creeds and an anemia of deeds. (*All right*)

Let us be dissatisfied (*Yes*) until the tragic walls that separate the outer city of wealth and comfort from the inner city of poverty and despair shall be crushed by the battering rams of the forces of justice. (*Yes sir*)

Let us be dissatisfied (*Yes*) until those who live on the outskirts of hope are brought into the metropolis of daily security.

Let us be dissatisfied (*Yes*) until slums are cast into the junk heaps of history (*Yes*), and every family will live in a decent, sanitary home.

Let us be dissatisfied (*Yes*) until the dark yesterdays of segregated schools will be transformed into bright tomorrows of quality integrated education.

Let us be dissatisfied until integration is not seen as a problem but as an opportunity to participate in the beauty of diversity.

Let us be dissatisfied (*All right*) until men and women, however black they may be, will be judged on the basis of the content of their character, not on the basis of the color of their skin. (*Yeah*) Let us be dissatisfied. [*applause*]

Let us be dissatisfied (*Well*) until every state capitol (*Yes*) will be housed by a governor who will do justly, who will love mercy, and who will walk humbly with his God.

Let us be dissatisfied [*applause*] until from every city hall, justice will roll down like waters, and righteousness like a mighty stream. (*Yes*)

Let us be dissatisfied (*Yes*) until that day when the lion and the lamb shall lie down together (*Yes*), and every man will sit under his own vine and fig tree, and none shall be afraid.

Let us be dissatisfied (*Yes*), and men will recognize that out of one blood (*Yes*) God made all men to dwell upon the face of the earth. (*Speak sir*)

Let us be dissatisfied until that day when nobody will shout, "White Power!" when nobody will shout, "Black Power!" but everybody will talk about God's power and human power. [*applause*]

And I must confess, my friends (*Yes sir*), that the road ahead will not always be smooth. (*Yes*) There will still be rocky places of frustration (*Yes*) and meandering points of bewilderment. There will be inevitable setbacks here and there. (*Yes*) And there will be those moments when the buoyancy of hope will be transformed into the fatigue of despair. (*Well*) Our dreams will sometimes be shattered and our ethereal hopes blasted. (*Yes*) We may again, with tear-drenched eyes, have to stand before the bier [coffin] of some courageous civil rights worker whose life will be snuffed out by the dastardly acts of bloodthirsty mobs. (*Well*) But difficult and painful as it is (*Well*), we must walk on in the days ahead with an audacious faith in the future. (*Well*) And as we continue our charted course, we may gain consolation from the words so nobly left by that great black bard, who was also a great freedom fighter of yesterday, James Weldon Johnson (*Yes*):

> Stony the road we trod (*Yes*),
> Bitter the chastening rod
> Felt in the days
> When hope unborn had died. (*Yes*)

Yet with a steady beat,
Have not our weary feet
Come to the place
For which our fathers sighed?
We have come over a way
That with tears has been watered. (*Well*)
We have come treading our paths
Through the blood of the slaughtered.
Out from the gloomy past,
Till now we stand at last (*Yes*)
Where the bright gleam
Of our bright star is cast.

Let this affirmation be our ringing cry. (*Well*) It will give us the courage to face the uncertainties of the future. It will give our tired feet new strength as we continue our forward stride toward the city of freedom. (*Yes*) When our days become dreary with low-hovering clouds of despair (*Well*), and when our nights become darker than a thousand midnights (*Well*), let us remember (*Yes*) that there is a creative force in this universe working to pull down the gigantic mountains of evil (*Well*), a power that is able to make a way out of no way (*Yes*) and transform dark yesterdays into bright tomorrows. (*Speak*)

Let us realize that the arc of the moral universe is long, but it bends toward justice. Let us realize that William Cullen Bryant is right: "Truth, crushed to earth, will rise again." Let us go out realizing that the Bible is right: "Be not deceived. God is not mocked. (*Oh yeah*) Whatsoever a man soweth (*Yes*), that (*Yes*) shall he also reap." This is our hope for the future, and with this faith we will be able to sing in some not too distant tomorrow, with a cosmic past tense, "We have overcome! (*Yes*) We have overcome! Deep in my heart, I *did* believe (*Yes*) we would overcome." [*applause*]

READING QUESTIONS

1. Use content from King's speech to explain why and how words contribute to the systemically oppressive challenges that black people face. Relatedly, can you think of an example of a sport team name or mascot or, similarly, a product name or image that should be changed according to King's reasoning? What would that argument for change be? Construct the argument and consider why someone might reject the argument. Which position has better reasons in favor of it? Why?

2. What is King's economic program for racial justice? Describe the details of it. Following that description, explain what kinds of positive results King predicts will result from the program he recommends. List and explain three of his predicted results in particular. Are his predictions compelling reasons in favor of the program? Is affordability for the government a case against it? Why or why not?

3. According to King, what success have riots had at bringing about racial justice? If riots are to be effective in the civil rights movement, then, King claims, certain conditions must be in place. What are those conditions? Were those conditions in place in the United States when King delivered this address in 1967? Are they in place today?

4. Consider King's statement, "Darkness cannot put out darkness. Only light can do that." Do you agree with this? What does it mean, in practice?

INSTRUCTIONS: Fill in the blanks with the appropriate responses listed below. (Answers at back of book.)

polis	logic of nonviolence	epochs of history	God
altruism	divisions	politics	Cold War
Leviathan	war	idolatry	rights
tyranny	axiology	alienation	Hegel
labor	nonviolent direct action	philosopher rulers	violence
Gandhi	inconveniences	imperialist racism	division of labor
class conflicts	love	John Locke	fiduciary role
consent	commonwealth	property	women
aristocracy	objective morality	artisans	

1. Political philosophy is not the same thing as _____ or political science.

2. Political philosophy, as a subdiscipline of philosophy, is often classified as a branch of _____ (the study of values).

3. For Plato, the ideal society was a form of _____.

4. The Greek term for city-state is _____.

5. Those responsible in Plato's Republic for looking after the material needs of society are called the _____.

6. In Plato's Republic, those ultimately responsible for the state's governance are called the _____.

7. According to Plato, the worst form of government is the _____.

8. _____ are treated as equals in the philosopher ruler and auxiliary classes.

9. According to Thomas Hobbes, _____ is not natural to human beings.

10. Hobbes argues that during the time human beings are without the sovereign authority of government in the state of nature, they are in a condition of _____.

11. In the state of nature, there is no _____.

12. The social contract, for Hobbes, requires that we deny our _____ to ourselves on the condition that others also do so, giving power to governmental authority.

13. Hobbes calls the coercive power that forces individuals to live by the social contract the _____.

14. The unity of persons in one governing body is called a _____.

15. The philosophy of _____ was to exert a great influence on Thomas Jefferson and the writing of the Declaration of Independence.

16. According to Locke, the architect of the natural law is _____.

17. Of all the rights embedded in the natural law, Locke attributes most importance to _____ rights.

18. What makes something "mine" when, at first, it belonged to everyone in principle is that my _____ mixes with it.

19. For Locke, some sort of government is necessary to avoid any _____ arising from individual transgressions of others when it comes to exercising power and punishing misdemeanors.

20. Locke does not give government supreme authority, but rather a _____.

21. Locke's social compact uses ⬚⬚⬚⬚⬚⬚⬚ as its rational foundation.

22. By allowing for certain ⬚⬚⬚⬚⬚⬚⬚ of power within government, Locke builds checks and balances into his system.

23. What can make an objective reading of Karl Marx difficult is a ⬚⬚⬚⬚⬚⬚⬚ hysteria hangover, and people continuing to confuse Marxist theory with military dictatorships claiming to be communist.

24. Marx's theory of historical social development is based on the notion of dialectic formulated by ⬚⬚⬚⬚⬚⬚⬚.

25. Apart from the ideal of the communist state, societies are characterized by their internal ⬚⬚⬚⬚⬚⬚⬚, according to Marx.

26. According to Marx, there are basically five ⬚⬚⬚⬚⬚⬚⬚.

27. In Marx's view, ⬚⬚⬚⬚⬚⬚⬚ is a byproduct of the capitalist mode of production.

28. When lifeless creations of man's labor are endowed with power and made objects of reverence and awe, ⬚⬚⬚⬚⬚⬚⬚ results, Marx argues.

29. For Marx, ⬚⬚⬚⬚⬚⬚⬚ within the capitalist mode of production is a major contributor to alienation.

30. Marx and ⬚⬚⬚⬚⬚⬚⬚ were significant influences on the philosophical thinking of Martin Luther King Jr.

31. Martin Luther King Jr.'s action-oriented philosophy is based on a ⬚⬚⬚⬚⬚⬚⬚.

32. King does not consider using ⬚⬚⬚⬚⬚⬚⬚ as a show of strength.

33. All of Martin Luther King Jr.'s speeches, writings, and activist endeavors were designed to terminate ⬚⬚⬚⬚⬚⬚⬚ from within.

34. To rectify social injustice stemming from poverty, racism, and militarism, King advocated a six-step program of ⬚⬚⬚⬚⬚⬚⬚.

35. For King, all inquiries into justice must be regulated by ⬚⬚⬚⬚⬚⬚⬚.

Key Terms

axiology: that division of philosophical inquiry dealing with matters of value   437

political philosophy: comprises theories or studies concerning basic questions about the state, government, politics, liberty, justice and the proper enforcement of legal codes by authoritative bodies   436

political science: study of the forms and functions of power systems   437

politics: that which deals with governance, power, and elections   436

Plato's *Republic*

aristocracy: for Plato, rule by the best   439

artisans (business class): merchants, shopkeepers, farm producers; driven primarily by appetite   442

auxiliaries: professional soldier class, police, and lower-level administrators functioning under the guidance of the philosopher rulers   443

city-state (*polis*): ancient Greek city that functioned more or less like an autonomous country (e.g., Athens, Sparta)   440

courage: distinguishing virtue of auxiliaries   443

democracy: anarchic form of society; equality and few restraints   445

division of labor: the separation of a work process into a number of tasks, with each task performed by a separate person or group of persons   441

eugenics: process by which people are selectively mated for the purpose of propagating specific, desirable hereditary traits   447

feminist: someone who advocates political, economic, and social equality between the sexes   446

guardian class: comprised of auxiliaries and philosopher kings/rulers   443

imperfect societies: societies that deviate from Plato's utopian aristocracy   445

individualism: the idea that personal autonomy should be favored over collectivism and state control   440

justice: virtue of the just state wherein everyone attends to his or her delegated function without interfering with the functions of others   444

meritocracy: a system wherein those with demonstrated knowledge, skills, or ability are put in positions of power and authority; positions of power must be earned   447

oligarchic state: the wealthy are in control   445

philosopher rulers: belong to guardian class; ultimately charged with the authority and control over the city-state   443, 444

Plato: Greek philosopher and founder of the Academy; student of Socrates and teacher of Aristotle   439

self-discipline: a primary virtue displayed by artisans   443

soul: the central part of a human (or, by extension, a society), determining its behavior, its essence, and its function   440

spirit: (for Plato) in an individual soul, the "part" which brings the thoughts of the rational "part" to action; in the state, by analogy, that which is to serve as the primary motivating force for auxiliaries   443

timocracy: military aristocracy   445

tyrannical society: oppressive use of power; use of violence against opposition   445

Thomas Hobbes and John Locke's Social Contract Theory

American Constitution: the supreme law of the United States of America   463

commonwealth: constitutes a multitude of citizens united in one person or governing body   460

consent: permission or give permission; agree to   468

Declaration of Independence: a statement by a nation's people asserting their right to choose their own government   463

egoistic rule of prudence: the selfish golden-rule; self-denial out of longer-term self-interest   458

executive: that which has the power to punish; appointed by individuals governed   467

fiduciary role: functioning in service of others and responsible for protecting their interests   468

God: creator and Supreme Being   464

individualism: an ideology that focuses on the rights of the individual   468

John Locke: Seventeenth-century British philosopher best known for his empiricist epistemology and metaphysics, as well as his defenses of liberty and property rights   463

law of nature: a kind of duty emanating from egoistic prudence; a condition of rational self-preservation   457

Leviathan: all powerful sovereign envisioned in Hobbes's commonwealth   458

majority rule: decisions for and against are made on the basis of the fact that most people want or do not want something   469

natural equality: the notion that humans are born equal by nature   454

natural law: "the workmanship of one omnipotent and infinitely wise Maker"—namely, God   464

natural rights: human rights independent of any state or legislation   464

political society: social organization with impartial and disinterested judges able to mete out punishments   467

prerogative power: special power given to the 'executive' (branch of government) when the legislative (branch) is not in session   470

property rights: a natural right to preserve lives, liberties, and estates   465

right of nature: the freedom to use our power in any way we wish for the purposes of self-preservation   457

right of self-preservation: a right to those things necessary to preserve life   466

Second Treatise of Government: one of John Locke's writings   463

social compact: notion that free and equal individuals consent to be subjected to political power   468

social contract: that which stipulates what is ultimately required by the laws of nature directing us toward peaceful coexistence   459

social contract theory: a conception of society where individuals form an agreement, either explicitly or implicitly, to live by certain commonly accepted rules and principles   453

state of nature (Hobbes): the primal condition, pre-societal, for humans; according to Hobbes, a situation of conflict or war, competition and distrust, in which every person is against every other person; a primal condition of competition and distrust   454

state of nature (Locke): for Locke, a condition whereby humans have freedom and reason teaching humankind that no individual has the right to harm another   464

tacit consent: giving permission indirectly or in an unspoken fashion, without direct or official formal means   469

Thomas Hobbes: British philosopher who defended a social contract theory of society   453

Karl Marx's Socialism

absolute idealism: philosophy which holds that the real is rational and the rational is real   478

Absolute Mind: also translated as 'Absolute Spirit'; truth as viewed by an undistorted rational mind; the state in which mind rises above all natural and institutional limitations   478

alienation: a feeling of separation, difference, or estrangement; produced by capitalist modes of production   482

bourgeois: capitalists; speculators and those owning the modes of production   481

capitalism: a higher synthesis of slave and feudal economies; this new synthesis produces conflict between the bourgeois and proletariat   481

class conflict: produces historical change; economic classes opposing each other (e.g., those who own the means of production versus those who don't)   479

communism: the final synthesis of historical development   481

dehumanization of capitalism: the psychological effect of a capitalistic mode of production; the retreat to animal functions; the state whereby animal becomes human and human becomes animal; alienation's retreat to the aesthetic mode of existence   488

dialectical materialism: sometimes called historical materialism; a materialist conception of history; the idea that human societies and their cultural institutions are the outgrowth of collective economic activity involving conflicts between opposing forces   479

dialectical process: elements include thesis, antithesis, and synthesis; a process of change in which opposite and conflicting ideas or forces (i.e., thesis vs. antithesis) create an outcome representing a new synthesis   478

division of labor: for Marx, a contributing factor to alienation; separation and division of work into smaller parts; process by which work becomes gradually more meaningless and the worker becomes more alienated from the products of their labor   486

epochs of history: historical periods reflecting different types of class conflicts (e.g., freeman versus slave, lord versus serf); different times having structurally different modes of economic production   480

fetishism of commodities: present when lifeless material things are endowed with power over the living subjects who should be their master   485

Georg Wilhelm Friedrich Hegel: Eighteenth-nineteenth-century German philosopher central to the movement known as "German Idealism"   478

handicraft: work that puts the working individual in charge of tools (the mode of production)   487

idolatry: the worship of idols   485

Karl Marx: nineteenth-century German philosopher, economist, and social reformer   474

manufacture: making articles from raw material   487

proletariat: the class of working people who do not own the modes of production; the class exploited by bourgeois capitalists.   481

surplus value: the profit used for further investment that comes from the difference between workers' wages and the worth or value of the products sold   487

Martin Luther King Jr.'s Philosophy of Nonviolence

color-line: visibly invisible barrier contributing to prejudice and discrimination   500

community of harmonizing equals: alternative to viewing society as a collection of mutually disinterested individuals often in conflict with each other over scarce resources   499

equality: pre-eminent value for King's logic of nonviolence; the state of being equal in terms of rights and opportunities; defined in relational, not individualistic, terms   499

ethic of love: incorporates an understanding of justice; aims at a revolution of conscience; a liberation from fear, anger, and hatred   496

freedom: lack of pressure, restraint, or sanction with respect to thought, word, or deed   499

justice: for King, related to love; deals with rights and equality   502

love: for King, love is a moral imperative that is closely related to justice   502

Martin Luther King Jr.: American minister, activist, and philosopher, whose methods of nonviolent resistance were central to the civil rights movement of the 1950s and 1960s   492

mass action: groups of people gathering to further a cause or to make a point in a public fashion   493

nonviolent direct action: needed to rectify structural inequalities in capitalistic liberal democracy; political action without resorting to violence   502

poverty: a condition of extreme lack of resources and money   500

power: strength or force; can be described as ideological, economic, or political   498

principled conscience: a motivating influence generating creative tension for change   498

racism: expressed as prejudice or discrimination against a person or persons on the basis of

their membership in a particular racial or ethnic group, usually one that is a minority or somehow marginalized   500

structural evil of racism: the "visibly invisible" barrier which prevents black people and other members of racial minorities from participating as full and equal members of society   500

structural inequalities: imbedded in US capitalist system; systemic requirement that some groups be placed in servitude to those who benefit by the system   500

structure: the social elements of society that extend beyond the individual, and which may give rise to structural inequality and structural racism   500

structure of racist imperialism: an organization comprising a combination of racism, poverty, and war; the subjugation of one people by another using 'race' as a basis for that subjugation   493

war: armed conflict between nations or between groups   500

Summary of Major Points

1. What is the nature of political philosophy?
▸ Different from politics and political science
▸ A part of axiology
▸ Overlaps with moral philosophy
▸ Divisible into classical and modern theories
▸ Political philosophers concerned with matters of justice, individual rights, freedom, state authority, political power, etc.

2. What are some classic and modern perspectives on political philosophy?
▸ Plato's Republic
▸ Hobbes's Leviathan
▸ Locke's Social Compact
▸ Karl Marx's Communist Utopia
▸ Martin Luther King Jr.'s Philosophy of Nonviolence

3. How does Plato conceptualize society?
▸ As a hierarchical class system
▸ Philosopher rulers govern (gold class)
▸ Auxiliaries execute and administer (silver class)
▸ Artisans produce and deliver materially (bronze class)
▸ Ideal society operates in harmonious balance

4. How, according to Plato, are societies corrupted?
▸ Through social imbalance
▸ Those who should follow lead and vice versa
▸ Passions and appetites are allowed to dominate
▸ The unwise assume control and people cease to perform their proper function
▸ Conflicts arise between rich and poor
▸ Disrespect for authority emerges

5. How were women treated in ancient Greece?
▸ Plato allowed women full equality in the guardian classes.
▸ Artisan women probably occupied traditional domestic roles.

6. How does Hobbes view human nature?
▸ People are equal by nature with respect to bodily and mental capacities.
▸ People are in constant competition and distrustful of each other.
▸ People without government are in a condition of war.
▸ Humans are solitary, nasty, selfish, and egoistic.

7. In what statements does Hobbes capture the natural laws of reason?
Basically two (though 19 are discussed in *Leviathan*):
1. "That every man ought to endeavor peace, as far as he has hope of obtaining it; and when he cannot obtain it, that he may seek and use all helps and advantages of war."
2. "That a man be willing, when others are so too, as far forth as for peace and defence of himself he shall think it necessary, to lay down this right to all things, and be contented with so much liberty against other men as he would allow other men against himself."

8. What is Hobbes's Leviathan?
▸ A coercive power to compel individuals to live by their covenant
▸ A strong sanctioning body
▸ Like a "Mortal God"

9. What is Locke's conception of the state of nature?
▸ In nature, humans are free, but not licentious.
▸ People are equal, independent, and possess the right to life, health, liberty, and possessions.
▸ The state of nature is pre-political but not pre-social.

10. To what natural right does Locke give special attention?
▸ Property rights: precede society
▸ State is created to protect property rights
▸ Property rights given to us by God
▸ Entitlements to property come from mixing our labor with objects

11. What function does the Lockean state play?

▸ Fiduciary role
▸ Protection of property rights
▸ Resolving disputes between citizens
▸ Avoidance of "inconveniences" regarding the punishment of wrongdoing

12. What are the basic structures of the state's power?

▸ Legislative branch: power to make laws
▸ Executive branch: power to enforce compliance to laws
▸ Federative branch: power to make war and peace

13. How or why is Karl Marx considered a revolutionary threat?

▸ His atheism is a threat to religionists and people of faith.
▸ His dialectical materialism threatens philosophers, charging that ideas are simply products of socioeconomic conditions.
▸ His theory threatens capitalism since he exposes its corruption and alienating effects.

14. Who influenced Marx's thinking?

▸ Hegel with his concept of dialectic
▸ Feuerbach and his materialism—reality is material, not spiritual (Hegel)
▸ Comte de Saint-Simon—economic conditions determine history (class conflict—rich versus poor)

15. What are the five historical periods of economic development according to Marx?

▸ Primitive/communal
▸ Slave
▸ Feudal
▸ Capitalistic
▸ Socialist/communist

16. What does 'alienation' mean? What role does it play in capitalistic modes of production?

▸ Alienation is the experience of separation, difference, estrangement, powerlessness (from oneself, others, one's species-being, work).
▸ One feels enslaved by machines originally made to serve humankind.

17. What contributes to alienation?

▸ The dehumanizing capitalistic mode of production
▸ Idolatry (making money your God)
▸ Fetishism of commodities (giving power to human-made objects and then adoring them)
▸ Division of labor (specialization)
▸ Making labor into a commodity that can be bought and sold

18. Who were some of the influences on King?

▸ Karl Marx, Gandhi
▸ African American activists: Frederick Douglass, W.E.B. Du Bois, A. Philip Randolph, Ralph J. Bunche, and Howard Thurman

19. What key concepts comprise King's logic of nonviolence?

▸ Equality
▸ Structure
▸ Nonviolent direct action
▸ Justice-love

20. In the end, what is King seeking?

▸ A revolution of conscience—an end to poverty, racism and militarism
▸ A new world order in which love motivates us to rectify injustices, and just actions are defined as those that are loving

21. What can be said about each key concept comprising King's logic of nonviolence?

▸ Equality
  · pre-eminent value
  · relational concept
  · points to a community of harmonizing equals
  · a notion perverted by white America

▸ Structure
  · racism is structural and systematic
  · racism is a structural problem perpetuating systematic injustice
  · poverty and war are two other structural evils which combine with racism to create injustice, e.g., the structure of racist imperialist capitalism perpetuates structural inequalities to maintain economic growth

- structural inequalities can only be eradicated with a revaluation of values

▸ Nonviolent Direct Action
- aims to establish true economic democracy
- based on principles of truth-telling, love, and courage which order protests, boycotts, etc.

▸ Justice-love
- Justice must be regulated by love
- Properly understood, 'justice' and 'love' are complementary and inextricably linked, not in opposition or contrary to each other.

Additional Resources

For interactive quizzes, stories, supplements, and other materials for study and review, visit:

sites.broadviewpress.com/experiencing-philosophy/chapter6
Passcode: w4822kj

Or scan the following QR code:

Answers to Progress Checks

CHAPTER 1

1. wisdom
2. Western rational tradition
3. knowledge
4. practical use
5. depth
6. therapeutic value
7. instrumental
8. liberate
9. Hellenistic tradition
10. epistemology
11. axiology
12. disciplinary
13. logic
14. ethics
15. social/political philosophy
16. rational
17. Medicine Wheel
18. irrational leap
19. historical periods
20. conceptual analysis

CHAPTER 2

1. factual, value
2. conceptual claims
3. groundless
4. arguments
5. rational disinterestedness
6. form, content
7. *modus ponens*
8. *modus tollens*
9. syllogisms
10. inductive
11. inductive generalization
12. necessary
13. sound
14. premises
15. logical fallacies
16. *ad hominem*
17. straw person
18. two wrongs
19. appealing to authority (of the majority)

CHAPTER 3

1. worldviews
2. Zeno
3. Socrates
4. Diogenes
5. ordered
6. synchronicity
7. courageous acceptance
8. nature
9. emotional detachment
10. existentialism
11. aphorisms
12. unorthodox
13. revolt
14. subjectivity, uniqueness
15. existence, essence
16. causal determinism
17. absurd

18. crowd
19. blame
20. Viktor Frankl
21. active engagement
22. meaningful life
23. psychological hedonism
24. ethical hedonism
25. Aristippus
26. pleasure
27. self-control
28. immediate
29. Epicurus
30. enduring
31. *ataraxia*
32. natural
33. fear
34. virtue
35. friendship
36. vain
37. limits
38. suffering
39. craving
40. *Nirvana*
41. Middle Path
42. ego

CHAPTER 4

1. epistemology
2. metaphysics
3. becoming
4. opinion
5. being
6. goodness
7. allegory of the cave
8. rationalist
9. Copernican revolution
10. deduction
11. methodological doubt
12. *cogito ergo sum*
13. wax example
14. John Locke
15. *tabula rasa*
16. complex idea, simple ideas

17. innate ideas
18. primary qualities, secondary qualities
19. wrecking-ball
20. impressions, thoughts
21. self
22. causality
23. synthesis
24. active construction
25. sensibility
26. categories
27. pure reason
28. socially situated, lived experiences
29. mind, body
30. ontological argument
31. Aristotle
32. natural theology

CHAPTER 5

1. teleology
2. soul
3. character
4. philosopher kings/rulers
5. democratic characters
6. *eudaimonia*
7. life of the intellect
8. Doctrine of the Mean
9. habit
10. utility
11. nature
12. sanction
13. hedonic calculus
14. is-ought
15. rational
16. good will
17. maxims
18. categorical imperative
19. ethical bias
20. post-conventional
21. care
22. rationality
23. similar
24. relation
25. God

26. will to power
27. slave morality
28. superman/*Übermensch*
29. revaluation
30. Muhammad
31. Allah
32. sacred texts
33. Arjuna
34. Krishna
35. Jesus Christ
36. deontology, revisionism, virtue ethics

CHAPTER 6

1. politics
2. axiology
3. aristocracy
4. *polis*
5. artisans
6. philosopher rulers
7. tyranny
8. women
9. altruism
10. war
11. objective morality
12. rights
13. Leviathan
14. commonwealth
15. John Locke
16. God
17. property
18. labor
19. inconveniences
20. fiduciary role
21. consent
22. divisions
23. Cold War
24. Hegel
25. class conflicts
26. epochs of history
27. alienation
28. idolatry
29. division of labor
30. Gandhi
31. logic of nonviolence
32. violence
33. imperialist racism
34. nonviolent direct action
35. love

A Note on Citations

When the original work (or its translation) that we quote from is not recent, we sometimes modernize the language a bit to help readers.

All bibliographical citations are indicated in the text by a superscript number corresponding to the notes at the end of this book.

Philosophical writing that is not recent is very often available in various book and online editions. Works quoted in this book by Plato, Aristotle, Cicero, Aquinas, Descartes, Hobbes, Locke, Hume, Bentham, and Marx are available free on the Internet.

To aid you in finding the place in an original larger work (or translation) from which a quotation was extracted, the end notes often give book, part, chapter, paragraph (etc.) numbers, and (for Plato and Aristotle) standard index numbers which are found in many editions of the same work.

Here's an example of one such note:

Aristotle, *Ethics*, 1.1 (1094a), 63

Here's how to decode that. Looking higher in that list of notes, you'll find that the full title of this book is *The Nicomachean Ethics*. That work is divided into books and parts, and '1.1' means Book 1, Part 1. The standard indexing system for all of Aristotle's works gives this location as '1094a.' Higher in the notes, you'll find a reference to the particular edition of this book that we have quoted from (J.A.K. Thomson and Hugh Tredennick, trans., London: Penguin, 1976), and the numeral '63' tells you what page number this excerpt is from.

A different example:

Locke, *Essay*, 2, 1, 4

Here, the original, Locke's *Essay Concerning Human Understanding*, was in English, so we mention no particular edition. We identify the location as Book 2, Chapter 1, Part 4.

Endnotes

CHAPTER 1

1. St. Teresa of Avila, *The Way of Perfection, The Collected Works* (Rockford, IL: TAN Books, 1997), 117–18.
2. John Passmore, "Philosophy," in *The Encyclopedia of Philosophy*, vol. 6 (New York: Macmillan and The Free Press, 1972), 216.
3. Plato, *Apology* (30e).
4. Anna More, "Introduction," in *Sor Juana Inés de la Cruz: Selected Works* (New York: Norton Critical Edition, 2016) and Alan S. Trueblood, "Introduction," in *A Sor Juana Anthology* (Cambridge, MA: Harvard University Press, 1988).
5. Sor Juana Inés de la Cruz, *Selected Works*, trans. Edith Grossman (New York: Norton, 2014), 185.
6. Sor Juana, *Works*, 161–72.
7. Sor Juana, *Works*, 145–46.
8. Brand Blanshard, "Wisdom," in *The Encyclopedia of Philosophy*, vol. 8 (New York: Macmillan, 1967), 322.
9. Martha Nussbaum, *The Therapy of Desire: Theory and Practice in Hellenistic Ethics* (Princeton: Princeton University Press, 1994), 4.
10. Nussbaum, *Therapy*, 4.
11. This selection was taken from a rough draft manuscript entitled *The New Stoics Book*. It has been altered and re-titled *Inner Resilience and Outer Results*. Go to Tom Morris's website to learn more: http://www.morrisinstitute.com/mihv_book_03.html.
12. Donald Simanek and John Holden, *Science Askew: A Light-hearted Look at the Scientific World* (Boca Raton, FL: Institute of Physics Publishing, CRC Press, 2001), 79–80.
13. For more about these initiatives, see http://www.newnarrativesinphilosophy.net/ and https://projectvox.org/about-the-project/.
14. Lee Hester and Jim Cheney, "Truth and Native American Epistemology," *Social Epistemology* vol. 15, no. 4 (2001): 319–34.
15. https://www.researchgate.net/figure/The-TL-of-Kabbalah-with-the-ten-sefirot-plus-sefira-Knowledge_fig1_220626476.
16. To learn how the enneagram has been used within Islam, see two books by Laleh Bakhtiar: *Traditional Psychoethics and Personality Paradigm* (Chicago: Kazi Publications, 1993) and *Moral Healer's Handbook: The Psychology of Spiritual Chivalry* (Chicago: Kazi Publications, 1994). To learn how the enneagram has been used outside of Islam, see Dan Riso and Russ Hudson, *Understanding the Enneagram*, rev. ed. (Boston: Mariner Books, 2000), 34–35.
17. Abu Hamid al-Ghazali, *Al-Munkidh min al-Dalal* (*Deliverance from Error*). Translation from *The Confessions of al-Ghazali*, trans. Claud Field (London: J. Murray, 1909), modernized by Jerome S. Arkenberg.

18. Adapted from *Meditation for Dummies* by Stephan Bodian (Foster City, CA: IDG Books, 1999).
19. Bertrand Russell, "Prologue: What I Have Lived For," in his *Autobiography* (New York: Routledge, 1998), 9.
20. Bertrand Russell, *The Problems of Philosophy* (Oxford: Oxford University Press, 1912), 46–50.

CHAPTER 2

1. Peter J. Ahrensdorf, *The Death of Socrates and the Life of Philosophy* (Albany: State University of New York Press, 1995), 9.
2. See Plato's defense speech at 21b–23b in *Apology*.
3. Plato, *Euthyphro*, in *The Apology and Related Dialogues*, ed. Andrew Bailey, trans. Cathal Woods and Ryan Pack (Peterborough, ON: Broadview Press, 2016) (5d–16a), 37.

CHAPTER 3

1. Quoted in Frederick C. Copleston, *A History of Philosophy*, vol. 1 (New York: Image Books, 1993), 392.
2. Copleston, *History*, 390.
3. Martha Nussbaum, *The Therapy of Desire: Theory and Practice in Hellenistic Ethics* (Princeton: Princeton University Press, 1994), 360.
4. Marcus Aurelius, *The Meditations of Marcus Aurelius*, trans. George Long (1862), revised by Robert M. Martin for this volume.
5. Albert Ellis, *Humanistic Psychotherapy: The Rational-Emotive Approach* (New York: McGraw Hill, 1974), 56.
6. See, for example, F.H. Sandbach, *The Stoics* (Indianapolis: Hackett Publishing, 1994), 59–60; also Douglas Soccio, *Archetypes of Wisdom*, 7th ed. (Boston: Cengage Learning), 226–27. Sandbach reminds us about Marcus Aurelius, who learned from Sextus to be entirely passionless, yet full of affection. Soccio quotes Seneca in claiming that Stoicism rejects all emotion, seeing it as a disease with no half-way cure.
7. Copleston, *History*, 433.
8. Marcus Aurelius, *The Meditations of Marcus Aurelius*, trans. George Long (1862), revised by Robert M. Martin for this volume. All footnotes were added by Anthony Falikowski.
9. For more on the *Meditations* of Marcus Aurelius, see P.A. Brunt, "Marcus Aurelius in His *Meditations*," *The Journal of Roman Studies*, vol. 64 (1974): 1–20.
10. See Harold Titus, Marilyn Smith, and Richard Nolan, *Living Issues in Philosophy*, 7th ed. (New York: D. Van Nostrand, 1979), 339.
11. David Zane Mairowitz and Alain Korkos, *Introducing Camus* (originally titled *Camus for Beginners*) (London: Icon Books, 1998).
12. Jean-Paul Sartre, *Existentialism Is a Humanism*, trans. Carol Macomber (New Haven: Yale University Press, 2007).
13. For more on de Beauvoir's contributions to "Existentialism Is a Humanism," see Kate Kirkpatrick, *Becoming Beauvoir: A Life* (London: Bloomsbury Publishing, 2019), 215.
14. University of St. Andrews, "CEPPA Chats—Susan Wolf Talks Moral Demands," *YouTube*, April 29, 2020, https://www.youtube.com/watch?v=-GXgxktJTTg.
15. Susan Wolf, "Moral Saints," in her book, *The Variety of Values: Essays on Morality, Meaning, and Love* (Oxford: Oxford University Press, 2015), 11.
16. Wolf, "Introduction," in *Variety*, 2.
17. Susan Wolf, *Meaning in Life and Why It Matters* (Princeton: Princeton University Press, 2010), 8.
18. John Martin Fischer, blurb for Susan Wolf, *Matters*, Princeton University Press, https://press.princeton.edu/

books/paperback/9780691154503/
meaning-in-life-and-why-it-matters.

19. Wolf, "The Meanings of Lives," in *Variety*.

20. "The Meanings of Lives," in Perry, Bratman, Fischer, eds., *Introduction to Philosophy: Classical and Contemporary Readings* (New York: Oxford University Press, 2007), 62–73.

21. David Wiggins, "Truth, Invention, and the Meaning of Life," *Proceedings of the British Academy* LXII (1976). Endnote added by Anthony Falikowski.

22. Richard Brandt, "Hedonism," in *The Encyclopedia of Philosophy*, vol. 3, ed. Paul Edwards (New York: Prentice-Hall, 1973), 432–35.

23. Epicurus, "Letter to Menoeceus" [from Diogenes Laertius, *Lives of Eminent Philosophers*, Book 10.121–34], in B. Inwood and L.P. Gerson, eds., *Hellenistic Philosophy: Introductory Readings*, 2nd ed. (Indianapolis: Hackett, 1998), 30.

24. P.H. DeLacy, "Epicurus," in *Encyclopedia*, vol. 3, 3–5.

25. Julia Annas, *The Morality of Happiness* (New York: Oxford University Press, 1993), 337.

26. Annas, *Morality*, 339–41.

27. Cicero, *De Finibus* I, 66–68.

28. Philodemus of Gadara, quoted in Nussbaum, *Therapy*, 134.

29. Epicurus (1997), "Letter to Menoeceus" [from Diogenes Laertius, *Lives of Eminent Philosophers*, Book 10.121–34], in Inwood and Gerson, eds., *Hellenistic Philosophy*, 28–36.

30. Theognis of Megara, quoted in *The Elegies of Theognis*, ed. T. Hudson-Williams (London: G. Bell and Sons, 1910), 425, 427. Endnote in Epicurus, "Letter," with additional information by Anthony Falikowski.

31. John Snelling, *The Buddhist Handbook: A Complete Guide to Buddhist Teaching and Practice*, 3rd ed. (London: Rider, 1998), 51.

32. The Dalai Lama, *The Four Noble Truths* (London: Thorsons, 1997), 6.

33. Lama Surya Das, *Awakening the Buddha Within: Tibetan Wisdom for the Western World* (New York: Broadway Books, 1997), 84.

34. Das, *Awakening*, 88.

35. Bhikku Bodhi, "The Buddha's Teaching," in Samuel Bercholz and Sherab Chodzin Kohn, eds., *Entering the Stream: An Introduction to the Buddha and His Teaching*s (Boston: Shambhala, 1993), 64.

36. Damien Keown, *Buddhism: A Very Short Introduction* (New York: Oxford University Press, 1966), 57.

37. John M. Koller, *Oriental Philosophies* (New York: Scribner, 1970), 141.

38. Das, *Awakening*, 98.

39. Quoted in Das, *Awakening*, 56–57.

40. Das, *Awakening*, 57.

41. Das, *Awakening*, 176.

42. Das, *Awakening*, 198.

43. This point is made in Manuel Velasquez, *Philosophy: A Text with Readings*, 6th ed. (Belmont, CA: Wadsworth, 1997), 495.

44. Velasquez, *Philosophy*, 496–97.

45. Koller, *Philosophies*, 144.

46. Das, *Awakening*, 266.

47. Das, *Awakening*, 335.

48. Koller, *Philosophies*, 142–44.

49. Nyanaponika Thera, "Karma and Its Fruits," in *Entering the Stream*, 123.

50. Thera, "Karma," 125.

51. Thera, "Karma," 127.

52. Thera, "Karma," 72.

53. *Dhammacakkappavattana Sutta* (*Setting in Motion the Wheel of Truth*), trans. from the Pali by Piyadassi Thera (1999). Available at https://www.accesstoinsight.org/tipitaka/sn/sn56/sn56.011.piya.html.

54. William McDonald, "Søren Kierkegaard," *The Stanford Encyclopedia of Philosophy* (Winter 2017 ed.), ed. Edward N. Zalta. Available at https://plato.stanford.edu/archives/win2017/entries/kierkegaard/.

CHAPTER 4

1. Peter A. Angeles, *The HarperCollins Dictionary of Philosophy* (New York: HarperPerennial, 1992), 184–85.

2. René Descartes, "Preface to the Reader," in *Meditations on First Philosophy*, trans. Ian Johnston, ed. Andrew Bailey (Peterborough, ON: Broadview Press, 2013).

3. Plato, *The Republic*, trans. G.M.A Grube, rev. C.D.C. Reeve (Hackett, 1992) (507–521), 180ff.

4. The only source for this is in Plato's dialogue *Cratylus* 402a.

5. Plato, *Republic* (507b–508e), 180–82.

6. Plato, *Republic* (514a–517b), 186–89.

7. Leon Roth, *Descartes's Discourse of Method* (Oxford: Clarendon Press, 1937), 3.

8. Descartes, "Letter to Newcastle, October 1645," *The Philosophical Writings of Descartes*, vol. III: *The Correspondence*, trans. John Cottingham et al. (New York: Cambridge University Press, 1991), 275.

9. Descartes, *Discourse on the Method*, trans. Ian Johnston, ed. Andrew Bailey (Peterborough, ON: Broadview Press, 2020) (4), 31.

10. See Descartes's description of the 'tree of philosophy' in *Oeuvres de Descartes*, 11 vols., ed. Charles Adam and Paul Tannery (Paris: Librairie Philosophique J. Vrin, 1983), vol. I, 186.

11. Descartes, *Discourse* (18–19), 41.

12. Descartes, *Meditations* (17–23), 41–45.

13. Descartes, *Meditations* (23–29), 46–49.

14. Descartes, "Second Set of Objections and Replies," in *The Philosophical Writings of Descartes* Vol. II, trans. John Cottingham et al. (New York: Cambridge University Press, 1984), 100.

15. Noel Moore Brooke and Kenneth Bruder, *Philosophy: The Power of Ideas*, 3rd ed. (Mountainview, CA: Mayfield, 1996), 82.

16. Descartes, *Meditations* (30–34), 50–52.

17. John Locke, "Introduction," in *An Essay Concerning Human Understanding* (1689).

18. Vere Chappell, *The Cambridge Companion to Locke* (Cambridge: Cambridge University Press 1994), 9.

19. Charlotte S. Ware, "The Influence of Descartes on John Locke. A Bibliographical Study," *Revue Internationale de Philosophie* vol. 4, no. 2 (1950): 211, 216.

20. Locke, *Essay*, 2, 1, 2.

21. Locke, *Essay*, 2, 1, 4.

22. Locke, *Essay*, 2, 1, 4.

23. Locke, *Essay*, 1, 2, 14.

24. Locke, *Essay*, 2, 8, 9.

25. Locke, *Essay*, 2, 8, 15.

26. Locke, *Essay*, 2, 8, 9.

27. Locke, *Essay*, 2, 23, 11.

28. Locke, *Essay*, 2, 31, 6.

29. Locke, *Essay*, 2, 23, 2.

30. Hume, Introduction, *A Treatise of Human Nature* (1739–1740). The language in this selection, and in the following selections by Hume, is slightly modernized for ease of reading and comprehension.

31. Hume, Introduction, *Treatise*.

32. David Hume, "My Own Life," April 18, 1776; https://www.econlib.org/book-chapters/chapter-my-own-life-by-david-hume/.

33. Eric Steinberg, "Introduction," in John Locke, *An Enquiry Concerning Human Understanding*, 2nd ed., ed. Eric Steinberg (Indianapolis: Hackett Publishing Company, 1993), xi.

34. J.Y.T. Grieg, *The Letters of David Hume*, vol. 2 (Clarendon Press, 1932), 18.

35. Hume, *An Enquiry Concerning Human Understanding*, II, 12.

36. Hume, *Enquiry*, II, 11.

37. Hume, *Enquiry*, II, 13.

38. Locke, *Essay*, 2, 23, Sections 2 and 5.

39. Hume, *Treatise*, I, IV, 6.

40. Hume, *Enquiry*, III, 19.

41. Hume, *Enquiry*, VII, I, 50.

42. Hume, *Enquiry*, VII, II, 59.

43. Hume, *Enquiry*, VII, II, 59.

44. Hume, *Enquiry*, IV, I, 20.

45. Hume, *Enquiry*, IV, I, 21.

46. Hume, *Treatise*, I, IV, 7.

47. Hume, *Enquiry*, IV, I, 20–27.

48. David Hume, *My Own Life* (1777).

49. Immanuel Kant, "Preface," in *Prolegomena to Any Future Metaphysics*, revised ed., trans. Gary Hatfield (New York: Cambridge University Press, 2004), 10.

50. This illustrative example and the following ones are taken from Anthony Falikowski, *Mastering Human Relations* (Scarborough, ON: Prentice Hall, Allyn and Bacon Canada, 1999), chap. 7.

51. Kant, *Critique of Pure Reason*, trans. Norman Kemp Smith (New York: St. Martin's Press, 1965), 41–42.

52. Kant, *Critique*, 22.

53. Kant, *Critique*, 93.

54. Kant, *Critique*, 67.

55. Kant, *Critique*, 68.

56. For a discussion of Kantian categories in a psychological cognitive-developmental context, see Anthony Falikowski, *Piaget's Kantianism and the Critique of Pure Knowledge* (Master's thesis, University of Toronto, 1979).

57. Kant, *Critique*, 75.

58. Kant, *Critique*, 61–62.

59. Kant, *Critique*, 136.

60. Justus Hartnack, *Kant's Theory of Knowledge*, trans. M. Holmes Hartshorne (New York: Original Harbinger Book, 1967), 55.

61. Kant, Preface, *Critique*, 29.

62. Kant, Preface, *Prolegomena*, 5–8, 10–12. Footnotes have been excluded here.

63. Descartes, *Discourse*, 111.

64. Patricia Hill Collins, *Black Feminist Thought: Knowledge, Consciousness, and the Politics of Empowerment*, 2nd ed. (New York: Routledge, 1999), 255–60.

65. Plato, *Phaedo*, 67e.

66. Plato, *Phaedo*, 67d.

67. Yasuo Yuasa, "Author's Introduction (English Edition)," in *The Body: T oward an Eastern Mind-Body Theory*, ed. Thomas P. Kasulis, ed. and trans. Shigenori Natatomo (Albany: SUNY Press, 1987), 24–26.

68. This summary is adapted from William F. Lawhead, *Voyage of Discovery: A Historical Introduction* (Belmont, CA: Wadsworth, 1995), 172–73.

69. Thomas Aquinas, *Summa Contra Gentiles*, 1, 7.

70. Frederick Copleston, S.J., A History of *Philosophy, Volume II: Augustine to Scotus* (London: Search Press, 1950), 338.

71. Aquinas, *Summa Theologica*, I, Second Question.

72. Aquinas, *Summa Theologica*, I, Second Question.

CHAPTER 5

1. Plato, *Phaedrus*, 253d.

2. Plato, *Republic*, trans. G.M.A Grube, rev. C.D.C. Reeve (Indianapolis, IN: Hackett, 1992), 4, (441c–445b), 117–21. The translations of Plato in this chapter are slightly modernized for ease of reading.

3. Anthony Falikowski, *Moral Philosophy for Modern Life* (Scarborough: Prentice Hall Canada, 1998), 23–27.

4. Plato, *Letters* 7, 326a–326b.

5. For a further discussion of this and related points, see Plato, *Republic* 6 (484a–502c), 157–85.

6. Plato, *Republic* 4 (442b), 118.

7. Plato, *Republic* 4 (442c), 118.

8. Plato, *Republic* 8 (553d), 224.

9. Plato, *Republic* 8 (554e), 225.

10. Plato, *Republic* 8 (561c–d), 232.

11. Plato, *Republic* 8 (559d–e), 230.

12. Aristotle, *Nicomachean Ethics*, trans. J.A.K. Thomson and Hugh Tredennick (London: Penguin, 1976), 1.1 (1094a), 63. (The translations of Aristotle in this chapter have been slightly modernized for ease of reading.)

13. Aristotle, *Ethics*, 1.7 (1097b), 75.

14. Slightly edited biography taken from Anthony Falikowski, *Moral Philosophy: Theories, Skills and Applications* (Scarborough: Prentice Hall, 1989), 17.

15. Jonathan Barnes, "Introduction," in Aristotle, *The Ethics of Aristotle*: *The Nicomachean Ethics*, trans. J.A.K. Thomson (Toronto: Penguin Books, 1976), 34.

16. Aristotle, *Ethics*, 1.7 (1098a), 76.

17. Aristotle, *Ethics*, 10.7 (1178a), 331.

18. Aristotle, *Ethics*, 1.7 (1098a), 76.

19. Aristotle, *Ethics*, 10.7 (1177b), 329.

20. Aristotle, *Ethics*, 1.8 (1099b), 80.

21. Aristotle, *Ethics*, 2.6 (1106b–1107a), 101–02.

22. Aristotle, *Ethics*, 2.3 (1104b), 95. For the reference to Plato, see *Laws* 653a–c and *Republic* 401e–402a.

23. Aristotle, *Ethics*. At 2.6 (1107b), 104; the translators provide this reconstructed table.

24. Aristotle, *Ethics*, 2.6–9 (1106b–1109b), 101–09. Footnotes here by Anthony Falikowski.

25. Jeremy Bentham, *An Introduction to the Principles of Morals and Legislation*, in *The English Philosophers from Bacon to Mill*, ed. E.A. Burtt (New York: Modern Library, 1939), 792. (Bentham's language has been slightly modernized for ease of reading.)

26. Bentham, *Principles* (1.1), 791.

27. Bentham, *Principles* (1.1), 791.

28. Bentham, *Principles* (1.1 and 1.6), 791, 804.

29. Bentham, *Principles* (1.1), 791. (Again, Bentham's language has been slightly modernized for ease of reading.)

30. Immanuel Kant, *Foundations of the Metaphysics of Morals*, trans. Lewis White Beck (Indianapolis, IN: Bobbs-Merrill Library of Liberal Arts, 1959), preface.

31. Kant, *Foundations*, 10.

32. Kant, *Foundations*, 16.

33. Kant, *Foundations*, 16.

34. Kant, *Foundations*, 13–14.

35. Kant, *Foundations*, 14.

36. Kant, *Lectures on Ethics*, trans. Louis Infield (Indianapolis, IN: Hackett Publishing, 1963).

37. Kant, *Lectures*, 117–18.

38. Kant, *Lectures*, 118.

39. Kant, *Lectures*, 121.

40. Kant, *Foundations*, 39.

41. Kant, *Foundations*, 47.

42. Kant, *Groundwork for the Metaphysics of Morals*, trans. James W. Ellington (Indianapolis, IN: Hackett Publishing, 1981), 31. This is a different translation of *Foundations*.

43. Kant, *Kant's Theory of Ethics*, trans. Thomas Kingsmill Abbott (London: Longmans, Green, 1879), 1–4. Abbott's book contains translations of *Fundamental Principles of the Metaphysics of Morals* and *Critique of Practical Reason*. The language of this translation has been slightly modernized for ease of reading. *Fundamental Principles* in this book is another translation of the same *Foundations*.

44. Kant, "On a Supposed Right to Lie Because of Philanthropic Concerns," in *Ethical Philosophy*, 2nd ed., trans. James W. Ellington (Indianapolis, IN: Hackett Publishing, 1983), 163.

45. Letter to Kant from Maria von Herbert, August 1791, in Rae Langton, "Duty and Desolation," *Philosophy* vol. 67, no. 262 (October 1992): 482.

46. Kant, "Right," 482.

47. Kant, "Right," 483.

48. Kant, "Right," 483.

49. Rae Langton, "Duty and Desolation," *Philosophy* vol. 67, no. 262 (October 1992): 504.

50. Sources: Langton, "Duty and Desolation"; Saniye Vatansever, "Theory Behind the Picture: Maria von Herbert," Bilkent Philosophy, 15 December 2018 (updated 22 March 2020): http://www.phil.bilkent.edu.tr/index.php/2018/12/15/story-behind-the-picture-maria-von-herbert/; Wikipedia, "Franz Paul von Herbert (patron)," https://de.wikipedia.org/wiki/Franz_Paul_von_Herbert_(M%C3%A4zen).

51. Carol Gilligan, *In a Different Voice: Psychological Theory and Women's Development* (Cambridge, MA: Harvard University Press), 1982.

52. Lawrence Kohlberg, "From Is to Ought: How to Commit the Naturalistic Fallacy and Get Away with It in the Study of Moral Development," in *Cognitive Development and Epistemology*, ed. Theodore Mischel (New York: Academic Press, 1971), 151–235. Also, Kohlberg, *Essays on Moral Development*, vol. 1, *The Philosophy of Moral Development* (San Francisco: Harper & Row, Publishers, 1981).

53. Ronald Duska and Mariellen Whelan, *Moral Development: A Guide to Piaget and Kohlberg* (New York: Paulist Press, 1975). Provides an easily understood description of Kohlberg's theory, which I have used in my own summary here. The quotation comes from p. 76.

54. For further discussion see, for example, Anthony Falikowski, *Moral and Values Education: A Philosophical Appraisal* (PhD thesis, University of Toronto, 1984); also Brian Crittenden, "The Limitations of Morality as Justice in Kohlberg's Theory," in D.B. Cochrane, C.M. Hamm, and A.C. Kazepides, *The Domain of Moral Education* (New York: Paulist Press, 1979). See also John Rawls, *A Theory of Justice* (Cambridge: Harvard University Press, 1971).

55. Rawls, *Justice*, 17–22.

56. Gilligan, *Voice*, 2.

57. Nancy Chodorow, *The Reproduction of Mothering* (University of California Press, 1978), 66–167.

58. Nancy Chodorow, cited in Carol Gilligan, *Voice*, 8.

59. Gilligan, *Voice*, 8.

60. Gilligan, *Voice*, 8–9.

61. Gilligan, *Voice*, 74.

62. Nel Noddings, *Caring: A Feminine Approach to Ethics and Moral Education* (Berkeley: University of California Press), 1986.

63. Noddings, *Caring*, 5.

64. Noddings, *Caring*, 5. Noddings's italics.

65. Noddings, *Caring*, 36.

66. Noddings, *Caring*, 37.

67. Noddings, *Caring*, 84.

68. Noddings, *Caring*, 6.

69. Noddings, *Caring*, 1–6.

70. Friedrich Nietzsche, *The Gay Science*, trans. Walter Kaufmann (New York: Vintage Books, 1974), §343, 279.

71. Nietzsche, *Science*, §125, 181–82.

72. Peter Berkowitz, *Nietzsche: The Ethics of an Immoralist* (Cambridge, MA: Harvard University Press, 1995), 67.

73. Berkowitz, *Nietzsche*, 68.

74. Berkowitz, *Nietzsche*, 70.

75. Nietzsche, *The Will to Power*, trans. Walter Kaufmann and R.J. Hollingdale (New York: Vintage Books, 1968), §200, 117.

76. Nietzsche, *Power*, §200, 117.

77. Nietzsche, *Beyond Good and Evil*, trans. Helen Zimmern, in *The Complete Works of Friedrich Nietzsche*, trans. Oscar Levy et al. (Edinburgh: Foulis, 1901–15), §284, 152.

78. Nietzsche, *Power*, §899, 474.

79. Nietzsche, *Power*, §983, 513.

80. Nietzsche, *Science*, §290, 232.

81. Besheer Mohamed, "New Estimates Show U.S. Muslim Population Continues to Grow," Pew Research Center, January 3, 2018.

82. Azim Nanji, "Islamic Ethics," in Peter Singer, ed., *A Companion to Ethics* (Oxford: Blackwell Publishers, 1993), 6–117.

83. *The Mathnawi*, vol. III, couplet 4129.

84. Hassan, Dr. Riffat. "Islamic View of Peace," from *Education for Peace: Testimonies from World Religions*, eds. Haim Gordon and Leonard Grob (Orbis Books, 1987), 96–98. Reproduced by permission of the author.

85. G.A. Parwez, *Lughat ul-Qur'ān* (Lahore: Idaru Tulu'-e-Islam, 1960), vol. 2, 894.

86. Ibid., vol. 1, 263.

87. Muhammad Ali, *The Holy Qur'ān* (Chicago: Specialty Promotions, 1973).

88. G.A. Parwez, *Islam: A Challenge to Religion* (Lahore: Idara Tulu'-e-Islam, 1968), 285.

89. M. Ali, *Holy Qur'ān*.

90. *Arabic-English Lexicon*, book 1, part 5, 1936.

91. See Surah 57.27.

92. Translation by Muhammad Asad, *The Message of the Qur'ān* (Gibraltar: Dar-Al-Andalus, 1980).

93. S. Abhayananda, *The Wisdom of Vedanta* (Olympia, WA: Atma Books, 1994), 5.

94. Ashok Kumar Malhotra, *Transcreation of the Bhagavad Gita* (Upper Saddle River, NJ: Prentice Hall, 1999) x, 1–4.

95. Brian Berry, "Roman Catholic Ethics: Three Approaches," http://theolibrary.shc.edu/resources/ligouri_berry.htm.

CHAPTER 6

1. Plato, *Protagoras* (319b–d). This and other translations of Plato are modernized for ease of reading.

2. Plato, *Republic*, trans. G.M.A. Grube and C.D.C. Reeve (Indianapolis: Hackett, 1992), 4 (432a), 202.

3. Desmond Lee, "Translator's Introduction," in Plato, *Republic*, trans. Desmond Lee (Middlesex, UK: Penguin Books, 1976), 42.

4. Plato, *Republic* 3 (416e), 93. This and further references to *Republic* are from the Grube/Reeve translation.

5. See Anne Applebaum, "How Stalin Hid Ukraine's Famine from the World," *The Atlantic*, October 13, 2017, https://www.theatlantic.com/international/archive/2017/10/red-famine-anne-applebaum-ukraine-soviet-union/542610/.

6. Plato, *Republic* 4 (433a, 434b–c), 109–10.

7. Plato, *Republic* 8 (545b ff.), 215ff.

8. Plato, *Republic* 5 (451d–457a), 125–31.

9. Aristotle allows for slavery in his conception of a well-ordered society. See his *Politics*, Book I, Chapters 4–7.

10. Thomas Hobbes, *Leviathan* (I, 13).

11. Hobbes, *Leviathan* (I, 13).

12. Source: Government of Canada, "Self-government," (Canada.ca), https://www.rcaanc-cirnac.gc.ca/eng/1100100032275/1529354547314.

13. Hobbes, *Leviathan* (I, 13).

14. Hobbes, *Leviathan* (I, 13).

15. Hobbes, *Leviathan* (I, 13).

16. Hobbes, *Leviathan* (I, 14).

17. Hobbes, *Leviathan* (I, 14).

18. Hobbes, *Leviathan* (I, 14).

19. Hobbes, *Leviathan* (I, 15).

20. Hobbes, *Leviathan* (I, 15).

21. Hobbes, *Leviathan* (II, 17).

22. Hobbes, *Leviathan* (II, 17).

23. Frontispiece by Abraham Bosse, with input by Hobbes, first published in the Latin version, *Leviathan, sive, De materia, forma, & potestate civitatis ecclesiasticae et civilis*) (Amsterdam: Joan Blaeu, 1668), and reproduced in many editions since.

24. Hobbes, *Leviathan* (II, 17).

25. Hobbes, *Leviathan* (II, 17). Note: The language of this text has been modernized for purposes of clarity and understanding.

26. John Locke, *The Second Treatise of Government* (II. 4). Locke's language here and in ensuing quotations has been modernized for ease of reading.

27. Locke, *Treatise* (II. 6).

28. Locke, *Treatise* (II. 6).

29. Frederick Copleston, *A History of Philosophy*, vol. 5 (New York: Doubleday, 1993), 129.

30. Copleston, *History* 5.

31. Locke, *Treatise* (III. 19).

32. Locke, *Treatise* (II. 8).

33. Locke, *Treatise* (II. 8).

34. Hobbes, *Leviathan* (I, 14).

35. Locke, *Treatise* (IX. 124).

36. Locke, *Treatise* (VII. 87).

37. Locke, *Treatise* (XV. 173).

38. Locke, *Treatise* (V. 32).

39. Locke, *Treatise* (V. 27 and 33).

40. Locke, *Treatise* (IX. 124).

41. Locke, *Treatise* (IX. 125).

42. Locke, *Treatise* (IX. 125).

43. Locke, *Treatise* (IX. 127).

44. Locke, *Treatise* (IX. 131).

45. Locke, *Treatise* (VIII. 102).

46. Locke, *Treatise* (VIII. 101).

47. Locke, *Treatise* (VIII. 97).

48. Locke, *Treatise* (XIII. 149).

49. Locke, *Treatise* (XII. 143).

50. Locke, *Treatise* (XII. 146).

51. Locke, *Treatise* (XIX. 211).

52. Locke, *Treatise* (IX. 123–31).

53. Locke, *Treatise*, Preface.

54. Ronald Reagan, "Address to the National Association of Evangelicals," March 3, 1983.

55. Erich Fromm, *Marx's Concept of Man* (New York: Frederick Ungar Publishing, 1976), vii.

56. Fromm, *Concept*, ix.

57. Quoted in Fromm, *Concept*, Preface to the first edition.

58. Neil McInnes, "Karl Marx," in *The Encyclopedia of Philosophy*, ed. Paul Edwards, vol. 5 (New York: Macmillan and Free Press, 1972), 173.

59. Karl Marx, *The German Ideology*, ed. C.J. Arthur (New York: International Publishers, 2004), 37, 47. The notion of "idealistic phantoms" in the context of Marx is explored by James Guillaume, "Michael Bakunin: A Biographical Sketch," in Sam Dolgoff, ed. and trans., *Bakunin on Anarchy* (New York: Vintage Press, 1971), 25–26.

60. Karl Marx, Preface, *A Contribution to the Critique of Political Economy* (Moscow: Progress Publishers, 1977).

61. Carl Schurz, *Reminiscences of Carl Schurz* (London: J. Murray, 1909), 138.

62. Erich Fromm, *Marx's Concept of Man* (New York: Frederick Ungar Publishing, 1976).

63. Quoted in Wallace Matson, *A New History of Philosophy*, vol. 2, 2nd ed. (Fort Worth: Harcourt College Publishers, 2000), 499.

64. A better translation of this slogan is probably "What is rational is actual and what is actual is rational." G.W.F. Hegel, *Hegel's Philosophy of Right*, trans. T.M. Knox (Oxford: Oxford University Press, 1952), 10.

65. A.J.P. Taylor, "Introduction," in Karl Marx and Friedrich Engels, *The Communist Manifesto* (Harmondsworth, UK: Penguin, 1967).

66. Marx, *Ideology*, 47.

67. Marx and Friedrich Engels, *Manifesto of the Communist Party*, in *Marx/Engels Selected Works*, trans. Samuel Moore in cooperation with Frederick Engels, vol. 1 (Moscow: Progress Publishers 1969), 98–137.

68. Marx and Engels, *Manifesto*.

69. Marx, *Critique of the Gotha Program*, in *Marx/Engels Selected Works*, I.3.

70. Marx, *Economic and Philosophic Manuscripts*, trans. Martin Milligan (Moscow: Progress Publishers, 1959), XXIV, 34.

71. *Toronto Star*, June 21, 2000, Section E, p. 3.

72. Nina Shapiro, "Under pressure, afraid to take bathroom breaks? Inside Amazon's fast-paced warehouse world," shortened and edited here, the complete Article was originally written by Nina Shapiro / *Seattle Times* staff reporter, for *The Seattle Times*, July 2, 2018.

73. Marx, *Capital*, trans. Samuel Moore et al. (Moscow: Progress Publishers, n.d.), (I.1.25.4), 451.

74. Cyrus Farivar, NBC News, "A Bathroom-Break Bill? California Looks to Make Sure Warehouse Workers Can Take a Break," July 2, 2020.

75. Fromm, *Concept*, 57.

76. Marx, *Capital* (I.4.15.4), 461–62.

77. Marx, *Manuscripts* (XXII), 29.

78. Marx, *Manuscripts* (XXIV), 48.

79. Marx, *Manuscripts* (XXIII), 30.

80. Thomas E. Wartenberg, film review of "American Beauty," *Philosophy Now* (June/July, 2000): 44.

81. Wartenberg, film review, 44.

82. Marx, *Manuscripts* (XXII), 30.

83. Marx, *Manuscripts* (XXIII and XXIV), 30–32.

84. Pieces of King's philosophy are scattered throughout his writings. Fortunately for us, Greg Moses has collected them in his *Revolution of Conscience: Martin Luther King, Jr., and the Philosophy of Nonviolence* (New York: The Guilford Press, 1996) and reassembled them in a fashion which allows

us to better understand the systematic and coherent nature of King's thought. Much of the interpretation provided in Section 6.5 is drawn from Moses's exegesis, and I acknowledge its valuable contribution here.

85. Martin Luther King Jr., *Stride Toward Freedom: The Montgomery Story* (New York: Harper, 1958), 94–95.

86. See Uma Majmudar, *Gandhi's Pilgrimage of Faith: From Darkness to Light* (SUNY Press, 2005), 138.

87. King, "Pilgrimage to Nonviolence," *Christian Century* 77 (April 13, 1960): 139–40.

88. King, speech, 28 August 1963, Lincoln Memorial, Washington, DC.

89. Moses, *Revolution*, 25.

90. King, *Where Do We Go from Here: Chaos or Community?* (Boston: Beacon Press, 1967), 57.

91. Moses, *Revolution*, 26–27.

92. King, *Where Do We Go from Here*, 95.

93. King, "The Role of the Behavioral Scientist in the Civil Rights Movement," *Journal of Social Issues* vol. 24, no. 1 (January 1968).

94. King, speech titled "America's Chief Moral Dilemma," 10 May 1967, Atlanta, GA.

95. See Moses, *Revolution*, 55.

96. King, *Where Do We Go*, 7.

97. King, *The Trumpet of Conscience* (New York: Harper & Row, 1968), 5.

98. King, *A Letter from the Birmingham City Jail*, 1963.

99. King, *Where Do We Go*, 196.

100. King, *Where Do We Go*, 85.

101. King, *Where Do We Go*, 186.

102. King, *Where Do We Go*, 188.

103. Mohandas K. Gandhi, *Yeravda Mandir* (Ahmedabad: Navajivan Press, 1935), 12, https://www.mkgandhi.org/sfgbook/two.htm.

104. Moses, *Revolution*, 186.

105. See Moses, *Revolution*, 186: "To Black Power advocates and white liberals alike, King argues the imperative of love. It is love that awakens perception to injustice and love that gathers strength for liberation."

106. Moses, *Revolution*, 188.

107. King, *Where Do We Go*, 37.

108. King, *Where Do We Go*, 37.

109. King, "Where Do We Go from Here?" Speech to the Eleventh Annual Southern Leadership Conference, Atlanta, Georgia, August 16, 1967. This quotation is from the speech, not from the book with the same title.

110. King, *Where Do We Go*, 12.

111. David J. Garrow, "Where Martin Luther King, Jr., Was Going: *Where Do We Go from Here* and the Traumas of the Post-Selma Movement," *The Georgia Historical Quarterly* vol. 75, no. 4 (Winter 1991): 720.

112. Coretta Scott King, "Foreword," in King, *Where Do We Go*, xxiv.

Sources

al-Ghazali, Abu Hamid. Excerpted from "Munkidh min al-Dalal [The Confessions, or Deliverance from Error]," *The Sacred Books and Early Literature of the East, Vol. VI: Medieval Arabia*, ed. Charles F. Horne (Parke, Austin & Lipscomb, 1917, pp. 99–133), a reprint of *The Confessions of al-Ghazali*, translated by Claud Field (J. Murray, 1909); with text modernized by Jerome S. Arkenberg (1996), *The Internet Medieval Source Book*, https://sourcebooks.fordham.edu/basis/1100ghazali-truth.asp.

Aquinas, Thomas. "Whether God Exists?" *The Summa Theologica*, translated by the Fathers of the English Dominican Province, originally published in 1911.

Aristotle. Book 2: "The Ethics," from *The Ethics of Aristotle*, published by Penguin Classics. Translation copyright 1953 by J.A.K. Thomson. Revised translation copyright © Hugh Tredennick, 1976 [excerpted, pp. 101–09]. Reprinted by permission of Penguin Books Limited.

Aurelius, Marcus. From Part V, *The Meditations of Marcus Aurelius*, trans. George Lang (P.F. Collier & Son, 1909–14) [excerpted].

Bentham, Jeremy. From Chapter 1, *An Introduction to the Principles of Morals and Legislation* (Oxford University Press, 1823) [excerpted].

Berry, Brian. Chapter 6: "Roman Catholic Ethics: Three Approaches." Theology Library at Spring Hill College. First published in *Catholic Practice*, March 1999.

Collins, Patricia Hill. "An Afrocentrist Standpoint Challenges the Tradition of Positivism," of Chapter 11: Black Feminist Epistemology, from *Black Feminist Thought: Knowledge, Consciousness, and the Politics of Empowerment*, 2nd ed. (Unwin Hyman). Copyright © 1990, 2000. Pp. 251–72 [excerpted]. Reproduced by permission of Taylor and Francis Group, LLC, a division of Informa plc, conveyed by Copyright Clearance Center.

Descartes, René. "First Meditation" and "Second Meditation, Parts 1, 2," from *Discourse on Method*, trans. Ian Johnston, ed. Andrew Bailey. Copyright © 2013 Broadview Press. Used with permission.

Dhammacakkappavattana Sutta (*Setting in Motion the Wheel of Truth*) (SN 56.11), translated from the Pali by Piyadassi Thera. *Access to Insight (BCBS Edition)*, 30 November 2013. Copyright © 1999 Buddhist Publication Society. Reprinted by permission of the Buddhist Publication Society. http://www.accesstoinsight.org/tipitaka/sn/sn56/sn56.011.piya.html.

Epicurus. "Letter to Menoeceus," from *Hellenistic Philosophy: Introductory Readings, Second Edition*, ed./trans. Brad Inwood and Lloyd P. Gerson, published by Hackett Publishing Company, 1998. Second edition copyright © 1997 by Brad Inwood and L.P. Gerson. Pp. 28–31 [excerpted]. Reprinted by permission of Hackett Publishing Company, Inc. All rights reserved.

Hassan, Dr. Riffat. "Islamic View of Peace," from *Education for Peace: Testimonies from World Religions*, ed. Haim Gordon and Leonard Grob (Orbis Books, 1987). Pp. 96–98. Reproduced by permission of the author.

Hester, Lee, and Jim Cheney. "Truth and Native American Epistemology," *Social Epistemology*, 15.4 (2001): 319–34 [excerpted]. Copyright © 2001 Taylor & Francis Ltd. Reprinted by permission of Taylor & Francis Ltd, http://www.tandfonline.com. https://doi.org/10.1080/02691720110093333.

Hobbes, Thomas. From Chapter XVII: "Of the Causes, Generation, and Definition of a Common-Wealth," Part II, *Leviathan* [1651], Library of Liberal Arts, Prentice-Hall, Inc. A Simon & Schuster Company, Englewood Cliffs, New Jersey. [excerpted]

Hume, David. From Part One, Section Four, *An Enquiry Concerning Human Understanding*, Harvard Classics, vol. 37. Copyright © 1910, P.F. Collier & Son. [excerpted]

Juana Inés de la Cruz, Sor. "Reply to Sor Filotea," from *Sor Juana Inés de la Cruz: Selected Works*, translated by Edith Grossman. Copyright © 2014 by Edith Grossman. Pp. 161–72 [excerpted]. Used by permission of W.W. Norton & Company, Inc.

Kant, Immanuel. "On Pure Moral Philosophy," *Kant's Theory of Ethics* [1879], trans. Thomas Kingsmill Abbott. "Preface," from *Prolegomena to Any Future Metaphysics*, trans./ed. Gary Hatfield, published by Cambridge University Press, 2004. Pp. 5–8, 10–11, 11–12 (4:255–4:258, 4:260–4:262) [excerpted]. Copyright © Cambridge University Press 1997, 2004. Reproduced by permission of Cambridge University Press, conveyed through PLSclear.

King, Martin Luther. "I Have a Dream," delivered August 28, 1963, Lincoln Memorial, Washington, DC. Copyright © 1963 by Dr. Martin Luther King, Jr. Renewed © 1991 by

Coretta Scott King. Reprinted by arrangement with The Heirs to the Estate of Martin Luther King Jr., c/o Writers House as agent for the proprietor New York, NY. "Where Do We Go from Here?" delivered August 16, 1967, Eleventh Annual Southern Leadership Conference, Atlanta, Georgia. Copyright © 1967 by Dr. Martin Luther King, Jr. Renewed © 1995 by Coretta Scott King. Reprinted by arrangement with The Heirs to the Estate of Martin Luther King Jr., c/o Writers House as agent for the proprietor New York, NY.

Locke, John. From Book II, Chapter IX: "Of the Ends of Political Society and Government," *Two Treatises on Government*. Published in London, 1690. Project Gutenberg, www.gutenberg.org/ebooks/7370. [excerpted]

Malhotra, Ashok Kumar. Chapter 1: "Arjuna's Moral Dilemma," from *Transcreation of the Bhagavad Gita*, 1st ed., published by the Library of Liberal Arts, Prentice Hall. Copyright © 1999 by Prentice-Hall, Inc. Pp. x, 1–4 [excerpted]. Reprinted by permission of Pearson Education, Inc.

Marx, Karl. "First Manuscript: Estranged Labor," Sections XXIII and XXIV, *Economic and Philosophic Manuscripts*, trans. Martin Milligan, first published in English by Progress Publishers, Moscow, 1959. Marxists Internet Archive, https://www.marxists.org/archive/marx/works/1844/manuscripts/labour.htm.

Nietzsche, Friedrich. Aphorism 125, "The Madman," Book Three, from *The Gay Science*, translated by Walter Kaufmann. Copyright © 1974 by Penguin Random House LLC. Pp. 181–82 [excerpted]. Used by permission of Random House, an imprint and division of Penguin Random House LLC. All rights reserved.

Noddings, Nel. "Introduction," from *Caring: A Feminine Approach to Ethics and Moral Education*, 2nd ed., published by University of California Press 1984, 2003. Copyright © 2013 The Regents of the University of California. Pp. 1–6 [excerpted]. Reproduced by permission of the University of California Press, conveyed by Copyright Clearance Center.

Plato. Book IV: "Virtue and Justice in the Individual and in the State," pp. 117–21 (441c–445b) [modified]; Book V: "The Nature of Woman," pp. 125–31 (451c–457b) [modified]; Book VI: "Simile of the Sun," pp. 180–82 (507b–509b) [modified]; Book VII: "Allegory of the Cave," pp. 186–89 (514a–517c) [modified], from *Republic*, trans. G.M.A. Grube, revised by C.D.C. Reeve. Copyright © 1992 by Hackett Publishing Company, Inc. All rights reserved. Used with permission. "Euthyphro," from *The Apology and Related Dialogues*, ed. Andrew Bailey, trans. Cathal Woods and Ryan Pack (Broadview Press, 2016). Copyright © 2016 Andrew Bailey, Cathal Woods, and Ryan Pack. Used with permission.

Russell, Bertrand. Chapter 2: "The Value of Philosophy," *The Problems of Philosophy* (Oxford University Press, 1912). Pp. 46–50.

Sartre, Jean-Paul. "Part I," from *Existentialism Is a Humanism*, translated by Carol Macomber. Translation copyright © 2007 by Yale University Press. L'Existentialisme est un humanisme © Éditions Gallimard, Paris, 1996. Pp. 20–25 [excerpted]. Reprinted in North America by permission of Yale University Press.

Shapiro, Nina. "Under Pressure, Afraid to Take Bathroom Breaks? Inside Amazon's Fast-Paced Warehouse World" [shortened and edited], complete article originally published in *The Seattle Times*, July 2, 2018. Copyright © 2018 The Seattle Times. Used under license.

Simanek, Donald, and John Holden. Chapter 10: "Mind Sciences," from *Science Askew: A Light Hearted Look at the Scientific World*, Institute of Physics Conference Series, CRC Press, 2001. Copyright © 2001 by Taylor & Francis Group, LLC. Pp. 79–80 [excerpted]. Reproduced by permission of Taylor and Francis Group, LLC, a division of Informa plc, conveyed by Copyright Clearance Center.

Van Alphen, Tony. "GM Suspends Worker for Going to Bathroom," *Toronto Star*, Section E, June 21, 2000 (p. 3). Copyright © 2000 Toronto Star Newspapers Limited. All rights reserved. Used under license.

Wolf, Susan. Chapter 6: "The Meanings of Lives," from *The Variety of Values: Essays on Morality, Meaning and Love*. Copyright © Oxford University Press 2015. Pp. 89–96 [excerpted]. Reproduced by permission of Oxford Publishing Limited (Academic), conveyed through PLSclear.

Yuasa, Yasuo. "Author's Introduction to the English Edition," from *The Body: Toward an Eastern Mind-Body Theory*, ed./trans. Thomas P. Kasulis, trans. Shigenori Nagatomo, published by the State University of New York Press. Copyright © 1987 State University of New York, pp. 24–26 [excerpted]. Reprinted by permission of the publisher.

Image Sources

CHAPTER 1

p. 29: *Wonderland* by Jaume Plensa. Photograph by Shafkat Alam/Unsplash.

p. 30: Bust of Socrates. Photograph by Jastrow.

p. 34: *Madame du Châtelet* by Maurice Quentin de La Tour. Photograph by RockMagnetist.

p. 36: *Portrait of Sor Juana Inés de la Cruz* by Miguel Cabrera. Photograph by Nameneko.

p. 42: *Existential Comics* © Existential Comics and Corey Mohler. Used with permission.

p. 43: Zora Neale Hurston. Photograph by Carl Van Vechten.

p. 50: Joseph Campbell. Photograph by Joan Halifax. Uploaded to flickr.com (https://www.flickr.com/photos/82431121@N00/196061673) by Joan Halifax. Image licensed under CC BY 2.0. Cropped from original.

p. 51: *Hagar the Horrible* comic © 2000 King Features Syndicate, Inc. Used with permission.

p. 61: Bertrand Russell. Unknown photographer.

CHAPTER 2

p. 73: Photograph by Milton Louiz/Shutterstock.

p. 81: John Stuart Mill. Photograph by the London Stereoscopic Company.

p. 82: John F. Kennedy. Photograph from the White House Press Office.

p. 85: Socrates. Line engraving by P. Pontius, 1638, after P.P. Rubens. Uploaded to commons.wikimedia.org (https://commons.wikimedia.org/wiki/File:Socrates._Line_engraving_by_P._Pontius,_1638,_after_Sir_P._P_Wellcome_V0005528.jpg) by Wellcome Images (http://wellcomeimages.org). Image licensed under CC BY 4.0.

p. 86: Randy Glasbergen comic © Glasbergen. Used with permission of Glasbergen Cartoon Service.

p. 110: Ludwig Wittgenstein. Photograph by Moritz Nähr.

p. 113: Elisabeth of Bohemia. Portrait by Gerard van Honthorst.

p. 119: *Dilbert* comic © 2013 Scott Adams, Inc. Used with permission of ANDREWS MCMEEL SYNDICATION. All rights reserved.

p. 252: John Locke. Portrait by Godfrey Kneller.

p. 259: David Hume. Portrait by Allan Ramsay.

p. 271: Immanuel Kant. Portrait attributed to Jean-Marc Nattier.

p. 287: Patricia Hill Collins. Photograph by Valter Campanato/Agência Brasil. Uploaded to commons.wikimedia.org (https://commons.wikimedia.org/wiki/File:PatriciaHillCollins.jpg) by Marcosfaria70. Image licensed under CC BY 3.0. Cropped from original.

p. 290: Yasuo Yuasa. Unknown photographer.

p. 292: Anselm of Canterbury. Unknown artist.

p. 294: Thomas Aquinas. Portrait by Gentile da Fabriano.

CHAPTER 5

p. 313: Schoolchildren. Photograph by Senior Airman Eboni Reams.

p. 314: Dante Alighieri. Portrait by Sandro Botticelli.

p. 316: *That's Life* comic © Mike Twohy. Used with permission of Mike Twohy and the Cartoonist Group. All rights reserved.

p. 332: *Priestess of Delphi*. Painting by John Collier.

p. 340: Bust of Aristotle. Photograph by Jastrow.

p. 343: John D. Rockefeller. Photograph by George M. Edmondson.

p. 355: Jeremy Bentham. Line engraving by C. Fox, 1838, after H.W. Pickersgill. Uploaded to commons.wikimedia.org (https://commons.wikimedia.org/wiki/File:Jeremy_Bentham._Line_engraving_by_C._Fox,_1838,_after_H._W._Wellcome_V0000462.jpg) by Wellcome Images (http://wellcomeimages.org). Image licensed under CC BY 4.0. Cropped from original.

p. 379: Maria von Herbert. Unknown artist.

p. 384: Carol Gilligan. Photograph provided by Carol Gilligan. Used with permission.

p. 387: Nel Noddings. Photograph by Jim Noddings. Uploaded to commons.wikimedia.org (https://commons.wikimedia.org/wiki/File:Nel_Noddings.jpg) by Esh77. Image licensed under CC BY-SA 4.0 license. Cropped from original.

p. 388: Blaise Pascal. Etching by J. Henriot after G. Edelinck after F. Quesnel, junior. Uploaded to commons.wikimedia.org (https://commons.wikimedia.org/wiki/File:Blaise_Pascal._Etching_by_J._Henriot_after_G._Edelinck_after_Wellcome_V0004510.jpg) by Wellcome Images (http://wellcomeimages.org). Image licensed under CC BY 4.0. Cropped from original.

p. 396: Friedrich Nietzsche. Photograph by Gustav-Adolf Schultze.

CHAPTER 6

p. 429: 1963 March on Washington © Leonard Freed/Magnum Photos. Used with permission.

p. 436: *Matt Wuerker Editorial Cartoon* © Matt Wuerker. Used with permission of Matt Wuerker and the Cartoonist Group. All rights reserved.

p. 436: Voltaire. Portrait by Maurice Quentin de La Tour.

p. 447: Sonia Sotomayor. Photograph by Steve Petteway.

p. 456: Thomas Hobbes. Line engraving by W. Humphrys. Uploaded to commons. wikimedia.org (https://commons.wikimedia.org/wiki/File:Thomas_Hobbes._Line_ engraving_by_W._Humphrys,_1839._Wellcome_V0002801.jpg) by Wellcome (http:// wellcomeimages.org). Image licensed under CC BY 4.0. Cropped from original.

p. 459: Frontispiece of *Leviathan* by Thomas Hobbes. Illustration by Abraham Bosse.

p. 476: Karl Marx. Photograph by John Jabez Edwin Mayal.

p. 481: Hannah Arendt. Photograph by Barbara Niggl Radloff. Uploaded to commons. wikimedia.org (https://commons.wikimedia.org/wiki/File:Hannah_Arendt_auf_ dem_1._Kulturkritikerkongress,_Barbara_Niggl_Radloff,_FM-2019-1-5-9-16.jpg) by Elya. Image licensed under CC BY-SA 4.0. Cropped from original.

p. 493: Malcolm X. Photograph by Marion S. Trikosko.

p. 494: Martin Luther King Jr. Photograph by Bob Fitch © Bob Fitch Photography Archive, Department of Special Collections, Stanford University Library. Used with permission.

p. 494: Rosa Parks, 1955. Unknown photographer.

p. 495: Martin Luther King Jr. on the steps of the Lincoln Memorial, August 1963. Unknown photographer.

p. 496: Frederick Douglass. Photograph by George Kendall Warren.

p. 498: Olympe de Gouges. Portrait by Alexander Kucharsky, photograph by Bonarov.

p. 499: Alicia Garza. Screen capture from Citizen University. Uploaded to commons. wikimedia.org (https://commons.wikimedia.org/wiki/File:Alicia_Garza.jpg) by PanchoS. Image licensed under CC BY 3.0. Cropped from original.

p. 500: W.E.B. Du Bois. Photograph by James Edward Purdy.

Index

Note: Page numbers in *italics* denote figures.

A

Abernathy, Ralph, 495
Abhayananda, S., 410
Abrahamic religious traditions, 52, 55, 394, 405–09, 424–25
  See also Christianity
absolute idealism, 478, 514
Absolute Mind, 478, 515
abstract universals, 155, 203
absurdity, 152, 203
Academy (school founded by Plato), 223
Acosta, Josephus, 468
active construction, perception as, 274, 306
active engagement, 163, 205
activity vs. state, 341
actual pleasures, 171, 205
act utilitarianism, 364–65, 423
ad hominem fallacy, 80, 118, 127
aesthetic phenomenon, life as, 404, 425
aesthetics, 49, 67
affirming the antecedent, 99–100, 127
affirming the consequent, 100, *104*, 127
African American philosophical approaches, 53, 287–89
  See also nonviolence
African philosophical approaches, 52–53
Albertus Magnus, 294, 295
Alexander the Great, 340
al-Ghazali, Abu Hamid, 56, 57–59, 67, 246
alienation, 44, 67, 482–85, 487–88, 490–92, 515

Allah, 406, 425
"Allegory of the Cave" (Plato), 230, *230*, 231–33, 304
Amazon (company), 484
America Day by Day (Beauvoir), 154
American Beauty (1999), 488
American Constitution, 463, 513
American Dream concept, 488, 503
analogy, arguments by, 111–12, 127
analytic philosophy, 52, 67
ancient philosophy, 52, 67
Angelou, Maya, 139, 382
Annas, Julia, 174, 177
Anselm of Canterbury, Saint, 292, 293, 307
antecedents, 99–100, 127
The Antichrist (Nietzsche), 396
anti-communist sentiment, 474
antinomies, 282, 306
anti-politics, 152, 203
Antisthenes (445–365 BCE), 139, 203
aphorisms, 153, 203
Apollonian dimension, 404
Apology (Plato), 85, 223
appealing to authority, fallacy of, 120–21, 127
appearance vs. reality, 324, 422
appetite, 323, 342, 422, *442*, *445*
a priori elements of knowledge, 275–77, *277*, 278–79, 366, 423
Aquinas, Thomas. *See* Thomas Aquinas, Saint
Arendt, Hannah, 481
argument from cause, 298, 307

argument from intelligent design, 299, 307
argument from motion, 297–98, 307
argument from necessity, 298–99, 307
argument from perfection and degree, 299, 307
arguments
    introduced, 74–76
    by analogy, 111–12, 127
    attitude adjustments for, 84–86
    benefits of, 86
    deductive, 98–107
    do's and don'ts for formulating, 123
    Euthyphro (Plato), 86–87, 88–97
    evaluating claims, 113–16
    by inductive generalization, 112–13
    informal logical fallacies, 118–22
    non-arguments vs., 81–84
    non-deductive, 109–13
    from past experience, 110–11, 127
    Know Thyself diagnostic: rational thinking, 77–80
    study guide, 127–31
Aristippus of Cyrene (430–350 BCE), 74, 170–71
aristocracy, 332, 422, 439, *447*, 513
Aristotle (384–322 BCE)
    historical philosophical approaches, 52
    influence on Epicurus, 172
    influence on St. Thomas Aquinas, 295
    medieval scholasticism and, 236–37
    Philosopher Profile, 340
    as student of Plato, 223, 340
    See also virtue ethics
artisan/business class, *442*, 442–43, 445, 513
asceticism, 141, 175, 189, 205, 207
Asian philosophical approaches, 52, 290–91,
    410–14
    See also Buddhism
ataraxia, 173–74, *175*, 175–76, 205
atheism, 152, 203, 322, 394–95, 474
    See also will to power
attachment, 185, 206
attainable ultimate ends, 341, 344, 422
Augustine, Saint, Archbishop of Canterbury, 52
Aurelius, Marcus (121–180 CE)
    The Meditations of Marcus Aurelius, 147–52
    Philosopher Profile, 144
    Stoicism and, 139, *141*, 143, 145, 203

authenticity, living with, 158, 205
autonomy, 373–76, 402, 423, 425
auxiliary/soldier class, *442*, 443–44, *445*, 513
Awakening the Buddha Within (Das), 192
axiology, 46, 49, 67, 437, 513

B

Bacon, Francis, 239
Bakunin, Mikhail, 477
balance, and the good life, 344–45, 422
Barnes, Jonathan, 341
Beauvoir, Simone de, 52, 153, 159, 205, 254, 503
becoming, 222, 304
Beeckman, Isaac, 235
begging the question, fallacy of, 119, 127
being, 226, 304
Being and Nothingness (Sartre), 154
Bentham, Jeremy
    act vs. rule utilitarianism, 364–65
    hedonic calculus, 356–59
    *An Introduction to the Principles of Morals and
        Legislation*, 362–64
    is-ought fallacy, 355–56
    Philosopher Profile, 355
    principle of utility, 354–55
    theory of sanctions, 357–61
    utilitarianism as consequentialism, 353–54
Berkowitz, Peter, 399
Berry, Brian, "Roman Catholic Ethics," 416–19
Beyond Good and Evil (Nietzsche), 396
Bhagavad Gita, 410, 425
Black activism, 495–96
    See also nonviolence
Black Feminist Thought (Collins), 287–89
Blanshard, Brand, 40
bodily health, 175, 205
The Body (Yuasa), 290–91
bourgeois capitalists, 481, 515
Brandes, Georg, 397
Brandt, Richard, 170
Bryant, William Cullen, 510
Buddha (Siddhartha Gautama), 135, 182–83,
    198–200

Buddhism
    characterized, 138, 181, 183–84, 206
    Four Noble Truths, 183–89
    meditative practices, 56
    Noble Eight-Fold Path, 189–97
    as non-Western philosophical approach, 52
    Philosopher Profile: Siddhartha Gautama, the
        Buddha, 182–83
    "The Setting in Motion of the Wheel of Truth"
        (Buddha), 198–200

C

Campbell, Joseph, 50
Camus, Albert, 153, 203
capitalism
    defined, 515
    alienation as byproduct of, 482–85, 487–88,
        490–92
    dehumanization of, 488–89
    division of labor within, 441
    Martin Luther King Jr. on, 492–93
    Marx's epochs of history and, 480–81
    post-capitalism, 489
    structural inequalities within, 500
care ethics
    characterized, 321, 424
    Caring (Noddings), 386, 391–93
    Gilligan's ethic of care, 384–86
    male bias in moral research, 379–83
    Nel Noddings on, 386–90
    Philosopher Profile: Carol Gilligan, 384
    Philosopher Profile: Nel Noddings, 387
Caring (Noddings), 386, 391–93
caring relation, 389
Cartesian method of doubt, 219, 239–43
Cartesian mind-body dualism, 290
Cartesian Rationalism, 219
categorical imperative, 371–73, 382, 424
categorical syllogisms, 105, 127
Categories (Aristotle), 340
cause, argument from, 298, 307
cause and effect, 262–65, 305
cause and substance, categories of, 277–79

certainty, 237, 304
chain arguments, 102–03
character ethics
    introduced, 321, 322
    functional explanation of morality, 324
    the ideal city-state (*Republic*, Plato), 325–28
    Plato's character types, 331–37
    Plato's teleology, 323
    vision of the soul, 323–24
    Know Thyself diagnostic: Platonic character
        index, 329–31
character types, Plato's, 331–37, 422
Cheney, Jim, 54
Choctaw Nation, 54
Chodorow, Nancy, 384
Christianity
    Christian ethics, 414–19
    morality and, 315, 405
    Nietzsche on, 401, 403
    science and, 236–37, 240
    See also God; nonviolence; religion and ethics
Chrysippus of Soloi (279–206 BCE), 139, 140,
    141, *141*, 203
Cicero, Marcus Tullius (106–43 BCE), 171, 177,
    205
circular reasoning, 119, 127
city-states, 325–28, 440, 513
civil rights movement, 495–96
claims, evaluating, 113–16
class conflict, 479–82, 515
Cleanthes of Assos (331–232 BCE), *141*
clear and distinct criterion of truth, 247, 304
cogito ergo sum ("I think therefore I am"), 156,
    203, 244–50, 260–62, 285–86
Cold War era, 474
Collins, Patricia Hill, *Black Feminist Thought*,
    287–89
color line, notion of, 500, 515
common antecedent, fallacy of, 103, *104*, 127
commonwealth, 434, 458, *459*, 460, 461–63, 514
communism
    introduced, 435, 515
    anti-communist sentiment, 474
    Marx's epochs of history and, 480–81
Communist League, 477

The Communist Manifesto (Marx and Engels), 477, 480, 481
community of harmonizing equals, 499, 515
complex ideas, 253, 305
concentration, and Noble Eight-Fold Path, 189, 193–95, 206
conceptual analysis, 41, 52, 67
conceptual claims, 116, 127
conclusions, in argumentation, 81, 127
Confucianism, 52
consensual democracy, 435, 468–69, 514
consequentialism, 354, 423
consequents, 99–100, 127
constant conjunction, 263, 264, 305
contemplative lifestyle, 343–45, 422
contemporary philosophy, 52, 67
content, of arguments, 98–99, 127
contiguity, 262, 263, 305
continental philosophers, 52
contingency and possibility, 158, 204
conventional level of moral development, 380–81, *381*
Copernican Revolution, 236, 274, 304
Copleston, Frederick, 296
cosmology, of Stoics, 142, 203
cosmos, 281–82, 306
courage, 142, 203, 443, 513
craving, 186, 206
critical-mindedness, 34–35, 67
Critique of Judgment (Kant), 271
Critique of Pure Reason (Kant), 271, 274, 276
Crito (Plato), 223
Cummings, E.E., 157
customary morality, 401–02
Cynicism, 139–40, 203
Cynosarges, 139, 203
Cyrenaic hedonism, 170–71, 205

D

Daoism, 52
Darwin, Charles, 395
Das, Surya, Lama, 192, 194, 195
Das Kapital (Marx), 477

Declaration of Independence (United States), 463, 464, 499, 514
deduction, knowledge through, 238
deductive arguments
    defined, *98*, 98–99, 127
    categorical syllogisms, 105, 127
    disjunctive syllogisms, 103–04, *104*
    hypothetical syllogisms/chain arguments, 102–03
    modus ponens, 99–101
    modus tollens, 101–02
    validity, truth, and soundness, 106–07
dehumanization of capitalism, 488, 515
Deliverance from Error (al-Ghazali), 57–59, 246
democracies, 445, 513
democratic character, 331, 336–37, 422
denial, as egoistic defense, 190, 206
denying the antecedent, 102, *104*, 127
denying the consequent, 101–02, 127
deontological ethics
    characterized, 321, 424
    autonomy vs. heteronomy of will, 373–76
    Brian Berry on, 416–17
    categorical imperative, 371–73, 382
    criticisms of, 377–78
    duty, 367–70
    the good will, 366–67
    Groundwork for the Metaphysics of Morals (Kant), 366, 371, 375–76
    maxims and moral behavior, 370–71
    Philosopher Profile: Maria von Herbert, 379
    rational basis of morality, 365–66
Descartes, René
    cogito ergo sum ("I think therefore I am"), 156, 203, 244–50, 260–62, 285–86
    First Meditation, 241–43
    Philosopher Profile, 235–36
    Second Meditation featuring the *cogito*, 245–46
    Second Meditation featuring The Wax Example, 249–50, 272
    See also rational method of doubt
descriptions vs. arguments, 82, 127
Dhammacakkappavattana Sutta (Buddha), 198–200
Dharma (Buddhist teaching), 184, 189, 206

dialectical materialism, 478–79, *479*, 515

dialectical process, 478, *479*, 515

dialogues, 153, 204

Dialogues Concerning Natural Religion (Hume), 259

Diogenes Laertius (180–240 CE), 139, 171, 205

Dionysian dimension, 404

direct seeing, 190

disagreement, 74, 127

Discourse on Method (Descartes), 235, 238–39, 286

disjunctive syllogisms, 103–04, *104*, 127

distinctive function (for humans), 342, 422

Divided Line Theory, *224*, 224–26, *225*, 304

divinity, 344, 422

division of labor, 441, 486–89, 513, 515

Dobson, Theodore, 380

Doctrine of Recollection, 223, 304

Doctrine of the Mean, 346–48, 422

do's and don'ts for argumentation, *123*

Dostoyevsky, Fyodor, 153, 204

Douglass, Frederick, 496

dualism, 219, 289, 290–91

Du Bois, W.E.B., 500

du Châtelet, Gabrielle-Émilie, 34, 113

Durant, Will, 44

duty, notion of, 367–70, 424

"Duty and Desolation" (Langton), 378

E

Eastern philosophical approaches, 52, 290–91, 410–14

    See also Buddhism

Economic and Philosophic Manuscripts (Marx), 477, 490–92

Education and the Social Order (Russell), 61

ego, 187–88, 206, 315

egoistic rule of prudence, 458, 514

egolessness, 189, 207

Eisai, Myōan, 290

"either...or" statements, 103–04, *104*

The Elements of Law, Natural and Political (Hobbes), 456

Ellis, Albert, 145, *145*, 203

emotion, and Stoicism, 145–46, 203

empirical self, 281, 306

empirical statements, 113

empiricism

    characterized, 219, 251, 252, 305

    criticisms of innate ideas, 253–54

    Philosopher Profile: John Locke, 252

    primary and secondary qualities of objects, 254–57

    tabula rasa, 253, 272

empty beliefs, 174, 206

enduring pleasures, 172, 206

Engels, Friedrich, 477, 480, 481

Enneagram symbol, 55–56, *56*

An Enquiry Concerning Human Understanding (Hume), 259, 267–69

An Enquiry Concerning the Principles of Morals (Hume), 259

entelechy, 338, 422

Epictetus (50–138 CE), 139, *141*, 145, 203

Epicureanism, 171, 172–77, *175*, 206

Epicurus (341–270 BCE), 45, 171–72, *175*, 178, 179–81, 206

epistemological objectivity, 286, 307

epistemology and metaphysics

    introduced, 46, 48, 67, 214–16, 220–21

    mind-body metaphysics, 289–91

    standpoint epistemology, 285–86, 307

    Know Thyself diagnostic: assumptions about knowledge, 217–19

    study guide, 304–11

    See also empiricism; God; metaphysical epistemology; radical skepticism; rational method of doubt; synthesis of reason and experience

epochs of history, 480, 515

equality, nonviolence and, 499, 515

An Essay Concerning Human Understanding (Locke), 251, 254, 256

essence vs. existence, 155–56, 159–60, 204, 394

    See also Existentialism

ethical hedonism, 170, 206

ethic of love, 496, 516

ethics and moral decision-making

    introduced, 46, 48, 314–18

ethics and political philosophy, 437–38
    Know Thyself diagnostic: ethical perspective
        indicator, 319–22
    study guide, 422–27
    See also care ethics; character ethics; deontolog-
        ical ethics; religion and ethics; utilitarian
        ethics; virtue ethics; will to power
The Ethics of Ambiguity (Beauvoir), 153
ethics of care. *See* care ethics
ethnocentrism, 43, 67
eudaimonia, 142, 203, 339–41
Eudemian Ethics (Aristotle), 340
eugenics, 447, 513
Euthyphro (Plato), 86–87, 88–97, 223
evaluating claims, 113–16
excessive passions, 146, 203
executive powers, 467, 514
existence vs. essence, 155–56, 159–60, 204, 394
existential atheism. *See* will to power
Existentialism
    defined, 204
    essence vs. existence, 155–56, 159–60, 204, 394
    existential freedom, 74, 138, 152, 157–58
    Existentialism Is a Humanism (Sartre), 159–60
    individuality and subjective experience, 156–57
    methods of, 153
    Philosopher Profile: Jean-Paul Sartre and Sim-
        one de Beauvoir, 154
    philosophers associated with, 153
    as revolt, 154–55
    See also will to power
Existentialism Is a Humanism (Sartre), 159–60
existential vacuum, 168, 205
experience, 271, 306
experimental confirmation, 190
explanations vs. arguments, 82, 127

F

factual statements, 113–14, 127
faculty of sensibility, 276, *277*, *280*, 306
faculty of understanding, 276, *277*, *280*, 306
fallacy of common antecedent, 103, *104*, 127
    See also informal logical fallacies

fascism, 152, 204
fate, 140–42, 203
faulty generalizations, 113
feelings of compulsion, 265, 305
feminist philosophical approaches, 53–54, 153,
        154, 287–89, 446, 513
    See also care ethics; women philosophers
Fernández de Santa Cruz, Manuel, 36, 37
fetishism of commodities, 485–86, 515
Feuerbach, Ludwig, 478
fiduciary role of government, 468, 514
fields of philosophy, 46–51
Filotea de la Cruz, Sor, 36, 37
final, ultimate ends as, 341
Five Ways, Aquinas's
    introduced, 295–97, *297*
    argument from cause, 298
    argument from intelligent design, 299
    argument from motion, 297–98
    argument from necessity, 298–99
    argument from perfection and degree, 299
forms
    of arguments, 98–99, 128
    of intuition, 276, 306
    Kantian vs. Platonic, 277
    Plato's theory of, 223, 226–27
foundational and disciplinary philosophies, 46,
        50, 67
Foundations of the Metaphysics of Morals (Kant),
        271
Four Noble Truths
    cessation of suffering, 188, 198–200
    craving, 186–88, 198–200
    prescription for *Nirvana*, 188–89, 198–200
    suffering, 185–86, 198–200
    See also Noble Eight-Fold Path
Frankl, Viktor, 168–69
freedom
    equality vs., 499
    Existentialism and, 74, 138, 152, 157–58, 204
    from physical need, 175, 206
Freedom within Reason (Wolf), 162
Freire, Paulo, 156
Freud, Sigmund, 178, 315
friendship, 177, 206

Fromm, Erich, 474–75, 476, 485
functional explanation of morality, 324, 422

G

Galbraith, John Kenneth, 112, 506
Galileo Galilei, 237, 238, 240
Gandhi, Mohandas K., 493–94, 502
The Garden (Epicurean school of philosophy),
      172, 177, 178, 206
Garza, Alicia, 499
The Gay Science (Nietzsche), 394–95, 398
generalized descriptions, 112, 128
General Motors Company (GM), 483
geocentric view of the universe, 236, 304
George, Henry, 506
Gilligan, Carol, 53, 379–86, 424
    See also care ethics
Glasser, William, 184
Glover, Jonathan, 74
God
    St. Anselm's ontological proof, 293, 307
    ataraxia and, 175–76
    as concept of pure reason, 282, 306
    Descartes's argument for, 247
    David Hume on, 261–62
    as innate, 253–54
    Locke's natural law and, 464
    meaning of life and, 163
    Nietzsche's existential atheism, 394–95
    property rights and, 466
    Stoicism and, 140
    Summa Theologica (Aquinas), 295, 296, 300–01
    St. Thomas Aquinas's Five Ways, 295–99
    See also Christianity; will to power
Godse, Nathuram, 494
the good life, 343, 422
goodness, 227, 228–30, 304
the good will, 366–67, 424
Gore, Albert, 74
Gouges, Olympe de, 378, 498
Grau, Christopher, Understanding Love, 162
Grisez, Germain, 416
grounds for opinions, 81, 128

Groundwork for the Metaphysics of Morals (Kant),
      271, 366, 368, 373, 375–76, 529
guardian class, 332, 422, 443, 513
guilt by association, fallacy of, 122, 128
Gurdjieff, George, 43

H

habit, 346, 423
handicraft, 487, 515
happiness, 339–42, 423
Hassan, Riffat, "Islamic View of Peace," 407,
      408–09
hasty conclusions, 111, 128
hasty generalizations, 113, 128
hedonic calculus, 356–59, 423
Hedonism
    characterized, 138, 169, 206
    Aristippus of Cyrene, 170–71
    ataraxia (tranquility), 173–74, 175, 175–76
    Epicurus, 171–72
    friendship in, 177–78
    kinetic vs. static pleasures, 173
    "Letter to Menoeceus" (Epicurus), 179–81
    momentary vs. enduring pleasures, 172–73
    natural desires, 174–75
    psychological vs. ethical, 169–70
    virtue and, 176–77
Hegel, Georg Wilhelm Friedrich, 154, 204, 476,
      478, 515
Heidegger, Martin, 153, 159, 204
Heine, Heinrich, 477
heliocentric theory of the universe, 236, 304
Hellenistic philosophy, 45–46, 67
Heraclitus of Ephesus (c. 500 BCE), 222, 304, 323
Herbert, Maria von, 377–78, 379, 424
herd morality, 401–02, 425
Hester, Lee, 54, 67
heteronomy of will, 373–76, 424
higher-order principle test, 115, 128
Hindu ethics, 410–14
Hinduism, 52, 425
historical approaches to philosophy, 52
History of England (Hume), 259

History of the Peloponnesian War (Thucydides), 456

Hitler, Adolf, 74

Hobbes, Thomas
  Leviathan, 457–58, 459, 461–63, 514
  Philosopher Profile, 456
  utilitarianism and, 353, 460
  See also social contract theories

Holden, John, *Science Askew*, 49

Hollingdale, R.J., 397

humanitarianism, 152, 204

Hume, David
  association of ideas, 262
  critique of causality, 262–65
  An Enquiry Concerning Human Understanding, 267–69
  influence on Immanuel Kant, 270
  on the origin of ideas, 260, 272
  Philosopher Profile, 259
  rejection of the *cogito*, 260–62
  types of reasoning, and Hume's "fork," 265–66, 305

Hurley, Kathleen, 380

Hurston, Zora Neale, 43

hypothetical fallacy, 103, *104*

hypothetical moral dilemmas, 382, 424

hypothetical syllogisms, 102–03, 128

I

Ibn Rushd, 407

Ibn Sina, 407

Ichazo, Oscar, 56

ideas, 253, 260, 262, 265, 305

identifying fallacies, 124–25

identity formation, 384, 424

idolatry, 485–86, 515

"if...then" statements, 99–103, *104*

ignoring an alternative disjunct, 104, *104*, 128

"I Have a Dream" (King), 497

imagination, 224, *224*, 262, 304, 305

immanence, 140, 203

imperfect societies, 445–46, 513, 514

impermanence, 189, 207

impressions, 260, 272, 305

In a Different Voice (Gilligan), 384, 385–86

inclination, actions performed out of, 368–69, 424

Indigenous peoples, philosophical traditions of, 53, 54

individualism, 440–42, 468, 513

individuality and subjective experience, 156–57

inductive arguments, *98*, 109, 128
  See also non-deductive arguments

inductive generalization, argument by, 112–13, 128

informal logical fallacies
  characterized, 118, 128
  ad hominem fallacy, 80, 118, 127
  appealing to authority, 120–21, 127
  circular reasoning/begging the question, 119, 127
  guilt by association, 122, 128
  identifying fallacies, 124–25
  red herring fallacy, 80, 121–22, 128
  slippery slope fallacy, 120
  straw person fallacy, 118–19, 129
  two wrongs fallacy, 80, 120

information age, philosophy and, 43–44

innate ideas, 253, 305

instrumental ends, 339, 423

instrumental value, 43, 67

intellectual virtue, 346, 423

intelligence, 40, 67

intelligent design, argument from, 299, 307

intelligible world, *224, 225,* 226, 304

intensity of pleasures, 170, 206

interior freedom, 142, 203

interlocutors, 87, 128

interpersonal, concept of, 152, 204

intimacy, 385, 424

intrinsic ends, 339, 423

intrinsic value of philosophy, 41, 67

An Introduction to the Principles of Morals and Legislation (Bentham), 354

intuition, knowledge through, 238, 305

Islamic ethics, 405–09

"Islamic View of Peace" (Hassan), 407, 408–09
is-ought fallacy, 44, 67, 355–56
I Think (Descartes's *cogito*), 271, 281

J

Jaggar, Alison, 53
Jalaluddin Rumi, Maulana, 407
James, William, 84, 155
Jaspers, Karl, 153, 159, 204
Jefferson, Thomas, 463, 499
Jesus Christ, 415
Johnson, James Weldon, 509–10
Juana Inés de la Cruz, Sor, 36, 37–39, 68
Judaism, 52, 55
Jung, Carl, 140
justice, 444, 502–03, 513, 515

K

Kabbalah (Tree of Life), 55, *55*
Kaczynski, Ted, 40
Kafka, Franz, 153, 204
Kant, Immanuel
    correspondence with Maria von Herbert,
        377–79
    Groundwork for the Metaphysics of Morals,
        375–76
    modern philosophy and, 52
    Philosopher Profile, 270, 271
    Prolegomena to Any Future Metaphysics, 283–85
    See also deontological ethics; synthesis of reason and experience
Kantian Structuralism, 219
karma, 195–97, 207
Keenan, James, 41
Kennedy, John F., 82
Kierkegaard, Søren, 55, 153, 205
kinetic vs. static pleasures, 173, 206
King, Martin Luther, Jr.
    "I Have a Dream" speech, 497
    influences on, 492–94, *494*
    Philosopher Profile, 495–96

"Where Do We Go from Here," 504–10
    See also nonviolence
kingdom of ends, 374, 424
knowledge, 40, 67, *224, 225,* 226, 304
    See also epistemology and metaphysics
Know Thyself diagnostics
    assumptions about knowledge and reality,
        217–19
    ethical perspective indicator, 319–22
    Philosophy of life preference indicator, 136–38
    Platonic Character Type Index, 329–31
    political outlook, 432–35
    preconceptions about philosophy, 32
    rational thinking for argumentation, 77–80
Kohlberg, Lawrence, 380–82, *381*
Kopernik, Mikolaj, 236, 238, 240, 274, 305

L

labor, division of, 441
Langton, Rae, "Duty and Desolation," 378
law of moral causation, 195, 207
law of nature, 457, 514
laws of association, 262, 305
League of the Just, 477
Lectures on Ethics (Kant), 369–70
Lee, George W., 496
Le Guin, Ursula K., 161
"Letter to Menoeceus" (Epicurus), 174, 179–81
Leviathan (Hobbes), 457–58, *459,* 461–63, 514
lifestyles, according to Aristotle, 342–45
Linda Brown et al. v. Board of Education of Topeka,
        495
literary forms, 153, 204
Locke, John
    consensual democracy, 435, 468
    criticisms of innate ideas, 253–54
    influence on Western democracy, 463
    Philosopher Profile, 252
    primary and secondary qualities of objects,
        254–57
    Second Treatise of Government, 472–73
    tabula rasa, 253, 272
    See also social contract theories

logic, philosophical branch, 46, 48, 67
logical fallacies. *See* informal logical fallacies
logical forms, in argumentation, 98, 128
logical self, 281, 306
logotherapy, 168, 205
love and justice, 502–03, 515–16
Lucretius Carus, Titus (94–55 BCE), 171, 206, 251
Luther, Martin, 240, *240*
Lyceum (school founded by Aristotle), 340
lying, impermissibility of, 377–78

M

Mahabharata, 410
majority rule, 469, 514
male bias in moral research, 379–83
Malebranche, Nicolas, 235
Malhotra, Ashok Kumar, *Transcreation of the Bhagavad Gita*, 412–14
The Mandarins (Beauvoir), 154
Manifesto of the Communist Party (Marx and Engels), 477, 480, 481
manufacture, 487, 515
Marcel, Gabriel, 153, 159, 204
Marriage and Morals (Russell), 61
Marx, Karl
   as anti-philosopher, 475
   Economic and Philosophic Manuscripts, 477, 490–92
   influence on Martin Luther King Jr., 492–93
   Philosopher Profile, 476–77
   See also socialism
Marxism, 152, 204
mass action, 493, 516
master vs. slave morality, 399–401, 424
mathematics and philosophy, 214–16, *224*, 227, 238, 247, 266
matters of fact, 265–66, 305
maxims and moral behavior, 367, 370–71, 424
McCarthy, Joseph, 474
McCormick, Richard, 417–18
meaningfulness, 164, 205
Meaning in Life and Why It Matters (Wolf), 162
meaning of life

Viktor Frankl and the will-to-meaning, 168–69
   meaningful lives, 162–64, 205
   The Meanings of Lives (Wolf), 165–67
   Philosopher Profile: Susan Wolf, 162
   pleasure and, 170–71
The Meanings of Lives (Wolf), 165–67
Medicine Wheel, 53, 68
medieval philosophy, 52, 68
medieval scholasticism, 236–37, 305
mediocrity and herd morality, 401–02
meditation, 60, 290
The Meditations of Marcus Aurelius (Aurelius), 144, 147–52
Meditations on First Philosophy (Descartes), 221, 236, 241–43, 245–50, 456
Memoirs of a Dutiful Daughter (Beauvoir), 154
Meno (Plato), 223
meritocracy, 447, 513
meta-ethicists, 48
metaphysical epistemology
   introduced, 221
   "Allegory of the Cave" (Plato), 230, *230*, 231–33, 304
   Divided Line Theory, 222, *224*, 224–26, *225*, 304
   "Simile of the Sun" (Plato), 227, 228–30, 304
   Theory of Forms, 223, 226–27, 304
metaphysics
   introduced, 46, 47, 68, 214–16, 220–21
   critiques of Western approaches, 285–91
   dialectical materialism and, 478–79, *479*
   as illusory, 280–81
   Immanuel Kant on, 279–82, *280*, 283–85
   John Locke's criticisms of, 251, 256–57
   Know Thyself diagnostic: assumptions about knowledge, 217–19
   study guide, 304–11
   See also empiricism; God; metaphysical epistemology; radical skepticism; rational method of doubt; synthesis of reason and experience
Metaphysics (Aristotle), 340
method of doubt, 239–43, 305
Middle Eastern philosophical approaches, 52, 55, 405–09
Middle Path of living, 181, 189, 198–200, 207

militarism, 500, 501–02
Mill, John Stuart, 52, 81, 111, 355
mind-body metaphysics, 289–91
moderation, 347, 423
modern Western philosophy, 52, 60–65, 68
modus ponens, 99–101, 128
modus tollens, 101–02, 128
momentary vs. enduring pleasures, 172–73, 206
monism, 140, 203, 221–22, 304
Monologion (Anselm of Canterbury), 292
Montaigne, Michel de, 153, 204
moral balance, 324, 422
moral certainty, 366, 424
moral development, 146, 380–82, *381*, 424
morality
    Christianity and, 315, 405
    functional explanation of, 324, 422
    herd morality, 401–02, 425
    Noble Eight-Fold Path and, 189, 191–93, 207
    Philosopher Profile: Susan Wolf, 162
    political philosophy and, 437–38
    rational basis of, 365–66
    See also ethics and moral decision-making
The Morality of Happiness (Annas), 174
moral sanctions, 360
moral virtue, 324, 346, 422, 423
Morris, Tom, 46
Moses, Greg, 499, 500, 503
motion, argument from, 297–98, 307
Murdoch, Iris, 163
My Own Life (Hume), 259

N

Naranjo, Claudio, 56
Native American peoples, philosophical approaches, 53, 54
natural caring, 389, 424
natural desires, 174–75, 206
natural equality, 454, 514
Naturalistic Empiricism, 219
natural law, 435, 464, 514
natural rights, 464

Nausea (Sartre), 154
necessary connections, 262, 264–65, 306
necessity, argument from, 298–99, 307
negation, 158, 204, 400, 425
new case test, 116, 128
Newton, Sir Isaac, 262
Nicomachean Ethics (Aristotle), 340, 343, 348, 350–53
Nietzsche, Friedrich Wilhelm
    evaluating values, 402–03
    as existentialist, 153
    The Gay Science, 394–95, 398
    God is dead, 394–95
    herd morality and revaluation of values, 401–02
    master vs. slave morality, 399–401
    Philosopher Profile, 396–97
    superman/*Übermensch*, 396, 403–05, 425
    will to power, 395–98, 425
nihilism, 403, 425
Nirvana, 188, 207
Noble Eight-Fold Path
    characterized, 189, 207
    karma and rebirth, 195–97
    training of concentration, 189, 193–95
    training of morality, 189, 191–93
    training of wisdom, 189–91
    See also Four Noble Truths
nobles (master moralists), 400, 425
Noddings, Nel, 386–93, 424
    See also care ethics
No Exit (Sartre), 154
non-arguments, 82–83
non-deductive arguments, 109–13
non-subjective values, 164, 205
non-traditional and non-Western philosophy, 52–53, 54
nonviolence
    characterized, 435, 496–99
    equality, 499, 515–16
    "I Have a Dream" (King), 497
    justice and love, 502–03, 515–16
    Martin Luther King Jr., influences on, 492–94, *494*

nonviolent direct action, 502, 516
Philosopher Profile: Martin Luther King Jr.,
495–96
structure, 500–02, 516
"Where Do We Go from Here" (King), 504–10
nonviolent direct action, 502, 516
noögenic neurosis, 168, 205
Notes from Underground (Dostoyevsky), 153
noumena vs. phenomena, 279–80, 306
Nussbaum, Martha C., *The Therapy of Desire*, 45,
178
Nyanaponika Thera, 196

O

Obama, Barack, 164
objectification of labor, 487
"Of Suicide" (Hume), 259
"Of the Ends of Political Society and
Government" (Locke), 472–73
"Of the Immortality of the Soul" (Hume), 259
oligarchic character, 331, 335–36, 422
oligarchic states, 445, *447*, 513
one caring and one cared for, 389–90, 424
On Education, Especially in Early Childhood
(Russell), 61
On the Genealogy of Morals (Nietzsche), 396, 399
On the Heavens (Aristotle), 340
On the Soul (Aristotle), 340
ontological argument, St. Anselm's, 292, 293, 307
opinion, 81–82, 128, 224, *224*, 304
ordered universe, concept of, 140, 203
the original position, 382
Original Sources
"Allegory of the Cave" (Plato), 231–33
Black Feminist Thought (Collins), 287–89
The Body (Yuasa), 290–91
Caring (Noddings), 391–93
Deliverance from Error (al-Ghazali), 57–59
Economic and Philosophic Manuscripts (Marx),
490–92
An Enquiry Concerning Human Understanding
(Hume), 267–69
Euthyphro (Plato), 88–97

Existentialism Is a Humanism (Sartre), 159–60
The Gay Science (Nietzsche), 398
Groundwork for the Metaphysics of Morals (Kant),
375–76
the ideal city-state (*Republic*, Plato), 325–28
"I Have a Dream" (King), 497
*An Introduction to the Principles of Morals and
Legislation* (Bentham), 362–64
"Islamic View of Peace" (Hassan), 408–09
"Letter to Menoeceus" (Epicurus), 179–81
Leviathan (Hobbes), 461–63
The Meanings of Lives (Wolf), 165–67
The Meditations of Marcus Aurelius (Aurelius),
147–52
Meditations on First Philosophy (Descartes),
241–43, 245–50
the nature of woman (*Republic*, Plato), 448–53
Nicomachean Ethics (Aristotle), 350–53
Prolegomena to Any Future Metaphysics (Kant),
283–85
Reply to Sor Filotea (Juana Inés de la Cruz),
37–39
"Roman Catholic Ethics" (Berry), 416–19
Second Treatise of Government (Locke), 472–73
The Setting in Motion of the Wheel of Truth (Bud-
dha), 198–200
"Simile of the Sun" (Plato), 228–30
Transcreation of the Bhagavad Gita (Malhotra),
412–14
"Truth and Native American Epistemology"
(Hester), 54
The Value of Philosophy (Russell), 62–65
"Where Do We Go from Here" (King), 504–10
original synthetic, 281

P

Padma Sambhava, 184
Pali Text Society, 183
Panaetius of Rhodes (185–110 BCE), *141*
parables, 153, 204
Parks, Rosa, 494, 495
Parmenides of Elea (c. 500 BCE), 221–22, 304
Pascal, Blaise, 153, 203, 388

Passions of the Soul (Descartes), 236
passive disengagement, 163, 205
Passmore, John, 34
past experience, argument from, 110–11, 127
perception, 224, *224*, 304
perennial wisdom, 41, 68
perfection and degree, argument from, 299, 307
perspective, sense of, 40, 68
Phaedo (Plato), 223, 289
Phaedrus (Plato), 223
phenomena vs. noumena, 279–80, 306
philosopher kings, 331, 332–33, *442*, 443, 444, *445*, 513
Philosopher Profiles
   St. Anselm of Canterbury, 292
   Aristotle, 340
   Marcus Aurelius, 144
   Simone de Beauvoir, 154
   Jeremy Bentham, 355
   René Descartes, 235–36
   Carol Gilligan, 384
   Maria von Herbert, 379
   Thomas Hobbes, 456
   David Hume, 259
   Sor Juana Inés de la Cruz, 36
   Immanuel Kant, 271
   Martin Luther King Jr., 495–96
   John Locke, 252
   Karl Marx, 476–77
   Friedrich Nietzsche, 396–97
   Nel Noddings, 387
   Plato, 223
   Bertrand Russell, 61
   Jean-Paul Sartre, 154
   Siddhartha Gautama, the Buddha, 182–83
   Socrates, 85
   St. Thomas Aquinas, 294–95
   Western philosophers, 34–35
   Susan Wolf, 162
philosophical counseling, 45
philosophical system-building, 154, 204
philosophies of life
   introduced, 46, 50–51, 68, 134–35
   Know Thyself diagnostic: philosophies prefer-
      ence indicator, 136–38

study guide, 203–10
See also Buddhism; Existentialism; Hedonism;
   meaning of life; Stoicism
philosophy
   introduced, 30–31, 68
   etymology of, 34
   feminist approaches, 53–54, 153, 154, 287–89,
      446, 513
   fields of, 46–51
   historical approaches, 52
   modern Western, 60–65
   non-traditional and non-Western, 52–53
   philosophers, characterizing, 33–39
   practical value of, 41–46
   spiritually-based traditions, 55, 55–59, *56*
   Western rational tradition, 51
   wisdom and, 34, 40–41
   Know Thyself diagnostic: Preconceptions
      about Philosophy, 32
   study guide, 67–70
   See also arguments; epistemology and meta-
      physics; ethics and moral decision-mak-
      ing; philosophies of life; political philos-
      ophy
Philosophy of Education (Noddings), 387
physical sanctions, 360
Physics (Aristotle), 340
Piaget, Jean, 272
Plato (c. 427–347 BCE)
   "Allegory of the Cave," 230, *230*, 231–33, 304
   Apology, 85
   Euthyphro, 86–87, 88–97
   historical philosophical approaches, 52
   on the ideal city-state, 325–28
   influence on Aristotle, 223, 340
   Kantian vs. Platonic forms, 277
   Immanuel Kant's criticisms of, 270
   on the nature of woman, 448–53
   Philosopher Profile, 223
   Platonic rationality, 154–55
   "Simile of the Sun," 227, 228–30, 304
   Socrates's influence on, 85, 223
   See also character ethics; metaphysical episte-
      mology; *Republic* (Plato)
Platonic Dualism, 219

pleasure, 170, 206

polis (city-state), 440

political conservatism, 152, 205

political philosophy
  introduced, 46, 50, 68, 430–31, 513
  politics and political science vs., 436–39
  Know Thyself diagnostic: political outlook, 432–35
  study guide, 513–20
  See also nonviolence; *Republic* (Plato); social contract theories; socialism

political sanctions, 360

political science, 437–38, 513

political society and government, 467–68, 514

politics, 436–37, 513

Politics (Aristotle), 340

Posidonius of Apamea (135–51 BCE), *141*

positivism, 287, 307

possibility and contingency, 158, 204

post-conventional level of moral development, 380–82, *381*

Posterior Analytics (Aristotle), 340

postmodernism, 52, 68

potential pleasures, 171, 206

poverty, 500, 516

power, nonviolence and, 498, 503, 516

powers of discrimination, 175, 206

The Practice and Theory of Bolshevism (Russell), 61

Prajna Paramita Sutras, 188

pre-conventional level of moral development, 380–81, *381*

premises, 81, 128

prerogative power, 470, 514

primary qualities of objects, 255–57, 305

principled conscience, 498, 516

principle of utility, 354–55, 423

The Principles of Mathematics (Russell), 61

Principles of Philosophy (Descartes), 236

Prior Analytics (Aristotle), 340

priority in time, 263–64, 306

The Problems of Philosophy (Russell), 62–65

Progress and Poverty (George), 506

Prolegomena to Any Future Metaphysics (Kant), 271, 283–85

proletariat, 481, 482, 485, 515

property rights, 465–66

Prophet Muhammad, 406

Proslogion (Anselm of Canterbury), 292–93

Proudhon, Pierre-Joseph, 477

prudence, 175, 206, 368, 424

psychological bias, 379, 424

psychological hedonism, 169–70, 206, 354

psychological honesty, 400, 425

Ptolemaic universe, 240, *240*

pure reason, *280*, 280–82, 306

Pyrrhus and Cinéas (Beauvoir), 154

Q

questions, in argumentation, 83–84

Quintus Junius Rusticus (100–170 CE), 144

Qur'an, 406, 425

R

racism, 500–02, 516
  See also nonviolence

radical skepticism
  characterized, 257–58, 306
  association of ideas, 262
  critique of causality, 262–65
  An Enquiry Concerning Human Understanding (Hume), 267–69
  the origin of ideas, 260, 272
  Philosopher Profile: David Hume, 259
  rejection of the *cogito*, 260–62
  types of reasoning, and Hume's "fork," 265–66, 305

Rand, Ayn, 169

rational capacities, 342, 423

rational disinterestedness, 84, 128

Rational-Emotive Behavior Therapy, 145, *145*

rationality
  as basis of morality, 365–66
  Existentialism as revolt against, 154, 204

rational method of doubt
  achieving certain knowledge, 237–39
  Cartesian method of doubt, 219, 239–43

cogito ergo sum ("I think therefore I am"), 156, 203, 244–50, 260–62, 285–86
    as father of modern philosophy, 236–37
    First Meditation (Descartes), 241–43
    on *Meditations*, 221
    Philosopher Profile: René Descartes, 235–36
    Second Meditation featuring the *cogito* (Descartes), 245–46
    Second Meditation featuring The Wax Example (Descartes), 249–50, 272
Rawls, John, *A Theory of Justice*, 382
reaction and negation, 400, 425
reality testing, 190, 207
reality vs. appearance, 324, 422
realm of forms, 155, 205, 333
reason, 34, 68, 280–82, 323–24, 365, *442*, *445*
rebirth, 195, 197, 207
receptive rationality of caring, 386
red herring fallacy, 80, 121–22, 128
reflection, 253, 305
regulative function of transcendental ideas, 281, 306
Reinhold, Karl Leonhard, 379
relation, as ethically basic, 389, 424
relations of ideas, 265–66, 306
relativism, 317
religion
    as life-denying, 401, 403
    morality and Christianity, 315, 405
    science and Christianity, 236–37, 240
    See also Buddhism; Christianity; God
religion and ethics
    Christian ethics, 414–19
    Hindu ethics, 410–14
    Islamic ethics, 405–09
    "Islamic View of Peace" (Hassan), 407, 408–09
    "Roman Catholic Ethics" (Berry), 416–19
    Transcreation of the Bhagavad Gita (Malhotra), 412–14
Religion and Science (Russell), 61
religious sanctions, 360
Reply to Sor Filotea (Juana Inés de la Cruz), 37–39
Republic (Plato)
    "Allegory of the Cave," 230, *230*, 231–33, 304
    aristocracy, 434, 439, *447*
    the ideal city-state, 325–28
    imperfect societies, 445–46
    individual and state, 440–42
    the nature of woman, 448–53
    Plato's class system, *442*, 442–45, *445*
    "Simile of the Sun," 227, 228–30, 304
    women, marriage, and family, 446–47, *447*
    See also Plato (427–347 BCE)
resemblance, 262, 306
resentment, of slave moralists, 400, 425
reversibility criterion, 382
revisionism, 417–18
Rhetoric (Aristotle), 340
right action, 192–93, 207
right concentration, 195, 207
right effort, 193–94, 207
right intention, 190–91, 207
right livelihood, 193, 207
right mindfulness, 194–95, 207
right of nature, 457, 514
right of self-preservation, 466, 514
right speech, 191–92, 207
right view, 189, 190
Rockefeller, John D., 343
role-exchange test, 115, 128
"Roman Catholic Ethics" (Berry), 416–19
Roman Catholicism, 415
Rules for the Direction of the Mind (Descartes), 238
rule utilitarianism, 364–65, 423
Russell, Bertrand
    contemporary philosophy, 52
    Philosopher Profile, 61
    relationship to John Stuart Mill, 355
    The Value of Philosophy, 62–65
Russell, Dora, 61

S

Saint-Simon, Claude-Henri de, 479
sanctions, 360, 423
Sartre, Jean-Paul
    contemporary philosophy, 52
    Existentialism Is a Humanism, 159–60
    as Existentialist, 153

on freedom, 74, 157
    Philosopher Profile, 154
satyagraha (truth force), 493
Schiller, Friedrich, 379
Schopenhauer, Arthur, 396
science and religion, 236–37, 240
Science Askew (Simanek and Holden), 49
Scott, Coretta, 495, 504
secondary qualities of objects, 255–57, 305
The Second Sex (Beauvoir), 153
Second Treatise of Government (Locke), 463, 470,
    472–73
seekers of truth, 35, 68
the self, 187, 207, 281, 306
self-diagnostics. *See* Know Thyself diagnostics
self-discipline, 443, 513
self-evident principle, 238, 305
self-mastery, 397, 425
self-overcoming, 397, 425
self-realization ethic, 338, 423
self-sufficiency, 175, 206, 341, 344
self-transcendence, 164, 168, 205
Seneca (4 BCE–65 CE), 139, *141*, 171, 206
sensation, 253, 305
sense perception, 155, 205
sensibility, faculty of, 276, *277*, *280*
sensible intuitions, 272, 306
separation, 385, 424
"The Setting in Motion of the Wheel of Truth"
    (Buddha), 198–200
Shaftesbury, Anthony Ashley Cooper, Earl of,
    252
shinjin ichinyo ("oneness of body-mind"), 290
A Short Tract on First Principles (Hobbes), 456
shugyō ("cultivation"), 290, 291
Siddhartha Gautama (the Buddha), 135, 182–83,
    198–200
Sign of the Presence of God (Wajh Allah), 56
Simanek, Donald, *Science Askew*, 49
"Simile of the Sun" (Plato), 227, 228–30, 304
simple ideas, 253, 305
simple tastes, 175, 206
slave vs. master morality, 399–401, 425
slippery slope fallacy, 120, 128–29
Smith, Adam, 259

Smith, Lamar, 496
Snelling, John, 190–91
social compact, 468–69, 514
social contract theories
    defined, 453, 514
    conditions on the sovereign, 460
    dissolution of government, 471
    divisions of power, 470–71
    Hobbes's Leviathan (commonwealth), 458,
        459, 460
    Hobbes's state of nature, 453–55
    laws of nature, 557–58
    Leviathan (Hobbes), 457–58, *459*, 461–63, 514
    limits on government, 469–70
    Locke's state of nature and natural law, 464–65
    Philosopher Profile: Thomas Hobbes, 456
    political society and government, 467–68
    property rights, 465–66
    Second Treatise of Government (Locke), 472–73
    social compact, 468–69
    social contract, 459–60
socialism
    alienation as byproduct of capitalism, 482–85,
        487–88, 490–92
    anti-communist sentiment and, 474
    class conflict, 479–82
    division of labor, 486–89
    Economic and Philosophic Manuscripts (Marx),
        477, 490–92
    fetishism of commodities, 485–86
    Marx as anti-philosopher, 475
    Marx's metaphysics and dialectical material-
        ism, 478–79, *479*, 532n63
    Philosopher Profile: Karl Marx, 476–77
    post-capitalism, 489
social philosophy. *See* political philosophy
Socrates (469–399 BCE)
    critical-mindedness of, 34
    influence on Plato, 223
    influence on Stoicism, 139–40
    Philosopher Profile, 85
    See also Plato (c. 427–347 BCE)
Socratic humility, 84–86, 128
Socratic method, 86–87
Socratic self-control, 171

solipsism, 247, 305

Some Thoughts on Education (Locke), 252

Sotomayor, Sonia, 447

soul, 323, 344, 422, 440–41, *442*, 513

sound arguments, 106, 129

soundness, 106, 129

space (*a priori* concept), 276, *277*, *280*, 306

spirit, 323, 422, *442*, 443, *445*, 513

spirit of scientific objectivity, 353, 423

spiritual effort, 193

spiritually-based traditions, 55, 55–59, 56

   See also religion

standpoint epistemology, 285–89, 307

state of nature, 453–55, 464–65, 514

statesman's lifestyle, 343, 423

state vs. activity, 341

static vs. kinetic pleasure, 173, 206

Stoic apathy, 142

Stoicism

   cynical origins, 139–40

   emotions and, 145–46, 526n6

   fate, 138, 140–42

   freedom and value, 74, 142

   The Meditations of Marcus Aurelius (Aurelius), 147–52

   moral development, 146

   periods and proponents of, *141*

   Philosopher Profile: Marcus Aurelius, 144

   purpose of life, 142–43

   Stoic universe, 140

   stress-management and, 145, *145*

   as therapeutic philosophy, 46

The Stranger (Camus), 153

straw person fallacy, 118–19, 129

structural evil of racism, 500, 516

structural inequalities, 500–02, 516

Structuralism, 219

structure of racist imperialism, 493, 516

subjective bias, 43, 68

subjective experience, 155, 156–57, 159–60, 205

substance and cause, categories of, 277–79

success, and concept of happiness, 341, 423

suffering, 185, 189, 198–200, 207

Sufism, 55, *56*, 57–59, 407

Summa Contra Gentiles (Aquinas), 295

Summa Theologica (Aquinas), 295, 296, 300–01

superman/*Übermensch*, 396, 403–05, 425

surplus value, 487, 515

syllogisms, 102–05, *104*, 127

symbolism, 55, 55–56, *56*

Symposium (Plato), 223

synchronicity, 140, 203

synthesis of reason and experience

   introduced, 270

   cause and substance, 277–79

   Copernican revolution in epistemology, 274–75

   Kantian vs. Platonic forms, 277

   metaphysics and transcendental ideas, 279–82, *280*

   modern philosophy and, 52

   Philosopher Profile: Immanuel Kant, 271

   a priori elements of knowledge, 275–77, *277*, 278–79

   Prolegomena to Any Future Metaphysics (Kant), 283–85

   sensory experience and knowledge, 271–74

T

tabula rasa, 253–54, 272, 305

tacit consent, 469, 514

tainin/taitoku ("body recognition"), 290, 291, 307

tarachai, 173, 206

teleology, 323, 338–39, 422

Teresa of Avila, Saint, 30

Theaetetus (Plato), 223

theism, 152, 205

   See also religion; religion and ethics

theology vs. philosophy, 296

Theory of Forms, 223, 226–27, 304

A Theory of Justice (Rawls), 382

theory of sanctions, 357–61

therapeutic philosophies, 44–46, 178, 184, 207

The Therapy of Desire (Nussbaum), 45, 178

things-in-themselves, 279–80, 306

Thomas Aquinas, Saint

   Christian ethics and, 415

   Five Ways, 295–99

medieval philosophy, 52

    Philosopher Profile, 294–95

    Summa Theologica (*Summary of Theology*), 295, 296, 300–01

Thoreau, Henry David, 493

Thucydides, *History of the Peloponnesian War*, 456

Thurman, Howard, 502

Thus Spoke Zarathustra (Nietzsche), 396

Till, Emmett, 496

timarchic character, 331, 334, 422

time (*a priori* concept), 276, *277*, *280*, 306

timocracies, 445, *447*, 513

Tolstoy, Leo, 493

traditional morality, 401–02, 425

tranquility, 173–74, *175*, 175–76, 205, 206

transcendental ideas, 279–82, *280*, 280–81, 306

transcendental unity of apperception, 281, 306

Transcreation of the Bhagavad Gita (Malhotra), 412–14

A Treatise of Human Nature (Hume), 258, 259, 261, 266

Treatise on Man (Descartes), 236

The Trial (Kafka), 153

Trudeau, Pierre Elliott, 474

truth, 106

"Truth and Native American Epistemology" (Hester), 54

Twilight of the Idols (Nietzsche), 396

Two Treatises of Government (Locke), 252

two wrongs fallacy, 80, 120

tyrannical character, 331, 337, 422

tyrannical societies, 445, 513

U

Übermensch/superman, 396, 403–05, 425

ultimate end in life, 339–441

understanding, faculty of, 276, *277*, *280*

Understanding Love (Wolf and Grau), 162

uniqueness and individuality, 155, 156–57, 205

United States Declaration of Independence, 463, 464, 499, 514

universal consequences test, 371

universalizability, 115, 371, 372, 387, 424

unorthodox methods, 153, 205

unsound arguments, 106, 129

Upanishads, 410

utilitarian ethics

    characterized, 321, 423

    act vs. rule utilitarianism, 364–65

    as consequentialism, 353–54

    hedonic calculus, 356–59

    An Introduction to the Principles of Morals and Legislation (Bentham), 362–64

    is-ought fallacy, 355–56

    Philosopher Profile: Jeremy Bentham, 355

    principle of utility, 354–55

    theory of sanctions, 357–61

utility, 354–55, 423

V

vain desires, 174, 206

validity, 106, 129

valid reasoning, 99, 129

value judgments, 114–16, 129

"The Value of Philosophy" (Russell), 62–65

values, 402–03, 501–02

The Variety of Values (Wolf), 162

Vedanta, 410

Vedas, 410

veil of ignorance, 382

virtue, 176–77, 206, 346, 423

virtue ethics

    characterized, 321, 423

    Aristotle's teleology, 338–39

    Brian Berry on, 418–19

    happiness and the ends of human life, 339–42

    kinds of lifestyles, 342–45

    Nicomachean Ethics (Aristotle), 350–53

    Philosopher Profile: Aristotle, 340

    virtue and the virtuous lifestyle, 345–49, *349*

visible world of becoming, *224*, 225, *225*, 304

Voltaire, 436

W

war, 500, 516
Wartenberg, Thomas, 488
weak analogies, 112, 129
Weil, Simone, 168
Weltanschauung (worldview), 214
Western rational tradition, 51, 68
Westphalen, Jenny, 476, 477
"Where Do We Go from Here" (King), 504–10
Whitehead, Alfred North, 223
Why I Am Not a Christian (Russell), 61
Wiggins, David, 165
willful blindness, 186, 207
will-to-meaning, 168–69
will to power
    characterized, 395–98, 425
    evaluating values, 402–03
    The Gay Science (Nietzsche), 394–95, 398
    God is dead, 394–95
    herd morality and revaluation of values, 401–02, 425
    master vs. slave morality, 399–401
    Philosopher Profile: Friedrich Nietzsche, 396–97
    superman/*Übermensch*, 396, 403–05, 425
wisdom
    characterized, 40–41
    Noble Eight-Fold Path and, 189–91, 207
    philosophy and, 34, 68
    practical wisdom and Epicureanism, 173
Wittgenstein, Ludwig, 110
Wolf, Susan, 162, 165–67, 205
women
    African American, 287–89
    in Plato's ideal society, 446–47, *447*
Women and Evil (Noddings), 387
women philosophers
    Simone de Beauvoir, 153, 154
    Patricia Hill Collins, 287–89
    Carol Gilligan, 379–86
    Riffat Hassan, 407, 408–09
    Maria von Herbert, 377–78, 379
    Sor Juana Inés de la Cruz, 36, 37–39
    Nel Noddings, 386–93

Susan Wolf, 162, 165–67
worldview, 46, 50–51, 214
    See also Buddhism; Existentialism; Hedonism; meaning of life; Stoicism

X

X, Malcolm, 493

Y

"Young Hegelians," 476
Yuasa, Yasuo, *The Body*, 290–91, 307

Z

Zeno of Citium (336–264 BCE), 139, *141*, 203

From the Publisher

A name never says it all, but the word "Broadview" expresses a good deal
of the philosophy behind our company. We are open to a broad range of
academic approaches and political viewpoints. We pay attention to the
broad impact book publishing and book printing has in the wider world;
for some years now we have used 100% recycled paper for most titles.
Our publishing program is internationally oriented and broad-ranging.
Our individual titles often appeal to a broad readership too; many are
of interest as much to general readers as to academics and students.

Founded in 1985, Broadview remains a fully independent
company owned by its shareholders—not an imprint
or subsidiary of a larger multinational.

To order our books or obtain up-to-date information, please visit
broadviewpress.com.

broadview press

www.broadviewpress.com

Fallacies of Reasoning

FORMAL FALLACIES (p. 104)

Affirming the Consequent

If p, then q
q
So, p

Denying the Antecedent

If p, then q
not p
So, not q

Hypothetical Fallacy (Fallacy of Common Antecedent)

If p, then q
If p, then r
So, if q, then r

Ignoring an Alternative Disjunct

Either p, q, or r
not p
So, q

INFORMAL FALLACIES

ad hominem **fallacy:** faulty reasoning whereby one attacks the person making an argument rather than properly dealing with the argument itself (**p. 118**)

circular reasoning: erroneous logic; assuming at the beginning of an argument what one hopes to prove in the end as the conclusion (**p. 119**)

fallacy of appealing to authority: inappropriately referring to the judgments, pronouncements, or teachings of an authoritative individual or body when there is no objective way of determining the truth, given the nature of the concern at hand, or when there is no consensus among authorities (**p. 120**)

fallacy of begging the question: circular reasoning; can also involve basing an argument on an assumption that is more problematic than the conclusion one hopes to prove (**p. 119**)

fallacy of common antecedent: error of reasoning in which two premises with a common antecedent are used to mistakenly derive an "if...then" conclusion that connects the premises' consequents. (**p. 103**)

guilt by association fallacy: inappropriately rejecting an individual or that individual's claim or argument by drawing an association between that individual and someone or something already discredited; the association does not exist, is distorted, or is not relevant to the acceptance or rejection of the individual or that individual's claim or argument (**p. 122**)

hasty conclusion: an inductive reasoning error arising from insufficient evidence (**p. 111**)

hasty generalization: results when using a biased, skewed, or unrepresentative sample to draw an inference about a larger group or population (**p. 113**)

is-ought fallacy: faulty reasoning based on the assumption that one can derive an 'ought' from an 'is'; incorrectly concluding that just because something 'is' the case, that it 'should' be the case (**p. 44**)

red herring fallacy: wrongly trying to defend a contentious or problematic claim by diverting attention to some other irrelevant matter and using it as a basis of support for the initial claim; can also be used to wrongly criticize a justifiable claim by directing attention away to something else more easily criticized and using that as a way of rejecting the original justifiable claim (**p. 121**)

slippery slope fallacy: a faulty argument with the built-in assumption that if we allow for something (A), it will lead to a necessary chain of events ending in something unwanted or undesirable (Z); since we don't want the undesirable endpoint of the chain (Z), we should not allow or be in favor of the original something (A); there is a break somewhere between (A) and (Z) (**p. 120**)

straw person fallacy: faulty reasoning whereby one criticizes an argument never made by a person to reject the argument that was actually and originally presented (**p. 118**)

two wrongs fallacy: inappropriately trying to justify one wrongdoing by pointing to other instances of the same wrongdoing that went unpunished (**p. 120**)

weak analogy: a faulty inference based on insufficient and/or insignificant similarities between or among two or more things; like comparing apples and oranges (**p. 112**)